G000109180

everybody's talkin'

The Top Films of 1965–1969

Barry Monush

APPLAUSE
THEATRE & CINEMA BOOKS | An Imprint of Hal Leonard Corporation
New York

Copyright © 2009 by Barry Monush

All rights reserved. No part of this book may be reproduced in any form, without written permission, except by a newspaper or magazine reviewer who wishes to quote brief passages in connection with a review.

This book is a work of scholarship, unrelated to any trademark status, and represents no venture of any films or television properties mentioned. Referential usage of related images is not to be construed as a challenge to any trademark status. The pictorial material that appears here is for the sole purpose of illustrating the creative processes involved in the making of the motion pictures discussed.

Published in 2009 by Applause Theatre & Cinema Books
An Imprint of Hal Leonard Corporation
7777 West Bluemound Road
Milwaukee, WI 53213

Trade Book Division Editorial Offices
19 West 21st Street, New York, NY 10010

All images in this book are from the personal collection of the author.

Printed in the United States of America

Book design by Mark Lerner

Library of Congress Cataloging-in-Publication Data

Monush, Barry.
  Everybody's talkin' : the top films of 1965-1969 / Barry Monush.
    p. cm.
  Includes bibliographical references.
  ISBN 978-1-55783-618-2 (alk. paper)
  1. Motion pictures--Plots, themes, etc. I. Title.
  PN1997.8.M66 2009
  791.43'75--dc22
                            2009019659

www.applausepub.com

EVERYBODY'S TALKIN'

In memory of
RICHARD VALLEY
whose quick wit, amazing knowledge of movies,
and heartfelt generosity continue to be an inspiration

contents

1966

1967

1968

1969

bibliography

those magnificent films on those cinema screens, or how i flew from new york to london to write about the sixties in 4 years, 10 months, 25 hours, 11 minutes

Everyone should have a favorite decade at the movies; mine is the '60s. This was the decade I first experienced going the movies, after all, which might have biased my enjoyment of the era; but looking back I see that this is not just a case of idealizing the past. I was privileged to witness a period that produced an incredibly diverse range of films in which a terrific selection of actors and filmmakers gave us some of their finest work.

For those who lament the passing of the old-fashioned, studio-bound era of filmmaking, it was still very much in evidence at this time, especially during the early part of the '60s. For those who were glad to see Hollywood throw off the shackles of mainstream storytelling and censorship restraints, this era was the beginning of all that independence and freedom. I think the films of that time represented the best of both worlds, something often taken for granted by both those who were unwilling to see things change and those who were so anxious to turn their backs on tradition that they failed to appreciate the value of anything that stuck to basics.

There were wonderfully probing dramas exploring important themes; westerns—traditional, epic, and radical; gloriously entertaining musicals; comedies of both a sophisticated and a bawdy nature; daring explorations of formerly taboo subjects; influential horror films that still retained some degree of restraint before this genre got so out of hand; ambitious science-fiction films that brought a wider degree of attention to this field; and war movies, both flag waving and critical. Seldom had so many followers of so many kinds of movies had such a great choice of what to see. As sex and violence were becoming more prevalent, attention was still being paid to what was relevant to the story line and what crossed the boundary into mere exploitation. Screenplays were given priority over high concepts; if a movie boasted a large budget, the costs were usually evident in the finished print. Films were allowed to roll out slowly rather than open in saturation bookings, giving moviegoers many chances to see them in theaters, where they belonged. There was a genuine sense of pride in much of the product being released; audiences took chances in what they chose to see; there was a feeling that all kinds of entertainment from different countries were being sampled. Novels and plays were looked to on a regular basis for source material; it was not common to depend on old television shows or flip through the pages of comic books for inspiration. Although there were occasional sequels, there were no numbers slapped on the ends of the titles (a horrid tradition that began in the '70s and continues to this day) and it was not a given to immediately put a spin-off or further chapter into development simply because a movie had done well at the box office. You could look down the list of Oscar nominees and pretty regularly find the very same titles showing up on that year's Top 25 Box Office list. Again, many people took this era for granted (and many still do), only realizing just how good things were in retrospect; but this holds true for pretty much any era of motion pictures.

Of course there were bad films, just as there are in any decade, but you did not get the impression that poor or mediocre pictures were the norm, with occasional gems slipping through. There was a sense of purpose and ambition to so much of what was being done—it made the industry seem admirable and something you wanted to be a part of, even when a film's reach exceeded its grasp. There was no falling back on cable television or home video; if you missed a picture in its theatrical run, you ended up seeing it cut and commercially interrupted on your television screen, a prospect that made it much more exciting to go out to the cinema and catch things before they were mutilated from their intended state. There were no video or digital devices to allow you to copy, download, or buy the same movie months if not weeks after its theatrical debut, so you didn't get the sense so prevalent today that a picture's run in cinemas was nothing more than a prelude to its appearance on a video monitor. For those brought up on the joys and conveniences of video and DVD consumption, this might seem like a negative aspect of the '60s, but it was not. During that time even people who settled for watching films on television knew they were missing out and that it was an inferior experience. This belief has become far less widely held, and as a result, the movies have lost much of their special luster.

There has been much written about how the late '60s and early '70s were some sort of second golden era of moviemaking—about how certain pictures from this period "saved" the movie industry from stagnation. Although I have great admiration for many of the pictures referred to as "breakthroughs," I believe that this is a whopping generalization. To insist that a handful of "independent-minded" films were trendsetting and therefore superior to those before them is an insult to a long list of fine motion pictures that appeared in cinemas throughout the '60s. To act as if movies had no value until *Bonnie and Clyde* and *The Graduate* came along is to denigrate such late '60s works as varied as *Alfie*, *The Sound of Music*, *The Fortune Cookie*, *Fantastic Voyage*, *The Pawnbroker*, *Georgy Girl*, *Shenandoah*, *A Thousand Clowns*, *A Man for All Seasons*, and *Who's Afraid of Virginia Woolf?*, to name but a few. The truth is that the decade was overloaded with fine films that need not apologize because they did not turn moviemaking on its head or fit into some sort of thesis about the countercultural revolution.

Setting out to write a book about half a decade of films is a daunting task, one that required some boundaries and rather strict criteria for exactly which titles would be selected. My idea from the start was to do a reference book highlighting a certain number of titles from each year that would represent what the decade really looked like had you actually been there, seeing them not so much in retrospect from a modern perspective, but according to what the dominant titles of the day were. It is very easy to choose favorite movies from the time and then act as if they were as important in their day as we might view them now, but this does not give a complete picture.

I also knew that I did not wish to simply include movies that I felt were good, because this would seem a bit repetitious in tone, praising one film after another. I finally struck upon the idea of giving a fairly thorough overview by focusing on two key areas: the Academy Awards and each year's top box-office moneymakers. The former would include the work considered worthy of accolades (those given by the movie industry itself, which has always been far more diplomatic, open-minded, and interesting in their choices than critics' awards, which often deliberately try to look away from commercial entertainment, as if to condemn a work for trying to appeal to the general public), while the latter would cover the chief pictures that the public paid to see. I was delighted to see how frequently both of these lists overlapped, not to mention how they included so many important and significant titles from the decade. I knew then that these lists would provide me with a pretty comprehensive overview of some of the best (and most varied) product the late '60s had to offer. It would also shed some attention on lesser-known pictures that had their brief moment in the '60s sun, either by having been listed somewhere on the Oscar-nomination roster or by having appealed to their paying customers because they reflected some fad or interest belonging strictly to the era. In any event, there are bound to be favorites missing (favorites of mine are missing. to be sure), but I think this does indeed give a pretty comprehensive look at the latter half of the decade.

I decided to include every movie that had won an Academy Award in all but the following categories: Short Subject—Live Action, Short Subject—Animated, Documentary—Feature, and Documentary—Short. The omission of the short films speaks for itself; this is a book about feature films, after all. As for the documentaries, not only are many of these films difficult to track down, but several were not even made publicly available to viewers at the time (a practice continued throughout Academy history) and don't really represent the sort of picture I was aiming to cover anyway. I also included all films to receive Oscar nominations in the following categories: Best Picture, the four acting slots, and Best Director.

For the box-office list I decided to cut it off at the top ten, those pictures with the highest attendance figures in their day. (I ranked the films according to the year they were released, not according to when they were making their money. In other words, if a movie arrived in theaters in December and made most of its money the following calendar year, I judged it according to how it performed alongside the titles from its own year, not any other year.) This is not a perfect system, and many might be inclined to feel that certain movies unjustly missed making the cut. I think those that remain are still very much worth a look.

My original intent was to look at a wide, wide range of movies from the entire decade. But because my ambitions exceeded my budget and my space, a compromise was made in which the decade was split in half and the criteria for making the cut made more restrictive, causing me to drop several titles I had been hoping to include. (Five titles I was obliged to drop according to my newly stated boundaries were thereafter reinstated, one from each year, when space became available.)

Not content to simply write about the 109 movies that made the list, I was adamant that I also wanted to track down the source material for any motion picture that had come from a novel, a short story, a play, a television play, or a magazine article. This was a challenge that entailed scouring out-of-print bookshops in Manhattan, Los Angeles, and throughout New Jersey, and it took me to all sorts of places and towns I had never been to before—itself a worthwhile offshoot of my project. Because used book-stores are yet another form of business that is losing its lure because of the Internet, I often found myself crossing out the names of shops on my preliminary list that had only recently closed or dropping in at others whose days may very well have been numbered. It was always a thrill to come across some of the titles in my search, even more so when I found the edition of the novel with the movie tie-in cover. Once or twice these places lived up to the traditional image of the cozy and cluttered old bookstore by includ-ing a cat sitting among the paperbacks. (I can only assume they were keeping guard over the novels *The Ballad of Cat Ballou* and *Undercover Cat*, both of which I needed for my project).

My project did not stop at books, however, which meant I went looking for magazines, sheet music, press books, LPs, and so forth, in all sorts of locations, from Long Beach to London, in order to represent most of the selected entries with an interesting bit of ephemera or memorabilia. I figured rather than always fall back on a still photo from the film, it would make the book more visually arresting to show something off the beaten track that represented other ways of merchandising or selling the films.

I have attempted to give some background on each of the titles because, frankly, even the worst mov-ies have backstories worth telling; and just how they were made, where, and why, is quite interesting. In order to locate such information, there were a number of books (listed in the bibliography) that were quite helpful, as well as Rebecca Cline at the Disney Archives, whose kindness and quick responses were an inspiration; the clipping files at the New York Public Library for the Performing Arts at Lincoln Cen-ter; the Library of the British Film Institute in London (where I discovered the fascinating *Kinemato-graph* weekly); and the Margaret Herrick Library in Los Angeles; my thanks to these establishments and those staff members who offered assistance. I would also like to thank the UCLA Archives (for the Twentieth Century-Fox titles) and the Warner Bros. Archives. In addition to the fulfillment of tracking down information that initially seemed out of my reach, it was great to return to each of these places just for the fun I had outside of doing research. (Alas, there was a smattering of folks along the way who were less than helpful or supportive, but they shall remain nameless.)

Since this is an overview of half a decade, I thought it only made sense to do the book chronologically, with each entry listed according to when it first opened in the United States. Being an East Coast boy, I have also listed when the movie first debuted in New York City, if the very first showing did not take place here. (Such films as *Inside Daisy Clover* and *You're a Big Boy Now* have often been chronicled in the New York area according to their openings here, 1966 and 1967, respectively, although their official debuts were in December of the preceding years). Each entry includes a quote from the film, which I hope captures its theme or tone; song lyrics are used for all official movie musicals from this period. The main credits and cast principals (and the roles they played) are followed by a brief plot summary, my observations on the movie, comparisons to source material, the background on how or why it was made, and whatever other information I was able to find. The more significant movies get the larger entries, of course.

thank you all very much

Of course all of this (and everything, for that matter) means so much more because of my life partner and best friend, Tom Lynch, who has been tremendously patient and supportive from the start, encouraging me to put my voice out there before the public, helping to smooth out the project's bumps along the way, taking great pleasure in seeing me collect memorabilia (filling our guest room with ten boxes of the stuff!), and giving advice while reading through the written entries. Because of him I will forever smile hearing the phrase "who ya brushin' . . . ?" (which requires too much explanation for the uninitiated). Like Sidney Poitier in *To Sir, with Love*, he is wise enough to know what is really important to learn in life, and like Paul Scofield's interpretation of Sir Thomas More in *A Man for All Seasons*, he is the admirable human being we should all strive to be.

I must make special mention of some people whose generosity in giving me or lending me material to make this project happen puts me forever in their debt. Thanks to: Larry Billman, whose Academy of Dance on Film will forever be an "Institute" to me; Dottie Burns, whose collection of film magazines from the era was helpful, not to mention a pleasure to flip through as well; Jim Hollifield; and Dave Torrey for finding *Lt. Crusoe*. A special posthumous thanks to Gene Massimo, who had access to pictures of celebrities and movies that *nobody* had heard of; and to Richard Valley, whose vast and varied knowledge of movies over the years will continue to astound me. I miss them both and thank them with all my heart for all their support and help.

Thanks to Michael Messina, who, when presented with the proposal for this book, actually thought it was a good idea and didn't toss me out of his office. And the same goes for Glenn Young and John Cerullo as well; and all those folks on the Applause staff who helped on this book along the way. Special thanks to Jessica Burr and Barbara Norton for their contributions.

I am eternally grateful to John Willis, who first opened up the path that led me here.

Thanks to Billy Hall for helping me fill in the holes in my Fox collection.

And thanks also go to Becky Paller, Craig Kelemen, Jim Howard, James Sheridan, Tim Johnson, Greg Rossi, and David Bushman, because they were among those who actually inquired with interest about this book over the years while it was in production. And grateful appreciation to Ron Simon and Diane Lewis for allowing me time off to get things done.

A nod to Alex Dawson because he not only graciously handed me a free copy of *Othello*, but looks up to all the great British punters of the '60s like Peter O'Toole, Richard Harris, Richard Burton, Albert Finney, and Oliver Reed.

Fond memories of those four people with whom I shared the bulk of my first decade of movies, my parents, my sister Michelle and my brother Bryan; as well as a very grateful memory of being taken, along with my sister, to the Paramount Theatre in Asbury Park by my cousin Hilda Kelemen and my aunt Olga Monush to see *The Sound of Music*. (My first movie with an intermission!)

Over the years the cinematic '60s have also been shared with such people as Nick Setteducato, without whom my world would be less Beatle-ridden; Doug Sulpy, who was just the right person to introduce me to the ultimate trip, *2001: A Space Odyssey*; Kimberly Scherling, who, I'm certain, knows the lyrics to every song in *Oliver!* and *Hello, Dolly!*, as well as musicals without exclamation points; George Scherling, who is more tolerant of the '60s than most, actually having good things to say about the beach party movies; Donna Deutchman, who was adventurous enough to meet me in New York just to see a revival of *Elmer Gantry*; Larry Deutchman, who had posters from three seminal '60s films on his dorm room wall when I first knew him: *The Great Escape*, *The Dirty Dozen*, and *The Wild Bunch*; Dave Zeliff, whose favorite movie remains *The Sound of Music*, which means he has a good heart; Paul Larkins, to whom I was most thankful for not telling me what was going to happen at the end of *Easy Rider* when we saw it together in a dumpy theater in Keansburg, New Jersey; Thomas Buxereau, who has not experienced his fill of Audrey Hepburn movies quite yet, as far as I am concerned; Robert Sleeman, whose reactions to watching *The Russians Are Coming* and *Thoroughly Modern Millie* at my home in Hazlet were almost exactly what I hoped they would be; and Brian Durnin, who, despite his appreciation of *Alfie* and *Seconds*, actually thinks the best movie ever made came from the '70s . . . go figure.

I hope looking through this book brings back some memories of late '60s cinema for you; it certainly did for me while putting it together.

EVERYBODY'S TALKIN'

1965

THE SOUND OF MUSIC

Academy Award Winner: Best Picture; Best Director; Best Sound; Best Scoring of Music—Adaptation or Treatment; Best Film Editing

Academy Award Nominee: Actress (Julie Andrews); Supporting Actress (Peggy Wood); Cinematography—Color; Art Direction-Set Decoration—Color; Costume Design—Color

Top 10 Box Office Film

Opening date: March 2, 1965.

Twentieth Century-Fox. A Robert Wise Production, Produced by Argyle Enterprises, Inc.

Director-Producer: Robert Wise. Screenplay: Ernest Lehman. Based on the 1959 musical play by Richard Rodgers and Oscar Hammerstein II, with book by Howard Lindsay and Russel Crouse. Suggested by Maria Trapp's story. Songs by Richard Rodgers (music) and Oscar Hammerstein II (lyrics): "The Sound of Music," "Dixit Dominus/Morning Hymn/Alleluia," "Maria," "Sixteen Going On Seventeen," "My Favorite Things," "Do-Re-Mi," "The Lonely Goatherd," "Edelweiss," "So Long, Farewell," "Climb Ev'ry Mountain." Song by Richard Rodgers (music and lyrics): "I Have Confidence." Song by Richard Rodgers (with uncredited contributions by Ernest Lehman and Saul Chaplin): "Something Good." Music Supervisor, Arranger, and Conductor: Irwin Kostal. Choreographers: Marc Breaux, Dee Dee Wood. Photography: Ted McCord. Production Designer: Boris Leven. Set Decorators: Walter M. Scott, Ruby Levitt. Costumes: Dorothy Jeakins. Associate Producer: Saul Chaplin. Editor: William Reynolds. Sound: Murray Spivack, Bernard Freericks. Puppets: Bil and Cora Baird Marionettes. Deluxe color. Todd-AO. 175 minutes (including entr'acte).

CAST: Julie Andrews (Maria), Christopher Plummer (Captain Georg von Trapp), Eleanor Parker (Baroness Elsa Schraeder), Richard Haydn (Max Detweiler), Peggy Wood (Mother Abbess), Charmian Carr (Liesl von Trapp), Heather Menzies (Louisa von Trapp), Nicholas Hammond (Friedrich von Trapp), Duane Chase (Kurt von Trapp), Angela Cartwright (Brigitta von Trapp), Debbie Turner (Marta von Trapp), Kym Karath (Gretl von Trapp), Anna Lee (Sister Margaretta), Portia Nelson (Sister Berthe), Ben Wright (Herr Zeller), Daniel Truhitte (Rolfe), Norma Varden (Frau Schmidt), Gil Stuart (Franz), Marni Nixon (Sister Sophia), Evadne Baker (Sister Bernice), Doris Lloyd (Baroness Ebberfeld).

PLOT: Told she does not have the strict dedication to become a nun, Maria is sent from her abbey to serve as governess to widower Captain von Trapp's seven children, teaching them the joy of music and bringing them closer to their stern and distant father.

Most of the world seemed to love the musicals of Rodgers and Hammerstein and had proven so time and again on Broadway during the 1940s and 1950s, where the two names had become household words by the time Oscar Hammerstein II died in 1960. The team's final collaboration, *The Sound of Music*, had earned praise for its score and less favorable comment for its book, most critics decrying it as saccharine and routine. This fazed the public not at all, for they lapped it up in a big way, the show running an impressive 1,443 performances, and making a movie sale inevitable. Twentieth Century-Fox, which had first dibs on buying anything the duo produced for the stage, snapped up the rights for $1.25 million in June 1960, a month before Hammerstein's untimely passing. Now came the difficult task of taking a potentially treacly property and making it soar onscreen.

It had all started with Maria Augusta Kutschera (1905–1987), an Austrian postulant who took a job tending to the seven children of a widowed retired navy captain, Georg von Trapp, and ended up marrying him in 1927. After discovering their musical abilities, the family became a singing group. This led to professional engagements in Austria and other parts of Europe until the Nazi regime forced them to escape to America. In 1948, a year after the Captain's death, Maria published an account of her life, *The Story of the Trapp Family Singers*, the rights to which were bought by German producer Wolfgang Reinhardt, who wanted to dramatize their tale as a motion picture. *Die Trapp Familie* (1956) proved so popular in Germany and Austria that a follow-up was ordered, *Die Trapp Familie in America* (1958), both of them directed by Wolfgang Liebeneiner and starring Ruth Leuwerik as Maria and Hans Holt as the Captain. Broadway director Vincent J. Donehue thought the movies could be adapted for the stage to accommodate the talents of Mary Martin. Originally he envisioned a dramatic play utilizing authentic Austrian folk songs, but this idea was wisely discarded in favor of an all-new score by Richard Rodgers and Oscar Hammerstein II. With a book by Howard Lindsay and Russel Crouse and a cast consisting of Martin, Theodore Bikel (as the Captain), Kurt Kasznar (Max Detweiler), Marion Marlowe (Elsa), Patricia Neway (the Mother Abbess), Lauri Peters (Liesl), and Brian Davies (Rolf), *The Sound of Music* opened at New York's Lunt-Fontanne Theater on November 16, 1959. It earned Tony Awards in five categories—Best Musical, Best Actress (Martin), Best Featured Actress (Neway), Best Music Direction, and Best Scenic Design—and finally ended its run at the Mark Hellinger Theatre (where it had transferred in November 1962) on June 15, 1963.

> "I go to the hills when my heart is lonely. I know I will hear what I've heard before. My heart will be blessed with the sound of music, and I'll sing once more."
> —Maria

There was much skepticism in Hollywood that *The Sound of Music*, with its mixture of religion, children, and unapologetic wholesomeness, could make the transition to the big screen without appearing square and overly cutesy. To make matters worse, Fox had purchased the two German Trapp films, stitched them together into one movie titled *The Trapp Family*, dubbed it in English, and opened it in the United States in March 1961 to complete public apathy, suggesting interest in the story was lower than anticipated. Writer Ernest Lehman, who had helped adapt *West Side Story* (United Artists, 1961) into an Oscar-laden motion picture, was one of the few who saw the possibility of something special in transferring the stage version to film and set about trying to restructure the show's problematic book. The two songs sung by the secondary characters of Max, the family's manager, and the captain's fiancée, Elsa—"How Can Love Survive?" and "No Way to Stop It"—were dropped, as was a love duet between Maria and Captain von Trapp, "An Ordinary Couple," which Rodgers claimed to have disliked anyway. "My Favorite Things," the song Maria sang to build up her confidence prior to going to the Trapp villa, was moved from the abbey to a scene in Maria's bedroom at her new place of employment, performed to comfort the children during a thunderstorm. In the play this scene had been where "The Lonely Goatherd" was sung, which now became part of a puppet show done by Maria and the children for the benefit of the Captain and Elsa. Rodgers was asked to write a new song for Maria to sing on her way to the Trapp residence, which resulted in the upbeat "I Have Confidence" (Rodgers supplying the lyrics as well, rather than finding a new partner to do this task). To replace "An Ordinary Couple," he wrote "Something Good," but nobody was particularly happy with the end result, so Lehman and the movie's musical supervisor and associate producer, Saul Chaplin, ended up providing additional lyrics and music, though they were uncredited.

There were further revisions in the characterization of the Captain, who had been perceived by pretty much everyone as a stiff onstage; and certain elements could now be enacted in a more fluid and cinematic fashion, notably the staging of "Do-Re-Mi," which allowed Maria and the children to traipse through the streets of Salzburg; the escape from the Nazis, which was relocated to a graveyard at the abbey; and, best of all, the opening. Now, rather than the whole thing being ushered in by the nuns' "Preludium," which had opened the play, the title song would be sung on those very hills described in the lyrics.

Because Lehman had done such an ace job in smoothing out the bumps in the script, he nearly got William Wyler committed to the project as director. However, after going so far as to scout locations, Wyler decided he simply didn't believe in the piece enough and opted to direct *The Collector* for Columbia instead. Another nonbeliever, Robert Wise, was also won over by the revisions but was hoping to get *The Sand Pebbles* into production at the time and had to pass. When Fox put *Pebbles* on hold, though, Wise was able to say yes, thereby reuniting Lehman with one of his *West Side Story* directors. With the production finally falling into place and getting closer to becoming a reality, Wise and Lehman managed to land the one actress

A nonmusical moment as governess Julie Andrews tends to the von Trapp children, as played by Debbie Turner, Angela Cartwright, Duane Chase, Kym Karath, Heather Menzies, Nicholas Hammond, and Charmian Carr.

they were most enthusiastic about playing Maria, Julie Andrews. Andrews had had great luck with her previous Rodgers and Hammerstein project, *Cinderella*, which had become one of television's best-loved and most highly acclaimed specials after its sensational first airing in March of 1957. At the time she was signed for *Music*, neither of her first two pictures, *Mary Poppins* (Disney, 1964) and *The Americanization of Emily* (MGM, 1964), had yet opened, but preview footage from the former convinced everyone that she had the makings of a great film star.

Far less willing to come aboard was Christopher Plummer, who was Wise's choice to play the Captain; the director believed the actor's edgy qualities would help make the character more interesting, sexier, more compelling. Once he was finally talked into it, Plummer comforted himself with the belief that he'd at least be able to sing onscreen, a dream that was not to come true. When he was told his vocals would be dubbed, he nearly walked off the picture, until Wise placated him by telling him he'd be allowed to record his tracks as a test to see if he was suitable. If he honestly believed he was up to the demands, they would go ahead with the Plummer pipes. Fortunately, Plummer realized he sounded hopelessly inadequate next to Andrews's gorgeous instrument and had to give in. He was ultimately "ghosted" by Bill Lee.

After considering two actresses who had not appeared before the cameras for years, Jeanette Mac-Donald and Irene Dunne, for the Mother Abbess, Wise went with Peggy Wood, who was best known for having reprised one of Dunne's roles on *Mama*, a television version of *I Remember Mama* (RKO, 1948) that ran on CBS from 1949 to 1957. Although she had once sung in such Broadway shows as *The Madcap Duchess* and *Maytime*, her vocal abilities were no longer what they had been, and she ended up being dubbed by Margery MacKay. Beating out such contenders as Mia Farrow and Lesley Ann Warren for the role of the oldest Trapp daughter, Liesl, was someone completely new to the business, Charmian Farnon, whose name was changed to Charmian Carr for her hoped-for new career in films. Popping up as one of the nuns was Marni Nixon, perhaps the most famous "ghost" singer in movie history, having filled in for Deborah Kerr in *The King and I* (Twentieth Century-Fox), Natalie Wood in *West Side Story*, and Audrey Hepburn in *My Fair Lady* (Warner Bros., 1964). As with Carr, this would be Nixon's only appearance in front of the cameras in a theatrically released picture.

Because Liesl was the only one of the von Trapp children to have a substantial role, the other six youngsters were cast principally for appearance, functioning more as a collective group than as individuals. (The stage version had come up with all new names for the children, who in the real life were called Rupert, Agathe, Maria, Werner, Hedwig, Johanna, and Martina.) All of their singing voices except Carr's were dubbed in the film.

Shooting began at the Twentieth Century-Fox studios on March 26, 1964, and continued there until the production traveled to Austria on April 23, where it would remain for over two months, returning to the Los Angeles soundstages on July 6. The interiors filmed in Los Angeles consisted of all the rooms in the Trapp villa, most of the abbey interiors (including the graveyard), and the pavilion on the grounds of the Trapp estate (used for both "Sixteen Going On Seventeen" and "Something Good"). The only indoor set that was built in Europe—at Dürer Studios in Parsch, when rainy weather kept the unit from filming outside—was the Mother Abbess's quarters, where she performed "Climb Ev'ry Mountain." All of the exteriors were shot in and near Salzburg, a decision that enhanced the movie in every way: the breathtaking backgrounds were just one reason the play suffered in comparison to the movie, especially in the eyes of later generations who had grown up on the film. The principal locales were comprised of the grounds and lake at the Bertelsmann estate, subbing for part of the Trapp property; Schloss Frohnburg, which served as the facade of the Trapp house (thereby necessitating cutting between the two locations, sometimes within the same scene); the exterior of the Nonnberg Abbey, where the real Maria had been cloistered; the imposing rock wall at the Rocky Riding School, which made for a stunning backdrop as the Trapp Family performed at the music festival; the St. Margarethen Chapel, where the nuns held service; Mondsee Cathedral, where the wedding of Maria and the Captain took place; Obersalzberg Mountain, which provided the inspiring final image of the family making their escape into Switzerland; and a montage of places around Salzburg, including Winkler's Terrace and the Mirabelle Gardens for the memorable "Do-Re-Mi," the latter locale providing the staircase for Andrews's sustained high note at the end of the song.

One location, however, surpassed all of these, simply because it was used for the moment that provided the movie with its defining image. Having created such a knockout opening for *West Side Story* by silently drifting over the streets of Manhattan from high above, Wise figured he could get away with something similar yet again and allowed his camera to descend from the snow-peaked Alps into the greenery of the Austrian countryside. But what capped the sequence was the helicopter shot that swept down toward Andrews as she spun about on a mountaintop before letting forth with the lyrics "The hills are alive with the sound of music." This was the sort of incredible and indelible filmic moment that was greeted with awe for the manner in which it plunged its audience so thoroughly and emotionally into the story. Filmed at a mountain called Mellweg near the Bavarian village of Schellenberg during the final week on location (June 28–July 2, 1964), the sequence would be cheered, parodied, talked about, and praised until it could rightly take its place as a part of cultural folklore.

Right about the time principal photography ended, something wonderful happened that caused Fox to breathe a sigh of relief about the future of its $8.5 million investment: Walt Disney's *Mary Poppins* had opened to rapturous notices, with critics proclaiming Julie Andrews the best thing to happen to the musical genre, or, indeed, movies in general, in years. The crowds lined up in record numbers, making this *the* event movie of 1964, and Andrews was one of the key reasons for its success. By the end of the year, *The Americanization of Emily* had earned her another avalanche of praise, and it seemed as if Andrews had become just about the best-known celebrity in town. Fox scheduled the road show engagement of *The Sound of Music* to open in early March 1965, which meant that *Poppins* would overlap with it in theaters, meanwhile continuing to rake in a small fortune for Disney. For a moment all of this build-up seemed for naught when the first reviews of *Music* came rolling in, pretty much blasting the picture for being everything that Wise and company had set out to avoid, accusing it of being saccharine and slight. And the mediocre-to-poor reviews kept arriving like black clouds, with only a sprinkling of favorable comment coming from select publications. Fortunately, in one of those miracles that all filmmakers pray for, nobody seemed to give a damn about the negative press, and audiences flocked to the film's exclusive engagements right from the start. Better yet, the audience kept growing and growing till the numbers were so staggering that even the naysayers started to wonder if they had missed something. As *Music* spread to more theaters during the summer and fall of 1965, the cash kept pouring into the Fox bank account until the movie had become the sort of phenomenon that comes along all too rarely. In time, *The Sound of Music* would zoom over the $100 million mark, passing the all-time record holder, *Gone with the Wind* (MGM, 1939), a feat that seemed unlikely at the time. Andrews had gone from superstar to household word and the whole world seemed to have an opinion of her and the movie, whether they'd seen it or not. Needless to say, the record attendance figures only caused certain reviews and champions of the cinema's more realistic, New Wave movement to denounce the picture more loudly and with greater venom. Because it was now the most popular motion picture of all time, the opposition pointed to it as the epitome of Hollywood sentimentality, the most caustic comments coming from those who weren't likely to enjoy musicals in the first place.

The millions who embraced the film obviously responded to its message of hope. *The Sound of Music* was a truly inspiring story about one triumph over the Nazi nightmare, whereas too many other true-life incidents had ended in unspeakable tragedy. Wise and Lehman had done a masterful job of storytelling, keeping the sugar to a minimum (despite what many declared) and creating people audiences genuinely cared about. Much of this success was due to Andrews's performance; the actress exuded a sense of comfort and love without ever once telegraphing her intentions in a manner that might be construed as self-conscious or false. It was, in many ways, the finest performance of her career, so it was only fitting that it be the one more audiences would see than any other. The beautiful Rodgers and Hammerstein score was another reason the film worked so well. As the airwaves and record sales figures were just on the cusp of being taken over by rock and roll, the soundtrack became the last of its sort to reach the number 1 spot on the *Billboard* charts, a position it held for two weeks in the fall of 1965. Nearly every song in the film became a standard, giving the impression that the traditional musical was *not* on its way out, as so many had predicted for years. As a direct result, every Hollywood studio in town found its share of Broadway musicals to adapt for the big screen, spending a lot of money, sometimes for the good, sometimes not. Big-budget musicals became the norm right into the early 1970s, when it suddenly became unfashionable to make this kind of entertainment in the midst of the cinema's crusade to establish a harder edged, uncensored, grittier style of filmmaking. Overnight, musicals seemed to bother everyone a great deal and were looked upon by certain factions as the squarest of the square, with *The Sound of Music* singled out as the worst offender.

Lehman, who had believed in the picture from the start, had been vindicated by its record-shattering success, which helped Twentieth Century-Fox find its legs after the crippling financial losses of *Cleopatra* (1963). *The Sound of Music* was an outstanding example of a movie attaining the status of a classic not because the reviewers were aware of its merits, but because the general public responded so passionately and treasured it in a way that few films ever were. It wound up with ten Oscar nominations, pitting it against the other big 1965 movie that had irked the critics and thrilled the public, *Doctor Zhivago* (MGM). It was *Music* that snatched up the Best Picture award to make its incredible triumph complete and thorough. The film was successfully reissued in 1973 and premiered to huge audiences on television in 1975, where it remained a staple of prime-time viewing for decades to come. Salzburg became a favorite vacation destination, and a "*Sound of Music* Tour" became a key attraction in which visitors were taken to the various locations used in the film, much to the chagrin of the locals. Austria was one of the few countries where the picture flopped. The film remains one of the great dividing lines of taste to this day, championed as an all-time favorite by millions who have kept it a constant seller on various home viewing formats, from VHS to DVD, while never failing to evoke a smirk of disdain from others. Even one of its stars, Christopher Plummer, took delight for years in making derisive comments about the role and film for which he remains best known. Andrews, on the other hand, was quick to point out all the joy it brought to so many people and was appreciative of the cinematic immortality it gave her.

THE PAWNBROKER

Academy Award Nominee: Actor (Rod Steiger)

Opening date: April 20, 1965.

Landau Releasing Organization–Allied Artists. An Ely Landau and Herbert R. Steinman Presentation.

Director: Sidney Lumet. Producers: Roger Lewis, Philip Langner. Executive Producer: Ely Landau. Screenplay: Morton S. Fine, David Friedkin. Based on the 1961 novel by Edward Lewis Wallant. Photography: Boris Kaufman. Art Director: Richard Sylbert. Set Decorator: Jack Flaherty. Costumes: Anna Hill Johnstone. Music: Quincy Jones. Editor: Ralph Rosenblum. Black and white. 116 minutes.

CAST: Rod Steiger (Sol Nazerman), Geraldine Fitzgerald (Marilyn Birchfield), Brock Peters (Rodriguez), Jaime Sánchez (Jesus Ortiz), Thelma Oliver (Ortiz's Girl), Marketa Kimbrell (Tessie), Baruch Lumet (Mendel), Juano Hernandez (Mr. Smith), Linda Geiser (Ruth Nazerman), Nancy R. Pollock (Bertha), Raymond St. Jacques (Tangee), John McCurry (Buck), Ed Morehouse (Oratory Award Owner), Eusebia Cosme (Mrs. Ortiz), Warren Finnerty (Savarese), Jack Ader (Morton), E. M. Margolese (Papa), Marianne Kanter (Joan), Marc Alexander (Rubin), Reni Santoni (Junkie with Radio), Charles Dierkop (Robinson).

PLOT: Sol Nazerman, an elderly Jewish pawnbroker plying his trade in Harlem, tries to run his business with as little human interaction as possible, having turned his back on mankind after witnessing the extermination of his wife and children in the Nazi death camps.

How to deal with something as unspeakable as the Holocaust? This event had scarred the world for all time and was ripe for reflection, criticism, and dramatization, but Hollywood wasn't too keen to venture into so explosive and potentially unnerving territory when it came to providing audiences with "entertainment." *Judgment at Nuremberg* (United Artists, 1961) had been one of the few movies to risk bringing up the subject, even going so far as to show actual footage shot within the concentration camps, but it had not dared to stage scenes of actors within the camps themselves. *The Pawnbroker* took that risk and moved motion pictures that much further ahead in confronting the monstrous nature of mankind and the numbed human beings left behind to forever confront the atrocities committed against them.

The source material was an excellent novel by Edward Lewis Wallant, who had been declared one of the most interesting and probing young writers of his generation but died in 1962 at the age of thirty-six. By that point Roger Lewis, a former vice president at United Artists, had bought the rights to the book, wanting to branch into independent film production with what he believed would be an unusual and adventurous property. MGM showed some interest, and Daniel Petrie was mentioned as a possible director. Lewis had wanted Rod Steiger to play the lead, Sol Nazerman, but MGM got cold feet about the commercial viability of this difficult piece, and Steiger's participation did not placate the studio where box-office business was concerned. The deal eventually fell apart, so Lewis brought in another producing partner, Philip Langner, who had received an associate producer credit on *Judgment at Nuremberg*. One studio after another turned them down. Finally, Ely A. Landau, whose only previous movie credit had been the blatantly noncommercial three-hour film version of Eugene O'Neill's *Long Day's Journey into Night*, offered to serve as backer and distributor on the picture, with Sidney Lumet (who had helmed *Long Day's Journey*) selected as director.

Two writers who worked mainly for television, David Friedkin and Morton S. Fine, were responsible for taking Wallant's book, which emphasized a lot of internalized feelings, and making it into something more cinematic. Although they were present in one of the earliest scenes in the film, Sol's sister and her family were given far less importance, which meant eliminating the relationship between Sol and his troubled, antisocial nephew Morton, who in the book was asked to help his uncle in the shop following the murder of Sol's apprentice, Jesus. Two other characters—a corrupt police officer who makes himself a nuisance at Sol's shop and a half-crazed Holocaust survivor who demands money for the Jewish Appeal from Sol's sex partner, Tessie—were dropped altogether. The ominous hood who rules over the pawnbroker's life from afar was changed from an Italian American named Murrillo to an African American called Rodriguez, with suggestions of a gay relationship between him and his blond housekeeper thrown in for good measure. Many of Sol's memories of his hellish internment were changed from nightmares to conscious memories triggered by present-day experiences. They included one pivotal sequence that wound up bringing the film the sort of attention and outcry that worked in its favor.

> "Survive? A coward's survival! And at what a price—no love, no passion, no . . . no pity. Dead! Sol Nazerman, the walking dead!"
> —Mendel

It was decided to take Sol's most unbearable memory—being forced to watch his wife submit sexually to a Gestapo officer—and intercut it with a desperate whore's efforts to trade her body to the pawnbroker for needed cash. Boldly, Lumet decided that in order to make this sequence truly ugly and gut-wrenching in its impact, he would photograph both the actress playing the hooker and the actress playing Sol's wife bare-breasted from the front, an unprecedented move for an American motion picture at the time. The nudity would thereby come off as unpleasant rather than titillating, and the full nature of his wife's degradation—and the crippling effect it had left upon Sol—would be made clear.

After nearly two years of trying to get the project off the ground, filming began on October 7, 1963, and continued over a schedule of fifty-six days. Lumet, who prided himself on having never filmed in Hollywood up to that point, kept to this credo by shooting entirely in the New York metropolitan area. The site for Nazerman's pawnshop was found near the southeast corner of Park Avenue and 116th Street, which meant that the elevated train loomed nearby for added atmosphere. Other locations, in addition to those near and around Harlem, included a glimpse of the newly erected Lincoln Center and an apartment housing project behind the complex; Connecticut, which would stand in for Germany; and a typical suburban home at 185 North Marginal Road in Jericho, Long Island, facing the Jericho Turnpike. Richard Sylbert's appropriately cluttered pawnshop set was constructed at the Fox Movietone Studios on West Fifty-fourth Street. The total budget was $1 million plus.

Whereas the previous Lumet and Landau collaboration, *Long Day's Journey*, had been able to get a distribution deal with Embassy Pictures, *The Pawnbroker* was simply too iffy a project to get even an established independent company to handle it. They took the movie to the Berlin Film Festival in June

1964, where it was hailed as the most stunning of all the new entries and brought Steiger a Best Actor award. Despite this acclaim and the buzz on just how stark, uncompromising, and ultimately shattering this film was, the nudity was still a problem. Submitted for the customary seal of approval by the Production Code authority, Lumet and Landau were told that their movie violated the code because of "indecent and undue exposure." The authority's head, Geoffrey M. Shurlock, did, however, realize the maturity and dramatic validity behind the offending scenes and saw fit to have the appeals board discuss the issue in depth in hopes of coming out in favor of Lumet's vision. Miraculously, it did just that and, in March 1965, granted *The Pawnbroker* an exemption from its standard regulations, voting to let the film be passed and released exactly as it was. The board did, however, make clear to other filmmakers hoping to use this ruling to their benefit that this exemption was being made solely for this particular movie. Lumet and Landau managed to retain the film they wanted, to be distributed directly by Landau's company under the banner of the Landau Releasing Organization. Thanks to this landmark ruling, their investment was a safer bet than they had even hoped, because the controversy only piqued the public's interest in seeing the finished product.

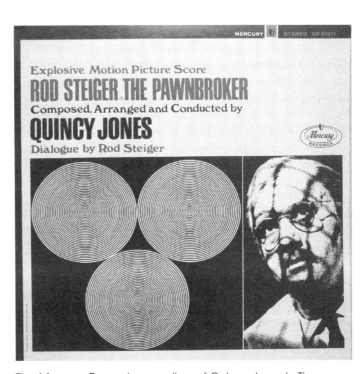

The Mercury Records recording of Quincy Jones's *The Pawnbroker* score includes a theme song by Jones and Jack Lawrence with vocals by Marc Allen that does not appear in the film itself.

No film had ever depicted so effectively and so relentlessly as *The Pawnbroker* the tawdry and hopeless side of urban living. Sol's motley customers were portrayed as dispirited, desperate, deluded, and sad. The movie was refreshingly honest in showing both the nonchalant day-to-day integration of the races as well as the unavoidable barriers erected between Caucasians, blacks, and Hispanics as the cultural overlap provoked tension, misunderstanding, and violence.

Always worth watching but never predictable when it came to how far he might extend his reach, Rod Steiger proved to be in every respect the perfect choice for the role of Sol Nazerman. The part called for a bulky actor who exuded the presence of someone older than his years, and Steiger certainly fit the bill physically, being able to convincingly play the character in his younger, happier years as well as in his latter, prematurely aged state. Knowing full well that a role this demanding and this good didn't come along every day, Steiger plunged so deeply into the self-induced lifelessness of this character that he was simply frightening to behold at times, painting the cinema's ultimate portrait of internalized despair, a being so emotionally destroyed by inhumanity that he has passed from bitterness into a resigned state of simply existing, unable to respond or wake up to the equally despondent beings around him until it is too late. It was by general consensus the pinnacle of his career, and whatever undisciplined trips into overemoting he would take later in life, *The Pawnbroker* was always around to remind people of the levels of greatness he could reach.

With some of the truly outstanding reviews of the year, *The Pawnbroker* became one of the top art-house attractions of 1965. But all that controversy spilled over into the mainstream venues as well, which meant that this important film was able to extend its reach outside the more exclusive bookings. There were plans, however, to get the to film play even wider. In 1966 American International Pictures took over distribution rights, but the studio compromised its most talked-about scene by taking the negative and blowing up the image so that both actresses were now seen from the shoulders up. Suddenly, because of this distortion, the once dreaded but increasingly ineffectual Catholic Legion of Decency could find satisfaction with the picture and lowered its "condemnation" classification to a less stringent A3, which meant Morally Objectionable. Apparently other religious organizations had looked beyond this puritanical carping: the National Catholic Office of Motion Pictures voted *The Pawnbroker* one of the best American films of 1965, securing a place for it on a list that didn't see fit to include George Stevens's expensive epic on the life of Christ, *The Greatest Story Ever Told* (United Artists).

CAT BALLOU

Academy Award Winner: Best Actor (Lee Marvin)

Academy Award Nominee: Screenplay—Based on Material from Another Medium; Song ("The Ballad of Cat Ballou"); Scoring of Music—Adaptation or Treatment; Film Editing

Top 10 Box Office Film

Opening date: May 7, 1965 (New York: June 24, 1965).

Columbia. A Harold Hecht Production.

Director: Elliot Silverstein. Producer: Harold Hecht. Screenplay: Walter Newman, Frank R. Pierson. Based on the 1956 novel *The Ballad of Cat Ballou*, by Roy Chanslor. Photography: Jack Marta. Art Director: Malcolm Brown. Set Decorator: Richard Mansfield. Miss Fonda's Gowns: Bill Thomas. Music: (Frank) DeVol. Songs by Mack David and Jerry Livingston: "The Ballad of Cat Ballou," "They Can't Make Her Cry," "They Made the Country Bleed/Round and Round They Rode," performed by Nat King Cole and Stubby Kaye; "All Your Tomorrows Were Yesterday," performed by Cole, Kaye, and Dorothy Claire. Choreographer: Miriam Nelson. Eastman Color by Pathé. 96 minutes.

CAST: Jane Fonda (Catherine "Cat" Ballou), Lee Marvin (Kid Shelleen/Tim Strawn), Michael Callan (Clay Boone), Dwayne Hickman (Jed), Nat King Cole (The Sunrise Kid), Stubby Kaye (Professor Sam the Shade), Tom Nardini (Jackson Two-Bears), John Marley (Frankie Ballou), Reginald Denny (Sir Harry Percival), Jay C. Flippen (Sheriff Cardigan), Arthur Hunnicutt (Butch Cassidy), Bruce Cabot (Sheriff Maledon), Burt Mustin (Accuser), Paul Gilbert (Train Messenger).

PLOT: While waiting to be hanged for murder, Cat Ballou looks back on how corruption and the murder of her father turned her into an outlaw, heading a misfit gang that included drunken gunman Kid Shelleen.

For a picture that relied so heavily on goofy laughs, slapstick, and broad ribbing, *Cat Ballou* had not even started out trying to be funny. The script derived from a straightforward novel by Roy Chanslor published nearly a decade before the release of the movie. The book included the title character, Kid Shelleen, Frankie Ballou, and Clay Boone, but it bore next to no resemblance to what ended up on film. Minus these names, it would be difficult for readers to equate what Chanslor put on the page with its cinematic adaptation. Chanslor's tale charted Cat's story from the meeting of her parents to her rescue from the gallows by her lover, Clay, and the women of Lariat, Wyoming. In the book, Cat's father, Frankie, is an outlaw who rides with Kid Shelleen; both men fall for Cat's mother, Cathy. Shelleen stays loyal to the Ballou family and joins on as a member of Cat's gang after her parents are killed during a stampede brought about by greedy land-grabber Adam Field. Field's hotheaded son, Abe, desires Cat, as does pretty much everyone else in the book, from

> "It's a hangin' day in Wolf City, Wyoming, Wolf City, Wyoming; 1894. They're gonna drop Cat Ballou through the gallows floor."
> —Professor Sam the Shade and the Sunrise Kid

Shelleen to a man of the cloth called Young Preach to ranch hand Jed French to Clay's spoiled, exasperating brother, Randy. Cat vengefully kills Adam and ends up falling in love with dashing outlaw Clay even before she meets him, prompting near-pathological jealousy from his sibling. Much blood is shed; Cat's grandfather, Old Doc, puts a bullet in bad guy Abe; Cat bears Clay's child, only to lose it while attempting to escape; and Randy is finally put out of his misery by the protective Kid. The novel had neither an affable Indian ranch hand nor a menacing twin brother for Kid Shelleen, both characters created for the film. It was, however, interrupted throughout by the lyrics of a ballad written about Cat and her gang, a device that proved helpful when it came to structuring the screenplay.

Despite Nat King Cole's many song interludes in *Cat Ballou*, Capitol Records chose to feature only two of them on the soundtrack album, filling the rest of the tracks with Cole vocals from such films as *Raintree County* and *In the Cool of the Day*.

The film rights had been purchased by the independent team of Harold Hecht, James Hill, and Burt Lancaster the same year as the book's publication, with the thought of filming it either as a serious western or even possibly as a musical; Tony Curtis was suggested as a costar for Lancaster. The project proved too difficult to adapt and was eventually abandoned, though Hecht hung on to the rights after the producing team dissolved their partnership. He eventually approached Columbia in 1964 with the idea of doing it as a comedy. Walter Newman's initial script was given a zanier spin by television writer Frank R. Pierson, who suggested another veteran of the tube, Elliot Silverstein, as the man to direct it. Hecht went with the novice director, who would receive for this film the best reviews of his mostly uneventful and undistinguished motion-picture career. Although she was initially skeptical about doing costume pictures, Jane Fonda agreed to play the heroine, greatly softened from her harder, more unrepentant counterpart in the novel, but Hecht got turned down by Kirk Douglas for the role of Kid Shelleen, changed from martyred soul into an outlandish drunk for the film. The part was instead filled by Lee Marvin (receiving $12,500 a week), who saw this as a great opportunity to do something completely unlike the mostly dramatic, often villainous parts he'd been mastering for over a decade. Just to make sure that he wouldn't be *too* far away from badman's territory, the revised story line required a terrifying villain who would turn out to be Shelleen's evil twin. This gave the actor a chance to have a showdown with himself.

There were two peripheral yet essential roles, and the addition of top-selling recording artist Nat King Cole and musical star Stubby Kaye (best known for playing Nicely-Nicely Johnson in *Guys and Dolls* on both stage and screen) as a pair of strolling balladeers who pop up throughout the film to sing directly to the audience about the events at hand yet are unseen by the other characters was a masterstroke that instantly established the movie as something engagingly out of the ordinary.

Cat Ballou was something of a quick shoot. Production started in and around Cañon City, Colorado, on September 28, 1964, with approximately two weeks of exteriors set against the magnificent mountain backdrops. These portions of the shoot included the use of Buckskin Joe Frontier Town, a re-creation of an old mining community that was a theme-park attraction in the state's Greenhorn Mountain area. The remainder of the movie used the Columbia soundstages and the Columbia Studio ranch, its western street standing in for Wolf City, Wyoming. Principal photography concluded on November 10.

For a movie that was often more fluffy and silly than surprising and witty, the critical response was very favorable, perhaps because it was not the norm for westerns to be played in a tone that was sometimes serious and downright cruel in nature (the heroine facing a noose, the abrupt and senseless murder of her father, the silver piece strapped across Tim Strawn's face to hide his missing nose, etc.) yet deliberately loony and unapologetically unsubtle. *Cat Ballou* had a lazy, engagingly winking sense of humor that produced mostly mild chuckles until the late arrival of Lee Marvin as a character so roasted by dangerous quantities of alcohol that his grotesquely unkempt appearance, with his glassy-eyed stare of confusion and his shock of unruly gray hair, was a sight gag in itself. Everything Marvin did, from being unloaded off the back of a stagecoach like a bundle of dirty laundry to literally not being able to hit the side of a barn until he can steady himself with a drink to his priceless appearance in the final rescue scene in which both he and his horse were propped against the side of a building, was outrageous to behold. It was the sort of scene-stealing comic role that few dramatic actors ever get a chance to sink their teeth into with such relish, and Marvin didn't let the opportunity pass without going for every possible laugh. After a while, his willingness to go the limit brought even the weakest moments of *Cat Ballou* into focus and elevated the picture into something sublime. The film became such a huge moneymaker during the summer of 1965 that Columbia very quickly found itself in the black for its very modest investment. Fonda (whose job it was to carry the picture by playing it relatively straight, which she did with underrated finesse) was now looked upon as one of the top female names in the business, and Marvin, after fourteen years as one of Hollywood's best character players, was at long last treated as a top-of-the-line star. He became the first (and to date the only) actor to win the Oscar for a genuine dual role in which he was portraying two different people in the same film.

SHENANDOAH

Academy Award Nominee: Sound

Top 10 Box Office Film

Opening date: June 3, 1965 (New York: July 28, 1965).

Universal.

Director: Andrew V. McLaglen. Producer: Robert Arthur. Screenplay: James Lee Barrett. Photography: William H. Clothier. Art Directors: Alexander Golitzen, Alfred Sweeney. Set Decorators: John McCarthy, Oliver Emert. Costumes: Rosemary Odell. Music: Frank Skinner. Editor: Otho Lovering. Technicolor. 105 minutes.

CAST: James Stewart (Charlie Anderson), Doug McClure (Sam), Glenn Corbett (Jacob Anderson), Patrick Wayne (James Anderson), Rosemary Forsyth (Jennie Anderson), Phillip Alford (Boy Anderson), Katharine Ross (Ann Anderson), Charles Robinson (Nathan Anderson), James McMullan (John Anderson), Tim McIntire (Henry Anderson), Eugene Jackson Jr. (Gabriel), Paul Fix (Dr. Tom Witherspoon), Denver Pyle (Pastor Bjoerling), James Best (Carter), George Kennedy (Col. Fairchild), Warren Oates (Billy Packer), Strother Martin (Engineer), Dabbs Greer (Abernathy), Harry Carey Jr. (Jenkins), Kevin Hagen (Mule), Tom Simcox (Lt. Johnson), Berkeley Harris (Capt. Richards).

PLOT: As the War Between the States rages on, widowed Virginia farmer Charlie Anderson refuses to take sides or join the battle, preferring to remain neutral and keep his family away from the conflict, a vow that becomes increasingly difficult as the altercation disrupts their once-peaceful existence, with tragic results.

When it came to plumbing drama from real-life tragedy, the Civil War was Hollywood's favorite American conflict. Having a nation battling itself meant that there was always an American hero on hand with whom audiences could sympathize, no matter which side they were on, and thanks to the era in which it was fought, the picture could always pass itself off as a western as well. When it came to depicting this bloody altercation and this most shattering lapse in democracy, it was customary to have

> **"It's like all wars—the undertakers are winnin' it."**
> **—Charlie Anderson**

Southerners or Northerners enthusiastically rally themselves up for fighting, only to discover down the line that they had lost far too much and too many of their brothers to find glory in victory. Writer James Lee Barrett wanted to approach the utter waste of war from a different angle. What about a story that focused on a man who most adamantly did *not* want to fight, did *not* see the benefit in war, and was proven all too tragically right in his resistance when the conflict erupts in devastation and crippling losses for everyone involved? In other words, Barrett very cleverly wanted to make an antiwar statement and figured retreating into history was the best way to do so, since Americans were notoriously sensitive when it came to seeing contemporary portrayals of war as futile and wasteful.

Barrett had written the original story treatment under the name *Fields of Honor*. It was purchased in May of 1963 by Universal, which had originally planned for Mervyn LeRoy to direct with a screenplay by John Lee Mahin. But following his first big box-office success at the helm of the John Wayne vehicle *McLintock!* (United Artists, 1963), Andrew V. McLaglen was sought in place of LeRoy, who was on the brink of retirement anyway. Barrett was promoted to screenwriter, while the perfect actor, James Stewart, was found to play the fiercely protective patriarch Charlie Anderson. Stewart's involvement in the picture shifted almost the entire emphasis of the story over to him, providing the actor, one of America's finest, with his very best role of the decade. While never less than fully dedicated to every part he played, *Shenandoah* was the rare property during the '60s that really gave Stewart a tremendous opportunity to tear into the very soul of so finely written a character, and he simply overpowered everyone else in his path with a heartfelt, often vibrantly caustic performance as this angry, unapologetically independent, impassioned, and heroic man.

Although the film emphasized intimacy above action, outdoor locales were needed to stage some Civil War battles, so Mohawk Valley, some twelve miles outside of Eugene, Oregon, was chosen. It had

The youngest (at least until the arrival of his niece) and oldest members of the Anderson family, as portrayed by Phillip Alford and James Stewart, respectively, share a quiet moment as the War Between the States rages on in *Shenandoah*.

the budgetary convenience for the studio of being West Coast based, yet to the undiscerning eye it could pass for the Shenandoah Valley in Virginia. Shooting began there on August 11, 1964, under Barrett's title, *Fields of Honor*. This was briefly changed to *Shenandoah Crossing* until someone realized that there was a more potent, simple eloquence in merely calling the film *Shenandoah*. To make sure that the conflicts onscreen looked sufficiently populated, some two hundred students from the nearby University of Oregon were engaged to don Confederate and Union uniforms to enact the battles. Once the location work was done, the rest of the picture was shot entirely on the Universal back lot, where the Anderson farm was constructed. The film was originally budgeted at $3 million, but McLaglen worked so fast and so efficiently that he brought the entire picture in for no more than $2.5 million.

McLaglen, whose work behind the camera would mostly prove rather ordinary, had found a property that was close to his heart, and he did the best work of his career on what he would always call his favorite among his pictures. Any danger of lapsing into false sentimentality was kept in check, and *Shenandoah* turned out to be not only grandly entertaining but surprisingly powerful and profound in dramatizing, as well as any picture before it, the heartbreaking destruction of peaceful lives and the ruination of the innocent wrought by war. The senseless and unexpected sniper attack on Jacob that prompts Anderson to berate his son's assailant and then leave him to live with his sinful deed, and the horrifying, unmotivated murder of James and Ann, caused audiences to bolt upright in their seats, deeply moved by the blunt injustice of these killings. This was one popular entertainment that really delivered the emotional goods, and the box-office response was terrific, landing the picture among the ten highest-grossing movies of the year and making it the biggest Universal hit since *That Touch of Mink* in 1962.

James Lee Barrett was convinced that this was not the end of the road for his property, of which he felt so proud that he was sure he'd be able to bring it to life yet again, this time as a stage musical. Working on the book with Peter Udell and Philip Rose, he managed to turn his original work into a surprisingly effective show, with lyrics by Udell and music by Gary Geld. Starring John Cullum as Charlie, *Shenandoah* premiered at the Alvin Theatre on Broadway on January 7, 1975, and ran 1,050 performances, earning Tonys for Cullum and for Barrett and his collaborators for their book. Having proven that his story could work equally well in two different incarnations, Barrett was fully rewarded for his faith in what would be his most enduring contribution.

THOSE MAGNIFICENT MEN IN THEIR FLYING MACHINES OR HOW I FLEW FROM LONDON TO PARIS IN 25 HOURS 11 MINUTES

Academy Award Nominee: Story and Screenplay—Written Directly for the Screen

Top 10 Box Office Film

Opening date: June 16, 1965.

Twentieth Century-Fox. A Ken Annakin Production.

Director: Ken Annakin. Producer: Stan Margulies. Screenplay: Jack Davies, Ken Annakin. Photography: Christopher Challis. Production Designer: Tom Morahan. Associate Art Director: Jim Morahan. Set Dresser: Arthur Taksen. Costumes: Osbert Lancaster. Music: Ron Goodwin. Title song by Ron Goodwin, performed by chorus. Editors: Gordon Stone, Anne V. Coates. Title Designer: Ronald Searle. Associate Producer: Jack Davies. Special Effects Supervisor: Ron Ballinger. Special Effects—Aircraft Mechanical Supervisor: Richard Parker. Todd A-O. Deluxe Color. 138 minutes (including entr'acte).

CAST: Stuart Whitman (Orvil Newton), Sarah Miles (Patricia Rawnsley), James Fox (Richard Mays), Alberto Sordi (Count Emilio Ponticelli), Robert Morley (Lord Rawnsley), Gert Froebe (Col. Manfred von Holstein), Jean-Pierre Cassel (Pierre Dubois), Eric Sykes (Courtney), Terry-Thomas (Sir Percy Ware-Armitage), Red Skelton (Neanderthal Man), Irina Demick (Brigitte/Ingrid/Marlene/Françoise/Yvette/Betty), Benny Hill (Fire Chief Perkins), Yujiro Ishihara (Yamamoto), Flora Robson (Mother Superior), Karl Michael Vogler (Capt. Rumpelstoss), Sam Wanamaker (George Gruber), Eric Barker (French Postman), Fred Emney (Elderly Colonel, Willie), Cicely Courtneidge (Colonel's Wife, Muriel), Gordon Jackson (MacDougal, a Pilot), Davy Kaye (Jean Pascal, Pierre's Chief Mechanic), John Le Mesurier (French Painter), Jeremy Lloyd (Lt. Parsons, a Pilot), Zena Marshall (Countess Sophia Ponticelli), Millicent Martin (Airline Hostess), Eric Pohlmann (Italian Mayor), Marjorie Rhodes (Waitress at Old Mill Cafe), William Rushton (Tremayne Gascoyne), Michael Trubshawe (Niven, Lord Rawnsley's Aide), Tony Hancock (Harry Popperwell, an Inventor), Norman Rossington (Assistant Fire Chief), Gerald Campion, Nicholas Smith, Graham Stark (Firemen), Jimmy Thompson (Photographer in Old Mill Cafe), Maurice Denham (Trawler Skipper), Ferdy Mayne (French Official), James Robertson Justice (Narrator).

PLOT: Hoping to bring together the best fliers from around the world to learn the craft of air travel from one another, Lord Rawnsley and his newspaper agree to sponsor an air race from London to Paris with a prize of ten thousand pounds.

In a year of planes (*The Flight of the Phoenix*), trains (*Von Ryan's Express*), and automobiles (*The Great Race*), Ken Annakin's lavishly lovely *Those Magnificent Men in Their Flying Machines* led the aerial parade by being both elegant and slapstick laden, a look at a bygone era that affectionately paid tribute to the pioneers who first took to the skies, sometimes in the most ridiculous of contraptions. It was these nutty machines that inspired writer Jack Davies in the first place. Upon seeing old newsreel footage of the early days of flight, he had been struck by how much comical mileage could be gotten simply out of the various designs of the planes. Meanwhile, director Ken Annakin had been hoping, as far back as the late 1940s, to do a film on John Alcock and Arthur Brown, the first Englishmen to fly the Atlantic. When he got wind of Davies's plans, he suggested they put their heads together and come up with something more universal in its appeal. This they certainly did. By envisioning an international air race that would attract various countries, and thereby various international stars to fill the roles, they assured interest from not only Great Britain, but also the United States, France, Italy, Germany, Scotland, and Japan. Since Twentieth Century-Fox agreed to bankroll the project, there was no doubt that a compromise of sorts would have to be made by the British writers when it came to scripting which of the countries would win the race.

The Davies-Annakin screenplay incorporated some real-life incidents that appeared at first glance to have been fabricated for the sake of humor but that had actually taken place, including the use of an anchor by one flier to try to stop his plane and a balloon duel using blunderbusses. (This latter was based on a true event from the Franco-Prussian War in 1870.) Brooklands Airfield, the hub of experimental flying in England in 1910, served as the inspiration for the film's Brookley Aerodrome. Searching for a

> "Trouble with these international affairs is that they attract foreigners."
> —Lord Rawnsley

location that had no anachronistic hindrances such as telephone wires or aerials, Annakin chose Booker Air Field, an abandoned Royal Air Force field located in Buckinghamshire, about forty miles from London. A good deal of the picture was shot here, and further location work took place in Southern England, including Dover, where a vintage day at the beach was spent by the fliers while mapping out the route across the English Channel. Only about 20 percent of the picture was filmed indoors, with sets for Heathrow Airport, the Old Mill Cafe, and Lord Rawnsley's mansion and office constructed at Pinewood Studios, along with a blue screen and hydraulic device for simulating close-ups of the actors flying their vehicles.

Of the total budget, $165,000 was allotted for the most essential attraction of the film, the planes, the construction of which was farmed out to various companies throughout England. They were to be built from scratch, using as models such real-life creations as the Antoinette (flown by Englishman Richard Mays), a Curtis biplane (Orvil's choice), and the most unusual of the flying machines, the Demoiselle (Frenchman Pierre's plane), a craft so delicate that it required someone very light to pilot it, hence the use of a female stunt flier. To assure that the filmmakers were covered should anything go wrong, each plane had two duplicates. The expense and attention to detail was well worth it, because some of the standout moments in the film were the simple, uncomplicated images of the handsome aircraft floating over the English landscape.

Shooting began on May 11, 1964, and continued throughout the summer of that year, with a planned road-show engagement set for the following summer—Fox knew that the movie would appeal greatly to children, which indeed it did, with very broad, Mack Sennett–like slapstick courtesy of Benny Hill's incompetent and frazzled fire brigade and Gert Froebe's bombastic, short-tempered German colonel. Alas, the screenplay never strayed too far from painting each of the nationalities in equally broad strokes to make sure the kids in the audience weren't subjected to too many complexities: the English were snooty and standoffish, the Americans were represented by a folksy cowboy, the

French flier was more interested in *amour* than racing, the Italian was given a large overbearing family, the deceptively quiet Japanese were seen shamelessly copying others' designs, and the Germans were portrayed as by-the-book, militaristic idiots. It was best not to dwell on such short-comings and sit back and enjoy the fun, the conflict in the plot being provided by the playful rivalries between the fliers as well as the more insidious plotting of Terry-Thomas's mustache-twirling villain (no doubt a homage to the silent-movie era in which the film was set). A brilliant concept in bracketing the film was the use of comedian Red Skelton, in his final movie role, representing different eras of man's attempts to fly, sequences cleverly intercut with real, oft-seen footage (some of it on display that same year in Disney's *The Monkey's Uncle*) of clodhopping planes failing to get any more than a few feet off the ground.

Four years later came Annakin and Davies's official follow-up, *Those Daring Young Men in Their Jaunty Jalopies* (Paramount, 1969). A British-French-Italian coproduction, it was released

The Gold Key comic book adaptation of *Those Magnificent Men in Their Flying Machines* omits, among other things, Red Skelton's delightful prologue depicting man's attempts to fly.

in the United Kingdom as *Monte Carlo or Bust* and had nearly a half hour sliced from its 122-minute running time for its American release. Substituting Tony Curtis for Stuart Whitman as the U.S. representative in the European auto race only brought to mind the superior *The Great Race* (Warner Bros., 1965), while Froebe, Eric Skyes, and, of course, Terry-Thomas were asked to do variations of their *Flying Machines* roles, with Terry-Thomas playing Sir Cuthbert Ware-Armitage, Sir Percy's brother. That film never came close to duplicating the success of the first, signifying that the genre of period slapstick was no longer of much interest to the public as the decade came to a close.

THE COLLECTOR

Academy Award Nominee: Actress (Samantha Eggar); Director; Screenplay—Based on Material from Another Medium

Opening date: June 17, 1965.

Columbia.

Director: William Wyler. Producers: Jud Kinberg, John Kohn. Screenplay: Stanley Mann, John Kohn. Based on the 1963 novel by John Fowles. Photography: Robert Surtees (in Hollywood), Robert Krasker (in England). Art Director: John Stoll. Set Decorator: Frank Tuttle. Men's Wardrobe: Jack Martell. Women's Wardrobe: Vi Alford. Music: Maurice Jarre. Editors: Robert Swink (Hollywood), David Hawkins (England). Technicolor. 119 minutes.

CAST: Terence Stamp (Freddie Clegg), Samantha Eggar (Miranda Grey), Mona Washbourne (Aunt Annie), Maurice Dallimore (Colonel Whitcomb, the Neighbor).

PLOT: Unhinged Freddie Clegg kidnaps art student Miranda Grey and imprisons her in a basement room in an isolated country house in hopes that she will grow to love him.

So audacious in premise that it stood out from all kidnapping stories told before or since, *The Collector* was the sort of risky, psychologically unnerving project that seemed tailor-made for the British New Wave of the '60s. Although it ended up with British leads, British locales, and a decidedly British flavor, it was in fact guided to the screen by one of America's leading directors, William Wyler, and shot principally on Hollywood soundstages. The source of this curious work was Englishman John Fowles's first novel, published in 1963, by which point it had already been bought for the screen by the London-based Blazer Films. This company's partners, Jud Kinberg and John Kohn, managed to sell Columbia executive Mike Frankovich on the property, picturing Terence Stamp, fresh from his Oscar-nominated debut in *Billy Budd* (Allied Artists, 1962), as the male lead, with Wyler at the helm. The veteran director had built a considerable reputation for his work with actors, and this film was principally a two-character piece that required a sure and steady hand. His only conditions for accepting the job were that he encounter as little meddling as possible from Kinberg and Kohn and that he receive final cut, making *The Collector* his to fashion to his satisfaction. Happy to have landed a man responsible for some of the most famous and lauded pictures of the past three decades, the producers agreed, even allowing the credit "A William Wyler Production" to appear onscreen.

Kohn worked on the screenplay in collaboration with Stanley Mann, hired on the strength of his adaptation of *The Mark*, which had dealt with the disturbing subject of child molestation. Fowles's original book was also challenging because of its intriguing structure: the first section was told entirely from the point of view of the kidnapper, Freddie Clegg, while the second and lengthiest section was the same series of events as chronicled by the victim, Miranda Grey, in her diary. The final two chapters returned to Clegg for a summing up of the tragedy. The script began and ended with Freddie's voice-over, making it appear as if the scenarists had chosen to adapt his part of the novel even though the rest of the film was devoid of his commentary. The character of Freddie's Aunt Annie was retained—she appeared ever so briefly in the person of the wonderful British character actress Mona Washbourne when she brought the news of her nephew's lottery winnings to his office—but her relationship to Freddie was not made overtly clear onscreen. In the book, she and Freddie's cousin (completely eliminated for the film) take off for a trip to Australia, adding the possibility of whether or not they would return to find Miranda incarcerated in the basement. A minor passage in the novel, when on his way to the village Freddie is confronted by a nosy neighbor about visiting his home, was built into a major suspense scene: the character actually shows up at the house while Miranda is bound and gagged in the bathroom.

> "This is death, don't you see? Nothing but death. These are dead. I'm dead. Everything here is dead. Is that what you love? Death?"
> —Miranda Grey

Certainly the most notable omission from the book was Miranda's older love interest, a cold and snobby artist, referred to by her as G. P.; their difficult relationship took up a good many of her diary entries. Wyler did in fact hire esteemed British actor Kenneth More to do this role, but his entire part (save for a glimpse from behind in a London pub) ended up on the cutting-room floor due to length. The often curt and spoiled behavior of Miranda was toned down considerably onscreen, making her far more sympathetic. Finally, the climax of the film was tightened and actually improved in the screen transition. On the page, Miranda had taken the blunt end of an ax to Freddie; that scene was followed by her misguided attempts to seduce him, and her eventual demise came another few days later after she has caught a cold from Freddie. Placing her unfortunate efforts to make love to her captive directly *before* her attack on him (here with a shovel) in a pouring rainstorm gave the scene more tragedy and impact: Miranda knows her timing has played an unfortunate part in her own demise once she is left bound and wet in her nightgown while Freddie goes to get his wound repaired.

Even before the screenplay was completed or the project had been given the go-ahead by Columbia, Kohn and Kinberg had asked Terence Stamp to play Freddie Clegg. The actor was resistant at first, simply because the strange, destructive behavior and motivations of this quirky and pathetic creation were so hard for him to grasp. Stamp's piercing eyes and the haunted, enigmatic quality he had displayed so well as Billy Budd were enough to convince Wyler and the rest that he was the right man for the part, and after considerable coaxing Stamp changed his mind. Once he was aboard he wanted to have some say in who would be sharing so much screen time with him. Samantha Eggar, who had been rising through the ranks in a handful of British films, was chosen for the female lead, a role that would prove as difficult to master as Stamp's. In fact, during rehearsals for the film, Wyler was so unhappy with her work that he fired her, shutting the production down while he decided how to rectify the situation. In a rare instance of second thoughts working to the benefit of a performer, he asked Eggar to do an entire reading of the screenplay with second unit director and editor Robert Swink so that he could judge whether he had been too hasty in his move. Wyler put Eggar back on the picture, but only under the condition that an established actress be present on the set to work as her drama and dialogue coach. This job went to Kathleen Freeman, the rubbery-faced character actress who would become best known for her many appearances opposite Jerry Lewis. Things did not get much easier for Eggar once the shooting began in mid-May of 1964 on the interior sets of the Clegg house and basement, built on the Columbia Pictures soundstages. Using the sort of mind games sometimes employed in the picture business to get a better performance out of a struggling actor, Wyler and Stamp decided to be both detached and unfriendly to the young actress, giving her the feeling of isolation and despair they felt necessary to bring out the terror and discomfort Miranda would be experiencing. It made for an unpleasant shoot, but their instincts were right, because Eggar rose to the occasion, matching Stamp scene for scene.

In late June the director and his two leads relocated to England for the exterior scenes, though Wyler left several of the American crew behind. A new cinematographer, Robert Krasker, was put in charge of photography, taking over from Hollywood's Robert Surtees, just as there were new craftspeople handling the sound, editing, and hairstyling. Shooting took place on the streets of London in the Hampstead area (the setting for the novel), with the actual kidnapping staged on a small lane called Mount Vernon, off Holly Hill. This was cho-

Maurice Jarre's score for *The Collector* as released on one of the more obscure record labels of its day, Mainstream.

sen because Stamp would be able to wedge his van in a tight alley near a wall, giving him the opportunity to abduct Eggar in broad daylight in a place that very convincingly could not be seen by a casual passerby. For the key location of Freddie's isolated home, a four-hundred-year-old farmhouse was found near Edenbridge in the western section of Kent. For scenes in the nearby village where Freddie gets his supplies while keeping Miranda under lock and key, the company shot in Westerham. Cast and crew returned to Columbia studios after this excursion, and filming wrapped in mid-July.

Aside from Freddie's memory flashback of his lottery win, brief moments of Miranda seen leaving her school, a quick scene of the injured Freddie pulling up to the hospital to seek help for his injury, and his final stalking of another innocent victim, the only scene requiring either of the leads to interact with another performer was Freddie's confrontation with his inquisitive neighbor, as played by Maurice Dallimore, a British actor chosen simply because he was based in Hollywood. The rest of the two-hour film required the audience to be engaged by the almost constant interaction of only two characters, mostly within the confines of a basement room—a major challenge to Wyler and his two leads. Stamp was nothing less than mesmerizing as the deluded and selfish but somehow pathetic abductor who firmly and cleverly takes command of the situation but hasn't a clue how to win another human being's trust or understanding through conversational give-and-take or empathy. Not being able to convey her inner thoughts through her diary musings as she had in the novel, Eggar was asked to alternate between fear, frustration, desperation, and a sense of power and managed to make some implausible situations thoroughly believable. Being very much from the old school, Wyler did not doll up the film with cinematic tricks or camera tics, but let the tone alternate between ominously discomforting, almost blackly comic in its absurdity, and serenely relaxed.

Because there was something so acceptable in the way that Freddie's actions were dramatized, it made the harrowing possibility of such a crime being carried out in the most seemingly timid of souls a very unsettling reality. When the film was over, just as many viewers were as enthralled as were maddened by the whole thing. Wyler insisted on keeping the dire and unhappy ending of the book despite Columbia's wishes to the contrary. Because of his decision, *The Collector* couldn't help but remain fixed in and haunt the minds of even those who were dismissive of it.

WHAT'S NEW PUSSYCAT

Academy Award Nominee: Song ("What's New Pussycat")

Top 10 Box Office Film

Opening date: June 22, 1965.

United Artists. A Charles K. Feldman Presentation of Famous Artists Productions and Famartists Productions, S. A.

Director: Clive Donner. Producer: Charles K. Feldman. Screenplay: Woody Allen. Executive Producer: John C. Shepridge. Photography: Jean Badal. Art Director: Jacques Saulnier. Set Dresser: Charles Mérangel. Costumes: Gladys de Segonzac. Miss Prentiss's Clothes: Fonssagrives-Tiel. Music: Burt Bacharach. Songs by Burt Bacharach (music) and Hal David (lyrics): "What's New Pussycat," performed by Tom Jones; "Little Red Book," performed by Manfred Mann, sung by Paul Jones; "Here I Am," performed by Dionne Warwick. Editor: Fergus McDonell. Titles: Richard Williams. Technicolor. 108 minutes.

CAST: Peter Sellers (Dr. Fritz Fassbender), Peter O'Toole (Michael James), Romy Schneider (Carole Werner), Capucine (Renée Lefebvre), Paula Prentiss (Liz Bien), Woody Allen (Victor Shakapopulis), Ursula Andress (Rita), Edra Gale (Anna Fassbender), Katrin Schaake (Jacqueline), Jess Hahn (Peter Werner), Eleonor Hirt (Sylvia Werner), Nicole Karen (Tempest O'Brien), Jean Paredes (Marcel), Jacqueline Fogt (Charlotte), Jacques Balutin (Etienne), Richard Burton (Man in Strip Club).

PLOT: Wanting to settle down with Carole Werner but worried that he can't stop making love to every beautiful woman he meets, Michael James seeks help from frustrated psychiatrist Fritz Fassbender, who is having no luck in wooing the patient of his dreams, Renée Lefebvre.

Whatever its shortcomings, the chaotic sex farce *What's New Pussycat* brought Woody Allen to the movies, for which devotees of irreverent and smart comedies are eternally grateful. As for his debut feature, which Allen both wrote and took a supporting role in (receiving an "introducing" credit in the opening titles), the great comedian-turned-filmmaker never minced words on how much he hated what director Clive Donner did with his screenplay, a factor that ultimately drove him to helming his own scripts in the future. Producer Charles K. Feldman had loved Allen's nightclub act and approached him with the idea of writing a screenplay to showcase Warren Beatty, who in his few short years as a Hollywood luminary had earned a reputation as quite a ladies' man (the very title of the film was, in fact, supposedly a favorite catchphrase of Beatty's). By the time production began, Beatty was long out of the picture, replaced by Peter O'Toole, who had become one of the hottest international stars of the time following leads in *Lawrence of Arabia* (Columbia, 1962) and *Becket* (Paramount, 1964). *Pussycat* would be his first big-screen comedy. This was certainly not for the case for the even hotter Peter Sellers, who had been so busy up

> "I can't help it, I'm a physical woman. I feel guilty about it, but I come from a family of acute nymphomaniacs. That includes my father and my two brothers."
> —Renée Lefebvre

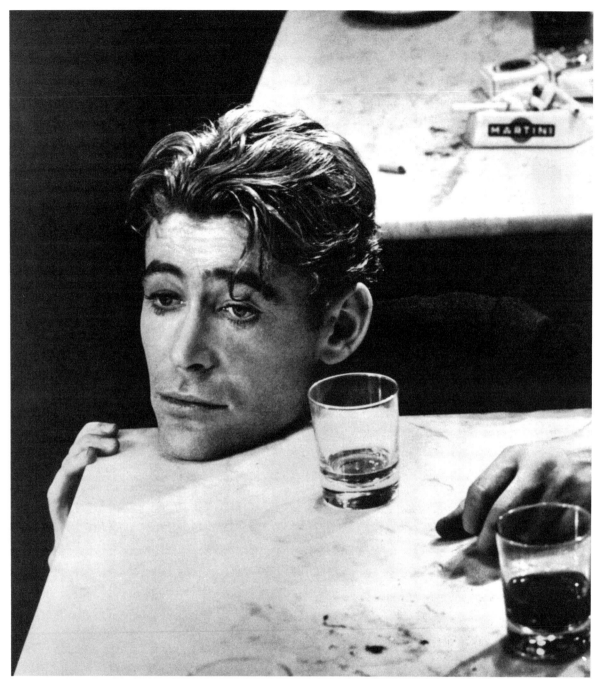

Peter O'Toole has had more than a few too many to drink in this scene from *What's New Pussycat.*

to this point that his strenuous workload had caused him to suffer a heart attack on the set of *Kiss Me Stupid* (Lopert) earlier in 1964. *Pussycat* marked his first time in front of the cameras since his recovery. O'Toole was more than willing to hold up production until Sellers was up and running once again so that he might have the opportunity to act opposite one of cinema's authentic comic geniuses.

Although the two men proved a definite boost to the box office, their involvement was a detriment to Allen, since some of his scenes were taken from his character and given to them, notably the strip-club confrontation with Sellers's Fritz (acted opposite O'Toole instead of Allen) and the drunken exploits beneath Miss Lefebvre's window (with Sellers subbing for Allen). In addition, the established stars didn't hesitate to change lines to their satisfaction, which further alienated Allen, who had long been an admirer of Sellers's ability to create multiple quirky screen personas. Allen remained a fan of Sellers, despite the strain of actually working with him, and instead blamed Donner for jazzing up the production with too many frills and for cranking up the broad level of the delivery, certainly a valid criticism in light of how thoroughly out of control the film became at times.

Filming took place in France, starting on October 5, 1964, and continued through the end of December. In addition to location work in Paris and Luzarches, the most notable site used in the film was the beautiful Château de Chaumontel, an eighteenth-century hunting lodge located between Paris and Chantilly that had been turned into a hotel in 1956. It stood in for the naughty "Chateau Chantel," the setting of the frantic climax which strove for a door-slamming frenzy worthy of Feydeau, but ended up being just another of too many sequences done in by clumsy timing and shameless mugging by many of the principals. Despite this anything-goes approach to the material, wisps of Allen's slyly off-kilter observations on life crept through, and cinema audiences were introduced to the writer's obsession with analysis, the film hinting at the deeper Allen to come with questions about humankind's futile pursuit of love, the validity of marriage, and monogamy versus random sexual encounters. It was all there, but it never seemed to be addressed in a manner that let you believe you were watching real human beings onscreen.

Indeed, *Pussycat*'s most praised and enduring contribution to pop culture turned out to be its thumping, irresistible title song, penned by the reliable Burt Bacharach and Hal David and sung full throttle by Welshman Tom Jones. Performed during Richard Williams's delightful, scrolling, animated credit designs, it got the movie off to a glorious and promising start with its unforgettable "whoa-o-o-o-o-oh!" refrains, suggesting something swinging and loose about to come. (Even Allen liked it!) It earned the film its one Oscar nomination and became a hit, reaching the number 3 position on the *Billboard* charts in July 1965 and helping usher in Jones's era of pop-idol fame.

VON RYAN'S EXPRESS

Academy Award Nominee: Sound Effects

Top 10 Box Office Film

Opening date: June 23, 1965.

Twentieth Century-Fox. A Mark Robson Production; a P-R Productions Picture.

Director: Mark Robson. Producer: Saul David. Screenplay: Wendell Mayes, Joseph Landon. Based on the 1964 novel by David Westheimer. Photography: William H. Daniels. Art Directors: Jack Martin Smith, Hilyard Brown. Set Decorators: Walter M. Scott, Raphael G. Bretton. Wardrobe: Mickey Sherrard. Music: Jerry Goldsmith. Editor: Dorothy Spencer. Special Photographic Effects: L. B. Abbott, Emil Kosa Jr. Deluxe color. CinemaScope. 117 minutes.

CAST: Frank Sinatra (Col. Joseph L. Ryan), Trevor Howard (Maj. Eric Fincham), Raffaella Carra (Gabriella), Brad Dexter (Sgt. Bostick), Sergio Fantoni (Capt. Oriani), John Leyton (Lt. Orde), Edward Mulhare (Capt. Costanzo), Wolfgang Preiss (Maj. Von Klemment), James Brolin (Pvt. Ames), John van Dreelen (Col. Gortz), Adolfo Celi (Major Battaglia), Vito Scotti (Italian Train Engineer), Richard Bakalyan (Corp. Giannini), Michael Goodliffe (Capt. Stein), Michael St. Clair (Sgt. Maj. Dunbar), Ivan Triesault (Von Kleist).

PLOT: After fleeing a prison camp abandoned by their Italian captors, Colonel Joseph Ryan and his fellow POWs seize control of a transport train in hopes of outwitting the Germans and reaching the safety of the Swiss border.

If nothing else, Frank Sinatra looked for diversity when it came to plotting out his film career, giving his public lighthearted comedies, dramas, musicals, and action films in equal doses, not only to display his ease in adapting to each genre, but to keep from falling into a routine pattern that would have bored the famously impatient actor-singer to death. Accepting an offer from Twentieth Century-Fox to appear in an adaptation of a recently published World War II novel, *Von Ryan's Express*, was a wise choice, because the finished film, despite the animosity between Sinatra and his director, Mark Robson, turned out to be the star's most satisfying credit in the action-adventure field. It was Robson who had latched onto the source material in the first place, buying the rights to David Westheimer's book, knowing he could

> "If you crab this, the Germans won't have to kill you, I'll do it myself."
> —Maj. Fincham

get one of the studios interested in a story of a massive prison camp break in light of the success of *The Great Escape* (United Artists, 1965). Fox agreed to produce the film and Robson hired Wendell Mayes and David Landon to adapt the work in time for the picture to start shooting by late summer of 1964, the same year of the novel's publication.

Despite Robson's desire to stick as closely to the original story line as possible, the scripters took many liberties with Westheimer's plot and characters. Although they retained the premise of a newly arrived, much-disliked American colonel leading a group of prisoners to safety by taking charge of a train, many

of the events needed more cinematic dash. To this end they let Ryan and his men actually get outside their Italian internment camp before being captured by the Germans (in the book they stayed put, having been fooled by a Nazi posing as an OSS major who issued orders from Allied Command), had the train rush dramatically through a raging fire caused by German mortar shells, allowed Ryan a more dangerous escape from his boxcar (crawling through a hole in the floor and dropping onto the tracks below), and gave the picture a smashing finale by having a trio of German fliers try to blast the locomotive as it races through the mountains in an attempt to outrun a troop train on its tail in hot pursuit.

None of this occurred in Westheimer's book, the latter half of which concentrated on Ryan and his men's efforts to dislodge each German guard perched atop the various train cars and to hold the major in charge of the train prisoner so he can get them safely past each railway stop. The film dispensed with the repetition of eliminating one guard after another by having the men take care of the bulk of their captors in one fell swoop, and it put the imprisoned major in a more subservient position, keeping him bound and gagged on the train while a German-speaking British officer gets the prisoners past the militaristic roadblocks—a far less plausible device because his accent would be easily detected by the enemy, though this revision brought more suspense to the proceedings. The film also eliminated Ryan's background shame of having

The front cover of the Signet edition of David Westheimer's novel *Von Ryan's Express* emphasizes the film's action and its star, Frank Sinatra, while the back cover contains an image of actress Raffaella Carra, whose character of Gabriella is nowhere to be found in the book.

caused his flight instructor's death, as well as his having played a part in the death of his camp assistant, Lt. Peterson, a character cut from the film altogether. To show how the Italians turned their alliance to the Americans after the takeover by Germany, the screenplay allowed a compassionate captain from the prison camp to accompany Ryan and his soldiers on their escape (in the novel the same character is responsible for blocking their initial escape). Similarly, the Italian train engineer gladly joins up with his hijackers, expressing disgust for the SS, whereas in the book he tried to sabotage the locomotive by allowing the water to run out.

Perhaps the most notable change from page to screen was one that emphasized Hollywood's need to put a sexual spin on a story that ran very well without one, changing a German radio operator to the major's Italian mistress. The other main rewrite involved the ending, which Sinatra himself insisted on. He felt that Ryan should be sacrificed just as he gets his men over the border to freedom. Overriding the protests of horrified studio executives, the star got his big death scene and gave the film one of its most memorable images as the heroic colonel is shot down on the tracks just inches from catching hold of the last car as it pulls away from its savior. This would be a rare (and unheralded) case of Hollywood's discarding a traditional happy ending in favor of a grimmer, more dramatically potent one.

Principal photography began on August 3, 1964, in such Italian locations as Cortina and Malaga before the cast and crew moved on to Spain. This was something of a surprise, for Sinatra had vowed to stay away from that country after his hellish experience shooting *The Pride and the Passion* (United Artists, 1957) there a decade earlier. The company then set up shop at the Twentieth Century-Fox Studios in October for interiors, scheduling that proved fortunate for Sinatra's personal life. Shooting on the lot at the same time was the television series version *Peyton Place*, which starred, among others, nineteen-year-old Mia Farrow. The supporting cast of *Von Ryan* included John Leyton, with whom Farrow had worked on her first picture, *Guns at Batasi* (Twentieth Century-Fox, 1964), and when she visited him on the set she met Sinatra. The two performers became one of Hollywood's most incongruous, highly publicized couples when they married in 1966.

THE SANDPIPER

Academy Award Winner: Best Song ("The Shadow of Your Smile")

Opening date: June 23, 1965 (New York: July 15, 1965).

MGM. A Filmways Presentation of a Martin Ransohoff Production, Filmways-Venice.

Director: Vincente Minnelli. Producer-Story: Martin Ransohoff. Screenplay: Dalton Trumbo, Michael Wilson. Adaptation: Irene Kamp, Louis Kamp. Photography: Milton Krasner. Art Directors: George W. Davis, Urie McCleary. Set Decorators: Henry Grace, Keogh Gleason. Costumes: Irene Sharaff. Music: Johnny Mandel. Song: "The Shadow of Your Smile," by Johnny Mandel (music) and Paul Francis Webster (lyrics), performed by chorus. Editor: David Bretherton. Laura's Paintings: Elizabeth Duguette. Redwood Sculpture: Edmund Kara. Metrocolor. Panavision. 117 minutes.

CAST: Elizabeth Taylor (Laura Reynolds), Richard Burton (Dr. Edward Hewitt), Eva Marie Saint (Claire Hewitt), Charles Bronson (Cos Erickson), Robert Webber (Ward Hendricks), James Edwards (Larry Brant), Torin Thatcher (Judge Thompson), Tom Drake (Walter Robinson), Doug Henderson (Phil Sutcliff), Morgan Mason (Danny Reynolds).

PLOT: Minister Edward Hewitt finds his marriage in jeopardy when he begins an affair with Bohemian beach artist Laura Reynolds, whose free-spirited lifestyle offers a respite from his staid existence.

In early 1964 Elizabeth Taylor and Richard Burton made the leap from being Hollywood's most famous lovers to its most famous (and overpublicized) married couple. Not only were they everywhere in the news and on the covers of the fan magazines, but they also seemed determined to spend as much time together on the big screen as they could. Producer Martin Ransohoff, hoping to cash in on their red-hot celebrity status, went so far as to pen his own screen story, one that he hoped would entice them—a glossy love triangle involving a married minister and a free-spirited beachcomber. The Burtons were excited not so much by the premise as by the money and managed to ensure a salary of $1 million for her and $500,000 for him, under the condition that they be provided with a director of stature who might be able to lift the material above its soap-opera superficialities. Vincente Minnelli agreed to step behind the camera, figuring it might be the right time to get involved in something that promised to make some big bucks—something no film of his had done in several years.

> "I still don't know much about your attitude towards marriage."
> —Edward
>
> "I'm withholding judgment until I see a happy one. How's yours? 'Adequate,' as they say?"
> —Laura

Armed with a screenplay that nobody involved in the project thought very highly of, the movie (under the name *The Flight of the Sandpiper*) started shooting on September 7, 1964, at some stunning California locations, including Big Sur. This gave cinematographer Milton Krasner ample opportunity to capture the crashing waves and steep hills in a rich Metrocolor glow, especially during the opening credits, which established a serene mood that the rest of the picture never lived up to. This picturesque area was where Taylor's beachside "shack" was built, which meant that credibility was already missing from the word go, since nobody barely making a living selling a piece or two of her amateur artwork could af-

ford a place with so magnificent a view. The company also shot at the Cypress Point Golf Course, along Highway 101, and in San Dimas, which provided the campus grounds of the San Simeon Episcopalian School that Laura's son is forced to attend. Rather than finish up the movie logically by shooting the interiors at the MGM studios in Culver City, the Burtons' contract demanded that they do part of the film outside of the United States to qualify for a tax cut. Therefore, the interiors of Laura's beach house, Dr. Hewitt's office, Judge Thompson's chambers, and other sets were constructed at the Studios de Boulogne in Paris, where the company relocated on October 10. This expensive move, added to the hefty star salaries, pushed the cost of this very small and intimate drama to a hefty $5.6 million.

Because he made no secret about being in it for the money, Burton hardly committed himself fully to the role, though he did, in fact, come off far better than his wife. Having just played a man of God in *Becket* (Paramount, 1964), as well as a former man of God in *The Night of the Iguana* (MGM, 1964), he seemed all too convincing as a stodgy minister, shaken by his unexpected carnal desires. Taylor, on the other hand, was far too glamorous for anyone to believe her as the sort of bohemian who stands barefoot on the shore, paints seascapes, and badmouths conformity. Very much out of her element, she was solely

The sheet music for *The Sandpiper's* Oscar-winning "The Shadow of Your Smile" contains more lyrics than are heard in the finished film, the introductory verse explaining how "You held a piper in your hand to mend its broken wing."

responsible for all the genuinely silly moments in the picture; her acting lost control and induced giggles during scenes that were supposed to be dramatically potent. In order to emphasize the fact that this was a woman who has lived life in her own way, Taylor was given a discreet seminude scene, meant to shock Burton's character as well as 1965 audiences, with the actress posing topless, her hands cupped around her breasts, while Charles Bronson carved her image from a tree trunk. There were also scenes of the unclothed Burtons resting under the sheets together, talk (but no displayed use) of marijuana and heroin (referred to here by Bronson as "h"), and the matter-of-fact friendship between a white woman and a black man. It was all very safe and superficial, and this story of forbidden love was allowed to go on much too long, considering it was very hard to really give a damn whether these two people did or didn't end up together. The critics trounced the picture, but Ransohoff's hunch was right, and *The Sandpiper* became one of the top grossers of 1965.

THE GREAT RACE

Academy Award Winner: Best Sound Effects

Academy Award Nominee: Cinematography—Color; Sound; Song ("The Sweetheart Tree"); Film Editing

Top 10 Box Office Film

Opening date: July 1, 1965 (New York: September 15, 1965).

Warner Bros. A Patricia–Jalem–Reynard Production.

Director: Blake Edwards. Producer: Martin Jurow. Screenplay: Arthur Ross. Story: Blake Edwards, Arthur Ross. Photography: Russell Harlan. Production Designer: Fernando Carrere. Set Decorator: George James Hopkins. Costumes: Don Feld. Miss Wood's Clothes: Edith Head. Music: Henry Mancini. Songs by Henry Mancini (music) and Johnny Mercer (lyrics): "He Shouldn't-a Hadn't-a Oughtn't-a Swang on Me," performed by Dorothy Provine; "The Sweetheart Tree," performed by Jackie Ward dubbing for Natalie Wood. Choreographer: Hermes Pan. Editor: Ralph E. Winters. Special Effects: Danny Lee. Sound: M. A. Merrick. Technicolor. Panavision. 160 minutes (including overture, entr'acte, and exit music).

CAST: Jack Lemmon (Professor Fate/Prince Hapnick), Tony Curtis (The Great Leslie), Natalie Wood (Maggie DuBois), Peter Falk (Max), Keenan Wynn (Hezekiah), Arthur O'Connell (Henry Goodbody), Vivian Vance (Hester Goodbody), Dorothy Provine (Lily Olay), Larry Storch (Texas Jack), Ross Martin (Baron Rolfe von Stuppe), George Macready (General Kuhster), Marvin Kaplan (Frisbee), Hal Smith (Mayor of Boracho), Denver Pyle (Sheriff), Frank Kreig (Race Starter).

PLOT: In the early 1900s, the Great Leslie and his archrival, the evil Professor Fate, agree to participate in the ultimate automobile race, taking them from New York City to Paris.

Blake Edwards had an idea for a comedy, but if executed properly it was going to cost an awful lot of money. What he had in mind was a grandiose, slapstick period romp about an elaborate automobile race between New York and Paris. Although the geographical obstacle of just how cars were supposed to cross the Bering Strait between Alaska and Russia gave the premise an outrageous slant, this concept was, in fact, based on a real incident. In 1908 the *New York Times* and *Le Matin*, a Paris-based newspaper, co-sponsored just such a competition, covering a 22,000-mile route. The drivers started from New York's Times Square on February 8 of that year; the winner, George Schuster, driving a Thomas Flyer auto, arrived at the finish line in Paris on July 30, 169 days later. Edwards and writer Arthur Ross, who had worked together on the CBS television series *Mr. Lucky* (1959–60), envisioned their leading characters as broad parodies of silent-movie heroes and villains, the former a too-good-to-be-true daredevil with teeth that genuinely sparkled and the latter a black-hatted, hissable bad guy with a mustache elaborate enough to

> "It's been my experience, General, that there is little advantage to winning if one wins too easily."
> —The Great Leslie

twirl. Producer Martin Jurow brought the idea of *The Great Race* (as it was to be called) to Warner Bros., which saw great potential for a rollicking road-show presentation.

Knowing that Edwards's concept required a good many overseas locations, as well as expensive pe-riod costumes and set designs, Warner Bros. insisted on some top stars to carry the film. For his scene-chewing villain, Professor Fate, Edwards wanted the very last actor anyone would accuse of authentic malice, the ever-likable Jack Lemmon, which was exactly what made his appearance in the role so much fun from the get-go. It was up to Lemmon to ham it to the hilt without sacrificing the laughs, huffing and puffing at dangerous levels, making the scheming professor more a buffoon than a threat. As if this weren't challenging enough, Lemmon was handed a second part with equal mugging potential, the ef-fete and deliriously dotty Prince Hapnick, an immature royal who appeared to be in a constant state of chemical alteration. As proof of his consummate genius as an actor, Lemmon was a delight in both roles; few performers ever seemed to be having so much fun letting go while knowing exactly how far to extend themselves and just when to hold back. Edwards had originally wanted Charlton Heston for the role of the heroic, self-assured "Great Leslie," and the actor found the script funny enough to want to do the part, only to be forced to pass when he discovered that the shooting schedule would conflict with his commitment to Fox's *The Agony and the Ecstasy* (1965). Just how someone with minimal experience in comedy would have fared in such a project remains an unsolved mystery. Instead, Tony Curtis, a far more able farceur and an actor whom Edwards had previously directed, was given the part and found the perfect balance between send-up caricature and genuine dashing man of action.

Jack Lemmon expresses his displeasure at sharing his bed with the royal Carpanian pugs as flunky George Macready looks on in this scene from *The Great Race*.

The third participant in this star trio was less enthusiastic. In order to get Warners to back her next project, *Inside Daisy Clover* (1965), Natalie Wood reluctantly agreed to sign on as *Race*'s crusading feminist reporter Maggie DuBois. Wood never could get in sync with this broadly played sort of material and was deeply unhappy during the whole seemingly endless shoot. Compared to her two shrill and miscalculated attempts at comedy that preceded and followed this film, *Sex and the Single Girl* (Warner Bros., 1964) and *Penelope* (MGM, 1966), her game performance brought forth some pleasing results; she looked beautiful in the decorative costumes, and she never fell completely behind any of her fellow actors in spirit, fully hiding whatever displeasure she felt offscreen.

The Great Race began filming on June 15, 1964, in Vienna, where the Karlskirche was used for the coronation ceremony in which Professor Fate is nearly crowned in place of the kidnapped Hapnick, and where the Hofburg, the Royal Winter Palace of the Habsburg monarchs, stood in for the prince's residence. From there the company moved on to Salzburg, where they filmed a chase through the streets that climaxed at a pie shop, and found an appropriately isolated lakeside castle (Schloss Anif) for the site of Hapnick's kidnapping and rescue. Next stop was Paris for the film's finale under the Eiffel Tower and for a stunt that had one of the eight Hannibal 8 autos built for the film bouncing down the steps in front of Sacre Cœur in Montmartre. Returning to the United States, Edwards used such northern California locations as Lone Pine, where a stranded Wood is rescued by Curtis, and Jamestown, where Fate's defective rocket sled was set up. The remainder of the filming was done back at the Warner Bros. studio, including the key set piece, a full-scale custard pie fight that was intended to be the final word on this sort of knock-down free-for-all that became synonymous with silent film comedy. Without the benefit of silence on his side, Edwards was taking a risk in aiming for something so thoroughly associated with a bygone era, but it paid off, thanks to the clever, slow building of the sequence and the precision timing of the shots. As future generations became less and less inclined to watch movies minus sound, the pie fight from *The Great Race* would be most viewers' first reference point at the mention of the subject.

With a final nerve-wracking cost of $12 million, *The Great Race* now had the dubious distinction of being the priciest comedy yet made. In slapping his name possessively before the title, Blake Edwards may have been hoping for a higher realm of recognition, but this sort of stature was considered acceptable for only a very few filmmakers and earned the picture a lot of unfavorable feelings before it even opened. The same was true for some of the ad copy, which none too modestly proclaimed the film "The Funniest Comedy of All Time," a tough assessment for *any* movie to live up to. Although the opulent production never once overwhelmed the grand fun the picture had to offer, the majority of the critics felt otherwise and slammed the farce for putting size before laughs. Nothing that hyped itself in advance this arrogantly was ever going to please reviewers, who preferred their laughs dark or subtle, so the film had an uphill battle overcoming the bad press in order to make back its enormous cost. Fortunately, *The Great Race* was just the sort of smashing entertainment that worked its spell on most family audiences, who were not looking for lacerating irony or dry wit, but simply an undemanding belly laugh or two. Edwards could run hot and cold with his staging of slapstick, but he was very much on the right track throughout most of the picture and delivered the goods. One of the highest-grossing pictures of 1965, *The Great Race* at least *looked* like a hit, though in truth Warners had to depend on later television sales and overseas bookings (some of which trimmed most of the sequences taking place at the newspaper office) for the movie to pay back all the money they had spent.

SHIP OF FOOLS

Academy Award Winner: Best Cinematography—Black and White; Best Art Direction–Set Decoration—Black and White

Academy Award Nominee: Picture; Actor (Oskar Werner); Actress (Simone Signoret); Supporting Actor (Michael Dunn); Screenplay—Based on Material from Another Medium; Costume Design—Black and White

Opening date: July 28, 1965.

Columbia. A Stanley Kramer Production.

Director-Producer: Stanley Kramer. Screenplay: Abby Mann, based on the 1962 novel by Katherine Anne Porter. Photography: Ernest Laszlo. Production Designer: Robert Clatworthy. Set Decoration: Joseph Kish. Costumes: Bill Thomas. Miss Leigh's Clothes: Jean Louis. Music: Ernest Gold. Songs: "Heute Abend, geh'n wir bummeln auf der Reeperbahn" and "Irgendwie, irgendwo, irgendwann," by Ernest Gold (music) and Jack Lloyd (lyrics), performed by José Ferrer. Editor: Robert C. Jones. Black and white. 149 minutes.

CAST: Vivien Leigh (Mary Treadwell), Simone Signoret (La Condesa), José Ferrer (Siegfried Rieber), Lee Marvin (Bill Tenny), Oskar Werner (Dr. Wilhelm Schumann), Elizabeth Ashley (Jenny Brown), George Segal (David Scott), José Greco (Pepe), Michael Dunn (Karl Glocken), Charles Korvin (Capt. Thiele), Heinz Ruehmann (Julius Lowenthal), Lilia Skala (Frau Hutten), Barbara Luna (Amparo), Christiane Schmidtmer (Lizzi Spockenkieker), Alf Kjellin (Freytag), Werner Klemperer (Lt. Huebner), John Wengraf (Graf), Olga Fabian (Frau Schmitt), Gila Golan (Elsa Lutz), Oscar Beregi (Herr Lutz), Stanley Adams (Prof. Hutten), Karen Verne (Frau Lutz), Charles de Vries (Johann), Lydia Torea (Pastora), Henry Calvin (Fat Spanish Laborer), Paul Daniel (Carlos), David Renard (Woodcarver), Rudy Carrella (Ric), Silvia Marino (Rac), Anthony Brand (Guitarist).

PLOT: A disparate group of passengers sailing from Veracruz to Bremerhaven, Germany, on the eve of the Nazi takeover, experience the growing insecurities, prejudices, and desperation of the changing political scene, while dealing with their own personal crises.

After proving he could go broad and comical for *It's a Mad Mad Mad Mad World* (United Artists, 1963), director-producer Stanley Kramer was back to more serious matters with his follow-up picture, *Ship of Fools*, a property he was already developing before *Mad World* went into production, having purchased the rights to Katherine Anne Porter's bleak novel prior to its 1962 publication. (The author, whose only novel this would be, was seventy-two at the time of its debut.) Porter claimed to have worked on her book over a thirty-year period, crediting a medieval poem, Sebastian Brant's 1494 satire *Das Narrenschiff* (Ship of Fools), as her inspiration. It tells of no fewer than 110 separate follies of the passengers aboard a ship bound for Narragonia, the island of fools. For her novel Porter pared down the number of passengers, though she still had quite a cast of characters, certainly more than could be dealt with in a manageable screenplay. Kramer hired Abby Mann, who had done such a splendid job for him on *Judgment at Nuremberg* (United Artists, 1961), to prune away at the lengthy book, giving a stronger emphasis to Porter's more engaging creations, relegating others to a few key scenes, deleting some altogether, and sometimes reassigning dialogue or scenes to those retained in the finished script. As a result, the snobby, diary-keeping Frau Rittersdorf; the Cuban medical students who alternately support and taunt the exiled Condesa; Señora Ortega and her Indian nursemaid; and the volatile Swede Arne Hansen were eliminated from the story line. The dog-obsessed Huttens were trimmed down considerably from their importance in the book, as were the Lutz family and their homely, socially awkward daughter Elsa (considerably Hollywoodized in looks for the film), and, most regrettably, Frau Schmitt, whose realization of her insignificance in light of her husband's death made her one of Porter's most subtly tragic figures. Once Kramer discovered that his favorite actor, Spencer Tracy, was too ill to take on the role of the disillusioned Dr. Schumann, the physician's age was lowered from sixty to the forties, making it suitable for Oskar Werner to take over the part. Scenes that had taken place on shore in Veracruz, Mexico, and in Tenerife, Spain, were omitted in order to keep a more claustrophobic atmosphere aboard ship.

> "Everybody on this ship is in love. Love me, whether or not I love you. Love me, whether I am fit to love. Love me, whether I am able to love. Even if there is no such thing as love, love me."
> —Mary Treadwell

Although there is no doubt that the completed film was a surprisingly downbeat one for a big-budgeted Hollywood production, Mann and Kramer knew they had to give audiences some breathing room amid all the sadness, despair, and unpleasant truths about mankind's failure to communicate and embrace one another, a theme Porter emphasized relentlessly in her book. To this end, the ship's captain was made far less hateful in his bigotry, and the one Jewish character, Lowenthal, was changed from being just as intolerant as his fellow passengers to a man so optimistic and reasonable that he became the most heartbreakingly misguided of all the characters. Mann also made the story's other principal outcast, hunchbacked dwarf Karl Glocken, our host of sorts, allowing him to speak directly to the camera at the outset and for the final scene of the movie. It was difficult enough to find an accomplished dwarf actor to carry this pivotal role, so Glocken's hump was, not surprisingly, disposed of. Most crucially, in order to give the growing menace of Nazism more urgency, the story was pushed forward from 1931 to the following year.

Like its literary source, *Ship of Fools* was not plot driven, but consisted of an often pessimistic series of vignettes. ("I wonder," theorizes Dr. Schumann, "if life is as stupid and meaningless as it seems to be on this ship.") It was therefore up to Mann to deliver a strong screenplay that could be played to the hilt by an exceptional cast. The initially disconnected pieces of each story line began to weave into an engrossing whole almost seamlessly after a drab beginning in which the actors, seated for dinner or lounging about on deck, reveal bits of information about themselves. Kramer's visual style was blatantly old-fashioned, the black-and-white photography adding to the feeling that this movie was not just set but actually taking place in 1932. Not unlike *Nuremberg*, this was a film fashioned to make some thought-provoking, often disturbing observations about humanity and to allow the actors to really sink their teeth into their parts.

Perhaps none seized this opportunity more impressively than did Oskar Werner, who had become an international name recently because of the art-house success of Francois Truffaut's *Jules et Jim* (Janus, 1962). Despite having made a considerable impression way back in the 1951, in the Oscar-nominated Twentieth Century-Fox drama *Decision before Dawn*, Werner had never actually shot a picture in Hollywood before (and never would again). Kramer was so satisfied with his work that they planned to reteam for a film about Andersonville Prison in Georgia, but the project never materialized. Just as he was able to handle the notoriously cranky Tracy, Kramer was just about the only person involved in *Fools* who could get along with Werner, because the actor's very moody and confrontational personality alienated him from most of the cast. In front of the cameras, however, he and Simone Signoret created magic in their incredibly nuanced portrayals of two people grasping for understanding and intimacy in the face of an utterly hopeless future. They were both so good in their performances that they formed the very backbone of the piece, riveting attention whenever the screenplay shifted focus to them. Both actors earned Oscar nominations for their work, as did the most unusual member of the cast, Michael Dunn (born Gary Neil Miller in Oklahoma), who had a congenital bone disease that

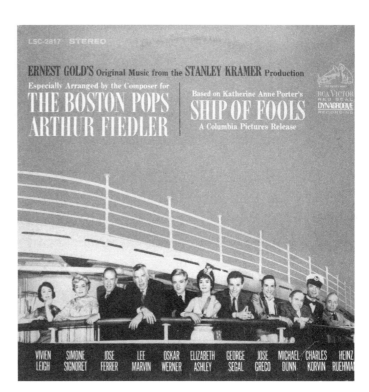

The RCA Dynagroove recording of Ernest Gold's score for *Ship of Fools* as performed by the Boston Pops contains such tracks as "Charleston for an Old Fool" and José Ferrer's interpretation of "Irgendwie, irgendwo, irgendwann (Somehow, Somewhere, Sometime)."

prevented him from growing. Kramer cast him in the crucial role of Glocken on the basis of his Tony-nominated performance in the 1963 Broadway adaptation of *The Ballad of the Sad Cafe*, and his astute, low-key work as the wizened misfit who has accepted his fate made him, if nothing else, the shortest actor (3'6") to ever be in the running for an Oscar.

The fine material on hand was instrumental in bringing Signoret to the project since she was reluctant to work in Hollywood, so far from her home base in France (like Werner, she never again returned there to make another film). The same was true of Vivien Leigh, who, since becoming a major name in the late 1930s, had never played anything less than a starring role. Here, in her first film in four years, she was part of an ensemble; she was compensated for her relatively small role by receiving top billing. Her cynical, beaten characterization of a woman who has destroyed her own happiness was nothing short of magnificent, and she boldly allowed herself to look less than her best, notably in a harrowing scene in which she smeared her face with makeup, wondering whether this curious custom was enough to attract a man. Leigh, whose ill-health had kept her from working frequently over the years, was very enthusiastic about the role, and it proved to be a worthy curtain to her all too short career; she passed away only two years after *Fool*'s release.

With production commencing on June 22, 1964, Kramer managed to shoot the whole film on the Columbia Pictures lot, using process shots and photos for the few distant images of the *Vera* at sea, as well as rear projection done by his second unit team. Because of its very pessimistic nature, *Ship of Fools* struggled to find a large audience outside of the major cities and was treated to the customary batch of mixed notices reserved for Stanley Kramer's unapologetically straightforward filmmaking style. Although Kramer himself was left off the list of nominations, *Ship* was rewarded for its uncompromising view of humanity with eight Oscar nominations, including the esteemed Best Picture spot.

DARLING (United Kingdom)

Academy Award Winner: Best Actress (Julie Christie); Best Story and Screenplay—Written Directly for the Screen; Best Costume Design—Black and White

Academy Award Nominee: Picture; Director

Opening date: August 3, 1965 (London: September 16, 1965).

Embassy. A Joseph E. Levine Presentation of a Joseph Janni Production for Vic Films.

Director: John Schlesinger. Producer: Joseph Janni. Screenplay: Frederic Raphael. Based on an idea by Frederic Raphael, John Schlesinger, and Joseph Yanni. Photography: Ken Higgins. Art Director: Ray Simm. Set Decorator: David Ffolkes. Costumes: Julie Harris. Music: John Dankworth. Editor: James Clark. Black and white. 122 minutes.

CAST: Laurence Harvey (Miles Brand), Dirk Bogarde (Robert Gold), Julie Christie (Diana Scott), Roland Curram (Malcolm), José Luis de Villalonga (Prince Cesare Della Romita), Alex Scott (Sean Martin), Basil Henson (Alec Prosser-Jones), Helen Lindsay (Felicity Prosser-Jones), Pauline Yates (Estelle Gold), Tyler Butterworth (William Prosser-Jones), Peter Bayliss (Lord Grant), Jean Claudio (Raoul Maxim), Ernest Walder (Kurt), Lucille Soong (Allie), Sidonie Bond (Gillian), Carlo Palmucci (Curzio), James Cossins (Basildon), Lydia Sherwood (Lady Brentwood), Georgina Cookson (Carlotta Hale), Brian Wilde (Willett), David Harrison (Charles Glass), Dante Posani (Gina), Ann Firbank (Sybil), Richard Bidlake (Rupert Crabtree), Trevor Bowen (Tony Bridges), Annette Carell (Billie Castiglione), John Schlesinger (Voice of Interviewer).

PLOT: Diana Scott looks back on how she reached her goal of fame and wealth, becoming a high-powered fashion model while leaving a trail of used and embittered men in her wake.

The idea for eviscerating the world of empty ambition came from one of England's brightest new talents, John Schlesinger, who, after years of working on television, had made a giant leap to the forefront of the British New Wave with his very first feature, *A Kind of Loving* (Governor, 1962), the story of a young newlywed feeling trapped by his marriage. Schlesinger confirmed every bit of the initial praise with his follow-up, *Billy Liar* (Continental, 1963), in which its protagonist chose fantasy as his preferred form of escape from his dead-end existence. It was while working on the latter that Schlesinger was told of a real-life scandal in which a promiscuous young woman who had been the mistress of several men in high places had jumped to her death, having grown tired of the sordid life she had been leading. He and his producer, Joseph Janni, had some ideas of how to shape this into a screenplay and called on Frederic Raphael to turn these suggestions into dialogue.

After several false starts, Raphael, Janni, and Schlesinger came up with Diana Scott, who would not be quite as tragic as the girl they had first envisioned. Although there would be satirical bite to the script, it was hardly a comedy, but more of a bitter, darkly unsettling look at a misguided, lost soul. As thoughtless as Diana would be at times, Schlesinger wanted to make sure that she was not so much hateful as pathetic. Raphael complied with Schlesinger's wishes as best he could but felt he was losing control of his work because of the director's insistence on having so much input into the screenplay. By the time shooting was ready to begin, Raphael still believed the script required much work and revisions. Feeling that a new voice was needed, Schlesinger hired Edna O'Brien, who had written the novel *The Lonely Girl*, which she had turned into the film *Girl with Green Eyes* (United Artists, 1964). O'Brien contributed ideas and changes to *Darling* while it was being made, but the final screenwriting credit went to Raphael, with Janni and Schlesinger listed in the opening titles along with Raphael for having provided the original story.

Part of the reason Schlesinger was so determined to create this character in the first place was that he had just the right actress in mind to embody her: Julie Christie. Christie had been cast as one of the two key women in the life of dreamer Tom Courtenay in *Billy Liar* and had made such an unforgettable impact in her part (her initial appearance, walking confidently through the streets of Bradford, became one of the great star entrances in '60s film lore) that the entire movie world was abuzz, wondering where this enchanting creature had come from and whether somebody was going to be smart enough to give her a vehicle of her own. Anglo Amalgamated, with which Janni had a distribution deal, was not so sure they'd be able to sell a picture starring a virtual unknown, so Schlesinger assured the studio that the principal male roles would be filled by "names." There was talk of Montgomery Clift or Paul Newman for the part of Diana's first married lover, Robert (initially written as an American), but those stars' lack of interest meant that things would stay firmly rooted in Great Britain, with a more suitable Dirk Bogarde cast in the closest thing to a sympathetic lead. Also ideal was the choice of Laurence Harvey as Miles, the very steely, wealthy sophisticate whom Diana latches on to, leaving Robert behind. For the part of Diana's clearly gay friend, Malcolm, Schlesinger turned to Roland Curram, whom he had known since his acting days back in the early 1950s. This was a breakthrough character for the mid-'60s, not because he did anything physical that might unsettle the censors, but simply because he was a homosexual who was not troubled or insidious, nor drawn in a grotesque, pitiable, or laughable manner. Although Malcolm had a smart tongue and a camp sensibility, he was loyal, comforting, and in possession of his own sexual interests, going off for a liaison with a waiter with whom Diana also sleeps. Word was out: many women had close gay friends with whom they got along better than they did with their hetero sex partners. This was not news to the industry or to insiders in the world portrayed in the film, but was likely something unheard of by the mainstream public.

> "Your idea of fidelity is not having more than one man in the bed at the same time."
> —Robert Gold

Darling began shooting on September 21, 1964, in London, with several locations in the Piccadilly area, including Fortnum and Mason, where Diana and Malcolm indulge in a bit of shoplifting; the Eros statue in Piccadilly Circus, in which a vagrant singing "Santa Lucia" provided the chillingly dotty final image (yesterday's *Darling*, perhaps?); and a newspaper stand outside of Swan and Edgar department store. Miles was seen bringing Diana into the ultramodern Sudbury House, part of the Paternoster Square development, where she catwalked for him on the boardroom table; Robert and Diana romped along the river at Strand-on-the-Green and were seen leaving the Computer House (standing in for Robert's television station) near Great West Road. There was also filming at Heathrow Airport, Paddington Station (where Robert and Diana use a phone booth to call their respective partners and lie about their whereabouts), and a fancy home on South End Road overlooking Hampstead Heath that stood in for Robert's house. The company also filmed in Florence, Italy for scenes at the villa Diana ends up marrying into and concluded the shoot with interiors done at Shepperton Studios. Because Schlesinger had won favor with his two previous movies (though not financial success in the United States) and because *Darling* sounded as if it was going to be very adult and possibly controversial, American distributor Joseph E. Levine offered a very pleasing $1 million to release the picture outside of the United Kingdom.

Darling, in fact, opened in the United States a full month before it premiered in its country of origin. Perhaps this was seen as a slight by the British critics, who were far less enthusiastic about the picture than were the American reviewers, many of whom expressed a degree of fervent excitement that ranked among the highest praise heaped upon any British film in recent memory. Everything about the look and style of *Darling* had a fresh, up-to-the-minute

The sheet music for a title song not heard in *Darling* features such lyrics by Gene Lees as "Just by saying 'Darling' she could fill my world with wonder," a sentiment that couldn't be more at odds with John Schlesinger's darkly satirical film.

feel, and there was much appreciation for the grown-up way in which it casually presented sex as something used for status and image, for advancement and career. The tone of the picture was blatantly unsentimental, harshly uncompromising, and terribly chic. It spoke of sophistication and maturity to recommend a movie that did not pander to safer commercial tastes, and for all its gloss there was a moral soul beating within, a potent warning of the terrible loneliness in store for those who placed possessions and wealth before humanity.

Despite the brilliance of Bogarde's portrayal of a smart man unwittingly brought down by a woman so clearly beneath him, all the attention went to Christie, who in a single film became the most important female name of the British New Wave. This was a difficult role to pull off: she had to make Diana ambitious yet uncalculating when it came to her intentions, fully aware of her own beauty without ever being arrogant about it, and she had to suggest a level of inner hurt while keeping the character generally shallow. Soon, everywhere you turned there were articles on and images galore of Christie, and she and her characterization of Diana Scott became a seminal part of the new British cinema, of London's youth-oriented changing scene, and of the jetsetting lifestyle emulated, envied, and deplored by the masses. By the end of 1965 Christie was starring in the blockbuster *Doctor Zhivago* (MGM), making it far and away her peak year at the movies. *Darling* did good business in the United States and was a flat-out smash in Britain, overriding any critical derision to become the sort of talked-about picture that stayed in everybody's mind come awards season, giving the impression that the U.K. press was a lot more supportive than it actually was.

Undoubtedly one of the landmark British pictures of its era, *Darling* remained highly cherished among the intelligentsia and continued to be looked upon as the signature role of its star throughout an impressive career. It had broken some taboos and shed some light on the lie behind celebrity obsession, and it did so with visual invention and verbal flair. For some, Schlesinger's portrait of the superficial and the heartless seemed just as empty as its heroine. The director himself insisted in later years that it was a movie all too pleased with itself and did not rank it among his personal favorites. But then Diana Scott was never an easy lady to love.

HELP! (United Kingdom)

Top 25 Box Office Film

Opening date: August 9, 1965 (New York: August 23, 1965; London: July 29, 1965).

United Artists. A Walter Shenson–Subafilms Production.

Director: Richard Lester. Producer: Walter Shenson. Screenplay: Marc Behm, Charles Wood. Story: Marc Behm. Photography: David Watkin. Art Director: Ray Simm. Costumes: Julie Harris. Songs by John Lennon and Paul McCartney: "Help!," "You're Gonna Lose That Girl," "You've Got to Hide Your Love Away," "Ticket to Ride," "She's a Woman," "The Night Before," "Another Girl." Song by George Harrison: "I Need You." Additional Music: "Ode to Joy" from the Ninth Symphony, by Ludwig van Beethoven. Music Director: Ken Thorne. Editor: John Victor-Smith. Eastmancolor. 90 minutes.

CAST: John Lennon, Paul McCartney, George Harrison, Ringo Starr (the Beatles), Leo McKern (Clang), Eleanor Bron (Ahme), Victor Spinetti (Foot), Roy Kinnear (Algernon), John Bluthal (Bhuta), Patrick Cargill (Superintendent), Alfie Bass (Doorman), Peter Copley (Jeweler), Golda Casimir (Cleaner in Temple, Clang's Mother), Bruce Lacey (Lawn Mower), Dandy Nichols, Gretchen Franklin (Neighbors), Jeremy Lloyd (Restaurant Patron), Warren Mitchell (Abdul), Durra (Belly Dancer), Mal Evans (Alpine Swimmer).

PLOT: Beatle Ringo Starr finds his life in danger when he gains possession of a valuable ring that requires its wearer to be sacrificed to the goddess Kaili.

By the end of 1964 the Beatles had not only turned the musical world on its ear, but, with *A Hard Day's Night* (United Artists) to their credit, were able to leave behind a worthy cinematic documentation of their importance to '60s culture. Box-office returns demanded some sort of follow-up, and, still convinced that all fads must end, United Artists was quick to enlist the world's most famous singing celebrities of the mid-'60s to carry their second feature one year later. To ensure that the magic would work a second time, the same producer, Walter Shenson, and director, Richard Lester, were assigned to the project, and a bigger budget (more than twice that of *Night*'s paltry $560,000) allowed them to film in color this time, with locations allotted outside of England as well, in the Austrian Alps and the Bahamas. (The latter locale was pretty much dictated as being included in the plot by the Beatles' business manager, who had established a tax shelter in the islands and would benefit from having his clients work there.) A pair of new screenwriters, Marc Behm (who had helped supply the story for the 1963 Universal hit *Charade*) and Charles Wood (who had most recently collaborated with Lester on United Artists' *The Knack . . . and How to Get It*, 1965) were given the task of actually coming up with something akin to a plot this time, but there would still be restrictions. The Beatles were, after all, the Beatles, amusingly deadpan personalities when it came to acting, and nobody was fooled into believing that they should stretch for their sophomore effort any more than they did for their first foray before the cameras. A quartet of sardonic, dry-witted lads with more than a bit of contempt for standard motion-picture acting was exactly what everyone had liked the first time around, and their mocking personas were retained for this romp. Though danger abounded in the form of a Middle Eastern cult and a mad scientist, John, Paul, George, and Ringo barely raised an eyebrow in concern, which was exactly what made them so funny to watch.

The Beatles themselves, however, were not so amused, complaining that the lion's share of the laughs were being handed to their more professional costars, Leo McKern, Victor Spinetti (the one supporting principal to return from *A Hard Day's Night*), Roy Kinnear, and Eleanor Bron. The most outspoken member of the group, John Lennon, would later badmouth the finished product, insisting that the Beatles came off as little more than extras in their own film. There was a smidgen of truth to this, insomuch as the supporting cast did indeed make a strong impression against four personalities that had already become iconic and indelible. Of the four Beatles, it was drummer Ringo Starr who received the greatest attention in the story line, simply because the plot revolved around his finger and the ring he couldn't seem to remove from it. Of all the band, Ringo had come off best in *A Hard Day's Night*, as far as reviewers were concerned, so this may have been the impetus for putting him at the center of attention this time out.

> "Help me if you can, I'm feeling down. And I do appreciate your being 'round. Help me get my feet back on the ground. Won't you please help me?"
> —The Beatles

With no title other than *Beatles 2* at the outset, filming began on February 23, 1965, on the island of New Providence in the Bahamas, where the final portion of the picture took place. In mid-March the crew moved on to the Austrian Alps, shooting in the town of Obertauern for scenes that included the delightful "Ticket to Ride" number, which showed the group cavorting on the slopes as they displayed their lack of skiing skills. Returning to England in late March, the company shot the remainder of the movie at various London locales, including the Thames towpath at Strand-on-the-Green, in front of the City Barge public house pub (where Ringo's entrapment with a tiger prompts the singing of Beethoven's Ninth Symphony), and Ailsa Avenue, which served as the exterior of the Beatles' connecting apartments, the interiors of which were shot, like most of the film, at nearby Twickenham Studios. Other locations included Asprey's, the famed jewelers on Bond Street ("even Royal House of Hanover had The Wheel"), the Dolphin Restaurant (subbing for the film's Rajahama Indian eatery) on Blanford Street, and Clivenden House in Berkshire, filling in for the one location even the Beatles weren't allowed to use—Buckingham Palace. During the first week of May the company moved southwest to Salisbury Plain, where the Fab Four were surrounded by real members of the 3rd Division Army while singing both "The Night Before" and George Harrison's one composition for the film, "I Need You," against a backdrop that included a glimpse of Stonehenge. Shooting finished on May 12, 1965, and Lester and his team raced against time (as they had with *A Hard Day's Night*) to have the whole thing edited and ready for the paying public in time for a midsummer London premiere.

Fourteen songs were provided by John Lennon, Paul McCartney, and George Harrison in hopes that Lester and his scripters would find places for them in the finished film, with seven numbers making the final cut. (One of those rejected, "If You've Got Trouble," would have given Ringo his own solo.) Although early on the title *Eight Arms to Hold You* was considered (a dual meaning that not only offered anxious Beatles fans the suggestion of being caressed by their heroes, but slyly made reference to the multilimbed goddess Kaili), it became obvious that there was one track in the film that was too perfect to pass up as a title. John Lennon's thrilling composition "Help!," punctuated by its repeated cry of the title word, became a Beatles classic and perfectly captured the manic, driving rhythm of the film. It was one of two number 1 chart hit singles to come from the movie. The other was McCartney's "Ticket to Ride,"

some editions of which included the erroneous *Eight Arms to Hold You* on its label, making it one of the great Beatles collector's items of the decade.

The film itself received enthusiastic notices from critics, a number of whom had declared themselves converts to the pop-music counterculture because of the first Beatles movie, though many couldn't help but point out that nothing Lester and the boys did was ever going to come close to the fresh surprise of *A Hard Day's Night. Help!* never stopped being a lively good time for Beatles fans, but it was disjointed, to say the least, in its patchwork plotting (why exactly were the Beatles even in the Alps?). It did, however, carry through on the Beatles' cinematic image as nonconformists and champions of surreal humor, with its loopy "intermission"

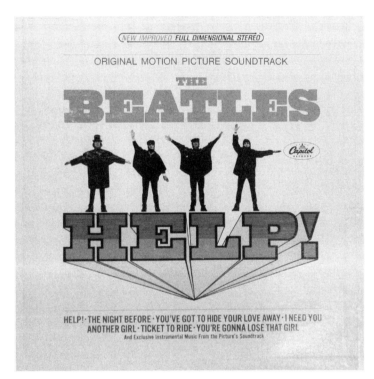

The *Help!* soundtrack released in the United States on Capitol Records features the Beatles making semaphores that in fact do *not* spell out the title of the film. The LP would stay in the number 1 spot on the *Billboard* chart for nine weeks.

sequence, deadpan throwaway bits (including a quick trip to the Battersea power station to replace the queen's faulty electrical system), priceless sight gags (the superintendent's introduction to the Nassau police force being one of the standouts), Paul's miniaturized romp on the floor of his flat, and deliberately silly dialogue along the lines of "take this hastily scribbled note. . . ."

Despite the not-unexpected box-office success of *Help!*, the Beatles' career as a team of film actors had come to an end. They would cameo at the climax of the animated *Yellow Submarine* (United Artists, 1968) and appear before the cameras to document the making of their *Let It Be* (United Artists, 1970) album, but there would be no more Beatles "acting" vehicles.

THAT DARN CAT!

Top 10 Box Office Film

Opening date: December 2, 1965.

Buena Vista. A Walt Disney Presentation.

Director: Robert Stevenson. Coproducers: Bill Walsh, Ron Miller. Screenplay: The Gordons, Bill Walsh. Based on the 1963 book *Undercover Cat*, by the Gordons (Mildred and Gordon Gordon). Photography: Edward Colman. Art Directors: Carroll Clark, William H. Tuntke. Set Decorators: Emile Kuri, Hal Gausman. Costumes: Bill Thomas. Music: Bob Brunner. Title song by Richard M. Sherman and Robert B. Sherman, performed by Bobby Darin. Editor: Cotton Warburton. Animal Supervision: William R. Koehler. Technicolor. 116 minutes.

CAST: Hayley Mills (Patti Randall), Dean Jones (Zeke Kelso), Dorothy Provine (Ingrid "Inky" Randall), Roddy McDowall (Gregory Benson), Neville Brand (Dan), Ed Wynn (Mr. Hofstedder), Elsa Lanchester (Kipp MacDougall), William Demarest (Wilbur MacDougall), Frank Gorshin (Iggy), Richard Eastham (FBI Supervisor Newton), Grayson Hall (Margaret Miller), Tom Lowell (Canoe Henderson), Richard Deacon (Drive-in Manager), Iris Adrian (Mrs. Tabin, Landlady), Syn (D. C.).

PLOT: When D. C., her Siamese cat, returns from his nightly rounds with a watch slipped under his collar and the word "help" scratched upon it, Patti Randall is certain her pet has made contact with kidnapping victim Margaret Miller and the criminals who have recently stolen $160,000 from the North Valley Bank.

That Darn Cat! **had double significance** for the Disney Studio. Like ships passing in the night, it featured the farewell performance for the company by Hayley Mills, while simultaneously marking the first time Dean Jones would appear for them. Mills had served the Mouse House well since her sparkling appearance in the title role of *Pollyanna* (1960), starring in a picture for Disney each year since and becoming one of its most adored attractions. At the time she completed her role in *Cat*, she was all of eighteen years old and ready to move on to other, more adult projects. Jones (who was thirty-four when shooting started on the film) had been showing up in movies since 1956 and eventually gained prominence in the stage and film versions of *Under the Yum Yum Tree* (Columbia,

> "Well, well, what will that dear, sweet, innocent cat be bringing home next? The Hope Diamond, I imagine."
> —Ingrid Randall

1963). Jones's jittery, likable comic style had a very nonthreatening, warm undercurrent to it that suited Disney's family target audience to a T, and Walt and his successors were so thrilled with him that over the next twelve years they made him the studio's premier "name."

Despite the charms of these two stars, their participation in *That Darn Cat!* was of secondary interest to most people who showed up for the picture, since it was the eponymous feline who was going to be pulling most if not all of the focus. For the starring role of D. C. (which did indeed stand for "Darn Cat"),

The only sin on a Disney set is a Siamese by the name of Syn, the star of *That Darn Cat!*, seen here with his human costars, Hayley Mills and Dean Jones.

Disney actually used a "contract player" who had already appeared in one of his pictures: Syn, a Siamese cat who had played Tao in the 1963 adventure *The Incredible Journey*. As with most movies requiring animals to be seen on camera throughout the majority of the picture, Syn had several stand-in pussycats as well, each one trained to do a particular feat (to avoid trying to instruct a single cat to do it all). Using a Siamese was a compromise; Disney suggested Syn not only because the cat had done commendable work for him previously, but because this breed was far more photogenic than mere black cats, which was what D. C. had been in the novel from which the picture was adapted, *Undercover Cat*. The D. C. of the book had been directly based on the real-life pet of the authors (Gordon Gordon and Mildred Gordon, who billed themselves simply as "the Gordons"), whose frisky troublemaking had led them to refer to him affectionately as "Damn Cat."

As if he had some special radar for suitable family source material, Walt Disney contacted the Gordons even before their book was finished, asking them to push him to the top of the list when it came time to sell their property to the movies. Although Disney hired the Gordons to work on the script, he also made sure one of his trusted studio writers, Bill Walsh, was on hand to give it that mandatory polish and turn it unmistakably into one of the company's offerings, hitting the exact buttons for maximum appeal to the young. The screenplay got rid of Patti Randall's twelve-year-old brother Mike (rightfully deemed superfluous) and made Patti the younger sister to grown-up Ingrid, reversing the ages of the book. There was now a surfer boyfriend, Canoe, for Patti, whereas it was a neighbor lawyer named Greg Balter who had caught her eye in the Gordons' version; pieces of Balter's story line (including D. C. stealing his prize duck) were kept for the newly devised character of snobby Gregory Benson, a mama's boy with designs on Ingrid. To make matters clearer to younger audiences, most of the word "Help" was scratched on the back of the watch, whereas in the Gordon version the FBI had made the connection to the kidnap victim by the jeweler's signature "Y" on the timepiece. Because D. C. was no longer black, there was no reason for anyone to dab his tail with phosphorescent paint in order to keep tabs on the tabby. A Beverly Hills–based feline psychiatrist, Dr. Faulkner, was dropped, as was a scene in which FBI agent Zeke Kelso attempted to dope the hyperactive cat, since Disney audiences would not have accepted that sort of animal abuse. To give the story more variety, a slapstick visit to a drive-in movie was now included during D. C.'s nocturnal roaming; Patti was allowed to participate in the final encounter at the hoodlum's hideout (it was Hayley Mills's film, after all); Canoe was seen stalking Patti in order to insert some patented Disney slapstick; and a sequence that brought Patti to the jeweler's shop that had sold the watch was put in mainly so that Disney could employ his dearly cherished Ed Wynn.

The movie began principal photography on October 19, 1964, the entire picture shot either on soundstages or on the generic small-town set standing on the Disney back lot. In order to keep things moving along (*Darn Cat* took a little less than two months to shoot, wrapping on December 16), scenes that involved the cat but not humans were often shot simultaneously on a nearby set, with a special camera built at a cat's level mounted on a track to glide along next to D. C. as he roamed the town. With his customary knack for knowing how to sell a movie to his loyal audience, Disney made sure that the relatively forgettable original book title was dropped in favor of one that instantly caught the eye and ear, *That Darn Cat!* Connecting this name (which was enhanced by a supercool title tune sung by Bobby Darin) with the concept of a self-reliant kitty accidentally working for the FBI was irresistible, and not only did the movie become one of the studio's top-grossing pictures of the decade, but its title came to symbolize, perhaps more than any other movie from this period, the sort of high-concept, gimmicky comedies that were a staple in this era, for better or worse.

A PATCH OF BLUE

Academy Award Winner: Best Supporting Actress (Shelley Winters)

Academy Award Nominee: Actress (Elizabeth Hartman); Art Direction–Set Decoration—Black and White; Cinematography—Black and White; Music Score—Substantially Original

Opening date: December 10, 1965 (New York: December 15, 1965).

MGM. A Pandro S. Berman–Guy Green Production.

Director-Screenplay: Guy Green. Based on the 1961 novel *Be Ready with Bells and Drums*, by Elizabeth Kata. Producer: Pandro S. Berman. Photography: Robert Burks. Art Directors: George W. Davis, Urie McCleary. Set Decorators: Henry Grace, Charles S. Thompson. Music: Jerry Goldsmith. Editor: Rita Roland. Black and white. Panavision. 105 minutes.

CAST: Sidney Poitier (Gordon Ralfe), Shelley Winters (Rose-Ann D'Arcey), Elizabeth Hartman (Selina D'Arcey), Wallace Ford (Ole Pa), Ivan Dixon (Mark Ralfe), Elisabeth Fraser (Sadie), John Qualen (Mr. Faber), Kelly Flynn (Yanek Faber), Debi Storm (Selina at age five), Renata Vanni (Mrs. Favaloro), Saverio LoMedico (Mr. Favaloro).

PLOT: Gordon Ralfe's friendship provides a ray of hope for Selina D'Arcey, a forlorn blind girl who knows no other world outside of tending to her sluttish, short-tempered mother and her alcoholic grandfather.

There was no denying that '60s audiences were drawn to the very decent nature of Sidney Poitier, and the fact that so many white moviegoers found themselves at ease with a black performer during this turbulent period was in a sense achievement enough. Despite his progress, there had been a somewhat safe quality to most of the roles Poitier had been given when it came to female interaction; he was either paired off with a black actress or rendered fairly neutral in the romance department. With *A Patch of Blue* he took a small step forward in suggesting a blossoming love between himself and a white girl, and although things didn't exactly get heated, passionate, or particularly physical, the relationship alone elicited controversy in certain areas of the country and thereby great interest elsewhere.

After British director Guy Green's wife brought a novel by Elizabeth Kata called *Be Ready with Bells and Drums* to his attention, he had optioned the rights, hoping to get somebody with influence in Hollywood to back the project. Green won over MGM producer Pandro S. Berman, who knew the one chance of getting the film made was to enlist the only bankable black actor in town. He therefore sent a copy of the book to Poitier, who owed Berman some degree of thanks because he'd been responsible for the actor's breakthrough part in *Blackboard Jungle* (MGM) ten years earlier. Poitier was willing to do the film if Berman and Green agreed to tone down the racism inherent in pretty much all of the white characters, since he was interested not so much in making a race-issue movie as a romance. He preferred to deemphasize the potentially uncomfortable interracial attraction and show the growing feelings between a man and a woman who happened to be of different colors. Once Poitier was on board, Berman managed to get the green light from MGM, which bought the rights to the book. Green, who had been a cinematographer prior to turning to directing, tackled yet another job, serving as the scriptwriter for the first and only time in his career.

Green followed the structure of most of Kata's novel and used some of her dialogue, or at least variations of it. The book had been told entirely from its blind heroine's point of view, which meant that the fact that the man with whom Selina had fallen in love, Gordon Ralfe, was black was not revealed until the final two chapters. This, of course, could not be done in a film, where the character would be visible to audiences from the moment he appeared onscreen, nor did Green want everything that happened to be witnessed or interpreted by Selina. She still had the largest role, but a few key moments would not include her, notably the discussions between Gordon and his worried brother Mark, who believes that "whitey" should be looking after his own kind, and a well-realized scene in which Mark attempts to "play blind" at his office in order to experience what Selina goes through every day. Knowing that the studio was already risking discomfort with its subject matter, Green felt it necessary to soften the physical deformity of Selina, who, in Kata's version, had had her eyes

> "I know you're good and kind. I know you're colored and I . . . and I think you're beautiful."
> —Selina D'Arcey

burned by acid to such a degree that she no longer had eyelashes, nor was she capable of shedding tears. Green solved this dilemma by having Selina be on the receiving end of a glass bottle instead. The makeup, therefore, emphasized only a mild disfigurement, which certainly put the nervous studio at ease. In order to placate Poitier's wishes that not all the whites be so outspokenly racist, it was no longer Ole Pa who had chased Selina's black friend Pearl away, but Selina's mother, Rose-Ann. Green also rewrote the ending so that Rose-Ann blurted out that Gordon was black after seeing him with her daughter, whereas Kata had shown the ugly side of Mr. Faber's seemingly affable son Janek by having him use a racial slur upon seeing Gordon try to help Selina after she'd fallen in a flowerbed.

Kata's book had included a most disturbing finale that left Selina realizing the terrible repercussions of her racist upbringing: Gordon was chased off by a hostile mob, leaving her alone in the park and knowing she had ruined her chance to get into the school for the blind Gordon had been kind enough to arrange for her. MGM just couldn't deal with this downbeat wrap-up, and so Selina was instead shipped off to her school after bidding Gordon goodbye. This allowed things to remain fairly chaste between the two, with only the hint of what might have been to serve as a small sign of progress. A gentle kiss was all that was shown to indicate that Gordon was experiencing affection for Selina. Kata had brought the two of them much closer by having them actually have sex—one giant step too many for what Metro had in mind. Although Poitier got his wish that a relationship develop between a white woman and a black man, he would not be given the satisfaction of breaking the final taboo.

In the fall of 1964 the picture was announced under the book's title, but it was wisely decided that there was something a bit too cumbersome (and perhaps too suggestive of a musical) about *Be Ready with Bells and Drums*, so not only was the title dropped, but all references to the Walter Bynner poem "The Pure-Hearted Girl," from which it came, were removed from the screenplay as well. With Poitier signed on for $80,000 plus 10 percent of the gross and Shelley Winters chosen to play Selina's repugnant mother, MGM was more than agreeable to Green's insistence that Selina be played by someone new. Green tested more than a hundred novice actresses, looking for someone who possessed the right degree of naïveté that would not come across as forced or affected. He found his ideal Selina in Elizabeth

Hartman, who had studied acting at Carnegie Mellon before joining the Kenley Players in Warren, Ohio. Prior to *Patch*'s scheduled March 15 start date in California, Hartman studied at the Braille Institute in order to feel at ease playing someone without sight.

A Patch of Blue was shot mostly on the MGM lot, and Green kept things rolling along so smoothly that a month and a half later the picture wrapped at a cost of $1.13 million—$65,000 under budget. Metro execs were pleased with the way Green had turning the movie into a highly emotional experience without lapsing into the maudlin. He did not, however, go very far out of his way to give deeper shading to the characters, any more than Kata had. As written, Gordon was a virtuous, helpful, and selfless being, which meant that audiences would respond instantly to him in a positive way. It was up to Poitier, through his customarily brilliant underplaying, to suggest the character's feelings of disgust toward racism and his unease about the situation he had gotten himself into. Likewise, Winters made a meal out of the flat-out villain role she was handed, turning Rose-Ann into one of the truly hateful mothers in screen history, a petulant, demanding slattern with no

This artistic ad for *A Patch of Blue* was preferable to some of the ickier ones MGM had devised for the Sidney Poitier drama.

regard for anybody's feelings but her own. It might not have been a multilayered performance, but it is doubtful anyone who saw the picture ever forgot it—for the young and impressionable her behavior was the stuff of nightmares. Given the task of having to carry the bulk of the picture, Hartman came off as no less accomplished than her experienced costars, hitting all the right notes of loneliness and wonder without letting Selina appear so guileless and forgiving as to be infuriating. Best of all, because of her acting and Green's controlled direction, the movie was extremely successful in capturing the experience of someone appreciating a newfound world that the rest of us have taken for granted, which was why it proved so moving.

Several critics found *Patch* condescending in its earnest intentions, giving the impression that the whole country had moved on from such backward attitudes. Needless to say, they were once again proven wrong when a downtown Memphis theater showing *Patch* was picketed by the Ku Klux Klan and a bomb threat was made in North Carolina. The more racist factions of the country were infuriated by Hollywood's first sanctioned black-on-white kiss scene, and certain theaters took it upon themselves to slice the "offending" footage out of their prints, thereby giving in to exactly the sort of stupidity the movie was speaking against. This offensive response was offset not only by *A Patch of Blue*'s five Oscar nominations, but by its increasingly potent box-office returns, which proved that what had left most critics cold was hitting the right nerve with filmgoers. The movie grossed $13.6 million in the United States, turning it into Poitier's biggest moneymaker to date.

A THOUSAND CLOWNS

Academy Award Winner: Best Supporting Actor (Martin Balsam)

Academy Award Nominee: Picture; Screenplay—Based on Material from Another Medium; Scoring of Music—Adaptation or Treatment

Opening date: December 13, 1965.

United Artists. A Harrell Productions, Inc. Presentation.

Director-Producer: Fred Coe. Screenplay: Herb Gardner, based on his 1962 play. Photography: Arthur J. Ornitz. Art Director: Burr Smidt. Set Decorators: Herbert Mulligan, George De Titta. Costumes: Ruth Morley, Bert Matthews. Music: Don Walker. Title song by Judy Holliday and Gerry Mulligan, performed by Rita Gardner. Song: "Yes Sir, That's My Baby," by Walter Donaldson and Gus Kahn, performed by Jason Robards and Barry Gordon. Editor: Ralph Rosenblum. Associate Producers: Ralph Rosenblum, Herb Gardner. Black and white. 119 minutes.

CAST: Jason Robards (Murray Burns), Barbara Harris (Sandra Markowitz), Martin Balsam (Arnold Burns), Barry Gordon (Nick Burns, aka Wilbur Malcolm, Theodore, Raphael Sabatini, Dr. Morris Fishbein, Woodrow, King, Rover, Lefty, Chevrolet, Big Sam Burns), Gene Saks (Leo Herman), William Daniels (Albert Amundsen), John MacMartin/John McMartin (Producer in Office), Philip Bruns (Jimmy Sloan).

PLOT: Murray Burns, a former comedy writer who has gladly left behind the grind of going to work on a daily basis, tries to raise his impressionable nephew Nick by his own unorthodox means until he is challenged by Social Services, who fear he might be a bad influence on the boy.

Writer Herb Gardner saw a great American tragedy sweeping the country and decided it was time to address the issue in a play. People were allowing their precious lives to slip away as they trudged obediently off to work. Casting aside the job that had brought him fame and money (writing a cartoon called "The Nebbishes"), Gardner sat down to pen his first full-length, three-act play, coming up with a comedy that was both drolly off-the-wall and heartbreakingly tragic, *A Thousand Clowns*. Thus was born one of the great nonconformist characters, Murray Burns. Just to show that Murray, despite his affably nutty approach to life, was indeed a man carrying a hefty emotional load, an actor who had been almost exclusively identified with heavyweight dramas was given the lead, Jason Robards. Supporting Robards in the cast of five were Sandy Dennis as Murray's love interest; Gene Saks, shortly before he turned to directing with the 1963 comedy *Enter Laughing*, as the garrulous children's show host Leo Herman; A. Larry Haines as Murray's patient brother and agent, Arnold; William Daniels, perfecting his patented stiff reserve, as Albert the social worker; and Barry Gordon, a squinty-eyed child actor with the demeanor of a Borscht Belt comic, as Murray's impressionable nephew, Nick. Apart from Robards, Gordon was probably the best-known cast member, having become something of a fifteen-minute celebrity back in 1955 when, at the age of seven, he landed on the pop charts with his rendition of the novelty song "I'm Gettin' Nuthin' for Christmas." Under the direction of Fred Coe, *A Thousand Clowns* opened at the

Eugene O'Neill Theater on April 5, 1962, and became one of the hits of the season, earning both a Tony and Theatre World Award for Dennis and running 428 performances. It closed on April 13, 1963.

The same year that *Clowns* hit the stage, Coe scored a success producing a film version of another play he had done on Broadway, *The Miracle Worker*, and he was anxious to see *A Thousand Clowns* turned into a movie as well. Coe chose to repeat his stage duty as director on the *Clowns* film, making this his first effort behind a motion-picture camera, though he had several directorial credits on programs such as *Philco Television Playhouse* and *Playhouse 90*. At one point Steve McQueen was announced for the lead, but that plan, thankfully, never materialized, and Coe wound up with Robards. Unlike so many theater actors, Robards was able to repeat yet another part he'd created, following his stage-to-screen depiction of James Jr. in *Long Day's Journey into Night* (Embassy, 1962). Although he was busy starring in not one but two plays at the time, *After the Fall* and *But for Whom Charlie*, at the Lincoln Center Repertory Theater, Robards made himself available during the day for filming, quitting at 5:30 P.M. This gave him just a two-hour gap in between shooting and his arrival at the theater, which meant he had three different scripts memorized during this period.

> "I wanna be sure he knows when he's chickening out on himself. I want him to get to know the special thing he is, or else he won't notice it when it starts to go. I want him to stay awake so he knows who the phonies are. I want him to know the sneaky, subtle reason he was born a human being and not a chair."
> —Murray Burns

Given the job of fashioning his script into something more cinematic, Garner did minimal trimming where the dialogue was concerned. An extensive phone conversation that took place in Arnold's office between an unseen, rambling Leo Herman (coming through on a speaker phone) and an increasingly impatient Murray was excised, as was the opening scene of Nick watching Leo's program and commenting on its sorry state. Garner made perhaps the most significant and beneficial change by taking Murray's final lines of dialogue from the second act closing, in which he lamented his inability to come up with his customarily nonsensical instructions for his neighbors, and moving them to the very end of the film, giving the whole finale a stronger and more emotionally devastating impact.

Filming began on May 11, 1964, at such locations as Battery Park and Front Street; the Liberty Island Ferry (the film crew was denied permission to actually shoot at the Statue of Liberty); Pier 40 north of Canal Street, where a ship from the Holland-American lines was used for the bon voyage departure scene; Grand Street; a junkyard at Pike Slip, where Murray purchases his latest eagle statue; the Union Carbide Building and the Lever Building on Park Avenue; a deserted Wall Street; and 530 Fifth Avenue, behind the statue of Atlas, which substituted for the entrance to an underlit restaurant. Coe's roving cameras also had the good fortune to capture Lincoln Center while it was under construction. The exterior for Murray and Nick's one-room apartment was found at 131 West Seventy-eighth Street. On May 29 the crew moved over to the Michael Myerberg Studio at Roosevelt Field, Garden City, Long Island, for interiors. The production wrapped on July 8, 1964, coming in under the $1 million mark.

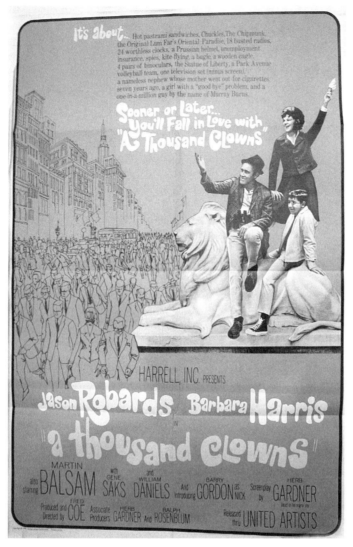

It's not your average movie that attempts to lure the customers with a poster drawing attention to "25 worthless clocks" and "the Statue of Liberty," but *A Thousand Clowns* was, blessedly, *not* your average movie.

Clowns did not surface on theater screens until the end of the following year—United Artists aimed for a December release date because it believed the movie, which was not an easy sell, would benefit from year-end awards. Their postponement paid off. First, word got out to fans of the original play that not only had *A Thousand Clowns* been lovingly preserved on-screen, but the choices for opening up the piece and allowing it to pour onto the streets of Manhattan made it something of a Valentine to the city, enhancing Gardner's work in the best way possible. Audiences responded to Murray's cry against conformity and his battle to stay true to himself as more and more Americans began to question the validity of surrendering the valuable time from nine to five to toil under an oppressive and uncaring bureaucracy. A word-of-mouth success, *Clowns* developed a substantial following in select areas—not enough to blossom into a full-scale top-10 hit, but enough to make it a favored film come award season. Gardner won the Writers Guild Award for Best Comedy, and the film scored one of the finalist spots for the Oscar for Best Picture, losing out to the year's runaway smash *The Sound of Music* (Twentieth Century-Fox).

Outside of the want ads being divided into male and female categories and the tendency for Murray and his fellow "clowns" to wear hats to work, the film and its message did not become dated. It was discovered and embraced by later generations as well, who loved its combination of easygoing laughs, giddy black-and-white montages of mid-'60s New York, skewering of show-business phonies (Saks was priceless in his egomaniacal ranting as the pathetic Leo Herman), unsentimental observations on the loss of freedom and innocence, and bittersweet but balanced decision to have one foot grounded in the real world. When productions of the play appeared decades later on Broadway, the critics carped that the work no longer had any relevance. That might be the viewpoint of someone who makes a living writing critiques of other people's work, but it was hardly true where the real world was concerned.

THE FLIGHT OF THE PHOENIX

Academy Award Nominee: Supporting Actor (Ian Bannen); Film Editing

Opening date: December 15, 1965 (New York: January 31, 1966).

Twentieth Century-Fox. An Associates and Aldrich Company Production.

Director-Producer: Robert Aldrich. Screenplay: Lukas Heller. Based on the 1964 novel by Elleston Trevor. Photography: Joseph Biroc. Art Director: William Glasgow. Set Decorator: Lucien Hafley. Costumes: Norma Koch. Music: (Frank) De-Vol. Song by Gino Paoli (music and Italian lyrics), and Alec Wilder (English lyrics): "The Phoenix Love Theme (Senza Fine)," performed by Connie Francis. Editor: Michael Luciano. Aerial Photographer-Pilot: Paul Mantz. Deluxe color. 143 minutes.

CAST: James Stewart (Frank Towns), Richard Attenborough (Lew Moran), Peter Finch (Capt. Harris), Hardy Kruger (Heinrich Dorfmann), Ernest Borgnine (Trucker Cobb), Ian Bannen (Crow), Ronald Fraser (Sgt. Watson), Christian Marquand (Dr. Renaud), Dan Duryea (Standish), George Kennedy (Mike Bellamy), Gabriele Tinti (Gabriele), Alex Montoya (Carlos), Peter Bravos (Tasso), William Aldrich (Bill), Barrie Chase (Farida), Chris Alcaide (Arab Leader).

PLOT: All seems lost after a sky truck crash-lands in the middle of the Sahara desert until one of the passengers comes up with the idea of building a smaller plane from the wreckage.

The plane-crash-survivor genre reached some sort of apex in 1965 with the release of two major studio offerings, Paramount's British-produced *Sands of the Kalahari* and Fox's stateside *The Flight of the Phoenix*. Both were set in Africa, the former in the southern part of the continent, the latter in the north. And although both explored the mounting tensions between the disparate and terrified survivors, as was the tradition with all such films, *Phoenix* added a plot twist to the mix that made it that much more interesting and, ultimately, more uplifting than any others of its ilk. For his source material, producer-director Robert Aldrich turned to a 1964 British novel authored by Elleston Trevor (born Trevor Dudley-Smith), who wrote under no fewer than ten pseudonyms during his fifty-year career. Trevor had been a flight engineer during World War II, and his understanding of the technical side of airplanes gave him his premise for *The Flight of the Phoenix*, in which a survivor of a plane wreck comes up with the outrageous plan to rebuild a smaller aircraft from the existing pieces and fly it to safety. Trevor's tale had been so grip-

> "You told Towns he was behaving as if stupidity was a virtue. If he's making it into a virtue, you're making it into a bloody science."
> —Lew Moran

pingly written that all implausibilities were cast aside as the reader began to believe that, despite the heat and physical exhaustion faced by the ragged crew, this could really be done. Building the plane becomes a symbol of hope to a group of men fast running out of it. It was up to Aldrich and his screenwriter, Lukas Haller, to present this plotline onscreen and make it fly, so to speak, with movie audiences.

Alec Wilder's
THE PHOENIX LOVE THEME
(SENZA FINE)

Since most of the male cast principals in *The Flight of the Phoenix* were constantly at odds or at each other's throats, one was hardly expecting to find sheet music of a love theme, though the tune does, in fact, pop up in the film.

The smart thing Haller did was to hardly veer at all from the outline of Trevor's book, retaining nearly all the events that took place on the page. What differences there were came in altering the names and characteristics of about half the protagonists in order to suit the actors filling the roles. The nervous and God-fearing Tilney became Standish, an accountant, and went from being the youngest of the novel's survivors to the oldest when Dan Duryea was cast in the role. The stoic and heartlessly determined aircraft designer Stringer was given an added edge of German efficiency in the person of Hardy Kruger and was therefore renamed Heinrich Dorfmann. The novel's Loomis, a Texas geologist rushing home to a wife he is certain will die before he sees her again, became Trucker Cobb's doctor, a Frenchman. Continuing to shift nationalities and monikers, the injured German Kepel became an Italian, Gabriele, while the monkey-toting Englishman Roberts became a Mexican named Carlos. The rest of the passenger list stayed faithful to the novel.

Searching for a location not too far from southern California, Aldrich chose Patton Valley, a section of the Imperial Sand Dunes Recreation Area north of Yuma, Arizona. Shooting took place between April 26 and August 13, 1965, with some interiors filmed at the Fox Studios. Unfortunately, *Phoenix* became one of those projects that suffered from tragedy on the set. Stunt pilot Paul Mantz, who had come out of retirement to take the controls of the Phoenix P-1 craft designed by Otto Timm and built by Tallmantz Aviation expressly for the film, was killed when the craft broke in two on July 8, 1965. For the remaining shots of the *Phoenix*, an observation plane of a somewhat different make was rented from an air museum.

The film offered James Stewart one of his best chances during the decade. He played a stubborn and guilt-racked man who must come to terms with losing his authority, a veteran confronting his possible obsolescence in the face of the a younger scientific mind as personified by the brainy and unfeeling aircraft designer portrayed with steely brilliance by Kruger. Theirs became a power play grounded in importance: Kruger possessed the technical knowledge to build the craft, but the final responsibility rested on the old-timer, the only survivor capable of piloting the plane. Giving the role of Moran deeper shadings than in the novel, Richard Attenborough made him not only the peacemaker between the sparring Towns and Dorfmann, but also a man quietly coping with his own personal alcoholic demons and his guilt over his own involvement in the crash. Despite the standout work from Stewart, Attenborough, and Kruger, it was Ian Bannen, curiously, as the one survivor whose outlook is less bleak than that of the others, who ended up with the sole Oscar nomination among the cast.

OTHELLO (United Kingdom)

Academy Award Nominee: Actor (Laurence Olivier); Supporting Actor (Frank Finlay); Supporting Actress (Joyce Redman); Supporting Actress (Maggie Smith)

Opening date: December 15, 1965 (New York: February 1, 1966; London: May 3, 1966).

Warner Bros. A B.H.E. Production from the National Theatre of Great Britain.

Director: Stuart Burge, based on the National Theatre staging by John Dexter. Producers: Anthony Havelock-Allan, John Brabourne. Based on the 1604 play by William Shakespeare. Photography: Geoffrey Unsworth. National Theatre Production and Costumes: Jocelyn Herbert. Wardrobe: William Walsh. Film Art Director: William Kellner. Music: Richard Hampton. Editor: Richard Marden. Technicolor. Panavision. 165 minutes.

CAST: Laurence Olivier (Othello), Frank Finlay (Iago), Maggie Smith (Desdemona), Joyce Redman (Emilia), Derek Jacobi (Michael Cassio), Robert Lang (Roderigo), Anthony Nicholls (Brabantio), Harry Lomax (Duke of Venice), Sheila Reid (Bianca), Michael Turner (Gratiano), Kenneth MacKintosh (Lodovico), Edward Hardwicke (Montano), Malcolm Terry, David Hargreaves (Senate Officers), Terence Knapp (Duke's Officer).

PLOT: Enraged that he has been passed over for a promotion to lieutenant in favor of Roderigo, Iago concocts a revenge scheme by playing upon his commander Othello's jealous feelings for his wife, Desdemona.

Laurence Olivier's reputation was such that his name had become synonymous with great acting, leading many to assume that he had played pretty much every significant male role in the works of Shakespeare. Olivier had certainly conquered most of the great Shakespearean parts, but one he'd always been nervous about tackling was Othello, claiming that the number of emotional peaks an actor must climb during the course of the play were insurmountable, and that, despite these acting highs, in the end it was the villain, Iago, who ended up with all the best notices. He had, in fact, played Iago, opposite his good friend Ralph Richardson, in a 1938 production for the Old Vic, interpreting the character as gay. This had not been one of his triumphs, and the lukewarm critical reception might have been another reason he avoided the play altogether for the next twenty-six years. It was not until he took charge of Britain's newly established National Theatre that he finally decided to take on the challenge of playing the Moor of Venice, in a production directed by John Dexter. As was his custom, Olivier did not just pick up the script and act out the lines, but submerged himself in the part thoroughly, carefully observing the modern-day black population of London, choosing to speak the role with a thick Caribbean accent, changing his walk to a rolling gait, and studying with a voice coach in order to deepen his pitch by an

> "Villain, be sure thou prove my love a whore! Be sure of it; give me the ocular proof; Or by the worth of man's eternal soul, thou hadst been better born a dog than answer my waked wrath!"
> —Othello

entire octave. He darkened his body completely with stage makeup and took on what he believed to be the mannerisms and look of a black man, a decision that was greeted with controversy, to say the least.

When the production opened in April 1964, the critics were astounded by his total transformation. Some of them hailed the sheer nerve it took to go this far and this fearlessly into choppy waters, while others accused the great actor of lapsing into an insensitive parody of a race of which he had only an outsider's view. Olivier stormed about the stage, bellowing in a voice so unlike his own that the viewer was completely unable to connect it to the previous roles this actor had played. Like it or hate it, this became another of Olivier's many peaks in the English theater. Because he had conquered this dangerous part against all odds, there was hope within the theatre community that somebody would preserve the performance on film.

When Warner Bros. expressed interest in distributing an *Othello* movie that could be produced quickly and cheaply, it was decided to take the same approach that had been done in recording the National Theatre's recently acclaimed *Uncle Vanya* for posterity, shooting in what appeared to be an actual theater with very minor changes in the staging and minimal editing of the text. That production had been directed for television by Stuart Burge and, although Olivier would have much preferred an actual filmic transformation of *Othello*, he reluctantly agreed to go ahead with a rushed movie version, trusting Burge to do a similarly solid job. All members of the theater cast were asked to repeat their roles, ensuring that this very rehearsed ensemble would be letter-perfect for the filming and thereby need very few takes. Although Burge still wanted three weeks of additional rehearsal to get everyone familiar with

The film adaptation of Laurence Olivier's stage triumph in *Othello* was treated, fittingly, like a play and held to minimal performances a day, as seen in this ad for its 1966 London engagement.

the camera set-ups, he wound up with only a day to pull things together before the shooting began at Shepperton Studios on July 12, 1965. The direction of the actors was Dexter's, but the shots were dictated by Burge, who used three cameras running at once, as if taping a television program. The actors arrived on set as if following stage directions, with minimal props and no furniture except for the bed in which Desdemona was murdered at the climax. Burge did not just plunk his camera down and allow the action to be played out in long shots, but actually went in close to get facial expressions and nuances. This was not always for the better, since the performances still seemed to be geared toward a theatrical presentation. The decision to shoot the picture in Panavision meant that movie audiences would be getting some idea of the scope of a proscenium stage during certain shots, while other compositions seemed all wrong for the wide-screen process. The picture wrapped after only three weeks of shooting.

Warner Bros. decided to follow the distribution pattern it had used when exhibiting the 1964 film version of Richard Burton's Broadway success in *Hamlet*, letting the picture play for four performances during two-day engagements in select cities and offering tickets on a reserved-seat engagement. The studio would start by opening the movie for Oscar consideration in Los Angeles in December 1965 and then let it work its way through various venues including such key cities as New York and London, in early 1966. The December release worked like magic, and the movie landed four Oscar nominations for its cast members: Olivier; Frank Finlay, in the most outstanding performance in the film, as the conniving Iago; Maggie Smith as the doomed Desdemona; and Joyce Redman as Iago's wife, Emilia. There were plenty of reservations when it came to judging *Othello* on its merits as a film per se, since it was missing more than a certain degree of cinematic excitement. There were those who complained that seen in close-up Olivier's bombastic performance as the Moor was too big, too ungainly, and his makeup too theatrical. His was, however, an unforgettable piece of acting, wildly out of hand as it seemed at times, turning the very dignified military leader into a bundle of insecurities as if watching a man collapse from civility into his most base nature. Orson Welles may have created a far more interesting cinematic interpretation of the play with his exciting 1952 movie *The Tragedy of Othello*, but whatever viewers thought of this newer stage transfer, it is doubtful that anyone could shake Olivier's acting in the role from his or her mind.

THE SPY WHO CAME IN FROM THE COLD

Academy Award Nominee: Actor (Richard Burton); Art Direction–Set Decoration—Black and White

Opening date: December 16, 1965 (New York: December 23, 1965).

Paramount. A Salem Films Production.

Director-Producer: Martin Ritt. Screenplay: Paul Dehn, Guy Trosper. Based on the 1963 novel by John le Carré. Photography: Oswald Morris. Production Designers: Hal Pereira, Tambi Larsen. Art Director: Edward Marshall. Set Dresser: Josie MacAvin. Costumes: Motley. Music: Sol Kaplan. Editor: Anthony Harvey. Black and white. 112 minutes.

CAST: Richard Burton (Alec Leamas), Claire Bloom (Nan Perry), Oskar Werner (Fiedler), Peter Van Eyck (Hans-Dieter Mundt), Sam Wanamaker (Peters), George Voskovec (East German Defense Attorney), Rupert Davies (George Smiley), Cyril Cusack (Control), Michael Hordern (Ashe), Robert Hardy (Dick Carlton), Bernard Lee (Patmore), Beatrix Lehmann (President of Tribunal), Esmond Knight (Old Judge), Niall MacGinnis (German Checkpoint Guard).

PLOT: Because Hans-Dieter Mundt has thwarted yet another effort to get a British agent safely over the Berlin Wall, a complicated plan is set in motion in which Alec Leamas will pretend to defect in order to gather damaging evidence on the enemy agent.

The dominance of James Bond over American and European pop culture during the mid-'60s was bound to get a lot of people angry, especially those who couldn't understand for the life of them what all the excitement was about. Some called the pictures silly or immoral, while others decried the fact that this wasn't what spying was really about at all. It was time to debunk the myths, and a former Eton schoolmaster named David Cornwell decided to do just that by writing about the life of a secret agent and all the boredom, depressing anonymity, morally questionable choices, and loneliness that surrounds it. Cornwall had not been employed just by the British education system—he had worked in Her Majesty's Foreign Service for nearly five years (1959–64) and therefore had some firsthand knowledge of the way the system worked. He chose the pen name of John le Carré, published a novel (his third) with the very evocative title *The Spy Who Came In from the Cold*, and found himself not only receiving thunderous acclaim for the reality of his tale but scoring a major hit with the public, who turned the book into one

> "You are a traitor! Does it occur to you? A wanted, spent, dishonest man; the lowest currency of the Cold War."
> —Alec Leamas

of the red-hot best sellers of 1964—it topped the *New York Times* best-seller chart for months. Working under the banner of their recently established company Salem Films, director Martin Ritt and actor Paul Newman snatched the rights to the novel away from several other interested parties, including Richard Burton. Burton needn't have fretted over the loss. The tired, resigned expression his face wore so well made him ideal for conveying Alec Leamas's sense of failure and disgust, and the part was his.

Preliminary work was done on adapting the novel by Guy Trosper, but his death in December 1963 necessitated a new writer. This brought the picture a James Bond connection in scenarist Paul Dehn, who had just worked on the recently released 007 adventure *Goldfinger* (United Artists, 1964).

Dehn's fairly close adaptation of *Spy* contained a few changes. These included getting rid of the character of the girlfriend of the agent killed at the Berlin War in the opening, whose presence suggested to Leamas that she had blown her lover's cover, which led thereby to her own death. Nan (Liz Gould in the book) was now present at Leamas's release from prison, whereas in the novel he had done the unlikely by agreeing to stay with Ashe, the agent Alec had already brushed off because of his homosexual inclinations. Le Carré had made it clear that Liz ended up in Berlin because of a fake letter, making it appear that the Communist Party wanted her there as part of an exchange program, whereas the movie kept her reason for being there vague. The book had included a sequence following the tribunal of Liz being interrogated by a brutish prison commissar and eventually being let out of her cell by Mundt, which allowed her to meet a waiting Alec outside. Not only was the commissar scene deleted, but the film script reversed the situation by having Alec find Liz/Nan waiting for him. Apparently believing that Leamas was in enough hot water at the end, Dehn chose not

A film as grim in nature as *The Spy Who Came In from the Cold* was hardly noted for its music score, though its theme by Sol Kaplan was available in sheet music form.

to include the scene of him murdering a guard during his incarceration, which had been an important aspect in the case against him.

Wisely shooting in black and white, Ritt began filming on January 11, 1965, with two weeks of locations in London, including Trafalgar Square (the exterior of the spy offices) and the entrance to Wormwood Scrubs Prison, where Burton was seen leaving after being jailed for throttling a grocer. This was followed by two months of interiors, shot at Ardmore Studios, outside of Dublin. Here the picture's very impressive, vividly grim recreation of Checkpoint Charlie and a piece of the Berlin Wall were constructed, the one standout set in a mostly drab-looking movie. The company also filmed in Amsterdam at the airport and at a private house where Burton was questioned by Wanamaker. Finally, there were scenes shot in both Garmisch and nearby Wallgau in southern Germany before the movie did some postproduction pick-up shots and process work at Shepperton, finally wrapping in April.

The Spy Who Came In from the Cold was released by Paramount right on top of the latest Bond picture, *Thunderball*, and there was no doubt which movie was preferred by the critics: *Spy* garnered Burton some of the best notices of his career. This enthusiastic need to condemn one entertainment in order to bring attention to the other seemed to overlook the fact that *Spy* went so far in the other direction to suck every ounce of life out of its undeniably depressing story that it was a bit of a slog to sit through, talky (though certainly intelligent), gloomy, and cold, both in atmosphere and in performance. Apart from Claire Bloom, it wasn't particularly easy to warm up to anybody in the film, and it all played like a very efficient espionage dossier full of specialized information, as would such future film adaptations of le Carré as *The Deadly Affair* (Columbia, 1967, from his book *Call for the Dead*) and *The Russia House* (MGM, 1990). Burton, who felt (rightly) that he wasted far too much of his movie career in inferior product or doing material for which he felt no admiration, always ranked this picture among his handful of proud achievements.

THUNDERBALL (United Kingdom)

Academy Award Winner: Best Special Visual Effects

Top 10 Box Office Film

Opening date: December 21, 1965 (London: December 29, 1965).

United Artists. An Eon Production, Presented by Albert R. Broccoli and Harry Saltzman.

Director: Terence Young. Producer: Kevin McClory. Screenplay: Richard Maibaum, John Hopkins. Based on an original screenplay by Jack Whittingham, based on an original story by Kevin McClory, Jack Whittingham, and Ian Fleming. (Uncredited: Based on the 1961 novel by Ian Fleming.) Photography: Ted Moore. Production Designer: Ken Adam. Art Director: Peter Murton. Wardrobe Designer: Anthony Mendleson. Sean Connery's Suits: Anthony Sinclair. Music: John Barry. Title song by John Barry (music) and Don Black (lyrics), performed by Tom Jones. Editor: Peter R. Hunt. Underwater Sequences Director: Ricou Browning. Main Title Designer: Maurice Binder. Action Sequences: Bob Simmons. Special Effects: John Stears. Technicolor. Panavision. 130 minutes.

CAST: Sean Connery (James Bond, 007), Claudine Auger (Dominique "Domino" Derval), Adolfo Celi (Emilio Largo), Luciana Paluzzi (Fiona Volpe), Rik Van Nutter (Felix Leiter), Guy Doleman (Count Lippe), Molly Peters (Patricia Fearing), Martine Beswick (Paula Kaplan), Bernard Lee (M), Desmond Llewelyn (Q), Lois Maxwell (Moneypenny), Roland Culver (Foreign Secretary), Earl Cameron (Pinder), Paul Stassino (Francis Derval/His Double), Rose Alba (Madame Boitier), Philip Locke (Vargas), George Pravda (Kutze), Michael Brennan (Janni), Leonard Sachs (Group Captain Pritchard), Edward Underdown (Air Vice Marshal), Reginald Beckwith (Kenniston), Harold Sanderson (Hydrofoil Captain), Bill Cummings (Quist), Mitsouko (Mademoiselle La Porte), Bob Simmons (Jacques Bouvar), Anthony Dawson (Ernst Blofeld, "Number One"), Eric Pohlmann (Voice of "Number One"), Suzy Kendall (Prue), Philo Hauser (Karlski).

PLOT: Emilio Largo hijacks a NATO bomber, on board which are two nuclear bombs, which SPECTRE plans to ransom for 100 million pounds' worth of uncut diamonds. The British Secret Service dispatches their top agent, James Bond, to Nassau to locate the hidden weapons and stop Largo's nefarious plan.

The first of the James Bond adventures to not give credit up front as being derived from a novel by Ian Fleming, *Thunderball* was, in fact, very closely based on a book in the series, though litigation dictated it be listed otherwise. Once upon a time, *Thunderball* was almost the very first James Bond opus to reach the screen, having been dreamed up a few years before Fleming sold the rights to his series of secret agent books to the production team of Albert R. Broccoli and Harry Saltzman. Fleming had hooked up with filmmaker Kevin McClory with the intention of bringing Agent 007 to cinemas, not by using one of the already published novels but by developing something from scratch. Ernest Cuneo had come up with a story outline that Fleming was then to turn into a film treatment. Several of the elements that would eventually find their way into the finished movie were present from the start, including the hijacking of a bomb and the setting of most of the action in Nassau, where the captured weapons were stashed. McClory hired Jack Whittingham to take Fleming's treatment and turn it into a screenplay, and the three men tossed around story ideas in order to come up with something they felt would play onscreen. After a while, Fleming began to lose interest and took off to work on what he did best, writing books. Whittingham had completed a first draft screenplay by early 1960, but during that year Fleming started turning these ideas into a novel, or what he would refer to as "a novel of the film." What he failed to take into consideration was that not all of what he was putting on the page came from him, so, not surprisingly, the publication of the book prompted legal action from McClory.

In the year of *Thunderball*'s publication, 1961, the Bond movie deal with Broccoli and Saltzman became a reality. The two men were confident in Fleming's claim on the property and decided that *Thunderball* would be the first of the screen adaptations, giving the task of turning the book into a script to Richard Maibaum. When it finally dawned on everyone that they had best let the *Thunderball* rights get cleared up before they went ahead with making a motion picture from it, *Dr. No* was chosen as the substitute Fleming property. In 1963 the court ruled in favor of McClory's retaining screen rights to the story, so he announced that he was going to commence with his own James Bond picture, without the input of the established Broccoli-Saltzman partnership. This did not seem like a good idea where the producing team was concerned, so they managed to come to an agreement in which McClory would receive sole "producer" credit, while Broccoli and Saltzman would be listed as "presenters." Maibaum's script, not Whittingham's, was selected as the starting point for the film, with revisions by John Hopkins. In

> "I forgot your ego, Mr. Bond; James Bond, who only has to make love to a woman and she starts to hear heavenly choirs singing. She repents, then immediately returns to the side of right and virtue. But not this one. What a blow it must have been to you, having a failure."
> —Fiona

the end, the opening titles read "Screenplay by Richard Maibaum and John Hopkins / Based on an original screenplay by Jack Whittingham / Based on an original story by Kevin McClory, Jack Whittingham, and Ian Fleming."

Although the screenplay bore a close resemblance to the details of Fleming's novel, there were a few attempts to veer away from the written page. According to Fleming, Domino's brother joined the forces of SPECTRE of his own greedy accord, but in the film this situation becomes more complicated: the villains replace him with a surgically altered lookalike to carry out the plane hijacking. The swap is brought to Bond's attention during a stay at the Shrublands spa, where he finds the real Derval's (called Palazzi in the book) body, thereby making the Secret Service branch aware of something fishy. Bond's identification of Derval gives him reason to go to Nassau in order to search out the dead man's sister. Rather than have the evil Derval double kill off his fellow fliers simply by tossing a gas canister on the floor of the plane, as described in the book, his actions are made more diabolical by having him surreptitiously pump cyanide through their oxygen system.

Thunderball found itself in a very lucky position chronologically in the still-continuing cinematic history of James Bond, coming at the very peak of "007 fever." With the three preceding films each building a larger audience, there was no denying that moviegoers just couldn't get enough of the superspy—*Goldfinger* (United Artists, 1964) was the height of the series's creativity—and they couldn't wait to see what the Bondsmen had in store for them next. United Artists had no qualms about laying out $5.6 million for the new film, knowing that its investment was a sound one. (It would also be the first entry to be shot in a wide-screen process.) Terence Young, who had guided the first two Bond films, was called back to direct, which was a good sign, but he somehow stumbled when it came to putting together the supporting cast, for *Thunderball* wound up with the least inspired line-up of performers of all the Connery 007s. Adolfo Celi looked menacing as the eye-patch-wearing Largo, but he lacked the eccentricities of the previous villains in the series and behaved more like an arrogant Eurotrash millionaire than a memorable threat to the world's safety. There was an extensive search to find the right beauty to play Domino. After rejecting such intriguing possibilities as Raquel Welch and Julie Christie, the filmmakers settled on a former Miss France, Claudine Auger, whose nationality prompted a change in her character's name, from Palazzi to Derval. There was very little spark in her screen personality, and like Celi, her voice was so thickly accented that she wound up having to be dubbed in the final print. The juiciest part, at least on

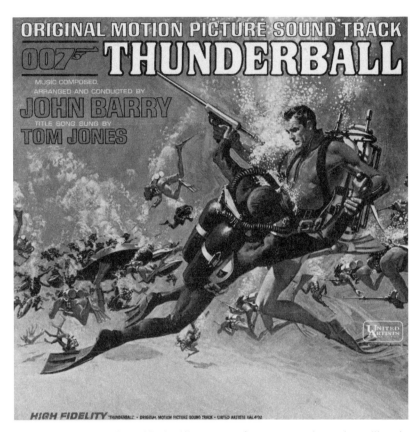

Leave it to James Bond to battle enemy frogmen underwater without an air mask, at least as depicted on the cover of the United Artists LP of John Barry's score for *Thunderball,* which only contains *some* of the music heard in the final film.

paper, was the deadly Fiona—a two-faced, unrepentant femme fatale—but the undeniably pretty Luciana Paluzzi was yet another disappointment in the charisma department.

Principal photography began on location outside of Paris on February 16, 1965, for Bond's fight with the cross-dressing Boitier (played by the film's chief action coordinator, Bob Simmons, once the actual battle began) and his memorable jet-pack retreat. These sequences were filmed at the Château d'Anet, followed by some brief work in Paris itself, where Largo was seen entering the offices of SPEC-TRE. The company then filmed interiors at the Pinewood Studios and at several sites in the United Kingdom: Chalfont Park House, Chalfont Park, Buckinghamshire, standing in for the Shrublands spa; Silverstone Racetrack, Northampshire, where the car chase and subsequent rocket blast by Fiona on her bike were staged; and Denham Quarry Lakes, South Harefield, Uxbridge, where Fiona submerged her cycle. The extensive Nassau shooting began on March 22, with Bond and Domino filmed dancing at the Café Martinique on Paradise Island, while most of the other locales were found on New

Providence Island, including Rock Point. There a lavish two-pool mansion on West Bay Street opened one of its swimming holes to a school of sharks and became Largo's Palmyra retreat. Also utilized were Love Beach, site of henchman Vargas's speargun demise; and the waters off Clifton Pier, where the undersea battle was shot. Once *Thunderball* finished its trip to the Bahamas, it was back to Pinewood to shoot most of the terrifically exciting fistfight in the engine room of Largo's combination hydrofoil and yacht, Disco Volante. Although most of the Bond gadgets were fairly tame, Largo's vessel was quite impressive, at least in the climactic scene when it broke into two pieces, leaving behind a hulking shell. The production designer had built this around an actual hydrofoil purchased for the film, which was then customized for maximum SPECTRE usage in Miami. The cast completed their obligations in May, and the production wrapped on July 9.

The publicity machine shifted into high gear as the Christmastime release of *Thunderball* approached and James Bond merchandizing and tie-in items flooded the stores, with both children and adults in mind. Just to show how important the American market had become for these pictures, *Thunderball* became the first of the series to premiere in the United States, opening one week *before* it debuted in Britain. Although United Artists had total faith that the film would outgross *Goldfinger*, even they were not prepared for the mobs that flocked to the theaters showing the film, and it was quickly decided that *Thunderball* would play around the clock in some of its venues. Records were indeed being broken. Where the box office was concerned, the film became the Mount Olympus of Bond movies, racking up more than $50 million at American theaters alone—one of the all-time moneymaking champs. This did not, alas, mean that it was the pinnacle for the Bond adventures in terms of quality. Quite the contrary, for, despite some fine set pieces, the film's pacing was often sluggish, and at times the ideas felt recycled, making this the weakest of the Connery Bonds. The much-publicized underwater sequences (the most in any production so far) were often stunning visually but were hampered by the lethargic pacing that hinders all underwater shots.

Because *Thunderball* remained one of two Bond-related titles (along with *Casino Royale*) that could be tampered with outside of the Broccoli-Saltzman regime, it was only a matter of time before it received a second big-screen adaptation. When McClory began toying with the idea in the late 1970s of doing a James Bond film with Connery involved as possible writer or director, United Artists quickly tossed water on their efforts by reminding them if they would be allowed to do so only if it somehow involved *Thunderball*. This meant that there was now a chance to sharpen and improve what hadn't entirely worked the first time out. The revamped script, once again bearing the credit "Based on an original idea by Kevin McClory, Jack Whittingham, and Ian Fleming," again involved the theft of destructive weapons (nuclear warheads), which led Bond to Nassau. Coming out a few months after the official Broccoli–Roger Moore Bond, *Octopussy* (United Artists, 1983), and proving to be the superior of the two pictures, *Never Say Never Again* (as it was cleverly titled) was indeed more fun than *Thunderball*, thanks to such casting improvements as Klaus Maria Brandauer as the villain and Barbara Carrera as a luscious femme fatale. It was a worthy farewell to his career-making role for Connery, who was still and forever the one and only James Bond where most of the moviegoing public was concerned.

DOCTOR ZHIVAGO

Academy Award Winner: Best Screenplay—Based on Material from Another Medium; Best Art Direction-Set Decoration—Color; Best Cinematography—Color; Best Music Score—Substantially Original; Best Costume Design—Color

Academy Award Nominee: Picture; Supporting Actor (Tom Courtenay); Director; Sound; Film Editing

Top 10 Box Office Film

Opening date: December 22, 1965.

MGM. A Carlo Ponti Production.

Director: David Lean. Producer: Carlo Ponti. Screenplay: Robert Bolt. Based on the 1957 novel by Boris Pasternak. Photography: Fred A. Young. Production Designer: John Box. Art Director: Terence Marsh. Set Decorator: Dario Simoni. Costumes: Phyllis Dalton. Music: Maurice Jarre. Song: "The Internationale," by Pierre De Geyter and Eugène Pottier, performed by chorus. Editor: Norman Savage. Metrocolor. Panavision. 197 minutes (including overture and entr'acte).

CAST: Omar Sharif (Yuri Zhivago), Julie Christie (Lara, Larissa Guishar), Geraldine Chaplin (Tonya Gromeko, later Tonya Zhivago), Rod Steiger (Viktor Komarovsky), Alec Guinness (Yevgraf, General Zhivago), Tom Courtenay (Pasha, Pavel Antipov, later General Strelnikov), Siobhan McKenna (Anna Gromeko), Ralph Richardson (Alexander Gromeko), Rita Tushingham (the Girl, Tonya Komarova), Adrienne Corri (Amelia Guishar), Geoffrey Keen (Prof. Boris Kurt), Jeffrey Rockland (Sasha Zhivago), Lucy Westmore (Katya), Noel Willman (Commissar Razin), Gerard Tichy (Military Chief Liberius), Klaus Kinski (Kostoyed Amourski), Jack MacGowran (Stationmaster Petya), María Martín (Gentlewoman), Tarek Sharif (Yuri at the age of eight), Mercedes Ruiz (Tonya at the age of seven), Roger Maxwell (Colonel), Inigo Jackson (Major), Virgilio Teixeira (Captain), Bernard Kay (Bolshevik, Leader of Deserters), Erik Chitty (Sergei, Old Soldier), José Nieto (Priest), Mark Eden (Young Engineer), Emilio Carrer (Sventytski).

PLOT: As revolution breaks out in Russia, tearing down the class order and causing ruin within the country, physician Yuri Zhivago falls in love with the beautiful Lara, only to find political and personal circumstances constantly thwarting their efforts to act on their passion and build a life together.

From sand to snow—director David Lean went the extreme opposite in temperature and atmosphere for the much-anticipated follow-up to his Oscar-winning desert epic *Lawrence of Arabia* (Columbia, 1962), choosing the chilly, snow-blanketed terrain of Russia to tell a tale of tragic love, *Doctor Zhivago*. The source material for his latest epic was controversial in its country of origin, where it was still banned at the time of the movie's release. Writer Boris Pasternak had spent a decade working on his lengthy novel, which dared to draw attention to the personal and economical destruction caused by the Russian Revolution, but it was promptly roadblocked by government authorities, who made sure that the book would not be published in Pasternak's homeland. Determined to have his work read, the author managed to smuggle the manuscript to an Italian publisher, who was responsible for its first printing in 1957.

Soon the rest of the world was aware of the epic novel, and it became one of the most talked-about publications of its time, earning a Nobel Prize for Pasternak in 1958, although he was forbidden to leave Russia to pick up the award. Producer Carlo Ponti quickly snatched up the film rights, seeing this as an ideal showcase for his wife, Sophia Loren. All he needed to do was get a studio interested. MGM eventually agreed to put up the money provided Ponti got the right person to direct it. There was hardly any filmmaker at the time who had been elevated to so lofty a level of acclaim and financial good fortune as David Lean, who could boast of having delivered back-to-back Academy Award winners for both Best Picture and Best Director that also happened to be two of the mightiest moneymakers in recent years, *The Bridge on the River Kwai* (Columbia, 1957) and *Lawrence*. Once he said yes to Ponti's offer, *Zhivago*

> "Feelings, insight, affections; it's suddenly trivial now. You don't agree. You're wrong. The personal life is dead in Russia. History has killed it."
> —Strelnikov

became MGM's priority prestige item of the day, with no expense spared in an effort to bring the company the sort of critical and monetary rewards that would hopefully top its recent colossus, next to which all others paled in comparison: the 1959 remake of *Ben-Hur*.

Lean knew from the start that he wanted many of the same people on the project who had been part of his winning *Lawrence* team. None of these was more crucial than Robert Bolt, who had crafted that movie's complex and literate screenplay. His main directive to Bolt was that he wasn't so much interested in making a political statement as he was a love story and told him to concentrate on adapting the book as such. It was a strenuous task to weed through Pasternak's long and winding tome, which meant discarding a great many characters and writing around the many philosophical musings and political theories presented throughout the work. These included criticism of the persecution of Russia's Jewish population, an issue that would be dealt with in the stage and screen versions of *Fiddler on the Roof*. Dropped were Zhivago's influential Uncle Nicolai, a priest-turned-writer who takes the boy under his wing after the death of his mother; Lara's gambler brother, Rodion; Pasha's father, who is arrested for helping organize a strike; revolutionary Tiverzin, who raises Pasha after his father's arrest; Yuri's childhood friend Misha Gordon; Galiullin, a janitor at the Tiverzin tenement, who becomes Pasha's nemesis during the revolution, taking charge of the White Army; the Mikulitsyn family, who provide Zhivago and his wife with housing when they arrive in Varykino; and Lara's friend Nadia, whose father shelters revolutionaries in his home.

In order to assure impatient audiences that this was a story about the eventual coming together of Zhivago and Lara, a prologue was created to have Yuri's half-brother, Yevgraf, tell the story to a young girl he is quite certain is the illegitimate child of the two lovers. Pasha's rabble-rousing qualities were presented earlier than in the book: he was made one of the principal instigators of a public demonstration that, for dramatic impact, was witnessed by Zhivago. Bolt and Lean made one of the key sequences in the first half of the picture Lara's shooting of the coarse Komarovsky, a far juicier event as enacted onscreen, in so much as Lara in the book had ended up firing her pistol at a public prosecutor who had denounced the railway worker's strike. Pasha was now included in the shooting scene as well, retrieving the shaken Lara after the incident, which meant that he was familiar to Zhivago. In the book, when

Zhivago meets up with Strelnikov (Pasha), he is not instantly aware that this man was Lara's husband. Pasternak had included a scene in which Strelnikov confronts Zhivago at Varykino once Lara has left, then shoots himself. Onscreen, Strelnikov's suicide, which he opts for as he is about to be executed, is described by Komarovsky rather than seen. Not surprisingly, Bolt eliminated much of the material from the concluding chapters, which found Zhivago taking up with a woman named Marina, with whom he has two children, and gave more romance to his demise by having him certain he has seen Lara from a passing trolley.

With all these cuts, changes, and distortions, Lean was sure he had the tale he wanted to tell and set about casting. He initially considered Max von Sydow for the lead, but MGM wasn't crazy about the idea and hoped they could coax him into using Paul Newman, whom Lean found totally unsuitable. Lean figured he would simply fall back on his *Lawrence* star, Peter O'Toole, until he discovered that producer Sam Spiegel would not release him from his contract. Instead, Lean found his Zhivago in another of *Lawrence*'s cast members, Omar Sharif, who had expressed interest in playing Pasha, never dreaming he'd be consider for the title role. A glimpse of Julie Christie in *Billy Liar* (Continental, 1963) convinced Lean that she was absolutely perfect to play the tormented Lara, and she was added to the cast even before the world had gotten to see her star-making turn in *Darling* (Embassy, 1965). Although he toyed briefly with the idea of Audrey Hepburn as Yuri's devoted wife, Tonya, Lean was enchanted with a magazine photo of Geraldine Chaplin, who at the time was known principally as the daughter of the great Charles Chaplin. Ponti loved the idea of playing up this angle and suggested Lean test her for the part. Although she had popped up along with her siblings in one of her father's pictures, *Limelight* (United Artists, 1951), *Zhivago* would be her official motion-picture debut.

Such locations as Finland, Yugoslavia (Ponti's choice), and Canada were considered until it was decided that the company did not want to establish production in a principally frozen locale, insomuch as four seasons were required for story purposes. Spain, where Lean had shot some scenes of *Lawrence*, seemed to fit the bill perfectly. Starting in August of 1964 the city of Moscow was constructed by production designer John Box and his crew on a ten-acre garbage dump in the Madrid suburb of Canillejas. It took some three months to complete the set, which included not only the exterior of the Gromeko house, but its interiors as well. Other interiors were created at the soundstages of nearby CEA Studios. The movie's most striking and famous set, the Ice Palace at Varykino, was built on a plain in Soria, some 150 miles north of Madrid. Because there was only so much fake snow that Lean and company could spread about with conviction, they were obliged to travel north to get the authentic feel of a numbingly cold Russia. Therefore, they ended up in Finland after all—Lake Pyhäselkä, less than ten miles from the Russian border—to shoot Yuri's escape from the Red Troops and several scenes involving the train ride out of Moscow. Filming began on December 28, 1964, and dragged on until October 7, 1965, costing MGM a whopping $15 million.

Knowing full well that MGM wanted *Doctor Zhivago* to be its big Christmas release for 1965, Lean and his editors spent a good deal of time banging the film into shape while shooting. They had a little more than two months to get the final cut in order for the December 22 opening. Because *Lawrence* had been hailed as just about the apex of '60s spectacles, anticipation was strong for *Zhivago*, which may have accounted for the general feeling of disappointment expressed by the majority of reviewers. Perhaps they were thrown by the fact that Lean's last two movies had pretty much dispensed with pivotal female characters altogether, while in this instance Lean proudly wallowed in romantic sentiment and melodrama. Lean was so stung by the negative comments that he swore this would be his swan song, but this declaration was soon forgotten once the box office began, unexpectedly, to ascend. Not unlike *The Sound of Music* (Twentieth Century-Fox), another big-budget film from 1965 that had triumphed over unfavorable press and become a runaway hit, *Zhivago* just kept attracting bigger and bigger audiences until it became one of the movie events not only of the year, but of the decade. Relieved, MGM realized that it would not only get back its costly investment, but have profits to spare, since *Zhivago* wound up second only to *Gone with the Wind* (1939) as the most highly attended motion picture ever distributed by the company.

"Lara's Theme from *Doctor Zhivago*," or "Somewhere My Love," as it became better known when Paul Francis Webster added lyrics to it, became one of the most famous songs never actually to be sung in the film from which it was derived. Indeed, the sheet music pictured here contains no lyrics whatsoever.

This must have come as a shock to many, considering the overwhelmingly downbeat nature of the film; for the most part it couldn't help but come off as more than somewhat gloomy, dwelling as it did on the people whose lives had been ruined by communism. The love story of Yuri and Lara was not only doomed, but also seemed hopelessly unfulfilling for the troubled protagonists: they were forced to spend their one chance to be together sitting in a freezing, ice-coated house, lamenting their sorry fate as howling wolves surround them. That audiences cared about a man who blithely arose from his mistress's bed so he could go home and sleep with his wife was no

small feat, so clearly Lean had done something right. *Zhivago* had taken audiences on a journey that was spectacularly engrossing for most of its epic length, presenting an intimate story of people uprooted by circumstances, while horrifying images of communist rule provided the sort of backdrop that gave the film a feeling of importance, though the issues hardly seemed as thoroughly explored as they could have been. Although coming attractions played up such moments as the Bolshevik attack on the demonstrators and the Red Army's charge from out of the woods, the film never presented itself as an action adventure per se; its most successfully executed set piece was the Moscow refugees' punishing train journey as it captured the oppressive misery of human beings forced into demeaning living conditions.

Fittingly, the two critically lambasted audience favorites went head to head at the Academy Award ceremony, with *Sound of Music* and *Zhivago* earning ten Oscar nominations apiece. They both ended up winning five trophies, although it was *Music* that took home the Best Picture prize. This seemed not to matter at all to fans of *Zhivago*; it continued to be spoken of by many moviegoers as one of the highlights of the decade, prompting it to pop up several times over the next ten years in reissues and return engagements. (It remains, with figures adjusted for inflation, the eighth-highest-grossing movie of all time.) A key feature in capturing the public's fancy was the film's Oscar-winning theme, composed by Maurice Jarre. Although the movie contained several glorious pieces of music, "Lara's Theme" took on a life of its own. With lyrics added, it was given the alternate name of "Somewhere, My Love" and covered by countless vocalists of the day. The most successful recording was that of the Ray Coniff Singers; their version reached number 9 on the *Billboard* charts in July 1966. Earlier that year the soundtrack had become one of the rare all-instrumental motion-picture albums to land in the number 1 position. "Somewhere, My Love" would rank as one of the most famous movie "songs" that was never actually sung in the motion picture from which it derived.

Pasternak's novel finally made it to the bookstores in his native Russia in 1988, thirty-one years after its unveiling and twenty-eight years after its author had passed away. The film's long-delayed Russian premiere took place in April 1994. By that time most people had long forgotten *Doctor Zhivago*'s soft critical reception and were referring to it as one of Lean's masterpieces. And to many it still towers above all the rest.

INSIDE DAISY CLOVER

Academy Award Nominee: Supporting Actress (Ruth Gordon); Art Direction–Set Decoration—Color; Costume Design—Color

Opening date: December 22, 1965 (New York: February 17, 1966).

Warner Bros. A Pakula–Mulligan Production; a Park Place Production.

Director: Robert Mulligan. Producer: Alan J. Pakula. Screenplay: Gavin Lambert, based on his 1963 novel. Photography: Charles Lang. Production Designer: Robert Clatworthy. Set Decorator: George James Hopkins. Costumes: William Thomas. Miss Natalie Wood's Wardrobe Designer: Edith Head. Music: André Previn. Songs by André Previn (music) and Dory Previn (lyrics): "You're Gonna Hear from Me" and "The Circus Is a Wacky World," performed by Jackie Ward dubbing for Natalie Wood. Musical Numbers Staged by Herbert Ross. Editor: Aaron Stell. Technicolor. Panavision. 128 minutes.

CAST: Natalie Wood (Daisy Clover), Christopher Plummer (Raymond Swan), Robert Redford (Wade Lewis), Roddy McDowall (Walter Baines), Ruth Gordon (Mrs. Clover, "The Dealer"), Katharine Bard (Melora Swan), Betty Harford (Gloria Goslett), John Hale (Harry Goslett), Harold Gould (Cop on Pier), Ottola Nesmith (Dolores, Old Lady in Hospital), Edna Holland (Cynara, Fortune Teller), Peter Helm (Milton Hopwood), Stanley Farrar (Doctor), Joseph Mell (Chauffeur), Dodo Denny, Peg Shirley (Gloria's Friends).

PLOT: Insolent teenager Daisy Clover is turned into an overnight movie star after her amateur record ends up in the hands of powerful Hollywood mogul Raymond Swan.

It was always fun to see Hollywood skewering itself for its crass pursuit of money, insensitivity to bona fide talent, and soulless manufacturing of artistically questionable product, but this sort of satire never went down very well when the movie doing the skewering was such a stinker. That's the best way to describe *Inside Daisy Clover*, one of the true A-picture misfires of the decade. Natalie Wood certainly could relate to what it was like to be a part of the movieland star-making machine, having been in front of the cameras since she was just six years old. When the heroine of Gavin Lambert's novel, cynical teen performer Daisy Clover, caught Wood's fancy, the actress figured a film version of the sour tale might relay some of her feelings about what it was like to be a slave to the studio system and give her a meaty role in the bargain. Wood had known Lambert

> "My mother says this world's a garbage dump and we're just the flies it attracts. Maybe she's right, but when I sing the smell doesn't seem so bad."
> —Daisy Clover

since he had served as personal assistant to Nicholas Ray, who had directed Wood in *Rebel without a Cause* (Warner Bros., 1955), and contacted the author to adapt his book. Producer Alan J. Pakula and director Robert Mulligan, the very same team that had served Wood so well with *Love with the Proper Stranger* (Paramount, 1963), were put in charge of the film.

Surprisingly, considering that the originator of the work was involved in the adaptation, there were a number of notable changes from page to screen. First, it was decided to give the movie a more nostalgic aura and set it in the 1930s, instead of the 1950s, as the book had been. Magnagram Pictures became Swan Studios, to reflect the name of its head, Raymond Swan, who now ended up sleeping with Daisy, though no such interaction had taken place in the novel. In the book, Daisy had submitted to the advances of pestering beachfront teen Milton, whom she definitely had no tolerance for in the film, and had also gone to bed with aspiring actor Ridge Banner, who had impregnated her after her disastrous, unconsummated marriage to Wade.

There was no Ridge in the film, no pregnancy, and no decision to chuck the film industry and move to New York, which had been Daisy's destiny on the written page, followed by a triumphant comeback concert in Atlantic City. For reasons unknown, or perhaps because they knew that they had screwed things up considerably, Lambert and the filmmakers chose to end the movie with the apocalyptic image of Daisy blowing up her beach house. Well, at least it was something different.

Shooting began at the Santa Monica Pier on March 2, 1965, before moving to the Convalarium, a rest home in Pasadena; off the coast of Ventura, for scenes on Wade's boat; Bel Air, where the Conrad Hilton estate on Bellagio Road became the Swan mansion; a dingy, isolated desert motel in Pearblossom, California, to accommodate Daisy and Wade's woeful wedding night; and the beach at Oxnard, to which a home once belonging to silent screen star Barbara LaMarr was transported from Venice and then dynamited as Wood walked away from it. The film then moved to the Warners lot, where several of the facility's office buildings were utilized,

The photograph of Natalie Wood that adorned the cover of the Bantam paperback edition of Gavin Lambert's *Inside Daisy Clover* was taken, appropriately, by one of the film's costars, Roddy McDowall.

in addition to its soundstages. It was in a recording booth on one of those soundstages that Lambert devised a scene that had not been in the book: Daisy begins to unravel while trying to synchronize her vocals to a big-screen image of herself. As shot by Mulligan, cutting between the silence outside the booth and the mute, onscreen Wood, it turned out to be a frighteningly good tour-de-force moment that made everything else in the picture look that much more pat and hollow in comparison.

Wood had trouble making anyone believe that this belligerent, eternally unhappy lowlife from the California beaches was, beneath it all, a magnetically talented screen personality, and her unconvincing performance set the tone for the entire caricatured mess, which never seemed to decide whether it was high melodrama or black comedy. Wood was deeply disappointed in the results but was thrilled enough with costar Robert Redford to request him for her next picture, *This Property Is Condemned* (Paramount, 1966), which, alas, turned out to be another negligible credit for them both. She also remained close friends with Gavin Lambert, who would go on to write a biography of her, *Natalie Wood: A Life* (2004).

1966

THE SHOP ON MAIN STREET (Czechoslovakia)

Academy Award Winner: Best Foreign Language Film (1965)

Academy Award Nominee: Actress (Ida Kaminska) (1966)

Opening date: January 24, 1966 (Prague: October 8, 1965, as *Obchod na korze*; released in the United Kingdom as *A Shop in the High Street*).

Prominent Films. A Marie Desmarais–Eurofilm Presentation.

Directors: Ján Kadár, Elmar Klos. Producers: Jaromír Lukás, M. Broz, K. Feix, Jordan Balurov. Screenplay: Ján Kadár, Elmar Klos, Ladislav Grosman. Based on the 1962 short story "The Trap" and the 1964 novel by Ladislav Grosman. Photography: Vladimír Novotný. Production Designer: Karel Skvor. Set Decorator: František Straka. Costumes: Marie Rosenfelderova. Music: Zdeněk Liška. Editors: Jaromír Janácek, Diana Heringova. Black and white. 126 minutes.

CAST: Josef Króner (Tono Brtko), Ida Kaminska (Rosalie Lautmann), Hana Slivková (Evelina Brtko), František Zvarik (Marcus Kolkotsky), Helena Zvaríková (Rose Kolkotsky), Martin Hollý (Imro Kuchar), Martin Gregor (Josef Katz), Adám Matejka (Piti Báci), Mikulas Ladizinsky (Marian Peter), Eugen Senaj (Blau), František Papp (Andoric), Gita Misurová (Andoricová), Luise Grossová (Eliasova), Alojz Kramar (Balko), Tibor Vadaš (Tobacconist).

PLOT: During World War II, Tono Brtko, a poor carpenter, is appointed Aryan Controller over a button shop owned by widow Rosalie Lautmann, an elderly Jew who remains oblivious to the danger she and the rest of the Jewish community are facing.

The United States had to wait until the mid-'60s to find out just what the Czechs had to offer in the way of cinema, and the first Czech motion picture to receive wide international distribution and make a major impact on the American market was simply one of the best pictures from *any* country, *The Shop on Main Street*. The movie, the title of which was *Obchod na korze* in its native land and was translated initially as *The Shop on High Street*, was one of those occasional features in which the directorial credit was a shared one, belonging to Ján Kadár and Elmar Klos. The two men came together in 1953 to serve as both writers and codirectors on the propaganda film *Unos* and continued as a collaborative filmmaking unit into the next decade. Kadár did the bulk of the work, actually guiding the actors and setting up the filming details on the set, while most of Klos's input came in the editing room, structuring the picture his partner had shot.

Kadár had read a short story, "The Trap," by Ladislav Grosman prior to its publication and purchased the rights to it, asking the author to do his own screenplay adaptation. After finishing his first draft, Grosman fashioned his ideas into a novel, which was published prior to the picture's release. Kadár and Klos then took a crack at what Grosman had written in order to shape it more naturally into a workable screenplay. The most notable aspect of their version was to give more prominence to the character of Kuchar, the "White Jew" to whom Tono had first gone to for advice after becoming Aryan Controller of Mrs. Lautmann's shop. In the screenplay Kuchar made additional appearances—coaching Tono along and giving him further ideas on how to cautiously keep both the Nazis and the ill-informed old Jewish woman happy as the imminent danger crept closer. Added to the film was the clever idea, on Kuchar's part, of fooling the Nazis into believing that Mrs. Lautmann's store was closed on the Sabbath not because she refused to open it, but because a stock inventory was being done. Further dramatic strength was added to Kuchar's inevitable capture by having him beaten in front of a helpless Tono while being carted away by the SS. In the book, Tono had been informed of Kuchar's fate after the fact. Placing more focus on the Aryan's attempts to aid the Jews and the awful repercussions of his acts helped to make Tono's tormented state of fear and indecision play more effectively to the audience.

The script did not bother to dwell on Grosman's mention of Mrs. Lautmann's two daughters, instead making it appear as if there was only a beloved husband in her past. It also provided some humor by having Tono make a shambles of his first day helping to run the shop, after which his good-hearted "boss" gives him a bonus fee for his noble efforts, and allowed Mrs. Lautmann to finally become aware of the horrific nature of her fate at the finale, rather than keeping her in the dark, as the book had done. Gone from the script was the character of Carny, an appointed official who demands to see the wares that Tono has gotten off Mrs. Lautmann. This forces Tono to give Carny rings and jewels, prompting the town blacksmith to spit in Tono's face for his betrayal of the woman he was sure Tono was looking out for. Carny had also played a part in another sequence not included in the film version, in which he berates Tono because his dog, Essence, is having sex with a Jewish dog, a situation that might have been simply too bizarre or seemingly clownish to stage on film, even if the censors could have been persuaded to go along with such a thing.

> "When the law persecutes the innocent, that's the end of it; of the lawmakers too."
> —Katz

The very difficult role of the ineffectual, tragically indecisive Tono was given to Josef Króner, who had actually appeared in the first feature that Kadár directed, *Katha*, back in 1949. Króner was required to pull off some semicomical moments, including his drunken outburst at his brother-in-law during a family party, and then turn about 180 degrees to invoke the naked cowardice of a man tossed into a situation requiring more strategy, bravery, and influence than he is capable of providing. Króner came off not unlike a sad-sack comic, whose uncomfortable handling of life goes from darkly humorous to simply dark. It was a flawless performance from start to finish, one that carried the picture but had a tendency to be overshadowed by all the attention given Króner's elderly costar, Ida Kaminska, who was, in truth, very much in support of him. Kaminska, who was sixty-five at the time of filming but very convincingly played an older woman in a more feeble state, had founded Warsaw's Jewish Art Theater, appearing for this company throughout Europe during the 1920s. After spending World War II in Russia, she returned to Warsaw to create the Jewish National Theatre. During this time she had made some sporadic, undistinguished movie appearances, though her heart truly belonged to the stage. When Kadár had trouble locating a suitable Czech actress, Kaminska's name came up, and because the drama in Grosman's story was so close to her heart, the actress having been as deeply involved in fighting anti-Semitism as she was in acting, she agreed to make her first motion-picture appearance since the late 1940s. In need of a small town that had not changed in the twenty years since the story took place, Kadár and Klos decided to film in Sabinov, located near the northeastern frontier, with many of the local citizens filling in the background as extras.

The Shop on High Street (as it was then titled) had its grand unveiling at the 1965 Cannes Film Festival, where it made so tremendous an impact with both reviewers and audiences that it became the key film of the Czech New Wave. It helped launch a brief period of prominence for its country's filmmakers that came to be known as the Prague Spring. Both Kaminska and Króner received special awards at the close of the festival, which ensured the picture a spot at that fall's New York Film Festival prior to its actual October release in Czechoslovakia. Unlike pretty much any other film around, good, bad, or indifferent, *The Shop on Main Street* (as it was now called) received almost unanimous raves for its incredible humanity, lack of unabashed sentimentality, and the way it personalized, in one relationship between a highly incongruous pairing, the most shameful event of the twentieth century, without ever having to set foot inside a concentration camp to bring to light the horror of the lives destroyed. Because this was clearly one of the most emotionally devastating of all foreign imports of the decade, United Artists decided to go as high as $100,000 for the distribution rights, only to discover that it had acted too late. A Canadian distributor, Marie Desmarais,

Because Mainstream waited until *The Shop on Main Street* made an impact to release Zdeněk Liška's score on record, the soundtrack is a rare one in that it includes the film's Academy Award win as part of the artwork.

head of Prominent Films, had seen the movie at Cannes and put forward a mere $2,000 for an option on both the American and Canadian rights, with a later, fuller payment of $20,000 agreed upon. Once the Czech government realized it could get more money out of United Artists, Desmarais was informed that they would not go through on the offer until she could match the $100,000 they would have gotten from the larger company. Desmaris managed to do so, and in the end, *The Shop* opened in New York and Los Angeles in January 1966. Three months later it became the first Czech entry to win the Best Foreign Language Film Oscar.

MORGAN! (United Kingdom)

Academy Award Nominee: Actress (Vanessa Redgrave); Costume Design—Black and White

Opening date: April 4, 1966 (London: May 15, 1966, as *Morgan: A Suitable Case for Treatment*).

Cinema V. A Quintra Films Presentation.

Director: Karel Reisz. Producer: Leon Clore. Screenplay: David Mercer, based on his 1962 television play *A Suitable Case for Treatment*. Photography: Gerry Turpin, Larry Pizer. Art Director: Philip Harrison. Costumes: Jocelyn Rickards. Music: John Dankworth. Editors: Tom Priestley, Victor Procter. Black and white. 97 minutes.

CAST: David Warner (Morgan Delt), Vanessa Redgrave (Leonie), Robert Stephens (Charles Napier), Irene Handl (Mrs. Delt), Arthur Mullard (Wally "the Gorilla" Carver), Bernard Bresslaw (Policeman), Newton Blick (Mr. Henderson), Nan Munro (Mrs. Henderson), Peter Collingwood (Geoffrey), Graham Crowden (Counsel), John Garrie (Tipstatt), John Rae (Judge), Angus Mackay (Best Man).

PLOT: Morgan Delt, a gorilla-fancying Marxist, refuses to give up his estranged wife, Leonie, causing havoc while trying to win her back with his eccentric schemes.

Morgan Delt fit right in with the British New Wave's pack of "angry young men," but, whereas most of those cinematic nonconformists were restless rebels in search of peace of mind and a possible escape from their dead-end lives, the gorilla-obsessed Morgan possessed hints of genuine insanity. This was no surprise, coming as he did from the mind of writer David Mercer (1928–1980), who had himself suffered from severe depression after parting from his wife, which had, in turn, led to a nervous breakdown and eventual analysis. Mercer decided to turn his misfortune into something with a comical edge and came up with an original television play about a blocked writer intent on wooing back the woman who has just divorced him by using his own eccentric idea of romance. Entitled *A Suitable Case for Treatment*, the program aired as part of the BBC's *Sunday Night Play* on October 21, 1962, with Ian Hendry as Morgan, Moira Redmond as Leonie, and Jack May as Charles Napier, under the direction of Don Taylor. Mercer got his chance to expand his teleplay when producer Leon Clore and director Karel Reisz expressed interest in a film version. This time Mercer would bring the character of Morgan closer to his own past by having him be a painter, which Mercer himself had tried to be, while Leonie's new lover, Charles Napier, was now the owner of the art gallery at which Morgan has displayed his works, rather than his publisher. Mercer also went to town making gorillas an

> "I do appreciate that living with a gifted idiot has its rewards. On the other hand, the function of a nursery in marriage is to be occupied by children, not by the husband and wife."
> —Charles Napier

important image in the story, going so far as to have his demented hero crash his ex-wife's wedding to Napier dressed in an ape costume, which he would therefore be wearing as he sped through the streets of London on a motorbike. Another "gorilla" added to the mix was a slow-witted, punch-drunk wrestler, Wally the Gorilla, who served as a companion to Morgan's Marxist mother. Finally, Mercer put his anti-hero in a psychiatric hospital at the finale, which had not been his fate on television.

Reisz and Clore made a distribution deal with British Lion that did not include a particularly large budget. This meant that they could go with the inexpensive casting ideas they had in mind. Looking for someone with both angst and the ability to play comedy, Reisz found the ideal actor when he spotted David Warner in the Royal Shakespeare Company's production of the American comedy *Eh?* Warner had done only one previous movie, but that movie happened to be *Tom Jones* (United Artists, 1963), which had turned into the biggest British export of the era. Warner's elongated features really did come across as marginally simian at times, his mop of unkempt blond hair suggesting an earthy sexuality and brooding quality that was alternately menacing and absurd—perfect for conveying Morgan's unrest and unpredictability. For Morgan's capricious, maddeningly indecisive ex-wife, Reisz selected one of

For its Mexican release, *Morgan!!* was given a subtitle that translates as "A Clinical Case," as seen on this lobby card.

England's hottest rising talents of the time, Vanessa Redgrave, who had been garnering just as much praise for her acting skills as for her stunning beauty ever since she made her stage bow in the late 1950s. Having built a reputation for doing classical theater, she loved the idea of playing someone as fluttery and instinctive as Leonie, and accepted the part after having turned down several other motion picture offers over the past few years.

Morgan: A Suitable Case for Treatment (as it would be called in the United Kingdom) began principal photography on March 29, 1965, with interiors shot at Shepperton Studios. A corner house was found at 13 Campden Hill Square in the Notting Hill section of London to serve as the digs of Morgan and his ex, the building surrounded by workmen's scaffolding. In addition to filming in the adjacent streets, Reisz took his cameras to the rooftop of the Dorchester Hotel on Park Lane for Leonie and Charles's crashed wedding reception; the entrance gates of Wormwood Scrubs Prison, where Morgan is seen fleeing his captors by heading inside instead of out; and Highgate Cemetery in northwest London, where Morgan and his mother pay their respects at the actual gravesite of Karl Marx, his imposing bust glaring from the top of his headstone.

Reisz shot parts of the movie in the freewheeling, tricky style that at the time was very much in vogue in British cinema, speeding up the camera for certain moments to stress the slapstick, but he was not as successful at making a laugh-out-loud funny movie as he was at presenting a dark, off-the-wall milieu for his protagonist to cavort in. While undeniably a comedy, *Morgan!* had a somewhat bitter, melancholy quality to it and challenged its audiences, who had trouble grasping just what its hero stood for. Morgan has been raised to champion communism but has clearly lost his grasp after marrying into the upper class; his struggle is not for the oppressed workers but for his own particular gain: getting his wife back no matter what the cost. A gorilla fancier, Morgan is most comfortable when following his animal instincts. This is most appealing to Leonie, who gets off on having a childlike, simian-assimilating lover to get her fires cooking. Two people all too oblivious to the world around them, Leonie and Morgan teetered on the brink of being too self-absorbed for words, but the wit of Mercer's dialogue and the expert playing of the two leads somehow made the whole thing seem like a jolly good lark for adults who liked their romantic comedies a bit skewed, chaotic, and determined not to play at an expected and obvious rhythm.

BORN FREE (United Kingdom)

Academy Award Winner: Best Song ("Born Free"); Best Original Music Score

Opening date: April 6, 1966 (New York: June 22, 1966; London: March 14, 1966).

Columbia. A Carl Foreman Presentation of an Open Road–Atlas Coproduction.

Director: James Hill. Producers: Sam Jaffe, Paul Radin. Screenplay: Gerald L. C. Copley (Lester Cole). Based on the 1960 book *Born Free: A Lioness of Two Worlds*, by Joy Adamson. Photography: Kenneth Talbot. Music: John Barry. Title song by John Barry (music) and Don Black (lyrics), performed by Matt Monro. Editor: Don Deacon. Chief Technical Advisor: George Adamson. Animal Supervisor: Peter Whitehead. Technicolor. Panavision. 95 minutes.

CAST: Virginia McKenna (Joy Adamson), Bill Travers (George Adamson), Geoffrey Keen (John Kendall), Peter Lukoye (Nuru), Omar Chambati (Makkede), Bill Godden (Sam), Bryan Epsom (Baker), Robert Cheetham (Ken), Robert Young (James), Geoffrey Best (Watson), Surya Patel (Indian Doctor), Ugas, Henrietta, Mara (Elsa).

PLOT: Finding three orphaned lion cubs, George Adamson, a senior game warden in the northern province of Kenya, and his wife, Joy, decide to raise the youngest of the cats, Elsa, on their own.

For reasons best explained by psychologists, motion pictures centered around animals have always been thought of as appropriate fare for children and families, even when they involve carnivorous beasts such as lions. It was a British picture of seemingly modest intentions that helped shake off this "youth" label to some degree. *Born Free* became not only the definitive motion picture where cinematic lions were concerned, but one of the rare entries of the animal-pic genre of which adults could speak admiringly without fear of condescension or judgmental looks from their peers.

The film was based on the sort of remarkable true story that simply cried out for dramatization on the big screen. The protagonists were Joy Adamson (born Friederike Victoria Gessner in Troppau, Austria-Hungary, in 1910), who had come to Africa to study wild animals and ended up marrying a game warden, George Adamson (born to a British mother and Irish father in India in 1906), her third husband. On February 1, 1956, Elsa the lion cub (along with her two sisters) walked into Joy and George's life and became their cherished pet, growing up alongside them as would a kitten. It was their seemingly hopeless but ultimately triumphant efforts to get Elsa to leave behind the life she knew and adapt to the wild life in which she should have grown up that made for so fascinating a story. It was first recounted to the rest of the world in a book written by Joy and published in 1960 under the title *Born Free: A Lioness of Two Worlds*. Joy went on to publish two more books about Elsa, *Living Free: The Story of Elsa and Her Cubs* (1961) and *Forever Free: Elsa's Pride* (1962), by which time writer-director-producer Carl Foreman had purchased the rights to make Adamson's first book into a motion picture, with Columbia Pictures attached as distributor. Although the blacklist period seemed a thing of the past by this point in time, the screenwriter hired to do the adaptation, Gerald L. C. Copley, was, in fact, not a real person but a fake name for one of the original Hollywood Ten, Lester Cole, who would not be given his actual onscreen credit for another thirty years. (A curious contradiction, in that Foreman had been a blacklist victim as well yet was allotted *his* onscreen credit.)

The intention was to stay faithful to the real events as they had happened, with as little fabricated drama as possible, and to use authentic and unstaged shots of the animals almost exclusively. Although it was believed initially that the filmmakers would have to use trained circus lions for safety and cooperation, these creatures proved quite unsuitable. They appeared false and unnatural on camera, prompting director James Hill to reject them in favor of several cats that had been found in the bush and raised by people, much as Elsa had been. Because the film required two actors to spend a great deal of time working with the lions, Hill and Foreman came up with the idea of casting a real-life acting couple, Virginia McKenna and Bill Travers. The pair, whose closest contact with a lion up to that point had been at a zoo, was game to

> "Elsa was full grown now. She had already been in season and was capable of having her own cubs. And she was beginning to realize that there was another life than the one we had been living together."
> —Joy Adamson

participate in the project to the fullest extent, going through an eight-week training period to familiarize themselves with the lions that played Elsa in order to make sure that they did not appear afraid or uncomfortable around the critters. Bravely, they insisted on never using stunt doubles, always appearing in the same frame with the cats, even though Hill and his camera crew spent most of the production shooting from behind a wire fence for their own safety.

The company arrived in Kenya in August 1964 to prepare for the following month's filming, which would take place in Naro Moru, some 120 miles north of Nairobi. Such locales as the Nanyuki area near Thomson's Falls, Maralal (scene of the elephant stampede); the shores of the Indian Ocean;

and Nairobi National Park provided settings that looked almost exactly like the places where the Adamsons had lived. While George Adamson provided technical assistance on the picture, Joy chose to stay away from the project altogether, even though it was she who enjoyed the vast publicity the couple had received from her book. The shooting schedule had called for thirty-six weeks on location, but it stretched out another six because of the unpredictability of working with the animals and the difficulty of getting them to do something akin to what was required for the story. In many instances, McKenna and Travers simply went walking with the Elsa stand-in and then contacted Hill and his crew by walkie-talkie when they thought something potentially dramatic or filmically exciting was about to happen. (Travers and McKenna later admitted they were lucky to get fifteen seconds of film a day.)

Although the filmmakers did not aim specifically to placate the family crowd, some concessions were made to make the story more accessible and comfortable. Much of the latter part of the book chronicled, in fairly graphic detail, Elsa's many meals, describing how she would pounced on the more vulnerable creatures of the wild and tear them open in order to get a satisfying dinner. This was left to the imagination onscreen, since the filmmakers knew that not only children but most adults would find it unsettling to watch so uncivilized an act of nature. Likewise, audiences were spared from witnessing how much pleasure Elsa derived from her habit of rolling in elephant dung. In order to relay the importance of getting Elsa into an environment in which she could thrive, a government official was made one of the few other supporting humans. Also, the death of Joy's beloved pet rock hyrax was moved earlier in the story in order to function as the principal reason George changes his mind about sending Elsa to a zoo, surprising his grieving wife with the lioness, who she thinks has been put on a transport plane. No such incident took place, Joy and George having decided straight off that Elsa would not be sent to the zoo with her sisters.

When the movie finally wrapped in the summer of 1965, two of the lionesses used onscreen were kept by the Adamsons themselves, while three others went to animal orphanages in Kenya; the rest were shipped off to various British zoos. The finished picture was deemed important enough to serve as the Royal Command Performance entry for March 1966, where it was greeted with much excitement by the customarily cynical press, who were pleased to see how free of sentiment and cutesy moments *Born Free* was. What's more, there was something stirring, almost inspiring, about the tale that cut close to the bone for any parent who struggled with that inevitable point in their lives when their children had to break away and move on, no matter how uncertain the future was for them. Africa was captured in all its dangerous glory, Travers and McKenna were praised for holding their own against the scene-stealing lions, and the film's depiction of a world so far removed from civilization was often intoxicating. The movie had no problem capturing American audiences as well, and in due time it became one of the most fondly remembered of cinematic

The sheet music for John Barry and Don Black's stirring *Born Free* title song quickly became a favorite of parlor pianists across the land.

experiences for many who grew up in the '60s. Adding tremendously to the movie's impact was John Barry's lovely score, which was capped, during the end credits, by a title song (sung by an uncredited Matt Monro) that was simple yet majestic in its power. Not only did the song "Born Free" make the Billboard charts (with Roger Williams's piano rendition reaching the number 7 position), but it was so widely heard (on several recordings and television variety shows) during the late 1960s that it's safe to say it is probably the most instantly recognizable of all the songs to win the Academy Award during that decade.

Born Free had a profound effect not only on the many who saw it, but on its stars, who became as devoted as their real-life counterparts were to the conservation of wildlife and the rights of animals. Not only were these the roles with which both McKenna and Travers would be most strongly identified for the remainder of their lives, but they seldom again bothered to do much work that *didn't* involve wild animals in one way or another. The real-life Adamsons both had tragic ends: Joy was shot to death by a vengeful fired employee on January 3, 1980, and George was killed by Somali poachers on August 20, 1989. As for Elsa herself, she was long gone before the media made her famous, having died of a tick-borne disease in 1961 after spending only two years in the wild. Per her wishes, Joy's ashes were spread over Elsa's gravesite.

THE RUSSIANS ARE COMING
THE RUSSIANS ARE COMING

Academy Award Nominee: Picture; Actor (Alan Arkin); Screenplay—Based on Material from Another Medium; Film Editing

Top 10 Box Office Film

Opening date: May 25, 1966.

United Artists. A Mirisch Corporation Presentation of a Norman Jewison Production.

Director-Producer: Norman Jewison. Screenplay: William Rose. Based on the 1961 novel *The Off-Islanders*, by Nathaniel Benchley. Photography: Joseph Biroc. Art Director: Robert F. Boyle. Set Decorator: Darrell Silvera. Costumes: Wesley Jeffries. Music: Johnny Mandel. Editors: Hal Ashby, J. Terry Williams. Special Effects: Daniel W. Hays. Deluxe color. Panavision. 126 minutes.

CAST: Carl Reiner (Walt Whittaker), Eva Marie Saint (Elspeth Whittaker), Alan Arkin (Rozanov), Brian Keith (Police Chief Link Mattocks), Jonathan Winters (Norman Jonas), Theodore Bikel (the Captain), Paul Ford (Fendall Hawkins), Tessie O'Shea (Alice Foss), John Phillip Law (Alexei Kolchin), Andrea Dromm (Alison Palmer), Ben Blue (Luther Grilk), Sheldon Golomb (Pete Whittaker), Cindy Putnam (Annie Whittaker), Guy Raymond (Lester Tilly), Cliff Norton (Charlie Hinkson), Richard Schaal (Oscar Maxwell), Philip Coolidge (Isaac Porter), Don Keefer (Irving Christiansen), Parker Fennelly (Mr. Everett), Doro Merande (Muriel Everett), Vaughn Taylor (Mr. Bell), Johnny Whitaker (Jerry Maxwell), Danny Klega (Polsky), Ray Baxter (Brodsky), Paul Verdier (Maliavin), Nikita Knatz (Gromolsky), Constantine Baksheef (Vasilov), Alex Hassilev (Hrushevsky), Milos Milos (Lysenko), Gino Gottarelli (Kregitkin), Michael J. Pollard (Stanley, Airport Mechanic), Peter Brocco (Reverend Hawthorne).

PLOT: Panic erupts among the locals of New England's Gloucester Island when a Russian submarine runs aground and members of the stranded crew come ashore seeking assistance.

The cold war had brought filmmakers a new, all-purpose villain, the Russians, who, in more extreme scenarios, could be held accountable for nefarious schemes suggesting world domination and destruction or, on a lighter note, were simply around to be poked fun at, principally for the stoically regimented, humorless characteristics Americans presumed them to possess. Either way, there was no denying that most Americans had a very uneasy feeling about the Soviets, and it was this fervent distrust that novelist Nathaniel Benchley (1915–1981; he was the son of the humorist Robert Benchley and the father of the future author of *Jaws*, Peter Benchley) attempted to satirize in his comic novel *The Off-Islanders*. The book, with its multiple story lines and screwball mishaps, clearly had cinematic possibilities, and the rights were purchased in September 1963 by Norman Jewison. Jewison had liked the premise of Benchley's book, but he knew that extensive revisions were needed to make it more emotional, more suspenseful, and funnier. Benchley's take had been sporadically humorous with some rather unpleasant misjudgments of physical cruelty that left a bad taste in the mouth, while the Russians' side of the situation was barely fleshed out, making them one-dimensional intruders. To rectify these problems, Jewison selected William Rose to do the screen adaptation. The choice was perfect: Rose's knack for building excitement through cross-cutting between a batch of stories and his ability to make average people look foolishly funny under pressure had been evident in his script for *It's a Mad Mad Mad Mad World* (United Artists, 1963) and was exactly what was needed here.

Benchley's main characters had been Barbara Hageman, a schoolteacher versed in Russian; Olin Leveridge, a painter who is treated as something of an outsider on the island by the longtime residents; and Roland Gurney, a garage mechanic. In the book Gurney and Barbara had eventually paired up as a budding love interest, but Rose scrapped these two, as well as Leveridge, and put a married couple with two young kids, the Whittakers, at the center of the story. Such characters as gung-ho townie Fendall Hawkins and Officer Norman Jones (renamed Jonas) were retained for the film, but Norman's second-in-command, Charles Palmer, Palmer's shrewish wife, and their large brood disappeared altogether except for their last name, which was given to the character of the Whittaker's babysitter, Alison. In the book, Emily Vardhall, an animal lover, had taken in a young Russian who was anxious to stay in the United States, but this plot thread was discarded in favor of giving Alison a tenuous relationship with a nervous Soviet lad, Alexei Kolchin. Leveridge had attempted to help one of the Russians, Zoltin, obtain U.S. citizenship, but none of this made it into the screenplay. Instead, a minor character from the book, Rozanov, was built up to become the one seemingly levelheaded sailor from the sub, who forms an unspoken bond of sorts with vacationing playwright Walt Whittaker. In Benchley's version the townspeople and the Russians ultimately found themselves engaged in a battle in the town dump, tossing garbage at each other. This had led up to the finale in which Barbara and Gurney attempted to sink the Russian sub; Gurney is trapped on board as the enemy tries to escape from the Coast Guard, which has come to the rescue, dropping depth charges in order to bring the vessel to the surface. Rose and Jewison both agreed that a far more potent statement about U.S.-Soviet relations could be made with a climax that was positive, hopeful, and nonconfrontational. Benchley's book, which had set out to rib cold war paranoia, turned its testy and fiercely protective Americans into heroes in the face of an unexpected invasion, although a gradual awareness of their narrow-mindedness and a condemnation of America's trigger-happy reaction at a perceived danger would have given the work more meaning. Jewison and Rose wound up giving the film just those aspects.

Having decided against using Benchley's original title in favor of the more blatantly crazy and memorable *The Russians Are Coming The Russians Are Coming*, Jewison got the okay for a $3.5 million budget from United Artists. Although Jewison was adamant about shooting most of his movie outdoors, the idea of filming in actual New England locations was deemed inconvenient because of the undependability of the weather. Chosen instead was a coastal area north of San Francisco. Both interiors and exteriors were

> "Remark to this, Whittaker Walt . . . we must have boat; even now may be too late. This is *your* island. I make your responsibility. You help us get boat quickly, otherwise there is World War 3 and everybody is blaming you!"
> —Rozanov

Carl Reiner bicycles into town in an effort to warn the locals that *The Russians Are Coming The Russians Are Coming.*

shot in Fort Bragg, Noyo, Westport, and Mendocino, with false fronts designed in the Cape Cod architectural style attached to standing buildings in order to give the impression that the action was indeed taking place in New England. The Whittaker house was built from scratch approximately three miles north of Fort Bragg. Because Jewison was not able to convince the navy to lend him a vessel that could be disguised as a Russian sub, a 140-foot-long, forty-ton fake submarine—made of Uni-Foam and plywood and constructed for the Twentieth Century-Fox film *Morituri* (1965)—was purchased for the production and transported to the location in eight sections. Stuffed with seventeen tons of Styrofoam to ensure that it would float, the sub spent most of the picture on a sandbar before making a grand entrance into the Noyo Bay harbor. The *Russians* location shoot began on September 3, 1965, and continued until the beginning of December, at which time the company returned to Hollywood, where the movie's only soundstage set, the interior of the submarine, had been constructed on the Paramount lot.

The Russians Are Coming The Russians Are Coming was sold with a deliberately nutty advertising campaign featuring broad caricatures by Jack Davis, but the nice surprise for those expecting something strictly for the slapstick crowd was just how richly fulfilling the picture was on so many levels. *Russians* certainly contained its share of physical comedy, most memorably Carl Reiner bound to hefty Tessie O'Shea as they attempt to hop to freedom; droll commentary on America's gun-happy society, with a ready firearm on hand for most of its principals; and a potent emotional payoff conceived by Rose in which all differences are set aside in order to perform a heroic, not to mention spectacularly staged, rescue of a hapless little boy from a church steeple (a set constructed specifically for the movie).

Jewison had great hopes of showing the picture in competition at the major Eastern European Film Festival of the time, the Karlovy-Vary (Czechoslovakian) Festival, and to that end had screened it in April 1966 for members of the Soviet embassy. Although the Russian officials expressed enjoyment overall, they were unhappy with Theodore Bikel's portrayal of the submarine captain as an irresponsible and possibly violent boob willing to level an entire American town. In any event, the picture was rejected by Karlovy-Vary, so the Berlin Festival intervened, allowing *Russians* to be their opening entry in June of that year. The Soviet Union, and therefore other communist countries, chose not to participate in that particular festival. By that point the movie had already opened in the United States to mostly enthusiastic notices. The negative opinions hardly mattered, because the film was a word-of-mouth hit, garnering growing crowds throughout the summer and beyond. It became *the* comedy to see in 1966, and the widespread appeal it nurtured among varying demographics was remembered at year's end as *Russians* ended up on several ten-best lists, won Golden Globes from the Foreign Press for Best Picture and Best Actor (Arkin), earned the Writers Guild Award for Rose, and brought Jewison his first nomination from the Directors Guild. That the film had achieved something by making people laugh *and* think without sacrificing the pleasure in favor of the lecture was obvious when it became one of the few slapstick comedies ever to receive a Best Picture nomination from the Motion Picture Academy of Arts and Sciences. *The Russians Are Coming The Russians Are Coming* earned Jewison a place on a list of the hottest directors in film and was looked back upon, decades later, as one of the most flat-out enjoyable pictures of its era.

WHO'S AFRAID OF VIRGINIA WOOLF?

Academy Award Winner: Best Actress (Elizabeth Taylor); Best Supporting Actress (Sandy Dennis); Best Cinematography—Black and White; Best Art Direction–Set Decoration—Black and White; Best Costume Design—Black and White

Academy Award Nominee: Picture; Actor (Richard Burton); Supporting Actor (George Segal); Director; Screenplay—Based on Material from Another Medium; Sound; Original Music Score; Film Editing

Top 10 Box Office Film

Opening date: June 22, 1966 (New York: June 24, 1966).

Warner Bros. An Ernest Lehman Production.

Director: Mike Nichols. Producer-Screenplay: Ernest Lehman. Based on the 1962 play by Edward Albee. Photography: Haskell Wexler. Art Director: Richard Sylbert. Set Decorator: George James Hopkins. Costumes: Irene Sharaff. Music: Alex North. Editor: Sam O'Steen. Miss Taylor's Makeup: Gordon Bau. Mr. Burton's Makeup: Ronnie-Berkeley. Black and white. 131 minutes.

CAST: Elizabeth Taylor (Martha), Richard Burton (George), George Segal (Nick), Sandy Dennis (Honey), Frank Flanagan (Roadhouse Proprietor), Agnes Flanagan (Waitress).

PLOT: History professor George and his vulgar wife Martha obligingly entertain new biology instructor Nick and his timid spouse Honey at their campus home, the drunken gathering turning into an explosive, all-night verbal battle of lacerating insults and bitter emotional truths.

An outstanding example that puts to rest the lie that Hollywood *always* distorts, ruins or misunderstands how to adapt a great stage work, *Who's Afraid of Virginia Woolf?* was one of the milestone theatrical events of the early 1960s and followed suit on the big screen, becoming one of the seminal motion pictures of the decade. This highly original drama came from the inventive and unpredictable mind of Edward Albee. The playwright had first made a name for himself with his 1959 one-act *The Zoo Story*, which helped introduce a new style of American absurdist drama to the public. It was followed in quick succession by several other one-acts, including *The Sandbox* (1959) and *The American Dream* (1961), which, like *Zoo*, played off-Broadway and made Albee a favorite of the intelligentsia, who knew damn well that most theatergoers out for an evening of reassuring pleasure weren't sure what the hell these dark and cryptic dramas were all about. Therefore, it was rather daring for Albee to make the leap, with *Virginia Woolf*, from smaller venues to the mainstream Broadway stage. At the time it was unheard of for the most important dramas to play anywhere *but* a Broadway house. Albee's move was in fact the right one, because his scorching and unnerving play very quickly took its place among the most mesmerizing works in the history of the American theater. Opening on October 13, 1962, at the

Billy Rose Theatre, under the direction of Alan Schneider and featuring Uta Hagen (Martha), Arthur Hill (George), George Grizzard (Nick), and Melinda Dillon (Honey), *Virginia Woolf* became the season's most hailed new production, inciting controversy and outrage, just as all groundbreaking works are supposed to. It won five Tony Awards—Best Play, Best Actor (Hill), Best Actress (Hagen), Best Director, and a trophy for its producers.

It was pretty much a given that any play that was able to chalk up 664 performances and receive so many honors would result in a bidding war among the Hollywood studios, but *Virginia Woolf* was not everyone's cup of tea. It was esoteric, harsh, and not easy to open up from its claustrophobic setting; most of all, it contained a lot of raw language that stood very little chance of getting past the censors. The only studio executive who saw the cinematic possibilities was Jack L. Warner, who purchased the rights for $500,000. His idea was to hire Ernest Lehman to serve as both producer and screenwriter, with George Cukor as director. Lehman, who had at one time expressed no desire to even see the play, had since become a great admirer of the piece and signed on, but the Cukor deal came to naught. Lehman set about trying to shape the script into something that would satisfy the Production Code officials, dropping the multiple uses of "goddamn" and "bastard" in favor of softer, less believable words and phrases. In an effort to give the movie a less stagy quality, he wrote George's speech about the boy killing his father in car accident as a flashback and had

> "George who is good to me, and whom I revile; who understands me, and whom I push off; who can make me laugh and I choke it back in my throat; who can hold me at night so it's warm, and whom I will bite so there's blood; who keeps learning the games we play as quickly as I can change the rules; who can make me happy and I do not wish to be happy, and yes I do wish to be happy. George and Martha: sad, sad, sad."
> —Martha

the foursome leave their campus confines for a stop at an empty roadside club. He even threw in a bit of none-too-subtle symbolism by having the movie start with a pair of dogs fighting with one another.

Albee had envisioned two of Hollywood's great old-time stars in the leading roles, Henry Fonda and Bette Davis—not a bad idea, though the latter's participation would have provoked instant chuckles in the opening scene, since the dialogue revolved around Martha's inability to remember the name of the Davis movie from which the immortal line "what a dump!" comes from. (The film in question, Warners' 1949 melodrama *Beyond the Forest*, was never actually identified by name.) Lehman had a more bankable idea for the movie: Elizabeth Taylor, who at thirty-two was far too young and beautiful for the frumpy, middle-aged Martha, though she certainly could suggest the bawdiness and coarseness, given enough coaching and the right makeup. Warners loved the idea and Taylor was thrilled to accept, getting a very tasty $1.1 million paycheck for the role. With a star of her magnitude as one of the leads, Warners wasn't so adamant about getting someone of equal importance to play George, though Jack Lemmon was, in fact, offered the part at one point and came close to committing to the film but eventually backed out. There was even talk of letting Arthur Hill repeat his stage role if it pleased Taylor. She did not, however,

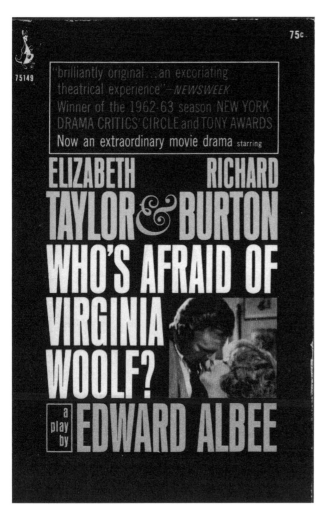

The published play script for *Who's Afraid of Virginia Woolf?*, released in conjunction with the movie version, gives its stars as much emphasis as the playwright, Edward Albee.

understand why the casting director needed to look any further than her own bedroom, believing that her husband, Richard Burton, was perfect to play the intellectual, browbeaten college professor who takes great glee in putting his brutish wife in her place. Burton wasn't as excited about the material as his wife was, but Taylor got her way, and Burton was given the role for a fee of $750,000. Jack Warner now had the security of the most famous Hollywood couple of the day to carry a very difficult property.

Although John Frankenheimer's name came up as a possible director, it was Taylor who chose Mike Nichols. Best-known at that point to most of America for his deadpan satirical routines with Elaine May, Nichols had recently made a career change to stage director with three comedy hits in a row, *Barefoot in the Park* (1963), *Luv* (1964), and *The Odd Couple* (1965). Trusting a man associated exclusively with humor and who had never been behind a motion-picture camera before was a risk that paid off in a big way. Once Nichols came on board he was adamant that Lehman bring the script back as close as possible to what audiences had experienced onstage. The fighting dogs and the flashbacks disappeared, although he agreed with the necessity of taking the principals away from the house for a spell. Most daringly, Nichols insisted that the majority of the off-color remarks be kept, with no "cover" words substituted for alternate takes. Nichols put his cast through a two-week rehearsal, and Taylor showed her dedication to the part by adding thirty pounds and lowering her voice an octave in order to appear older and less glamorous.

The Burtons flew from their European residence to southern California to begin filming on July 26, 1965, on the Warner Bros. soundstages. There was a break in shooting toward the end of August so the company could head east for the exteriors, which were shot at the Northampton, Massachusetts, campus of Smith College. The outside of the Tyler Annex, at 48 Green Street, stood in for George and Martha's campus home, while the parking lot of the Red Basket restaurant in Southampton was the site of the bickering couple's argument following their altercation within the eatery itself. Problems on location stretched the shooting schedule out a month longer than anticipated, and the cast and crew finally finished up back at Warners on December 13, 1965. At a surprisingly high cost of $7.5 million, *Virginia Woolf* trailed only the more physically spectacular *The Longest Day* (Twentieth Century-Fox, 1962) as the most expensive black-and-white motion picture ever made.

With the movie in the can, the question remained as to whether there was going to be opposition to the frank language. Knowing he had an esteemed work on his hands, Warner appealed to the Production Code office for an exemption and, surprisingly, got it. *Virginia Woolf* proved a landmark in the fall of motion-picture censorship, for better or worse, because of the amount of explicit language that would be heard, with such phrases as "hump the hostess" and "up yours" spewed forth, not to mention multiple mentions of "son of a bitch" and "bastard." Needless to say, word quickly spread that Hollywood's most overexposed media couple, the Burtons, were appearing in a "dirty" movie, and suddenly the must-see level for the picture began to climb higher than Warners had anticipated. The casting had been a masterstroke, insomuch as a movie this challenging and difficult might otherwise have been passed over by the bulk of the general public, even with actors as revered as Davis and Fonda.

Movie critics were caught off guard, expecting a bowdlerization of the searing theatrical work only to find that Nichols and company had been uncompromising in the layer-by-layer peeling away of the relationship between this caustic married couple. George and Martha were incapable of expressing their need for one another without hiding behind lacerating insults and games of torment. To some it seemed like a heightened form of reality, albeit one full of brilliant wordplay, while others detected an

For variety, Elizabeth Taylor takes her bickering outside the house and over to a nearby eatery in this scene from *Who's Afraid of Virginia Woolf?*

unremittent, bracing honesty in how it captured the way far more marital partners behave than most people were willing to admit. Again, the casting of America's most talked-about married couple only worked in the film's favor; their incendiary remarks were as believably conveyed as the enormous love inherent underneath.

For those who believed that Richard Burton had been pulled down from his mantle as one of the theater's potentially great actors into a world of shallow show-business hype by his media-frenzied nuptials with the world's ultimate movie star, his performance as the wounded but vengeful George was better than anyone might have hoped. His work here, for which he adapted a mild-mannered, modulated control under which simmered a brilliant mind, the character calculating his next move like a great chess player, quieted all detractors. Not only was it the pinnacle of his motion-picture career, but it also ranked among the truly great performances of the decade. Yet as much a triumph as *Woolf* was for him, it was his wife who turned out to be the real eye-opener. Taylor was certainly one of the great stars of her day, but her abilities as an actress had always been open to debate. Customarily more game than accomplished in many of her dramatic efforts, she managed to win an Oscar for a performance most people (including the actress herself) hadn't even cared for, in *BUtterfield 8* (MGM, 1960). For *Virginia Woolf* she not only rose to the occasion but delivered way beyond anyone's wildest expectations, giving so fiercely full-bodied and galvanizing a performance as the slatternly but vulnerable Martha that it seemed as if an exciting new actress had appeared on the scene. With Nichols's help and the awareness that she was sinking her teeth into genuinely great material, she dug more deeply into a character's pain than she ever did before or since. This time her Academy Award was much applauded by both the press and the industry. It would mark her last nomination, and she never again seemed to express herself in her craft with such stimulating results.

Helped by its adults-only label and the suggestion that theater owners do their own degree of regulating this rule, audiences flocked to the film. Viewers certainly came away with strong opinions, even if the average person who knew Liz Taylor from the tabloid stories on the movie-magazine rack probably hadn't the slightest idea how to interpret Albee's riveting dissection of the American dream. What exactly Martha and George's make-believe child meant, or just how to respond to Martha's haunting final response to the play's seemingly flippant title ("I am") was wide open for interpretation and made for an exciting discussion. *Virginia Woolf* just the sort of thrilling experience a motion picture could be under the right circumstances, and it remains one of the best-ever stage-to-screen adaptations in film history.

LT. ROBIN CRUSOE, U.S.N.

Top 10 Box Office Film

Opening date: June 29, 1966 (New York: July 13, 1966).

Buena Vista. A Walt Disney Production.

Director: Byron Paul. Coproducers: Bill Walsh, Ron Miller. Screenplay: Bill Walsh, Donald Da Gradi. Based on a story by Retlaw Yensid (Walt Disney). Photography: William Snyder. Art Directors: Carroll Clark, Carl Anderson. Set Decorators: Emile Kuri, Frank R. McKelvy. Costumes: Bill Thomas. Music: Bob Brunner. Editor: Cotton Warburton. Special Effects: Peter Ellenshaw, Eustace Lycett, Robert A. Mattey. Technicolor. 110 minutes.

CAST: Dick Van Dyke (Lt. Robin Crusoe), Nancy Kwan (Wednesday), Akim Tamiroff (Tanamashu), Arthur Malet (Umbrella Man), Tyler McVey (Captain), P.L. Renoudet (Pilot), Peter Duryea (Co-Pilot), John Dennis (Crew Chief), Nancy Hsueh, Victoria Young, Yvonne Ribuca, Bebe Louie, Lucia Valero (Native Girls), Richard Deacon (Survival Guide Narrator).

PLOT: During a routine flight mission in the Pacific, navy pilot Lt. Robin Crusoe ends up stranded on a seemingly deserted island where he sets up house with a long-lost astro-chimp whose capsule had earlier ended up on the same desolate spot.

Although the film owed its jokey title to Daniel Dafoe's immortal literary castaway, the creators of *Lt. Robin Crusoe, U.S.N.* more likely had two other enormously successful Disney properties in mind at the time: *Swiss Family Robinson* (1960) and *Mary Poppins* (1964). The *Crusoe* script did, after all, adhere closely to the outline of *Swiss Family*. The opening scenes showed its protagonist being washed up on a seemingly abandoned island, establishing his base and survival tactics through ingenuity, and then brought a woman into the plot. Finally, there was an attack by outside forces. *Crusoe* was also built around the fact that *Poppins* had proven Dick Van Dyke to be an ideal Disney star, broadly exuberant, affable, comically inventive, and highly accessible to young kids. A vehicle that would give the star a perfect showcase was needed as a follow-up, and none other than Walt Disney himself supplied the story, making this a milestone in the history of the studio. *Lt. Robin Crusoe, U.S.N.* marked the one and only time that he actually took onscreen credit in the writing department for one of his feature presentations, but he didn't want to draw attention to that fact. Instead, Disney simply spelled out his first name and then flipped both names backward so that the credit read "Based on an original story by Retlaw Yensid," which very soon became one of the year's worst-kept secrets.

> **"Okay, Admiral Honey, you boss."**
> **—Wednesday**

To enhance the look of the movie, Disney had his company shoot most of the exteriors on the island of Kauai in Hawaii. Poipu Beach was used for Van Dyke's arrival, while the curving shoreline at Waiohai Beach figured into Akim Tamiroff's disembarkation and the ensuing retreat at the climax. Lawai Kai,

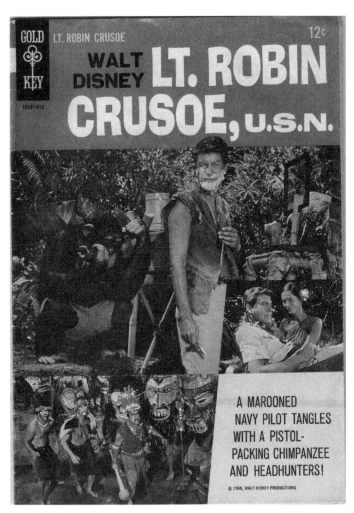

If nothing else, the Gold Key comic book adaptation of Disney's *Lt. Robin Crusoe, U.S.N.* made good on its promise to feature a "pistol-packing chimpanzee."

the former estate of Hawaii's last reigning monarch, Queen Liliuokalani, was seen in all other beach scenes; while the estate's Allerton Gardens provided the dense jungle foliage. Tons of sand and several palm trees were shipped back to the Disney Studio to create some island interiors, including the site of the Kapuna stone idol, built on stage 2. The crew of the U.S.S. *Kitty Hawk* allowed the company to shoot the bracketing scenes of Van Dyke's rescue on their deck, figuring there was nothing harmful or antimilitary in the script. *Crusoe* was filmed between May 10 and July 30, 1965, during the summer hiatus of Van Dyke's television series before it entered its last season.

The reunion of Van Dyke and Disney had box office written all over it, no matter what the critical reception. Van Dyke was allowed to hold the screen solo for a good chunk of the picture, acting opposite only a monkey during the first forty-five minutes. This was the best part of *Crusoe*; Van Dyke showed his deft comic touch, overcoming material that wasn't always first rate and creating a very comfortable mood. Once Nancy Kwan showed up things became a bit sillier, while the final scenes with Tamiroff lapsed into the sort of over-the-top, juvenile nonsense that made Disney's detractors point to this sort of thing as an example of children's entertainment at its most puerile.

Surprisingly, the screenplay actually took a progressive step in bringing up women's rights at a time when the country was beginning to discuss such things quite seriously. Such clear thinking did not mean, however, that the island girls were portrayed as anything more than a bunch of giggling bubbleheads whose main goal was to name Van Dyke their chief and carry him about on a litter.

A MAN AND A WOMAN (France)

Academy Award Winner: Best Foreign Language Film; Best Story and Screenplay—Written Directly for the Screen

Academy Award Nominee: Actress (Anouk Aimée); Director

Opening date: July 12, 1966 (Paris: May 27, 1966, as *Un homme et une femme*).

Allied Artists. A Les Films 13 Presentation.

Director-Photography(-Producer-Editor): Claude Lelouch. Screenplay: Claude Lelouch, in collaboration with Pierre Uytterhoeven. Music: Francis Lai. Song: "Samba Saravah," by Baden Powel (music) and Vinicius de Moraes (lyrics), performed and adapted by Pierre Barouh. Art Director: Robert Luchaire. Costumes: Richard Marvil. Assistant Editor: Claude Barrois. Eastmancolor/black and white. 102 minutes.

CAST: Anouk Aimée (Anne Gauthier), Jean-Louis Trintignant (Jean-Louis Duroc), Pierre Barouh (Pierre Gauthier), Valérie Lagrange (Valerie Duroc), Antoine Sire (Antoine Duroc), Souad Amidou (Françoise Gauthier), Simone Paris (Headmistress), Yane Barry (Yane, Jean-Louis's Mistress), Henri Chemin (Jean-Louis's Co-Driver).

PLOT: After dropping their children off at the same private school, Anne Gauthier and Jean-Louis Duroc find themselves falling in love.

Despite having made five features, filmmaker Claude Lelouch had created next to no impact on the movie landscape by the mid-1960s—certainly not in America, where none of his pictures had been imported, and not even in his native France, where he couldn't even get that fifth film, *Les grands moments*, a distributor. In debt and eager to be heard, Lelouch figured he would aim for something very direct and simple with his next project, quickly knocking off an outline for a screenplay about two widowed single parents who fall in love. For the male lead he had Jean-Louis Trintignant in mind and managed to coax him into doing the picture even before Lelouch had a finished screenplay in hand. Enthusiastic about Lelouch's ideas and his plan to do a good deal of improvisation, Trintignant was further pleased when the filmmaker agreed to his suggestion of turning his character from physician to race-car driver. For the female lead, Lelouch considered either Romy Schneider or Anouk Aimée, opting for the latter because Trintignant knew her

> **"When something's not serious, we say it's like a film. Why aren't films taken seriously do you think?"**
> **—Jean-Louis**

personally and could therefore help convince her to join such an underdeveloped project. Lelouch's technique was to give his actors key dialogue to read but allow them to ad lib or run in all kinds of directions according to their instincts as long as the main thrust of the scene was addressed. Despite her initial reservations, Aimée was intrigued enough by this unorthodox setup to say yes.

The British ad for that country's 1967 release of *A Man and a Woman* prefers to use its French title, *Un homme et une femme.*

With a small guerilla filmmaking unit of no more than ten, no trailers, no constructed sets, and a minuscule budget, Lelouch gave himself a month's worth of preparation and another month for filming. (Shooting at a furious pace, Lelouch managed to get the entire movie done in only three weeks during January 1966.) Because the story line had come to him while driving between Deauville and Paris, these were chosen as the central locations, with additional shooting at the Montlhery Racetrack and during the actual Monte Carlo Rally. Lelouch had originally intended to film the whole thing in black and white to save money but was assured some distribution deals if he would do it in color. Meeting them halfway, he chose to shoot all the exteriors in color and the interiors in black and white, which came off as simply puzzling to some and cryptically engaging to those on the lookout for abstract meaning in anything French. Wanting to keep the set in a constant state of creative tension and movement, Lelouch's approach was to pick up the camera and let the scene roll (he served as his own official cinematographer), usually opting for the first take for spontaneity and then quickly moving on to the next scene before things got too relaxed or lazy.

In a reversal of the customary technique of recording a score after a movie is completed, it was Lelouch's habit to have the music ready prior to filming so he could play it on the set and have his camera and actors react to it. The background score, by then-unknown Francis Lai, became just one of the many elements that turned the movie into something special. Lai's rapturously haunting main theme, punctuated by a chorus vibrantly chiming in with its repeated "dabba-dabba-dap, dabba-dabba-dap" not only added immeasurably to the mood and timing of the picture, but took on a life of its own. Something about it came to represent everything romantic and giddily infectious about French music of the period, and people began buying the soundtrack album even if they hadn't bothered to see the film. The LP did the unthinkable: it broke into the top 10 on the *Billboard* charts, and the theme remained instantly recognizable for generations to come.

A Man and a Woman became the sensation of the 1966 Cannes Film Festival, taking home the Grand Prize that year. Lelouch had finally gotten the attention he had so fervently desired. Critics marveled at the way he let his camera capture the feelings being conveyed by his two actors through glances and thoughts, keeping the dialogue secondary to the sense of mood and rhythm. Many scenes unfolded as montages, the music playing over the moment with no on-set sound recorded. Very quickly this technique became so overused that the first response by many future viewers would be to equate it with a perfume ad, but at the time it seemed daringly spontaneous and ever so romantic.

ALFIE (United Kingdom)

Academy Award Nominee: Picture; Actor (Michael Caine); Supporting Actress (Vivien Merchant); Screenplay—Based on Material from Another Medium; Song ("Alfie")

Top 10 Box Office Film

Opening date: August 24, 1966 (London: March 24, 1966).

Paramount. A Sheldrake Films Presentation.

Director-Producer: Lewis Gilbert. Screenplay: Bill Naughton, based on his 1963 play. Photography: Otto Heller. Art Director: Peter Mullins. Set Dresser: Terence Morgan. Costumes for Miss Winters: Jack Dagemais. Wardrobe Supervisor: Jean Fairlie. Music: Sonny Rollins. Title song by Burt Bacharach (music) and Hal David (lyrics), performed by Cher. Editor: Thelma Connell. Technicolor. Techniscope. 114 minutes.

CAST: Michael Caine (Alfie Elkins), Shelley Winters (Ruby), Millicent Martin (Siddie), Julia Foster (Gilda), Jane Asher (Annie), Shirley Anne Field (Carla), Vivien Merchant (Lily), Eleanor Bron (Doctor), Denholm Elliott (Mr. Smith, the Abortionist), Alfie Bass (Harry Clamacraft), Graham Stark (Humphrey), Murray Melvin (Nat), Sydney Tafler (Frank), Bryan Marshall (Perce), Tony Shelby (Lace), Queenie Watts (Pub Singer).

PLOT: Alfie Elkins callously bounces from one woman's bed to the next, determined to have his share of fun while avoiding emotional attachments of any kind.

"What's it all about, Alfie?" became one of the preeminent catchphrases of the '60s, tossed about cheekily and glibly by many who had no idea that it was connected to a film that was just about the peak of the decade's British New Wave working-class dramas—a lacerating, disturbing, often blackly funny cautionary tale about the repercussions of cruelty and indifference toward one's fellow man, or, in this case, woman. *Alfie* was the crowning achievement of Bill Naughton (1910–1992), who had made a fair name for himself writing plays for television, radio, and the theater. His most notable contribution before *Alfie* was *June Evening* (1960), which marked him as yet another impressive contributor to the "kitchen-sink" dramas that were dominating Britain at the time. Two years later, the character of womanizing, self-involved Alfie Elkins first appeared on radio in *Alfie Elkins and His Little Life*, which starred character actor Bill Owens in the lead (the medium hid the fact that, like the author, Owens was in his second half century). Naughton knew he had latched onto something special that he wanted to expand for wider audience consumption and set about revising the work for the stage.

With its title now wisely shortened and its story line updated from the 1950s to the present, *Alfie* made its West End debut at the Mermaid Theatre on June 19, 1963, with John Neville as its star. Courting controversy with its central character's cavalier way of bedding women and its inclusion of a postabortion scene, *Alfie* rankled as many theatergoers as it enthralled and was considered saleable enough to send over to New York. The play's producers, believing they had a sure hit in the making by hiring the hot young U.K. newcomer Terence Stamp as their lead, opened *Alfie* at Broadway's Morosco Theatre on December 17, 1964, only to see it very quickly chased out of town, closing after only twenty-one performances. This hardly put an end to Naughton's work, because plans were already under way for bringing *Alfie* to the big screen.

Among those who had seen the West End production was director Lewis Gilbert, who credited his wife with convincing him to buy up the rights and transfer the play to celluloid. Gilbert immediately enlisted Naughton to do the screenplay, knowing that there was no point in dropping him from the mix. Naughton's expansion of his piece included a scene for Siddie's cuckolded husband, a very amiable fellow, whose kind nature made the deception played upon him that much more poignant; a visit to the maternity ward following the birth of Gilda and Alfie's child; an initial meeting between Alfie and the predatory American Ruby at Tower Hill; a fight scene at a pub indirectly caused by Alfie; and the actual events leading up to Alfie's seduction of Lily, which had been summarized in a monologue onstage. The famous question "What's it all about?," asked by Alfie at the end of the film, was new—the line had made no appearance in the stage version. Eliminated was the character of Joe, a retired cabbie Alfie meets at the sanitarium who relates the story of an opportunity he had missed to go on holiday with his wife before she died.

> "My understandin' of women only goes as far as the pleasure. When it comes to the pain, I'm like any other bloke—I don' wanna know."
> —Alfie Elkins

Naughton also decided to drop the idea of having Ruby's younger lover be the very same fellow, Lofty, from whom Alfie had stolen Annie away and made him a random young rocker instead. To emphasize Alfie's pathetic, self-induced solitude at the finale, Siddie no longer agreed to go off for a quick hookup as she had in the play, but rejected the Lothario in favor of meeting up with her husband. Most surprisingly, two risky elements were retained from the play: the very theatrical concept of having Alfie speak directly to the audience and the abortion episode.

Although the stage dialogue had been careful to point out that engaging someone to perform an abortion was against the law, there was still a frank unpleasantness behind the sequence that brought home how very ugly Alfie's life was, which on the surface had appeared to be a randy bit of fun and games. It was this scene that stopped the viewer short, stripped Alfie bare, and exposed the selfish and destructive nature of this deluded satyr. Up to that point many an actor might have been able to get by on sheer surface charm, but it seemed a bit of a risk to be associated with something that could lapse dangerously into bad taste. As a result, Gilbert was turned down by Anthony Newley, Laurence Harvey, and James Booth. Figuring he could fall back on the Broadway *Alfie*, Terence Stamp, Gilbert was surprised to be greeted by an adamant no from that actor as well, who felt burned by the New York reception. He did, however, recommend Gilbert give his former roommate a look. Michael Caine had been acting in films for eight years, popping up mostly in unbilled bits, before his breakthrough role in *Zulu* (Embassy, 1964), as a snooty lieutenant, and his first lead, as stoic secret agent Harry Palmer in *The Ipcress File* (Universal, 1965). Caine was very interested in playing Alfie—he had already done one of Naughton's radio plays, *Looking for Frankie*, back in 1963—and Gilbert figured the relative high-profile of Caine's previous pictures boded well for his casting selection. Gilbert had already penciled in a deal with Paramount Pictures to do a project that eventually fell by the wayside and offered *Alfie* as a substitute. He therefore found himself in the enviable position of proceeding with a tricky British property with the support of a major American distributor.

Given a budget of 350,000 pounds, of which 75,000 pounds went to Caine (who opted for an up-front fee instead of a percentage deal), Gilbert began filming on June 7, 1965, at Twickenham Studios, where interiors were shot over the next three weeks. In July Gilbert took his company on location around London, sometimes using hidden mikes and cameras to speed things along. Featured were Vauxhall Bridge, where the film opens; Camley Street behind Kings Cross Station, the site of Alfie and Siddie's tryst in the car; Waterloo Station, for the scene in which Siddie meets up with her husband; 22 Stephen's Street near Chepstow Road in Notting Hill, where Alfie makes Annie scrub his flat; St. Mary's Battersea Parish Church in Battersea Park, where Alfie sees Gilda and Humphrey tie to knot; the Twickenham Town Hall, which stood in for the convalescent home; the Thames River embankment outside of the Tower of

This posed shot on the set of *Alfie* brings together four actresses who share no scenes in the film itself: Vivien Merchant, Jane Asher, Julia Foster, and Shelley Winters. Instead they share their laps with star Michael Caine.

London, in the shadow of the Tower Bridge, for the initial meeting between Alfie and Ruby; the Elephant and Castle, in South London, site of the pub fight; and London Bridge, for the final moment of Alfie's epiphany about his empty life. The film wrapped in late August after an eleven-week schedule.

Not unexpectedly, *Alfie*'s highly adult subject matter earned it an X certification in England and a good deal of condemnation from various religious and moralizing groups, who seemed to miss the point that nothing in Alfie's ghastly self-absorption was being condoned. Yet another step forward in dealing openly with promiscuity, adultery, and human need, *Alfie* was already provoking talk prior to its U.K. opening in March 1966. Two things made the picture work from the word go: Alfie talking straight to the camera, and Caine. Starting with the flippant line "I suppose now you think you're gonna see the bleedin' titles," this potentially coy or annoying device, whereby more than half the dialogue was delivered, clicked instantly. It became evident that there was no better way to contrast Alfie's deliriously misguided philoso-

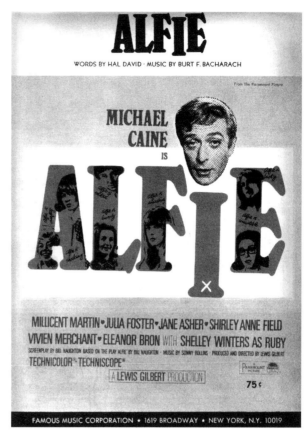

The sheet music of Burt Bacharach and Hal David's title song from *Alfie*, which brought the decade one of its great catchphrases, "What's it all about, Alfie?," and resulted in a none too successful record for Cher and a hit for Dionne Warwick.

phies on how to deceive the opposite sex and shake off all risk of lasting contact with the visible discomfort he causes by turning a blind eye to pain. Scripting whole scenes by having Caine break within a single line to address the audience before returning his attention to his fellow cast member was bold and groundbreaking and became probably the best example of how to pull this technique off with flying colors. This might not have been the case had Caine not been so effortlessly disarming in spinning his cockney slang, laying down the law, and trumpeting his independent spirit. This was nothing short of a miraculous acting job. Alfie was undeniably charming despite his misogynistic, borderline loathsome nature, and ultimately sad. For some, Caine became the symbol of "Swinging London" cool thanks to this role, certainly one of the iconic characterizations of the period. As far as Hollywood was concerned, he became England's most desirable new import. Offers began rolling in, and they never ceased.

FANTASTIC VOYAGE

Academy Award Winner: Best Art Direction–Set Decoration—Color; Best Special Visual Effects

Academy Award Nominee: Cinematography—Color; Film Editing; Sound Effects

Opening date: August 24, 1966 (New York: September 7, 1966).

Twentieth Century-Fox.

Director: Richard Fleischer. Producer: Saul David. Screenplay: Harry Kleiner. Adaptation: David Duncan. Based on a story by Otto Klement, Jay Lewis Bixby. Photography: Ernest Laszlo. Art Directors: Jack Martin Smith, Dale Hennesy. Set Decorators: Walter M. Scott, Stuart A. Reiss. Men Costumes: Bruce Walkup, Truman Eli. Women's Wardrobe: Ollie Hughes. Music: Leonard Rosenman. Editor: William B. Murphy. Special Photographic Effects: L. B. Abbott, Art Cruickshank, Emil Kosa Jr. Sound: Bernard Freericks, David Dockendorf. Technical Advisor: Fred Zendar. Flying Sequences: Peter Foy. Deluxe color. CinemaScope. 100 minutes.

CAST: Stephen Boyd (Grant), Raquel Welch (Cora Peterson), Edmond O'Brien (General Carter), Donald Pleasence (Doctor Michaels), Arthur O'Connell (Colonel Donald Reid), William Redfield (Captain Bill Owens), Arthur Kennedy (Doctor Duval), Jean Del Val (Jan Benes), Barry Coe (Communications Aide), Ken Scott (Secret Service Man), Shelby Grant (Nurse), James Brolin (Technician), Brendan Fitzgerald (Wireless Operator).

PLOT: A team of scientists is shrunk to the size of microbes in order to travel inside the body of a comatose patient and remove a deadly blood clot.

Science fiction took a giant step forward with a movie about miniaturization, *Fantastic Voyage*, one of the most fondly remembered films of the genre to come out of '60s Hollywood. Although there had been quality pictures in this field that received more attention than was customary from the studios and larger budgets than were usual (MGM's *Forbidden Planet* in 1956; Fox's *Journey to the Center of the Earth* in 1959), it was safe to say that sci-fi was more often treated as a bastard second cousin to pretty much every other genre. This area was more likely to be handled by the B unit or by independent companies that were looking to attract teenagers and less demanding audiences. Twentieth Century-Fox, therefore, was taking a gamble on *Fantastic Voyage*, which the studio decided would be given an across-the-board A-treatment when it came to crafting the script, filming it, publicizing it, and distributing it. Producer Saul David, who had just delivered a top-notch war film to Fox, *Von Ryan's Express* (1965), came up with the idea of a team of scientists being shrunk to the size of germs and sent on a trip through the human body. He hired sci-fi writer Jerome Bixby (here working as Jay Lewis Bixby) to develop a story outline, which he did in collaboration with producer Otto Klement. Their treatment, which went under such titles as *Microscopia*, was then given to David Duncan to turn into a screenplay, mainly because he had written one of the best-known sci-fi films of recent years, *The Time Machine* (MGM, 1960). Saul, however, was not pleased with the results and hired someone *not* associated with the field, Harry Kleiner, to do a rewrite. Kleiner, knowing that he would be under great scrutiny where authenticity and accuracy were concerned, even with something as fanciful as this, worked closely with physicians and anatomy instructors to produce the final script. Duncan retained a credit for the adaptation.

The production design team faced the challenge of filling the Fox soundstages with oversized reproductions of the inside of the human body that were both plausible and visually stunning at the same time. Dale Hennesy, Jack Martin Smith, Stuart A. Reiss, and Walter A. Scott, plus a few uncredited others, were responsible for creating four main "interior" sets: the capillaries, the lungs, the heart, and the brain. The capillaries and lung sacs were made of a combination of flexible resin and fiberglass. Cinematographer Ernest Laszlo then came up with the terrific idea of washing the set with an amber light, then placing color wheels behind the translucent material to simulate cell movement. This way, the set possessed a properly abstract "inner-body" feeling that would never have been possible simply with painted props and sets. The heart set was sculpted in Styrofoam by artist Jim Casey, its muscle and valves made of rubber, and the entire organ was coated with latex. The brain, a set measuring 200 by 100 feet, was filled with spun fiberglass, hand-sprayed from floor to ceiling of the soundstage. Here the dangerous blood clot for which the scientists had entered the body in the first place would be eliminated by a special laser device. Outside of the body the CMDF control area, which included the shrinking room and the operating amphitheater, was built for an extremely costly $1.25 million, more than four times the budget of most sci-fi pictures of the time. The film's key prop, the nuclear-powered sub that transported the tiny surgical team, was designed by Harper Goff, who had created Captain Nemo's *Nautilus* for *20,000 Leagues under the Sea*. Called the *Proteus*, it measured 42 feet long and 23 feet wide, weighed four tons, and cost $100,000 to build.

> "The only danger of . . . uh, turbulence is in the heart . . . and we're not going through it."
> —Doctor Michaels

Filming of the acting scenes took place at Fox Studios starting on January 25, 1965, with a side trip off the lot to the Los Angeles Sports Arena on South Figueroa Street. The circular ramps and corridors of this facility, considered the most modern of all arenas when it opened in 1959, were used to represent the interior of the underground miniaturization facility. Once shooting with the actors had concluded in the spring of 1965, the special effects team, working under the supervision of Art Cruickshank, toiled for months to smooth out the visual look of the picture and perfect the matte and model work. Because it had been decided that having the actors swim around inside an actual tank of water was unconvincing, all scenes meant to show them swimming through the body were filmed dry. Therefore the cast was dangled from wires designed by flying expert Peter Foy, who had made Mary Martin airborne in *Peter Pan*. Once the cast was suspended in the air, their movements were shot at three times the normal speed; diffusion and trick lighting further giving the impression that they were submerged in liquid. Unfortunately, while the effects team did a mostly outstanding job of plunging viewers into another world, the wires that kept Stephen Boyd and Raquel Welch afloat were all too visible in certain shots, spoiling the illusion.

Finally released in late summer of 1966, *Fantastic Voyage* was a rare film that lived up to its title. Certainly nothing like it had ever been attempted on so grand a scale, and even the critics, who were often

A demonstration of how to unshrink the cast principals of *Fantastic Voyage*, features large and small versions of Stephen Boyd, Raquel Welch, Arthur Kennedy, and Donald Pleasence.

reluctant to give much attention to sci-fi, had to admit that the movie was outlandish without lapsing into camp, intelligent without boring the audience with too many scientific details, and great fun overall, plunging right into its story line without a moment to spare and keeping viewers enthralled by its inventive design scheme and eye-popping visuals. *Voyage* had just the sort of crossover appeal that Fox had hoped for, offering thoughtful stimulation to science-fiction fans, who appreciated having an adventurous subject matter treated with the utmost seriousness. The movie presented a fantastical and outrageous premise that could be accepted on a certain screwy level by those who were impressed with the sheer chutzpah it took to dream up such a concept, and it possessed the necessary number of memorable images and level of wonderment that could be embraced by children. Few people who turned up for the picture during its initial run ever forgot the experience, and when its very title was mentioned to future generations, they instantly connected it with its premise. So significant was *Fantastic Voyage* to the 1966 film year that it scored no fewer than five Oscar nominations, the most to date for a sci-fi picture.

THE BIBLE (United States–Italy)

Academy Award Nominee: Original Music Score

Top 10 Box Office Film

Opening date: September 28, 1966 (Rome: 1966, as *La Bibbia*).

Twentieth Century-Fox. A Dino De Laurentiis Production, Produced in Association with Seven Arts.

Director: John Huston. Producer: Dino De Laurentiis. Screenplay: Christopher Fry. Assistants on Screenplay: Jonathan Griffin, Ivo Perilli, Vittorio Bonicelli. Special Consultant: Professor the Rev. W. M. Merchant. Photography: Giuseppe Rotunno. Art Director: Mario Chiari. Set Decorators: Enzo Eusepi, Bruno Avesani. Costumes: Maria De Matteis. Miss Gardner's Costumes: Sorelle Fontana. Music: Toshiro Mayuzumi. Editor: Ralph Kemplen. Choreographer: Katherine Dunham. Special Effects: Augie Lohman. Deluxe color. Dimension 150. 174 minutes (including overture, entr'acte, and exit music).

CAST: *The Creation*: John Huston (Narrator/Voice of God/Voice of the Serpent), Michael Parks (Adam), Ulla Bergryd (Eve); *Cain and Abel*: Richard Harris (Cain), Franco Nero (Abel); *Noah's Ark*: John Huston (Noah), Eric Leutzinger (Japheth), Angelo Boscariol (Ham), Peter Heinze (Shem), Pupella Maggio (Noah's Wife), Gabriella Pallotta (Ham's Wife), Rossana Di Rocco (Japheth's Wife), Anna Maria Orso (Shem's Wife); *The Tower of Babel*: Stephen Boyd (Nimrod), Claudie Lange (Queen); *The Story of Abraham*: George C. Scott (Abraham), Ava Gardner (Sarah), Peter O'Toole (Three Angels), Gabriele Ferzetti (Lot), Eleonora Rossi Drago (Sarai, Lot's Wife), Zoe Sallis (Hagar), Luciano Conversi (Ishmael), Adriana Ambesi, Grazia Maria Spina (Lot's Daughters), Alberto Lucantoni (Isaac), Robert Rietty (Abraham's Steward).

PLOT: The Book of Genesis follows the creation of the Earth, Adam and Eve's expulsion from the Garden of Eden, Cain's slaying of Abel, the great flood and the building of Noah's Ark, the doomed efforts to construct the Tower of Babel, the destruction of Sodom and Gomorrah, and Abraham's willingness to make a sacrifice to God.

During the fifteen-year heyday (1951–66) of the biblical spectacle, it seemed as if Hollywood and European filmmakers had pretty much covered whatever epic tales from the Good Book lent themselves to dramatization. But as far as prolific Italian producer Dino De Laurentiis was concerned, they had all missed out on the obvious: filming the Bible itself. De Laurentiis envisioned a massive production that would bring various stories from the Book of Genesis to life, with a different director assigned to each sequence. On his wish list were such prestigious names as Luis Buñuel, Orson Welles, and John Huston. In the end, only Huston stuck around, so the multidirectorial approach was abandoned. Huston, who did not consider himself a religious man, found the project appealing simply because he thought the Bible was full of great myths and legends that had wonderful cinematic possibilities. To keep the project on a more manageable level, he decided that the film would stretch from the Creation to the story of the sacrifice

> "Go forth of the Ark . . . bring forth with thee every living thing that is with thee . . . that they may be fruitful, and multiply upon the earth."
> —God

of Abraham, the first biblical figure of whose existence there was evidence. The theme, therefore, as far as Huston was concerned, would be man's emergence from mythology into history.

The Bible (officially subtitled *In the Beginning . . .*) went into production on May 11, 1964, with interiors shot at the De Laurentiis Studio outside of Rome, utilizing four soundstages, two of them the largest in the world. The city of Sodom was constructed on the slopes of Mount Etna; a crater of Vesuvius was used for the section depicting Cain's murder of Abel; and the Sahara desert provided the location for the Abraham and Sarah story, as well as the top of the Tower of Babel. The base of the tower was built back at the studio, in addition to a miniature used for long shots. The Garden of Eden scenes were shot at a zoological compound in Rome that had fallen into disrepair. Sparing no expense, a two-hundred-foot long, fifty-foot high replica of Noah's Ark was constructed, as well as a second partial ark. The menagerie of animals needed for the scene was shipped to Rome and then housed, trained, and fed by no fewer than fifty trainers. This impressive sequence, hands down the best executed and most enjoyable one in the movie, was filmed over a five-month period at a cost of $3 million.

There are no statistics available on how many unsuspecting bookstore shoppers, looking for a copy of the real thing, accidentally ended up with Pocket Book's published version of Christopher Hampton's screenplay for *The Bible*.

Still photographer Ernest Haas was dispatched to various parts of the globe, including Ecuador, the Galápagos Islands, and Iceland to film the opening montage that suggested the creation of the Earth. Shooting dragged on well into 1965, and it was more than two years from the start of shooting till the finished film finally arrived in theaters. During that time De Laurentiis had rented a billboard in Times Square that announced the coming of his spectacular event, which had soared in cost from $13 to $18 million by the time production was completed.

Needless to say, a movie that merely dramatized a few chapters from the Holy Bible in a respectful manner ran the risk of being episodic, disjointed, and detached from true emotional involvement, which was indeed the case. After a nature documentary–type opening, the Garden of Eden segment kept one's attention because the extensive nudity on hand made it so undeniably naughty for its day. However, once Richard Harris, as Cain, showed up to kill off Franco Nero, as Abel (a year before the two men clashed onscreen in Warner Bros.' *Camelot*), it became evident that a good deal of the picture would consist of visual miming while John Huston's narration supplied the explanation and dramatic texture (hopefully) of what the audience was seeing. Everything worked fine for the Deluge sequence, which was followed by the curiously abrupt Tower of Babel, which looked spectacular but didn't really add up to much. Following the intermission, whatever the film had accomplished thus far was negated by the endless and heavy-handed Abraham and Sarah episode, which featured George C. Scott emoting to the heavens in an effort to convince himself that he was enacting material the equal of *King Lear*. This lifeless chapter soon collapsed under its own self-important weight, sending the crowds out in a very dissatisfied mood. Only Peter O'Toole's mystical appearance as three angels out to destroy the city of Sodom (whose annihilation resembled an atomic blast) kept the latter half of the epic from putting viewers to sleep altogether. Amazingly, *The Bible* managed to triumph over its mostly negative reviews to take in a substantial amount of cash, making it one of the top five attractions of 1966—helped, no doubt, by the religious majority, who considered it their duty to patronize something with such lofty spiritual aspirations. Although this seemed to signal that the Bible was still viable film fare, Huston's grand spectacle actually marked the end of an era. It was the last major motion picture of its kind for many years.

SECONDS

Academy Award Nominee: Cinematography—Black and White

Opening date: October 5, 1966.

Paramount. A Douglas & Lewis Productions Presentation.

Director: John Frankenheimer. Producer: Edward Lewis. Screenplay: Lewis John Carlino. Based on the 1963 novel by David Ely. Photography: James Wong Howe. Art Director: Ted Haworth. Costumes: Jack Martell, Pete Saldutti. Music: Jerry Goldsmith. Editors: Ferris Webster, David Newhouse. Main Title Designer: Saul Bass. Black and white. 106 minutes.

CAST: Rock Hudson (Antiochus "Tony" Wilson), Salome Jens (Nora Marcus), John Randolph (Arthur Hamilton), Will Geer (Old Man), Jeff Corey (Mr. Ruby), Richard Anderson (Dr. Innes), Murray Hamilton (Charlie Evans), Karl Swenson (Dr. Morris), Khigh Dhiegh (Davalo), Frances Reid (Emily Hamilton), Wesley Addy (John), John Lawrence (Texan), Elisabeth Fraser (Plump Blonde), Dody Heath (Sue Bushman), Robert Brubaker (Mayberry), Dorothy Morris (Mrs. Filter), Barbara Werle (Secretary), Frank Campanella (Man in Station), Ned Young (Henry Bushman).

PLOT: Unhappy with his routine and empty life, middle-aged businessman Arthur Hamilton submits to an operation giving him the body of a younger man and a brand new identity.

Some movies are destined to be cult items, which means they are required to fail upon initial release and go through a certain period of neglect or lack of overall appreciation until they are finally unearthed and proclaimed misunderstood gems, if not masterpieces. Director John Frankenheimer's *Seconds* fit the bill in all respects. It was the sort of unsettling experience that seemed an unlikely property for a major studio like Paramount to release, had so prestigious a name as Frankenheimer or so potent a box-office attraction as Rock Hudson not been attached to it. It was while Frankenheimer and Kirk Douglas were working on *Seven Days in May* during the summer of 1963 that they had come across the galleys of *Seconds*, David Ely's stark novel about rejuvenation and a second chance at life. The two believed that this could be an intriguing showcase for Douglas, and along with Edward Lewis (previously Douglas's producing partner at Bryna, who now officially joined forces with Frankenheimer with this film) they convinced Paramount (which was distributing *Seven Days*) to buy the rights to the book prior to publication for $75,000. The movie would be a coventure of Douglas's Joel Productions and Frankenheimer's company, with the idea of filming it in the spring of 1964. This scheduled start date never materialized, and Douglas eventually dropped out because he had too many other commitments, although he still received partial producing credit. Now on the lookout for a new star, the idea arose to get Rock Hudson, which might have seemed at first like mere pandering to money but was in fact a brilliant choice. If a man was hoping to start life anew and change his outward appearance, wouldn't he prefer to look like someone as ruggedly handsome as Hudson? Hudson, always hoping to prove that he was more than a lightweight, was willing to do the movie only under the condition that he not be required to play the older version of himself, which he believed he would not be able to pull off convincingly. This decision turned out to be superior to the initial idea of the same performer doing the before-and-after versions of the protagonist. If indeed Arthur Hamilton was going to be reborn as someone else, he should look like a whole new person. Frankenheimer agreed to Hudson's proposal, which meant the star would not appear onscreen until some forty minutes into the picture, but Paramount now had a saleable name and was happy to proceed.

To adapt the novel, Frankenheimer opted for a playwright who had never before written anything for the screen, Lewis John Carlino. His script unfolded chronologically, whereas Ely's book had Hamilton show up for his appointment with the Company at the outset and then explain how he got there. Carlino's approach started the film off with a greater sense of mystery by having Hamilton be handed a note in Grand Central Station without any clear explanation of why. Another wise decision was made to keep Wilson's place of relocation a secret until the party scene, when it is made clear that he is living in a community of reborns. In the book this fact was told to him earlier, making his drunken outburst far less ef-fective. Eliminated, no doubt to avoid censorship problems, were a passage in which Hamilton was comforted with sex by a nurse at the Company and the idea of giving Wilson a teenager for the nude model who offers him sex (although he is incapable of carrying out the performance). The film had Wilson attempt to follow through on the relationship established with the girl on the beach (in the book he had rejected her), taking them to a newly invented moment of frolicking naked at a wine festival, a key step in Wilson's learning to unwind. Gone too was the appearance of Char-lie's widow, Sue, at Wilson's party; in the film her new mari-tal status was later revealed by Wilson on the phone to her

> "I had to find out where I went wrong. The years I've spent trying to get all the things I was told were important . . . that I was supposed to want . . . things . . . not . . . people, or meaning, just . . . things."
> —Antiochus Wilson

devastated "late husband." Time was saved in depicting Wilson's flight from the reborn community by cutting out a scene in which he spoke to a woman in a dive club, finding out that her husband had died in much the same way as the man whose body he has claimed, and eliminating his stopover at the home of his daughter, where Wilson is made uncomfortable by how little the woman misses her "late" father. Finally, the climax was heightened dramatically by making Wilson resistant to his inevitable demise, whereas in Ely's version he had accepted his fate more passively.

The film began shooting on June 14, 1965, at several Manhattan locations, including Grand Central Station. Outside of New York, the unit used the New Haven–Hartford train line for scenes of Arthur Hamilton's commute and the exterior of a white clapboard house on Lockwood Lane in Scarsdale for the Hamilton residence. Heading west, a cheap and simple solution was found for Wilson's posh beachfront digs: Frankenheimer gave up his own house in Malibu for the setting. For the wine vat scene, Franken-heimer used participants in the Feast of Bacchus in Santa Barbara for what turned out to be one of the most startlingly provocative sequences to yet appear in a major motion picture. So much nudity was captured by the handheld camera (controlled by Frankenheimer himself) that only the European print featured all of the footage intended—Americans missed approximately a minute, which was restored during the video era. Interiors were shot at Paramount Studios, including the Daliesque dream, with a set concocted by Frankenheimer himself. A stunning Saul Bass title montage, James Wong Howe's

This ad for the British release of *Seconds* was heightened by the creepy image of a bandaged Rock Hudson, which, alas, was enough to turn away his mainstream fans.

frequent use of wide-angle lenses and of a seemingly floating camera in the opening Grand Central scene, and a soundtrack that was mostly dubbed in after the shoot contributed to the overall disturbing nature of the piece.

The picture was not an easy sell. Paramount managed to get it accepted at the Cannes Film Festival in the spring of 1966, only to find out that a good portion of the audience wasn't pleased with what it saw. *Seconds* was not to be taken lightly. It was not a flippant satire on plastic surgery, but a shattering meditation on just how difficult it is to escape life's rut, even when given a second chance to do it right. This uneasy feeling that middle-aged men everywhere were crying out for a change and were unable to achieve lasting happiness no matter how high a price they paid for it really left a sting. Frankenheimer's vision was nightmarish and uncompromising, with Wilson's final, hopeless journey into death enough to leave the toughest audiences numb. Paramount figured it'd best sell the movie as a horror entry, which was not the sort of thing the typical Rock Hudson fan wanted to see. Likewise, those on the lookout for something bleak and avant-garde felt put off by the inclusion of Hollywood's ultimate box-office-friendly male attraction. As if to punish Hudson for catching them off balance, the actor's reviews were not as supportive as they should have been, which was a shame, for he had committed himself fully, giving a heartbreakingly good performance, effectively conveying the longing of someone who can't feel comfortable with his good fortune. It was among the best acting of his career, and the actor remained justifiably proud of what he had accomplished in the role.

HAWAII

Academy Award Nominee: Supporting Actress (Jocelyne LaGarde); Cinematography—Color; Sound; Song ("My Wishing Doll"); Original Music Score; Costume Design—Color; Special Visual Effects

Top 10 Box Office Film

Opening date: October 10, 1966.

United Artists. A Mirisch Corporation Presentation of the George Roy Hill–Walter Mirisch Production.

Director: George Roy Hill. Producer: Walter Mirisch. Screenplay: Dalton Trumbo, Daniel Taradash. Based on the 1959 novel by James A. Michener. Photography: Russell Harlan. Production Designer: Cary Odell. Art Director: James Sullivan. Set Decorators: Edward G. Boyle, Ray Boltz Jr. Costumes: Dorothy Jeakins. Music: Elmer Bernstein. Song: "My Wishing Doll," by Mack David (lyrics) and Elmer Bernstein, performed by Julie Andrews. Editor: Stuart Gilmore. Sound: Robert Martin, Bert Hallberg. Special Photographic Effects: Film Effects of Hollywood, Linwood G. Dunn, James B. Gordon. Special Effects: Paul Byrd. Deluxe color. Panavision. 189 minutes (including overture, entr'acte, and exit music; later cut to 171 minutes).

CAST: *The Leading Players*: Julie Andrews (Jerusha Bromley Hale), Max von Sydow (Abner Hale), Richard Harris (Captain Rafer Hoxworth); *The Bromley Family*: Carroll O'Connor (Charles Bromley), Elizabeth Cole (Abigail Bromley), Diane Sherry (Charity Bromley), Heather Menzies (Mercy Bromley); *The Missionaries*: Torin Thatcher (Reverend Thorn), Gene Hackman (John Whipple), John Cullum (Immanuel Quigley), Lou Antonio (Abraham Hewlett); *The Hawaiians*: Jocelyne LaGarde (Queen Alii Nui Malama), Manu Tupou (Keoki), Ted Nobriga (Kelolo), Elizabeth Logue (Noelani), Lokelani S. Chicarell (Iliki); *The Hale Family*: Malcolm Atterbury (Gideon Hale), Dorothy Jeakins (Hepzibah Hale); *Ship's Company— "Thetis"*: George Rose (Captain Janders), Michael Constantine (Mason), John Harding (Collins), Robert Crawford (Cridland); *and*: Don Dolittle (Fredericks), Robert Oakley (Micah, four years), Henrik von Sydow (Micah, seven years), Clas S. von Sydow (Micah, twelve years), Bertil Werjefelt (Micah, eighteen years), Bette Midler (Seasick Passenger).

PLOT: In 1819 Reverend Abner Hale and his new wife, Jerusha, sail from New England to Hawaii, where Hale and the other missionaries plan to bring civilization to the islanders and teach them the word of God, thereby putting an end to long-established traditions and customs.

The very year in which it became, amid great fanfare, the fiftieth and final state to enter the union, Hawaii received a loving valentine in the form of author James A. Michener's most ambitious and longest novel to date, itself called *Hawaii*. A combination of the timeliness of its publication and the fact that Michener had become not only a favorite writer since his 1948 Pulitzer Prize winner *Tales of the South Pacific*, but something of a household name through his many tomes exploring the people and the islands of the South Seas, turned the novel into one of the most widely read books of its era. Perhaps sensing that great things were to happen to *Hawaii*, the Mirisch Corporation wasted no time in shelling out a very hefty figure for the rights, $600,000 against 10 percent of the eventual film gross; among the highest fees ever paid for a work of literature. One reason the Mirisches were so fast in their negotiations was that they already had a director lined up for the project, Oscar-winner Fred Zinnemann, who had just received some of the best reviews of his career for the unexpected moneymaker *The Nun's Story* (Warner Bros., 1959). Zinnemann intended to produce the picture as well, through his Highland Films production, and hired his *From Here to Eternity* (Columbia, 1953) scriptwriter, Daniel Taradash, to come up with not one but two screenplays, the idea being to concentrate on only two portions of the massive work, "From the Sun-Swept Lagoon," which had dealt with the islands' first settlers, and "From the Farm of Bitterness," about the New England missionaries who traveled to Hawaii with the intention of forcing their ways upon the "heathens."

During the eighteen months Taradash labored on his scripts, Zinnemann announced that Audrey Hepburn would be playing the genteel missionary's wife, Jerusha, and that Alec Guinness would fill the role of the stubbornly self-righteous reverend, Abner Hale. The Mirisches began to worry about the cost of producing a pair of three-hour movies, especially in light of all the financial hardships Twentieth Century-Fox was enduring with *Cleopatra* (1963), which had been similarly planned as two gargantuan halves. Dalton Trumbo was therefore called in to revise what Taradash had been working on. Zinnemann asked him to concentrate on the earlier chapter about the settlers. This, however, was not feasible from the point of view of the box office, as far as the Mirisches were concerned, because it meant that the principals would all be Asians, which Hollywood was regrettably short

> "A disease . . . despair . . . our lack of love . . . our inability to find them beautiful . . . our contempt for their ways . . . our lust for their land . . . our greed . . . our arrogance. That is what kills them, Abner. And that's what you must save them from."
> —Jerusha Hale

of where star names were concerned. By August 1963 some $2 million had already been spent preparing the picture, with nothing to show for it. The Mirisches put a $10 million cap on the budget, which Zinnemann thought was unrealistic. It became apparent that the director and his financiers were no longer on the same plane where *Hawaii* was concerned, and Zinnemann decided to take a job at Fox directing *Behold a Pale Horse* (1964) instead.

Chapter 3 of the book, "From the Farm of Bitterness," certainly had enough material for a full-length feature, although it would make for a challenging film because its chief protagonist, Reverend Abner Hale, was so insufferably priggish and intolerant. The final script, which was credited to both Trumbo and Taradash (in that order), began with a brief prologue culled from material from the now abandoned chapter 2 about the settling of Hawaii by inhabitants from Bora Bora. The film otherwise concentrated on a great many of the events from the two-hundred-page third chapter, with some revisions being made mainly for the purpose of compressing the time frame. These included no longer having Reverend Thorn arrive in Marlboro to interrogate both the townspeople and Abner's parents about the young man's missionary qualifications and dispensing with the correspondence between Jerusha and Abner's sister Esther prior to their meeting. Perhaps because the writers sensed that they were already struggling to build sympathy for Abner, the Reverend Hale no longer withheld Bibles from the crew of the *Thetis* because they had dared to assist his sickly wife rather than stay and listen to his sermon. This cruel and unreasonable act was replaced by a display of drunkenness by one of the men, which took the blame away from poor Jerusha's suffering. Rafer Hoxworth now appeared in the story at a later time, showing up on the island rather than meeting up with the Hales while at sea as he had in Michener's version. This meant that the scene in which he tosses Abner overboard in hopes of his being eaten by sharks now took place in Hawaii itself. Indeed, Hoxworth's anger was toned down so as not to make him too maniacal, no longer having him murder a policeman over Malama's new laws and following this act by trying to blast the Hales' house to pieces with cannon fire.

Also missing from the book was a hurricane that destroyed the whaling ships following the death of Malama and Abner's realization that he has lost some of his converts after Noelani uses the traditional Pele stone to stop a volcanic flow on Hilo. The ending of the chapter had seen Hoxworth marry Noelani after Keoki had perished from the measles; their daughter ultimately married Hale's eldest son, an act that invokes the usual bigoted ire from Abner—hardly a fitting way to end a motion picture. Instead, the character of a birthmarked baby saved by Jerusha returned for the final scene in order to give audiences

Jocelyne LaGarde makes her memorable entrance in *Hawaii*, welcoming the missionaries who have come to the islands with the intention of "civilizing" her people.

some hope for Abner's greater acceptance of the islanders, whose customs he has been instrumental in destroying. As crucial as it had been to point out the occasional "good" done by the outsiders, notably in teaching the Hawaiians the evil in killing babies unwanted by their families, it was more important to bring attention to Western civilization's misguided, thoughtless self-justification in forcing a single-minded religious way upon a culture unlike themselves, as if the beliefs or customs of others were worthless in the eyes of God. Unfortunately, most of the criticism that had been leveled at Abner and his religion by the far more levelheaded and open-minded Dr. Whipple was trimmed down for the film script when it should have been emphasized more.

Once the picture looked as if it would finally get ready to sail, the Mirisches decided on George Roy Hill as the new director. Hill very pointedly wanted Julie Andrews to play Jerusha, a choice that couldn't have made the Mirisches happier, considering her palpable heat at the time in the wake of the phenomenon of *Mary Poppins* (Buena Vista, 1964). Not bothering to stick to the book's frequent description of Abner Hale as a small man, Hill went with Sweden's leading star, Max von Sydow, who had recently made his English-language debut in the about-to-be-released spectacle *The Greatest Story Ever Told* (United Artists, 1965). Having just finished portraying Jesus, von Sydow was a bit hesitant about going the religious route yet again, until he realized that Abner couldn't have been further from Christ in his lack of compassion and stubborn refusal to see his fellow human beings in a loving light. For the four pivotal Hawaiian roles, Hill went with not only unknowns but nonactors. Among these, the real gem was Jocelyne LaGarde, a three-hundred-pound, six-foot-tall descendant of an ancient Tahitian royal family. LaGarde spoke only French at the time she was cast and learned her lines phonetically; yet she captured the very heart and goodness, as well as the melancholy and domineering ire, of the richly eccentric but commendably proud ruler Malama.

The first stage of the *Hawaii* shoot took place in February 1965 and did not involve any of the principals; instead, footage of Norway was captured by the second unit to fill in for the Straits of Magellan. Filming proper commenced on April 19, with Old Sturbridge Village in Massachusetts standing in for Walpole, New Hampshire. The unit then found itself on the Samuel Goldwyn Studios soundstages for four weeks from May to June, where the big set piece from the first third of the movie, the ocean storm sequence, was done. The next four months brought cast and crew to Hawaii itself. Makua Beach on the island of Oahu served as the entrance to Lahaina, while the village itself, shown in various stages of growth between 1820 and 1848, was constructed on Maui. In the Pearl City area of Honolulu, a former naval warehouse was transferred into a soundstage where several interiors were done, notably the inside of the Hale home, where Andrews enacted her big scene enduring the pain of childbirth.

Hill delivered a three-hour-plus epic to United Artists and the Mirisches at a nerve-racking cost of $14 million. The studio believed deeply in the movie, however, not only because it seemed as if Hill had kept things together and handed in a winner, but because their source material was simply too well-known by this point for people not to be eager to see how it (or rather, a portion of it) had made it to the big screen. They also had the added lure of having some bare-breasted women in the film. This costuming decision was not only accurate for the period and customs, but was even sanctioned by the National Catholic Office of Motion Pictures, making this the first mainstream feature to get the OK in this department. *Hawaii* was scheduled for its road-show, two-performances-a-day, reserved-seat-engagement debut in

October 1966, approximately a year after photography had ended. (In the interim, Andrews had made Universal's *Torn Curtain*, which had already been released in July 1966).

Interest in snapping up tickets prior to opening was encouraging, but the reviews were not. The lukewarm ones were fairly easy to take, but the downright hostile ones were far more rancorous and destructive than anyone could have imagined. Despite a literate screenplay, a general fidelity in spirit and incident to Michener's intentions, and an engrossing story, the general critics' consensus was that *Hawaii* was little more than a lumbering travelogue, which certainly sold an imperfect but commendable accomplishment short. Andrews, despite taking a back seat to von Sydow in screen time, proved once again that she fit pretty much any part effortlessly. She instilled great heart and gentle wisdom into the film without seeming pious or timid. Von Sydow had the tougher task of not making Abner an absolute ass, and he did not shy away from the more infuriating traits of this man, while never playing him as an out-and-out villain. The best reviews, however, were for LaGarde, who made one of the screen's great entrances, hoisted aboard ship on a sling customarily used for cattle and afterward bestowing a comforting series of "alohas" on her startled but fascinated passengers. (In the book she had stripped naked for them.) She was the sole cast member to net an Oscar nomination, making her (to date) the only acting nominee in Academy history to have never performed before or after her nomination in *anything*, screen, stage, or television, since LaGarde swore off the profession even while filming. She died on September 12, 1979, in her native Tahiti at the age of fifty-five.

Andrews's participation in *Hawaii* proved to be a crucial one when the Mirisch Corporation began to realize that her huge fan base had mostly ignored the negative press and kept buying tickets, bringing U.S. grosses up to the $31 million mark. That meant the producers just about broke even on their investment. As the picture moved from exclusive to general engagements, United Artists made sure it was able to squeeze more showings into theaters by trimming away at the movie, first shaving off about eight minutes, and then lopping off another ten, mostly from the preliminary material in New England and from the ocean voyage. *Hawaii* ended up as the highest-grossing 1966 release, though this didn't keep its many detractors from continually writing it off as a big-budget flop—the habit of critics who wanted their distaste for a movie verified somehow through profits. The reception was certainly good enough as far as the Mirisch Corporation was concerned, because it dusted off the old idea of filming multiple chapters of the Michener epic, though it didn't intend to go backward in the story by shooting chapter 2, as Zinnemann had once planned, but figured the best approach was to proceed to the fourth chapter, "From the Starving Village." Entitled *The Hawaiians*, the new picture starred Charlton Heston, Geraldine Chaplin, and John Phillip Law as descendants of a union between the Whipple and Hoxworth families, with Mako, Tina Chen, Keye Luke, and Virginia Ann Lee representing the Chinese inhabitants. Released in 1970, the 132-minute movie was less costly than the first, and even more critically disliked.

A FUNNY THING HAPPENED ON THE WAY TO THE FORUM

Academy Award Winner: Scoring of Music—Adaptation or Treatment

Opening date: October 16, 1966.

United Artists. A Melvin Frank Production.

Director: Richard Lester. Producer: Melvin Frank. Screenplay: Melvin Frank, Michael Pertwee. Based on the 1962 musical with music and lyrics by Stephen Sondheim, book by Burt Shevelove and Larry Gelbart. Photography: Nicolas Roeg. Production and Costume Designer: Tony Walton. Songs by Stephen Sondheim: "Comedy Tonight," "Lovely," "Everybody Ought to Have a Maid," "Bring Me My Bride," "The Dirge." Musical Director and Incidental Music: Ken Thorne. Musical Conductor: Irwin Kostal. Choreographers: Ethel Martin, George Martin. Editor: John Victor-Smith. Deluxe color. 99 minutes.

CAST: Zero Mostel (Pseudolus), Phil Silvers (Marcus Lycus), Buster Keaton (Erronius), Jack Gilford (Hysterium), Michael Crawford (Hero), Annette Andre (Philia), Patricia Jessel (Domina), Michael Hordern (Senex), Leon Greene (Captain Miles Gloriosus), Pamela Brown (High Priestess), Inga Neilsen (Gymnasia), Myrna White (Vibrata), Lucienne Bridou (Panacea), Helen Funai (Tintinabula), Jennifer Baker and Susan Baker (Geminae), Janet Webb (Fertilla), Beatrix Lehmann (Domina's Mother), Alfie Bass (Gatekeeper), Roy Kinnear (Gladiator Instructor), Jon Pertwee (Crassus), John Bluthal (Roman Chief Guard).

PLOT: In exchange for his freedom, Pseudolus, a wily Roman slave, agrees to help his master, Hero, win the girl of his dreams, a courtesan from the whorehouse next door, who has already been promised to a powerful general.

High on pretty much everyone's list of the funniest Broadway musicals, *A Funny Thing Happened on the Way to the Forum* owed a great deal of its success to its intricately crafted script by Burt Shevelove and Larry Gelbart and to its powerhouse leading performance by Zero Mostel, who, because of this show, became a prized figure of the musical genre. It was only in later years, when he took almost godlike status as one of the twentieth century's foremost contributors to the art of musical theater, that people began to worship *Forum* as a "Stephen Sondheim musical" and acknowledge the composer's role in its success. Indeed, at the 1963 Tonys, although *Forum* took home six awards, Sondheim was not even nominated in the composer and lyricist category. While there was no denying that he had come up with some very witty material, even one of his fellow collaborators, Shevelove, felt that many of the songs lacked a sort of show-biz panache and were around merely for audiences to take a breather from the laughs, rather than to keep the plot rolling along. That put them at odds with the rollicking book that

> "Old situations, new complications; nothing portentous or polite. Tragedy tomorrow, comedy tonight."
> —Pseudolus

surrounded them. When it came time make a movie of *Forum*, it shouldn't have surprised anyone that fidelity to the score would not be a priority.

In mid-January 1964 it was announced that United Artists had paid $300,000 plus a percentage of the film profits for the screen rights to *Forum*, which was still having a healthy run in New York. (The show, which had premiered on May 8, 1962, would close on August 29, 1964, having run 964 performances at three different theaters, the Alvin, Mark Hellinger, and Majestic.) The idea was for the team of Melvin Frank and Norman Panama to adapt, produce, and direct the piece. By the time the film was ready to go into production in 1965, United Art-ists was having second thoughts about Frank directing the picture and now preferred to engage Richard Lester, who had just become one of the most in-demand new talents in the indus-try for the fresh and freewheeling way he helmed the Beatles' first movie, *A Hard Day's Night* (United Artists, 1964). United Artists did, however, ask Frank to stay on as producer and writer, only he would not be collabo-rating with Panama. Instead, Eng-lishman Michael Pertwee, who had worked with Frank on *Strange Bedfel-lows* (Universal, 1965) and with Lester on *The Mouse on the Moon* (United Artists, 1963), was brought on board to help on the script. Lester and Frank immediately clashed on how to adapt

The two cast principals retained from the Broadway original, Zero Mostel and Jack Gilford, enjoy one another's company on the set of *A Funny Thing Happened on the Way to the Forum.*

the farce. The latter revised the original script to include many comical anachronisms, which the Broad-way show had never once fallen back upon and which Lester correctly believed were at odds with the play's humor. By the time the movie started filming on September 1, 1965, Lester and Frank weren't even on speaking terms.

The casting of the film could not be faulted. It was decided pretty much from the get-go that Zero Mostel be asked to repeat his part, to which he happily agreed. He had not acted in front of a motion-picture camera since 1951, when he fell victim to the Hollywood blacklist. *Forum* would mark his first starring role in a film. Mostel suggested to Frank that he also get Jack Gilford to reprise his stage part of Hysterium, the nervous slave who becomes Mostel's unwilling partner in deception. Like Mostel, he too had suffered from the communist witch hunts of the '50s and had been away from movies nearly as long (a few months before filming began on *Forum* he shot a small role in MGM's *Mister Buddwing*), his last credit being an unbilled bit as a box-office attendant in MGM's *Main Street to Broadway* (1953). For the part of whorehouse proprietor Marcus Lycus (John Carradine had done the role on Broadway),

Phil Silvers was hired, an ironic bit of casting, in that the comedian had turned down the Pseudolus role in the stage musical, which had actually been written with him in mind. Rather than cast some neutral presence to play Hero, the male love interest, Lester brought aboard his *Knack* star, Michael Crawford, whose gulping hesitancy and expertise at pratfalls made the character just as funny as the older farceurs on hand. For the role of the half-senile old citizen who spends most of the story line running around the Seven Hills of Rome, legendary silent-film comedian Buster Keaton was chosen. Keaton, who had spent most of the last thirty-five years of his professional life trying to regain the glory that had evaporated with the coming of sound, made much of his few moments of screen time but couldn't help but come off as yet again having been criminally wasted.

Although the original intention was to shoot in England, *Forum* wound up being made entirely in Spain. Initially, the idea had been to use the mammoth Roman forum set left over from Samuel Bronston's epic *The Fall of the Roman Empire* (Paramount, 1964), but Lester found it too pristine in appearance. Wanting Rome to be seen in all its cluttered squalor, he had Tony Walton construct shabbier buildings in Las Matas, thirty miles south of Madrid. Because his style was so kinetic and visual, Lester worked more closely with his cameraman, future director Nicolas Roeg, to map out the script than with his writers, having pretty much banned Melvin Frank from the set. Knowing that Keaton was not in the best of health, Lester was forced to replace him with an ex-jockey during many of the long shots in which the character was seen running. A gag in which Keaton was required to hit his head on a tree branch proved near-disastrous when the seventy-year-old miscalculated the impact and knocked himself out cold. This was to be Buster's final appearance before the cameras; the great comedian died of cancer on February 1, 1966, only a few months after the movie finished shooting.

Held back from release until October of that year, *Forum* found a smattering of favorable notices—not even a fraction of the acclaim it had received on the stage. The very people who had recently championed Lester's exuberant, flashy shooting style condemned it here, while there was much complaining about the cutting of so many of the songs. Only five were retained in the transfer; gone were "Love, I Hear," "Free," "Pretty Little Picture," "Impossible," "I'm Calm," "That'll Show Him," and "That Dirty Old Man." Most of the original creators, including Larry Gelbart and Stephen Sondheim, made no secret of their dislike of the finished picture, so it became quite acceptable for supporters of the New York theater community to dismiss the *Forum* movie without a second thought.

Although Silvers's role had to be built up in order to justify casting him, the script additions in no way harmed the structure of the farce, as Gelbart had complained. With Mostel and Gilford working at full throttle, plus Lester's penchant for throwaway humor and sight gags (an inserted scene of a warm-up at a gladiator school was priceless), some deftly executed bits of slapstick by Crawford, and a rapid pace that never lagged for a minute, the film of *Forum* was far funnier than most of its detractors gave it credit for being. Despite the come-on of United Artists slapping a "Suggested for Mature Audiences" label on all its advertising, *Forum* couldn't work up enough public interest outside of select metropolitan engagements, and the distributor chalked it up as a money-loser. Frank, no doubt, was gloating, having done his own cut of the picture, which United Artists had rejected in favor of Lester's.

GEORGY GIRL (United Kingdom)

Academy Award Nominee: Actress (Lynn Redgrave); Supporting Actor (James Mason); Cinematography—Black and White; Song ("Georgy Girl")

Opening date: October 17, 1966 (London: October 13, 1966).

Columbia. A Robert A. Goldston–Otto Plaschkes Production.

Director: Silvio Narizzano. Producers: Robert A. Goldston, Otto Plaschkes. Screenplay: Margaret Forster, Peter Nichols. Based on the 1965 novel by Margaret Forster. Photography: Ken Higgins. Art Director: Tony Woollard. Miss Rampling's Clothes: Mary Quant. Music: Alexander Faris. Children's Dance Music: Brian Hunter. Title song by Tom Springfield (music) and Jim Dale (lyrics), performed by the Seekers. Additional Songs: "Whole Lot of Woman," by Marvin Rainwater, performed by Lynn Redgrave; "You Look a Little Lovelier Every Day," by William Hill Bowen; "Deep in My Lonely Heart," by Alexander Faris (music and lyrics) and Barry Noble (lyrics). Editor: John Bloom. Black and white. 99 minutes.

CAST: James Mason (James Leamington), Alan Bates (Jos Jones), Lynn Redgrave (Georgina, "Georgy"), Charlotte Rampling (Meredith Montgomery), Bill Owen (Ted, Georgy's Father), Clare Kelly (Doris, Georgy's Mother), Rachel Kempson (Ellen Leamington), Denise Coffey (Peg), Peggy Thorpe-Bates (Hospital Sister), Dandy Nichols (Hospital Nurse).

PLOT: Georgy, a frumpy girl who has resigned herself to being one of life's misfits, finds herself the unexpected object of affection of two men, Josh, the boyfriend of her selfish roommate Meredith, and James Leamington, the millionaire for whom Georgy's parents work.

As the defining female representative of the mostly male-dominated British New Wave of the '60s, plump, frumpy, highly sensitive, and defensively witty Georgy Girl became a heroine to anyone subjected to the world's harsh condemnation of those not fortunate enough to be born popular, desirable, and hopelessly beautiful. Of course the character was far more complex than just a nice, overweight lady enduring the cruel put-downs of the world, so hung up on mothering everyone around her that she winds up leaving her own degree of pain in her wake, unable to see what all the fuss is about sex, marriage, and love. This outstanding creation came from the mind of Margaret Forster, an Oxford graduate who had taught school in Islington, in North London, prior to embarking on a writing career. A newly established production company, Everglades, purchased *Georgy Girl*, Forster's second published book, with the idea of having the author work solely on the screenplay and hiring one of most talked-about new actresses in London theater, Vanessa Redgrave, to play the leading role.

Forster initially had no desire to adapt her own work to the screen; having no experience whatsoever in screenwriting, she believed the job was best left to others. Everglades persisted, so the author basically handed in a massive stack of papers that consisted of the entire book, every scene and line of dialogue kept intact. Everglades knew that this would never do but liked so many of her words that it decided to keep a good many of them. To pare down her draft and shape it into something filmable that would run at an acceptable length, the studio hired playwright Peter Nichols, two years before his most famous work, *A Day in the Death of Joe Egg*, was first produced on the London stage.

Although the screenplay adhered closely to Forster, especially in the early part of the film, Nichols felt the need to leave some elements out and add a few of his own scenes. Jos no longer was present at Georgy's outrageous vamp performance during the Leamington party, which certainly made more sense; James's offer to have Georgy be his mistress took place not at her flat, which had allowed the millionaire to meet Jos, but at his mansion; the first sex scene between Georgy and Jos was moved to make it less distasteful—in the book it occurred while Meredith was in labor in a nearby bedroom, but now it took place when she was away in hospital; Jos was no longer seen actually signing an agreement to have his baby adopted; and the idea of having Meredith return to the flat to live while Jos and Georgy continue their relationship, only to be driven out by them, was dropped in favor of having the stridently independent Meredith leave of her own choice, running off with her latest lover. Nichols added a risky sequence that had Jos shedding his clothing while running through the streets of London to tell Georgy how much he loves her, a moment that could have lapsed into the cute or grotesque but turned out delightful, against

> "The absolute story of my life—no matter what I try, God's always got a custard pie up his sleeve."
> —Georgy

all odds; wrote a pungent scene in which Meredith shows her true colors when she accepts a date by phone, showing that she thinks nothing of the fact that she and Georgy are on their way out to eat and defining Meredith's selfish nature brilliantly; and allowed Georgy a terrific moment to tell Meredith off at the hospital, when she cannot believe that the hedonistic bitch would be so callous as to give her baby to someone else. The character of Georgy's neighbor, Peg, an overweight and socially inept woman who reflects the very worst potential future for Georgy, which does *not* happen, was kept for the film, but most of her participation in the story was eliminated, including her lesbian crush on Georgy. Finally, knowing that such a gesture might cause the audience to feel less enchanted with their heroine, Nichols dropped Georgy's angry confrontation with her parents at the book's end, which led to her asking James to sack them so that they can finally stop living exclusively for the Leamingtons. When Nichols was told that as good as his work was, the intention was to combine both his efforts and what Forster had written, he nearly walked off the picture. In the end the two writers received up-front credit, Forster listed *before* Nichols.

Vanessa Redgrave agreed to take on the leading role, having recently finished her first motion picture lead in *Morgan!* (Cinema V, 1966). Talented as she was and no doubt committed to delving deep into this characterization, she was also a stunningly beautiful woman, which made her casting as the admittedly unlovely Georgy rather a stretch. Because Redgrave was a movie newcomer at the time, it was decided to hire recognizable stars as the men in her life, hoping to entice some name actors who were pleased enough with the material to take a lower salary in order to keep the budget down. Fortunately, James Mason was interested in playing Georgy's befuddled, somewhat lecherous older suitor, and his compensation for a cut in pay was to receive top billing for what was clearly a supporting role. One of the seminal young British actors of the moment, Alan Bates, was also willing to sign on, and although his part was bigger than Mason's but nowhere near as substantial as Georgy's, he rated second billing. Redgrave had casting suggestions for some of the smaller roles, which included her mother, Rachel Kempson, as Mason's ailing wife, and her younger sister Lynn as Peg. Silvio Narizzano, a Canadian who had done mostly television work up to that point and a single theatrical feature, the Tallulah Bankhead horror opus *Fanatic/Die! Die! My Darling!* (Columbia, 1965), was selected as director, receiving a mere $5,000 up front for his services. Once he saw Lynn Redgrave in action, he started to wonder if the studio had not, indeed, picked the wrong Redgrave sister for the star spot. Whether or not this was on her mind all along is not clear, but it turned out that Vanessa also came to the realization that it was Lynn who should be playing Georgy and announced that she was backing out of the film, allowing her sibling to claim the lead. Fortunately, the participation of Mason and Bates was enough to keep Columbia Pictures interested in distributing the movie, so Everglades did not lose its American support.

Being given a budget of less than half a million pounds with which to work, Narizzano was obliged to film as fast as possible and to get Mason's scenes done first so he could go off to do another picture. Shooting began on December 6, 1965, with interiors done at Shepperton Studios. During the studio filming, Narizzano took his cast out on the streets of London, using the underground tunnels at Hyde Park Corner, Little Venice, and a sightseeing boat on the Thames.

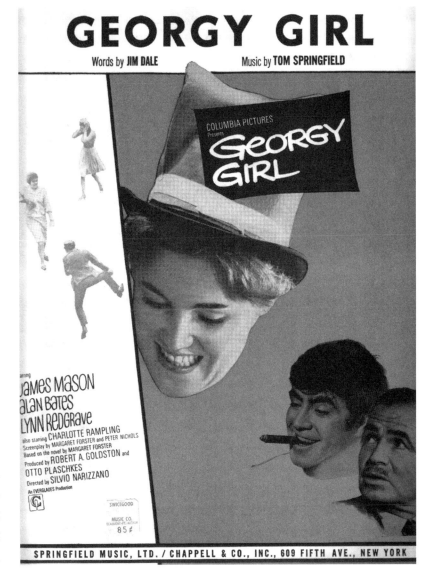

The sheet music for the undeniably catchy title song from *Georgy Girl*, which had the distinction of containing lyrics by British actor Jim Dale.

The Maida Vale section of London, at 449 Edgware Road, provided the exterior of the flat shared by Georgy and Meredith; the Hampstead Town Hall in Rosalyn Hill at Belsize Avenue became the registry where Jos and Meredith reluctantly exchange their very inconvenient marital vows; and 7 Harley Road in Hampstead was the outside of the Leamington mansion. The chilly winter shoot wrapped in mid-February 1966. Soon afterward, Vanessa was winning raves for her role in *Morgan!*, with reviewers and industry notables predicting big things for her as a motion-picture star (this time they were correct). This was nothing, however, compared to the enthusiasm that greeted Lynn when *Georgy Girl* made its bow at the Berlin Film Festival (where Narizzano would pick up an award for his work). Giving the character a mock flamboyance and a self-effacing quick wit that just barely masked her underlying insecurity and heartache, Redgrave was so good that for a moment it looked as if she were going to zip so far ahead of not only her sister, but her father, Michael, and her brother, Corin, as well, that she would leave them all in the dust. The excitement over a brand new, unique star was very much in the air by the time the movie made its debut in both England and the United States in mid-October 1966.

Narizzano's direction had the flashy, loose style one had come to expect of the British New Wave, but he never forfeited feeling or emotion in pursuit of a skittishly trendy camera angle. *Georgy Girl* was something that so many others of its ilk was not—readily accessible to mainstream American audiences—so it broke from the art houses (it would play at a single New York theater for a six-month straight run) and crossed into smashing commercial success, ringing up some $15.2 million in grosses in the United States alone. One aspect that helped to raise awareness of the movie was the title song, penned by Tom Springfield (brother of singer Dusty Springfield) and actor Jim Dale, and sung by an Australian pop group, the Seekers, led by Judith Durham. With its whistling beat, snappy tempo, and instantly memorable opening phrase, "Hey, there, Georgy girl," it became one of those songs that were quickly embraced by both young and old listeners. The Capitol single hit the number 2 spot on the *Billboard* charts by year's end and earned an Oscar nomination as well.

Lynn Redgrave took home the New York Film Critics Award (in a tie with Elizabeth Taylor) and found herself competing with sister Vanessa for the Oscar (which went to Taylor). In the end, Lynn had far more difficulty finding suitable roles than Vanessa did, but she retained her stardom over the succeeding decades, no matter how far beneath her the assignment. Despite her often marvelous work, she would forever be Georgy to most people. But since the role and film were among the high points of British cinema, it was not a bad lifelong association to have.

THE FORTUNE COOKIE

Academy Award Winner: Best Supporting Actor (Walter Matthau)

Academy Award Nominee: Story and Screenplay—Written Directly for the Screen; Cinematography—Black and White; Art Direction-Set Decoration—Black and White

Opening date: October 19, 1966.

United Artists. A Mirisch Corporation Presentation of a Phalanx-Jalem Production.

Director-Producer: Billy Wilder. Screenplay: Billy Wilder, I. A. L. Diamond. Photography: Joseph La Shelle. Art Director: Robert Luthardt. Set Decorator: Edward G. Boyle. Wardrobe: Chuck Arrico, Paula Giokaris. Music: André Previn. Song: "You'd Be So Nice to Come Home To," by Cole Porter. Associate Producers: I. A. L. Diamond, Doane Harrison. Editor: Daniel Mandell. Black and white. Panavision. 126 minutes.

CAST: Jack Lemmon (Harry Hinkle), Walter Matthau (Willie Gingrich), Ron Rich (Luther "Boom Boom" Jackson), Cliff Osmond (Chester Purkey), Judi West (Sandy), Lurene Tuttle (Mother Hinkle), Harry Holcombe (O'Brien), Les Tremayne (Thompson), Marge Redmond (Charlotte Gingrich), Noam Pitlik (Max), Harry Davis (Dr. Krugman), Ann Shoemaker (Sister Veronica), Maryesther Denver (Ferret-Faced Nurse), Lauren Gilbert (Kincaid), Ned Glass (Doc Schindler), Sig Ruman (Prof. Winterhalter), Archie Moore (Mr. Jackson), Dodie Heath (Nun), Herbie Faye (Maury, the Equipment Man), Billy Beck (Maury's Assistant), John Todd Roberts (Jeffrey Gingrich), Lisa Jill (Ginger Gingrich), Bill Christopher (Young Intern), Bartlett Robinson, Robert P. Lieb, Martin Blaine, Ben Wright (the Four Specialists), Howard McNear (Mr. Cimoli), Judy Pace (Elvira), Bob DoQui (Man in Bar), Helen Kleeb (the Lawyers' Receptionist).

PLOT: While covering a football game, television cameraman Harry Hinkle is accidentally knocked down by Cleveland Browns halfback Boom Boom Jackson and ends up with a mild concussion. Harry's brother-in-law, ambulance-chasing lawyer Willie Gingrich, seizes the opportunity to benefit financially from the incident by convincing Harry to pretend that a childhood spinal injury is a direct result of the accident.

Still licking his wounds from the (unjustified) trouncing he had received from both the critics and the public over his stingingly funny sex comedy *Kiss Me, Stupid* (Lopert, 1964), Billy Wilder retreated to safer ground with his next feature, *The Fortune Cookie*, a tale in which integrity overrode avarice. Part of his safety strategy included reuniting with Jack Lemmon, who had, after all, been the star of Wilder's three biggest box-office hits, *Some Like It Hot* (United Artists, 1959), *The Apartment* (United Artists, 1960), and *Irma La Douce* (United Artists, 1963), and was the sort of audience-friendly actor who could always take the potential bad taste out of any script. Although Lemmon got top billing in *The Fortune Cookie*, he was well aware that he was not getting the best-written role in the picture—that of the gleefully amoral shyster Willie Gingrich. For this part Wilder had his sights set on Walter Matthau, with whom he had wanted to work for more than a decade. Wilder had originally selected Matthau for the lead in *The Seven Year Itch* (Twentieth Century-Fox, 1955), but the studio had insisted he go with the originator of the role on Broadway, Tom Ewell. At the time that Wilder was ready to commence work on *The Fortune Cookie*, Matthau was scoring his biggest acting triumph to date in the original Broadway production of Neil Simon's classic *The Odd Couple*, which had been playing to sold-out houses since it opened in March 1965. Visiting Matthau backstage at a performance of Simon's play, Lemmon and Wilder offered him the part of Willie. Matthau was smart enough to know that this packaging of talents was reason enough to say yes and agreed to do the film without even reading the script.

> "What's the matter—you feel sorry for insurance companies? They've got so much money they don't know what to do with it—they've run out of space—they have to microfilm it."
> —Willie Gingrich

Because a genuine football game was required for the opening scene of the movie, Wilder managed to secure the cooperation of the Cleveland Browns and Cleveland Municipal Stadium, where he shot Lemmon's sideline injury before the packed arena on October 31, 1965. After a few

other glimpses of the city were captured, the rest of the production moved west to the Samuel Goldwyn Studios, where Wilder had shot scenes for all of his movies since *Witness for the Prosecution* (United Artists, 1957). A good deal of *Fortune Cookie* took place in two cramped settings, Lemmon's hospital room

Billy Wilder directs the opening football game that leads to Jack Lemmon's accident in *The Fortune Cookie*.

and his shabby apartment, but Wilder was so skillful a filmmaker and the dialogue he and I. A. L. Diamond had written was so on the mark that the picture never came off as stagy or dull. The shooting continued through January, when Matthau suffered a mild cardiac infarction, causing the movie to shut down temporarily. There was simply no way that Wilder was going to replace his prized actor. Not only had most of his scenes been completed, but Matthau's performance was proving to be every bit as smashing as Wilder had predicted; putting someone else in the part would hinder the work overall. Insofar as Wilder and Lemmon (through his Jalem Productions) were coproducers on the picture (along with the Mirisch Corporation), there was no questioning of their decision to halt any further shooting for a three-month period until Matthau could return, in improved health, to finish his role. During that time he dropped approximately thirty-five pounds, so Wilder had him wear a heavy topcoat to cover the change in weight. The picture's final cost was $3.7 million.

Because Wilder had lost a lot of critical supporters with both *Kiss Me, Stupid* and, before that, *Irma La Douce*, the reaction to *The Fortune Cookie* went in both directions. Some dismissed it as another disappointment from a onetime master, a minor addition to his résumé, while others were thrilled to see that he was back on track with a morality tale that possessed touches of the same brilliance that had made *The Apartment* one of the best movies of the decade. There was no denying that the film was well worth the effort, if only for the knockout performance of Matthau, who grabbed every witty, acerbic line and made it that much funnier. This was one of the screen's great morally bankrupt characters, a charlatan very much in the tradition of W. C. Fields, and just as lovable. It was, plain and simple, a great piece of acting, and because of it Matthau moved up the scale from a class-A supporting player to a genuine star. *The Fortune Cookie* brought Matthau a much-applauded Academy Award, the actor showing up at the Oscar ceremony bruised and in a cast, having just broken his elbow falling off a bicycle. Despite his injuries, he was the only one of the four acting winners that night to be present; Elizabeth Taylor, Paul Scofield, and Sandy Dennis were all otherwise engaged.

This window card from *The Fortune Cookie* bills Walter Matthau above the title, although he ended up winning his Academy Award in the supporting category.

THE PROFESSIONALS

Academy Award Nominee: Director; Screenplay—Based on Material from Another Medium;
Cinematography—Color

Top 10 Box Office Film

Opening date: November 2, 1966.

Columbia. A Pax Enterprises Production.

Director-Producer-Screenplay: Richard Brooks. Based on the 1964 novel *A Mule for the Marquesa*, by Frank O'Rourke. Photography: Conrad Hall. Art Director: Edward S. Haworth. Set Decorator: Frank Tuttle. Wardrobe: Jack Martell. Music: Maurice Jarre. Editor: Peter Zinner. Special Effects: Willis Cook. Technicolor. Panavision. 118 minutes.

CAST: Burt Lancaster (Bill Dolworth), Lee Marvin (Henry "Rico" Fardan), Robert Ryan (Hans Ehrengard), Jack Palance (Jesus Raza), Claudia Cardinale (Maria Grant), Ralph Bellamy (J. W. Grant), Woody Strode (Jake Sharp), Joe De Santis (Pascual Ortega), Rafael Bertrand (Fierro), Jorge Martinez de Hoyos (Eduardo Padilla), Marie Gomez (Chiquita), Jose Chavez, Carlos Romero (Revolutionaries), Vaughn Taylor (Banker).

PLOT: Weapons expert Rico Fardan, scout Jake Sharp, horse master Hans Ehrengard, and explosives specialist Bill Dolworth are hired by wealthy J. W. Grant to travel a hundred miles across the desert into Mexico to bring back his young wife, Maria, who has been kidnapped and held for ransom by the bloodthirsty bandit Jesus Raza.

It was mighty impressive the way Burt Lancaster had defied typecasting over the years, becoming a major presence in American motion pictures on his own terms and appearing in some of the top dramas for more than a decade while leaving behind the early image he had cultivated of the ever-smiling, limber man of action in a series of lighthearted adventure tales. It was time to return to that field before age dictated otherwise, and this was clearly on his mind when he signed up for *The Professionals*, a rip-roaring western proudly offering solid, male-dominated entertainment and containing some implausible plot twists, a very butch camaraderie between its principals, and sweaty action scenes. The film also served as the long-overdue reunion between Lancaster and the man who had guided him to his Academy Award, Richard Brooks. Brooks was the director and writer of the 1960 hit *Elmer Gantry*, which had given the star not only that much-coveted trophy but a signature role as well.

> "Maybe there's only one revolution, since the beginning: the good guys against the bad guys. Question is, who are the good guys?"
> —Bill Dolworth

Brooks had discovered a novel by Frank O'Rourke, *A Mule for the Marquesa*, which had all the makings of the sort of lean adventure he was looking to do, although that title would have to go. (Not only did the title go, but so did all references to its meaning; the kidnap victim no longer held the title of marquesa, and no big deal was made about bringing her precious mule to her to ride away on.) The novel had brought together five men of varying attributes or specialties, though one of them, the glib Bill Dolworth, seemed to be along just so someone from group leader Fardan's past could remind him of his prior glories and past mistakes. Brooks therefore took the book's explosives expert, Bisley, gave his "talent" to Dolworth, and tossed the former out of the story altogether. Although Brooks retained the names of Fardan, Dolworth, and Ehrengard for three of his principals, the casting of towering, muscular black actor Woody Strode as the fourth member of the team meant that the equivalent character in the novel, the weapons expert with a particular knack for shooting arrows, was no longer a mestizo named Rios.

Brooks followed the set-up of the novel very closely for the first part of his film but restructured things once his heroes arrived at their destination, having them be followed by a team of trackers after they have scoped out Raza's hacienda. This sequence in O'Rourke's version had led to Dolworth's splitting from the team in order to fend off their pursuers, which Brooks figured would make for a better set piece at the climax, giving Lancaster the chance to enact some heroic gunplay that reminded audiences, after all, just who was top billed. In order to keep the plot focused on a single villain, Brooks also eliminated the twist that had revealed the head of the trackers to be a former ally of Fardan's named Cruz, who is then accidentally killed in an unexpected explosion while taking the team captive. He also made Raza the lover of the kidnap victim, Maria (called Angelica in the book), whereas one of his men, Torres, had been her partner in the original. Brooks greatly improved the finale of the picture by giving it a more complex turn of events, having the heroes insist on giving Maria back to Raza right in front of her aghast husband once they realize who the real bad guy is.

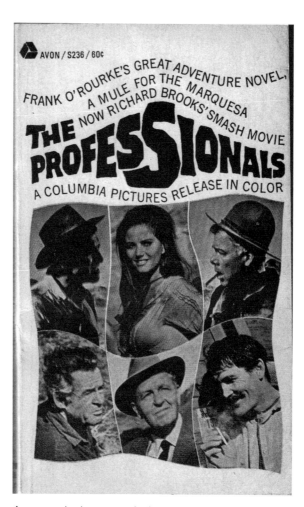

A somewhat groovy design adorned the cover of the tie-in Avon paperback upon which *The Professionals* was based, Frank O'Rourke's *A Mule for the Marquesa*.

In O'Rourke's version, Raza had been shot dead while the mercenaries were on the run from him, causing his men to retreat and allowing the heroes to reach safe ground. Brooks also tossed in a rollicking escape by a mining cart (though he left it vague as to how it was able to operate and outrun the enemy seemingly on its own) and, by having his adventurers commandeer a locomotive, allowed them to flee from their pursuers backward (!).

Bypassing Mexico altogether; *The Professionals* started principal photography on October 20, 1965, with location work in Death Valley; the Valley of Fire, fifty miles north of Las Vegas, which filled in for

Dead Man's Canyon and Coyote Pass, and where Palance's hacienda was located; and Idio, California, where the train sequence was shot. In early January 1966 the company retreated from the often blistering heat of these desolate areas for Los Angeles to shoot interiors at the Columbia Pictures lot and to use a western street set at the Warner Bros. facility for Lancaster's daring escape from a lady's bedroom. Columbia had a great deal of faith that the movie would appeal to the general public, but the studio was unprepared for its superb critical reception. Brooks was highly praised for taking a pretty standard plotline and giving it a fresh coat of paint, so to speak, keeping the picture moving briskly and creating a Saturday-matinee feel to the whole thing. *The Professionals* ended up among the year's top ten highest-grossing movies, making some $17.6 million in the United States alone.

YOU'RE A BIG BOY NOW

Academy Award Nominee: Supporting Actress (Geraldine Page)

Opening date: December 9, 1966 (New York: March 20, 1967).

Seven Arts Pictures. A Phil Feldman Production.

Director-Screenplay: Francis Ford Coppola. Based on the 1963 novel by David Benedictus. Producer: Phil Feldman. Photography: Andrew Laszlo. Art Director: Vassilis Photopoulos. Set Decorator: Marvin March. Costumes: Theoni V. Aldredge. Music: Robert Prince. Amy's and Miss Thing's Themes Composed by John B. Sebastian. Songs by John B. Sebastian: "Girl, Beautiful Girl (Barbara's Theme)," "Darling, Be Home Soon," and "You're a Big Boy Now," performed by the Lovin' Spoonful. Editor: Aram Avakian. Pathécolor. 97 minutes.

CAST: Elizabeth Hartman (Barbara Darling), Geraldine Page (Margery Chanticleer), Peter Kastner (Bernard Chanticleer), Rip Torn (I. H. Chanticleer), Michael Dunn (Richard Mudd), Tony Bill (Raef Delgado), Julie Harris (Miss Nora Thing), Karen Black (Amy Partlett), Dolph Sweet (Patrolman Francis Graf), Michael O'Sullivan (Kurt Doughty).

PLOT: Deciding to strike out on his own, shy nineteen-year-old Bernard Chanticleer leaves behind his overprotective parents and falls under the spell of self-involved actress Barbara Darling.

For someone who was going to change the course of filmmaking in 1972 with his epic masterpiece *The Godfather* (Paramount), Francis Ford Coppola had a very strange, spotty, and not always promising list of credits during the previous decade. One of these, *You're a Big Boy Now*, he adapted from a 1963 novel by British author David Benedictus, the rights to which Coppola had purchased with $1,000 of his own savings. He convinced Seven Arts Productions to back the film, but the company offered him just $8,000 for writing and directing, was willing to put up no more than $250,000 for the budget, and asked if the picture could be shot in a little more than two weeks. Coppola accepted the challenge and was ultimately rewarded when Seven Arts decided to up the budget to $800,000.

For the leading role of the mother-dominated, ill-at-ease Bernard Chanticleer, Coppola chose the Canadian actor Peter Kastner, who had made a favorable impression playing an alienated teen in his native country's *Nobody Waved Goodbye* (1964; United States: Cinema V, 1965). The gap-toothed Kastner, who bore a certain resemblance in manner and looks to star-to-be Richard Dreyfuss, was certainly affable, making Bernard's desires and hormonal unrest both amusing and empathetic.

Although the novel took place in London with British characters, Coppola managed to retain not only the principals and their idiosyncratic characteristics, but also key incidents, dialogue, and even

> "Now, don't eat too much, don't stay out late, don't go to suspicious places or play cards. And stay away from girls. But most of all, Bernard, try to be happy."
> —Mrs. Chanticleer

sight gags, often echoing author Benedictus's glib tone about the destructive nature of obsession and love but going for a more upbeat and hopeful ending. In the book, Bernard not only fails to leave behind his feelings for Barbara, but loses Amy as well after she is cruelly killed off in a bus accident. Coppola also changed the workplace for Bernard and his father. He made the father a curator at the New York Public Library instead of a department store manager on Oxford Street, while Bernard, instead of selling shoes in the same establishment, was given the drab job of retrieving books from the building's basement, a task made colorful by the fact that all such employees roller-skated from shelf to shelf. In place of Bernard's making off with the store's foot measure, as he had in the novel, Coppola had him dash off with a rare Gutenberg Bible. Benedictus had followed this incident with a trial and Barbara's subsequent wedding to Bernard's snooty (and seemingly gay) coworker, Raef. Barbara's background as a sexually abused preadolescent was changed to an absurdist flashback in which a decidedly more mature Barbara is pursued and seduced by an albino hypnotherapist with a wooden leg, which was stolen by Barbara in vengeance (in the book, the wooden leg had belonged to Barbara's real father, not the doctor). This sequence, tasteless in its own way, was an example of Coppola's desire to keep the film on a freewheeling, often deliberately grotesque level. To this end he

The Kama Sutra LP of *You're a Big Boy Now* looks more like a Lovin' Spoonful album than a soundtrack, which was no doubt deliberate.

also tossed in a rooster with a distaste for young girls, an exasperating scene in which Miss Thing freaks out thinking Bernard's father is trying to seduce her in a library vault, and a chaotic chase through a department store.

Somehow, by guilting Mayor John Lindsay into standing by his recent pledge to make it easier to film in New York City, Coppola managed to override the New York Public Library's initial refusal to allow him to shoot there. *Big Boy* therefore became one of the rare pictures to actual film scenes in the hallowed Fifth Avenue institution. Using high-speed film, Coppola was able to shoot night scenes in Times Square without lights, often riding in the back of a convertible while Kastner and Karen Black walked the streets. In doing so he managed to capture the feel of the area at the time, with its peep-show theaters, adult boutiques, and shimmering movie marquees. There were also scenes filmed at the Forty-second Street automat, Central Park, and a branch of May's department store. Coppola shot his frantic chase scene there one morning without bothering to alert any of the paying customers, which might explain why the sequence came off so choppy and undernourished. Best of all, during Bernard's joyous roller-skating jaunt through the city, after he has received Barbara's encouraging letter, a bit of history in the making was shown in the background, as Kastner zipped past the old Penn Station while it was being dismantled, the skeleton of the new Madison Square Garden looming behind it.

Principal photography began on June 1, 1966, adhering to a very tight schedule that lasted about a month. Coppola delivered an energetic romp that Seven Arts thought might capture a young audience who could relate to the protagonist's efforts to release himself from his parents' selfish grip. Opening the picture in Los Angeles in late 1966 to qualify for Oscar consideration seemed like wishful thinking, and yet Geraldine Page did manage to end up among the supporting nominees for her often funny, often out-of-control turn. In fact, the entire picture could best be described in the same way, hitting some bright and very witty notes and just as often landing some discordant ones, with an often exhausting sense of hectic activity. Undeniably, though, a director of talent was at work here, and many critics championed the film simply because it was aiming at something that sympathized with the young. Coppola went so far as to hire a then-popular rock band, the Lovin' Spoonful, back when it was unusual and rare to pepper the soundtrack with pop records. (One song, "Darling, Be Home Soon," reached number 15 on the *Billboard* charts in February 1967.) Despite the encouragement, the unexpected Oscar nomination, and the studio support, *You're a Big Boy Now* failed to find an audience, which only helped secure the reputation it eventually acquired as a cult item once Coppola came to prominence.

A MAN FOR ALL SEASONS (United Kingdom)

Academy Award Winner: Best Picture; Best Actor (Paul Scofield); Best Director; Best Screenplay—Based on Material from Another Medium; Best Cinematography—Color; Best Costume Design—Color

Academy Award Nominee: Supporting Actor (Robert Shaw); Supporting Actress (Wendy Hiller)

Top 10 Box Office Film

Opening date: December 12, 1966 (London: March 30, 1967).

Columbia. A Fred Zinnemann Production.

Director-Producer: Fred Zinnemann. Screenplay: Robert Bolt, based on his 1960 play. Executive Producer: William N. Graf. Photography: Ted Moore. Production Designer: John Box. Art Director: Terence Marsh. Set Dresser: Josie MacAvin. Costumes: Elizabeth Haffenden, Joan Bridge. Music: Georges Delerue. Editor: Ralph Kemplen. Make Up: George Frost, Eric Allwright. Hairdressers: Gordon Bond, Helen Bevan. Technicolor. 120 minutes.

CAST: Paul Scofield (Sir Thomas More), Wendy Hiller (Alice More), Leo McKern (Thomas Cromwell), Robert Shaw (King Henry VIII), Orson Welles (Cardinal Wolsey), Susannah York (Margaret More), Nigel Davenport (Duke of Norfolk), John Hurt (Richard Rich), Corin Redgrave (William Roper), Colin Blakely (Matthew), Cyril Luckham (Archbishop Cranmer), Jack Gwillim (Chief Justice), Thomas Heathcote (Boatman), Yootha Joyce (Averil Machin), Anthony Nicholls (King's Representative), John Nettleton (Jailer), Eira Heath (Matthew's Wife), Molly Urquhart (Maid), Paul Hardwick (Courtier), Michael Latimer (Norfolk's Aide), Philip Brack (Captain of the Guard), Martin Boddey (Governor of the Tower), Eric Mason (Executioner), Matt Zimmerman (Messenger), Vanessa Redgrave (Anne Boleyn).

PLOT: Sir Thomas More invokes the ire of Henry VIII when he refuses to support his majesty's wish to divorce his first wife in order to marry Anne Boleyn, thereby prompting the monarch's controversial decision to appoint himself Supreme Head of the Church of England.

Every so often, if perhaps by accident, a literate motion picture of impeccable taste slips out of the restrictive realm of the art-house circuit and manages to cultivate a wider and more enthusiastic audience among the general public than expected. Such was the case with *A Man for All Seasons*, a movie that proudly emphasized words over action and wound up with not only a mantle full of accolades, but money in the bank.

Although Sir Thomas More achieved much fame during his lifetime as a lawyer, government official, and author, notably of the fictional work *Utopia* (1516), his final notoriety came by way of martyrdom, having gone to the chopping block for putting his loyalty to God before his allegiance to his king. It was this noble sacrifice that Robert Bolt chose to dramatize, bringing his play *A Man for All Seasons* to the Globe Theatre in London on July 1, 1960, where it was greeted with great acclaim, particularly for Paul Scofield's subtle yet commanding portrayal of More. Bolt had painted More as a pillar of virtue and common sense. This was only half the truth, for the real man was more than somewhat intolerant of any religion outside the Catholic Church, an opinion he expressed many times in writings that particularly condemned the Protestant faith. Although the play (and film) did have More using the word "heretic" to describe his prospective son-in-law's allegiance to Lutheranism, this, in fact, was somewhat inaccurate, chronologically speaking; William Roper did not actually take up that faith until *after* he was married to More's daughter. As for the More family, it seemed more compact to dramatize his strong bond with his loyal and intelligent daughter Margaret as if she were his one and only child, so his three other offspring were eliminated altogether. There were also some dramatic liberties taken in the depiction of both Thomas Cromwell and Richard Rich, the chief villains of the piece; their animosity toward the Mores became somewhat more pronounced as written by Bolt; in truth, the former was considered close enough to the family that he was asked to be godfather to Margaret's child.

Bolt's play was enough of a sensation in London that it was brought to America, opening at the ANTA Theatre on November 22, 1961, and running for 637 performances. Scofield was asked to repeat the role he originated and won a Tony Award for Best Actor. Additional Tonys went to the play itself, to Bolt as author, to producers Robert Whitehead and Roger L. Stevens, to director Noel Willman, and to stage technician Michael Burns. The original cast included Albert Dekker as the Duke of Norfolk, Leo McKern as Cromwell (he had started as the Common Man in the London version), and Keith Baxter as King Henry VIII. The screen rights were purchased for $100,000, with such names as Laurence Olivier as More, Alec Guinness as Cromwell, and Peter O'Toole as the king mentioned as possible box-office insurance to help sell a potentially

> **"I think that when statesmen forsake their own private conscience for the sake of their public duties, they lead their country by a short route to chaos."**
> **—Thomas More**

uncommercial project. Once Oscar-winner Fred Zinnemann came aboard as both producer and director, he announced that Scofield and nobody else would be considered for More since the great stage actor had been so crucial to the success of the play. Like many busy theater actors in England, Scofield had no great fondness for motion pictures and was perfectly content to ply his trade on the boards. He did not, however, wish to pass up an opportunity to preserve the role that had made him famous and happily accepted Zinnemann's offer. He and the rest of the cast agreed to a salary cut in order to keep the picture under the $2 million budget.

Robert Bolt was asked to do the adaptation of his play. Not surprisingly, the first aspect of the stage version to be dropped was the Common Man character, who not only served as narrator but had also taken on such other roles as the servant Matthew, the boatman, and the executioner. This device was strictly theatrical, so the narration was dispensed with (save for the final epilogue, which had been spoken earlier in the play, prior to More's questioning by Cromwell and his cohorts), and all the other Common Man parts were filled, of course, by different actors. Another key figure from the play was eliminated: the Spanish diplomat Chapuys, who was around to condone More's silence on the Act of Succession. He and his fellow countrymen had construed the act as emblematic of Henry's desire to dispose of his first wife, Catherine of Aragon, who was, after all, the daughter of Spain's king and queen, Ferdinand and Isabella.

Bolt did a good job of rewriting many lines of dialogue, sometimes for the better (in the film, when Thomas is told by Norfolk, "Your life is in your own hands, just as it's always been," he calmly retorts, "Then I'll keep a good grip on it," a response that does not appear in the play), and sometimes at the expense of some intriguing character developments (in the play, after Matthew is discharged by More, he offers his services to Rich, for whom he had previously expressed his distaste, thereby suggesting a lack of principles on the servant's part). In the film, More is shown receiving the bribery cup, which plays a pivotal role in his downfall, and is even seen dumping it in the Thames on the way home from Hampton Court, whereas in the play it had already been given to him before the action began, which somewhat lessened the impact of its ominous nature. Richard Rich, as oily and duplicitous onscreen as he had appeared onstage, was given one added piece of dialogue in the film that made him that much more hateful: when Cromwell laments his failure to get a confession from More, Rich suggests that Cromwell put the prisoner on the rack, though in the play it is Cromwell himself who suggests the torture device and then promptly rejects it.

The movie began shooting at Shepperton Studios on May 2, 1966, where such sets as More's cell, Wolsey's chamber, the Towpath, the Richmond interrogation chamber, and the Hampton River Steps were built. The company then moved on to Studley Priory in Oxfordshire, which stood in for the Thomas More house and grounds, and then on to the Beaulieu River for all scenes involving the many barge and boat trips made during the story. Once the production finished at Shepperton in late July, it moved over to Pinewood Studios, where the scenes of Cromwell meeting Rich at the dockside pub and More's execution, among others, were filmed. The movie wrapped in mid-August. Zinnemann and his team worked diligently to get the completed footage edited and ready for a December release. Columbia hoped to present *A Man* as its chief year's-end release (its other big Christmas opening, *Murderers' Row*, qualified as *A Man*'s polar opposite), figuring the one way to earn back its cost was to sell it as a "must-see" quality item and hope for accolades to instill further interest.

A Man for All Seasons was so prestigious an offering that RCA released a two-record LP featuring all of Robert Bolt's magnificent dialogue.

By getting rid of the artifice of its theatrical presentation, Bolt brought a clearer and more powerful focus to More's futile but gallant attempt to prove that conscience must come before public office. It mattered not whether one agreed with the character's religious convictions; More's steadfast belief in his principles could not help but be admired and interpreted as an act of heroism and honor of the sort too seldom seen in the average man, let alone true-life government figures. The very fact that his adversaries were depicted as fully aware that they lacked the decency and nerve to commit to their own beliefs, if indeed they even had the capacity to develop beliefs of their own, gave the work an added bite and irony. Thomas More had to die so that weaker leaders could live with their own shame of mindlessly following their ruler, protecting their own necks and accommodating themselves to whatever cause should bring them power as well as immunity from a stronger man's wrath. Through dramatic license, Bolt had created a hero for all time, thereby bringing greater attention to Thomas More than he had ever received. Indeed, as Zinnemann theorized, the majority of moviegoers were probably not the least bit aware of who this man was prior to the release of *A Man for All Seasons*.

Facing his final hours, Paul Scofield (*front left*) ends up comforting his concerned family (Susannah York, *front right*; Wendy Hiller and Corin Redgrave, *rear*) in this scene from *A Man for All Seasons*.

With the sort of glowing reviews that even the best movies could only hope to receive, *A Man for All Seasons* became one of the most talked-about releases of the Christmas season. It took home both Best Picture and Best Actor awards from the National Board of Review, the Golden Globes, and the New York Film Critics. Zinnemann received the Directors Guild Award and won his second Academy Award (his first had been for *From Here to Eternity*, Columbia, 1953). Despite stellar work from the entire cast, it was Scofield who riveted the audiences' attention with the most cerebral and gentle of performances. Calmly debating his enemies with wit and logic, he made every phrase, every word, every pause come off like poetry of the most majestic sort. Bolt's already brilliantly conceived script sounded that much better coming from Scofield, and *A Man* was one of the most glorious celebrations of the spoken word on film. A curious public turned out to see what all the fuss was about and came away amply rewarded. The movie marched home with six Academy Awards, which meant Columbia could congratulate itself on reluctantly complying with Zinnemann's wishes to do things his way.

BLOWUP (United Kingdom–Italy)

Academy Award Nominee: Director; Story and Screenplay—Written Directly for the Screen

Opening date: December 18, 1966 (London: March 16, 1967).

Premiere Productions Co. Inc. (MGM).

Director-Story: Michelangelo Antonioni. Producer: Carlo Ponti. Executive Producer: Pierre Rouve. Screenplay: Michelangelo Antonioni, Tonino Guerra. English Dialogue in Collaboration with Edward Bond. Inspired by the short story *Las babas del diablo* by Julio Cortázar. Photography: Carlo Di Palma. Art Director: Assheton Gorton. Dress Designer: Jocelyn Rickards. Music: Herbert Hancock. Song: "Stroll On," by the Yardbirds. Editor: Frank Clarke. Photographic Murals: John Cowan. Metrocolor. 111 minutes.

CAST: Vanessa Redgrave (Jane), Sara Miles (Patricia), David Hemmings (Thomas), John Castle (Bill), Jane Birkin (the Blonde), Gillian Hills (the Brunette), Peter Bowles (Ron), Verushka (Herself), Julian Chagrin, Claude Chagrin (Mimes), Susan Broderick (Antiques Shop Owner), Tsai Chin (Thomas's Receptionist), Harry Hutchinson (Shopkeeper), Mary Khal (Fashion Editor), Chas Lawther (Waiter), Ronan O'Casey (Jane's Lover in the Park), Reg Wilkins (Reg, Thomas's Assistant), the Yardbirds (Themselves).

PLOT: After developing and enlarging some photographs he has taken in a London park, Thomas is certain he has evidence that someone has been murdered.

***Blowup* was a misleading title** for those not aware that it was a photographic reference, the incendiary implications suggesting to the unenlightened something explosive or dramatically scorching, in the manner of *Who's Afraid of Virginia Woolf?* (Warner Bros., 1966). What appeared onscreen was, in fact, very much the opposite, a reflective, deliberately paced mood piece with long takes, extended silent pauses, and cryptic occurrences that may or may not have meant something. It was just the sort of alternately daring and maddening bit of filmmaking that sharply divided audiences, as had been the case with pretty much everything directed by Michelangelo Antonioni since he first caused a stir in certain critical circles with *L'avventura* (United States: Janus, 1961). In 1965 Antonioni announced that his next project not only would be his first English-language feature, but would be set in England as well. Fans had reason to be wary, so many acclaimed foreign directors having fared so badly away from their native countries.

What Antonioni ultimately decided upon for inspiration was a short story by Belgian-born Spanish writer Julio Cortázar entitled *Las babas del diablo*, which translated roughly as *The Drivel of the Devil*. It concerned a photographer who became obsessed with an unidentified woman in a photograph he had taken, only to realize that the same photo contained a cryptic image that seemed to be a body. From this idea Antonioni and his collaborator, Tonino Guerra, put together an outline and created characters, scouting London locations even before finishing their concept. Once they had fashioned their story line, they brought in playwright Edward Bond to supply the English-language dialogue.

In an effort to further capture the feel of the '60s scene in Great Britain, Antonioni went for two of the most exciting up-and-coming actresses around: Vanessa Redgrave, whose first big-screen starring role, in *Morgan: A Suitable Case for Treatment* (Cinema V, 1966), was about to open in the United Kingdom; and Sarah Miles, who had created an impression in two of the more somber British pictures of the day, *Term of Trial* (Warner Bros., 1962) and *The Servant* (Landau, 1964). Redgrave, who received top billing despite what was clearly a supporting role, was asked to spend a portion of one of her scenes topless, albeit with her arms strategically wrapped about her breast. The image was so alluring that it was used in some of the bolder advertising. Not unexpectedly, for a celebrity who was already making her name as not only one of the best new actresses around, but one who championed individuality and courted controversy, Redgrave spoke in defense of the nudity in the film, proclaiming it artistically relevant to the story and intentionally cold in its lack of sensuality. Miles, on the other hand, wasn't too enchanted with the picture or Antonioni's method of working and departed before it was completed, which might explain her

> "I'm only doing my job. Some people are bullfighters, some people are politicians. I'm a photographer."
> —Thomas

aborted role as David Hemmings's part-time love interest. With a part even tinier than Redgrave's, she still rated billing *over* the real star of the film, Hemmings, who was onscreen consistently throughout the picture. Despite her brief participation, Miles did find herself involved in one of the moments that got the censorship board all riled up, when she engages in sex with John Castle. Although some sources claimed that Antonioni agreed to remove a few of the more explicit frames of this scene, the actual suggestion of intercourse remained far more vivid than in any other film up to that time.

With great fanfare that the cryptic Italian filmmaker was about to make his statement on "Swinging London," *Blowup* (or rather *The Blow-Up*, as it was called during production) began filming in the U.K. capital on April 24, 1966. Antonioni wanted to avoid studio shooting as much as possible (what few fake interiors the film had were done on the soundstages of the MGM British Studios) and chose an actual photographer's studio for the main setting, that of real-life picture snapper John Cowan, located in the Holland Park section of London at 49 Princes Place (the outside of the building, however, was filmed elsewhere, at 77 Pottery Lane). Antonioni began his film in the austere and personality-free courtyard of the building that housed the *Economist* magazine, at St. James's Street, with a carload of happy, white-faced youths disembarking to run through the streets of the city. The pub used for Hemmings's meeting with his agent was the El Blason, on Blacklands Terrace near Sloane Square, and the antiques shop at which Hemmings purchased an airplane propeller (another piece of the puzzle) was a converted grocery store in Cleverley Clove, located at the northwest corner of the movie's most famous site, Mayron Park, off Woolrich Road. Great care was taken in putting up false house fronts, painting paths, and decorating the area with greenery to get the right feel. More importantly, the very lonely-looking park was made all the more hypnotically desolate by the sound of the wind rustling through the trees, an effect that made the sequence in which Hemmings stalks Redgrave and her lover all the more memorable.

Once shooting ended in August of that year, MGM decided it would slot the picture into a pair of East and West Coast theaters in December in order to qualify for Oscar consideration. Not surprisingly,

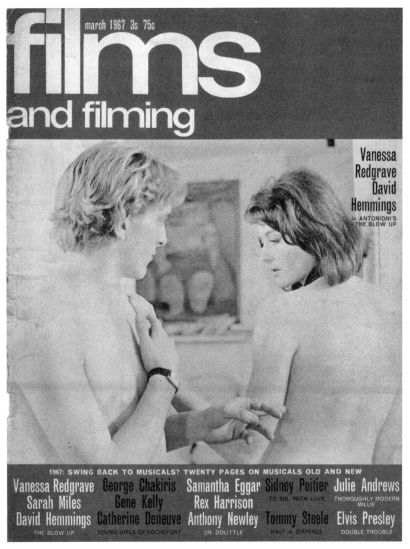

march 1967 3s 75c

films
and filming

Vanessa
Redgrave
David
Hemmings
in ANTONIONI'S
THE BLOW UP

1967: SWING BACK TO MUSICALS? TWENTY PAGES ON MUSICALS OLD AND NEW

Vanessa Redgrave	George Chakiris	Samantha Eggar	Sidney Poitier	Julie Andrews
Sarah Miles	Gene Kelly	Rex Harrison	TO SIR, WITH LOVE	THOROUGHLY MODERN MILLIE
David Hemmings	Catherine Deneuve	Anthony Newley	Tommy Steele	Elvis Presley
THE BLOW UP	YOUNG GIRLS OF ROCHEFORT	DR. DOLITTLE	HALF A SIXPENCE	DOUBLE TROUBLE

One of *Blowup*'s most notorious scenes, featuring stars David Hemmings and Vanessa Redgrave, adorns the cover of Britain's *Films and Filming*, a magazine known for its provocative choice of photos.

once the Production Code got a look at the movie, it demanded some edits, specifically in the aforementioned Miles-Castle sex scene and during Hemmings's romp around his studio with a pair of forthright ladies who offer their services as "models." The latter scene contained quick glimpses of their breasts and behinds and was deemed utterly unacceptable by the board. Initially MGM was willing to comply with the request, but Antonioni certainly was not. In order to stay on the director's good side, and to ensure that a picture this singular and risky would now have a selling point, MGM made the bold move of going ahead without the designated revisions. Because this meant putting out a film under the studio banner with a "condemned" seal that would hurt bookings, the company decided to create a subsidiary distributor on the spot, calling it Premier Productions. *Blowup* received its condemnation seal and was therefore advertised as "Suggested for Mature Audiences." Public interest outside of the Antonioni cult was suddenly growing.

The picture was helped immensely by the amount of favorable response it received from certain critical factions, who championed the director's customary decision to leave things open-ended and opaque. Discussions ran in the papers over just what it all meant, and suddenly every prop, every gesture, every silence was deemed symbolic and meaningful. Because it seemed like something provocative that *should* be seen so that everyone could put in his or her two cents' worth, MGM was delighted to have a crossover box-office hit on its hands. Needless to say, a movie this deliberately devoid of drama was going to leave plenty of people cold, and indeed it did. Antonioni set out to take the "swing" out of "swinging London," much as Fellini had wanted to decimate Rome's similar scene in *La dolce vita* (Rizzoli, 1961), showing it as a bleakly unattractive place full of passive participants who expressed as little feeling for their rituals of sex, drugs, and rock and roll as they did over the possibility of someone's having been killed. The concept of uncovering and possibly solving a murder was raised as an intriguing plot point, only to dissolve in a haze of ennui. It may have made for a statement on a shallow society, but it also felt like a good deal of build-up to nothing.

Blowup earned a pair of Oscar nominations for Antonioni, including one for Original Screenplay despite the credit to Cortázar's story. For one brief shining moment, Antonioni was on top, having delivered a moneymaker that was declared by some to be one of the defining works of the decade. The picture's perplexing, often dull nature, however, meant that never again would there be a vast public ready to dissect and theorize about Antonioni's themes and intentions. *Blowup* retained a degree of lasting fame, which meant that future filmmakers as varied as Mel Brooks (*High Anxiety*, Twentieth Century-Fox, 1977) and Brian De Palma (*Blow Out*, Filmways, 1981) would pay tribute to it, but for some it forever represented self-indulgence at its worst, as might be expected of any movie that dared to end with something as eye-rolling and pretentious as a pair of mimes playing tennis with a nonexistent ball.

THE SAND PEBBLES

Academy Award Nominee: Picture; Actor (Steve McQueen); Supporting Actor (Mako); Cinematography—Color; Art Direction–Set Decoration—Color; Sound; Original Music Score; Film Editing

Top 10 Box Office Film

Opening date: December 20, 1966.

Twentieth Century-Fox. An Argyle-Solar Production; a Robert Wise Production.

Director-Producer: Robert Wise. Screenplay: Robert Anderson. Based on the 1962 novel by Richard McKenna. Photography: Joseph MacDonald. Production Designer: Boris Leven. Set Decorators: Walter M. Scott, John Sturtevant, William Kiernan. Costumes: Renié. Music: Jerry Goldsmith. Editor: William Reynolds. Deluxe color. Panavision. 196 minutes (including overture, entr'acte, exit music; later cut to 179 minutes).

CAST: Steve McQueen (Jake Holman), Richard Attenborough (Frenchy Burgoyne), Richard Crenna (Captain Collins), Candice Bergen (Shirley Eckert), Marayat Andriane (Maily), Mako (Po-han), Larry Gates (Jameson), Charles Robinson (Ensign Bordelles), Simon Oakland (Stawski), Ford Rainey (Harris), Joe Turkel (Bronson), Gavin MacLeod (Crosley), Joseph di Reda (Shanahan), Richard Loo (Major Chin), Gus Trikonis (Restorff), Beulah Quo (Mama Chunk), James Hong (Victor Shu), Barney Phillips (Chief Franks), Shepherd Sanders (Perna), James Jeter (Farren), Tom Middleton (Jennings), Paul Chinpae (Cho-jen), Tommy Lee (Chien), Stephen Jahn (Haythorn), Jay Allan Hopkins (Wilsey), Glenn Wilder (Waldron), Steve Ferry (Lamb), Ted Fish (CPO Wellbeck), Loren Janes (Coleman), Henry Wang (Lop-eye Shing), Ben Wright (Outscout, Englishman on Steamer), Walter Reed (Bidder).

PLOT: Machinist Jake Holman joins the crew of the *San Pablo*, a U.S. gunboat assigned to patrol China's backwaters in the midst of a civil war in which nationalist leader Chiang Kai-shek hopes to rid the country of any American presence.

Having finished his adult ghost story *The Haunting* (MGM, 1963), director Robert Wise was not scheduled to do the motion picture for which he would become best known, *The Sound of Music* (Twentieth Century-Fox, 1965), but something altogether different: *The Sand Pebbles*, a story of the United States' futile involvement in China on the eve of the communist takeover by Chiang Kai-shek. Wise's original choice to head the project, Paul Newman, had turned him down, while his second casting idea, Steve McQueen, was thought to be more of a financial risk by Fox Studios. By the end of 1963 McQueen had proven himself not only a bona fide motion-picture star, but a box-office draw as well, helping both *The Great Escape* (United Artists, 1963) and *Love with the Proper Stranger* (Paramount, 1963) to more than respectable figures. Once Wise realized he had a chance to direct *The Sound of Music* after William Wyler dropped out of the project, *Pebbles* was put on hold for more than a year. Following *Music*'s awesome worldwide success, Fox not only was glad to let Wise do pretty much whatever film he wanted, but said an eager yes to McQueen. The studio put up a hefty budget of $8.3 million, hoping to treat *The Sand Pebbles* as its prestigious Christmas release for 1966, with road-show prices and, hopefully, awards and millions to follow. *The Sand Pebbles* (which had been originally purchased by United Artists for $300,000 but ended up being sold to Fox) was the first and only novel by Richard McKenna (1913–1964), who had spent twenty-two years in the navy, two of them on a gunboat on the Yangtze River, albeit in the decade following the one during which the book took place (the 1920s).

The three-year lapse between the 1962 publication date and the 1965 starting date for the film version only worked in the movie's favor. During that time the parallels between China's hostility toward American involvement in their country, as depicted in the book, and the situation the United States was facing in Vietnam had become even more pronounced. Once the bombing of North Vietnam had commenced in 1965 and the actual conflict officially began, there was no getting away from the fact that *The Sand Pebbles* could be used to make a topical statement against the futility of a foreign military power meddling in a conflict it could not hope to come away from with any glory. Considering how anti-American this stance could seem to more conservative thinkers, it is surprising that Fox not only OK'd the project, but was willing to cough up

> "Apparently we're being blamed for everything. The foreign devils! Oh, it's an old trick, Mr. Bordelles, to unify people by getting them to hate something or someone. Well, we're it."
> —Collins

a great deal of cash for a picture so critical of American arrogance. Robert Anderson was given the difficult task of shaping the vast and very busy novel into a marketable picture that could be sold as part spectacle, part action film, and part love story. Ultimately, its chief strength would lie in the intimate and compassionate manner in which it dealt with a handful of principal characters, most of whom ended up destroyed or victimized by a situation they themselves did not create and barely understood.

The relationship between Jake Holman and the doomed engine-room "coolie," Po-han, dominated the first half of the picture, while the hopeless marriage of Frenchy and his Asian bride, Maily, was a pivotal part of the second act. Outside of the brutish Stawski (Simon Oakland), few of the other sailors (the "Sand Pebbles") aboard the *San Pablo* were presented as fully drawn characters onscreen in the way they had been in the book. The novel had also emphasized the presence of similar gunboats in the province, chiefly those commanded by the British, and the appearance of Russian aircraft in support of the Chiang Kai-shek regime, but the screenplay downplayed all of this to focus on the American-Chinese unrest. Po-han no longer had a family waiting for him on shore, as he had in the McKenna story, and many plotlines were reworked so that Jake was now accused of having killed Maily though the real killers were the Kumiang soldiers, whereas her fate had remained unclear on the written page. Surprisingly, the film script chose to make the fateful climax at the besieged China Light even unhappier by having Captain (Lieutenant in McKenna's book) Collins killed as well; in the novel the officer had been injured and carried back to the ship.

Shooting in the novel's actual locations in the Hunan province of Mainland China was impossible, so most of the movie was done in Taiwan and Hong Kong. Filming began on November 22, 1965, in the port of Keelung, which was decorated to look like Shanghai circa 1926 for the opening scene introducing Jake Holman; many of the ancient ships were built to order for the picture. The most important vessel, and, according to much publicity, at $250,000 the single most expensive prop ever constructed for a motion picture, was the *San Pablo* itself. The bulk of the picture was shot at the village of Tam Sui, which filled in for the city of Changsha, including an area called Paoshan for the startling sequence in which Po-han is tortured before Jake comes to his aid. After additional filming in Taipei (including a studio where cover sets were shipped from the Fox lot in southern California), the unit moved on to Hong

Steve McQueen does the expected beefcake shot for the photographer on the set of *The Sand Pebbles*.

Kong, where most of the river filming occurred, including the picture's big action set piece (using the waters of Sai Kung), the battle between the *San Pablo* and the Chinese blockade on the Chin River. The sequence took an entire month to complete. Because of the unpredictable weather, overseas shooting ran far beyond its original schedule, finally coming to a close on May 15, 1966. From there the company headed back to California, where they filmed some interiors on the Fox soundstages. They then staged the suspenseful showdown in the courtyard of the China Light mission on a huge set constructed on the Fox Malibu Ranch. The production had taken eight and a half months to complete and the final cost had come close to $12 million, making this yet another movie the studio had let get financially out of hand.

Fortunately, Wise handed the nervous studio a picture it could be proud of, one that combined male-dominated action with thought-provoking issues about racism, war, and political beliefs foolishly placed above human lives. Wise never let the film lapse into standard war posturing and kept the story compelling and personal, with Steve McQueen's central performance giving it all the stature and complexity it required. Although the notoriously independent actor and Wise clashed repeatedly over the character and the script, the head-butting seemed to have worked, because this ranks as perhaps the actor's most subtly moving work, a portrait of a fiercely noncommittal loner whose heart is cracked open by the injustice he witnesses around him. McQueen received some of the best notices of his career and ended up with his one and only Oscar nomination. The response to the movie itself was more divided. There were just as many reviewers who championed the intelligence and engrossing presentation of the epic tale as there were who found it long-winded and simplistic. The public opinion seemed more on the side of the positive: *The Sand Pebbles* racked up some impressive figures throughout most of its engagement, especially considering its bleak and deglamorized presentation of a touchy issue. It became the fourth-highest-grossing 1966 release, with a take somewhere in the vicinity of $27 million.

Despite the fact that *Pebbles* was doing its share of business, Twentieth Century-Fox still saw fit to trim away at the three-hour-plus epic, feeling that it had the potential to play better at a shorter length. By the time the movie went into general release, it had been cut from 196 to 179 minutes. Deletions included a political discussion between Jake and Shirley, although the image of the two in a rowboat together remained one of the principal stills in the advertising for the movie. These cuts had not been sanctioned by Wise himself, but until the 2007 DVD presentation most prints of the movie remained at this length. At the time of its original release, McQueen had expressed dissatisfaction with his own performance (as was so often the case with the notoriously flinty, critical actor) but proclaimed *The Sand Pebbles* the best picture with which he had been associated.

GRAND PRIX

Academy Award Winner: Best Sound; Best Film Editing; Best Sound Effects

Top 10 Box Office Film

Opening date: December 21, 1966.

MGM.

Director: John Frankenheimer. Producer: Edward Lewis. Screen Story and Screenplay: Robert Alan Aurthur. Photography: Lionel Lindon. Production Designer: Richard Sylbert. Costume Supervisor–Hairstyles–Makeup: Sydney Guilaroff. Music: Maurice Jarre. Song: "Take a Chance," by Larry Kusik and Eddie Snyder. Supervising Film Editor: Fredric Steinkamp. Editors: Henry Berman, Stewart Linder, Frank Santillo. Sound: Franklin Milton, Roy Charman. Racing Advisors: Phil Hill, Joakim Bonnier, Richie Ginther. Racing Camera Mounts Executed by Frick Enterprises. Technical Consultant: Carroll Shelby. Second Unit Cameramen: John M. Stephens, Jean-Georges Fontenelle, Yann Le Masson. Visual Consultant–Montages–Titles: Saul Bass. Metrocolor. Super Panavision (shown in Cinerama). 179 minutes (including overture, entr'acte, and exit music).

CAST: James Garner (Pete Aron), Eva Marie Saint (Louise Frederickson), Yves Montand (Jean-Pierre Sarti), Toshiro Mifune (Izo Yamura), Brian Bedford (Scott Stoddard), Jessica Walter (Pat Stoddard), Antonio Sabato (Nino Barlini), Françoise Hardy (Lisa), Adolfo Celi (Agostini Manetta), Claude Dauphin (Hugo Simon), Enzo Fiermonte (Guido), Geneviève Page (Monique Delvaux-Sarti), Jack Watson (Jeff Jordan), Donal O'Brien (Wallace Bennett), Jean Michaud (Children's Father), Albert Rémy (Surgeon), Rachel Kempson (Mrs. Stoddard), Ralph Michael (Mr. Stoddard), Alan Fordney, Anthony Marsh, Tommy Franklin (Sportscasters), Lorenzo Bandini, Bob Bondurant, Jack Brabham (Drivers), Phil Hill (Tim Randolph), Graham Hill (Bob Turner), Evans Evans (Mrs. Randolph), Bernard Cahier (Journalist).

PLOT: American Pete Aron, Frenchman Jean-Pierre Sarti, and Englishman Scott Stoddard are among those willing to risk their lives in the world of professional auto racing as they compete at a number of European locations to win the Grand Prix.

Director John Frankenheimer was a car enthusiast who had a dream of bringing an auto racing story to cinematic life, only his vision was grander and more adventurous then most. For one thing, he didn't see why he and his filmmaking team couldn't take that extra step and actually put the audience right *in* the driver's seat, or at least give them the feeling that they were cramped inside a Formula 1, pedal to the floor, taking every hairpin turn of the track as they came careening down each winding bend within an inch of their competitors. Frankenheimer, who had actually competed in some amateur racing events, found his enthusiasm for the sport reaching a fever pitch during a trip he took to Le Mans in France while filming *The Train*

> "Maybe to do something that brings you so close to the possibility of death and to survive it is to feel life and living so much more intensely."
> —Pete Aron

(United Artists, 1965). Sensing the tremendous excitement experienced by the vast crowds at this major event, he felt sure that he could turn it into an epic motion picture that would put all previous such films to shame. Although his producing partner, Edward Lewis, did not share his love of the sport, he certainly could see the box-office potential and arranged a deal with MGM. Frankenheimer juggled with two possible ideas: the story of a racing car from development to its victory on the track, and a multicharacter tale in the tradition of *Grand Hotel* (MGM, 1932). He ultimately settled on the latter. The racing spectacle

at the center of the story would be the Grand Prix, which dated back to 1906, when the first competition was held at Le Mans. (The official world championship would not become a reality for another forty-three years.) Because this event involved a good deal of globetrotting, *Grand Prix* required a hefty budget. And an international cast was required in order to ensure that the film would have global appeal and recoup what became a $9 million investment.

Frankenheimer was adamant that his stars really compete in the races and sent his leads on extensive driving courses for three weeks, eight hours a day, at Jim Russell's auto school in England. Dispensing with special effects and with the customary rear projection that had always been a detriment to such movies, and falling back on stunt drivers as little as possible, the director actually photographed James Garner, Yves Montand, and Antonio Sabato in such a way that audiences could tell that these men were indeed piloting their own vehicles. Garner even went so far as to risk getting singed during the dramatic scene in which his car catches fire, forcing him off the track

This ad for the 1967 London engagement of *Grand Prix* offered reserved seats at the city's first Cinerama theater, which has since reverted back to the Prince Edward.

before it explodes in a ball of flames. For maximum excitement, director of photography Lionel Lindon covered each race with two Panavision sound cameras, eighteen handheld cameras stationed around the course, and a 360-degree swivel camera from a hovering helicopter. The opening race, at Monaco, was perhaps the most thrilling in the film, the cameras (some of which were strapped to the drivers' helmets) careening wildly through the streets of Monte Carlo. Music was completely absent from the scene; the ever humming car engines provided the background "score." Frankenheimer made an innovatively extensive use of split screens, giving multiple images of different angles and often of the very same visual—a technique he had copied from the World's Fair presentation *To Be Alive*. Additional competitions were filmed at Clermont-Ferrand, Brands Hatch in England, Spa Francorchamps in Belgium and, for the climax, Monza in Italy. The four-and-a-half-month shoot lasted from May 15 to October 1, 1966.

Approximately three-quarters of the way through shooting, Frankenheimer was informed by MGM that it wanted to schedule *Grand Prix* as its big Christmas attraction, with road-show prices and special reserved seating. Once filming wrapped, the director put four teams of editors on the picture to pull it into shape as quickly as possible. They couldn't have done a better job visually, creating some exciting cuts and montages that really gave a feeling of what it felt like to be there at the event.

Outside of its technical triumphs, there was not a lot good to be said about the movie. After three hours, there was a sense of exhaustion by the time the picture ended. Each trip around the track was interspersed with a good many hackneyed and predictable personal traumas, most of which involved women who can't get a grasp on just what it is that drives their men to put their lives at risk. (No doubt there were more than a few audience members who shared the bewilderment of Eva Marie Saint's character, who asked how exciting it could be to sit in the grandstands and see so little of what was happening.) Despite all the efforts to make *Grand Prix* something more than the traditional racing melodrama, the pacing seemed to have the exact sort of engine trouble all such movies of this genre experienced, plowing ahead in fits and starts and shifting gears awkwardly from visual stimulation to intimate storytelling.

Grand Prix was presented in its first-run engagements in the Cinerama format. Audiences had a reason to rush to it, simply because there was little to compare it to. Once it found its way into general release, the excitement diminished somewhat and had pretty much fallen off altogether once the picture made its inevitable journey to the small screen. Ending up as one of the year's top ten–grossing pictures and picking up three Academy Awards, *Grand Prix* was looked upon by its studio as a worthwhile investment, while the director, who certainly had done and would do far better movies, always held it dear to his heart as his personal favorite among his pictures.

1967

THOROUGHLY MODERN MILLIE

Academy Award Winner: Best Original Music Score

Academy Award Nominee: Supporting Actress (Carol Channing); Art Direction–Set Decoration; Sound; Song ("Thoroughly Modern Millie"); Scoring of Music—Adaptation or Treatment; Costume Design

Top 10 Box Office Film

Opening date: March 21, 1967.

Universal. A Ross Hunter Production.

Director: George Roy Hill. Producer: Ross Hunter. Screenplay: Richard Morris. Photography: Russell Metty. Art Directors: Alexander Golitzen, George C. Webb. Set Decorator: Howard Bristol. Costumes: Jean Louis. Music: Elmer Bernstein. Musical Numbers Arranger and Conductor: André Previn. Songs: "Looking at the World thru Rose-Colored Glasses," by Jimmy Steiger and Tommy Maile; "Thoroughly Modern Millie," by Jimmy Van Heusen (music) and Sammy Cahn (lyrics); "Stumbling," by Zez Confrey; "I Can't Believe That You're in Love with Me," by Jimmy McHugh and Clarence Gaskill; "The Tapioca," by Jimmy Van Heusen (music) and Sammy Cahn (lyrics), "Baby Face," by Benny Davis and Harry Akst; "Hallelujah Chorus," by George Frideric Handel; "The Jewish Wedding Song (Trinkt Le Chaim)," by Sylvia Neufeld; "Jazz Baby," by Blanche Merrill and M. K. Jerome; "Jimmy," by Jay Thompson; "Ah! Sweet Mystery of Life," by Victor Herbert (music) and Rida Johnson Young (lyrics); "Do It Again," by George Gershwin (music) and Buddy DeSylva (lyrics); "Poor Butterfly," by John L. Golden and Raymond Hubbell; "Rose of Washington Square," by James F. Hanley and Ballard MacDonald; "Japanese Sandman," by Ray Egan and Richard A. Whiting. Choreographer: Joe Layton. Editor: Stuart Gilmore. Technicolor. 153 minutes (including overture, entr'acte, and exit music).

CAST: Julie Andrews (Millie Dillmount), Mary Tyler Moore (Miss Dorothy Brown), Carol Channing (Muzzy Van Hossmere), James Fox (Jimmy Smith), John Gavin (Trevor Graydon), Beatrice Lillie (Mrs. Meers), Jack Soo (Oriental Number 1), Pat Morita (Oriental Number 2), Philip Ahn (Tea), Cavada Humphrey (Miss Flannery), Anthony Dexter (Juarez), Lou Nova (Cruncher), Michael St. Clair (Baron Richter), Albert Carrier (Adrian Huntley), Victor Rogers (Gregory Huntley), Lisabeth Hush (Judith Tremaine), Herbie Faye (Taxi Driver), Ann Dee ("Rose of Washington Square" Singer), Benny Rubin (Waiter), Mae Clarke (Woman in Office), Christopher Riordan ("Jazz Baby" Dance Partner).

PLOT: Millie Dillmount arrives in New York City with plans of becoming secretary to a rich boss she will one day marry, little aware that the hotel she is residing in is a front for a white-slavery operation.

In the wake of *The Sound of Music*'s worldwide sensation, Universal's most successful producer, Ross Hunter, became anxious to work with Julie Andrews, preferably in an adaptation of her first stage success, *The Boy Friend*, but was not too keen to cough up the hefty price MGM wanted for the rights. As luck would have it, Richard Morris, who had just adapted Meredith Willson's *The Unsinkable Molly Brown* (MGM, 1964) into a popular film, had the idea for a tongue-in-cheek 1920s spoof in the *Boy Friend* vein that he was developing with Carol Channing in mind. Although Channing had just become the darling of the Great White Way with her Tony Award–winning performance in *Hello, Dolly!*, nobody was fooled into believing that Hollywood was going to start making starring vehicles around this very individualistic, rarified performer, whose broad style was not everyone's cup of tea. Morris had no such delusions, knowing that his script stood a better chance of getting made with Andrews in the lead and Channing in a scene-stealing supporting part. Andrews requested the services of George Roy Hill, who had just directed her in an entirely different sort of film, the epic drama *Hawaii* (United Artists, 1966), and the project now became one of Universal's elite productions of the decade.

Morris's script made room for a batch of tunes from the past, as was the initial concept. However, it was wisely decided that some new songs be thrown into the mix, hence the addition of Jimmy Van Heusen and Sammy Cahn's smashing title number, a bouncy, winking ode to the liberated women of the '20s that was the sort of tune that was impossible to shake from your head even after a single hearing. Channing was given two standards to showcase her goofy, energetic charms, "Jazz Baby" (made famous by Marion Harris's 1919 recording), which included a tap dance atop a xylophone, and, from the 1922 West End revue *Mayfair and Montmartre*, "Do It Again," which began with the actress being shot out of a cannon (prompting the priceless line "What a *full* life she leads!" from an envious Andrews).

> "There are those, I suppose, think we're mad, heaven knows. The world has gone to rack and to ruin. What we think is chic, unique, and quite adorable, they think is odd and Sodom and Gomorrah-ble."
> —Millie

Andrews chimed in on a version of "Baby Face" (thereby making this one of the anachronistic features of the film; the title song clearly designating the action as taking place in 1922, whereas Benny Davis and Harry Akst wrote this tune in 1925) that threw in pieces of the "Hallelujah Chorus" and the plaintive "Poor Butterfly" (from the New York Hippodrome's *The Big Show*, 1916). An uncredited Ann Dee appeared in the background of one scene, doing a rendition of "Rose of Washington Square" (specially written for and introduced by Fannie Brice in the 1920 *Ziegfeld Midnight Frolic*); and snatches were heard of "I'm Looking at the World thru Rose Colored Glasses" (sung by Jackie Ward, with ukulele accompaniment by an uncredited actress at the start of the film; another anachronism, since it had been written for the 1926 show *A Night in Paris*); *Naughty Marietta*'s immortal "Ah! Sweet Mystery of Life" (dubbed by Bill Lee, who had provided the vocals for Captain von Trapp in *Sound of Music*); and "I Can't Believe That You're in Love with Me." The film used a lyric-free version of the 1922 novelty hit "Stumbling" to serve as the music for Andrews's elevator dance with Mary Tyler Moore, while Jack Soo and Pat Morita got their chance for a brief soft-shoe in the same contraption to the strains of "Japanese Sandman" (originally introduced by the Orpheus Trio in 1920).

In order to give the film a quaint, old-fashioned quality that in no way suggested reality, nearly the entire production was shot for maximum artificiality on soundstages and around the Universal back lot, where standing sets were dressed to suggest the façade of the Priscilla Hotel for Single Young Women and the crowded streets of Chinatown. A journey over to the Warner Bros. studio was needed in order to find the right building to pass for the front of the Sincere Trust Company, and the cast and crew utilized one nonstudio location, the Riviera Country Club, which stood in for the landing field of Muzzy's Long Island estate. Universal's most famous standing set, the interior of the Paris Opera House, originally created back in 1925 for *Phantom of the Opera*, was redressed to play the Hippodrome Theatre at which Muzzy and her acrobats do their leaps through the air. Filming of *Millie* started on May 18, 1966, and went on throughout the summer, wrapping on September 2, 1966. Although the finished film ran about 139 minutes, Universal wanted it to play like the other road-show musicals of the day and made sure it included an overture, an intermission, and exit music, which unnecessarily elongated one of the more modest offerings of this genre.

Although Hill often lost his grip on the material and allowed the whole hectic film to lapse into mere nonsense (notably in its slapstick Chinese-acrobat finale), *Thoroughly Modern Millie* was, for the most part, packed with the sort of deftly satirical touches and winking awareness of good-natured kitsch most comedies of the day lacked. This was one film that set out from the get-go to be campy, rather than later being proclaimed as such, like too many movies that couldn't stay in sync with changing attitudes. It was broad, purposefully arch, and self-referential, and it never for a minute lost sight of the fact that this was all a great big send-up of a bygone era, with white-slavery rings, sinister Orientals, a building-scaling homage to Harold Lloyd, stoic heroes, and pinheaded heroines holding onto their purity. There were deadpan line deliveries of deliberately ludicrous dialogue and an occasional silent-movie subtitle thrown

Who says audiences in 1967 only wanted to listen to rock? Containing such 1920s chestnuts as "Poor Butterfly" and "Baby Face," the Decca soundtrack for *Thoroughly Modern Millie* reached number 16 on the *Billboard* charts.

in to express Millie's feelings, never more hilariously than her reaction to being greeted with scornful frowns as she goes for her first job interview at the Sincere Trust Company ("I can't *wait* for the Christmas party!"). With *Millie*, Andrews displayed yet another side of her talents: her ability to parody a genre without the slightest lapse into self-consciousness. Her comic timing was letter-perfect, even in scenes that ultimately did not pay off, keeping the entire frenetic hodgepodge afloat.

Despite the fact that the script ended up giving in to the outdated beliefs of the era it was making fun of, having its heroine forsake her crusade for women's equality and modernity to sacrifice all for her man, *Millie* was very much what audiences wanted to see in 1967, an unapologetically studio-bound musical comedy of the sort that was fast disappearing. Its success was such that Andrews now could lay claim to having starred in the highest-grossing movie for three different studios: *Mary Poppins* for Disney, *The Sound of Music* for Fox, and now *Thoroughly Modern Millie* for Universal.

TWO FOR THE ROAD

Academy Award Nominee: Story and Screenplay—Written Directly for the Screen

Opening date: April 27, 1967.

Twentieth Century-Fox. A Stanley Donen Production.

Director-Producer: Stanley Donen. Screenplay: Frederic Raphael. Photography: Christopher Challis. Art Director: Willy Holt. Wardrobe Coordinator: Sophie Issartel-Rochas. Miss Hepburn's Clothes: Ken Scott, Michèle Rosier, Paco Rabanne, Mary Quant, Foale and Tuffin. Miss Hepburn's Wardrobe Supervisor: Clare Rendelsham. Mr. Finney's Clothes: Hardy Amies. Music: Henry Mancini. Editors: Richard Marden, Madeleine Gug. Production Supervisor: Christian Ferry. Titles: Maurice Binder. Deluxe color. Panavision. 112 minutes.

CAST: Audrey Hepburn (Joanna Wallace), Albert Finney (Mark Wallace), Eleanor Bron (Cathy Manchester), William Daniels (Howard Manchester), Claude Dauphin (Maurice Dalbret), Nadia Gray (Françoise Dalbret), Georges Descrieres (David), Gabrielle Middleton (Ruthie Manchester), Kathy Chelimsky (Caroline Wallace), Carol van Dyke (Michelle), Karyn Balm (Simone), Mario Verdon (Palamos), Roger Dann (Gilbert, Comte de Florac), Irène Hilda (Yvonne de Florac), Dominique Joos (Sylvia), Libby Morris (American Lady), Yves Barsacq (Police Inspector), Hélène Tossy (Madame Solange, Hotel Proprietor), Jean-François Lalet (Boat Officer), Albert Michel (Customs Officer), Jackie Bisset/Jacqueline Bisset (Jackie), Judy Cornwell (Pat), Joanna Marie Jones, Sofia Torkely, Patricia Viterbo, Olga Georges-Picot, Clarissa Hillel (Joanna's Touring Girlfriends).

PLOT: Joanna and Mark Wallace look back on how several trips through France became pivotal moments in their initially happy relationship that led to their presently unfulfilling marriage.

If there was one thing movies gave attention to on a fairly regular basis it was relationships, marital and otherwise. It was, after all, the very foundation of what made most story lines spin. Only a handful of movies, however, have ever explored the growth, stagnation, disintegration, rebirth, and ever-puzzling mystery of marriage with such thorough honesty, bitterness, humor, and sophistication as did *Two for the Road*. Certainly no others took this picture's unique approach. The whole idea behind the film came from a random bit of self-reflection screenwriter Frederic Raphael had had while driving through the South of France, wondering what it would be like to pass his younger self, traveling the same spot a decade earlier. This led to the time-hopping premise of his story. Raphael got wind of Stanley Donen's admiration for his work (including his Oscar-winning script for *Darling*) and presented his idea (at this point referred to as *Four Times Two*) to the director, who was very intrigued. Donen figured if he could get some solid star names interested, he'd be able to get studio financing, so he suggested the possible pairing of Audrey Hepburn and Paul Newman. Newman said no, believing that the picture sounded like a gimmick that

> **"They don't look very happy."**
> **—Joanna**
> **"Why should they?**
> **They just got married."**
> **—Mark**

would allow the director to look good, but not the actors. (Because of Newman's refusal, Universal decided to pass on financing the film.) Although Hepburn, who'd worked with Donen twice before, was a safer bet to join the project, she was nervous, initially, because the jumping about in the story reminded

her of one of her biggest failures, *Paris When It Sizzles* (Paramount, 1964), and because the script included such adult themes as marital infidelity and also called for suggestions of nudity.

Once Raphael had completed his first draft (which, surprisingly, remained pretty close to what ended up being filmed), Hepburn found herself becoming more enthusiastic about participating in something that seemed both clever and audacious. Once Hepburn had committed, Donen figured he had his bankable name, and therefore he felt less restricted as to his choice of leading man. The name of Albert Finney came up, which excited Hepburn (who had costar approval), the actress having been won over by him, as had most of the movie industry, by his performance in the 1963 Oscar-winner *Tom Jones* (United Artists). If there was any doubt as to whose was the bigger name on the picture, it was evident in the paychecks: Hepburn received $750,000 for her work, Finney $300,000. The script was so thoroughly and completely focused on these two characters that there was less concern over who filled the supporting roles, though the inclusion of a pricelessly dry William Daniels and a haughtily self-involved Eleanor Bron, as the friends with whom Finney and Hepburn share a disastrous vacation, was inspired, to say the least.

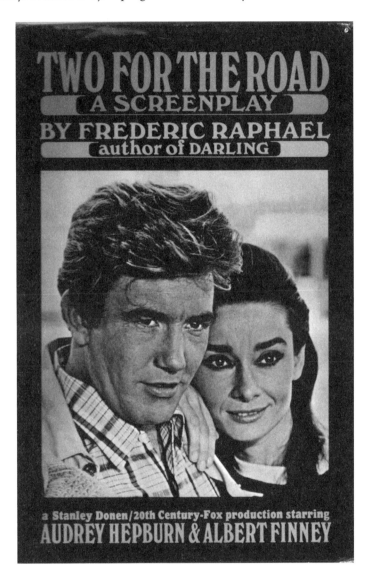

So highly regarded was Frederic Raphael's screenplay for *Two for the Road* that Holt, Rinehart and Winston published it in hardcover.

Donen made a deal with Twentieth Century-Fox to finance and distribute the movie and was persuasive enough to negotiate for a $5 million-plus budget, knowing that all the moving around from place to place required by the story, as well as the necessity of changing costumes and settings to indicate the different periods of time, would stretch the shooting out for almost a full four months. To maximize on the warmest possible weather, filming was scheduled from May 3 to August 23, 1966. The shooting commenced in Nice at the Quay du Commerce for scenes on and involving the cross-Channel steamer (using the S.S. *Cyrnos*). During May the company filmed at La Colle sur Loup, a hotel in Abbeville, for the vacation accommodations for Joanna and her girlfriends; Hôtel du Golf in Beauvallon, as the low-rent establishment where Joanna and Mark stay happily in 1954 and then, more miserably, with their daughter, Caroline, in 1963; Plage de Beauvallon, for beach scenes set in 1963 and 1966; the Restaurant des Mouscardins, as the St. Tropez Restaurant, where Joanna and her lover, David, observe the silent couple at a nearby table; Castle Grimaud, to play the Restaurant de L'Abbaye in 1963; the roads and beaches at Gigaro; the beach at the Penede Hotel in St. Tropez; Villa L'Oumède in St. Tropez-Ramatuelle for the Dalbert's villa and swimming pool; and Col de Canadel, where Joanna and Mark end up inside a piece of tubing. Starting in June, interiors of the Abbeville Clinic were done at Franstudio in Paris, while other interiors—of the Hôtel St. Just; the Abbeville hotel lobby; the inside of the Dalbert Villa; the Florac Villa, during which the blackout occurs; and the plane—were shot at Studio St. Maurice. The Hôtel Chaumontel was the elegant 1966 hotel; Frisy les Platres provided the 1954 street market; and the Château de la Villette became the site of the couple's memorable mosquito-infested stay.

Shockingly, the critical response to *Two for the Road* was not unqualified praise, but ran the gamut from ecstatic to rude dismissal. It was left to audiences to keep the picture from falling off the radar screen. As it happened, the more mature and self-analytical moviegoers were astounded by how perceptively Raphael and Donen had captured the very flexible, roller-coaster path experienced by couples of all kinds, be they married, unmarried, gay, or straight. The giddy highs of early courtship gave way to obligations and seriousness in a way that was made all the more powerful by having earlier scenes of happiness placed back-to-back with latter-day moments of dissension at the very same locales. The ingenious cross-cutting, which allowed Joanna and Mark's vehicles to literally pass their earlier (or later) cars on the very same road, fully realizing the cinematic equivalent of Raphael's original idea, made *Two for the Road* a masterful piece of cinema that flew from sequence to sequence like a train of thought, key occurrences leading to similar moments in time, just as our minds would think of them, in stream-of-consciousness fashion. Both Hepburn and Finney were magnificent, she plumbing unexpected depths of insecurities and doubt to create one of her finest performances, he entirely convincing as a man leaping between randy immaturity and a wearied sense of defeat without ever losing his appeal.

Fox wasn't at all happy with the soft box-office reaction, considering the picture's high cost, while the Academy shortchanged it with a sole nomination for Raphael's undeniably brilliant script. A movie this good simply refused to slink away in defeat, and more and more admirers would talk it up over the passing years as one of the truly special treasures of its era, one of the most innovative, witty, and distinctive pictures ever to shed light on just how difficult and fulfilling it is to spend years knowing and loving a person so thoroughly that it sometimes hurts to do so.

BAREFOOT IN THE PARK

Academy Award Nominee: Supporting Actress (Mildred Natwick)

Opening date: May 25, 1967.

Paramount. A Hal Wallis Production, Produced in Association with Nancy Productions, Inc.

Director: Gene Saks. Producer: Hal B. Wallis. Screenplay: Neil Simon, based on his 1963 play. Associate Producer: Paul Nathan. Photography: Joseph LaShelle. Art Directors: Hal Pereira, Walter Tyler. Set Decorators: Robert Benton, Arthur Krams. Costumes: Edith Head. Music: Neal Hefti. Title song by Neal Hefti (music) and Johnny Mercer (lyrics), performed by chorus. Editor: William Lyon. Technicolor. 106 minutes.

CAST: Robert Redford (Paul Bratter), Jane Fonda (Corie Bratter), Charles Boyer (Victor Velasco), Mildred Natwick (Ethel Banks), Herbert Edelman (Harry Pepper, Telephone Man), James F. Stone (Lord & Taylor Delivery Man), Ted Hartley (Frank), Mabel Albertson (Aunt Harriet), Fritz Feld (4 Winds Restaurant Proprietor).

PLOT: Tensions arise between newlyweds Corie and Paul Bratter after they move into a cramped New York apartment, leading Corie to wonder if the man she married is nothing more than a stuffed shirt incapable of enjoying life.

Few writers ever connected with the public as strongly as Neil Simon did for more than three decades, giving theatergoers just the sort of lighthearted, quip-filled, none-too-challenging evenings of laughs and romance that seemed to reach a surprisingly diverse demographic. He made the leap from television comedy writer to established playwright with the popular, semiautobiographical *Come Blow Your Horn* (1961) and then took a giant step into the rarefied world of behind-the-scene names that sell tickets with his second produced play, *Barefoot in the Park*. This very mild, gently amusing, mostly pleasing look at the first struggling steps taken by a pair of newlyweds as they move into a cramped apartment in Manhattan struck just the right chord, no doubt, appealing to everyone who had both fond and horrific memories of their first rented living quarters away from home, all those who had been uncertain about the decision to marry, and anyone coping with the love-hate relationship one develops with a doting parent. This sort of lark was a dime a dozen on Broadway in the early '60s, but Simon had the knack to manipulate the laughs with the correct balance of situation comedy know-how and a dollop of humanity, so that average playgoers believed they too could be this bright, attractive, and funny. *Barefoot* arrived on Broadway at the Biltmore Theatre on October 23, 1963, under the guidance of Mike Nichols, here making the transition from sketch comedy performer to director. Starring as the newlywed Bratters, Paul and Corie, were Robert Redford and Elizabeth Ashley. Mildred Natwick played Mrs. Banks, Corie's widowed mother, and Kurt Kasznar portrayed flirtatious foreigner Victor Velasco.

> **"Paul, if the honeymoon doesn't work out, let's not get divorced, let's kill each other."**
> **—Corie Bratter**

The critics were appreciative, and the audience couldn't snap up tickets fast enough, making *Barefoot in the Park* the must-see play of the season and beyond. It chalked up an incredible 1,350 performances, making it the eleventh-longest-running show in Broadway history when it closed on June 25, 1967. Simon had no idea at the time just how high he had already reached. Despite cranking out one money-maker after another, *Barefoot* remained his longest-running play, with *Brighton Beach Memoirs*, at 1,299 play dates, coming closest to its predecessor's record tally.

One of Hollywood's top producers, Hal B. Wallis, purchased the rights to *Barefoot* even before its New York premiere. Wallis had a distribution deal with Paramount Pictures, the very same company that had released the 1963 movie adaptation of *Come Blow Your Horn*. That was *not* a selling point as far as Simon was concerned. The playwright had been very unhappy with that stage-to-screen transfer, for which he was not invited to do the adaptation. Wallis rectified that error by allowing Simon to do the screenplay, assuring that *Barefoot* would sound pretty much the way it did on the stage.

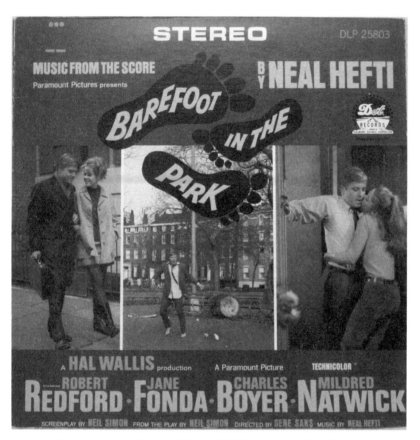

The Dot Records soundtrack of Neal Hefti's score for *Barefoot in the Park* buries the name of the other significant Neil behind the film, writer Neil Simon.

Although his appearance in the Broadway version had garnered Robert Redford several movie offers, each of those pictures had gone belly-up at the box office, which meant that he might have been passed over for the *Barefoot* film in favor of a more proven name. In the end his very personable charm and golden-boy looks helped immensely in convincing Wallis and Saks that he was the right man for the job, one with movie-star potential that had not yet been fully realized—a decision that turned out to be most astute. Although such women as Faye Dunaway, Geraldine Chaplin, and Yvette Mimieux were tested for the role of Corie, a far better choice was made in Jane Fonda, who had become one of the most interesting actresses of the '60s, albeit one who, like Redford, often had trouble finding the right property to reflect her range. (The two had, in fact, already appeared together in a movie, Columbia's *The Chase*, in 1966.) Her biggest hit had been the western spoof *Cat Ballou* (Columbia, 1965), in which she had pretty much essayed the straight role; *Barefoot* would allow her to show that she could play light comedy with the utmost ease. Happily, the wonderful Mildred Natwick was asked to repeat her stage role (as she had also done in the London production), which meant she would be returning to the big screen for the first time since *Tammy and the Bachelor* (Universal) ten years earlier. Her dry reactions to being shown her daughter's minuscule apartment for the first time were alone worth the price of admission. This performance ranked among the highlights of her movie career, bringing the veteran actress her one and only Oscar nomination.

The opening up of the play included a prologue that turned out to enhance the piece in every way, showing Corie and Paul being driven through Central Park in a horse-drawn carriage during the opening credits and taking them to their honeymoon at the Plaza Hotel. This not only established a very romantic image of Manhattan, but gave audiences a necessary glimpse of the couple in a state of happiness before their new living conditions began to rock their relationship. Simon moved their location from East Forty-eighth Street (as it had been in the Broadway show) to 49 West Tenth Street, putting them in close proximity to Washington Square Park. Now there could be an actual scene showing Paul running barefoot in a park, which had merely been alluded to onstage. The screenplay also showed Corie, Paul, Mrs. Banks, and Victor having their meal at the Albanian Restaurant on Staten Island; set the previous scene of the four experimenting with "knichi" in Victor's attic apartment, where it made more sense; allowed brief onscreen moments for some of the other oddballs in the apartment house; and even gave Mrs. Banks a pratfall on the front stoop. Velasco was no longer a deadbeat with his rent; now he had key trouble, which made it necessary for him to crawl through the Bratters' bedroom to get to his own apartment; and some feminist progression was evident in cutting Corie's line about desiring a husband who "tells me how much I can spend." Despite this nod to women's liberation, Simon did not consider it necessary to give Corie a job or even the ambition to go out and get one, which might have helped her save money toward getting a home with an actual bedroom in it.

Filming began at the Paramount studios on October 31, 1966 and continued there for another three and a half weeks. Starting November 26, location shooting took place in Manhattan with scenes shot in Central Park, the Plaza Hotel (before this landmark establishment made it its policy not to open its doors to movie companies), Washington Square Park (looking suspiciously empty for the "barefoot" scene), and Tenth Street and Fifth Avenue, where Fonda was seen racing toward the park to find Redford. The actual exterior of the Bratter's apartment building was not on Tenth Street, as indicated in the script, but instead used 111 Waverly Place, off the northwest corner of Washington Square. For night scenes, a Paramount back-lot mock-up was used. Returning west, *Barefoot* wrapped after another month of shooting, at the end of December. Being just the sort of sunny, audience-pleasing entertainment that the Radio City Music Hall was built for, *Barefoot in the Park* made its East Coast debut there in May 1967 and proved right from the start that the tremendous interest that had turned it into a Broadway sensation hadn't evaporated in the least when the picture broke all of the Hall's previous box-office records. Fonda and Redford were a sparkling pair; the latter especially benefited from the picture's success, which made him at last a certified film star. *Barefoot* had a relaxed, friendly feel, though the comedy seemed to grow thin by the home stretch, making this the sort of film to induce frequent smiles rather than big laughs. It did its job, however, in proving that Simon's comedy could make the transition from the proscenium arch to a soundstage, and Paramount wound up with its biggest moneymaker for 1967.

YOU ONLY LIVE TWICE (United Kingdom)

Top 10 Box Office Film

Opening date: June 13, 1967 (London: June 18, 1967).

United Artists. An Eon Production.

Director: Lewis Gilbert. Producers: Harry Saltzman, Albert R. Broccoli. Screenplay: Roald Dahl. Additional Story Material: Harold Jack Bloom. Based on the 1964 novel by Ian Fleming. Photography: Freddie Young. Production Designer: Ken Adam. Art Director: Harry Pottle. Set Decorator: David Ffolkes. Music: John Barry. Title song by John Barry (music) and Leslie Bricusse (lyrics), performed by Nancy Sinatra. Main Title Designer: Maurice Binder. Second Unit Director and Supervising Editor: Peter Hunt. Editor: Thelma Connell. Action Sequences Director: Bob Simmons. Special Effects: John Stears. Technicolor. Panavision. 116 minutes.

CAST: Sean Connery (James Bond, 007), Akiko Wakabayashi (Aki), Mie Hama (Kissy Suzuki), Tetsuro Tamba (Tiger Tanaka), Teru Shimada (Mr. Osato), Karin Dor (Helga Brandt), Donald Pleasence (Ernst Stavro Blofeld), Bernard Lee (M), Lois Maxwell (Miss Moneypenny), Desmond Llewelyn (Q), Charles Gray (Dikko Henderson), Tsai Chin (Ling, Chinese Girl in Hong Kong), Peter Fanene Maivia (Car Driver), Burt Kwouk (SPECTRE 3), Michael Chow (SPECTRE 4), Ronald Rich (Hans, Blofeld's Bodyguard), Jeanne Roland (Bond's Masseuse), David Toguri (Assassin in Bedroom), Robert Hutton (President's Aide), Alexander Knox (American President), Mai Ling, Yasuko Nagazumi, Yee-Wah Yang (Bath Girls), John Stone (Submarine Captain).

PLOT: After a U.S. capsule is captured in space by an unidentified rocket, Secret Agent James Bond is sent to Japan to find out from where the mysterious craft was launched and put a stop to any future such abductions.

By the late '60s James Bond was no longer the only secret agent in town. Owing to the phenomenal financial success of the first four 007 adventures, the whole film industry was going spy crazy, searching for other properties to compete with the real thing and to cash in on the overflow of wealth. To some degree, the public was responding to pretty much whatever was being offered, good or bad. The year 1966 had been the first since the premiere Bond effort, *Dr. No* (United Artists; United Kingdom, 1962; United States, 1963), that there had been no new Sean Connery Bond adventure released, and both of Columbia's Matt Helm flicks, *The Silencers* and *Murderers' Row*, as well as Fox's *Our Man Flint*, had picked up the slack in his absence. All three pictures performed well enough to suggest that you didn't have to be 007 to succeed. In 1967 Connery had to keep up not only with these upstarts but also with another James Bond movie made elsewhere without his participation—Columbia's over-the-top send-up *Casino Royale*. And there was still another, one starring his own sibling, Neil, who up to that point had been a laborer with no acting aspirations whatsoever; this was the shamelessly titled rip-off *Operation Kid Brother* (United Artists). Clearly producers

> "Chasing girls will be the end of you, Bond-san. I told you so."
> —Tiger Tanaka

Harry Saltzman and Albert R. Broccoli had to keep upping the ante, and the newest official Bond, *You Only Live Twice*, was designed to be bigger and more exciting than any entry before it. The money was rolling in to a spectacular degree, so why not throw some of it back up there on the screen?

You Only Live Twice had been the twelfth James Bond novel and the last one to be entirely written by Ian Fleming, who died in the summer of 1964, the year of the book's publication. The plot had Bond sent to Japan to kill Guntram Shatterhand, who has designed a suicide center at a remote castle. When Shatterhand is ultimately revealed to be none other than SPECTRE's diabolical Ernst Blofeld, Bond carries out the execution before losing his memory and setting up his new life in Japan, having been presumed dead by the home office back in London. Broccoli and Saltzman wanted to retain the Japanese setting but weren't crazy about the plot, which they felt would not translate into an exciting cinematic experience since too much of the book involved 007's absorption of Japanese culture. American writer Harold Jack Bloom was hired to come up with a new story, and British journeyman director Lewis Gilbert was invited to take control of the project. It was Gilbert who, while scouting locations in Japan, came up with the idea of having Blofeld's secret hideaway concealed inside a dormant volcano. Scripter Bloom was then dropped in favor of a more intriguing name, Roald Dahl, who with his tales of the dark and the whimsical had become one of Britain's foremost writers. Dahl stuck for the most part to what had become the basics in plotting and dialogue, so this particular movie was not instantly identifiable as the work of this unique and gifted author.

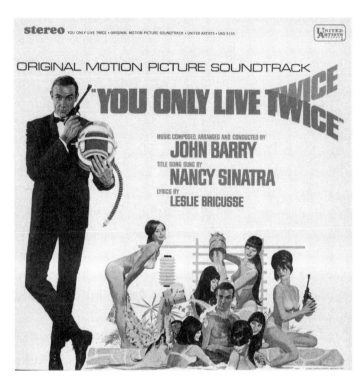

A familiar pose and familiar surroundings for Sean Connery are found on the United Artists LP cover for the fifth official James Bond epic, *You Only Live Twice*.

You Only Live Twice began production on July 4, 1966, at the usual Bond base of operations, Pinewood Studios, filming select interiors, while Ken Adams's most spectacular set, the volcano, was being erected on the back lot. While that was being finished, the company moved on to Japan. There Connery found that the lack of privacy he had been experiencing in England on account of his motion-picture fame was nothing compared to what he had to confront in Japan, where he'd become something of a folk hero, constantly being hounded by press and public. It was just this sort of obnoxious behavior that drove him to announce that the new Bond film would be his last—he was leaving the series behind to concentrate on other roles. In the meantime, the Japan filming took him to Tokyo, where the recently opened Hotel New Otani served as the Osato Chemical building; to the docks of Kobe, where Bond's waterfront fight took place; and then on to the fishing village of Akime. The ninja training school, where Bond "turns

Japanese" (with the usual none-too-convincing eye makeup given Caucasians), was the Himeji Castle in Himeji, and the extinct volcano was found in Kirishima National Park, at the southern tip of Kyushu, Japan's southernmost island. The helicopter battle started filming over Elbino but was halted after an accident that cost aerial photographer Johnny Jordan a leg. This sequence was completed in Torremolinos, Spain, by second unit director Peter Hunt after principal photography had been finished. Hunt also supervised the "burial" of Bond (filmed in Gibraltar Harbor), his subsequent undersea rescue (shot in the clear waters of the Bahamas), and the crash landing of Helga's plane, filmed in Finmere, Scotland. Prior to this, in the fall of that year, the company moved back to Pinewood for the interior volcano scenes. This incredible set, which included a helicopter launch pad and a working monorail, was arguably *the* masterpiece of designer Ken Adam, who really outdid himself this time. The structure pretty much stole the film, setting the standard for all the dazzling villain hideouts that became a staple of the series for decades to come. Principal photography was completed by Christmas of 1966 at a cost of $9.5 million.

Having been told that this would be Connery's farewell to the role that had made him one of the icons of the decade, audiences flocked to *You Only Live Twice*, though not to the degree that they had for *Thunderball* (United Artists, 1965), the series's financial peak. What they got was a goofy plot made palatable by its larger-than-life presentation: the capturing of the first space capsule in the precredit scene was both ominous and spectacular. (It was also a clever idea to link the futuristic technology of the Bond films with the most significant scientific event of the decade, the space race, here portrayed with historical accuracy as a tense competition between the United States and Russia, both of which seem to operate in a perpetual state of distrust.) There was a terrific piece of gadgetry on hand, a mini-helicopter, styled after a real-life model and enhanced by various missiles and rockets by way of Q branch. The actual designer of the craft, Wing Commander Ken Wallis, was engaged to do the onscreen piloting for Connery. *Twice* gave Bond his first wedding (albeit a bogus one) prior to his actual nuptials in the follow-up picture, *On Her Majesty's Secret Service* (United Artists, 1969), and the odd sight of Connery in semi-Asian makeup as he went through the ritual Japanese conversion in order to fulfill his mission with a team of ninjas, another aspect of the novel that was at least to some extent retained. The smashing assault on Blofeld's volcano was everything the creative team had envisioned from the start; the sight of the Japanese attack force shimmying down their ropes from the sliding ceiling of the fortress was one of the outstanding images in the series's history.

Although Connery really seemed to have sworn off Bond with *You Only Live Twice*, he was to have second thoughts twice more in his career, much to the delight of the series's 'growing number of admirers. After his predecessor, George Lazenby, had proven such a washout in *On Her Majesty's*, Broccoli and Saltzman were thrilled to be able to get the "real" Bond back before the cameras for *Diamonds Are Forever*, after which all the money in the world couldn't seem to change his mind about returning to work for the two men who had changed his life. Although *Diamonds* marked his final assignment for the producing team, his true Bond adieu came in 1983 with Warner Bros.' *Never Say Never Again*, a semi-remake of *Thunderball*, that was produced by different parties altogether.

TO SIR, WITH LOVE (United Kingdom)

Top 10 Box Office Film

Opening date: June 14, 1967 (London: October 29, 1967).

Columbia. A James Clavell Production.

Director-Producer-Screenplay: James Clavell. Based on the 1959 book by E. R. Braithwaite. Executive Producer: John R. Sloan. Photography: Paul Beeson. Art Director: Tony Woollard. Set Decorator: Ian Whittaker. Wardrobe Supervisor: John Wilson Apperson. Music: Ron Grainer. Songs: "To Sir, with Love," by Mark London (music) and Don Black (lyrics), performed by Lulu; "Stealing My Love from Me," by Mark London (music) and Don Black (lyrics), performed by Lulu; "Off and Running," by Toni Wine and Carole Bayer, performed by the Mindbenders; "It's Getting Harder All the Time," by Charles Albertine (music) and Ben Raleigh (lyrics), performed by the Mindbenders. Editor: Peter Thornton. Technicolor. 105 minutes.

CAST: Sidney Poitier (Mark Thackeray), Judy Geeson (Pamela Dare), Christian Roberts (Denham), Suzy Kendall (Gillian Blanchard), Faith Brook (Grace Evans), Christopher Chittell (Potter), Geoffrey Bayldon (Weston), Patricia Routledge (Clinty Clintridge), Adrienne Posta (Moira Jackson), Edward Burnham (Headmaster Florian), Rita Webb (Mrs. Joseph), Fiona Duncan (Euphemia Phillips), Lulu (Barbara Pegg), Grahame Charles (Fernman), Gareth Robinson (Tich), Ann Bell (Mrs. Dare), Fred Griffiths (Vendor), Mona Bruce (Josie Dawes), Marianne Stone (Gert), Dervis Ward (Mr. Bell), Peter Attard (Ingham), Michael Des Barres (Williams), Anthony Villaroel (Seales), Lynne Sue Moon (Miss Wong), Roger Shepherd ("Fats" Buckley), Cyril Shaps (Mr. Pinckus), Ric Rothwell, Bob Lang, Eric Stewart (the Mindbenders).

PLOT: Having made no progress with his belligerent working-class students at London's Quay Secondary School, novice schoolteacher Mark Thackeray dispenses with standard book learning and decides instead to teach these teens the social skills they will need to make it as adults in the real world.

It was time for Sidney Poitier to go back to school. In 1955 he had played a pivotal early film role as a very cool, unflappable student in Glenn Ford's class in the most important school-set motion picture of the '50s, *Blackboard Jungle* (MGM, 1955). Twelve years down the line, an ideal role was found for him when Columbia Pictures bought the rights to E. R. (Edward Ricardo) Braithwaite's autobiographical novel *To Sir, with Love*, about a black teacher who manages to break through to a pack of uncouth white East End secondary schoolers by treating them as adults. Published in 1959, two very important events had taken place over the seven years it took for the film to roll: Poitier had won an Oscar and become the sole bankable black actor in the business, and the British Invasion had swept America, making the book's London setting now more appealing to Hollywood and making it easier to get the studio to cough up some cash. Poitier's agent, Martin Baum, turned to one of his other clients, Australia-born, U.K.-raised James Clavell, not only to adapt the script, but to direct and produce the picture as well. To placate the skeptical studio, which still wasn't sure about the financial prospects of the property, both Clavell and Poitier agreed to work on *To Sir* for percentage points. The budget was kept to a very low $750,000. Shooting started on May 31, 1966, with three weeks of locations. Street scenes took place mainly in

Wapping; the actual Braithwaite school, St. George-in-the-East, was located not far from the spot where the funeral flower sequence was filmed. The disused Victoria Barracks in Windsor became the exterior of the school, and an effective montage (designed and executed by George White) chronicled a school trip to the Victoria and Albert Museum. The remaining six weeks of filming took place at Pinewood Studios.

Braithwaite had been the star of his own book, but rather than have the movie be thought of as a true story, the protagonist received a name change of "Mark Thackeray," as did the name of the school, Glensdale Secondary, which was now "New Quay Secondary." Although there were passing mentions of Poitier's race, this very important theme of the book was toned down considerably. This aspect had been the chief reason for Braithwaite's shift from engineering to teaching: he had been subjected to a great deal of discrimination while hunting for a job in his first field. A suggestion raised during a chance conversation in a park with an elderly gentleman led him to take up a new profession. Another very important part of the book was also eliminated, Braithwaite's interracial romance with his fellow instructor Gillian Blanchard, which erupts in dissension between the two because she feels that he is allowing himself to be derided and dismissed by bigotry. While the idea that Thackeray/Braithwaite and Gillian might be feeling something stirring was hinted at by the performances of Poitier and Suzy Kendall, the two remained platonic friends onscreen, this role being yet another of Poitier's "chaste" characterizations.

> "I suddenly realized that you are not children; that you will be adults in a few weeks, with all the responsibilities that implies. So, from now on, you will be treated as such by me and by each other; as adults . . . responsible adults."
> —Mr. Thackeray

A handful of racial barriers remained, notably the resistance of the students to be seen delivering funeral flowers to a black household, a declaration that causes Thackeray/Braithwaite to react with monumental disappointment at the lack of hoped-for progress his mere presence was supposed to have triggered. Clavell dropped a story line in which one of the students, Fernman, is arrested for stabbing another boy, with the subsequent trial allowing a barrister to admonish the school for its lack of discipline; and a sequence in which a news magazine hopes to build a story around the novelty of a black teacher at the school, a stunt in which Braithwaite refuses to participate. Because the film would not be seen entirely through Thackeray's eyes as the book had been, a handful of scenes with the students at recess were added; the bullying gym teacher, Mr. Bell, no longer rose to the occasion by apologizing to the boys for his cruelty, as he had in the book; and a more fitting climax was found by having Thackeray nearly quit, only to change his mind at the year-end graduation dance, whereas in the novel he had no such plans to leave. Clavell's one crossover into implausibility was to have Thackeray dispose of schoolbooks in favor of oral education, while no such leap was made by Braithwaite. It was perhaps the single aspect most damned and questioned by critics.

Of the supporting cast, it was Lulu (born Marie Lawrie in Glasgow, Scotland, in 1948) who became a temporary sensation in the United States thanks to her singing of the title tune, which Michael

London and Don Black had penned for her. A very distinctive, haunting song to begin with, it was wailed no fewer than four times during the course of the picture, so audiences couldn't shake it from their heads. Lulu's recording of it very quickly climbed the *Billboard* charts to stay at the number 1 spot for five straight weeks in the fall of 1967. (It also helped the soundtrack album reach the number 16 position later that year.) The tune, in fact, stayed at number 1 longer than any other song that year and become one of the indelible anthems of the mythical "swinging London" era.

While a good many critics brushed the picture off as fluffy, sentimental, and highly improbable, it is no exaggeration to say that *To Sir, with Love* struck so emotional a chord with movie audiences that whatever negative commentary the picture had provoked was quickly forgotten. Poitier became just about everybody's ideal of what an educator should be, and yet another barrier was smashed in a small way through another of the actor's cleverly conceived performances, one that made racism unthinkable to anyone with an open mind. Looked upon as a highly effective piece of commercial filmmaking, *To Sir* captured the imagination of an entire

You knew you were in the '60s when the copy made reference to miniskirts, as does this London ad for *To Sir, With Love*.

generation in such a way as to become the rare movie perceived as "inspiring" where the teaching profession was concerned. It was the one to top in this genre for years to come.

THE DIRTY DOZEN

Academy Award Winner: Best Sound Effects

Academy Award Nominee: Supporting Actor (John Cassavetes); Film Editing; Sound

Top 10 Box Office Film

Opening date: June 15, 1967.

MGM. A Kenneth Hyman Production.

Director: Robert Aldrich. Producer: Kenneth Hyman. Screenplay: Nunnally Johnson, Lukas Heller. Based on the 1965 novel by E. M. Nathanson. Photography: Edward Scaife. Art Director: W. E. Hutchinson. Set Designer: Tim Hutchinson. Music: (Frank) DeVol. Songs: "Einsam," by Frank DeVol and Sibylle Siegfried; "The Bramble Bush," by Frank DeVol and Mack David, performed by Trini Lopez. Editor: Michael Luciano. Special Effects Supervisor: Cliff Richardson. Metrocolor. 149 minutes.

CAST: Lee Marvin (Major John Reisman), Ernest Borgnine (General Worden), Charles Bronson (Joseph Wladislaw), Jim Brown (Robert Jefferson), John Cassavetes (Victor Franko), Richard Jaeckel (Sergeant Clyde Bowren), George Kennedy (Major Max Armbruster), Trini Lopez (Pedro Jiminez), Ralph Meeker (Captain Stuart Kinder), Robert Ryan (Colonel Everett Dasher Breed), Telly Savalas (Archer Maggott), Clint Walker (Samson Posey), Robert Webber (General Denton), Donald Sutherland (Vernon Pinkley), Tom Busby (Milo Vladek), Ben Carruthers (Glenn Gilpin), Stuart Cooper (Roscoe Lever), Robert Phillips (Corporal Carl Morgan), Colin Maitland (Seth Sawyer), Al Mancini (Tassos Bravos), George Roubicek (Private Arthur Gardner), Thick Wilson (Captain Haskell, Worden's Aide), Dora Reisser (German Girl), Dick Miller (MP at Hanging).

PLOT: Major John Reisman is ordered to select twelve military prisoners, train them, and lead them in an attack upon a chateau in Brittany, where a conference of important Nazi generals will be taking place.

The reality of the conflict in Vietnam might have been enlightening people to the cold fact that war wasn't quite as glorious as it had been portrayed in the movies, but that didn't stop Hollywood from falling back on an occasional slam-bang war film to please the paying customers, even if it did have to return to the seemingly less complicated backdrop of World War II to do so. MGM saw some great possibilities in a novel about to be published by E. M. Nathanson, and the studio snatched up the rights to his lengthy and gritty tale of a batch of condemned prisoners trained to kill for a reason even before the first copies hit the shelves. It didn't hurt that the name of the book, *The Dirty Dozen*, was so unapologetically coarse and unforgettable that the average customer would stop and smile at the very sound of it. Producer Kenneth Hyman originally thought that the lead character of the hard-assed captain, who whips his cons into fighting shape, would make an ideal vehicle for John Wayne, then at the top of his box-office powers. After demanding some script changes, Wayne passed on the project. He decided that if he was going to fight another cinematic war it would be the current one, hence his participation in the controversial *The Green Berets* (Warner Bros., 1968). His replacement, Lee Marvin, was, in truth, a superior choice: the rugged, deep-voiced actor was younger and no less commanding a screen presence. Because Marvin had won an Oscar only days before shooting on the new picture was to commence, MGM felt pretty good about the $350,000 it had agreed to pay him.

Robert Aldrich, who had just done a first-rate job with his mostly male cast in Fox's *The Flight of the Phoenix* (1965), was hired to direct. He had helmed a different kind of war picture back in the '50s, the downbeat *Attack*, which also featured Lee Marvin among its cast. Veteran Nunnally Johnson was enlisted to work on *The Dirty Dozen* script, along with Lukas Heller, who had already collaborated several times with Aldrich. The adaptation of Nathanson's massive novel required a good deal of pruning to fit into an acceptable motion-picture length of two and a half hours, which meant several characters and background stories had to go. Surprisingly, considering Hollywood's reputation for creating love stories from sources that had none, the women were among the edits. In the book, Captain Reisman developed a relationship with a British waitress to whom he runs on several occasions as a form of release from his tense training sessions. Cut too was a disagreeable aristocrat, Lady Margot Strathallan, who reluctantly relinquishes a portion of her property to Reisman and his men for use as their training compound. The invasion of her privacy is eventually justified when it is revealed that her secret lover is a Nazi. The only women who made it into the movie were a German maid attacked by the lecherous Archer Maggott (though the scene from the book that might have inspired this moment had involved another character altogether, Roscoe Lever), a group of anonymous Nazi wives who were simply around to be disposed of during the brutal climax, and a truckload of whores sneaked into camp to bring pleasure to the Dozen. The last-mentioned was a compromise of sorts: the men had been allotted a single prostitute to share among themselves in Nathanson's story, a set-up that would have been deemed too sordid for movie audiences used to seeing their hookers pair off with one partner at a time.

> ## "Donald Duck's down at the crossroads with a machine gun."
> —Samson Posey

The Johnson-Heller script also tossed out Reisman's conflicted Jewish–Roman Catholic upbringing, not to mention the past criminal act that tormented him and made him feel close to the men he trained (as a sixteen-year-old he had killed a Chicago mobster in self-defense). Although most of the actual names for the Dirty Dozen were retained, they were not always attached to the same characters from the book. Samson Posey, whose Indian background was frequently emphasized in the novel, now became a hulking white man with a suggestion of Native American blood in the person of taciturn Clint Walker. The one black character, Napoleon White, had his justified hatred for the white race, not to mention his superior intelligence in comparison to the other prisoners, toned down considerably for the film, and his name was changed to Robert Jefferson. (The great idea of having him shoot the most bigoted of the prisoners, Maggott, unbeknownst to the others, during the attack was thought up for the movie.) Victor Franko remained a volatile hothead for the movie, but even he was softened; his constant desire to murder Reisman and his eventual death during the mission at the hands of Sergeant Bowren, who prevents the con from killing the captain, were eliminated to make him a team player during the big siege. Wladislaw's character was built up for the film in order to accommodate the casting of Charles Bronson.

Twenty-two years after the end of World War II, having an ad inform audiences that their heroes were going to kick Nazi butt was still an incentive to get them to buy tickets, as was the case with *The Dirty Dozen*.

And there were two new names, Milo Vladek and Tassos Bravos, given to two of the more underdeveloped characters to compensate for the dropping of the novel's religious fanatic Calvin Smith and unhinged introvert Myron Odell. Nathanson had given Smith perhaps the most developed story line of the Dozen, detailing his unhappy upbringing, his own uncertainty about his manhood, the fatal incident that led to his death sentence, and his escape from Glasgow after being brought there by Reisman in order to relive the crime he believed he did not commit. The omission of this character was an unfortunate choice, though his inclusion might well have thrown the ensemble feel of the picture off track. Finally, the screenplay called for Reisman and his aide, Sgt. Bowren, to survive, with all but one of the Dozen (Wladislaw) killed off, whereas the body count in the novel was more complicated: Bowren was the sole accounted-for survivor; Odell, Lever, Smith, Gilpin, and Victor were the confirmed casualties; and Reisman, Posey, Maggott, Jiminez, White (Jefferson), Sawyer, Wladislaw, Pinkley, and Maggott were reported missing in action.

Inasmuch as the original story took place mostly in England, MGM saw fit to have all of *The Dirty Dozen* shot there. The production rolled on April 25, 1966, with sixteen weeks of filming anticipated at a budget of $4 million. The Ashbridge Management College near the village of Little Goddesden, Hertfordshire, was chosen to stand in for the imposing Marston-Tyne Prison from which Reisman chooses his team. The nearby village of Aldbury was used for scenes involving the military maneuvers, during which the Dozen pull a surprise attack on Colonel Breed; and the Hendon Aerodrome became Breed's paratrooper training base. Further shooting took place at Beechwood Park School in Markyate, and interiors were done at MGM's Borehamwood Studios. On the back lot, the movie's most spectacular set was built from scratch: W. E. Hutchinson designed a 2,400-foot-long, 50-foot-high French château that needed to be bombarded and ultimately dynamited by the attack force for the fiery climax. The film dragged on well beyond its allotted shooting time and finally wrapped in the fall of 1966, the cost having reached close to $5 million.

MGM had no qualms about the time and money spent because it was certain it had a hit on its hands, trumpeting *The Dirty Dozen* as its big summer attraction of 1967. What it was not expecting was the outcry from certain members of the press over the level of violence, which seemed to get too out of hand even for a war movie. The unrelenting executions of the German generals and their party guests (trapped in a basement while hand grenades are dropped into their airshafts) were served up in so ugly a manner that the more squeamish critics started feeling sorry for the Nazis. Audiences felt otherwise. *Dozen* had a terrific premise that it really made the most of, offering the requisite macho high jinks and gunplay while building up to a superbly executed, action-laden set piece (even if the editing team was so eager to keep things moving that they didn't bother to include Clint Walker's death scene in the final cut, leaving it to the subsequent death roll to verify his demise). Moviegoers were lining up to see the picture from the word go, and it was doubtful a better visceral thrill could be found in theaters that summer. *The Dirty Dozen* became the highest-grossing movie of its genre to be released during the 1960s, passing even the blockbuster *The Longest Day* (Twentieth Century-Fox, 1962).

THE WHISPERERS (United Kingdom)

Academy Award Nominee: Actress (Edith Evans)

Opening date: July 31, 1967 (London: August 24, 1967).

Lopert Pictures (United Artists). A Seven Pines Production.

Director-Screenplay: Bryan Forbes. Based on the 1961 novel by Robert Nicolson. Producers: Michael S. Laughlin, Ronald Shedlo. Photography: Gerry Turpin. Art Director: Ray Simm. Set Decorator: Peter James. Costumes: Julie Harris. Music: John Barry. Editor: Anthony Harvey. Black and white. 106 minutes.

CAST: Edith Evans (Margaret Ross), Eric Portman (Archie Ross), Nanette Newman (Girl Upstairs), Ronald Fraser (Charlie Ross), Avis Bunnage (Mrs. Noonan), Gerald Sim (Mr. Conrad), Robin Bailey (Psychiatrist), Kenneth Griffith (Mr. Weaver), Leonard Rossiter (Assistance Board Officer), Harry Baird (Man Upstairs), Margaret Tyzack (Hospital Almoner), Clare Kelly (Prostitute), Michael Robbins (Mr. Noonan), Max Bacon (Mr. Fish), Jack Austin (Police Sergeant), Lionel Gamlin (Mr. Conrad's Colleague), George Spence (Caretaker), Penny Spencer (Mavis Noonan), Kaplan Kaye (Jimmie Noonan), Robert Russell (Andy).

PLOT: Margaret Ross, a lonely senior citizen living in a dingy flat, finds her uneventful life interrupted by the sudden reappearance of her criminal son and her deadbeat estranged husband, both of whom cause the old woman their share of problems.

If the working-class dramas that made up the bulk of the British New Wave cinema were simply too grim, too uncompromising in their unsentimental view of life's hardships for some viewers, then Bryan Forbes's adaptation of Robert Nicolson's sad little novel *The Whisperers* took this bleakness to a whole new level. From its opening montage capturing the desolate urban blight of a nameless Northern England city to its surprisingly downbeat conclusion, this was one movie that could not be accused of sidestepping the seriousness of its subject: the neglect of the elderly. Forbes had been intrigued by the challenge of dramatizing this very touchy and uncommercial topic from the time his wife, Nanette Newman, told him about how, as a struggling actress, she had lived in the same apartment building as an old woman whose eventual death had gone unnoticed for several days, simply because there was no one who cared enough to keep track of her day to day. It was a pair of aspiring American producers, Michael S. Laughlin and Ronald Shedlo, who brought Nicolson's book to Forbes's attention, contacting him about the possibility of adapting it into a film that would serve as their maiden venture into the world of moviemaking. Once Forbes read the book, he was hooked and thought immediately of Dame Edith Evans in the role of the nearly senile Mrs. Ross. That somebody was hoping to build an entire film around the esteemed actress at the age of seventy-eight was inconceivable and undeniably flattering.

> "You poor old bitch. You're on your own again."
> —Archie Ross

Forbes sat down to write his screenplay and found that Nicolson had made his story so easily adaptable, with brief chapters that kept the story moving almost cinematically, that he had the whole script written in two weeks' time. Forbes had taken nearly every description and line of dialogue and simply transposed it onto the screen. His changes or omissions were minimal at best, and his script missed only the following scenes from the book: Mr. Conrad returning the one-pound note Mrs. Ross has mailed to him, explaining that it is against the policy of the Assistance Board to accept charity; Mrs. Noonan arguing with an N.A.B. employee prior to taking Mrs. Ross home to rob her; and Archie Ross faking a stutter to ensure that he will not be offered a job at a cinema. Mrs. Noonan's young wastrel boys

were upped in age and turned into a brother and sister, and it became the Girl and Man Upstairs who were now responsible for getting the sickly Mrs. Ross to the hospital after they found her passed out in the alley where the Noonans had dumped her. In the novel it was Mr. Conrad's concern for the old woman that brought the police to break down the door of her flat and find her near death, lying in her own bed. Certainly the image of the frail old lady slumped in the grubby back alley as if tossed out with the garbage was more powerful and cinematically more interesting. Beyond these adjustments, this was certainly one of the most faithful translations of a novel to the big screen.

Typing a dedication page to Edith Evans at the front of the screenplay, Forbes sent it off to the legendary actress and received a response within twenty-four hours. Evans simply adored the character and had no trouble relating to the theme of loneliness: she had lived alone since losing her husband back in 1935, more than thirty years ago. Having secured the services of England's most esteemed senior thespian, Forbes presented the idea to United Artists, which, surprisingly, was keen on banking the project. There were a few stipulations, one being that the novel's original Glasgow setting had

London's once-popular entertainment guide *What's On in London* gave its cover over to Edith Evans in her starring role in *The Whisperers*.

to go—a movie loaded with Scottish accents would be too hard to sell. So Forbes was obliged to relocate the whole thing to England's North Country. The studio also asked that the budget be kept on the exceedingly low side, offering only $400,000 to cover the entire cost. *The Whisperers* began filming at Pinewood Studios on May 9, 1966, before moving to the Moss Side area of Manchester for exteriors. This proved to be the perfect, hideously ugly backdrop for the story, since several buildings in the area had recently been flattened in preparation for a series of high-rise tenements.

The Whisperers was almost relentless in driving home the point that old age was not something to march into alone, especially in a dire financial state. There were no hopeful endings, no loving family reunions or scenes of forgiveness and understanding. Mr. and Mrs. Ross were even unhappier together than they had been apart, suggesting that perhaps a numbing daily routine adding up to next to nothing and an overwhelming paranoia that there were voices whispering in your walls was preferable to spending one's life with a loveless, lying lout whose every breath smacked of insincerity. Evans dropped all the imperial *grande dame* vocal intonations for which she was famous and really tossed herself into the part, suggesting with frightening conviction a lady only half aware of her surroundings. No doubt many viewers assumed this was not acting at all but an almost cruel cinema verité glimpse into the actual state of mind of a great actress in her declining years—Evans was that effective in the role. Being perhaps the most depressing movie ever made about the plight of the elderly was not going to win *The Whisperers* a huge following, but Evans did find herself nominated for an Oscar in the leading category. At the time she was the oldest nominee ever.

This souvenir booklet was included with RCA's best-selling soundtrack for Rodgers and Hammerstein's *The Sound of Music* which, surprisingly, only stayed in the number 1 spot on the *Billboard* charts for two weeks despite the movie's unparalleled success.

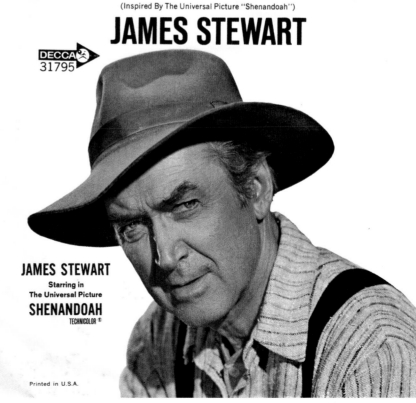

A most unusual tie-in to Universal's Civil War saga *Shenandoah* was star James Stewart's spoken-word recording "The Legend of Shenandoah," released on Decca Records as a 45.

The cover of Dell's adaptation of *The Great Race* emphasizes the comic-book nature of the film by giving its two leading men, Tony Curtis and Jack Lemmon, the format's traditional "speech bubbles" with which to converse.

stereo WHAT'S NEW PUSSYCAT?

ORIGINAL MOTION PICTURE SCORE

WHAT'S NEW PUSSYCAT?

MUSIC BY BURT BACHARACH

UNITED ARTISTS RECORDS
© UAR, Inc.

FEATURING

TOM JONES singing "WHAT'S NEW PUSSYCAT?"

MANFRED MANN singing "MY LITTLE RED BOOK"

DIONNE WARWICK singing "HERE I AM"

LYRICS · HAL DAVID

The United Artists soundtrack for *What's New Pussycat* captures the film's strongest asset, Burt Bacharach's bouncy score. The LP would reach number 14 on the *Billboard* charts, while Tom Jones's unforgettable rendition of the title song would hit the number 3 spot and become one of the defining pop tunes of the decade.

Owing to contractual ties elsewhere, Bobby Darin's recording of the title song was *not* heard on the Buena Vista soundtrack of *That Darn Cat!*, but was replaced by versions performed by both Louis Prima and Bobby Troup & Trio.

The United Artists soundtrack of Johnny Mandel's score for *The Russians Are Coming The Russians Are Coming* includes Peggy Lee's lyrics for the song "The Shining Sea," as sung by Irene Kral, though it was excluded from the release print of the film.

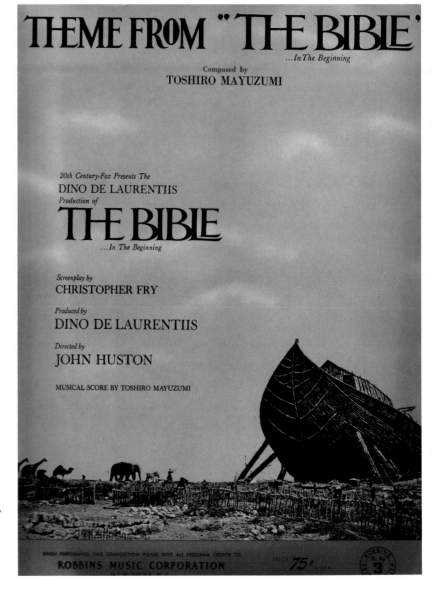

Produced by an Italian, directed by an American, and written by an Englishman, *The Bible* further extended its world reach by hiring a Japanese composer to write the music, as seen in the sheet music for Toshiro Mayuzumi's theme.

The soundtrack for *The Sand Pebbles* on the Twentieth Century-Fox Records label featured a score by Jerry Goldsmith, who would earn the third of his eighteen Oscar nominations for his efforts.

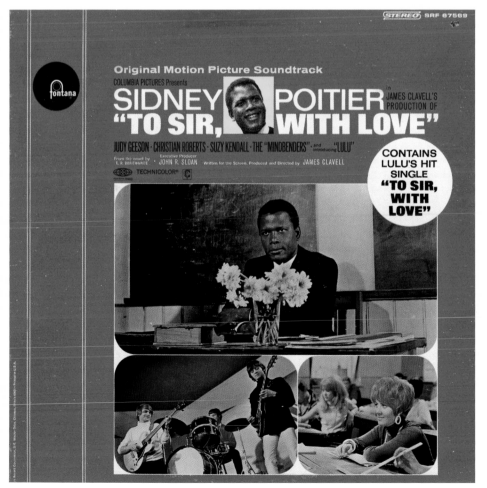

The Fontana Records soundtrack for *To Sir, with Love* gave no credit on the front cover to Ron Grainer's instrumental scoring but certainly made mention of the real reason everybody was purchasing the LP: Lulu's memorable rendition of the title track.

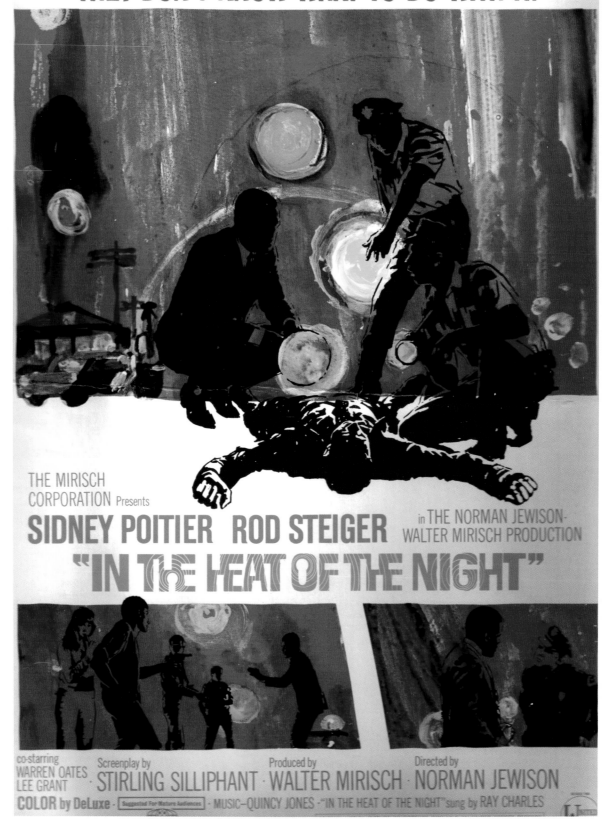

United Artists' striking artwork for the year's Best Picture Oscar winner, *In the Heat of the Night*.

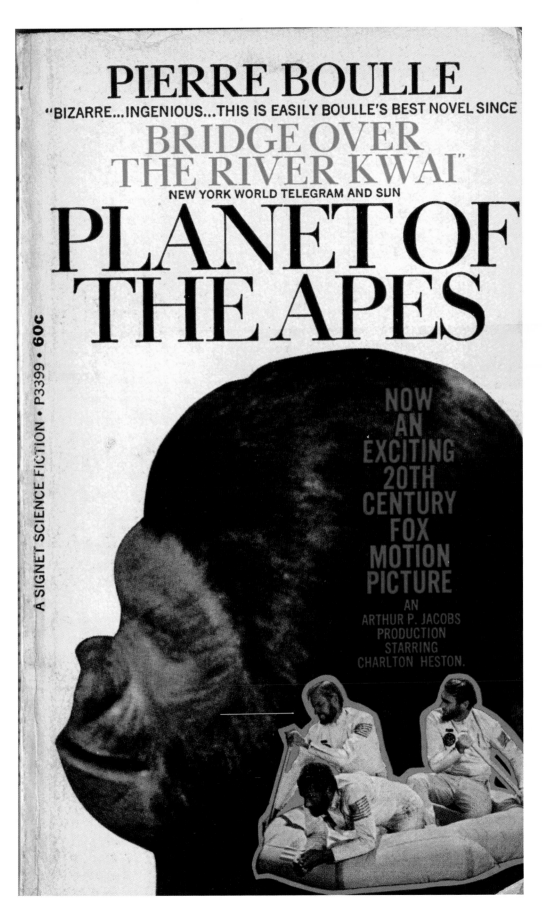

Signet's science-fiction branch issued this tie-in paperback of Pierre Boulle's *Planet of the Apes* and made sure to mention the author's connection to one of the great motion-picture hits of the previous decade, *The Bridge on the River Kwai.*

The MGM Records soundtrack of *2001: A Space Odyssey* made a whole generation of moviegoers think of Johann Strauss's "Blue Danube" waltz and Richard Strauss's *Also sprach Zarathustra* in a way they had never done before.

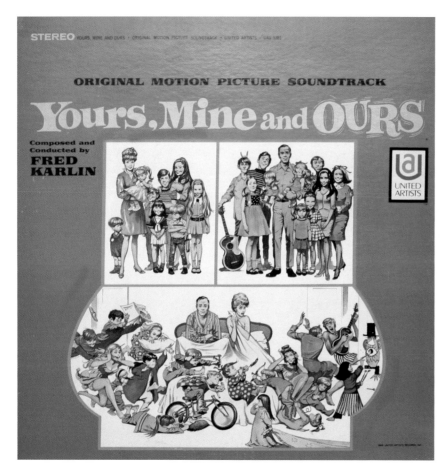

The cover of the United Artists Records soundtrack for *Yours, Mine and Ours* demonstrates how to add two families together for maximum box-office results.

A simple but effective image adorns the cover of the *War and Peace* souvenir booklet, sold during the film's reserved-seat, two-part engagement.

The Scholastic paperback movie tie-in edition of the original play script for Neil Simon's *The Odd Couple* features images of its stars, Jack Lemmon and Walter Matthau, that perfectly capture their contrasting personalities.

Although Lionel Bart's splendid songs for *Oliver!* hardly received stellar treatment, in terms of the audio on this hastily processed Colgems recording, their presentation in the film itself could not be faulted.

Who better to provide the narration of a children's tie-in record for *The Love Bug* than one of its stars, Buddy Hackett, who always seemed ideally suited to the Disney Studio despite his naughty nightclub persona.

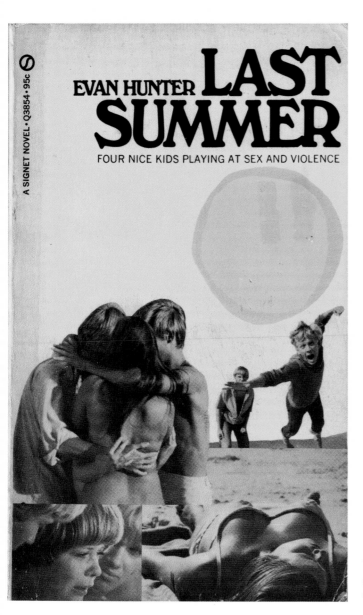

The Signet paperback of Evan Hunter's *Last Summer* includes some intriguing images of its youthful cast that helped sell the film as something highly provocative.

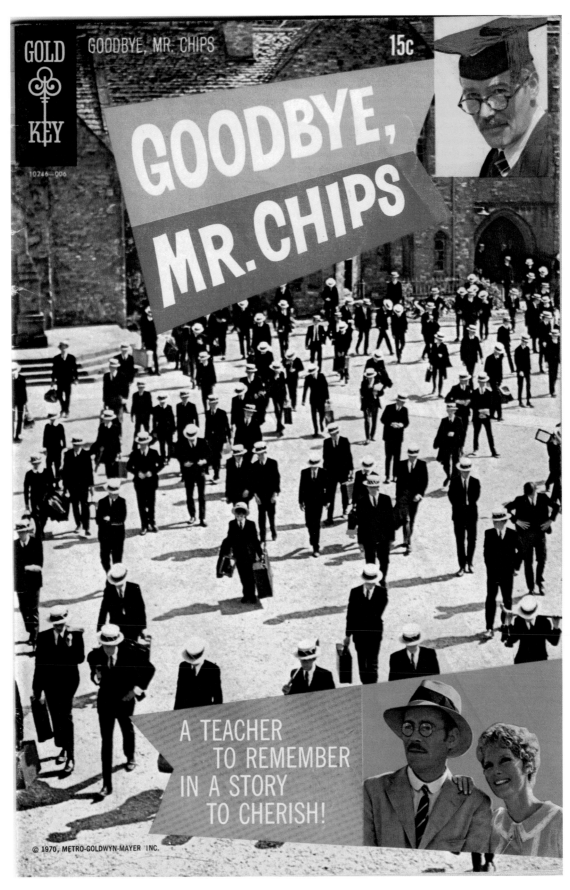

No doubt stumped on how to make the musical version of *Goodbye, Mr. Chips* interesting to comic book readers, the writers of this Gold Key adaptation included a subplot about a misplaced school bell.

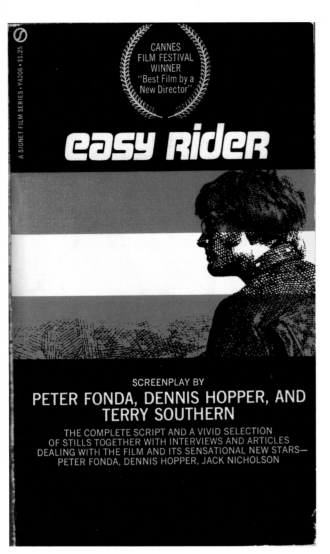

Documenting every camera angle and every "man" uttered by star Dennis Hopper is the Signet screenplay for *Easy Rider*, as written by Hopper, costar Peter Fonda, and Terry Southern.

The soundtrack album of Quincy Jones's score for *Cactus Flower* is adorned with images of Ingrid Bergman and Walter Matthau for the traditionalists and Goldie Hawn in a very mod pantsuit to let younger audiences know that this old-fashioned farce has its hip side as well.

The Twentieth Century-Fox Records soundtrack for *Hello, Dolly!* was a rare Barbra Streisand album *not* on the Columbia Records label, and what is more curious—even though the rendering of the Jerry Herman score is terrific—is that it was one of her few LPs not to chart in the top 40.

This very cheeky image of a shaggier-than-usual Steve McQueen was all *The Reivers* needed to sell this pleasant comedy-drama.

IN THE HEAT OF THE NIGHT

Academy Award Winner: Best Picture; Best Actor (Rod Steiger); Best Screenplay—Based on Material from Another Medium; Best Sound; Best Film Editing

Academy Award Nominee: Director; Sound Effects

Opening date: August 2, 1967.

United Artists. A Mirisch Corporation Presentation of a Norman Jewison–Walter Mirisch Production.

Director: Norman Jewison. Producer: Walter Mirisch. Screenplay: Stirling Silliphant. Based on the 1965 novel by John Ball. Photography: Haskell Wexler. Art Director: Paul Groesse. Set Decorator: Robert Priestley. Men's Costumer: Alan Levine. Film Editor–Assistant to the Producer: Hal Ashby. Music: Quincy Jones. Songs by Quincy Jones (music) and Alan and Marilyn Bergman (lyrics): "In the Heat of the Night," performed by Ray Charles and the Ray Charles Singers; "It Sure Is Groovy," performed by Gil Bernal; "Bowlegged Polly," performed by Glen Campbell; "Foul Owl," performed by Boomer & Travis. Deluxe color. 109 minutes.

CAST: Sidney Poitier (Virgil Tibbs), Rod Steiger (Police Chief Bill Gillespie), Warren Oates (Deputy Sam Wood), Lee Grant (Mrs. Leslie Colbert), James Patterson (Purdy), Quentin Dean (Delores Purdy), Larry Gates (Eric Endicott), William Schallert (Mayor Webb Schubert), Beah Richards (Mama Caleba, aka Mrs. Bellamy), Scott Wilson (Harvey Oberst), Jack Teter (Philip Colbert), Matt Clark (Packy Harrison), Anthony James (Ralph Henshaw), Kermit Murdock (H. E. Henderson), Khalil Bezaleel (Jess), Peter Whitney (George Courtney), William C. Watson (Harold Courtney), Timothy Scott (Shagbag Martin), Michael LeGlaire, Larry D. Mann, Stewart Nisbet (City Council), Eldon Quick (Charlie Hawthorne), Fred Stewart (Dr. Stuart), Arthur Malet (Ted Ulam, Mortician), Peter Masterson (Arnold Fryer), Alan Oppenheimer (Ted Appleton), Philip Garris (Engineer), Jester Hairston (Henry, Endicott's Butler), Clegg Hoyt (Deputy).

PLOT: Passing through the sleepy town of Sparta, Mississippi, Virgil Tibbs, a black police officer from the North, reluctantly agrees to help bigoted police chief Bill Gillespie find out who murdered a prominent businessman.

Apparently, where Hollywood was concerned it was up to Sidney Poitier and him alone to pretty much carry the weight of the civil rights movement on his shoulders. The film industry had been doing its part to condemn racism against the black population as far back as the late 1940s, before Poitier had even made his first picture (Fox's 1950 release *No Way Out*), but once it had found a star of his magnetism, talent, good looks, and box-office appeal, any film that brought up the subject of prejudice and the black population's fight for acceptance was his for the asking. By the late 1960s his résumé was already full of worthwhile projects, including some, like *Lilies of the Field* (United Artists, 1963) and *To Sir, with Love* (Columbia, 1967), where the color of his skin was irrelevant to the drama at hand. Now *that* was progress. However, this approach (looking past an issue rather than confronting it) also offered a safety net of sorts for the nervous movie industry, which loved Poitier but worried about how far it could allow him (and other performers of his race) to advance and how honestly it wanted to show just how steeped in inequality and internalized hatred the country was during this turbulent decade. If Poitier was looking for that final word on the subject, the one that would indicate that the African

American population not only was around to be accepted as equals but could also show themselves to be superior to many a white man, then he got it with *In the Heat of the Night*, which proved to be the crowning achievement of his illustrious career.

It was independent film producer Walter Mirisch who first happened upon John Ball's book, which had earned the author an Edgar Award as the Outstanding Mystery Novel of 1965. Ball had taken what might have been a conventional whodunit and cleverly commented on prejudice, having a quick-think-ing black police officer from Pasadena, California, get involved with a murder that had taken place in a hostile hotbed of racism somewhere in the Deep South. Mirisch hired writer Stirling Silliphant to adapt the book so the producer would have a solid script to show whichever director he hoped to attach to this potentially touchy project. Mirisch presented the screenplay to Norman Jewison, who had just helmed a very successful comedy/message picture for the producer, *The Russians Are Coming The Russians Are Coming* (United Artists, 1966), and he jumped at the chance of making his cinematic statement on a cause very dear to him. There was no doubt in anyone's mind that the character of Virgil Tibbs had Poitier's name written all over it, and he accepted the role without hesitation. The first actor considered for the part of Police Chief Gillespie was George C. Scott, but Jenkins finally settled on Rod Steiger, hot off a pair of 1965's major releases, *The Pawnbroker* (Landau) and

> "Because you're so damn smart. You're smarter than any white man. You're just gonna stay here and show us all. You got such a big head that you could never live with yourself unless you could put us all to shame. You wanna know something, Virgil? I don't think that you could let an opportunity like that pass by."
> —Bill Gillespie

Doctor Zhivago (MGM). Silliphant had already made some major alterations in his adaptation, and once Jewison and his cast were assembled, even more revisions, additions, and cuts were made, eliminating the somewhat pulpy, often superficial tone of Ball's book and fashioning a more subtle and potent work. This was one instance in which Hollywood took a literary property and improved it in every way.

Aside from clearly designating where the action was taking place (Mississippi), the first thing that was strengthened in the script was the background of the murder victim. In the book he had been an Italian orchestra conductor named Mantoli who had come to the sleepy town of Wells in order to establish a music festival. In a brilliant stroke, the film changed him to an industrialist whose intention of build-ing a factory in the economically strapped town is brought to a halt by his senseless death. The need for industry rather than high culture played more believably in light of the unsophisticated nature of the citizens. Tibbs's base of operations was now Philadelphia, an urban center with a large black population, rather than Pasadena, which would have indicated that he had escaped to the more liberal shores of Southern California rather than establishing himself in the freethinking cities of the North. The mae-stro's daughter was disposed of in favor of a grieving widow, which gave Lee Grant a terrific opportunity to emote as an open-minded Northerner appalled by the racial insensitivities around her. This also meant that the somewhat hokey romance between the victim's daughter and Deputy Sam was discarded, keeping the focus on the mystery and on the tension between Tibbs and Gillespie. In a prime example of Hollywood's being braver than its source novel, sluttish Delores Purdy's age was lowered to sixteen in order to bring up the issue of statutory rape, whereas she had been lying about her years in the novel (she was actually eighteen when she became pregnant). Purdy's guardian became her ignorant brother (not her pigheaded father), and the climax was strengthened to include a character who had not appeared in the book, Mama Caleba, an illegal abortionist who holds the name of the murderer. Two additions to the script Jewison credited to Poitier. A scene in which Tibbs is taunted by tailgating rednecks who bump his car from behind was based on a real-life experience that Poitier and fellow entertainer Harry Belafonte had had earlier in the decade when campaigning for civil rights in Mississippi. The other addition was more monumental and gave the film its greatest single moment.

In the Ball novel, the character of wealthy businessman Endicott was a somewhat peripheral one; he played host to the maestro's daughter at his mansion and cooperated fully with Tibbs and his investigation, showing none of the pent-up hostility toward the detective that most of the townspeople do. But in the film, Endicott became a chief suspect because he was seen as a rival for the victim's industrial plans,

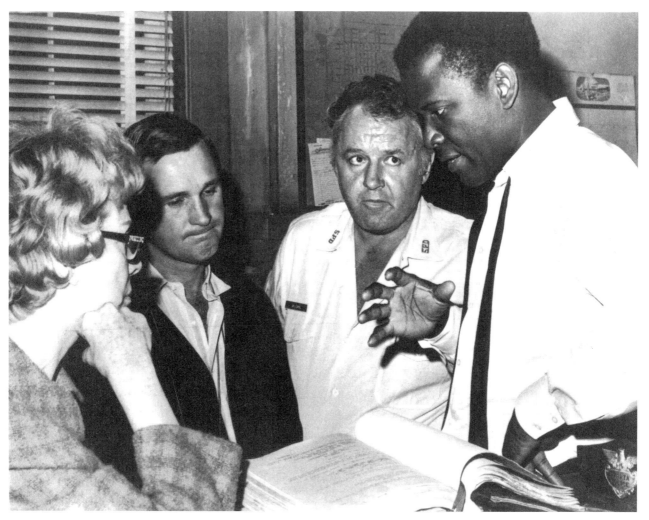

Rod Steiger seems to stay in character as a skeptical Southern sheriff, as he watches costar Sidney Poitier discuss the *In the Heat of the Night* script with director Norman Jewison.

and his position as Sparta's most influential and powerful citizen was emphasized by his arrogance and sense of entitlement. But most significant, the film's Endicott was an unapologetic racist, even more dangerous than the white-trash townies in his insistence on adhering to antiquated traditions and class distinctions based on color. Therefore, the pivotal scene in the picture became Poitier's confrontation with the millionaire (as played by Larry Gates) in his greenhouse. Gillespie tags along in order to put Endicott at ease, and Endicott's black servant hovers in the background, presenting a subtle contrast between his servility and Tibbs's authority. Endicott feels fully justified in slapping the black police officer for having the audacity to suggest that a man in his position should be questioned by someone he considers an inferior, so he is mortified and enraged when Tibbs instinctively strikes him right back in retaliation for the lack of respect the white man has shown *him*. This was plainly and simply Poitier's most powerful and physical cinematic comment on the whole race issue. Putting behind all the polite and accommodating characteristics he had previously displayed as a man eager not to rock the boat but to merely fit in or be accepted on the basis of his capabilities rather than his color, this was an outburst of rage that spoke volumes. With this single gesture the message was made clear: the imbalance would no longer be accepted, past prejudices would have to be laid to rest, and violence just might be answered with violence. The scene was superbly enhanced by the mix of stunned disbelief and subtle hint of admiration registered on Steiger's face and the tears of humiliation that Gates sheds once the others have left the room. This was without a doubt one of the towering motion-picture moments of the decade.

It was just such moments that made the Mirisch Corporation hesitant to spend too much money on something that was a risk in terms of bringing in substantial audiences, since the film clearly took no prisoners when it came to condemning the South specifically. The Mirisches gave Jewison a budget that capped off at $2.6 million. At Poitier's instance, Jewison looked for a place to film that was *above* the Mason-Dixon line: the star believed that the incendiary subject matter could expose the cast and crew to danger. Therefore, a very sleepy town in southern Illinois by the name of Sparta was chosen. It was close enough to the Mississippi River that the crew could film scenes of Scott Wilson's attempted escape by and over the fabled river, remaining somewhat true to the intended locale. In order to save themselves the trouble of changing signs, the name of the story's setting became Sparta. This was the biggest thing to ever happen to this town, and the citizens were only too happy to accommodate the folks from Hollywood, who filmed most of the exteriors there or nearby during the fall of 1966, starting on September 19.

But it was the build-up to the aforementioned Endicott scene that posed a problem as far as location was concerned. Silliphant's script called for Endicott to rule over a cotton plantation, which meant Jewison needed to capture the real thing: Tibbs and Gillespie were supposed to drive their vehicle among the black sharecroppers, who represented a shameful and backward step in Tibbs's eyes. A suitable field was found in Dyersburg, in western Tennessee, and Poitier reluctantly agreed to journey there for a few days in order to get this telling moment preserved onscreen. Once the bulk of the picture was finished shooting in these far-off places, the production headed west to Hollywood, where some interior sets, including the police station, were built on the soundstages of the Samuel Goldwyn Studio.

In the Heat of the Night succeeded in pulling viewers into its mystery while never missing an opportunity to shade a scene with an underlying gesture or passing comment that suggested Virgil's efforts to see justice done were nearly thwarted at every turn by stupidity and bigotry. The pacing, writing, directing, and almost uniformly superb acting never banged home the point too blatantly or stridently, which was why the picture continued to play so well as progress was made in subsequent decades. There is no doubt that many viewers found themselves coming around, slowly, some resistant, much in the manner of Steiger's character, until they had to concede, if only to themselves, that a black character was clearly the hero, the levelheaded voice of reason, the protagonist to root for, the man to admire. *In the Heat* became one of the runaway hits of the season.

By the time the Oscar nominations were announced in the winter of 1968, Jewison's picture had become somewhat overshadowed by the tremendous public and critical response to a pair of films that would become perhaps the two most seminal motion pictures of their era, *Bonnie and Clyde* (Warner Bros.) and *The Graduate* (AVCO Embassy). *In the Heat of the Night* found itself competing with these movies, which seemed to bode none too well for its chances at capturing the top prize. What's more, somehow Poitier had been left out of the running, Steiger being the only cast member to get a nomination. When the awards were handed out on April 10, 1968, *In the Heat*'s overall excellence won out, and the Mirisch Corporation was thrilled to receive its third Best Picture Oscar that decade (following *The Apartment* and *West Side Story*). As *Bonnie and Clyde* and *The Graduate* continued to rise in stature over the years, many were predisposed to come down hard on the film that had "robbed" them of their Academy accolade, only to find out just how marvelous the victor truly was.

BONNIE AND CLYDE

Academy Award Winner: Best Supporting Actress (Estelle Parsons); Best Cinematography

Academy Award Nominee: Picture; Actor (Warren Beatty); Actress (Faye Dunaway); Supporting Actor (Gene Hackman); Supporting Actor (Michael J. Pollard); Director; Story and Screenplay— Written Directly for the Screen; Costume Design

Top 10 Box Office Film

Opening date: August 13, 1967.

Warner Bros.–Seven Arts. Tatira-Hiller Productions.

Director: Arthur Penn. Producer: Warren Beatty. Screenplay: David Newman, Robert Benton. Photography: Burnett Guffey. Art Director: Dean Tavoularis. Set Decorator: Raymond Paul. Music: Charles Strouse. Additional Music: "Deep Night," by Charlie Henderson and Rudy Vallee, performed by Rudy Vallee; "Foggy Mountain Breakdown," by Earl Scruggs, performed by Lester Flatt and Earl Scruggs; "We're In the Money," by Harry Warren and Al Dubin, performed by the film chorus, reprised by Faye Dunaway. Editor: Dede Allen. Technicolor. 111 minutes.

CAST: Warren Beatty (Clyde Barrow), Faye Dunaway (Bonnie Parker), Gene Hackman (Buck Barrow), Michael J. Pollard (C. W. Moss), Estelle Parsons (Blanche Barrow), Denver Pyle (Frank Hamer), Gene Wilder (Eugene Grizzard), Evans Evans (Velma Davis), Dub Taylor (Malcolm Moss), Clyde Howdy (Deputy), Garry Goodgion (Billy), Ken Mayer (Sheriff Smoot), Ernest Edgar Parker (Farmer at House), Roy Heard (Man at House), Martha Adcock, Sadie French (Bank Customers), James Stiver (Butcher), Mark Jackman III (Okie Boy), Raymond Schacherl, Jack E. Garrett (Okie Men), Patricia Garrett (Okie Woman), Ada Waugh, Frances Fisher (Bonnie's Aunts), Ann Palmer (Bonnie's Sister), Harry Appling (Bonnie's Uncle), Mabel Cavitt (Bonnie's Mother), J. J. Lemmon Jr. (Sheriff).

PLOT: During the Depression Bonnie Parker joins Clyde Barrow in pulling off a series of bank robberies that turn them into notorious criminals to some and symbols of rebellion to the downtrodden.

By the mid-1960s Warren Beatty realized he needed to seriously reassess his Hollywood career. He had started off on a high note, landing the lead in one of the major dramas of 1961, *Splendor in the Grass* (Warner Bros.), but had followed this star-making debut with a series of miscalculations, including his feeble Italian gigolo impression in *The Roman Spring of Mrs. Stone*, the pretentious *Mickey One* (Columbia, 1965), and the moronic sex comedy *Promise Her Anything* (Paramount, 1966). To most moviegoers he was better known at this point for his fan-magazine persona as a handsome lothario with a knack for dating some of the movie industry's best-known and best-looking women. Beatty wanted to be taken seriously and believed that he had found just the right property to establish him as an industry figure to be reckoned with.

David Newman and Robert Benton, *Esquire* writers eager to break into the movie industry, had written a script treatment about real-life Depression-era criminals Bonnie Parker and Clyde Barrow that they hoped François Truffaut would direct. Truffaut was not available, but the script made its way to

Beatty, who fell in love with the novice writers' work and tracked them down. He purchased the rights for $10,000 and became determined to see the picture made, initially intending to serve expressly as producer. After several other rejections, Beatty contacted his *Mickey One* director, Arthur Penn (who had already passed on the property previously), and managed to convince the skeptical filmmaker that they could create something special out of this project, which Beatty had finally decided he would star in as well as produce. He went to the company that had launched him in the first place, Warner Bros., and wound up talking Jack L. Warner into putting up the $1.8 million budget, though the veteran studio boss was not a fan of Beatty's, nor did he have a great deal of faith in something he considered just another "gangster picture." Beatty managed to negotiate a deal in which he would receive a $200,000 fee up front (as actor and producer) and 40 percent of the profits under his company's banner, Tatira (a composite of his parents' names).

> "One time I told ya I was gonna make you somebody. That's what you done for me— you made me somebody they're gonna remember."
> —Clyde Barrow

Since Hollywood had never been known to adhere to total accuracy, nobody seemed too concerned that there were plenty of factual errors in the screenplay. Bonnie Parker (born 1910) had first met Clyde Barrow (born 1909) in 1930, after which he was sent to prison, escaped, and rejailed. The two met up again in 1932. The script condensed the time period by having them first make contact in 1931, with no mention made of Bonnie's having already been wed and divorced by that point. Shortly after Barrow's return from jail, Bonnie herself was arrested and spent three months behind bars, but the film gave no impression that she had ever served any time. Rather than complicate the picture with too many extraneous characters, the writers created a composite, C. W. Moss, of two Barrow gang members, William Daniel "W. C." Jones and Henry Methvin. The climax had Bonnie and Clyde caught unawares in the middle of an ambush, when in truth they were armed and prepared to fight back when they were mowed down along the highway near Gibsland, Louisiana, on May 23, 1934. The original draft had brought attention to Barrow's indecisive sexuality by having the Moss character be a football player who bedded both Bonnie and Clyde. Penn and Beatty both believed this was too complex for audiences to handle, not to mention unconvincingly developed, and insisted that it be dropped in favor of giving Clyde a problem with impotency instead. Although less than a decade had passed, the filmmakers were hoping that few people remembered *The Bonnie Parker Story* (American International Pictures, 1958), a poorly conceived cheapie starring Dorothy Provine in the title role and Jack Hogan as "Guy Darrow," a name change necessitated by legal issues.

Although Jack Warner had wanted the movie to be done on the back lot, Penn and Beatty were insistent on filming in Texas, where the Barrow bunch hailed from and where they had spent most of their time. The interiors were shot in Dallas, while the company went on location to such small towns as Midlothian, where Bonnie and Clyde first meet as he's attempting to steal her family car; Ponder, site of the bank that Clyde cannot rob because business has failed; Pilot Point, at the Farmer and Merchants Bank Building in the town square, where Clyde refuses to rob the poor farmer of his own money; Waxahachie, where C. W. Moss leaves his filling station behind for a life of crime; Red Oak, where Moss's insistence on parking the getaway car leads to the shooting of a bank employee; and the Burkhart Farm east of Rowlett, where Bonnie and Clyde meet up with the owner of the foreclosed property while doing some target practice. Shooting began on October 11, 1966 and continued to January 6, 1967, with the movie filmed as much as possible in sequence. Still adamant about doing their project without interference from the unsupportive studio, Penn oversaw the editing in New York rather than Warners' Burbank headquarters. When Beatty finally screened the picture for Jack Warner, the reaction was not encouraging. The veteran studio chief made no secret of the fact that he hated the movie, and he predicted a quick demise in the theaters. He wasn't all that concerned with the future of the company that bore his name; he was selling his share of ownership to the Seven Arts Corporation and would soon be stepping down from his position of power.

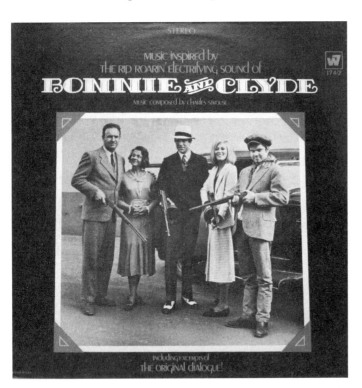

The Warner Bros.–7 Arts soundtrack for *Bonnie and Clyde* was a curious hybrid of original background scoring by Charles Strouse, snatches of dialogue from the film, and a nutty "title song" intended to capture the style of the period.

Even if Jack Warner didn't care much for *Bonnie and Clyde*, the picture had its share of supporters at the studio who felt this was not just box-office material but something fresh and exciting that could win the company critical notice. Things did not bode well when *New York Times* critic Bosley Crowther weighed in with a scathingly bad review, calling the picture smugly irresponsible in its glorification of these hardened criminals and its graphic depiction of violence. Fortunately, this was not the consensus shared by all critics, and when *Newsweek*'s Joe Morgenstern went so far as to retract his earlier bad notice and admit he was wrong, it was clear that something miraculous was happening. What's more, enough moviegoers found value in the film to write to the *Times* and inform the paper that Crowther had missed the boat on this one. Crowther's insistence on the movie's lack of merit began a debate that brought further attention to the film, the best sort of free publicity a movie could ask for. By the time *Bonnie and Clyde* opened in Europe in September, the controversial picture had gotten a considerable amount of advance buzz, and business was brisk. Beatty kept badgering the studio to give his movie more bookings.

There was no mistaking that Warners' had something hot on its hands when *Time* magazine put the film on its cover in December to illustrate a story exploring the exciting new strides the cinema was taking. What had once sneaked into town so quietly was soon taking the country by storm. Some audiences found themselves considerably put off by the unexpectedly dark mix of humor and bloodshed. Others felt that they had witnessed a boldly original piece of filmmaking that offered violence, satire, and social commentary in a way that had never been seen before. Whatever the reaction, people could not easily wipe *Bonnie and Clyde* from their minds.

Just as during the Depression some of the poorer citizens looked upon the real Bonnie and Clyde as folk heroes who thumbed their noses at the capitalists who were wrecking the lives of the oppressed, select '60s audiences found something to champion about these free-spirited outlaws, who were lashing out at authority and creating their own community on their own terms. The very fact that *Bonnie and Clyde* upset as many people as had the actual criminals made the picture very "cool" in the eyes of the young, and it had enough forbidden elements (not only the amount of blood, but the frank sexuality that included barely covered glimpses of a nude Faye Dunaway in its opening scene) that it became the sort of picture that gave a person status to be able to say they had seen it. Penn had dared to establish an unexpectedly comic feel in the early portions of the picture, notably by using Lester Flatt and Earl Scruggs's rollicking 1949 recording of "Foggy Mountain Breakdown" (the piece had inspired Newman when he was writing the script), its plucky, runaway banjo rhythms suggesting a good-time air about robbing banks and shooting guns. Slowly and cleverly the script began to shift tone, sometimes within the same scene, as the inevitable doom of these characters became clearer, notably in what started out as its funniest sequence, in which an engaged couple is kidnapped by the robbers who seduce them with their joie de vivre, only to have a pall fall over the fun when it is revealed that one of their "guests" is an undertaker.

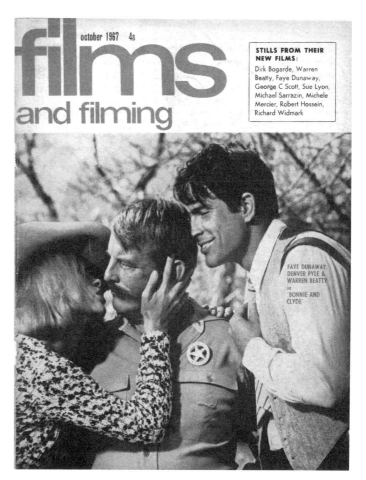

The picture seemed like a sure Oscar hopeful and indeed wound up with ten nominations, tying with *Guess Who's Coming to Dinner* (Columbia) for most nominations received that year. Estelle Parsons and cinematographer Burnett Guffey came away the only winners, but the movie's impact was far from over. Hollywood took the cue that it was okay to be more explicit about violence. There was no doubt that, for better or worse, *Bonnie and Clyde* would be held responsible for upping the ante in this area, letting the floodgates open wide, good taste be

Its growing status as a worldwide phenomenon was reflected in the fact that *Bonnie and Clyde* made the cover of an issue of Britain's *Films and Filming* magazine.

damned. The movie also led to such similar-in-tone gangster pictures as *Bloody Mama* (American International Pictures, 1970) and *Dillinger* (American International Pictures, 1973) though nobody else but Penn ever really got the balance of mordant humor and gunplay right.

Beatty had achieved everything he had hoped to with this movie and more. He became an iconic figure in Hollywood, one with an eye for both prestige and financial smarts when it came to producing pictures. Penn, who had previously proven himself a fine director with the excellent job he did transferring *The Miracle Worker* (United Artists, 1962) to screen, was now hailed as one of the auteurs of modern cinema and would be studied and revered for the rest of his career, no matter how ordinary or disappointing the results of his subsequent work.

THE BATTLE OF ALGIERS (Italy–Algeria)

Academy Award Nominee: Foreign Language Film (1966); Director (1968); Story and Screenplay—Written Directly for the Screen (1968)

Opening date: September 21, 1967 (Rome: September 8, 1966, as *La battaglia di Algeri*; Los Angeles: April 12, 1968).

Rizzoli Films.

Director: Gillo Pontecorvo. Producers: Antonio Musu, Yacef Saadi. Screenplay: Franco Solinas. Original Story: Gillo Pontecorvo, Franco Solinas. Photography: Marcello Gatti. Art Director: Sergio Canevari. Costumes: Giovanni Axerio. Music: Gillo Pontecorvo, Ennio Morricone. Editors: Mario Morra, Mario Serandrei. Special Effects: Aldo Gasparri. Black and white. 122 minutes.

CAST: Jean Martin (Colonel Mathieu), Yacef Saadi (Saari Kader), Brahim Haggiag (Ali La Pointe), Tommaso Neri (Captain Dubois), Fawzia El-Kader (Halima), Samia Kerbash (Fathia), Mohamed Ben Kassen (Petit Omar), Ugo Paletti (Captain), Michele Kerbash (Fathia).

PLOT: The National Liberation Front rallies the people of Algiers to end 130 years of colonial oppression and gain independence from the French, leading to a explosive battle for control of the Casbah.

Gillo Pontecorvo's resume might have been short, but it did contain one motion picture that was spoken of with such enthusiasm by audiences, critics, and fellow directors that it gave him a degree of respect and status that carried him over an otherwise erratic output. His name was often mentioned as one of Italy's greatest of all directors, exclusively on the strengths of *The Battle of Algiers*.

Wanting to make a film about the efforts of the Algerian people to win their independence from French colonialism, Pontecorvo visited Algiers in the early 1960s (prior to its independence) to get a feel for the city and its people. Meanwhile, Yacef Saadi, a participant in the revolution and a member of the National Liberation Front, was anxious to find a director of some note to film the story of the Battle of Algiers with the utmost accuracy and give the world some idea of the hellish nature of what he and his countrymen went through. His small list of directors, all of them Italian, consisted of Francesco Rosi, who was unavailable; Luchino Visconti, who could not come to an agreement on the concept; and Pontecorvo, who was, of course, the perfect choice because of how much time he had already invested in the subject matter. Saadi gave him a rough "script" of how he envisioned the picture, and although neither Pontecorvo nor screenwriter Franco Solinas cared for this novice's amateurish attempts at storytelling, they knew that Saadi had ideas and firsthand information that could point them in the right direction. The more stories he told of the battle, the more the filmmakers became convinced that they wanted to steer as far away from fiction as a fictional film could.

The screenplay for what would become *The Battle of Algiers* began to cover a larger canvas as Pontecorvo came to realize that he wanted to wrap the event not around one or two central characters, but around an ensemble, teaming with people on both sides of the battle lines. Background stories and long explanations of motives or characterizations were dispensed with as the Algerians became a collective force, with individuals brought to life not so much by dialogue as by action and the looks of those chosen to play them. Pontecorvo again returned to the Casbah in Algiers to speak directly to those who had lived through the siege, getting thorough descriptions of guerilla tactics used by the oppressed Algerians and the military strategy and reliance on torture used by the French. Although there was no doubt toward whose side the picture was slanted, Pontecorvo insisted that he was not out to paint the French as one-dimensional villains. Instead, he wanted to show how ugly the brutality and bloodshed was from both directions. He would often state that his film was not anti-French but anticolonial.

> "You know, Ali, it's hard enough to start a revolution, even harder to sustain it, and hardest of all to win it. But it's only afterwards, once we've won, that the real difficulties begin."
> —Ben M'Hidi

Enthusiastic over the project, Saadi persuaded his government to clear the way for Pontecorvo to have complete access to every location necessary in the city of Algiers. After Pontecorvo, Solinas, and their producer, Antonio Musu, put together most of the budget by pooling their own funds, the Algerians agreed to cover the rest of the cost, approximately 45 percent of the total, making *Algiers* an Italian-Algerian coproduction. Inspired by his role model, Roberto Rossellini, and the two films from that director that had been pivotal in establishing the Italian neorealism movement, *Open City* (1945; United States: Mayer-Burstyn, 1946) and *Paisan* (1946; United States: Mayer-Burstyn, 1948), Pontecorvo decided to cast the picture almost entirely with nonprofessionals, making the movie that much more authentic. There was one role, however, that required fairly lengthy speeches explaining the French position, and rather than risk leaving these big scenes to an amateur, Pontecorvo cast the ensemble's sole professional, Jean Martin, as the coolly militaristic French leader Colonel Mathieu.

Pontecorvo was adamant about shooting *The Battle of Algiers* in black and white, knowing full well that it would give the movie an almost newsreel-like sense of urgency, as if he were capturing current events in action. Not wanting the cinematography to look crisp and clear, he and photographer Marcello Gatti came up with the idea of duplicating the positive film that they shot, giving it the grainier feel of a second-generation print. It was a masterstroke that made *Algiers* deliberately crude and often ugly to look at, and the harshness became a part of its power. Although he worked with a relatively small behind-the-scenes crew and often used a handheld camera, the shooting was not rushed. Pontecorvo did a great many rehearsals and takes, although the camera angles and set-ups were often improvised on the spot. All the locations were exactly as they had appeared during the period being covered, 1954–57, with the exception of the two buildings seen being dynamited in the movie: the Casbah house blown up by French terrorists and the apartment where La Pointe and his cronies meet their fate. *Algiers* was filmed between July 25 and December 3, 1965, with a mounting sense of excitement that something very kinetic was being captured for the cameras.

Wanting to launch their movie where it would garner sufficient attention, Pontecorvo and Musu secured it
a spot at the Venice Film Festival of 1966. The favorable
reaction was tremendous. The picture's stark nature, the
exciting feeling of being in the middle of the event, and
the terrifying lack of sentiment in depicting the cruel retaliation used on both sides had people not only talking
with great enthusiasm, but even tossing about words like
"masterpiece" and "groundbreaking." The movie rolled
like a juggernaut through further festivals, picking up one
award after another while opening to the general public in
Italy in September 1966.

When it did finally make its U.S. debut, *Algiers* served
as the opening-night attraction of the New York Film Festival in September 1967. The movie did not lose an iota of
the excitement that had been building over the course of
a year; American critics turning it into one of the most
highly praised pictures, foreign or otherwise, to play in
cinemas during the decade. When word arrived that the
movie had not yet opened in France, where authorities
were intent on banning it as blatant propaganda that unfairly portrayed their countrymen in a negative light, it
made the intelligentsia love it all the more. *The Battle of*

This ad for *The Battle of Algiers* appeared late in
the movie's long run, once the distribution was
taken over by Allied Artists.

Algiers turned up on one ten-best list after another and became essential viewing for anyone interested
in studying filmmaking at it most nakedly raw. Finally, five years after it was first shown in Venice, the
film had its long-delayed premiere in Paris, where it became the target of a much-publicized bomb
threat, further proving that Pontecorvo had touched a nerve.

CLOSELY WATCHED TRAINS (Czechoslovakia)

Academy Award Winner: Best Foreign Language Film

Opening date: October 15, 1967 (Czechoslovakia: November 18, 1966, as *Ostře sledované vlaky*; known in the United Kingdom as *Closely Observed Trains*).

Sigma III. A Carlo Ponti Presentation of a Czechoslovak Films—Bohumil Smída—Ladislav Fikar Production Group Production.

Director: Jiří Menzel. Producer: Zdeněk Oves. Screenplay: Bohumil Hrabal, Jiří Menzel. Based on the 1965 novel by Bohumil Hrabal. Photography: Jaromír Šofr. Art Director: Oldrich Bosák. Sets: Jiří Cvrček. Costumes: Olga Dimitrovová. Music: Jiří Sust. Editor: Jiřina Lukešová. Black and white. 89 minutes.

CAST: Václav Neckář (Miloš Hrma), Josef Somr (Train Dispatcher Ladislav Hubicka), Vladimír Valenta (Max Lanska, the Station Master), Libuše Havelková (Mrs. Lanska, His Wife), Jitka Bendová (Masha), Alois Vachek (Station Assistant Novak), Ferdinand Kruta (Masha's Uncle Noneman), Vlastimil Brodský (Councillor Zedniček), Jiří Menzel (Dr. Brabec), Jitka Zelenohorská (Virginia Svatá, the Telegraphist), Kveta Fialová (Countess), Nada Urbánková (Victoria Freie), Pavla Maršálková (Mother), Milada Jezková (Virginia's Mother).

PLOT: In German-occupied Czechoslovakia, timid Miloš Hrma gets a job as an apprentice dispatcher at a small railway station where the employees are warned not to make any efforts to sabotage the German war effort.

Jiří Menzel's *Closely Watched Trains* became 1967's front runner for the Foreign Film Oscar, not because it was so clearly an outstanding piece of art, but because it happened to sneak in during a particularly uninspired run of international offerings. Many critics had been less than thrilled by it, while others hailed it as a sort of unpretentious masterpiece, a combination of deeply black humor and tragedy that made an unpreachy comment against war. After winning the Grand Prix award at the Mannheim Festival, the film opened in the United States in the autumn of 1967, pulling in a good-sized crowd whose reactions were just as varied as those of the critics. There was much to admire in Menzel's deadpan, simple approach to the everyday lives of train station workers during the end of Nazi Germany's occupation of Czechoslovakia, but there was also much to complain about in the way his pacing meandered to the point where the picture didn't seem to be about very much of anything. When it did finally build to its sad and tragic finale, the impact was far less powerful than it might have been with a more focused story line.

> "I have just finished a training course to be a station guard. It is common knowledge in our town that, like all my family, my one desire is to stand on a platform and avoid hard work."
> —Miloš Hrma

The film was based on a very slim novel by Bohumil Hrabal, who, like his protagonist, had worked at a train station during the war. The book had caught the eye of filmmaker Menzel, who was interested in adapting it for the first feature-length motion picture to be directed entirely by him. Previously he had contributed segments to a pair of episode films, including *Perlicky na dne (Pearls of the Deep)* (1965), for which his chapter, "The Death of Mr. Batasar," had been cowritten by Hrabal. Menzel asked Hrabal to write a rough screen treatment of *Trains* to which he in turn would contribute ideas, along with rewriting dialogue and converting it to more cinematic terms. The most significant change Menzel made to the original story was having it take place in chronological order, whereas the book had made frequent references to events that had already occurred, including the stamping of the posterior of Virginia, the telegraphist, and Miloš's attempt to slit his wrists. In the film, Miloš was seen reporting to work for the first time, in contrast to the book, which had him returning to his job after a three-month hiatus he had spent recuperating from his failed suicide attempts. These changes worked for the better, but the distortion of the climax seemed like an unfortunate (and possibly political) choice. Hrabal had documented the aftermath of the bombing of the town of Dresden by describing the German survivors, defeated and devastated by their loss, as they passed through Miloš's station. Miloš had shown no compassion for the suffering of his enemies until he shot a German on the train, who, in turn, put a bullet in Miloš. The two wounded men fell off the train and ended up side by side. The situation finally brought

Once *Closely Watched Trains* earned the Academy Award for Best Foreign Film, Grove Press was able to reissue Bohumil Hrabal's novel with a special mention of its honor.

Miloš to the realization that his enemy's pain was not something he had sought, and he was forced to put the dying German out of his misery. In the film, Menzel has Miloš's shooting take place while Virginia's distraught mother argues with the train officials about the assault on her daughter's derrière by the station dispatcher, Hubicka---a darkly comical contrast to Miloš's death. As rewritten, there was no demonstration of compassion for the Germans, which seemed to indicate that Menzel, unlike Hrabal, was unwilling to forgive their desecration and dominance of his homeland during World War II.

Filmed in 1966 principally at the Loděnice Station, *Closely Watched Trains* was a very low-budget affair, financed and owned by the Czech-run motion picture industry, with mostly unknowns filling the roles. Menzel himself took on the part of the psychiatrist who helps Miloš over his depression about his "manhood." For his lead, Menzel selected Václav Neckář, who was known in his country as a jazz singer, not an actor. Neckář turned out to be the best thing about the movie. He possessed just the right degree of innocence, and his bugged-out eyes and bat ears made him endearingly funny looking---perfect for both the comedic aspects of the story and the sadder ones. Although Menzel was hailed as the next big find in foreign cinema, his fame here was short-lived. In 1968 the Soviet invasion of his country imposed new restrictions on its filmmakers, and suddenly the rest of the world no longer heard much from Czechoslovakia.

THE JUNGLE BOOK

Academy Award Nominee: Song ("The Bare Necessities")

Top 10 Box Office Film

Opening date: October 18, 1967 (New York: December 22, 1967).

Buena Vista. A Walt Disney Presentation.

Director: Wolfgang Reitherman. Story: Larry Clemmons, Ralph Wright, Ken Anderson, Vance Gerry. Inspired by Rudyard Kipling's Mowgli stories, featured in *The Jungle Book* (1894). Directing Animators: Milt Kahl, Frank Thomas, Ollie Johnston, John Lounsbery. Character Animation: Hal King, Eric Larson, Walt Stanchfield, Eric Cleworth, Fred Hellmich, John Ewing, Dick Lucas. Music: George Bruns. Songs by Richard M. Sherman and Robert B. Sherman: "Colonel Hathi's March," "I Wanna Be like You," "Trust in Me," "That's What Friends Are For," "My Own Home." Additional Song by Terry Gilkyson: "The Bare Necessities." Editors: Tom Acosta, Norman Carlisle. Technicolor. 79 minutes.

VOICE CAST: Phil Harris (Baloo the Bear), Sebastian Cabot (Bagheera the Panther), Louis Prima (King Louie of the Apes), George Sanders (Shere Khan the Tiger), Sterling Holloway (Kaa the Snake), J. Pat O'Malley (Colonel Hathi the Elephant/Buzzie), Bruce Reitherman (Mowgli the Man-Cub), Verna Felton (Winifred), Clint Howard (Young Elephant), Chad Stuart (Flaps, a Vulture), Tim Hudson (Dizzy, a Vulture), Digby Wolfe (Ziggy, a Vulture), John Abbott (Akela, a Wolf), Ben Wright (Rama, a Wolf), Darleen Carr (Shanti, the Girl).

PLOT: Bagheera the Panther believes it is time to bring young Mowgli, who has been raised in the Indian jungle since infancy, back to civilization to ensure the boy is safe from the clutches of a deadly man-eater, Shere Khan the Tiger.

Arguably Rudyard Kipling's most famous creation, Mowgli, the man-cub raised by wolves, had first been introduced in a short story called "In the Rukh," which appeared in an 1893 compilation published under the name *Many Inventions*. The very next year came *The Jungle Book*, seven short stories (interspersed with corresponding poems, or "songs"), four of which featured Mowgli. There was also a follow-up, *The Second Jungle Book* (1895), which featured an older Mowgli in five of its eight tales. Down the line the two books were paired up under the name *The Jungle Books*, which was how most readers came to know them. Since the stories featured both talking animals and a child as their human protagonist, they seemed a perfect match for the Walt Disney animation factory. In fact, in a 1961 essay by Marcus Cunliffe, written to accompany a reprinting of the tales, the author made a passing reference to how Kipling's animals were not unlike those found in Disney cartoons. Very soon after that essay, Disney's staff set to work on an adaptation of the classic tales, with which, not surprisingly, they took major liberties.

> "I wanna be a man, man-cub, and stroll right into town. And be just like the other men. I'm tired o' monkeyin' around."
> —King Louie

The Disney story team, Larry Clemmons, Ralph Wright, Ken Anderson, and Vance Gerry, decided to stick pretty much to the earlier book, when Mowgli was small, with most of the details from the screenplay coming from the three opening stories, "Mowgli's Brothers," "Kaa's Hunting," and "Tiger-Tiger!" The writers then chose which animals to include from the book while also creating a few of their own. Bagheera the Panther and Baloo the Bear were kept on as Mowgli's mentors and closest jungle allies, although the latter received an extensive overhaul in characterization. Kipling had referred to Baloo specifically as "serious" and the teacher of the Jungle Law to the wolf pack. The cinematic Baloo couldn't be further from this, being gleefully lazy, irresponsible, and anything but serious. Bagheera, not the wolves, was now the one responsible for discovering Mowgli as a baby; and Kaa became a conniver out to devour Mowgli, although in the stories he had been another of the boy's friends, helping to save him from the kidnapping monkeys. A leader for the apes, King Louie, was added, as were a trio of Vultures, one of whom sounded suspiciously like Beatle Ringo Starr. The movie's climax had Mowgli returning to civilization, for the better, though in the Kipling stories his first trip back to mankind had been a disaster: the lad was driven from the village for suspected sorcery after killing (and skinning!) Shere Khan.

Although in the past Disney had not gone for star power when casting actors to voice its animated features, *The Jungle Book* became something of a first in changing all that. This time much was made of the fact that such personalities as Phil Harris, Louis Prima, George Sanders, and Sterling Holloway were behind the jungle creatures. Harris and Prima, in fact, were such inspired choices that these became the consummate big-screen assignments for both of them. As

The Disney soundtrack for *The Jungle Book* contained not only the songs, but also dialogue highlights and an illustrated story booklet.

good as these talents were, they didn't stand a chance against George Sanders, whose deceptively comforting, self-satisfied, and insinuating line readings as the villain of the piece, Shere Khan, were nothing short of brilliant.

After having come up short with their tunes for *The Sword in the Stone*, Disney's chief songwriting team of the decade, the Sherman Brothers (Robert B. and Richard M.), rose to the occasion with *The Jungle Book*, penning one true gem, "I Wanna Be like You," that fitted Louis Prima's talents to a T; a lovely ballad, "My Own Home"; and revising one trunk song, "Trust in Me," cleverly refashioned from a number intended for a never-filmed sequence of *Mary Poppins* to sound just the way a snake would sing it. Ironically, even the best of the Shermans' work wound up taking a back seat to the one additional song that was provided by Terry Gilkyson for Baloo to sing. "The Bare Necessities" was so deliriously catchy, with its bouncy, butt-shaking presentation, that it became the score's breakout hit, getting all the raves and an Oscar nomination in the bargain.

As for the film itself, those expecting a faithful rendering of Kipling's much more serious and often dark tales of survival and violence in the Indian jungles were more than taken aback by Disney's off-the-cuff, "cool" approach to the material. It was this "swinging," irreverent tone, however, that caught 1967 audiences in exactly the right way. Unlike many of Disney's live-action features in those days, *The Jungle Book* seemed to be fashioned to be very "with it," taking its cue from the growing free-spiritedness of the era. It was also, unlike *The Sword in the Stone*, utterly devoid of heavy-handedness, pretensions, or weak characterizations. Because of this very loose fidelity to its source material, the movie became one of the company's highest grossing of all its features.

CAMELOT

Academy Award Winner: Best Art Direction–Set Decoration; Best Costume Design; Best Scoring of Music—Adaptation or Treatment

Academy Award Nominee: Cinematography; Sound

Top 10 Box Office Film

Opening date: October 25, 1967.

Warner Bros.–Seven Arts.

Director: Joshua Logan. Producer: Jack L. Warner. Screenplay: Alan Jay Lerner. Based on the 1960 musical play, with book and lyrics by Alan Jay Lerner, music by Frederick Loewe, directed by Moss Hart, from the 1958 novel *The Once and Future King*, by T. H. White. Photography: Richard H. Kline. Costumes, Scenery and Production Designer: John Truscott. Sets and Art Direction: Edward Carrere. Set Decorator: John W. Brown. Editor: Folmar Blangsted. Music: Frederick Loewe. Music Supervisor and Conductor: Alfred Newman. Music Associate: Ken Darby. Orchestrations: Leo Shuken, Pete King, Jack Hayes, Gus Levene. Songs by Frederick Loewe (music) and Alan Jay Lerner (lyrics): "Guenevere," "I Wonder What the King Is Doing Tonight," "The Simple Joys of Maidenhood," "Camelot," "C'est Moi," "The Lusty Month of May," "Take Me to the Fair," "How to Handle a Woman," "If Ever I Would Leave You," "What Do the Simple Folk Do?," "Follow Me," and "I Loved You Once in Silence." Technicolor. Panavision. 180 minutes (including overture, entr'acte, and exit music).

CAST: Richard Harris (King Arthur), Vanessa Redgrave (Guenevere), Franco Nero (Lancelot Du Lac), David Hemmings (Mordred), Lionel Jeffries (King Pellinore), Laurence Naismith (Merlyn), Pierre Olaf (Dap), Estelle Winwood (Lady Clarinda), Gary Marshal (Sir Lionel), Anthony Rogers (Sir Dinadan), Peter Bromilow (Sir Sagramore), Sue Casey (Lady Sybil), Gary Marsh (Tom of Warwick), Nicolas Beauvy (Arthur as a Boy), Fredric Abbott (Sir Geoffrey), Leon Greene (Sir Turloc).

PLOT: King Arthur's dream of building a perfect society in Camelot is challenged when his queen, Guenevere, falls in love with Arthur's bravest new knight, Lancelot.

Having conquered Broadway and the American musical theater in general with *My Fair Lady*, Alan Jay Lerner and Frederick Loewe chose as their follow-up the legendary love triangle of King Arthur, Queen Guenevere, and the noble knight Sir Lancelot, with T. H. White's definitive interpretation of the tale, *The Once and Future King*, credited as their source material. With *Fair Lady*'s Eliza Doolittle, Julie Andrews, leading the cast as Guenevere, and Richard Burton chosen to carry on the talking-singing vocalizing style established by Rex Harrison's Henry Higgins, all the elements were in place for a surefire hit. *Camelot*, featuring newcomer Robert Goulet as Lancelot and Roddy McDowall as the villainous Mordred, opened on December 3, 1960, at New York's Majestic Theatre to mixed reviews. Most of the criticism centered on the shift in tone from the pageantry and romance of the first act to more serious matters, when the utopian society King Arthur has envisioned begins to crumble because he hadn't counted on matters of the human heart to destroy it. Even though Richard Burton took home a Tony Award for his performance and the play had additional wins for scenic design, costumes, and music direction, the show itself did not even compete in the Best Musical category. Nevertheless, *Camelot* ran on Broadway for over two years, closing on January 5, 1963, after 873 performances.

It would be six years from the Broadway opening of *Camelot* before the cameras started rolling on Warners' lavish movie version, by which time both Richard Burton and Julie Andrews had become two of the biggest motion-picture stars in the world. The director selected to helm the picture, Joshua Logan, however, had no interest in casting either of these two performers, nor did he want Robert Goulet, who had become both a top recording artist and one of the most ubiquitous television entertainers of the decade. Logan, believing the title was the selling point, went looking for fresher names. He opted for Andrews's *Hawaii* (United Artists, 1966) costar, Richard Harris, for Arthur, in part because Logan preferred Harris's singing voice to Burton's. And he chose relative newcomer Vanessa Redgrave for Guenevere, having found her Oscar-nominated performance in *Morgan!* (Cinema V, 1966) rife with the naughty sexuality he didn't see in Andrews. Despite the fact that Harris's and Redgrave's vocals would ultimately have to be pieced together from multiple takes, both actors were, in fact, very good in their roles dramatically, stressing the tormented passion and emotion necessary to bring these characters to life. Logan's casting mistake, however, came with his choice of Franco Nero for Lancelot. Struggling with his English at the time of his casting, Nero was subjected to additional language lessons before and during the making of the film. His fractured accent was a further hindrance to his already stiff performance, and being forced to mouth his vocals to the dubbing voice of Gene Merlino caused him to come off as awkward in the finished print. The bad lip-synching suggested that Nero was still uncertain about some of the lyrics.

> "What else do the simple folk do, to perk up the heart and get through? The wee folk and the grown folk who wander to and fro, have ways known to their own folk, we throne folk don't know."
> —Guenevere

Although Jack L. Warner wanted *Camelot* to look as sumptuous as the studio's Oscar-winning adaptation of *My Fair Lady* (1964) and to be treated with equal importance, he was reluctant to let it go off the back lot. Logan, however, thought otherwise and managed to convince the stubborn producer to let him shoot sequences among the castles of Spain. Starting in late August 1966, Logan used the castle of Coca to stand in for Camelot, the imposing structure glimpsed in the background in several scenes, including Lancelot's confrontation on the road with Arthur. For Lancelot's Joyous Gard, which appeared most majestically on the hill behind Arthur in the opening and closing scenes, Logan opted for the striking Alcázar of Segovia. After shooting other sequences involving the summoning of the various knights to Camelot, the crew returned to the Warner Bros. lot to film the remainder of picture. Designer John Truscott did an exceptional job, giving the film a deliberately less glamorous look than the standard sword-and-pageantry epic, but making it beautiful nonetheless. On the back lot was built the courtyard on which the jousting scenes, among others, took place, while the studio's largest facility, Stage 7, housed the Great Hall and the Throne Room set.

Mordred's solo number from the play, "The Seven Deadly Virtues," was omitted, as were Guenevere's "Before I Gaze at You Again," the knights' defiant "Fie on Goodness!" (the most regrettable loss), and the lyrics to "The Joust," which, logically, were no longer needed because the scene could now be dramatized before the viewers' eyes rather than having to be commented upon by the onlookers.

By the time the film was released, the country's desire for a world free of disharmony was at an all-time high, which boded well for *Camelot*'s box-office appeal. The film did, in fact, rank high on the lists of most-attended 1967 releases, but it had great difficulty in breaking even because of its staggering $15 million cost. What's more, unlike *Fair Lady*, the critics were none too supportive of what they found to be a turgid and overlong rendering of a story that should have been told with a lighter hand. There were no qualms about the stunning look Truscott had brought to the film (he ended up with two Academy Awards, for costumes and sets), or for the lush adaptation of Loewe's gorgeous melodies (which brought an Oscar to conductor Alfred Newman for film scoring). There *were* complaints about Logan's extensive use of close-ups (which resulted in constant scrutiny of Harris's pronounced eye makeup) and the often uninspired staging of the songs. Few movie musicals ever suffered so clearly from an undisciplined audio track, with distracting shifts in tone very evident in the final film. *Camelot* continued to have its share of detractors over the years, many unfavorably comparing the soaring vocals of An-

So loved was the score of *Camelot* that even a soundtrack starring nonsingers climbed to number 11 on the *Billboard* charts. Within the next year one of the movie's stars, Richard Harris, would find himself with a hit single, "MacArthur Park."

drews on the original cast album to Redgrave's more breathy, weaker renditions. Harris, however, was eventually accepted as having given King Arthur his own individual stamp when he returned to the piece in the 1980s, filling in for Richard Burton during a revival of the stage show.

WAIT UNTIL DARK

Academy Award Nominee: Actress (Audrey Hepburn)

Opening date: October 26, 1967.

Warner Bros.–Seven Arts.

Director: Terence Young. Producer: Mel Ferrer. Screenplay: Robert Carrington, Jane-Howard Carrington. Based on the 1966 play by Frederick Knott. Photography: Charles Lang. Art Director: George Jenkins. Set Decorator: George James Hopkins. Music: Henry Mancini. Title song by Henry Mancini (music) and Jay Livingston and Ray Evans (lyrics). Editor: Gene Milford. Technicolor. 108 minutes.

CAST: Audrey Hepburn (Susy Hendrix), Alan Arkin (Roat, "Harry Roat Sr.," "Harry Roat Jr."), Richard Crenna (Mike Talman), Efrem Zimbalist Jr. (Sam Hendrix), Jack Weston (Carlino), Samantha Jones (Lisa), Julie Herrod (Gloria), Jean Del Val (Old Man), Frank O'Brien (Shatner), Gary Morgan (Boy on Stoop).

PLOT: Three hoods terrorize blind woman Susy Hendrix, who has unwittingly come into the possession of a doll filled with heroin.

In early 1966 Warner Bros. offered Audrey Hepburn the starring role in a juicy thriller that would not only allow her to spend a good deal of the story in a state of anxiety but to play a blind woman as well, always an intriguing challenge for an actor. The property in question was a theatrical thriller, *Wait until Dark*, written by Frederick Knott. Knott was best-known for his 1952 play *Dial M for Murder*, which Alfred Hitchcock had filmed successfully for Warner Bros. back in 1954.

> **"Pick up the cane. And tap on the floor, right where you are, so I know where you are. Go on, tap. Tap. Keep tapping . . . keep tapping . . . keep tapping . . . tap."**
> **—Susy Hendrix**

Warners was, in fact, so sure that Knott had another winner of his hands that the studio purchased the rights (at a price ranging from $350,000 to a whopping $1 million, depending on the source) several months *before* its February 2, 1966, Broadway opening, with Hepburn already announced for the part. This meant that Lee Remick took the role in the play knowing full well that no matter how good she was (and she earned a Tony nomination for her performance), she would not be asked to re-create the part onscreen. The rest of the New York stage cast consisted of Robert Duvall (Roat), Mitchell Ryan (Talman), Val Bisoglio (Carlino), James Congdon (Sam), and Julie Herrod (Gloria), with William Jordan and Richard Kuss showing up at the finale as a pair of policemen. Only child actress Herrod was invited to be in the movie, which turned out to be the only picture she would ever make. Directed by Arthur Penn, *Wait until Dark* was a solid hit in New York and played at no fewer than four different theaters (Ethel Barrymore, Shubert, George Abbott, and the Music Box) for its 374-performance run. It closed on December 31, 1966.

Jack L. Warner, pleased to have the star of his studio's top blockbuster of the decade, *My Fair Lady* (1964), working for him again, had no qualms about agreeing to the same $1 million salary Hepburn had received for the earlier film. Hepburn already had a director in mind, Terence Young, for whom she had auditioned prior to her leap to stardom. The first two choices to play the villain of the piece, the psychotic Roat, were George C. Scott (who had already been fired from a previous Audrey Hepburn movie, *How to Steal a Million*, Twentieth Century-Fox, 1966) and Rod Steiger, but when neither of these proposals happened, the part was offered to Alan Arkin, who had just charmed the world playing the good-hearted Russian officer in the hit comedy *The Russians Are Coming The Russians Are Coming* (United Artists, 1966). This 180-degree turn from levelheaded hero to reprehensible killer was just the sort of opportunity to display one's range that most actors could only dream of, and Arkin eagerly accepted.

Rather than hiring Knott to do the adaptation himself (as he had done for *Dial M*), Young asked the husband-and-wife team of Robert and Jane-Howard Carrington to write the script. Clearly this was the

Cast and crew principals, including estranged real-life couple Mel Ferrer and Audrey Hepburn, cram into the apartment set for a friendly photo during the making of *Wait until Dark*.

sort of thriller that achieved a good deal of its tension from the small space in which it took place, so only the most logical choices of "opening" it up for the cameras were necessary. A prologue was added in which Lisa was seen receiving the heroin-filled doll and handing it off to an unsuspecting Sam Hendrix at the airport, which meant that the company actually flew to Montreal to film the first few minutes of the picture and then to Kennedy Airport in Queens to shoot Lisa and Sam's arrival in New York. This sequence also suggested that Lisa and Roat were very much aware of one another, since he met her at the airfield, whereas Knott's play had Roat insisting that he had first met the girl in the Hendrix apartment. Similarly, Talman and Carlino now arrived at the designated rendezvous together, though the stage version had them showing up separately, each believing the other to have arranged the meeting. The screenplay also saw fit to change Susy's means of memorizing phone numbers from stacking sugar cubes to a (less theatrical) punchboard; had her toss sodium thiosulfate (hypo) in Roat's face instead of a mix of ammonia and vegetable oil; made Roat quietly clip the phone wire and wrap it around the stair railing, rather than having Talman yank it out in front of Susy; and came up with the far better idea of having Susy make Roat tap to signal his location, not by banging his hand on a table, as Knott had written, but with her cane. These very minor tweaks and alterations were barely noticeable, for this was the sort of motion picture that was unmistakably yet unapologetically derived from a play.

The sheet music for the title song from *Wait until Dark* includes lyrics like "Who cares how cold and gray the day may be; wait until dark and we'll be warm," which in no way capture the essence of this tense thriller.

Starting with the Montreal scenes, *Wait until Dark* began shooting on January 16, 1967. The location work in New York was done almost exclusively at St. Luke's Place in Greenwich Village, where the entrance to the Hendrix apartment was located in the basement at number 4. The rest of the filming took place at the Warners Studio in Burbank.

Wait until Dark proved a triumph for Hepburn, who was the perfect heroine, alternately vulnerable and cleverly resilient. With the help of much study at the Lighthouse for the Blind, where she practiced with blind masks to get the sense of just what it felt like to be devoid of sight, and contact lenses to give her eyes more of a blank look, Hepburn was effortlessly convincing, giving one of her most accomplished performances. Arkin's nasally tones added just the right weird touch to this unflappable and very deadly character, even if those looking for a "comfortable" chiller carped that he was simply too far out there. There were the expected complaints about staginess and plot holes—most critics questioned why Arkin needed to disguise himself to fool a blind person (since they failed to notice that this was done when Gloria was around, who would otherwise have noticed that Roat Sr. and Roat Jr. were one and the same person) or why Susy didn't lock the door (which indeed she did, which was why Talman picked the lock in order to enter at the climax). Realizing there was a lot of talk going on, Young kept the picture playing at a very smooth pace, knowing exactly where and when to keep the camera moving to give as much of a cinematic sense without resorting to fancy tricks, building slowly but surely to an undeniably tense finale that really delivered the goods.

Wait until Dark broke house records at the Radio City Music Hall and continued to do excellent business, thanks in large part to a gimmick suggested by the marketing department at Warners. Distributors were asked to heighten the suspense of Susy and Roat's final altercation by actually turning off the house lights at their theater during the last eight minutes (the legal limit on how long such a thing could be done). This meant that audiences were plunged into the same degree of darkness that the characters were, which added a marvelous "you are there" feeling to the tension. Better yet, there was one riveting, genuinely heart-stopping moment during the climax that was so well timed it not only guaranteed an audience full of patrons gasping or screaming in unison, but managed to scare even after repeated viewings and full awareness of when it was going to happen.

COOL HAND LUKE

Academy Award Winner: Best Supporting Actor (George Kennedy)

Academy Award Nominee: Actor (Paul Newman); Screenplay—Based on Material from Another Medium; Original Music Score

Opening date: November 1, 1967.

Warner Bros.–Seven Arts. A Jalem Production.

Director: Stuart Rosenberg. Producer: Gordon Carroll. Screenplay: Donn Pearce, Frank R. Pierson. Based on the 1965 novel by Donn Pearce. Photography: Conrad Hall. Art Director: Cary Odell. Set Decorator: Fred Price. Costumes: Howard Shoup. Editor: Sam O'Steen. Music: Lalo Schifrin. Song: "Plastic Jesus," by Bruce Phillips, performed by Paul Newman. Technicolor. Panavision. 126 minutes.

CAST: Paul Newman (Lucas Jackson, "Cool Hand Luke"), George Kennedy (Clarence, "Dragline"), J. D. Cannon (Society Red), Lou Antonio (Koko), Robert Drivas (Loudmouth Steve), Strother Martin (Captain), Jo Van Fleet (Arletta, Luke's Mother), Clifton James (Carr), Morgan Woodward (Boss Godfrey), Luke Askew (Boss Paul), Marc Cavell (Rabbit), Richard Davalos (Blind Dick), Robert Donner (Boss Shorty), Warren Finnerty (Tattoo), Dennis Hopper (Babalugats), John McLiam (Boss Kean), Wayne Rogers (Gambler), Dean Stanton/Harry Dean Stanton (Tramp), Charles Tyner (Boss Higgins), Ralph Waite (Alibi), Anthony Zerbe (Dog Boy), Buck Kartalian (Dynamite), Joy Harmon (The Girl), Jim Gammon (Sleepy), Joe Don Baker (Fixer), Donn Pearce (Sailor), Norman Goodwins (Stupid Blondie), Chuck Hicks (Chief).

PLOT: Lucas Jackson is sentenced to serve time on a road gang, where his stubborn resistance to authority and determination to maintain his independence makes him a hero to his fellow prisoners.

Prison pictures have always held an undeniable fascination for movie audiences, and there is something even more riveting about ones set in the rather backward correctional camps in which men are shackled like animals, forced to live by the whip, and made to endure punishment in the form of a tiny box in which they are placed in order to atone, with only their reeking sweat for company. Warners' Depression-era picture on the subject had been titled, unforgettably, *I Am a Fugitive from a Chain Gang* (1932), but that had been just one stop along the road to hell by its protagonist, as played by Paul Muni. Thirty-five years down the line, the same studio released *Cool Hand Luke*, which took place almost entirely within such a prison facility and, through the skill of an exceptional cast, director, and writer, became the final word on cinematic road gangs.

> "That's my darlin' Luke.
> He grin like a baby . . .
> but he bites like a gator."
> —Dragline

The authenticity of the tale came from the fact that the author of the original novel, Donn Pearce, had indeed done two years of hard labor, starting in 1949, at the Tavares Road Prison no. 5758 on SR 19, south of the Florida town of Tavares, for stealing $100 worth of tools in Tampa. More than a decade after his release, Pearce decided to write a fictional account of his stay, an episodic piece that, for the sake of grit, didn't even bother to put quotes around any of the dialogue. Despite its title, Luke was initially a very vague character. There was no introductory prologue about the crime that landed him in the camp, as the film would have, and the loner disappeared for a good portion of the book after arriving at camp.

Pearce himself was hired to do the first screenplay draft, which he completed in November 1965. Knowing that someone with more movie experience was needed to give it an overhaul, Frank Pierson came on board. Between them they rectified the emphasis, placing Luke at the center of attention from the get-go—after all, the script was being fashioned for Paul Newman. There would no longer be narration from an inmate named Sailor (Pearce's surrogate), but as a sort of compensation, Pearce himself was placed in the cast as one of the prisoners, unbilled in the credits but listed in the studio paperwork as portraying "Sailor." There was a boxing match written into the action so that Luke could show his stubborn streak and win the favor of Dragline, his opponent, not to mention the admiration of the other

men. A contrast to Luke's resigned attitude to being locked up in a sweatbox was shown by having a weaker prisoner, one of the concurrent new arrivals, break down like a child at having to endure this harsh punishment. In Pearce's story, Luke's first escape attempt had prompted the warden to make a statement by tossing several of the other men into the sweatbox, but this too was dropped from the picture, as was a competition between Luke and an inmate named Curly to see who would be declared the camp's biggest eater. (It was a draw.) It was replaced by Luke's memorable efforts to consume a record number of eggs. Because Luke's wartime experience was played down in the picture, a scene was cut in which he told the other men of the atrocities in World War II, including rapes he had participated in, a terrible fact that would have killed audience sympathy. It was also decided to make something cinematic and exciting about the arduous task of tarring a new road, so this sequence was edited and underscored in such a way that it built thrillingly to a sense of achievement, something that had not happened on the written page. Finally, just to give the audience a dose of unapologetically chauvinistic humor, the sexy girl who had merely sunbathed in Pearce's version now became part of the single most exploitive and undeniably funny car-wash scene in movie history.

Art director Cary Odell and his team took photos of the actual site of the prison camp in Florida, which they were then asked to re-create down to the tiniest detail in an empty field near Thornton Road, north of Stockton,

Paul Newman's image dominates the paperback tie-in for *Cool Hand Luke,* although the title character is just one of the ensemble in Donn Pearce's original novel.

California. Following a week of rehearsals, the $3,457,500 production began principal photography on October 3, 1966, filming in and around Stockton in such areas as Roberts Island, where the rural village at which Luke manages to chop off his shackles was constructed from scratch; and both Davis Road

Charles Tyner takes aim at an offending snapping turtle while convicts Paul Newman and George Kennedy look on in this scene from *Cool Hand Luke*.

and Stark Road for scenes of the road gang's daily work. Behind schedule, the company journeyed to the Warner Bros. studio on November 17, where the interiors of the barracks were filmed on Stage 6-A and the scene of Luke cutting the heads off the parking meters was shot on standing sets on the back lot. Photography was completed on December 14, 1966.

Anticipating Oscar gold, Warners delayed the opening until November of the following year so that the movie would be fresh on the voters' minds. This was one of those pictures in which even a director whose output would prove to be sometimes dreadful in the extreme could come through magnificently, Stuart Rosenberg creating a gritty character study that was devoid of sentimentality and sensationally entertaining in the bargain. *Cool Hand Luke* was full of rousing set pieces like the boxing match, Luke's two escape efforts, the "torturous" car washing, the road tarring, and, most unforgettably, the egg-eating contest, which ranked among the most robust, pricelessly comical scenes of the decade. At the center of it all, commanding the screen with one of the most assured performances of his career, was Paul Newman, creating yet another antihero and loner who was perhaps the most solitary and defiant in his gallery of independent men. Not heroic on account of any particular deeds, but commendable in his resistance to authority, Luke became a life force simply for realizing that the only way to face his inevitable doom was to try and resist it, whatever the penalty. Moviegoers discovered another counterculture rebel to whom they could relate, and as a result, Luke became one of the iconic figures of the era, turning the picture into a box-office winner. In a very short time *Cool Hand Luke* was recognized as one of the "quiet" classics of the decade, never ranked as "important," seldom analyzed for great social significance, always left off those many lists of the greatest pictures, and yet never less than superb in pretty much everything it set out to accomplish.

THE PRODUCERS

Academy Award Winner: Best Story and Screenplay—Written Directly for the Screen (1968)

Academy Award Nominee: Supporting Actor (Gene Wilder) (1968)

Opening date: November 22, 1967 (New York: March 18, 1968).

AVCO Embassy. A Joseph E. Levine Presentation.

Director-Screenplay: Mel Brooks. Producer: Sidney Glazier. Photography: Joseph Coffey. Art Director: Charles Rosen. Set Decorator: James Dalton. Costumes: Gene Coffin. Music: John Morris. Songs by Mel Brooks: "Have You Ever Heard the German Band?," performed by Zale Kessler; "Springtime for Hitler," performed by Michael Davis and Company; "Prisoners of Love," performed by Prison Inmates. Song by Norman Blagman (music) and Herb Hartig (lyrics): "Love Power," performed by Dick Shawn. Choreographer: Alan Johnson. Editor: Ralph Rosenblum. Pathécolor. 88 minutes.

CAST: Zero Mostel (Max Bialystock), Gene Wilder (Leo Bloom), Kenneth Mars (Franz Liebkind), Dick Shawn (LSD, Lorenzo St. DuBois), Estelle Winwood ("Hold Me, Touch Me" Old Lady), Renée Taylor ("Eva Braun"), Christopher Hewett (Roger De Bris), Lee Meredith (Ulla), Andreas Voutsinas (Carmen Ghia), William Hickey (Drunk in Theater Bar), Michael Davis ("Springtime for Hitler" Tenor), John Zoller (*New York Times* Critic), Madlyn Cates (Concierge), Frank Campanella (Bartender), Shimen Ruskin (Landlord), David Patch ("Goebbels"), Barney Martin ("Goering"), Brutus Peck (Hot Dog Vendor), Arthur Rubin ("A Wandering Minstrel, I"), Zale Kessler (Jason Green, "Have You Ever Heard the German Band?"), Bernie Allen ("The Little Wooden Boy"), Rusty Blitz ("Beautiful Dreamer"), Anthony Gardell (Auditioning Hitler, Blows Raspberry), Mary Love, Amelie Barleon, Nell Harrison, Elsie Kirk, Anne Ives (Little Old Ladies), Mae Crane, Diana Eden (Showgirls), Tucker Smith, David Evans (Lead Dancers), Josip Elic (Violinist in Restaurant), Hank Garrett (Stagehand), Patrick Owens (Conductor), Bill Macy (Jury Foreman), Bud Truland (Bar Patron), Mel Brooks ("Don't Be Stupid, Be a Smarty" Vocal).

PLOT: Having fallen on hard times, Broadway producer Max Bialystock schemes with accountant Leo Bloom to deliberately stage a surefire flop, *Springtime for Hitler*, with the intention of absconding with the investors' cash when the show folds.

Despite having earned an Oscar for writing and narrating the 1963 animated short subject "The Critic," Mel Brooks had not yet been able to get involved in feature films as he had hoped. For years he had wanted very badly to direct an original idea he had developed about a desperate Broadway producer who comes up with an outlandish idea to create a musical guaranteed to flop in order to swindle its backers out of their money. If there was one key element that kept the movie companies from handing Brooks the money to make his film, it might have been the title he was pushing: *Springtime for Hitler*. It took another relative novice to the picture industry to finally get things rolling. Sidney Glazier, who also had an Oscar on his mantle, had produced the 1965 documentary *The Eleanor Roosevelt Story*, a movie that did not immediately suggest an imminent partnership with Brooks. He loved Brooks's concept, however, and was determined to see the film made.

As Brooks was finishing up his screenplay, Glazier shopped the property around, finally landing a deal with a friend of his, independent producer Joseph E. Levine. Because Brooks was not a proven name and the subject matter didn't exactly guarantee a hit, the budget was kept somewhere in the $1 million range. The only real star hired was the bombastic Zero Mostel, who was better known for his Broadway work than for his scattered movie appearances. His costar, Gene Wilder, had played stuttering Billy Bibbett in the short-lived original 1962 Broadway adaptation of *One Flew Over the Cuckoo's Nest* and acted in support of Anne Bancroft in a production of *Mother Courage and Her Children* the year before the actress became Mrs. Mel Brooks. Wilder, with his sponge-like mop of hair and put-upon, kicked-puppy look, was an inspired choice and adapted to Brooks's sense of humor so thoroughly that the two teamed together twice more, for *Blazing Saddles* (Warner Bros., 1974) and *Young Frankenstein* (Twentieth Century-Fox, 1974).

> **"That's exactly why we want to do this play. To show the world the true Hitler, the Hitler you knew, the Hitler you loved, the Hitler with a song in his heart."**
> **—Max Bialystock**

The film, which was indeed announced to the press in November 1966 under the title *Springtime for Hitler*, began shooting on May 22, 1967, at the Production Center, a facility at 221 West Twenty-sixth Street usually reserved for television commercials. These soundstages housed such sets as Max Bialystock's cluttered office (the walls decorated with the posters of actual Broadway flops) and its more presentable later incarnation; Roger DeBris's white-carpeted townhouse; and Franz Liebkind's grungy apartment, complete with an eight-by-ten glossy of Hitler on the kitchen wall. Brooks then took his cameras around Manhattan to such sites as Central Park, the observation deck of the Empire State Building, and, most memorably, the fountain in the plaza of Lincoln Center, where jets of water were made to leap upward at the precise moment Leo decides to join Max in a life of crime, making for one of the visual highlights of the picture and one that was hard to shake for anyone visiting the site from then on. Needing an actual Broadway theater to house Bialystock's grotesque Nazi musical, Brooks selected the Playhouse on West Forty-eighth Street, a venue on its last legs that was slated for the wrecking ball (it finally came down in 1969).

Stars Zero Mostel and Gene Wilder are nowhere to be found on the cover of RCA's soundtrack for *The Producers,* a sexy lady with a Hitler mustache apparently being considered a surer selling point.

Although Levine had posited no restraints on how far Brooks's imagination could go, it was finally decided that slapping *Springtime for Hitler* on a movie could well be the kiss of death, so the more benign, to-the-point title *The Producers* took its place. When at last the movie had its official Manhattan unveiling (following test engagements in a few markets in November 1967), the critics weighed in with mixed notices, as would be expected for something so unabashedly wild and so deliberately tasteless. Although Brooks never crossed the line where language, sex, or violence was concerned, he found pretty much every other opportunity to walk the boundary between screwy and flat-out offensive. There were Jews eagerly hoping to make money by subjecting the public to a glorification of Adolf Hitler; decrepit old ladies getting on the casting couch with an overweight, self-loathing theatrical impresario; a busty, dim-witted secretary whom Bialystock, and thus the audience, ogled as if they were in a burlesque skit; and a pair of homosexuals so flamingly effete that one of them was introduced wearing a dress. The amazing thing was that through sheer combustible energy, or perhaps because everyone and everything onscreen came off as larger-than-life nutty, there wasn't any time to really take offense. Brooks's dialogue was genuinely laugh-out-loud hilarious, and the level of sheer outrageousness at which the whole farce was played seemed to be something that hadn't been attempted before. For everyone who turned their noses up at the very concept, someone else dragged his or her friends to the cinema, pretty sure

This British ad for *The Producers* placed special emphasis on countryman Peter Sellers's enthusiastic endorsement, which helped draw attention to the film.

that anyone with even a marginal sense of humor was going to surrender to the lunatic gusto on hand. Not surprisingly, the New York theater community found the most to love about the film, recognizing the screw-loose types that Brooks had created as not too far removed from the real self-involved folks who made show business so much fun to be a part of.

If *The Producers* couldn't drum up more than average business outside of the major cities, it hardly mattered, because the comedy was finding a very appreciative degree of word-of-mouth praise within the entertainment industry. When the Oscar nominations for 1968 were announced, Brooks found himself in the running for original screenplay and came away the winner. In due time, this choice would seem even more justified, because *The Producers* became the sort of movie that future generations kept "discovering" and quoting lines from. The little movie that most average Americans weren't all that aware of back in 1968 had become one of the most revered comedies of all time, held dear as the increasingly erratic filmmaker's most assured work.

GUESS WHO'S COMING TO DINNER

Academy Award Winner: Best Actress (Katharine Hepburn); Best Story and Screenplay—Written Directly for the Screen

Academy Award Nominee: Picture; Actor (Spencer Tracy); Supporting Actor (Cecil Kellaway); Supporting Actress (Beah Richards); Director; Art Direction–Set Decoration; Scoring of Music—Adaptation or Treatment; Film Editing

Top 10 Box Office Film

Opening date: December 11, 1967.

Columbia. A Stanley Kramer Production.

Director-Producer: Stanley Kramer. Screenplay: William Rose. Photography: Sam Leavitt. Production Designer: Robert Clatworthy. Set Decoration: Frank Tuttle. Costumes: Joe King. Wardrobe Supervisor: Jean Louis. Music: (Frank) De Vol. Song: "The Glory of Love," by Billy Hill, performed by chorus, reprised by Jacqueline Fontaine. Editor: Robert C. Jones. Technicolor. 108 minutes.

CAST: Spencer Tracy (Matt Drayton), Sidney Poitier (John Prentice), Katharine Hepburn (Christina Drayton), Katharine Houghton (Joanna "Joey" Drayton), Cecil Kellaway (Monsignor Mike Ryan), Roy E. Glenn Sr. (John Prentice Sr.), Beah Richards (Mary Prentice), Isabell Sanford (Tillie Binks), Virginia Christine (Hilary St. George), Alexandra Hay (Car Hop), Barbara Randolph (Dorothy), D'Urville Martin (Frankie, Driver in Drive-in Parking Lot), Tom Heaton (Peter), Grace Gaynor (Judith), Skip Martin (Delivery Boy), John Hudkins (Cab Driver), Jacqueline Fontaine (Singer).

PLOT: Diehard liberals Matt and Christina Drayton find their principles put to the test when their daughter, Joey, arrives home with her fiancé, John Prentice, a well-to-do doctor who happens to be black.

Although producer-director Stanley Kramer had come to embody Hollywood at its most liberal, it was not his idea to do a film about an interracial couple. That was the brainchild of writer William Rose, with whom Kramer had previously collaborated on something far more lighthearted, *It's a Mad Mad Mad Mad World* (United Artists, 1963). Rose had written the outline for his script, about a black man and a white woman facing opposition in their decision to wed, and set the drama in South Africa. He approached Kramer at just the right time, since the director's latest project for Columbia, about the Civil War prison Andersonville, had been scuttled by the nervous studio, which decided that the picture would be too expensive to produce. They still wanted Kramer to fulfill his contractual obligation, but only if he could come up with something that could be financed for no more than $3 million. He sat down with Rose and began throwing around ideas for the interracial script, insisting it be relocated to America to expand the commercial possibilities. Kramer realized that the subject matter would still be a tough selling point to the studio, but if he could back it up with a solid cast, he could get Columbia's blessing.

First, he knew he would have to enlist the sole bankable black motion-picture name of the '60s, Sidney Poitier, in order to give the movie credibility and make it thoroughly appealing from all angles.

Fortunately Kramer had already endeared himself to the star, having directed Poitier in his Oscar-nominated role in *The Defiant Ones* (United Artists, 1958), and the actor was very interested in hearing about anything the director wanted to pitch his way. Kramer also saw this as an opportunity to give his friend Spencer Tracy one last chance to shine onscreen in a great role. The actor had been ill the past several years and incapable of much physical activity, so he had declared himself retired from acting. To entice the notoriously obstinate Tracy to agree to the film, Kramer offered Katharine Hepburn the role of his wife. She would be working in front of a movie camera for the first time in five years, having slipped out of the spotlight to serve as Tracy's "nurse." Once Kramer had Tracy on board, he was told by Columbia that the company was resistant to insuring the ailing star, whose precarious health meant he could die in mid-production and Columbia could end up with an unfinished picture. As a result, both Kramer and Hepburn put up their fees in escrow until the picture was finished, serving as a form of insurance should Tracy not be able to perform.

> **"You and your whole lousy generation believes the way it was for you is the way it's got to be. And not until your whole generation has lain down and died will the dead weight of you be off our backs!"**
> **—John Prentice**

Filming commenced in San Francisco on March 20, 1967. Because of his fragile health, Tracy was not required to participate in any of the location shooting. Instead, he worked exclusively on the soundstages at Columbia Studios, and no later than noon on the days he was scheduled, with a minimum of exertion. Kramer shot Tracy's lengthy and important final speech from multiple angles on different days, so it would be less taxing for the actor than having to do it all at once. Not an ounce of his declining spirits was evident in the finished product, and it proved to be the last hurrah for one of the giants of the film industry. He filmed his final scene on May 24, 1967, two days before the picture wrapped altogether. Tracy was elated that he had withstood the challenge and would go out on a film with an important topical message. Two and a half weeks later he suffered a massive heart attack and died on June 10, 1967. By the time the film was released at Christmas, the public devotion to the Tracy-Hepburn legacy (this was their ninth teaming), along with the fact that Poitier was riding the peak of his popularity with a pair of huge moneymakers released earlier that year, *To Sir, with Love* (Columbia) and *In the Heat of the Night* (United Artists), made *Guess Who's Coming to Dinner* one of the most eagerly awaited film events of the year.

Of course Kramer was hoping for controversy to entice the public to see his film, but nobody anticipated how much of the discussion would surround not the topic at hand, but Kramer and Rose's "drawing-room comedy" approach to it. While the general public was lining up around the block in the sort of record numbers that made the Columbia honchos pat themselves on the back for having gotten behind the property, the critics were slamming the film for what they perceived to be a naive take on a delicate subject, accusing the filmmaker of softening a serious issue by making Poitier's character nothing short of a saint, which robbed the story line of any genuine conflict. Of course, this was what enlightened reviewers were writing who perceived themselves as having long since moved on from such issues. Their attitude was itself naive, or at least deeply self-involved, for the majority of the American public was still having trouble waking up to the realities of the civil rights movement.

Kramer's interracial tale certainly seemed quaint, especially because it looked like a stage-bound series of discussions rather than a motion picture, but the filmmaker was far smarter and more forward-thinking in the way he put it together than most people gave him credit for. Knowing he wanted his message to reach a vast commercial public and not the sort of tiny, specialized audiences who had shown up for the acclaimed independent drama *One Potato Two Potato* (Cinema V, 1964), which dealt with the same topic, the director had purposely made the whole package accessible and comfortable rather than raw and harsh. He wanted the masses to sit up and listen, and there were few blacks in 1967 who had done more to awaken the world to black equality than had Poitier, who couldn't help but come off as the voice of reason and understanding. If anything, part of the angry reaction was a feeling of resentment among those who declared themselves liberals in thought as opposed to action, since the film challenged the notion of tolerance, asking how far one would take his or her beliefs when the issue cut so close to the bone. Despite being looked upon as the antithesis of the "youth movement" film that was rising through the ranks at the time, *Guess Who's Coming to Dinner* presented one of the more boldly outspoken tirades against the oppressive and backward thinking of the older generation. The film emphasized the necessity of disposing of inherited prejudices and limitations as the only hope for the next generation if

Hearing the lyrics to the discarded title song from *Guess Who's Coming to Dinner* on the Colgems Records soundtrack ("It's true there are many colors in every rainbow. My friend, let's blend") makes it obvious why Stanley Kramer opted to use Billy Hill's 1936 pop hit "The Glory of Love" as the theme.

it were to move on to a more enlightened way of looking at racial issues. Whatever its virtues or faults, *Guess Who's Coming to Dinner* continues to be one of those films that never fails to provoke a thorough response. Even its detractors might be inclined to think of it as an important work from its era, at least one worth an argument or two.

IN COLD BLOOD

Academy Award Nominee: Director; Screenplay—Based on Material from Another Medium; Original Music Score; Cinematography

Opening date: December 14, 1967.

Columbia. A Pax Enterprises Production.

Director-Producer-Screenplay: Richard Brooks. Based on the 1966 book by Truman Capote. Photography: Conrad Hall. Art Director: Robert Boyle. Set Decorator: Jack Ahern. Wardrobe: Jack Martell. Editor: Peter Zinner. Music: Quincy Jones. Black and white. Panavision. 135 minutes.

CAST: Robert Blake (Perry Smith), Scott Wilson (Dick Hickock), John Forsythe (Alvin Dewey), Paul Stewart (Jensen, Reporter), Gerald S. O'Loughlin (Harold Nye), Jeff Corey (Mr. Hickock), John Gallaudet (Roy Church), James Flavin (Clarence Duntz), Charles McGraw (Mr. Smith), Will Geer (Prosecutor), John McLiam (Herbert Clutter), Ruth Storey (Bonnie Clutter), Brenda C. Currin (Nancy Clutter), Paul Hough (Kenyon Clutter), Vaughn Taylor ("Good Samaritan"), Duke Hobbie (Young Reporter at Hanging), Sheldon Allman (Reverend Jim Post), Sammy Thurman (Mrs. Smith), Raymond Hatton (Old Hitchhiker), Sadie Truitt (Herself, Postmistress), Myrtle Clare (Herself), Teddy Eccles (Young Hitchhiker), Al Christy (Sheriff), Don Sollars (Luke Sharpe).

PLOT: Perry Smith and Dick Hickock's attempted robbery at a Kansas farm results in the savage and senseless slaughter of the Clutter family, their crime becoming one of the most-talked about murders of the century.

Already considered one of the foremost writers of the postwar era, Truman Capote surpassed all previous accomplishments and created his literary masterpiece, *In Cold Blood*, by turning to a most atypical subject matter, a senseless and brutal real-life crime. Following the November 15, 1959, murders of four members of the well-to-do and well-liked Clutter family in the peaceful farming community of Holcomb, in western Kansas, Capote traveled to the out-of-the-way locale to get the scoop on exactly what happened and, more important, why. He began interviewing anyone and everyone even peripherally linked to the victims, to the murderers, and to the police investigation as he tried to piece together the psychology behind what would drive someone to commit such a heinous act. Capote researched and wrote his observations over a five-year period, during which time he was allowed to visit the killers, Dick Hickock

> "Who would kill four people in cold blood for a radio, a pair of binoculars, and forty dollars in cash?"
> —Alvin Dewey

and Perry Smith, in their cells on Death Row at Kansas State Penitentiary. After many long delays, they were finally executed on April 14, 1965 (or five years, four months, and twenty-eight days after the killing, as the flap of the published book informed its readers). As one of the must-read books of 1966, *In Cold Blood* brought Capote the sort of celebrity status the author craved, making him more famous than ever. Columbia Pictures was thrilled at the excitement the book was creating, having already purchased the film rights for a figure that was estimated to be somewhere in the vicinity of $400,000 to $500,000, plus a profit percentage for the author.

Capote's prized work ended up in the hands of the very capable director-writer Richard Brooks, who had coaxed Capote into selling the book for a lower price than he had expected, simply by convincing the author that he would have some say in what was going to be done with the material. Capote had ideas of which parts of his book Brooks should consider for inclusion in his screenplay and actually sent him an annotated copy with underlined passages and lines of dialogue, many of which Brooks would later claim were exactly the scenes and situations he himself had already intended to concentrate on. The screenplay had to sacrifice many of the background details about the Clutters and the backstories of the killers. Instead, occasional flashbacks were used to fill in some details, principally for Perry Smith, who was seen as the more conflicted and complex of the two criminals. There would be no side trip to Florida for Smith and Hickock, as had happened following the killings; no scene of the investigators tracking down Smith's terrified sister; no mention of Smith's devotion to friend and fellow convict Willie-Jay; no correspondence between Smith and ex-army-buddy-turned-religious-fanatic Cullivan; beyond a summation by an angered prosecutor, no trial scene; and no retrial, as had actually happened after Hickock protested that he should not be required to die since it was Smith who had pulled the trigger. Brooks did not submit a finished script to the authorities in Kansas, fearing too much meddling and intervention, and worked pretty much on a day-to-day basis, handing the pages to be filmed to cast and crew just before shooting commenced. Capote was there on the set to witness a good deal of the filming.

The Colgems Records soundtrack captured Quincy Jones's pulsating score for *In Cold Blood,* which earned him one of two Oscar nominations that year.

As good luck would have it, Brooks managed to secure as much cooperation from the Kansas State Prison Commission and the state department as he had hoped for. Therefore he was able to film in the exact locations where the events had taken place, including, most surprisingly, the actual Clutter farmhouse (called River Valley Farm at the time of the killings). Brooks also filmed in the Hickock home in

Edgerton; the Kansas Bureau of Investigation offices in the State Building at Topeka; the Finney County Court House (where the trial took place) in Garden City; a hotel in Olathe; Hartman's Café in Holcomb; the Hanes Hardware Store in Emporia, where Smith and Hickock had purchased the rope and rubber gloves used during the crime; and in Kansas City, at the bus station, a pawnshop, and Shepherd's Men's Store. Tracing the killers' trek to and from Kansas included filming in Missouri; El Paso, Texas; and Ciudad Juárez, Mexico. There was a stopover in Las Vegas to film the capture of the criminals as well as their interrogation, using the actual cells where the questioning took place at the city jail. The only location that posed a problem was the Kansas State Penitentiary at Lansing, the Security and Isolation building where Smith and Hickock awaited their execution having since been demolished. It was instead re-created in a studio, and the remaining prison scenes were shot at Colorado State Penitentiary in Cañon City. Working with a budget just short of $1 million, Brooks filmed from February 28 to early June 1967.

Columbia saved a key Christmas-season slot for the movie's opening, figuring this would serve it well come awards season. Although there were critics who were put off by the grim nature of the picture, as well as those who had insisted from the start that Capote's vision could never be preserved on film, there were as many reviewers who were stunned by just how good the picture was. The decision to go for a very straightforward, documentary-like approach removed any feeling of sensationalism, and Brooks directed in a tight, no-nonsense fashion that got right to the facts, sprinkling in moments of humanity and introspection with such subtlety that the movie never sounded preachy, didactic, or sentimental. His fluid style of allowing one scene to flow uninterruptedly into the next seemingly unrelated one by using a connecting thread (for example, a glance at the road from the Clutter farm brought the viewer a glimpse of the approaching killer's car, miles away) was a terrific cinematic equivalent of the leaping back and forth between the killers and their victims that Capote had done so effectively in his writing. In the end, even the notoriously hard-to-please Capote went on record as saying he was very happy with the film, as well he should have been. Although no film of his book was ever going to cram in all the backstory, minutiae, and multitude of reflections from various interview subjects, Brooks's picture had fully captured the shattering and lasting effect of the crime and served Capote well in making a worthy cinematic companion piece to his work, one that would forever be spoken of with high praise in relation to its enduring source material.

VALLEY OF THE DOLLS

Academy Award Nominee: Scoring of Music—Adaptation or Treatment

Top 10 Box Office Film

Opening date: December 15, 1967.

Twentieth Century-Fox. A Mark Robson–David Weisbart Production.

Director: Mark Robson. Producer: David Weisbart. Screenplay: Helen Deutsch, Dorothy Kingsley. Based on the 1966 novel by Jacqueline Susann. Photography: William H. Daniels. Production Designer: Philip M. Jefferies. Art Directors: Jack Martin Smith, Richard Day. Set Decorators: Walter M. Scott, Raphael G. Bretton. Gowns: Travilla. Makeup Supervisor: Edith Lindon. Songs by André Previn (music) and Dory Previn (lyrics): "Theme from 'Valley of the Dolls,'" performed by Dionne Warwick; "Give a Little More," performed by Gail Heideman dubbing for Patty Duke; "It's Impossible," performed by Gail Heideman dubbing for Patty Duke; "Come Live with Me," performed by Tony Scotti, reprised by Scotti and Patty Duke; "I'll Plant My Own Tree," performed by Margaret Whiting dubbing for Susan Hayward. Choreographer: Robert Sidney. Editor: Dorothy Spencer. Deluxe color. Panavision. 123 minutes.

CAST: Barbara Parkins (Anne Welles), Patty Duke (Neely O'Hara), Paul Burke (Lyon Burke), Sharon Tate (Jennifer North), Susan Hayward (Helen Lawson), Tony Scotti (Tony Polar), Martin Milner (Mel Anderson), Charles Drake (Kevin Gillmore), Alex Davion (Ted Casablanca), Lee Grant (Miriam Polar), Naomi Stevens (Miss Steinberg), Robert H. Harris (Henry Bellamy), Jacqueline Susann (First Reporter), Robert Viharo (Director), Joey Bishop (Telethon Host), George Jessel (Grammy Awards Host), Richard Angarola (Claude Chardot), Robert Street (Choreographer), Barry O'Hara (Stage Manager), Richard Dreyfuss (Assistant Stage Manager), Margot Stevenson (Anne's Mother), Judith Lowry (Aunt Amy), Darryl Wells (Willie).

PLOT: Egomaniacal singer Neely O'Hara, secretary Ann Welles, and aspiring actress Jennifer North resort to pills to cope with the turbulent world of show business.

As a book, Jacqueline Susann's *Valley of the Dolls* made history as the best-selling novel of all time, with some 22 million copies sold to eager readers who devoured every overbaked plot development and randy exchange of dime-store dialogue as it purported to lay bare the backstabbing world of show business. As a film, *Valley of the Dolls* became known by many as the worst major motion picture to be released during the 1960s, the most appallingly over-the-top collection of melodramatic clichés ever assembled. The self-deluded Susann went on record as saying the filmmakers had "ruined" her work, as if Hollywood had taken a literary masterpiece and brought shame upon it.

Twentieth Century-Fox pounced on the movie rights and got the project rolling within the same year that the book was published, hiring Mark Robson to direct it. The studio hoped that lighting would strike again as it had ten years earlier, when the same man had guided Fox's 1957 adaptation of the best selling novel of *that* decade, Grace Metallious's *Peyton Place*, not only to huge box-office figures, but to a surprising degree of respectability, earning mostly favorable notices and nine Oscar nominations. But the difference began in the source. Metallious's original novel was a potboiler, to be sure, but an engrossing one of more literary merit than most critics gave it credit for. *Dolls*, on the other hand, presented more of a challenge. Only a miracle could have turned a faithful adaptation into something of value. In a way, anything of higher quality might have made some quick cash and passed quietly into obscurity. Instead, the movie of *Dolls* came to be looked upon as some sort of pinnacle of motion-picture camp, giving it a lasting immortality, albeit of the most blush-inducing kind.

Screenwriters Helen Kingsley and Helen Deutsch kept the separate career paths of the novel's three female protagonists pretty much intact, with a few alterations, chronological liberties, and edits in order to keep things down to a manageable two hours. Gone were Anne Welles's millionaire suitor, Allen Cooper, and his equally rich papa, Gino, who breaks the heart of man-hungry and admittedly lonely superstar Helen Lawson after she scopes him out as her next prospective husband. Lawson's role in the film was diminished considerably, discarding her dependency on Anne altogether, which made the part something akin to an extended guest appearance. Rather than have Neely O'Hara get her big break by moving up into a vacated role in one of Lawson's shows, the scripters made them instant enemies by having the insecure Helen insist that the newcomer be fired from the cast, thereby giving more motivation for the big powder-room confrontation between the two women.

> "They drummed you out of Hollywood, so you come crawling back to Broadway. But Broadway doesn't go for booze and dope."
> —Helen Lawson

(This scene climaxed in perhaps the most celebrated ludicrous moment in the picture, if not '60s film history, when Neely tosses Helen's wig in the toilet.) Rather than have the depressed Jennifer abort her baby, as she had in the book, the screenplay skipped right to her suicide, for brevity's sake. In fact, children were very much absent from the screen: neither Neely nor Anne gave birth, though in Susann's story both had. Although the *Dolls* movie went out of its way to keep in a few utterances of "bitch" and flashes of skin filmed from discreet angles, it wasn't ready to go the lesbian route and cut out Jennifer's passionate affair with a woman while living in Switzerland. Tony's illness, a neurological disease, was deemed not photographically interesting, so he was given loss of muscular control instead. Surprisingly, despite wallowing in pill-taking excesses, as the book had done, the film opted for some degree of integrity for its ending, at least where Anne was concerned. It allowed her to turn her back on the whole stinking show-business scene, Lyon Burke included, rather than spinelessly accept her fate as a betrayed wife downing Seconals to ease the pain.

As if to compensate for a mostly uninspired cast, Fox announced that no less than Judy Garland would be playing the coarse and dynamic Helen Lawson. This came as a bit of surprise, considering many readers had theorized that the novel's Neely O'Hara could be looked upon as an unflattering portrait of Garland herself. No matter—the great entertainer was in need of money and figured it was beneficial to get involved with a big A-list project that would be seen by many. After costume fittings and prerecordings of the André and Dory Previn number "I'll Plant My Own Tree," Garland finally got wise to the tripe she had gotten herself attached to and refused to leave her dressing room. Fox had no choice but to fire her and replace her with Susan Hayward, who was more at home in this sort of soap opera milieu, having recently carried such nonsensical sudsers as *Back Street* (Universal, 1961) and *Where Love Has Gone* (Paramount, 1964). Although the dismissal brought the beleaguered Garland yet more bad press, nothing better could have happened to her: the finished movie wound up being a black mark on the careers of everyone involved.

Taking advantage of the winter weather, Robson began shooting in upstate New York and New England, on February 20, 1967, to chronicle Anne's journey from Massachusetts to New York City (one of the more pictorially lovely moments in the film) and

for scenes set at the Lawrenceville Inn (filmed in Bedford, New York), Anne's old-fashioned colonial house (shot in Redding Center, Connecticut), and a train station (in Katonah, New York). In mid-March the unit moved to New York City, utilizing Rockefeller Center, Gracie Square, Grand Central Station, a rehearsal hall on West Fifty-first Street, the Martha Washington Hotel on Twenty-ninth Street, and the soon-to-be-demolished Forty-eighth Street Playhouse. The company then finished up in Los Angeles, with interiors on the Fox soundstages and scenes shot at the newly built Music Center (where Tony has his first public collapse, a distraught Jennifer at his side), the International Ballroom of the Beverly Hilton Hotel (for the Grammy Awards, hosted by George Jessel), the Santa Monica Court House, and private homes in Malibu and Westwood. André and Dory Previn's five songs included one of the few pluses of the film: the title track, sung hauntingly by Dionne Warwick over the opening credits and throughout the picture.

The Previns, André and Dory, came up with a haunting title tune for the otherwise tawdry *Valley of the Dolls*. The movie's key ad image of its three leading ladies warming the same bed was featured on the song's sheet music cover.

Word quickly leaked out that Fox had turned a stinker of a book into a stinker of a movie, and the critics had a field day coming up with adjectives to describe its combination of dated melodramatic posturing and "shocking" words and phrases, the favorite of which seemed to be "fags," which Susann had used ad nauseam in her book. Despite the condescending and homophobic tone present on both the page and onscreen, the movie was adapted as a favorite by certain members of the gay community, who seemed to take these derisive jibes with far better humor than the film deserved. Not surprisingly, the moviegoing public couldn't care less about the reviews, and Fox had a massive hit on its hands, making good on its investment and even backing an unrelated sequel directed by the notorious junk-filmmaker Russ Meyer, *Beyond the Valley of the Dolls* (1970), which evoked a lawsuit from Susann and actually managed to be worse than the first film.

DOCTOR DOLITTLE

Academy Award Winner: Best Song ("Talk to the Animals"); Best Special Visual Effects

Academy Award Nominee: Picture; Cinematography; Art Direction–Set Decoration; Sound; Original Music Score; Scoring of Music—Adaptation or Treatment; Film Editing

Opening date: December 19, 1967.

Twentieth Century-Fox. An Arthur P. Jacobs Production.

Director: Richard Fleischer. Producer: Arthur P. Jacobs. Screenplay: Leslie Bricusse. Based upon the *Doctor Dolittle* stories, by Hugh Lofting. Songs by Leslie Bricusse: "My Friend the Doctor," "The Reluctant Vegetarian," "Talk to the Animals," "At the Crossroads," "I've Never Seen Anything Like It," "Beautiful Things," "When I Look in Your Eyes," "Like Animals," "After Today," "Fabulous Places," "I Think I Like You," "Doctor Dolittle," "Something in Your Smile." Music Scored and Conducted by Lionel Newman and Alexander Courage. Dance and Musical Numbers Staged by Herbert Ross. Photography: Robert Surtees. Production Designer: Mario Chiari. Art Directors: Jack Martin Smith, Ed Graves. Set Decorators: Walter M. Scott, Stuart A. Reiss. Costumes: Ray Aghayan. Editors: Samuel E. Beetley, Marjorie Fowler. Special Photographic Effects: L. B. Abbott, Art Cruickshank, Emil Kosa Jr., Howard Lydecker. Animals and Birds Supplied and Trained by Jungleland, Thousand Oaks, California. Deluxe color. Todd-AO. 152 minutes (later cut to 144 minutes).

CAST: Rex Harrison (Dr. John Dolittle), Samantha Eggar (Emma Fairfax), Anthony Newley (Matthew Mugg), Richard Attenborough (Albert Blossom), Peter Bull (General Bellowes), Muriel Landers (Mrs. Blossom), William Dix (Tommy Stubbins), Geoffrey Holder (William Shakespeare X), Portia Nelson (Sarah Dolittle), Norma Varden (Lady Petherington), Ginny Tyler (Voice of Polynesia) .

PLOT: In nineteenth-century England, John Dolittle, an eccentric veterinarian who is able to talk to animals, hopes to raise money by exhibiting the rare Pushmi-Pullyu, thereby enabling him to finance a voyage to track down the fabled Great Pink Sea Snail.

Twentieth Century-Fox's costly musical fantasy *Doctor Dolittle* was a direct result of the tremendous financial success of Walt Disney's *Mary Poppins* (Buena Vista, 1964). If Disney could create box-office gold out of a series of children's books involving an eccentric British character with unusual attributes, then why couldn't Fox do the same? To that end, producer Arthur P. Jacobs managed to purchase the rights to the fourteen Dolittle books written by Hugh Lofting (1886–1947). Lofting had first introduced the gentle physician, who taught himself to speak to animals, back in 1920 with *The Story of Doctor Dolittle*, which had spawned nine more adventures over the next twenty-seven years.

Jacobs decided that *The Story of Doctor Dolittle* (as it was initially called) would be a lavish musical with lyrics by the esteemed Alan Jay Lerner and Rex Harrison playing the title role. The picture was scheduled to roll in August 1965 at a projected budget of $6 million, only to have Lerner bail out of the project, leaving Harrison in the lurch. The actor got cold feet and threatened to quit until Fox placated him by raising his $500,000 fee to $750,000.

Jacobs hired Leslie Bricusse not only as the replacement songwriter, but to pen the script as well. Bricusse liberally borrowed elements from many of the Lofting stories, taking the Pushmi-Pullyu from the first book, although the creature's exhibition in the Blossom circus came from the fourth book, *Doctor Dolittle's Circus*. He also made Tommy Stubbins and Matthew Mugg essential characters from the outset,

> "We would converse in polar bear and python, and we would curse in fluent kangaroo. If people asked us 'can you speak rhinoceros,' we'd say 'of courserous, can't you?'"
> —Doctor Dolittle

although they were not introduced in the series until the second and third books, *The Voyages of Doctor Dolittle* and *Dolittle's Post Office*, respectively. The Giant Lunar Moth came from the seventh book, *Doctor Dolittle's Garden*, and the character of Emma Fairfax was simply created out of whole cloth, because it was deemed necessary that the two male leads have a woman to fall in love with, at least for appearance's sake—it might look strange for two men to go on a long ocean voyage with a young boy and a shipload of animals.

Although for tax purposes Harrison had hoped to stay out of England during filming, director Richard Fleischer and company had found the perfect village there to fill in for Dolittle's place of residence, Puddleby-on-the-Marsh. It was a picturesque spot near Bath called Castle Combe, which boasted of having been voted Great Britain's prettiest town in 1962. Following the June 27, 1966, start date, the filmmakers sat out most of the summer in Castle Combe waiting for the rain to cease; they got clear weather for all of five days during a two-month period. Already behind schedule and over budget, the company then journeyed to southern California on August 15, where several interior sets had been built on the Twentieth Century-Fox soundstages, although Dolittle's home was erected on the studio's Malibu Ranch. (The Blossom Circus sequence was shot there as well.) Because the introductory scene of the good doctor involved his being surrounded by a vast menagerie, it was deemed unhealthy and unwise to work on the shuttered stages. Therefore, a raked set was constructed outdoors so it could be hosed down following each take, after the uncontrollable animals had made a mess of it. Harrison endured the smell and an occasional nip or bite, but it made singing his numbers live (which he wanted to do, as he had done in *My Fair Lady*) not always feasible, and he wound up prerecording some of his tracks. The third location was Saint Lucia, a remote island in the British West Indies (where the company moved on November 5) that served as Sea Star Island, where Dolittle and his cohorts come to seek the Great Pink Sea Snail. Needless to say, it rained there as well, and the shooting stretched on even longer than anticipated. After another trip back to the Fox soundstages, the picture finally wrapped on February 10, 1967, nearly three months behind schedule. By the time *Doctor Dolittle* was in the can, the nervous studio had $18 million invested in its property, which meant that it was going to treat the film as *the* single most important release of 1967, no matter what the quality of the finished product. A staggering $11 million was spent on merchandising, advertising, and advanced product placement and ballyhoo.

No movie could withstand the amount of overhype that *Dolittle* received. It was talked up as the must-see family film of the decade, with an astronomical number of product tie-ins (ranging from dolls and lunchboxes to cookies and coloring books) licensed and an unprecedented first pressing of 500,000 copies of the soundtrack, the largest up to that time. There may have been a lot of excitement for *Dolittle* in theory, but there was far less for the movie itself. Early previews got a polite but less than thrilling response, so a prologue, in which Dolittle is seen riding a giraffe to visit a crocodile who is suffering from a toothache, was excised. This left the problem of what to do with the image of Dolittle atop the giraffe, which was designated the key visual for the ad campaign. A snippet of the moment was therefore moved to a later part of the film. Along the way, an entire Anthony Newley song, "Where Are the Words?," sung aboard the *Flounder* to the sleeping Samantha Eggar, was dropped, although it stayed on the soundtrack, which had already been pressed; the instrumental version could be heard during the overture. Regrettably, a prettier Newley tune, "Beautiful Things," was sliced down from its original length as well. The movie finally opened at a running time of 152 minutes, which even the kinder critics felt was still far too long for something based on books that were short and sweet. Eventually, once the road-show engagement had come to an end, another eight minutes were snipped out, including Harrison's brief recitation of the letter he is writing to Eggar, "Something in Your Smile," an important number in that it showed that the doctor had changed his antihuman ways and was eager to return to civilization.

Doctor Dolittle may have suffered from being too faithful to the genteel tone of Lofting's books. Many of its songs played out quietly rather than aiming for a big bang. Furthermore, the picture was episodic in nature and simply ambled along good-naturedly rather than creating any great excitement. It did have an exceptionally strong central presence in Harrison, who, admittedly, was far less befuddled a fellow than his literary counterpart, but brought along an infectious sense of individualism all his own and turned Bricusse's best song, "Talk to the Animals," into another talking-singing tour de force, as he had done on so many of his *Fair Lady* numbers. This clever, elongated explanation of the joys of conversing with various species was a standout in a score that was often too sophisticated to entrance the younger audiences, and it ended up winning the Academy Award. This was about the only Oscar that was not going to upset too many of the picture's many enemies, who were stunned when the movie itself ended up as one of the five finalists for the Best Picture award, helped, no doubt, by the countless Academy screenings

So high were expectations for *Doctor Dolittle* that Twentieth Century-Fox produced a record number of soundtrack albums, only to have the LP fail to reach the *Billboard* charts.

held by the cautious studio, which was witnessing its bank account being drained away by the agreeable but unexceptional box-office response to the film. That *Doctor Dolittle* managed to land a spot on the exalted nominees list was the chief reason for the continuing and scathing backlash against the picture by future generations, who were even less inclined to find the merits in what was, in fact, an expensive but dramatically modest, occasionally pleasant, sometimes tedious diversion that was chastised for not being something more special than it was.

THE GRADUATE

Academy Award Winner: Best Director

Academy Award Nominee: Picture; Actor (Dustin Hoffman); Actress (Anne Bancroft); Supporting Actress (Katharine Ross); Screenplay—Based on Material from Another Medium; Cinematography.

Top 10 Box Office Film

Opening date: December 21, 1967.

AVCO Embassy. A Joseph E. Levine Presentation of a Mike Nichols–Lawrence Turman Production.

Director: Mike Nichols. Producer: Lawrence Turman. Executive Producer: Joseph E. Levine. Screenplay: Calder Willingham, Buck Henry. Based on the 1963 novel by Charles Webb. Photography: Robert Surtees. Production Designer: Richard Sylbert. Set Decorator: George Nelson. Costumes: Patricia Zipprodt. Songs by Paul Simon: "Sounds of Silence," "April Come She Will," "The Big Bright Green Pleasure Machine," "Scarborough Fair/Canticle," "Mrs. Robinson," performed by Simon and Garfunkel. Additional Music: Dave Grusin. Editor: Sam O'Steen. Technicolor. Panavision. 105 minutes.

CAST: Anne Bancroft (Mrs. Robinson), Dustin Hoffman (Benjamin Braddock), Katharine Ross (Elaine Robinson), William Daniels (Mr. Braddock), Murray Hamilton (Mr. Robinson), Elizabeth Wilson (Mrs. Braddock), Brian Avery (Carl Smith), Walter Brooke (Mr. McGuire), Norman Fell (Mr. McCleery), Elisabeth Fraser (Second Lady), Alice Ghostley (Mrs. Singleman), Buck Henry (Hotel Desk Clerk), Marion Lorne (Miss De Witte), Eddra Gale (Woman on Bus), Richard Dreyfuss (Berkeley Student at Boarding House), Buddy Douglas, Mike Farrell (Bellhops in Lobby), Harry Holcombe (Minister), Jonathan Hole (Mr. Singleman), Lainie Miller (Stripper), Ben Murphy (Shaving Student), Noam Pitlik (Gas Station Attendant).

PLOT: Uncertain of his future and looking to fill the empty void in his life, recent college graduate Benjamin Braddock plunges into an affair with Mrs. Robinson, the unhappy wife of his father's business partner.

If one could choose a single movie to exemplify the seismic shift into a whole new way of thinking about how to present motion pictures and just exactly whom they were reaching, there would be very little debate over *The Graduate*'s being *the* representative film of the '60s. It was not the highest grossing (Fox's *The Sound of Music* claimed that honor), nor was it the most unanimously praised (if indeed it would be possible to gauge such a thing), though it came pretty close in both departments. It was among the most analyzed, enthusiastically discussed, endlessly copied and parodied, excitedly championed, cross-culturally embraced, and stylistically brilliant pictures to come from any period of film history. Unlike so many "important" achievements in cinema that meant something on an expressly aesthetic, coldly artistic, or wholly technical level to a select group of people, *The Graduate* was nothing short of a cultural landmark. It was taken to heart by an entire generation (and future generations) who believed that, more than any other movie before (or since), it spoke of the societal unrest, generational discomfort, and deep-rooted fear facing anyone who ever questioned empty materialistic values and the predestined lives they were asked to surrender to by the previous generation, who hadn't gotten any of it right for themselves. But the power of *The Graduate* certainly didn't end with the youth. Any movie this successful would have to appeal as well to their elders, who got a kick out of seeing the status quo sought by themselves, and so many like them, deflated so deftly. *The Graduate* was sold and bought as a comedy, but those willing to admit it knew that between all the laughs this was one very sad movie, one that didn't present any easy answers to the question of how to escape from what seemed so inevitable for us all.

Interestingly, what would turn out to be arguably the most famous movie of its era derived from a book that hadn't made any great impression on the world at large when it was first published in 1963. Charles Webb (born in San Francisco in 1939), was a recent graduate of Williamstown College in Massachusetts when he wrote a twelve-page short story that he turned into a full-length novel in 1960, when he was all of twenty-one years of age. Another three years passed before he actually got it published, and within a year (in March 1964) it had been bought for the relatively paltry sum of $20,000 by producer Lawrence Turman. In October of 1964 Turman made a deal with Joseph E. Levine's company to distribute the movie with the intention of starting production in the autumn of the following year. The screenplay was to be written by William Hanley, who had received attention that year for his Broadway play *Slow Dance on the Killing Ground*. By February 1965, Hanley was out, and Calder Willingham (*End as a Man*, *Paths of Glory*) was announced as the new scriptwriter.

> "Oh, no, Mrs. Robinson.
> I think . . . I think you're the
> most attractive of all my
> parents' friends. I mean that.
> I find you desirable."
> —Benjamin Braddock

In the meantime, Turman's first choice for director, Mike Nichols, had actually gotten another offer to make his motion-picture directorial debut when Elizabeth Taylor suggested him for *Who's Afraid of Virginia Woolf?* (Warner Bros., 1966), so Turman put *The Graduate* on hold for a spell. When Willingham presented him with his draft of the script, Nichols was not pleased and decided that somebody with more experience in humor was needed to brush it up. He hired Buck Henry to do the job.

Nichols would credit Henry and himself for what eventually ended up onscreen, but there was no denying that tons of dialogue had been taken directly from the book, which had been Willingham's decision when he first took a crack at the job. Because so much of this material stayed in the script, Nichols had no choice but to abide by the Screenwriters Guild ruling that anyone who supplied at least 15 percent of the dialogue was to be allotted onscreen mention. In contrast, Nichols was not permitted to share screenwriting credit unless he could prove he had written 55 percent of the script, which was simply not the case. In the end, the opening titles listed a screenplay by Calder Willingham and Buck Henry, and no one else. Although great chunks of the movie were scrupulously faithful to Webb's words, there were some well-thought-out omissions. In the book, Benjamin's hapless scuba scene was followed by a sequence in which he hitchhiked north to try his hand at odd jobs, including firefighting, while getting hit on by "queers." Nichols instead did a masterfully funny overlap of Benjamin standing in his wetsuit at the bottom of the Braddock pool while his phone call setting up his hotel rendezvous with Mrs. Robinson is heard on the soundtrack, indicating that next to no time has passed between the two events. The movie also dispensed with a series of correspondences: Benjamin writing a letter to Mrs. Robinson in which he tried to call off the affair; Elaine receiving a letter at college from her father explaining her mother's immoral behavior and announcing that he plans to inform Ben's parents and end his law partnership with Mr. Braddock; Benjamin getting a harsh telegram from Mrs. Robinson commanding him to leave Berkeley; and Benjamin finding a note at Carl Smith's apartment from a friend, which tips him off on where the wedding is to take place. Other smart changes included removing Mr. Robinson from the scene in which Benjamin desperately returns to the Robinson house seeking Elaine; and having Benjamin drive frantically up to Berkeley and later to the climactic wedding for maximum suspense, whereas in the book he had already sold his car by this point.

An unexpectedly old-fashioned posed shot from one of the decade's most decidedly new-fashioned films, *The Graduate*, with Katharine Ross and Dustin Hoffman.

Nichols decided to test somebody relatively new for the part of Benjamin Braddock while going with an established name for the predatory Mrs. Robinson. He toyed with the idea of using Jeanne Moreau, a suggestion Levine hated because it would have given the character an exotic foreign touch entirely at odds with the bored, creatively stunted American wife Webb had created. Instead, the job went to Anne Bancroft, who had established herself as one of the truly versatile actresses of the decade, with an Oscar for *The Miracle Worker* (United Artists, 1962) and a nomination from the Academy for *The Pumpkin Eater* (Columbia, 1964), in which she played another wife searching for fulfillment, though an emotionally unhinged one, the polar opposite of the ultracool Mrs. Robinson.

Nichols's concept of Benjamin was different from what Webb had created on the page. The book's version was a more WASPishly handsome sort, while Nichols thought that the whole thing would work far better with somebody less conventionally good-looking—someone capable of a dry, deadpan, introverted way with a line that would bring out the laughs. Theater actor Charles Grodin was considered, but Nichols was keen on testing Dustin Hoffman, whom he had recently seen in an off-Broadway comedy with the unforgettable title *Eh?* Nichols was quite taken with Hoffman's hesitancy and wittily monotonal line readings, certain he could convincingly play the sort of self-effacing young man who was unsure about his sexual capabilities but still attractive enough for someone to try to coax into bed. Nichols was sure the actor was going to raise the picture to a whole new level, simply because he didn't seem like anyone else who'd appeared onscreen before. Hoffman comfortably pulled off playing someone fresh out of college, even though he was twenty-nine years old at the time of filming—all of six years younger than Bancroft. Her hair streaked with gray to give her the appearance of an older woman, Bancroft still ended up looking sensational and got top billing, so it is doubtful she had any qualms about playing someone old enough to be Hoffman's mother.

Budgeted at $3.1 million, *The Graduate* started principal photography on April 24, 1967, with select interiors shot at Paramount Studios. Over the next several months Nichols moved to such southern California locations as Beverly Hills, for the exterior of the Braddock home; the Ambassador Hotel on Wilshire Boulevard, to fill in for the fictional Taft Hotel, where Benjamin carries on his affair with Mrs. Robinson; the campus of the University of Southern California, posing as Berkeley, with the Von Kleinsmid Center of International and Public Affairs used as Elaine's dorm and the fountain in front of the Edward L. Doheny Jr. Memorial Library providing the setting for one of the movie's most famous images, in which Hoffman sits longingly on the rim of the fountain as a dissolve takes him from solitude to being surrounded by a horde of students; the Sunset Strip, for Elaine and Benjamin's disastrous first date; a gas station at Winchester Canyon, north of Santa Barbara, for the scene in which Benjamin tries frantically to make a phone call, looking for the church; and the United Methodist Church of La Verne at 3205 D Street in the town of La Verne, for the famous climax, with Hoffman banging on the window of its upper level shouting "Elaine!" Actual filming up north included Berkeley's Sproul Plaza, the Theta Delta Chi frat house on Durant Avenue, and a side trip to the San Francisco Zoo, where Benjamin would be introduced to Elaine's square fiancé, Carl Smith (Brian Avery). The picture finished shooting by August 8, Hoffman's thirtieth birthday.

Although Nichols had originally planned to use a new score by André Previn, he had a brainstorm while cutting the picture, throwing on some tracks by Paul Simon and Art Garfunkel to help him get some ideas. Nichols then made a decision that turned out to be another masterstroke: playing Simon and Garfunkel tunes over certain sequences rather than use background

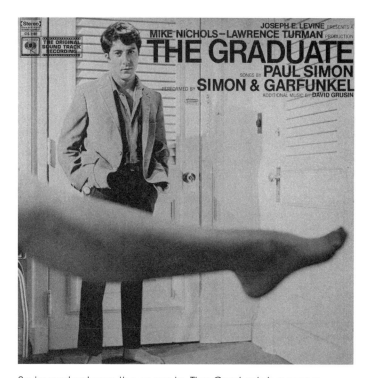

So important was the score to *The Graduate*'s success that the Columbia soundtrack became the first Simon and Garfunkel album to hit the number 1 position on the *Billboard* charts, remaining there for nine weeks until the duo's next LP, *Bookends*, knocked it from the top spot.

scoring, a move that enhanced the film immeasurably. Although films like *A Hard Day's Night* (United Artists, 1964) and *You're a Big Boy Now* (Seven Arts, 1966) had already used pop tunes for a movie score, they had chosen to shape scenes around songs written specifically for the movie. Nichols's approach was downright revolutionary and set the tone for how movies would be scored for decades to come, using already established songs on the soundtrack to create mood through association.

AVCO Embassy was so convinced it had a winner on its hands that the distributor scrapped the idea of releasing another of its comedies, *The Producers*, at the end of 1967, wanting all the attention to go to *The Graduate*. Even with such faith the company could not have been prepared for just how much attention the movie would receive. The good reviews were rapturous, the less favorable ones very quickly forgotten and, over time, often revised in subtle ways by those who had written them. Everything about the picture seemed so fresh and exciting that the word of mouth was galvanizing, to put it mildly. The spot-on, deadpan timing of the laughs was nothing short of priceless. The frankness of the sexuality was titillating but elegant in execution, and this alone guaranteed enthusiastic crowds for its exclusive engagements during the 1967 Christmas holidays.

The excitement did not abate one bit in the months that followed, and articles began talking about the one picture that had gotten the whole exasperating fact of the widening generation gap so perfectly and exactly right. This declaration amused and puzzled Nichols, who claimed that he had no inkling that such a gap existed, nor did he feel that he had made a movie that favored the youth while pointing a hostile finger at their parents. It was true, in fact, that Benjamin and Elaine were not in any way presented as rebellious or hell-bent on cultural upheaval; that was evident from their very conservative dress and manners, not to mention their disdain for raucous music that interrupts them on their night out. The sense of dissatisfaction over buying into the American dream was felt by *all* the characters, regardless of their ages, which was exactly why the movie started to reach so many with its message.

The Graduate simply *would not* stop making money. This sort of mass cultural effect on the public went beyond mere entertainment, making the movie an important statement about the mind-set of the population at the time. The audiences had voted: this was precisely the sort of movie they wanted to see. Hollywood would fall all over itself for years trying to come up with seemingly simple, humanistic comedies they hoped would touch a nerve in the way this movie had. By July 1968 the picture had already grossed $50 million, and the end was still nowhere in sight. Eventually, its $86 million take at the U.S. box office would place it (for a brief while) in the number 3 spot, after *The Sound of Music* and *Gone with the Wind* (MGM, 1939), as the biggest moneymaker in motion-picture history.

The Graduate put AVCO Embassy on the map. The company stuck around until the early 1980s, when it finally called it quits, simply because after *The Graduate* everything went downhill financially. The movie was reissued with great success in 1972, and nobody was the least bit surprised to see that nothing about the picture seemed to be dated. As the years passed , younger fans searched it out, blown away by it just as the previous generations had been, quoting lines and repeating moments to the point where much of the film became a part of pop-culture lore. The unforgettable image of a nervous Dustin Hoffman, the shot framed by Anne Bancroft's bent leg, and the accompanying "Mrs. Robinson, you're trying to seduce me" was embedded in the general public's subconscious in a way that made subsequent filmmakers, hoping to make their mark, truly envious.

1968

PLANET OF THE APES

Academy Award (Special): Makeup Design

Academy Award Nominee: Original Score—For a Motion Picture (Not a Musical); Costume Design

Top 10 Box Office Film

Opening date: February 8, 1968.

Twentieth Century-Fox. An Arthur P. Jacobs Production.

Director: Franklin J. Schaffner. Producer: Arthur P. Jacobs. Screenplay: Michael Wilson, Rod Serling. Based on the 1964 novel *La planète de singes* (*Planet of the Apes*), by Pierre Boulle. Photography: Leon Shamroy. Art Directors: Jack Martin Smith, William Creber. Set Decorators: Walter M. Scott, Norman Rockett. Costumes: Morton Haack. Music: Jerry Goldsmith. Editor: Hugh S. Fowler. Special Makeup Designer: John Chambers. Special Photographic Effects: L. B. Abbott, Art Cruickshank, Emil Kosa Jr. Deluxe color. Panavision. 112 minutes.

CAST: Charlton Heston (George Taylor), Roddy McDowall (Cornelius), Kim Hunter (Zira), Maurice Evans (Dr. Zaius), James Whitmore (President of the Assembly), James Daly (Honorious), Linda Harrison (Nova), Robert Gunner (Landon), Lou Wagner (Lucius), Woodrow Parfrey (Maximus), Jeff Burton (Dodge), Buck Kartalian (Julius), Norman Burton (Hunt Leader), Wright King (Dr. Galen), Paul Lambert (Minister).

PLOT: Thousands of years in the future, astronaut George Taylor crash-lands on a planet populated by a superior race of intelligent, speaking apes that treat humans as inferior creatures.

Long before Hollywood made "high concept" the norm, producer Arthur P. Jacobs came across one hell of an outlandish premise when he read the translated galleys of a book written by French author Pierre Boulle, *La planète des singes* (published here in 1963 as *Planet of the Apes*), about a world in which speaking, civilized apes rule over mute humans, who are kept in cages and treated as little more than wildlife to be hunted, studied, and experimented upon. Jacobs thought this could make a terrific motion picture—not a cheapjack sci-fi thriller, but something high-budgeted and important.

Boulle's book described a world populated by actual apes (not a hybrid of human and ape, as in the film) who drove cars, flew planes, and otherwise operated in a modern urban environment. Jacobs knew that the cinematic equivalent would require a revision of sorts, allowing for actors to play the parts in specially and carefully conceived makeup. To give more plausibility to the concept,

> "I can't help thinking, somewhere in the universe there has to be something better than man . . . has to be."
> —Taylor

it was also agreed that the look of the film should be a cross-pollination of the modern with the old, since the idea of apes building themselves a town and wearing clothing was bizarre enough. Michael

Wilson was hired to adapt the Boulle book along with one of the most respected writers in the business, Rod Serling, whose series *The Twilight Zone* had made him revered by lovers of the fantastic.

Allotted an impressive budget of $6 million, *Planet of the Apes* followed in the footsteps of Fox's *Fantastic Voyage* as one of the rare multimillion-dollar science-fiction adventures of the era to be backed by a major Hollywood studio and given the same prominence as any of its other features. Although the film would prove to have great appeal for children, *Apes* was not packaged or scripted expressly as an action film or fantasy, but deftly combined elements of adventure with social satire while slipping in a condemnation of nuclear war. A further factor in making *Apes* viable for adults was the inclusion of fleeting nudity. In Boulle's book the humans were constantly naked, as indeed they had to be in order to accurately turn the distinction between man and ape on its head. Although moviegoers were treated to glimpses of Charlton Heston's bare behind (making him one of the first American superstars to show his derriere on the big screen), the humans were given loincloths and makeshift scraps of clothing in order to make the story filmable for a general audience. Similarly, whereas the lead character of the novel (called Ulysse Merou) needed to teach himself the ape language in order to communicate with his captors, this potentially awkward device

Knowing the California sun can be hot enough *without* chimpanzee makeup, Maurice Evans finds shelter from the rays on the set of *Planet of the Apes.*

was easily dispensed with by having the apes speak English.

Filming began in the town of Page, in northern Arizona, on May 22, 1967. The location expanded into southern Utah's Glen Canyon National Recreation Area as Heston and his fellow astronauts were filmed trekking across the desert. Once the production moved to the Fox soundstages in June, the major undertaking of providing makeup for some 205 ape characters was met by a team of more than forty makeup artists, using John Chambers's stunning and unforgettable creations, under the supervision of Ben Nye and Daniel C. Striepeke. A staggering $1 million of the budget was allotted for this crucial aspect of the film. For the principals and any apes required to do more than fill the background, it was decided that the actors could not simply wear a mask, which would hinder their ability to project facial expressions. Instead, it was necessary to apply onto each individual's face pieces of foam rubber, plastic noses, hair, and an extra set of teeth in fake jaws that turned him or her into a convincing chimpanzee, orangutan, or gorilla while never fully obscuring the actor. This application took between three and four hours each morning; Chambers spent some six months coming up with a design that allowed the skin to breathe.

Requiring a manageable location at which to build the ape village, the company chose Fox's Malibu Ranch, where art directors William Creber and Jack Martin Smith designed a set that was both primitive and futuristic, with what appeared to the viewer's eye to be stone structures (actually made of polyurethane foam). The famous finale, in which Heston drops to his knees after realizing where he has been all along, was shot just north of Malibu, at Point Dune Beach. Production wrapped in August 1967, leaving the cast, director Franklin J. Schaffner, and his behind-the-scenes team with a generally optimistic sense that they had all created something so unusual that there was every reason to believe that *Planet of the Apes* would be a major moneymaker for Fox. When the film was launched in February 1968, the studio did indeed have on its hands one of the greatest must-see properties of the entire decade. It was helped in great measure by the critical support it received, reviewers praising the welcome bits of humor and wit that made the movie tremendous fun without ever sending itself up altogether. *Apes* became one of the touchstone science-fiction pictures of its time and, ultimately, of all time.

2001: A SPACE ODYSSEY

Academy Award Winner: Best Special Visual Effects

Academy Award Nominee: Director; Story and Screenplay—Written Directly for the Screen;
Art Direction–Set Decoration

Top 10 Box Office Film

Opening date: April 2, 1968 (New York: April 3, 1968).

MGM.

Director-Producer-Special Photographic Effects Designer and Director: Stanley Kubrick. Screenplay: Stanley Kubrick, Arthur C. Clarke. Based on the 1948 story "The Sentinel," by Arthur C. Clarke. Photography: Geoffrey Unsworth. Additional Photography: John Alcott. Production Designers: Tony Masters, Harry Lange, Ernest Archer. Art Director: John Hoesli. Set Decorator: Robert Cartwright. Wardrobe: Hardy Amies. Adaptations of Music by Richard Strauss, Johann Strauss, Aram Khachaturian, György Ligeti. Editor: Ray Lovejoy. Special Photographic Effects Supervisors: Wally Veevers, Douglas Trumbull, Con Pederson, Tom Howard. Metrocolor. Super Panavision 70 (also shown in Cinerama). 139 minutes (cut from 161 minutes).

CAST: Keir Dullea (Dr. David Bowman), William Sylvester (Dr. Heywood Floyd), Gary Lockwood (Dr. Frank Poole), Daniel Richter (Moon-Watcher, Main Ape), Douglas Rain (Voice of HAL 9000), Leonard Rossiter (Dr. Andrei Smyslov), Margaret Tyzack (Elena), Robert Beatty (Dr. Ralph Halvorsen), Sean Sullivan (Dr. Bill Michaels), Frank Miller (Mission Controller Voice), Penny Brahms, Edwina Carroll, Heather Downham (Stewardesses), Alan Gifford (Poole's Father), Ann Gillis (Poole's Mother), Vivian Kubrick ("Squirt" Floyd), Edward Bishop (Lunar Shuttle Captain), Richard Wood (Ape Killed by Moon-Watcher).

PLOT: A monolith discovered on the moon emits a piercing signal directed at Jupiter, prompting the United States to send a team of astronauts to the planet to explore the possibility of extraterrestrial life.

A motion picture so staggeringly unprecedented in approach and execution that it took on an almost mythic level in the annals of science fiction, *2001: A Space Odyssey* was one of the true milestones of the '60s and helped to turn Stanley Kubrick from a great director into the sort of filmmaker spoken of in reverent tones. During the theatrical run of his brazenly original satire *Dr. Strangelove* (Columbia, 1964), he announced that he was searching for a science-fiction story to develop into his next picture. It was recommended that he get in touch with Arthur C. Clarke, one of the foremost names in the field. Clarke was excited by the prospect and thought a short story of his, "The Sentinel," might be ideal for an adaptation. Kubrick liked the choice and began adding his own ideas in order to expand the brief tale into a full-length screenplay. To ensure that what they were concocting was of interest to the money men, Kubrick asked if Clarke would turn their script into a full-length novel, which the author began writing in 1964. The first screenplay draft was presented to the brass at MGM, who, on the basis of what they read, agreed to finance the project for the very high figure of $6 million. In February 1965 it was official: Stanley Kubrick's new picture, then given the very ordinary B-movie title of *Journey beyond the Stars*, would begin shooting in England by the end of the year, with a projected release date of December 1966. Little did the studio realize that Kubrick did not have a traditional filming schedule in mind and would take his sweet time perfecting what he envisioned would be his masterpiece. More than three years would pass between the press announcement and the actual opening of the movie.

In the summer of 1965 sets began rising at MGM's Borehamwood Studios, where the bulk of the picture would be shot. Although Kubrick and company took over much of that facility, there was one particular set that was simply too big for MGM to accommodate: the TMA-1 excavation site where the astronauts encounter the monolith. This was erected instead over at Shepperton Studios, on Stage H, the second-largest soundstage in Europe. To carry the first segment of the movie, which consisted entirely of performers in ape costumes (designed by Stuart Freeborn), Kubrick hired a collection of mimes and dancers to enact simian movements, which they did with an incredible degree of grace and conviction. Daniel Richter was chosen for the central ape role, referred to in the screenplay as "Moon-Watcher." This character was given the task of tossing a bone skyward, starting one of the most famous and unexpected transition scenes in movie history. The one actor who ended up making a greater impact than any of the others was never even seen onscreen (nor did he ever appear on the set). Douglas Rain, a Canadian performer, was chosen to provide the gentle, lulling voice of the computer, HAL, and gained something of a following for this credit. As spoken by Rain, HAL came off as the most three-dimensional and interesting character in the picture.

> "The 9000 series is the most reliable computer ever made. No 9000 computer has ever made a mistake or distorted information. We are all, by any practical definition of the words, fool-proof and incapable of error."
> —HAL

Kubrick soon discarded his original proposed title in favor of something very odd and infinitely more intriguing, *2001: A Space Odyssey*. (Clarke's original story had been set in 1996.) As Clarke continued to revise his novel under the new title, Kubrick set to work; principal photography began on December 29, 1965, at the Shepperton soundstage. The company shot the excavation sequence (which required pouring ninety tons of dyed sand onto the set) first so the cast and crew could move over to their designated headquarters at Borehamwood. Filming that required actors went on for another seven months, including scenes utilizing the movie's most impressive set, the centrifuge (the interior of the *Discovery-1*) in which the astronauts, played by Gary Lockwood and Keir Dullea, are first seen going about their daily lives in space. This enclosed structure, built so it could be rotated like a bicycle wheel at three miles per hour, required that Kubrick direct from outside the wheel by closed circuit. This amazingly detailed forty-foot-high contraption cost a whopping $750,000 to build. Kubrick was so dead set on keeping his project behind closed doors that he even came up with the idea of filming the opening "Dawn of Man" scene indoors, using a newly developed front screen projection system that allowed for the use of still photographs as backdrops before which actors could be filmed in a relatively convincing fashion. Another technical advancement was the "slit-scan machine," created to produce a fast-moving tunnel of lights; it helped to achieve the psychedelic effect of Dullea racing through his trip into "the Unknown" toward the climax of the movie. Most of the images used for this scene were shot by the second unit crew over Monument Valley in Utah and the Hebrides in Scotland. Once all the human beings (including the "apes") were out of the way, Kubrick and his team spent the remainder of 1966 and all of 1967 toiling on the special effects. By the time Kubrick declared *2001* finished, some $10.5 million had been invested in this risky property, $6.5 million of it for the visual effects.

Prior to spending more than a year on his special effects, Stanley Kubrick directed *2001: A Space Odyssey*'s two human stars, Keir Dullea and Gary Lockwood.

Kubrick decided to reject a totally original score (from Alex North) in favor of classical music—by two nineteenth-century composers (coincidentally with the same last name) who thereby gained the appreciation of a new generation. A memorably poetic use of Johann Strauss's "Blue Danube" waltz played to a series of floating and interlocking spacecraft that at times suggested hardware intercourse, while the eerie, majestic beginning of Richard Strauss's 1896 tone poem *Also sprach Zarathustra* was used to open and close the movie, an effect so brilliant and thrilling that the piece was parodied over and over. From then on these few measures of *Zarathustra* have been used time and again to evoke an opulent degree of magnitude or wonder, or outer space itself.

Ever the perfectionist, Kubrick kept tinkering with the movie right up to its premiere—and beyond. Shortly before it opened, he decided to excise a prologue, a sequence of Dr. Floyd purchasing a "bush baby" for his daughter (something still referred to in the release print), and other scenes of the astronauts' families. He also eliminated all of the voice-over narration, which was a bold move; this was one film that certainly left many viewers confused and in need of some clarity. The final cut clocked in at 156 minutes (161 minutes with entr'acte and overture), and MGM planned to release it as a road-show attraction with a break, to be viewed in the Cinerama format. This version played for the first batch of reviewers and paying customers for all of three days at the Capitol Theatre in New York. Kubrick then decided that he was uncomfortable with how the picture was unfolding at this length and trimmed another seventeen minutes, shaving down the "Dawn of Man" opening and further scenes within the centrifuge to bring the footage down to 139 minutes. This version reopened on April 6, 1968, at Manhattan's Cinerama and became the accepted final cut of the movie.

Belying the classic status the picture achieved in due time, *2001* was not, in 1968, a critical favorite for the most part, garnering some pretty harsh condemnations from certain critics who found it hard to follow and dull. MGM might have had good reason to worry about having spent so much money, were it not for the fact that audiences seemed to be ignoring the bad press and showing up in large numbers at the select venues exhibiting the picture. This was the sort of movie that wasn't going to please everyone, but those it did were enthusiastic in such a way that *2001* was looked upon as something akin to a religious experience. It was also a case of perfect timing in terms of distribution. In the three years since the project was first announced, the U.S. space program had become something of a national obsession, and the upcoming moon landing, which would take place the year after *2001*'s release, was a landmark event that had most of the world wondering and theorizing about interplanetary travel and exploration. Soon enough word got around that this movie was so unlike anything else that had ever been attempted, so visually awesome, and so "out there" that it had to be seen only on a big screen, which meant that it became the event picture MGM had envisioned. For many, this heralded the long-awaited arrival of the science-fiction film as an intellectual experience, devoid of laser guns and men in rubber monster suits—a picture that stressed the "science" and considered the very plausible possibilities of advanced civilizations from other worlds in an earlier period of history. For every excited endorsement the film got, just as many admirers of old-fashioned, low-budget, fast-moving sci-fi couldn't help but look at it with disdain for taking itself too seriously and placing thought before action. Kubrick's *2001* kept audiences sharply divided, but even some of its detractors couldn't help but concede that it was an undeniably important achievement.

By the end of its initial run, *2001: A Space Odyssey* had managed to take second place (after Columbia's comparatively old-fashioned *Funny Girl*) as the highest-grossing 1968 release. The picture had a multitude of theories and arguments written about it and quickly entered the public consciousness as the final word in science fiction—or "the ultimate trip," as some of MGM's ad copy had proclaimed, in a barely coded nod to the drug culture that had helped champion the film.

YOURS, MINE AND OURS

Top 10 Box Office Film

Opening date: April 24, 1968.

United Artists. A Robert E. Blume Presentation of a Desilu-Walden Production.

Director: Melville Shavelson. Producer: Robert F. Blumofe. Screenplay: Mort Lachman, Melville Shavelson. Story: Bob Carroll Jr., Madelyn Davis. Photography: Charles F. Wheeler. Designer: Arthur Lonergan. Set Decoration: James Payne. Costumes: Frank Cardinale, Renita Reachi. Music: Fred Karlin. Songs: "Yours, Mine and Ours" and "It's a Sometimes World," music by Fred Karlin, lyrics by Ernie Sheldon. Editor: Stuart Gilmore. Technicolor. 111 minutes.

CAST: Lucille Ball (Helen North Beardsley), Henry Fonda (Frank Beardsley), Van Johnson (Officer Darrel Harrison), Louise Troy (Madeleine Love), Sidney Miller (Dr. Ashford), Tom Bosley (Family Doctor), Nancy Howard (Nancy Beardsley), Walter Brooke (Howard Beardsley), Ben Murphy (Larry); *The Beardsley Children*: Tim Matthieson/Tim Matheson (Mike), Gil Rogers (Rusty), Nancy Roth (Rosemary), Suzanne Cupito/Morgan Brittany (Louise), Gary Goetzman (Greg), Holly O'Brien (Susan), Michele Tobin (Veronica), Maralee Foster (Mary), Tracy Nelson (Germaine), Stephanie Oliver (Joan); *The North Children*: Jennifer Leak (Colleen), Kevin Burchett (Nicky), Kimberly Beck (Janette), Mitch Vogel (Tommy), Margot Jane (Jean), Eric Shea (Phillip), Greg Atkins (Gerald), Lynnell Atkins (Teresa).

PLOT: Frank Beardsley, a naval commander whose late wife has left him in charge of ten children, and widowed Helen North, a mother of eight, fall in love and marry, requiring them to adapt to a whole new lifestyle to accommodate their enormous combined brood.

By 1967 Lucille Ball had become so identified with television that few expected to see her on motion-picture screens on a regular basis. She was, however, always on the lookout for suitable big-screen properties and had found one back in 1961, when the marriage of Frank Beardsley to Helen North made newspaper headlines because of the staggering number of children they were combining through their nuptials: eighteen total. (And they later had two more together.) Ball had her company, Desilu, buy the rights to the Beardsley-North story years before the real Helen Beardsley decided to tell her tale in book form and publish it as *Who Gets the Drumstick?* (1965). Ball relied on her trusted writing team from her smash hit series *I Love Lucy*, Bob Carroll Jr. and Madelyn Davis, to come up with a story outline, which was then scripted by Mort Lachman and veteran writer-director Melville Shavelson. Although the screenplay did not alter the names or number of children, efforts were made to give audiences a more comedic and confrontational spin on the situation than the relatively stress-free one described by Beardsley. Whereas the real Helen and Frank met through his sister, a nun, who encouraged them to correspond by letter, the scripters wisely removed almost all references to

> "Let's get one thing straight—there's no more 'mine' and there's no more 'yours.' From now on everyone and everything is 'ours.'"
> —Frank Beardsley

religion or spirituality. Instead, Helen and Frank enacted the standard cinematic meet-cute of colliding shopping carts. Leaving out the nun as middleman also meant the writers could get some comic mileage out of Frank and Helen attempting to conceal the number of their offspring from one another, something the real couple told each other up front. Since Helen insisted their union was greeted with wholehearted support by all of their children, this aspect most definitely needed to be fictionalized. The uncomfortable feelings between the movie's North and Beardsley kids provided Ball with a typical "Lucy" set piece: during her first meeting with Fonda's brood, they spike her drink, and she becomes increasingly tipsy. Also fictionalized was the Beardsley home. Rather than moving into a new house altogether as depicted in the movie, the Beardsley-Norths chose to add on to Frank's residence in Carmel, California.

Filming of *Yours, Mine and Ours* (originally called *His, Hers and Theirs*) took place during the hiatus between seasons five and six of *The Lucy Show*, beginning on July 10, 1967, with location shooting in San Francisco, at the Alameda Naval Station and aboard the aircraft carrier U.S.S. *Enterprise*. Because the film was a coproduction of Desilu, Ball had a lot of say in how the picture was fashioned. She enlisted one of her favorite actors and a former costar (of Fox's 1942 melodrama *The Big Street*), Henry Fonda, to

What better way to fall love than a game of bocce ball, as Lucille Ball and Henry Fonda discover in *Yours, Mine and Ours*.

play Frank and hired her close friend Van Johnson (her costar from MGM's 1945 comedy *Easy to Wed*) for the fictional role of Fonda's best buddy. The real-life Frank was about twenty years younger than Fonda, and Ball was further stretching credulity by asking audiences to believe that she was capable of having yet another child at the age of fifty-six. But since all of America was crazy about "Lucy" and couldn't have felt more comfortable spending time with anyone else in the part, all strains on believability were tossed aside.

Not surprisingly, a majority of critics carped over what they perceived as a mere sitcom extended for the big screen, safe, squeaky clean, and extolling family values. They were looking for something radical and cutting-edge to reflect the changing attitudes of the era; what they found was a film that made offhand comments reminding people not to "question the workings of a democracy" and made it seem only natural that a young man would happily accept being drafted to fight in Vietnam. Although Louise Troy, as the archly named "Madeleine Love," got her chance to speak out for any childless citizen who ever had to endure listening to people swap stories about their offspring, there was no doubt that any lifestyle outside the family unit was under suspicion.

Remarkably, *Yours, Mine and Ours* avoided falling into the cutesy zone more often than not. For the first half of the film a refreshing amount of time was given over to the dating lives of a middle-aged (or beyond) man and woman, with charming performances by the two leads and a very relaxed, credible tone given to the potentially sticky situations on hand.

WAR AND PEACE (Soviet Union)

Academy Award Winner: Best Foreign Language Film

Academy Award Nominee: Art Direction–Set Decoration

Opening date: April 28, 1968 (opened in the Soviet Union as *Voyna i mir*, in four sections: *Andrey Bolkonskiy* in 1966; *Natasha Rostova* in 1966; *1812 god* in 1967; and *Pierre Bezuhkov* in 1967).

Continental. A Walter Reade Organization and Satra Presentation of a Mosfilm Production.

Director-Producer: Sergei Bondarchuk. Screenplay: Sergei Bondarchuk, Vasily Solovyov. Based on the 1869 novel *Voyna i mir* (*War and Peace*), by Leo Tolstoy. Photography: Anatoly Petritsky. Art Directors: Mikhail Bogdanov, Gennady Myasnikov. Costumes: Mikhail Chikovany. Music: Vyacheslav Ovchinnikov. Editor: Tatiana Likhacheva. Choreographer: Vladimir Burmeister. (English-Language Version: Dialogue Adaptation and Direction: Lee Kressel, for Titan Productions; Supervising Editor: Sidney Katz; Narration Written by Andrew Witwer; Narrator: Norman Rose.) Sovocolor/Deluxe. Sovoscope 70. 373 minutes (shown in two parts in the United States, part 1 at 195 minutes, part 2 at 178 minutes; cut from the 484-minute Soviet print).

CAST: Ludmila Savelyeva (Natasha Rostova), Sergei Bondarchuk (Pierre Bezukhov), Vyacheslav Tihonov (Andrei Bolkonsky), Hira Ivanov-Golovko (Countess Rostova), Irina Gubanova (Sonya Rostova), Antonia Shuranova (Princess Maria Bolkonsky), Victor Stanitsin (Count Rostov), Oleg Tabakov (Nikolai Rostov), Anatoly Ktorov (Prince Nikolai Bolkonsky), Anastasia Vertinskaya (Princess Liza Bolkonsky), Nikolai Kodin/Seryozha Yermilov (Petya Rostov), Boris Smirnov (Prince Vasily Kuragin), Irina Skobtseva (Helene Kuragin), Vasily Lanovoi (Anatole Kuragin), Oleg Yefremov (Dolohov), Angelina Stepanova (Anna Scherer), Boris Zahava (Kutuzov), Vladislav Strzhelchik (Napoleon).

PLOT: In the early eighteenth century, as Napoleon attempts to conquer Russia, Prince Andrei Bolkonsky and his friend Pierre Bezukhov find their lives and those around them shattered by the conflict.

Aside from its place as the most famous and revered Russian-language book of all time, Leo Tolstoy's epic novel *War and Peace* had the distinction of being the title that came most frequently to mind when anybody wanted to stress great length and size in literature, or to emphasize a depth and density of content that was impressive to wade through for some, eminently impenetrable for others. The novel first appeared between 1865 and 1869 and soon became one of the most widely read books not only in its homeland but throughout the world. Recognized as a complex masterpiece about the devastation of war, it combined the historical background of the 1812 conflict between France and Russia with a series of heavily detailed, fictionalized personal stories that kept readers enthralled through more than a thousand pages. Most fittingly, it was the Soviet Union that decided if anybody was going to do the definitive film adaptation, it would be them.

Director-actor Sergei Bondarchuk's plan was to get the government of the Soviet Union to cooperate in putting together a motion picture that would stand as that country's most important contribution to world cinema to date, one that would indicate the scope and power of Soviet filmmaking. Furthermore, he hoped to put as much of the novel up on the screen as he could. This meant dividing the film into four individual sections that could play on their own in their initial engagements and then be fitted together for some sort of special showing once they were all completed. Trusting Bondarchuk's talent and personal vision, the Soviet government allowed its army to cooperate fully in order to ensure that the battle sequences were every bit as spectacular as they were described by Tolstoy. It also offered unlimited funding so that the movie would look great and not suffer from any artistic compromises. Production began in September 1962 and continued over an unprecedented five-year period, including postproduction on each quarter of the movie. This passage of time was a great help when it came to aging each of the principals, who required little makeup to indicate their maturing. Some one hundred indoor sets were built in the four large soundstages at Mosfilm Studios, the most impressive of them the massive ballroom in which Natasha and Andrei discover their feelings for one another. There were no fewer than 168 outdoor locations as well, chief among them Borodino itself, where the intense and mostly accurate staging of the fateful battle of the same name was shot during 1964. In the end, it took up some forty-five minutes of screen time and was so loaded with smoke, blood, artillery fire, and chaos

> "War is not a polite sport, but the vilest thing in life. We must understand that and not play at war. This fearful necessity must be taken sternly and seriously. Don't lie about it. Let war be war and not a game."
> —Andrei Bolkonsky

that a shocking number of horses were sacrificed in the name of art. Bondarchuk shot the stunning sequence of Moscow in flames at Volokolamsk, and the hunting scene in the village of Boguslavskiy, near Kashira. By the time Bondarchuk had finished putting it all on celluloid, something akin to $100 million (approximately $600 million in today's dollars) had been spent, making this by a wide margin the most costly motion picture ever produced, a record it continues to hold with inflation taken into consideration.

The opening installment, supposedly centering on Andrei but featuring many of the principals, was first screened as part of the Moscow Film Festival in 1965; its official Russian distribution took place the following year. Judging from this two-and-a-half-hour introduction, Bondarchuk seemed to know exactly what he was doing: putting some grand artistic flourishes to the tale with slow motion, overlapping scenes, freeze-frames, silent-movie-like dream sequences that involved matte work, and poetic recitations on immortality and the nature of war. The film was large and opulent but extremely intimate as well, giving great attention to its three leads, though less to such characters as Natasha's brother Nikolai and Princess Maria. Part 2, concentrating on Natasha, was certainly the most soap-opera-like portion of the film. It too arrived in 1966, and the Russian public kept showing up in huge numbers, eagerly shelling out the fifty kopecks (approximately fifty-five cents) for admission. The next year, 1967, saw the arrival of *1812 god*, which was dominated by the Borodino sequence, and *Pierre Bezuhkov*, which contained perhaps the most visually smashing and emotionally wrenching sequence in the film: the looting and burning of Moscow, captured with a sweeping camera crane as one of civilization's lowest moments unfolded.

The Soviet Union proudly noted that more than 98 million filmgoers had turned out to watch the four-part epic. Along the way, U.S. distributor Walter Reade Jr. was keeping abreast of the creation and distribution of the picture, wanting very badly to do something with it here in America. Confronted with the dilemma of selling an eight-hour-plus movie to as many customers as possible, he knew that some compromises were needed. After shelling out $1.5 million for all Western Hemisphere rights, he convinced Bondarchuk that he needed to lop some footage off the movie, bringing the running time down by nearly two hours. He also felt (wrongly) that it would be better to present the picture in a dubbed version, assigning this task to Lee Kressell, who had handled such other international attractions as *Divorce Italian Style* and *The Shop on Main Street*, although in both of those cases the pictures were allowed to be exhibited first in their original language with subtitles.

The release strategy for *War and Peace* in New York, at the DeMille Theatre on Broadway, meant that customers paid between $5.00 and $7.50 to see both parts of *Peace*. The first was shown at three hours and fifteen minutes plus a ten-minute intermission; the second, two minutes shy of three hours and including a ten-minute break as well. Part 1 would screen in the afternoon, followed by a two-and-a-half-hour break, with the second half showing that evening. From that point on, there would be alternate viewings, with parts 1 and 2 trading off afternoon and evening showings to ensure that those who actually worked for a living could be on hand for consecutive evening viewings. This

It was certainly an impressive achievement, but this ad for the British engagement of *War and Peace* is immodest even in the annals of film hyperbole.

sort of time commitment needed tremendous critical support to assure the public that this was something well worth the sacrifice of six hours of one's life. Despite the shabby dubbing, the U.S. critics did indeed get behind the movie 100 percent, proclaiming it every bit as good as one could hope an adaptation of this seemingly unadaptable work could be. This acclaim helped the film become a stellar art-house attraction in its big-city engagements. But its unwieldy length made finding acceptable venues in which to play it throughout the rest of the country much too difficult. Those who made the effort were amply rewarded with a stirring and sumptuous motion picture, its antiwar message wholly relevant in the era of the much-debated Vietnam debacle.

THE ODD COUPLE

Academy Award Nominee: Screenplay—Based on Material from Another Medium; Film Editing

Top 10 Box Office Film

Opening date: May 2, 1968.

Paramount. A Howard W. Koch Production.

Director: Gene Saks. Producer: Howard W. Koch. Screenplay: Neil Simon. Based on his 1965 play. Photography: Robert B. Hauser. Art Directors: Hal Pereira, Walter Tyler. Set Decorators: Robert Benton, Ray Moyer. Costumes: Jack Bear. Men's Wardrobe: John Anderson. Music: Neal Hefti. Editor: Frank Bracht. Technicolor. Panavision. 106 minutes.

CAST: Jack Lemmon (Felix Ungar), Walter Matthau (Oscar Madison), John Fiedler (Vinnie), Herbert Edelman (Murray), David Sheiner (Roy), Larry Haines (Speed), Monica Evans (Cecily Pigeon), Carole Shelley (Gwendolyn Pigeon), Iris Adrian (Waitress), Heywood Hale Broun (Sportswriter at Shea).

PLOT: Tossed out by his wife after driving her crazy with his perfectionism and hypochondria, Felix Ungar moves in with his slovenly divorced friend Oscar Madison, only to have their contrasting habits and personalities take its toll on their relationship.

With *The Odd Couple*, playwright Neil Simon struck upon a simple premise so universal in its appeal that its very title would become a part of the lexicon, its lead characters popping instantly to mind when describing either slovenly or fastidious behavior. It might not have been Simon's best or funniest play, but it had more staying power than any of the others in the public consciousness, achieving success not only in its original theatrical format but as a motion picture and a television sitcom. Simon knew there was great humor in putting polar opposites together (he later admitted that he was inspired to write the piece after visiting his brother, Danny, who was living on his own following his divorce). Although he had not set out to write anything particularly profound, Simon's play did indeed capture just how impossible it is for most of the human race to spend any extended amount of time in the same dwelling with another of the same species, even best of friends and lovers eventually put off by too much up-close cohabitation.

Opening on March 10, 1965, at the Plymouth Theatre, with Walter Matthau and Art Carney in the leads, *The Odd Couple* was hailed as Simon's best work yet and became an instant box-office smash. It won Tony Awards for Matthau, director Mike Nichols, its scenic design, and Simon (as best author, *not* best play, since the organization made a distinction between the two at this period in its history), and continued at its original venue until switching over to the Eugene O'Neill in August 1966. When it closed on July 2, 1967, it had run for 966 performances.

By the time of its Broadway closing, the film version of *The Odd Couple* had already completed principal photography, Paramount having paid Simon for the rights prior to its Broadway bow. The original pre-stage deal had given Simon a $175,000 advance that would escalate to $500,000 along the way. In April 1965, the first casting announcement stated that Jack Lemmon would be taking on the role of Felix, with Frank Sinatra as Oscar. If Matthau was worried that he had missed his chance of repeating his stage role, fate intervened in the person of Billy Wilder, who had wanted to work with the actor as far back as 1954 when he was casting *The Seven Year Itch* (Twentieth Century-Fox), only to end up, reluctantly, with Tom Ewell in the lead. Wilder offered Matthau the part of Jack Lemmon's shady brother-in-law in his comedy *The Fortune Cookie* (United Artists, 1966), which Matthau eagerly accepted; that meant he would have to vacate his Tony Award–winning role in October 1965 to make the picture. *The Fortune Cookie* not only earned Matthau the best notices of his motion-picture career to date, but won him a much-applauded Academy Award for Best Supporting Actor. Because of this triumph, he was promoted to leading man for Twentieth Century-Fox's adultery comedy *A Guide for the Married Man*, proving himself a box-office draw and ensuring that the *Odd Couple* movie would be his, not Sinatra's.

Simon didn't see much reason to change his words, although several pop-culture references from the play (ranging from *Maverick* and Bulldog Drummond to Pepto-Bismol and the Marx Brothers) were discarded. Also gone was dialogue about Oscar's having injured himself while on a drinking binge after the collapse of his marriage and Felix's confession of having looked at other women while still married to Frances, these two passages being deemed per-

> "Something wrong with this system, that's what's wrong. I don't think that two single men living alone in a big, eight-room apartment should have a cleaner house than my mother."
> —Oscar Madison

haps too adult in tone for what was to be marketed as a family-friendly comedy and booked to play Radio City Music Hall. For clarity, a bit of dialogue was added indicating that Felix had no intention of going upstairs to join Oscar at the Pigeon Sisters' apartment (act 2 of the play left this vague until it was clarified in the opening of the third act), and any suggestion of cruelty to fish was absent, since a line about Oscar's accidentally letting his son's goldfish die was cut. Some discussions from the show were staged outside of the apartment for a cinematic change of scenery, while bits were added just to remind people that they were no longer sitting in a Broadway house. These included an extended (perhaps too extended) opening that had Felix trying to kill himself and then crimping his neck at a strip club; a bit of padding that showed Felix shopping for the big dinner with the Pigeon sisters; and a superfluous bit that had Oscar and his buddies searching the Upper West Side for Felix. Best of the added scenes was one of Felix phoning Oscar at Shea Stadium to report on dinner, causing his roommate to miss a rare triple play.

Paramount allotted a very generous $4 million budget to the production, which included a three-week rehearsal period. Principal photography began on April 25, 1967, at Paramount Studios in Hollywood. In early June the company arrived in New York for three weeks of location shooting at Central Park and the Soldiers and Sailors Monument on Riverside Drive, both used for part of Oscar and Felix's late-night discussion (which now included a timely reference to "muggers"); the Metropole Cafe in Times Square, where Felix would hurt his neck; Bohack's supermarket; the Flanders Hotel on West Forty-seventh Street (a return to harsher times for Lemmon, who had actually stayed there years earlier while trying to break into the business) for Felix's aborted suicide attempt; and Shea Stadium itself, where an actual triple play was staged with real ballplayers from the Mets and the Pirates. For Oscar's apartment the filmmakers, wanting the exterior to come as close as possible to the description in Simon's original script for the play, chose the Dorchester at 131 Riverside Drive at East Eighty-fifth Street. The rooftop argument between Lemmon and Matthau was shot a bit further uptown, however, atop 190 Riverside Drive at West Ninety-first Street.

Very strategically, *The Odd Couple* was planned to open in May in the same theater (Radio City) in which the film of Simon's previous hit play, *Barefoot in the Park*, had debuted a year earlier. The reviewers picked sides: some decided that the laughter that had rocked Broadway just could not be repeated on a movie screen, while others guaranteed audiences that not a single iota of fun had been lost in the stage-to-screen transfer. The Radio City attendance records for *Barefoot* were quickly smashed, and the latest Simon comedy became the highest-grossing movie in the hall's history. *The Odd Couple* soared past its predecessor at the box office once it opened to the general public, becoming not just a solid hit but a flat-out sensation, more than doubling the earlier picture's grosses to rack up an astounding $40 million in America alone. That made it the third-highest-grossing comedy of the decade, following *The Graduate* (AVCO

Carrying a cigar that does not exactly fit the character of Felix Ungar, Jack Lemmon makes tracks from an angry Walter Matthau in this rehearsal photo from *The Odd Couple*.

Embassy, 1967) and *It's a Mad Mad Mad Mad World* (United Artists, 1963). The teaming of Lemmon and Matthau, already so evidently on the mark in *The Fortune Cookie*, was even more glorious this time out. Allowed equal playing time, Matthau again came out that much further ahead with his droll line readings, strangely stooped posturing, and priceless slow burns. The film's humor ran the gamut from mildly amusing to dryly observant to belly-laugh funny, the comic highlight being Lemmon's incessant "moose calls" in an effort to clear his sinuses in the middle of a crowded late-night diner. *The Odd Couple* became one of the year's most-quoted movies, and its tremendous response assured future adaptations of almost all of Neil Simon's stage hits for years to come.

ROSEMARY'S BABY

Academy Award Winner: Best Supporting Actress (Ruth Gordon)

Academy Award Nominee: Screenplay—Based on Material from Another Medium

Top 10 Box Office Film

Opening date: June 12, 1968.

Paramount. A William Castle Production.

Director-Screenplay: Roman Polanski. Based on the 1967 novel by Ira Levin. Producer: William Castle. Photography: William Fraker. Production Designer: Richard Sylbert. Art Director: Joel Schiller. Set Decorator: Robert Nelson. Costumes: Anthea Sylbert. Music: Christopher Komeda. "Rosemary's Lullaby," performed by Mia Farrow. Editors: Sam O'Steen, Bob Wyman. Technicolor. 136 minutes.

CAST: Mia Farrow (Rosemary Woodhouse), John Cassavetes (Guy Woodhouse), Ruth Gordon (Minnie Castevet), Sidney Blackmer (Roman Castevet), Maurice Evans (Edward "Hutch" Hutchins), Ralph Bellamy (Dr. Abraham Sapirstein), Angela Dorian/Victoria Vetri (Terry Gionoffrio), Patsy Kelly (Laura-Louise McBirney), Elisha Cook (Mr. Nicklas), Charles Grodin (Dr. C. C. Hill), Emmaline Henry (Elise Dunstan), Marianne Gordon (Joan Jellico), Phil Leeds (Dr. Shand), Hope Summers (Mrs. Gilmore), Wendy Wagner (Tiger), Hanna Landy (Grace Cardiff), D'Urville Martin (Diego), Tony Curtis (Voice of Donald Baumgart), William Castle (Man outside Phone Booth).

PLOT: Young mother-to-be Rosemary Woodhouse fears for her unborn child when evidence leads her to believe that her next-door neighbors are members of a witch coven using her for their own diabolical means.

Ira Levin earned his stripes by writing a pretty nifty suspense novel, *A Kiss before Dying*, that had been made into a moderately successful film (United Artists, 1956), and by adapting Mac Hayman's comic novel *No Time for Sergeants* both for television and for the Broadway stage. These commendable credits suddenly became mere blips on his résumé after the impact of his 1967 novel, *Rosemary's Baby*, which offered so brilliant a premise that the very title became a part of twentieth-century horror folklore. Knowing that a woman is never more vulnerable or frightened than during her first pregnancy, Levin created a nightmarish tale of witchcraft in modern-day Manhattan in which a frail young mother-to-be is tricked by a coven of Satanists into bearing the devil's child. By the time the book hit the stands, Hollywood producer William Castle had paid

> **"I dreamed someone was raping me . . . someone inhuman."**
> **—Rosemary Woodhouse**

$150,000 for the rights, hoping to direct a film version for Paramount Pictures. Castle was known for his cheaply made gimmick thrillers, like *The Tingler* (Columbia, 1959) and *Homicidal* (Columbia, 1961); but Robert Evans, then head of production at the studio, thought *Rosemary's Baby* had greater possibilities and needed a firmer directorial hand to bring it to life. He suggested Roman Polanski, who had created a stir on the art-house circuit with two psychological thrillers, *Knife in the Water* (Kanawha, 1963) and the British-made *Repulsion* (Royal Films International, 1965). In order to get Castle to give up his directorial reins, Evans agreed to let him stay on board as producer and to receive 50 percent of the profits.

Although Polanski had just suffered an unpleasant experience with the handling of his first studio-released picture, *The Fearless Vampire Killers* (MGM, 1967), he was anxious to do the film, under the condition that he himself write the screenplay. Thankfully, he envisioned a script that pretty much used the original source as a blueprint, sometimes taking dialogue and action directly from the book. Indeed, what few moments were eliminated were more a decision of time than content. The film discarded any reference to the actual November 1965 New York blackout, which Rosemary and Hutch discuss in the book in order to bring up Minnie's use of exclusively black candles; the birth of the baby of Rosemary's sister a few months before Rosemary's child is born; and Guy's deceiving Rosemary by sending her to see *The Fantasticks* in order to keep her out of the building, a sequence actually filmed and then cut though still referred to at one point in the finished movie. Polanski also chose to play down the irony of the pope's visiting New York (as the pontiff really did in the fall of 1965) during Rosemary's pregnancy. All of these seemed minor sacrifices in light of how true to its source the film turned out to be, certainly one of the most letter-perfect and faithful renderings of a novel ever made.

The Dot Records soundtrack for *Rosemary's Baby* contained Mia Farrow's greatest musical contribution to cinema, her eerie rendition of the Christopher Komeda lullaby that bracketed the film.

When the film began shooting in New York on August 21, 1967, it was evident from the start what a difference hiring Polanski in place of Castle had made. Whereas Castle would have had the picture done in a few weeks' time, Polanski was meticulous and precise about every camera angle, every gesture, every nuance. While in Manhattan, he and his company shot brief scenes at such locales as Tiffany's, Park Avenue (for the exterior of the doctor's office), and the Doubleday Book Shop on Fifth Avenue. The most important New York location was the Dakota apartment building, a magnificent 1884 structure designed by Henry J. Hardenbergh on Seventy-second Street and Central Park West, subbing for the film's Bramford. Following the Manhattan shoot, the cast and crew moved west to Paramount Studios, where the interiors of the Bramford/Dakota were brilliantly recreated by designer Richard Sylbert. While in

California there was a brief diversion away from the soundstages to film Rosemary's bizarre dream sequence on a yacht at the Playa del Rey marina.

There was little doubt that public interest would be high by the time *Rosemary's Baby* opened in June 1968, but few could have anticipated how wonderfully Levin's story played out onscreen. The depiction of the seemingly everyday and normal constantly surrounded by a sense of menace and dread and the encroaching fear born of Rosemary's realization that she has no safe haven to turn to were all the more unnerving and horrific because Polanski did *not* resort to gore or cheap thrills for effect. Polanski's atmospheric use of the Bramford's unfriendly, cavernous hallways; the murmurs of coven incantations seeping through the walls; the sudden and cruel victimization of Terry, Hutch, and Baumgart; the comical presentation of such meddlesome characters as Minnie and Laralouise, masking the true evil of their intentions—all this made *Baby* one of the cinema's most masterful depictions of paranoia and unrest. Of course the film had its detractors, not unexpectedly the Catholic Legion of Decency, which was no doubt horrified at the film's matter-of-fact depiction of Satanism (the upside-down crucifix tied to the baby's bassinette at the finale was just one of many blasphemous images dramatized from the novel), the suggested absence of God (an authentic *Time* magazine cover asking "Is God Dead?" was glimpsed), and the utter hopelessness of Rosemary's plight, which was instrumental in the gut-level shock that stunned and stayed with patrons long after they had left the theaters.

Baby accomplished everything it set out to do: it established Roman Polanski as one of the most important contemporary directors and one of the rare foreign filmmakers to cross over into American motion pictures with total success; it turned Mia Farrow into a star; it raked in enough cash to make it one of the top moneymakers of the year; and it set the tone for all future mature, intelligent cinematic forays into psychological horror. Within a few short years *The Exorcist* (Warner Bros., 1973) would present mankind's battle with the devil in a more graphic and gory manner that, unfortunately, became the more expected and preferred way for audiences to see their horror. None of these movies came close to suggesting the sort of terror that *Rosemary's Baby* did, and it came to be looked upon as one of the true masterpieces of its genre.

THE GREEN BERETS

Top 10 Box Office Film

Opening date: June 19, 1968.

Warner Bros.–Seven Arts. A Batjac Production.

Directors: John Wayne, Ray Kellogg. Producer: Michael Wayne. Screenplay: James Lee Barrett. Based on the 1965 novel by Robin Moore. Photography: Winton C. Hoch. Production Designer: Walter M. Simonds. Set Decorator: Ray Moyer. Costumes: Jerry Alpert. Music: Miklós Rózsa. Song: "Ballad of the Green Berets," by Robin Moore and Staff Sgt. Barry Sadler, performed by chorus. Editor: Otho Lovering. Special Effects: Sass Bedig. Technicolor. Panavision. 141 minutes.

CAST: John Wayne (Col. Mike Kirby), David Janssen (George Beckworth), Jim Hutton (Sgt. Petersen), Aldo Ray (Sgt. Muldoon), Raymond St. Jacques (Doc McGee), Bruce Cabot (Col. Morgan), Jack Soo (Col. Cai), George Takei (Capt. Nim), Patrick Wayne (Lt. Jamison), Luke Askew (Sgt. Provo), Irene Tsu (Lin), Edward Faulkner (Capt. MacDaniel), Jason Evers (Capt. Coleman), Mike Henry (Sgt. Kowalski), Craig Jue (Hamchunk), Chuck Roberson (Sgt. Griffin), Eddy Donno (Sgt. Watson), Rudy Robbins (Sgt. Parks), Richard "Cactus" Pryor (Collier).

PLOT: Col. Mike Kirby and his Special Forces unit of Green Berets take charge of a strike camp near Da Nang, where they work alongside the Asian Honor Guard to fight the Vietcong.

Everybody in Hollywood knew that John Wayne was one of the industry's most outspoken right-wingers, a defender of the conservative faction, a fervent anticommunist, and a supporter of war. Few, however, realized he was willing to put his reputation on the line by concocting a motion picture that actually made it appear that it was a *good* idea for the United States to get itself involved in the Vietnam War, the most protested, most unnecessary, and most abhorred military conflict of the century. Wayne announced in the fall of 1965 that he would be making a film based on Robin Moore's recent best seller, *The Green Berets*, in order to make a statement about the importance of supporting a war against communism. Around the same time, three other major studio pictures about Vietnam were reportedly being prepared, but one by one each of these projects fell by the wayside as the real situation began to tear the U.S. population apart, leading to emotional protests and condemnations of the situation of an intensity never before seen in this country. Not one to be told he was on the wrong side of an issue, Wayne insisted that not only would his picture get made, come hell or high water, but, just to prove how crucial it was to get it produced, he would seek the support and cooperation of the Pentagon.

The problem was, the Pentagon had not been too pleased with Moore's novel, feeling that he showed the military in a bad light by writing about immoral dealings within the superior command. Wayne assured them that his screenwriter, James Lee Barrett, would take every precaution to ensure that the movie version portrayed the American forces with the utmost respect. Barrett therefore did not do a direct adaptation of Moore's book, which had been, after all, a collection of stories rather than a continuous narrative. The connection between the tales had been a nameless narrator, clearly Moore himself, who had been allowed to go behind enemy lines to write a firsthand account of what he witnessed. Moore had pulled no punches in writing about the good and bad of what he saw, but Barrett smoothed over this controversial angle by inventing another journalist, George Beckworth, who strongly condemned the war at first, only to be swayed to the opposing side after coming face to face with the evil of the Vietcong. Barrett concentrated on two incidents from the book: the attack on a U.S. base by the Vietcong that was saved from certain obliteration by a last-minute air strike, and the use of an embittered Vietnamese woman, whose family had been brutally killed by the Vietcong, to help the United States and its allies capture an important Vietcong military leader. Around these two set pieces Barrett wrote entirely new characters, including a dominant one for Wayne that allowed him to take charge in the manner his fans had come to expect.

Wayne managed to secure weaponry, artillery, helicopters, and military vehicles from the army; he was also allowed to film at Fort Benning, in western Georgia. Knowing he couldn't go anywhere near Vietnam itself, Wayne decided to shoot nearly the entire picture in this southern location, even though the surrounding area looked more like a forest than it did the jungles of Vietnam. At Fort Benning he spent $150,000 to build a Vietnamese village, which he pledged to leave up for the soldiers at the base to use for military training, and recruited a platoon of Hawaiians, brought down from Fort Devens in Mississippi, to play the Vietnamese. Photography began on August 9, 1967, with Wayne sitting in the director's chair for the first time since his last big personal project, *The Alamo* (United Artists, 1960),

even though the lumbering pace of that long-winded epic had proved that he was none too adept at directing. Perhaps sensing that it was better to allow someone else to share the reins, Wayne asked second unit director Ray Kellogg to take over some of the directorial duties, allowing work to proceed faster. Wayne did not, however, work fast enough, as far as his distributor, Warner Bros., was concerned, and when the $6 million production began to lag behind and escalate in cost, veteran Mervyn LeRoy was sent to oversee the production in order to get it back on track. After some three months in Georgia, the company was forced to relocate to the Warners back lot, where a twenty-acre jungle

> "No sir, Mr. Beckworth, it doesn't take a lead weight to fall on me, or a hit from one of those weapons to recognize that what's involved here is Communist domination of the world."
> —Sgt. Muldoon

was constructed to compensate for the loss of the forest at Fort Benning after a premature frost there had turned all the trees brown. Shooting finished in mid-November 1967, about $1 million over the original estimated cost.

Although Wayne shortened the picture by entirely excising the character of Kirby's wife (played by Wayne's costar from Paramount's 1962 release *The Man Who Shot Liberty Valance*, Vera Miles), he still allowed it to run way too long, the finished print clocking in at close to two and a half hours. Furthermore, Wayne often lost a good deal of clarity in the narrative, once again proving that he was no ace in the directorial department. He still had great faith in the movie and scoffed at the protestors who stood in front of the select theaters where *The Green Berets* opened in June 1968. The mostly liberal press, which already had its daggers ready for the movie, simply because of what it stood for, was relieved to discover

With the movie already running far too long, *The Green Berets'* star and codirector John Wayne was obliged to leave Vera Miles's entire role as his wife on the cutting-room floor.

that it didn't even have to stress the political angle in order to come down hard on the picture, so cliché ridden, foolishly simplistic, and numbingly dull it was on its own terms. Wayne, however, had been pretty impervious to media criticism for most of his career, and *The Green Berets* was no exception. It took in more than $19 million at the U.S. box offices, turning it into one of the top ten attractions of the year and proving that not all moviegoers in the late '60s were as tired of old-fashioned, conservative filmmaking as much of the media tried to make readers believe. While hawks could look to the picture as confirmation that Wayne was some sort of promilitary cinematic icon, peace supporters seemed vindicated in their opinion that Wayne was a dangerous influence on the population, with his pigheaded politics and backward patriotism.

Because Wayne was genuinely a great star and an important moneymaker, Hollywood felt highly ambivalent about him at this point in history, as he became the brunt of all kinds of criticism, fair and unfair. Not unexpectedly, Wayne couldn't care less about his detractors and was only too happy to speak on a platform unpopular in a generally liberal industry. He seemed not at all aware that he had been more than somewhat irresponsible in the way he had presented the Vietnam War in *The Green Berets*, the sole commercial studio release up to that time to deal with it. It took some distance and the passage of time for filmmakers to finally shed a very critical light on the conflict with such pictures as *The Deer Hunter* (Universal, 1978), *Apocalypse Now* (United Artists, 1979), *Platoon* (Orion, 1986), and *Full Metal Jacket* (Warner Bros., 1987). Each of these depicted the horror of the Vietnam War so powerfully that there was no chance anyone would ever again dare to try and present it as naively as Wayne had.

THE THOMAS CROWN AFFAIR

Academy Award Winner: Best Song ("The Windmills of Your Mind")

Academy Award Nominee: Original Score—For a Motion Picture (Not a Musical)

Opening date: June 19, 1968 (New York: June 26, 1968).

United Artists. A Mirisch Corporation Presentation of a Norman Jewison Production; a Mirisch–Simkoe–Solar Production.

Director-Producer: Norman Jewison. Screenplay: Alan R. Trustman. Photography: Haskell Wexler. Art Director: Robert Boyle. Set Decorator: Edward Boyle. Miss Dunaway's Wardrobe Designer: Thea Van Runkle. Mr. McQueen's Wardrobe Consultant: Ron Postal. Music: Michel Legrand. Song: "The Windmills of Your Mind," by Michel Legrand (music) and Alan and Marilyn Bergman (lyrics), performed by Noel Harrison. Editors: Hal Ashby, Ralph E. Winters, Byron Brandt. Associate Producer: Hal Ashby. Deluxe color. 102 minutes.

CAST: Steve McQueen (Thomas Crown), Faye Dunaway (Vicky Anderson), Paul Burke (Lt. Eddy Malone), Jack Weston (Erwin Weaver), Yaphet Kotto (Carl), Biff McGuire (Sandy), Astrid Heeren (Gwen), Todd Martin (Benjy), Sam Melville (Dave), Addison Powell (Abe), Sidney Armus (Arnie), Jon Shank (Curley), Allen Emerson (Don), Harry Cooper (Ernie), Johnny Silver (Bert), Carol Corbett (Miss Sullivan), John Orchard (John, Butler), Gordon Pinsent (Jamie McDonald), Patrick Horgan (Danny), Peg Shirley (Honey Weaver), Leonard Caron (Jimmy Weaver), Bruce Glover (Bank Manager).

PLOT: Insurance investigator Vicky Anderson tries to figure out how and why millionaire Thomas Crown managed to steal $2.6 million from the Boston Mercantile Bank.

Steve McQueen knew he was Hollywood's ambassador of cool during the '60s, but he also knew that it was wise to vary that persona, so he decided that for his next picture he'd like to be cool in a suit. When he got word of a script about a wealthy Bostonian who plans a bank heist principally for the fun of it, he contacted Norman Jewison, who had gotten his hands on the property, to campaign for the part. Jewison already had a working relationship with McQueen, having guided him through *The Cincinnati Kid* (MGM, 1965), but he wasn't anxious to resume the relationship at this point, worried that this unconventional bit of casting might hurt the picture. (He would later refer to McQueen as the most difficult actor he ever worked with.) Finally he relented,

> **"Every crime has a . . . personality, a something like the mind that planned it."**
> **—Vicky Anderson**

though screenwriter Alan R. Trustman was quite unhappy with the choice, having envisioned Sean Connery in the part from the get-go.

It was Jewison's wish to make a very loose, very stylish caper picture that had a great deal of flash, little real substance, and made its two leads look highly desirable in their sexual foreplay and handsome attire. Like so many other filmmakers of the day, he had seen a short film at Montreal's Expo 67 fair, "A Place to

The sheet music for Michel Legrand and Marilyn and Alan Bergman's whirligig of a song "The Windmills of Your Mind," which proved to be the undisputed highlight of *The Thomas Crown Affair.*

Stand," in which Pablo Ferro and his team had compressed forty minutes of footage into a seventeen-minute span by projecting multiple images on the screen at the same time. Jewison rightly believed that this gimmick would help cover up the lack of story material in the picture and filmed a good deal of it with the idea of piecing scenes together in this showy manner. *The Crown Caper* (as it was initially called) began shooting in Boston on June 6, 1967, and continued there for twelve weeks. It was filmed on the fifteenth floor of a building at 80 Federal Street (where Crown's office was created so that there could be an authentic city backdrop and not a studio-built one); at the National Shawmut Bank (both interior and exterior); at the Boston Police Station; along the Charles River; at the Cambridge Cemetery (where McQueen was seen picking up the money dropped off by Jack Weston); at the Belmont Country Club (for the golf sequence); at the Myopia Hunt Club (for the polo game); at Logan Airport; and at the Greyhound Bus Station. McQueen and Dunaway were also seen racing about in a dune buggy in Provincetown (back before this sort of recreation was considered dangerous for the environment and outlawed) and relaxing at an unfinished house at Crane's Beach in Ipswich. Adhering to Trustman's original conception of setting the story in Boston gave the movie (whose title was changed along the way to *Thomas Crown and Company*) a fresh look, if nothing else, and it made for the most extensive use of the Massachusetts capital yet put on film.

Jewison worked closely and extensively with his usual editor, Hal Ashby, and with Pablo Ferraro in order to give the movie a very complex, interlocking look of concurrent events popping up on the screen at the same time, montages set to Michel Legrand's plucky score, and an overall sense of very beautiful people living the high life, through the very artistic lensing of Haskell Wexler. Launching the whole thing was a whirligig of a song, "The Windmills of Your Mind," penned by Legrand with the husband-and-wife team of Alan and Marilyn Bergman, and sung by Rex Harrison's eldest son, Noel. This haunting tune was reprised later in the picture, during a sequence in which McQueen flew his glider over the outskirts of Boston, and really stood out as the movie itself fell apart from its lack of solid action and lazy pacing. It went on to win the Academy Award for Best Song of 1968 (it was Dusty Springfield's recording, not Harrison's, that cracked the *Billboard* charts, reaching number 31 nearly a year after the picture's release). *The Thomas Crown Affair* had genuine star power working in its favor, so audiences showed up to the tune of some $14 million in the summer of 1968 just to see McQueen and Dunaway flirt, look swanky in their costly wardrobes, and make it seem like there was no better way for a bored millionaire to entertain himself than to commit a robbery.

THE HEART IS A LONELY HUNTER

Academy Award Nominee: Actor (Alan Arkin); Supporting Actress (Sondra Locke)

Opening date: July 31, 1968.

Warner Bros.–Seven Arts.

Director: Robert Ellis Miller. Producers: Thomas C. Ryan, Marc Merson. Screenplay: Thomas C. Ryan. Based on the 1940 novel by Carson McCullers. Executive Producer: Joel Freeman. Photography: James Wong Howe. Art Director: LeRoy Deane. Costume Designer: Albert Wolsky. Music: David Grusin. Editor: John F. Burnett. Technicolor. 124 minutes.

CAST: Alan Arkin (John Singer), Sondra Locke (Mick Kelly), Laurinda Barrett (Mrs. Kelly), Stacy Keach Jr. (Blount), Chuck McCann (Spiros Antonapoulos), Biff McGuire (Mr. Kelly), Percy Rodriguez (Dr. Copeland), Cicely Tyson (Portia), Jackie Marlowe (Bubber Kelly), Johnny Popwell (Willie), Wayne Smith (Harry), Pete Mamakos (Spirmonedes), John O'Leary (Beaudine), Hubert Harper (Brannon), Robbie Barnes (Ralph Kelly), Gavin Paulin (Spareribs), Richard Fingar (Sucker), Sherri Vise (Delores), Horace Oates Jr. (Himself), Don Swafford (Dr. Gordon).

PLOT: Hoping to gain legal custody of his retarded friend Spiros after the latter is placed in a state hospital, John Singer, a deaf mute, takes up residence near the institution at the Kelly home, where he befriends awkward teenager Mick.

Four times Hollywood took a crack at adapting the delicately sad works of Carson McCullers. It got closest to her intentions with *The Heart Is a Lonely Hunter*, though the book certainly took its time making it from page to screen. McCullers (born Lula Carson Smith in Columbus, Georgia, in 1917) published the novel, her first, when she was all of twenty-two years old, receiving raves for her compassionate and enlightened examination of mankind's eternally aching soul. Although the novel sold well, there were enough touchy elements in the text, including deafness, mental retardation, suggestions of homosexuality, racial injustice, and pro-Marxist statements, to keep it from being obvious movie material. That was just as well, since these matters would most certainly have been excised or misinterpreted in any commercial adaptation done at the time. Once McCullers's third book, *The Member of the Wedding*, was successfully transformed into a Broadway play, interest was reawakened in *Heart*, and the rights to the novel were purchased in 1950 by an independent company called Film Documents. Things got no further than the planning stages, and for more than a decade there was no more mention of turning *Heart* into a movie. In 1961 José Quintero told the press that he had bought the rights to the book for his J/Q Productions with the intention of making it his second movie (following Warner Bros.' *The Roman Spring of Mrs. Stone*), to be filmed in the summer of 1962 with a screenplay by Gavin Lambert. His dream cast was Paul

> "I'll think about you, Singer. I could talk to you. And you listened. You ol' dummy, you really listened. S'times I think you're the only one who ever did."
> —Blount

Scofield as the deaf mute, John Singer; Zero Mostel as his brain-damaged pal, Antonopoulos; and Montgomery Clift as the philosophical alcoholic, Blount. Yet again this intriguing possibility curled up and died, only to be resurrected to some degree in 1963 when David Susskind, having paid $100,000 for the rights, decided *Heart* would be one of his next projects. Mostel and Clift were still being sought, only this time the latter was to be cast as Singer, since Blount's contribution to the story line had been minimized

The Warner Bros.–Seven Arts Records soundtrack for *The Heart Is a Lonely Hunter,* starring Alan Arkin as a deaf mute, whose affliction requires Sondra Locke to attempt to describe music to him through pantomime.

in Thomas C. Ryan's adaptation. Sidney Lumet was engaged to direct the picture, which was to be shot not in the South, but in the New York area, starting in September 1963, for the Landau Company. Once *Heart* was pushed back to the end of the year, Lumet was instead given the task of directing *The Pawnbroker*. By the time he finished that film, plans for putting *Heart* onscreen had been scrapped yet again.

Ryan had already gotten the blessing to proceed with his script from McCullers herself, who had read it and loved it. Determined not to let the project sit in storage much longer, he found a producing partner in Marc Merson. Merson, it turns out, had just done a TV drama, *The Love Song of Barney Kempinski*, which featured Alan Arkin, who was crazy about the McCullers book and had expressed interest in playing Singer. Once Arkin found himself Oscar-nominated for the hit comedy *The Russians Are Coming The Russians Are Coming* (United Artists, 1966), making him one of the most in-demand performers around, Merson and Ryan used his

name as the selling point in shopping the project around to the studios. Warner Bros. agreed to the do the picture with Arkin in the lead, provided the cost did not exceed $1 million. Any consideration of setting the movie during the book's original late 1930s time period was no longer valid, as this would have wreaked havoc with the budget. Instead, *The Heart Is a Lonely Hunter* would be set in the present, with nearly all of the filming to take place in Selma, Alabama. Selma had become famous in 1965 as the starting point of the Peace March to Montgomery, official response to which had made it one of the decade's many disturbing racial incidents. Therefore, the city more than welcomed the good publicity a movie about human understanding would bring. The principal site of filming (rented for $124 a month) was a deserted, thirteen-room, eighty-year-old Southern Gothic house located at 620 Mabry Street, which served as the Kelly home. Additional scenes were shot in Marion, Demopolis, and Birmingham.

Merson and Ryan decided upon Joseph Strick as director, which was certainly tempting fate. Strick was not a conventional filmmaker, to say the least, having done two of the most audience-unfriendly pictures of recent years—adaptations of Jean Genet's *The Balcony* (Continental, 1963) and James Joyce's *Ulysses* (Continental, 1967)—both of which he helmed with a heavy hand. Scheduled to begin filming on September 19, 1967, *The Heart Is a Lonely Hunter* got off to a rocky start when Ryan and Strick found themselves clashing over the script. Strick was adamant that the homosexual aspects of the relationship between Singer and his simple Greek friend be stressed, which Ryan absolutely could not fathom. One of the producers as well as the screenwriter, Ryan stood his ground, causing Strick to quit. Production was delayed while a replacement was found in Robert Ellis Miller, a far less experimental filmmaker than Strick and one who would make the picture more accessible to audiences. In the interim, between Strick's departure and the actual commencement of shooting on October 2, McCullers died in Nyack, New York, on September 29, 1967, at the age of fifty.

Despite McCullers's favorable reaction to the script, the film was hardly a letter-perfect rendering of her book. Aside from the updated time period, the movie shunted into the background one of the five main protagonists from the novel, restaurant owner Biff Brannon, who is left to grieve after his wife's unexpected death. Less surprisingly, Mick's two older sisters and older brother Bill were rightly deemed superfluous and eliminated altogether, as was the idea of the Kellys housing other boarders in addition to Mr. Singer. Feeling that the depiction of Dr. Copeland's stubbornly uneducated daughter, Portia, was dangerously close to offensive stereotyping, she was written with far more smarts and dignity and portrayed as such by Cicely Tyson, and was no longer working for the Kellys, as she had been in the book. The script also sidestepped both Copeland's and Blount's enthusiastic support of communism, as well as the controversial criticism McCullers had raised over the black community's refusal to better themselves in the light of white domination and racism. Gone, too, was the accidental wounding of neighbor Baby Wilson by young Bubber Kelly, an incident that had plunged the Kelly family into deeper debt after they were forced to pay his medical bills. Playing it safe in order to engender greater sympathy for the character, Willie (now Portia's husband instead of her brother) ended up in jail after being falsely accused of assaulting a white woman, whereas in the book he had gotten into a fight at a whorehouse. Likewise, although Copeland would suffer the indignity of being ignored while waiting to speak to the judge, the film did not make his plight any more horrid by having him slapped and unjustly tossed into jail as well, as had happened on the page. For all the softening of some of the harsher elements of the novel, the film did have the guts to retain the sad demise of Singer, but it did not keep Blount around for the event, having him abandon his deaf friend earlier.

With all of these changes, champions of McCullers's book were bound to carp, though the film was certainly faithful to the very melancholy tone of her work, capturing the inherent feeling of loss, loneliness, and lack of communication that the author had conveyed so well. Arkin, who did not play the part for sympathy or self-pity, did a beautiful job enacting the man's sense of dignity, loyalty, and empathy, even adding a touch of humor along the way. Anyone not yet convinced that this actor was one of the most important new performers to enrich the current movie scene had to have been simply floored by the contrast between this and the roles he had just pulled off in *Russians* and *Wait until Dark* (Warner Bros., 1967). In the central role of tomboyish Mick, Sandra Locke carried her share of the picture in what ranked as one of the most impressive debuts of the decade.

The Heart Is a Lonely Hunter touched on the theme of the importance of human compassion in a delicate and incisive manner that built up to one of the most genuinely heartbreaking final lines uttered in the annals of powerful motion-picture dramas. Good reviews, rather than great ones, were compensated for by a very steady word of mouth, turning the film into a surprise moneymaker for Warners. This was a relief to the studio, which had been stung at the box office the year before with its release of another McCullers adaptation, *Reflections in a Golden Eye*, which had lapsed into the grotesque in a way that *Heart* never did. With a Writers Guild nomination for Ryan as a reward for his faith in getting the movie on the screen, much-deserved Oscar mentions for both Arkin and Locke, and a win from the New York Film Critics for Arkin, *The Heart Is a Lonely Hunter* made the long journey to the screen well worthwhile.

RACHEL, RACHEL

Academy Award Nominee: Picture; Actress (Joanne Woodward); Supporting Actress (Estelle Parsons); Screenplay—Based on Material from Another Medium

Opening date: August 26, 1968.

Warner Bros.–Seven Arts. A Kayos Production.

Director-Producer: Paul Newman. Screenplay: Stewart Stern. Based on the 1966 novel *A Jest of God*, by Margaret Laurence. Photography: Gayne Rescher. Art Director: Robert Gundlach. Set Decoration: Richard Merrell. Costumes: Domingo Rodriguez. Music: Jerome Moross. Songs by Jerome Moross (music) and Stewart Stern (lyrics), performed by the Phaetons. Editor: Dede Allen. Technicolor. 101 minutes.

CAST: Joanne Woodward (Rachel Cameron), James Olson (Nick Kazlik), Kate Harrington (Mae Cameron), Estelle Parsons (Calla Mackie), Donald Moffat (Niall Cameron), Terry Kiser (Preacher), Frank Corsaro (Hector Jonas), Bernard Barrow (Leighton Siddley, Principal), Geraldine Fitzgerald (Reverend Wood), Nell Potts (Rachel as a Child), Shawn Campbell (James Dougherty), Violet Dunn (Verla), Izzy Singer (Lee Shabab).

PLOT: Rachel Cameron, a thirty-five-year-old unmarried schoolteacher living a lonely existence in a small New England town, hopes that her empty life has found some meaning when she begins an affair with former schoolmate Nick Kazlik, who has returned home for the summer.

When you're looking to get a difficult film project off the ground, it helps to have a husband who has box-office clout in the industry, which was what happened to Joanne Woodward when she came upon a property that offered her sublime acting opportunities but was also uncompromising in its truths about human frailty and loneliness, and often so unbearably sad that it seemed a risk to expect large audiences to spend money to see it. Margaret Laurence's novel *A Jest of God* first appeared in the author's native Canada in 1966 and went on to win the Governor-General's Award for Fiction (that country's equivalent of the Pulitzer Prize). This was an encouraging sign, because Woodward's agent had already come across the book in galley form and passed it along to his client, seeing the role of thirty-four-year-old spinster teacher Rachel Cameron (Woodward was thirty-five the year the book was published) as tailor-made for her talents. Woodward agreed wholeheartedly, as did her friend, writer Stewart Stern, who was chosen to do the adaptation for the screen.

In making adjustments and edits from the book, Stern dispensed with the idea of having Rachel narrate the tale, as she had in Laurence's novel, figuring that her innermost thoughts would be best expressed instead through Woodward's performance. Stern created more of an uneasy feeling between Rachel and fellow teacher Calla following the latter's unbridled display of affection, having them steer clear of one another, whereas in the book they had continued to socialize, simply choosing not to speak of Calla's having kissed her colleague. In the book Rachel finally declared that she would break off contact with Calla for good only after the latter lapsed into the curious practice of speaking in tongues, but Stern eliminated this scene as something that might come off as too bizarre onscreen. The screenplay added a scene in which Calla and Rachel try to capture a canary that has gotten loose in their schoolhouse and one in which Rachel's love interest, Nick, is tossed out of a movie theater after opening a beer. There was no dwelling on the rocky relationship between Nick and his father, nor past memories of Rachel's sister; and a potent scene in which Rachel, out to pick flowers, is made to feel inadequate and embarrassed after coming across a pair of two teenagers engaged in a hot embrace was unfortunately dropped as well. The finished script was very much in keeping with the unsentimental spirit of the novel; it contained a love story that didn't end happily, and it didn't flinch from dwelling on the emptiness of human existence. Not surprisingly, it proved a hard sell.

Rescue came in the form of Woodward's husband, Paul Newman, who wasn't all that crazy about the book but was willing to serve as producer in order to get the film made. After a while he found himself becoming more and more attracted to the property and wondered if this might not be the ideal opportunity for him to fulfill his long-contemplated wish to direct a motion picture. This announcement suddenly made the whole industry sit up and take notice of the tiny project. It now had

> "I'm exactly in the middle of my life. This is my last . . . ascending summer. Everything else, from now on, is just . . . rolling downhill into my grave."
> —Rachel Cameron

a strong selling point: one of Hollywood's best and most popular actors was about to show a whole different side of his talents. Warner Bros. let Newman know that it would back the picture if it could be made on a tight budget—somewhere between $700,000 and $780,000. This in itself offered another challenge. It meant that Newman had to work pretty fast and that both he and Woodward would make the ultimate show-business sacrifice by agreeing to work at no salary to ensure that the budget could be met. There were other strings attached. Warners, wanting still further commitments from the couple, negotiated a deal in which Newman would do two more pictures for the studio at half his regular salary and Woodward would sign up for a project for a fraction of the fee she normally commanded.

To ensure that *Rachel, Rachel*, as the film was eventually retitled, would be shot without studio interference, Newman set up shop basically in his own backyard, in southwestern Connecticut in a trail of small towns located north of the Newman home in Westport. The bulk of the location work was done in Danbury, where a gymnasium served as a makeshift studio for the company, and additional footage was shot in Georgetown, Redding, and Bethel. Shooting began on September 11, 1967.

Newman found himself very excited by the experience of directing, keeping his editor nearby while he set up shots, so he had a pretty clear idea of how scenes were going to look when they were stitched together down the line. There were no raised tempers on the set, and the actors appreciated the close attention paid to their performances by someone who knew the field so intimately. Warners expected a minor payback on its investment but suddenly saw the possibility of greater things when *Rachel, Rachel* earned some of the most enthusiastic praise of the year. Critics were highly impressed by Newman's avoidance of melodrama and false sentiment. He instead concentrated on a very natural quality in the acting, a leisurely pacing of the scenes, and the often unpleasant, and therefore very honest, interplay between

human beings who all seemed unsure of themselves, terrified of being
alone, and unable to connect, just as
in real life. Woodward's portrayal of a
self-effacing, needy, frightened woman who has watched life pass her by,
was faultless, never coming off as self-
pitying or dour yet believable in suggesting that there were extraordinary
possibilities within a seemingly very
ordinary lady. It was as great a piece of
acting as one would expect from this
exceptional actress, a triumph made
all the more thrilling by the equally
fine work Newman had done. In a
single picture he had proved himself
to be one of the most sensitive and
lyrical of directors, showing the sort
of subtlety that had been his hall-
mark as one of the best actors of his
generation. The raves meant that the
picture attracted vast attention in its
initial city engagements, but Warners
couldn't help but be surprised that the
movie did better-than-expected business in wider release. The often dis-
turbingly bleak nature of the material

Once Paul Newman decided to sit in the director's chair for *Rachel, Rachel,* his wife Joanne Woodward's "small" movie became one of the big events of 1968.

was a challenge, but some audiences didn't seem to mind, and *Rachel, Rachel* performed well enough at the box office that Warners did not hold the Newmans to their original bargain to do other films for the studio at cut-rate salaries.

FUNNY GIRL

Academy Award Winner: Best Actress (Barbra Streisand)

Academy Award Nominee: Picture; Supporting Actress (Kay Medford); Cinematography; Sound; Song ("Funny Girl"); Score of a Musical Picture—Original or Adaptation; Film Editing

Top 10 Box Office Film

Opening date: September 19, 1968.

Columbia. A Rastar Productions Presentation of a William Wyler—Ray Stark Production.

Director: William Wyler. Producer: Ray Stark. Screenplay: Isobel Lennart. Based on the 1964 musical with book by Lennart. Songs by Jule Styne (music) and Bob Merrill (lyrics): "If a Girl Isn't Pretty," "I'm the Greatest Star," "Roller Skate Rag," "His Love Makes Me Beautiful," "People," "You Are Woman, I Am Man," "Don't Rain on My Parade," "Sadie, Sadie," "The Swan," "Funny Girl." Additional songs: "I'd Rather Be Blue Over You (Than Happy with Somebody Else)," by Fred Fisher (music) and Billy Rose (lyrics); "Second Hand Rose," by James F. Hanley (music) and Grant Clarke (lyrics); "My Man," by Maurice Yvain, with English lyrics by Channing Pollock (adapted from the French lyrics by A. Willemetz and Jacques Charles). Photography: Harry Stradling. Production Designer: Gene Callahan. Art Director: Robert Luthardt. Set Decorator: William Kiernan. Streisand's Costumes: Irene Sharaff. Music Supervisor and Conductor: Walter Scharf. Orchestrations: Jack Hayes, Walter Scharf, Leo Shuken, Herbert Spencer. Musical Numbers Director: Herbert Ross. Supervising Editor: Robert Swink. Film Editors: Maury Winetrebe, William Sands. Technicolor. Panavision. 155 minutes (including overture, entr'acte, exit music).

CAST: Barbra Streisand (Fanny Brice), Omar Sharif (Nick Arnstein), Walter Pidgeon (Florenz Ziegfeld), Kay Medford (Rose Brice), Anne Francis (Georgia James), Lee Allen (Eddie Ryan), Mae Questel (Mrs. Strakosh), Gerald Mohr (Tom Branca), Frank Faylen (Keeney), Mittie Lawrence (Emma), Gertrude Flynn (Mrs. O'Malley), Penny Santon (Mrs. Meeker), John Harmon (John, Company Manager), Tommy Rall (Prince in *Swan Lake* Ballet), Lloyd Gough (Bill Fallon, Lawyer).

PLOT: Fanny Brice looks back on how she became one of the top attractions of the New York stage, only to experience constant heartbreak in her personal life when she fell in love with dashing but irresponsible gambler Nick Arnstein.

Belying the cliché, Ray Stark was one man who actually wanted to *celebrate* his mother-in-law. Stark, who was married to Fanny Brice's daughter, Fran, saw great possibilities in a motion-picture biography of Brice (1891–1951), one of the best loved of all the Ziegfeld Follies stars, a lady who ran the gamut from knockabout comedy to impassioned torch singing and later achieved fame on radio, playing an overgrown brat who went by the name of "Baby Snooks." Stark hired Isobel Lennart, who had helped script many an MGM musical, to fashion a screenplay based on Brice's life, Lennart blatantly whitewashing many of the facts in order to leave the performer's name unblemished. Stark, a former agent, successfully turned to film producing in 1960 with the hit *The World of Suzie Wong* (Paramount, 1960) but had trouble convincing anyone in Hollywood that '60s audiences cared to see Brice's story, fictionalized or not. Instead, he managed to interest Broadway director Vincent J. Donehue, who thought Brice's story could make a worthwhile stage vehicle for Mary Martin, even though the Broadway icon bore no resemblance whatsoever to Brice in either manner or looks. What had been conceived as a straightforward drama naturally evolved into a musical, with composer Jule Styne and lyricist Stephen Sondheim chosen to follow their recent success, *Gypsy*. Eventually, Martin and Donehue backed out of the deal, as did Sondheim, who was replaced by Bob Merrill. Anne Bancroft and Carol Burnett were seriously considered for the lead until Styne suggested Barbra Streisand, who had been causing a sensation in New York nightclubs and had made a name for herself on Broadway with a scene-stealing supporting role in *I Can Get It for You Wholesale.*

Streisand, whose kook-and-heartbreak style of performing was closer to Brice than any of the other ladies under consideration, certainly could sing the role, but there was some trepidation about whether she could carry a show on her own. After a rocky tryout period, *Funny Girl* finally opened on Broadway at the Winter Garden Theatre on March 26, 1964 and, although there were quibbles over Lennart's book, there was no denying that Streisand had thoroughly and fully arrived as one of the great stars of her time. She would stay with the show through December 1965 and then return to the part when the musical opened in London on April 23, 1966.

Although *Funny Girl* continued to run in New York after Streisand's departure (finally closing on July 1, 1967, with 1,348 performances to its credit), it was clear that this was one case where a star had so thoroughly dominated a role and made it her own that there was little point in considering anyone else for the movie version. By the time the film began principal photography on August 7, 1967, Streisand had starred in two television specials, released nine solo albums, and become a highly desirable casting choice. Aside from Kay Medford, who had played Fanny's mom, no one else was retained from the original Broadway cast.

Since this was one musical most people did not appear to hold sacred, detractors of Hollywood adaptations of Broadway shows seemed to have no qualms about changes being made to the original book. And there were several. Whereas Nick Arnstein's song list onstage had been whittled down to two numbers, the screen version was even less generous, keeping only his participation in "You Are Woman" and dropping "I Want to Be Seen with You Tonight" altogether. Fanny's mama was allowed to sing an aborted version of "If a Girl Isn't Pretty," but all other songs that involved characters from the old neighborhood—"Henry Street," the catchy "Who Taught Her Everything She Knows?," and "Find Yourself a Man"—were cut. Substituting for "Cornet Man" was "Roller Skate Rag," and "The Swan," a send-up of ballet, now took the place of Broadway's "Rat-Tat-Tat-Tat," a comical military bit. If there was one song that was in no danger of being eliminated, it was "People," which had not only become the breakout standard from the show, but also brought Streisand her first top-ten single (reaching number 5 on the *Billboard* charts in May 1964) and became her signature tune. Whereas the play had confined itself to a new score, the filmmakers now had the opportunity to include actual standards Brice had done in her lifetime. Therefore, "I'd Rather Be Blue Over You" and "Second Hand Rose" were added to the mix, both presented anachronistically. The former was seen winning over audiences

> "Don't tell me not to live, I simply have to. If someone takes a spill, it's me and not you. Don't bring around a cloud to rain on my parade."
> —Fanny Brice

prior to Brice's fame, when in fact it was not sung by the star until 1928, when she introduced it in the motion picture *My Man*, its lyrics credited to her future husband, Billy Rose. "Second Hand Rose" was interpolated in the film as a kind of audition for Ziegfeld, when in actuality Brice first sang it long af-

Although the cover of the Columbia Records soundtrack for *Funny Girl* might lead one to think that Omar Sharif was given equal time on the vocals, the LP belonged very much to Barbra Streisand, save for a duet on "You Are Woman, I Am Man."

ter she was established as a star of the famous showman's revues in *Ziegfeld Follies of 1921*. This show had also introduced the most important Brice standard interpolated into the film, "My Man." Stark had wanted to include this number onstage but faced too many obstacles in obtaining the rights to use it. With this greatest of torch songs now available for the important final number, "The Music That Makes Me Dance" was discarded so that Streisand could put her own special touch on "My Man." It was this moment, the camera remaining stationary on her face against a black backdrop as she poured her heart out lamenting the loss of her love, that became arguably *the* defining moment of Streisand's movie career.

Fanny Brice may have had no relevancy to the late '60s, but Barbra Streisand certainly did, and Columbia was ecstatic when the crowds started lining up for what was really a blatantly old-fashioned motion picture, one that pretty much looked and played like a dozen other moldy backstage show-business stories of yore. When *Funny Girl* became the studio's second-biggest moneymaker of the decade and the highest-grossing 1968 release, there was no denying that the property's gigantic public success rested on the shoulders of Streisand.

Streisand went on to share the Academy Award for Best Actress of 1968 (with Katharine Hepburn for AVCO Embassy's *The Lion in Winter*), making this only the second time in Oscar history that two performers tied the vote. (Wallace Beery for MGM's *The Champ* and Fredric March for Paramount's *Dr. Jekyll & Mr. Hyde*, in 1931–32, were the first.) Since Hepburn did not bother to show up for the ceremony and Streisand did, the spotlight was all hers that evening. Streisand put so strong a stamp on her interpretation of Fanny Brice that there seemed to be no point in ever reviving the stage version without her. As part of a contractual obligation to Columbia and Ray Stark, Streisand reluctantly reprised Fanny for the 1975 sequel *Funny Lady*, which covered the lady's next unhappy marriage, to impresario Billy Rose, as played by James Caan, with Omar Sharif showing up for a token appearance as Arnstein.

CHARLY

Academy Award Winner: Best Actor (Cliff Robertson)

Opening date: September 23, 1968.

Cinerama. A Selmur Pictures in Collaboration with Robertson Associates Presentation.

Director-Producer: Ralph Nelson. Screenplay: Stirling Silliphant. Based on the 1966 novel *Flowers for Algernon*, by Daniel Keyes, expanded from his 1959 short story of the same name. Executive Producer: Selig J. Seligman. Photography: Arthur J. Ornitz. Production Designer: John DeCuir. Art Director: Charles Rosen. Set Decorator: Clint Marshall. Costumes: Hazel Roy. Music: Ravi Shankar. Editor: Fredric Steinkamp. Technicolor. Techniscope. 104 minutes.

CAST: Cliff Robertson (Charly Gordon), Claire Bloom (Alice Kinian), Lilia Skala (Dr. Anna Strauss), Leon Janney (Dr. Richard Nemur), Ruth White (Mrs. Apple, the Landlady), Richard Van Patten (Bert), Skipper McNally (Gimpy), Barney Martin (Hank), William Dwyer (Joey), Dan Morgan (Paddy), Frank Dolan (Eddie), Ralph Nelson (Convention Speaker).

PLOT: Thirty-year-old mentally retarded bakery employee Charlie Gordon gets a chance at improving his lot in life when he consents to a medical experiment that will greatly accelerate his mental development.

Having had a successful, albeit mostly unremarkable career that seemed devoid of a signature role, actor Cliff Robertson was sure that he had found a part he could spin into something pretty special when he was cast in a live *U.S. Steel Hour* presentation called *The Two Worlds of Charlie Gordon*. This had been derived from a short story, "Flowers for Algernon" (originally titled "The Genius Effect"), published by Daniel Keyes in the April 4, 1959, edition of *The Magazine of Fantasy and Science Fiction*. Although the idea behind the tale (told in the first person, through journal entries), of a scientific experiment temporarily turning a retarded man into a genius, was indeed fanciful enough to qualify as fantasy, both the story and the subsequent television production played more like a gentle drama with an unusual twist. *Charlie Gordon* aired on CBS on February 22, 1961, with Mona Freeman as Charlie's teacher, Jane Rawlins (a name change from the story's Alice Kinian). Under the routine direction of Fielder Cook, it was hardly more than a sincere but uninspired rendering of a fascinating work, but it earned an Emmy nomination for Robertson, who was not anxious to let go of the role.

> "I was wondering why people that would never dream of laughing at a blind or a crippled man would laugh at a moron."
> —Charly Gordon

Two months after the broadcast, Robertson purchased the rights to Keyes's work with the intention of getting it made into a full-length motion picture, with Maria Schell as his costar. In 1962 there was some negotiation with Columbia, with the idea of having Carol Reed direct, and Warners expressed some interest the following year, but Robertson simply could not get things rolling.

Fortunately for him, Keyes was also having trouble letting go of Charlie Gordon. He wanted to expand his story into a novel, but because he had sold the rights, he needed permission from Robertson to do so. Robertson, figuring he would have even more material from which to derive his dream project, consented to the expansion but continued to try and get a screenplay out of the original story. In March 1966, Keyes's all-new *Flowers for Algernon* appeared in print for the first time, and a month later Stirling Silliphant was hard at work trying to come up with the latest screenplay for the Robertson film. Although Robertson's movie would state that it was based not on the short story but on the novel, next to nothing that Keyes added was inserted into the film script. (One of the few aspects it carried over from the novel was changing Charlie's place of employment from a plastic box manufactory to a bakery.)

A full six years after buying the rights to *Algernon*, Robertson finally found a company that was willing to do business with him, Selmur Pictures, a subsidiary of ABC that was hoping to branch out from television into motion-picture production. Just as the television version had rejected Keyes's original title, so would the movie, going so far as to change the spelling of Charlie's name to the deliberately awkward "Charly," with the "R" printed backward in the advertising and opening credits, though this spelling had never appeared in either version of Keyes. Anne Heywood was supposed to fill the role of Miss Kinian. She made it as far as actually appearing on the set for the start of principal photography on September 25, 1967, but then decided that her interpretation of the part was not what director Ralph Nelson and Robertson were looking for and walked off the picture. Claire Bloom came in at the end of the month as a last-minute replacement. The screenplay had transported the story from its original New York City setting to the less frequently used Boston and was so intent on showing off the city that it included both a bus tour and a walking tour to encompass such historical sites as Faneuil Hall, Bunker Hill, and the Freedom Trail leading up to the Old North Church. The Boston City Hospital lent its building for some of the clinic scenes, the Dorothy Quincy Suite at John Hancock Hall on Berkeley Street provided the auditorium at which Charly lashes out at the scientists near the finale, and a house on G Street near East Seventh, heading toward Dorchester Bay, was used as the location of Charly's shabby apartment.

The backward "R" and the unusual spelling of the character's first name, as seen here in the British ad for *Charly*, was an idea created expressly for the film—there is no such spelling in Daniel Keyes's original source material.

Although it was a distinct improvement over the television adaptation, *Charly* did very little to enhance what had already been done so nicely in the original story and even made some grievous mistakes in attempting to update the material and give the picture a modern look, like incorporating the very trendy multiscreen device that had been such a sensation at the Expo 67 fair and a downright embarrassing montage that suggested a rebellious Charly had become a hippie and taken to riding a motorcycle. The picture benefited from whatever it decided to keep from the source material, but it stumbled with such additions as having Charly absentmindedly play in dough that has been stuffed in his locker at work as a prank, or a conversation with his batty landlady, who instructs him to love Algernon because pets are loyal. Silliphant also erred in not dramatizing Charly's slow relapse back into mental retardation, thereby robbing the story of a real emotional payoff. As for Robertson's performance, he wisely did not overact Charly's retarded characteristics, which had been and always would be the danger for any actor portraying the mentally handicapped. He did not, however, submerge himself so deeply that he was ever more than solid when he should have been superb. His reviews were good enough that he felt justified in his faith in the property, and so he refused to let it end at that. Trade ads were run championing his performance to a degree that had never been witnessed before in the annals of Oscar campaigning. It was no surprise when he was nominated, but there was no certainty as to whether his heavy push for the Academy Award would pay off or backfire. Amazingly, Robertson ended up trumping Peter O'Toole, Ron Moody, and Alan Arkin for the finest performances of their careers, turning *Charly* into the signature role the actor always hoped it would become.

ROMEO AND JULIET (United Kingdom–Italy–United States)

Academy Award Winner: Best Cinematography; Best Costume Design

Academy Award Nominee: Picture; Director

Top 10 Box Office Film

Opening date: October 8, 1968 (London: March 4, 1968).

Paramount. A BHE Film made with Verona Produzione Sr.l and Dino De Laurentiis Cinematografica, SpA.

Director: Franco Zeffirelli. Producers: Anthony Havelock-Allan, John Brabourne. Screenplay: Franco Brusati, Masolino D'Amico, Franco Zeffirelli. Based on the 1584 play by William Shakespeare. Photography: Pasqualino De Santis. Production Designer: Renzo Mongiardino. Art Directors: Luciano Puccini, Emilio Carcano. Set Decorator: Christine Edzard. Costumes: Danilo Donati. Music: Nino Rota. Song: "What Is a Youth," by Nino Rota (music) and Eugene Walter (lyrics), performed by Bruno Filippini. Editor: Reginald Mills. Technicolor. 138 minutes.

CAST: Olivia Hussey (Juliet Capulet), Leonard Whiting (Romeo Montague), Milo O'Shea (Friar Laurence), Michael York (Tybalt), John McEnery (Mercutio), Pat Heywood (Nurse), Natasha Parry (Lady Capulet), Robert Stephens (Prince of Verona), Keith Skinner (Balthazar), Richard Warwick (Gregory), Dyson Lovell (Sampson), Ugo Barbone (Abraham), Bruce Robinson (Benvolio), Paul Hardwick (Lord Capulet), Antonio Pierfederici (Lord Montague), Esmeralda Ruspoli (Lady Montague), Roberto Bisacco (Count Paris), Roy Holder (Peter), Laurence Olivier (Chorus).

PLOT: In fifteenth-century Italy, Romeo Montague and Juliet Capulet defy their warring families by falling in love.

As far as the wide world was concerned, the joined names of William Shakespeare's star-crossed lovers, Romeo and Juliet, represented love at its most passionate, its most pure, its most tragic—indeed, it represented romantic couplings of any sort. Given this level of familiarity, it only made sense that the cinema should have its own definitive version of *the* definitive love story. As the youth of the '60s became increasingly restless and disillusioned with the adult world, the time couldn't have seemed more perfect for a *Romeo and Juliet* told pretty close to the way it was meant to be seen and heard.

The man to do the job was Franco Zeffirelli, who had made his name directing opera prior to his much-heralded transition to professional legit theater with a 1960 adaptation of *Romeo and Juliet* for the West End's Old Vic. Starring John Stride and Judi Dench in the title roles, there was much debate over Zeffirelli's insistence that his actors *not* emphasize the poetry and verse but instead speak their lines in as casual and natural a manner as possible. Also, large chunks of the dialogue were sacrificed to make sure that the play did not lag. For every purist who complained about this approach, there were others who found it refreshing and progressive. With scenic design also done by Zeffirelli, it became one of the major events of the London theater season, and the production was considered important enough to tour, stopping off on Broadway at New York's City Center in February 1962 with Stride reprising his role and Joanna Dunham taking over as Juliet. Zeffirelli directed two additional productions of the play for the Italian stage over the next several years, making this his defining work in the theater.

Although Zeffirelli was anxious to bring his vision to the cinema, he opted instead for a version of *The Taming of the Shrew* (Columbia, 1967) as his debut feature, since he had the commitment of two of the biggest stars in the business, Richard Burton and Elizabeth Taylor. His very cinematic, often hectic, always colorful take on *Shrew* proved that he had a keen eye behind the camera, and the surprisingly good payoff at the box office made this the first Shakespeare movie since Laurence Olivier's Oscar-winning *Hamlet* (Universal, 1948) not to turn patrons away. Certainly the appearance of the Burtons had been a tremendous asset, but Zeffirelli's plan for *Romeo* would take quite the opposite tack. Not only was he insistent on avoiding established stars, but he also wanted to use actors who were pretty close to the ages Shakespeare had described. This was considered risky on the outset; the shared opinion was that no teenagers had the acting chops to pull off these difficult roles, hence the tradition of Romeo and Juliet being played by (hopefully) youthful-looking but considerably older performers of some experience. The director's decision to cast such young actors was a masterstroke that turned his picture from art-house item into a crossover event.

> "See what a scourge is laid upon your hate, that heaven finds means to kill your joys with love? And I, for winking at your discords too, have lost a brace of kinsmen. All are punished. *All* are punished!"
> —The Prince

Although he was set on teens, Zeffirelli still wanted his leads to know how to act, so he scoured the English theater scene, purportedly running through a thousand possible candidates. His Romeo, sixteen-year-old Leonard Whiting, he found at the National Theatre playing a page in a production of *Love for Love*. He had no motion-picture credits to his name when he was selected to fill Romeo's tights. But Zeffirelli's choice for Juliet did. Olivia Hussey, who at the time she was cast was playing one of the schoolgirls in the West End presentation of *The Prime of Miss Jean Brodie*, had shown up on the big screen as one of the youngsters in a feature aimed at the same, *Cup Fever* (1965), prior to getting a part in a Hollywood production, *The Battle of the Villa Fiorita* (Twentieth Century-Fox, 1965), in which she had portrayed the offspring of Rossano Brazzi. Although there was much press about her being fifteen years old at the time she won the part, all biographical sources on the actress list her year of birth as 1951, which would have made her sixteen at the start of production.

Because he planned to shoot the movie in his native Italy, Zeffirelli was required to fill certain roles with Italian thespians, including those of Lord and Lady Montague, whose dialogue was whittled down enough that it was hardly noticeable that their voices were dubbed by other actors into English. The fact that there were not enough principal roles filled by Italians caused some dissension with the government, which was reluctant to provide any funding for the picture. In the end, the bulk of the upfront money for the $1 million budget came from the British studio BHE, which had also backed Olivier's *Othello* (Warner Bros., 1965). A deal was sealed with Paramount, which was happy to distribute as long as the cost could be kept low. Zeffirelli coached his young leads extensively prior to filming, ensuring that they spoke and behaved as if they were residing in fifteenth-century Italy. Working with Franco

Brusati and Masolino D'Amico, Zeffirelli remained more faithful to the play's structure than he had *Shrew*'s, where he had taken great liberties with its elements and dialogue.

Although it hardly pleased the actors playing some of the supporting roles, most of the cuts in the text helped to keep Romeo and Juliet at the center of things, since Zeffirelli deleted any extraneous material that might have caused interest to wane or lessen the powerful impact of their plight. Trimmed were the opening exchange between Sampson and Gregory prior to the initial fight, since these characters had no further importance in the story; Lord Montague's discussion with Benvolio over Romeo's curious behavior before the latter's first appearance; the speech by Mercutio while he is looking for Romeo prior to the balcony scene; Juliet's monologue before the nurse brings her the bad news about Tybalt's death; Friar Laurence and Romeo's lengthy discussion of the latter's banishment; the entire scene in which the Capulets give Paris their blessing to marry their daughter; Juliet's dialogue with the nurse informing her she will lie alone the night she takes the potion; the extensive "woe"-ing by the family and Laurence following Juliet's "death"; Romeo summoning an apothecary to get his own dose of poison; and the appearance of Paris at the tomb, which had led to his being killed by Romeo. There would be no death for Paris, nor would Lady Montague die of grief, as she had in Shakespeare's version, according to a line of dialogue delivered by her husband at the tomb.

The undeniably eye-catching image of Leonard Whiting and Olivia Hussey naked in bed together was instrumental in drawing attention to *Romeo and Juliet* and therefore ended up on two of three soundtracks connected with the film, this one containing music and dialogue highlights.

Gone too were the typical "comic" exchanges of the day, done by some servants and musicians, the latter having delivered some most inappropriate jokes after the Capulet family thinks their daughter has gone to her maker. Juliet's drinking of the potion encompassed a single line, written for the picture—"Love, give me strength"—and it was deemed necessary to have Balthazar explain to Romeo more directly that Juliet has taken her own life by inventing the line "She's dead, my lord" for him. Interestingly, the writers also chose to deemphasize Romeo's infatuation with Rosaline prior to meeting his true love, and they did not have Juliet pretend to denounce Romeo in front of her mother. This kept their devotion more true and unspoiled.

Following a rehearsal period (a portion of which was captured live by satellite television for a June 25, 1967, broadcast to twenty-four countries on the program *Our World*), the picture began shooting four days later in the town of Tuscania, some thirty miles northwest of Rome, where the Romanesque church of San Pietro provided Friar Laurence's cell, as well as the setting for Romeo and Juliet's marriage. On that very first day of filming, June 29, Leonard Whiting turned seventeen. Shooting continued in the town of Pienza, where the three-story, fifteenth-century Piccolomini Palace (currently a museum) was used as the interior and most of the exteriors of the Capulet house. This town also supplied the setting for Mercutio's nocturnal "Queen Mab" speech before the masked ball. Because the play's original setting, Verona, had been far too modernized over the years, the stony streets and alleyways of Gubbio were used for the skirmishes between the Capulets and Montagues. The setting for the play's most famous scene, the nighttime meeting at Juliet's balcony, took place not outside Piccolomini, but in the village of Artena, twenty miles outside of Naples. The town's sixteenth-century Palazzo Borghese, with its massive wall, steps, and overgrown gardens, was deemed perfect for the look Zeffirelli desired. After a break in August, shooting picked up again, with remaining interiors done at Cinecitta Studios. Along the way money ran out, and Zeffirelli was forced to turn to Paramount to foot the bill. Once executives got a glimpse of the magnificence of what the director was turning out, they allowed him an increase that brought the cost up to $1.9 million. Filming ended in mid-October. Zeffirelli was already locked into delivering a finished movie in time for the Royal Command Performance in early March, *Shrew* having gone over so well as the choice to fill this illustrious spot the previous year. Zeffirelli screened the picture in London at a length of 152 minutes, which was not to his liking; he announced almost immediately that he would be shortening it by some twelve minutes or so.

Romeo and Juliet had gotten favorable mention in the British press, but there was much hesitancy over praising such untested leads, despite their excellent command of the verse. This did not stop the movie from performing well, which did not ensure that Americans were going to take to it with equal enthusiasm. Fortunately, the Paramount marketing department had no qualms about telling moviegoers that what the studio was presenting was not the stuffy Shakespeare they had come to dread from years of inadequate English courses. It placed an image of Leonard Whiting and Olivia Hussey, clearly naked in bed together, at the center of its marketing campaign, and the buzz started immediately that, if nothing else, this version of the tale promised to be sexy.

Opening at New York's Paris Theatre with an intermission and a souvenir booklet on sale in the lobby, the picture was treated by Paramount with respect and importance from the word go, exactly as it deserved. Once again, many critics refused to admit that Whiting and Hussey had done the roles justice, but there was no denying that Zeffirelli had topped his production of *Shrew* with an adaptation of Shakespeare that treated the verse with great clarity and respect, kept things moving along excitingly and most fluidly, and brought it all to life in so pictorially vivid a way that it was certainly the most handsome cinematic rendering of the bard to date. Zeffirelli staged his street duels and brawls with a thrilling sense of movement, and the flirtation between Juliet and the masked Romeo at the ball leading up to their first exchange, as these two undeniably beautiful young actors went slack-jawed with awe in expressing their first real encounter with true love, was so poetically conceived and executed as to become one of the most romantic sequences yet committed to film. The outstanding work that was expected of such talents as Milo O'Shea as Friar Laurence, Natasha Parry as Juliet's mother, and Robert Stephens, in a few brief but magnetic scenes as the "moved" prince, in no way eclipsed the heartfelt and truly lovely readings of the verse by Hussey and Whiting.

Thanks to their youth, the two stars made an undeniable and fierce connection with audiences their own age. This did the trick, and soon the youth of America started supporting the film, believing it represented their own discordant relationships with their elders and showed how impossible it was to lead your own life in a world hell-bent on destroying inner peace. *Romeo and Juliet* was soon declared very "mod" and very important to see.

Zeffirelli was now hailed as one of the masterful directors of the era, though most of his subsequent work would pale in comparison. He finally returned to Shakespeare in 1990 with his version of *Hamlet* (Warner Bros.), featuring Mel Gibson and Glenn Close, with *Romeo*'s Mercutio, Peter McEnery, showing up as Osric. Hussey got a pretty steady career out of her participation in *Romeo*, though she would never again receive a role to equal this one. Leonard Whiting did not fare even half as well; his list of credits is spotty, the best-known being a TV adaptation of *Frankenstein* in which he played the doctor. By the mid-1970s his acting career had come to an end, and he later took up writing children's books. This hardly mattered; he would always have to his name one of the genuine masterpieces of '60s cinema and the hands-down best adaptation of a Shakespeare work ever committed to celluloid.

FINIAN'S RAINBOW

Academy Award Nominee: Score of a Musical Picture—Original or Adaptation; Sound

Opening date: October 9, 1968.

Warner Bros.–Seven Arts.

Director: Francis Ford Coppola. Producer: Joseph Landon. Screenplay: E. Y. Harburg and Fred Saidy, based on the 1947 Broadway musical with book by Harburg and Saidy, lyrics by Harburg and music by Burton Lane. Songs by E. Y. Harburg and Burton Lane: "Look to the Rainbow," "This Time of the Year," "How Are Things in Glocca Morra?," "Old Devil Moon," "Something Sort of Grandish," "If This Isn't Love," "That Great Come-and-Get-It Day," "When the Idle Poor Become the Idle Rich," "When I'm Not Near the Girl I Love," "Rain Dance Ballet," "The Begat." Music Supervisor and Conductor: Ray Heindorf. Associate Music Supervisor: Ken Darby. Choreographer: Hermes Pan (uncredited: Claude Thompson). Photography: Philip Lathrop. Production Designer: Hilyard M. Brown. Costumes: Dorothy Jeakins. Editor: Melvin Shapiro. Technicolor. Panavision. 148 minutes (including overture, entr'acte, and exit music).

CAST: Fred Astaire (Finian McLonergan), Petula Clark (Sharon McLonergan), Tommy Steele (Og the Leprechaun), Don Francks (Woody Mahoney), Keenan Wynn (Senator Billboard Rawkins), Al Freeman Jr. (Howard), Barbara Hancock (Susan the Silent), Ronald Colby (Buzz Collins), Dolph Sweet (Sheriff), Wright King (District Attorney), Louis Silas (Henry), Avon Long, Jester Hairston, Roy Glenn (Passion Pilgrim Gospeleers).

PLOT: Arriving in Rainbow Valley with a crock of gold he has stolen and transported from Ireland, Finian McLonergan and his daughter Sharon are pursued by a determined leprechaun who hopes to retrieve the item in order to prevent himself from turning mortal.

Because splashy adaptations of Broadway musicals were all the rage during the '60s, the studios went scrambling to find not only recent properties to transfer into motion pictures, but also those from bygone eras that had somehow skipped the journey from stage to screen. One such was *Finian's Rainbow*, which had opened way back on January 10, 1947, at the Forty-sixth Street Theatre and become one of the solid hits of the season, eventually tallying up 725 performances. The decidedly unstarry cast had consisted of Albert Sharpe (who would act opposite Fred Astaire in MGM's 1951 musical *Royal Wedding*) as Finian, Ella Logan as his daughter Sharon, Donald Richards as Woody Mahoney, Anita Alvarez as the silent Susan, and newcomer David Wayne in

> "On the day I was born, said me father said he, I've an elegant legacy waitin' for ye. 'Tis a rhyme for your lips and a song for your heart, to sing it whenever the world falls apart."
> —Sharon

the scene-stealing part of the excitable leprechaun Og. The show had introduced a handful of hit tunes, including "How Are Things in Glocca Mora?" and "When I'm Not Near the Girl I Love," which was reason enough for Hollywood to take sufficient interest in shaping the show for the screen; but there was a catch. *Finian* was not just a pleasing evening's worth of Irish blarney and beautiful music, but a statement against racism: its supporting cast included a bigoted white senator who is turned black by an act of willful magic. Book writers Fred Saidy and E. Y. Harburg were perfectly willing to let a movie be made of their show, but only under the condition that the story line not be distorted or altered, a demand that left Hollywood of the late 1940s in a bit of a quandary. Despite the fact that such movies as *Intruder in the Dust* (MGM, 1949) and *Pinky* (Twentieth Century-Fox, 1949) had made potent statements against bigotry toward blacks, presenting this incendiary topic under the guise of a musical entertainment was much trickier to pull off.

It took the civil rights movement to convince Hollywood that a Finian film could finally get done correctly, and Warner Bros. teamed up with Seven Arts in the late '60s to do the job. Figuring it needed a younger eye to keep the twenty-year-old piece fresh, Warners sought twenty-eight-year-old Francis Ford Coppola, who'd just done a low-budget comedy for Seven Arts, *You're a Big Boy Now* (1966), and was considered one of the most promising of the new filmmakers to come from the film-school sect of directors. Coppola, hoping to get financing from the studio for his own screenplay, *The Rain People*, agreed, knowing that his father, conductor Carmine Coppola, would be delighted at the prospect of his son directing a big-screen musical. Although other companies were spending big bucks without hesitation in hopes of finding the next *Sound of Music* (Twentieth Century-Fox, 1965), Warners wanted *Finian's Rainbow* done pretty quickly and on a relatively tight budget, allotting it a mere $3.5 million. Coppola took on the challenge but surprised the studio by rejecting the initial script, which had been updated with such very '60s additions as having Woody Mahoney be a hippie folk singer from San Francisco. The original authors were instead engaged to stick as closely as possible to what they had created onstage (an intrusive subplot about a botanist creating a mentholated cigarette and a barn burning at the wedding were two aspects created for the movie), although one drastic change was necessary after it was decided who would be playing the leading role. Onstage Arlen and Harburg had not bothered to put Finian McLonergan at center stage in any of the musical numbers, thereby making it one of the true curios of the genre: a musical in which the title character doesn't get a song. Somebody had the terrific idea of hiring Fred Astaire to play Finian onscreen, which meant that the script needed to be tinkered with to bring him into the numbers and, most important, to allow the greatest of all dancers to dance.

The *Finian* cameras rolled on June 26, 1967, with filming stretching through the end of September. Although Warner Bros. had encouraged Coppola to shoot the entire movie on their Burbank lot, he found that with this restriction it would be impossible to capture what was essentially a very outdoorsy piece. The studio would not bend to his wishes to film in Kentucky, but he managed to talk them into allowing him to travel north to do exteriors in the vicinity of Modesto, Carmel, and Monterey, with Tuolomne County's Sierra Railroad utilized for part of the "This Time of the Year" number. Coppola also dispatched Carroll Ballard (long before his breakthrough success as the director of United Artists' *The Black Stallion*, which was produced by Coppola) to shoot the imaginative opening title montage, in which a pair of stand-ins for Sharon and Finian are seen trekking past such American landmarks as the Statue of Liberty, the Grand Canyon, and Mount Rushmore. Unfortunately, Coppola made a grievous error when he fired choreographer Hermes Pan during the shoot (although his cameo, in which he tossed a towel into Astaire's face, was kept in the completed movie), and the final film was made up of dances by Claude

Thompson, staging ideas devised by Coppola himself (the director would often rethink a number to fit the camera tracks already laid, rather than the other way around), and some seemingly improvisational steps with the cast prancing about on fields and hills. For every creative move that Coppola made—for example, setting "The Begat" in a variety of locations as Keenan Wynn and his cohorts motor around the countryside—he made some miscalculations in his refusal to simply let certain numbers play fully with a minimum of editing interruptions.

This was most notable in Astaire's one big dance moment, "When the Idle Poor Become the Idle Rich" (a song that had belonged to Sharon in the play), which included some wince-inducing close-ups of Astaire's feet, something the performer had been successful in eliminating from all of his movies since *The Gay Divorcee*. Needless to say, he was none too happy with the finished film.

Although Warners had been loath to treat the movie like a blockbuster when it was being filmed, it suddenly decided the film was good enough to release as a reserved-ticket road-show attraction. In order to meet this qualification, the studio took the 35mm print and blew it up to 70mm, adding an overture, intermission, and exit music. Despite its two-and-a-half-hour length, the movie still had to sacrifice one of the stage show's

The Warner Bros.–Seven Arts soundtrack for *Finian's Rainbow* brought together one of the top vocalists of the era, Petula Clark, with one of the movies' great interpreters of song, Fred Astaire.

numbers, "Necessity," sung by Brenda Arnau and a batch of sharecroppers, which had been filmed and was intended to come shortly before Wynn's transformation scene. (Fortunately, the tune was retained on the soundtrack album.) Petula Clark promoted *Finian*'s upcoming release on her April 1968 special *Petula*, which inadvertently made its mark on television history because of a nervous executive's racist reaction to the singer's making physical contact with guest Harry Belafonte. Curiously, despite this indication that the United States was not yet comfortable about equality when it came to the races, many critics denounced *Finian* as naive and dated when it finally premiered in October 1968.

Notwithstanding the popularity of most of the road-show musicals of the era, audiences really couldn't work up a great deal of enthusiasm for this particular musical, and, despite the historical significance of its being the final Astaire vehicle in this genre (his last actual onscreen dancing was done in MGM's 1976 *That's Entertainment II*, a documentary), it fell far short of expectations at the box office. Coppola's ascent to the pantheon of revered directors of the '70s with the phenomenal success of *The Godfather* (Paramount, 1972) would only hurt *Finian*'s reputation in the eyes of certain hardened film students who found it hard to believe that the same man who served up the grit of the *Godfather* saga and *Apocalypse Now* (United Artists, 1979), had "squandered" his talents on something so fluffy as a musical. On the other hand, there were just as many factions who came to realize that *Finian's Rainbow* had more than its share of pleasures (including those Coppola himself brought to the film), a sprightly degree of unpretentious fun, and a gorgeous roster of songs that made it anything but a disgrace.

THE SUBJECT WAS ROSES

Academy Award Winner: Best Supporting Actor (Jack Albertson)

Academy Award Nominee: Actress (Patricia Neal)

Opening date: October 13, 1968.

MGM. A Coproduction of Edgar Lansbury Productions, Inc.–T.D.J. Productions, Inc.–Delos Productions, Inc.

Director: Ulu Grosbard. Producer: Edgar Lansbury. Screenplay: Frank D. Gilroy, based on his 1964 play. Photography: Jack Priestley. Art Director: George Jenkins. Set Decorator: John Godfrey. Costumes: Anna Hill Johnstone. Music: Lee Pockriss. Songs: "Albatross," written and performed by Judy Collins; "Who Knows Where the Time Goes?," by Sandy Denny, performed by Judy Collins; "Sun Bonnet Sue," by Will D. Cobb, performed by Jack Albertson. Editor: Gerald B. Greenberg. Metrocolor. 108 minutes.

CAST: Patricia Neal (Nettie Cleary), Jack Albertson (John Cleary), Martin Sheen (Timmy Cleary), Don Saxon (Nightclub M.C.), Elaine Williams (Woman in Club), Grant Gordon (Man in Restaurant).

PLOT: Following military service, Timmy Cleary returns home to the Bronx, only to be expected to take sides as his parents continue to spar over past pains and disappointments.

The unfulfillment so evident in Patricia's Neal's face as it filled the screen in the opening shot of *The Subject Was Roses* was a testament to a great actress, here being given the film role of a lifetime in the sort of emotionally powerful dialogue- and character-driven drama she deserved but seldom received. It was very fortunate that Neal had survived to do the picture at all. In 1965, as she was about to begin work on MGM's *7 Women*, she suffered a stroke that put her in a coma for two and a half weeks and left her future uncertain. For the next two years she struggled courageously to recover her speech and movement, determined not only to function normally once again, but to return to her profession. Believing that she was indeed ready, it was Neal's husband, author Roald Dahl, who said yes to producer Edgar Lansbury's offer for Neal to play Bronx housewife Nettie Cleary in his planned film of *Roses*, the part having been written for her in the first place by Frank D. Gilroy. At the time Gilroy's play was being prepared for Broadway,

> "I asked you if you loved her. You nodded. I asked you to say it. You hesitated. I got hysterical. To quiet me you finally said 'I love her.'"
> —Timmy Cleary

Neal had just suffered another personal setback with the death of her daughter and was feeling far too depressed to accept the grueling responsibility of acting in front of an audience. The box office could have benefited from her presence, as the advance sales on the drama were a paltry $162 prior to its May 25, 1964, opening at the Royale Theatre. The cast consisted of Irene Dailey, Jack Albertson, and Martin

Sheen, none of whom were considered draws of any sort. Thanks to the superlative reviews, business began to build, and by the following year the play had been awarded a Pulitzer Prize, a New York Drama Critics' Award, and Tonys for Best Play and for Albertson as Supporting or Featured Actor (competing against Sheen, though both men were clearly leads). As the sort of intimate drama that was championed in this era, *Roses* stayed on Broadway for two years, running at no fewer than four other theaters: the Winthrop Ames, the Helen Hayes, the Henry Miller, and the Belasco. Gilroy was now hailed as one of the important playwrights of the era.

Lansbury and the same team that had converged onstage decided to put together the movie pretty much on their own terms. Gilroy formed his own production company, T.D.J. (named for his three sons, Tony, Dan, and John), in conjunction with Lansbury and their original director, Ulu Grosbard, with MGM footing the bill for distribution rights. Neither Grosbard nor Lansbury had any previous experience in motion pictures, but one would never have suspected, given the sure hand both men displayed in getting the job done. With Neal on board as their star name (although she was not considered a box-office draw per se, she did have a recent Academy Award to her name for her splendid work in Paramount's searing 1963 drama *Hud*), Grosbard and Lansbury were able to employ their original male cast members, Albertson and Sheen.

Because the whole production was pretty much Grosbard and Lansbury's to present as they pleased, it was decided that Gilroy would do the script, and furthermore he was encouraged to keep it as close to what had appeared onstage as possible. There were next to no alterations in the dialogue, with most of the film taking place in the Cleary apartment just as it had in the theater. For Timmy and John's discussion about how John and Nettie met, a side trip to the family's summer house was included in order to keep the single setting from getting too claustrophobic, while Nettie's monologue about losing her job and giving up another man for John, was restaged on the roof of the apartment building. An additional scene charting the family's night on the town was added to include a song for Jack Albertson and an uncomfortable

This striking image of a shattered vase of flowers captured the unhappiness so palpable in *The Subject Was Roses*.

meeting with one of John's sideline pickups. Whereas in the play there had been no explanation of where Nettie had disappeared to during her twelve-hour "escape" from the Bronx, the film followed her to the Jersey seashore for a bit of moody soul searching that worked quite well and added to the piece considerably.

Staying on the east coast, *The Subject Was Roses* filmed its interiors at the Production Center Studio on West Twenty-sixth Street. Because the piece was so blatantly autobiographical (like Timmy in the play, Gilroy had returned from military service following World War II at the age of twenty-one), the Cleary apartment was decorated and laid out to resemble Gilroy's own Bronx home as closely as possible. For further authenticity, the brief glimpse of the outside of the building was the real thing, the Gilroy residence at 116 West 176th Street. There was also a quick location shot of the front of Manhattan's legendary Latin Quarter and side trips across the state line to northwestern New Jersey (for the family lake house) and down the shore at Spring Lake (for Nettie's day trip). Filming took place over a ten-week period starting on February 19, 1968. Much was made of Neal's return to the screen, which became the focus of most of the articles surrounding the making and release of the picture. While her performance was something close to perfection, wearied, aching with pain and regret, stubborn, and nakedly vulnerable, her costars were every bit as good. Albertson acted his heart out, knowing that his chances of getting roles this well written and sharply defined would be few and far between. Alternately exasperating, self-involved, and needy, this was a marvelous portrait of a man on whom all and none of the blame must be placed for his family's misfortunes. Reading every line with a knowing sadness about his own shortcomings as well as those of his parents, Sheen proved himself to be one of the most effective new actors to arrive during the '60s. Although his later work ran the gamut from outstanding to ill-advised, his performance in this film was a reminder of the heights he could reach at his very best. Some critics felt the need to remain unimpressed by something so unapologetically uncinematic, but there was no doubt that this was an exemplary preservation of an affecting work, an exploration of the subtle battles waged in families that have pushed one another away because of their own personal disappointments. Hearing Gilroy's rich words spoken by three fine actors in their greatest screen roles was a pleasure to behold.

BULLITT

Academy Award Winner: Best Film Editing

Academy Award Nominee: Sound

Top 10 Box Office Film

Opening date: October 17, 1968.

Warner Bros.–Seven Arts. A Solar Production.

Director: Peter Yates. Producer: Philip D'Antoni. Screenplay: Alan R. Trustman, Harry Kleiner. Based on the 1963 novel *Mute Witness*, by Robert L. Pike. Executive Producer: Robert E. Relyea. Photography: William A. Fraker. Art Director: Albert Brenner. Set Decorators: Phillip Abramson, Ralph S. Hurst. Costumes: Theadora Van Runkle. Music: Lalo Schifrin. Editor: Frank P. Keller. Technicolor. 114 minutes.

CAST: Steve McQueen (Lt. Frank Bullitt), Robert Vaughn (Walter Chalmers), Jacqueline Bisset (Cathy), Don Gordon (Detective Delgetti), Robert Duvall (Weissberg), Simon Oakland (Captain Sam Bennett), Norman Fell (Captain Baker), Georg Stanford Brown (Dr. Willard), Justin Tarr (Eddy), Carl Reindel (Detective Stanton), Felice Orlandi (Renick), Victor Tayback (Pete Ross), Robert Lipton (First Aide), Ed Peck (Wescott), Pat Renella (Johnny Ross/Albert Renick), Paul Genge (Mike, Hired Killer), John Aprea (Second Hired Killer), Al Checco (Desk Clerk), Bill Hickman (Phil).

PLOT: Johnny Ross, a key witness set to testify against his Mafia associates, is shot by gunmen at a San Francisco hotel while under guard, leading police lieutenant Frank Bullitt to investigate how and why the assault happened so easily.

Every great star deserves a signature part, and Steve McQueen got his playing the title role in one of the seminal cop movies of its time, *Bullitt*. It was not his greatest film (that honor would most likely go to *The Great Escape*, United Artists, 1963), nor did the part offer complexities on the level of those inherent in the character of Jake Holman in *The Sand Pebbles* (Twentieth Century-Fox, 1966), but San Francisco cop Frank Bullitt was just about the epitome of male cool, and in the late '60s it was very "in" to be cool. Therefore, McQueen and this character became, quite simply, one of the iconic figures of the era.

Ironically, the movie had not originally been considered as a vehicle for this star. The source novel, *Mute Witness*, by Robert L. Pike (whose real name was, in fact, Robert L. Fish), had been purchased years earlier by Bill Nantony, who failed to get it made. The property eventually ended up with Philip D'Antoni, a former television producer, who wanted to turn it into a vehicle for Spencer Tracy. Tracy's ill-health during the mid-'60s made it highly unlikely that he would be able to do something as physically demanding as this, and it seemed like the property would end up nowhere until D'Antoni managed to interest McQueen's company, Solar, in doing it. Initially McQueen wasn't too enthusiastic about the idea; he'd made a career playing men who defied authority and the law, and here he was being asked to portray a policeman. Good sense prevailed, and Solar bought the rights. Rather than opt for an established American filmmaker, it was decided to go with someone new to U.S. films, an English director named Peter Yates, hired on the strength of the job he had done on *Robbery* (1967), which featured a tense car chase.

A car chase was something McQueen was dead set on having, although no such thing had occurred in Pike's original novel. The Pike book hadn't even featured a leading character named Bullitt—the cop was called Clancy—but using a deliberate misspelling of "bullet" as the name of the coolest of cool cops was a stroke of brilliance. The script also took the original story out of its New York City setting and transferred it to San Francisco (an earlier draft had taken place in Boston), the screenwriters figuring that cop thrillers set in Manhattan were a dime a dozen. The northern California city supplied a somewhat fresher backdrop and allowed for some exciting possibilities once that car chase was developed. The screenplay got rid of the more obvious Italian origins of the crime organization simply by dropping the letter "i" from the name of the "mute witness" in question, Johnny Rossi; gave "Bullitt" a girlfriend who is none too sure about being a part of such a hazardous way of life (this small addition brought a degree of unrest to the cop's life, making him far more real, more unsure, and less

> "Come on now, don't be naive, Lieutenant. We both know how careers are made. 'Integrity' is something you sell the public."
> —Walter Chalmers

one-dimensional than the unappealing know-it-all Pike had created); and played down the participation of Ross's brother, Pete, who had actually confronted the cop at one point in the book, demanding to know the whereabouts of his wounded (as he thought) sibling. A sequence in which Clancy, having tracked down a potential clue to the shooting, questioned Ann Renick was cut as well; the character was retained as a key figure in the plot twist but showed up onscreen only as a corpse. Pike's book had Ross(i) being stabbed by a nervous intern *after* he has died from his earlier gunshot wounds, in order to prevent any possible retaliation by the Organization. The movie replaced this sequence with the arrival at the hospital of one of the hired killers, who attempts to stab the witness but fails, leading to a pursuit through the building with Bullitt on his tail. The novel's climax, which had taken place at a Hudson River pier with the criminals hoping to leave the country by booking passage on a freighter, was relocated to an airport, which allowed for yet another chase.

Not unexpectedly, McQueen, who had always been vocal about how his films should be developed, even when he wasn't in charge, was adamant about how everything in the movie would proceed. He insisted that *Bullitt* be shot entirely on location, away from the all too obviously artificial environs of a studio soundstage or back lot. Given a $5 million budget, the picture began shooting in San Francisco on February 12, 1968, and continued filming there until late May. Among the principal locations used were the famed Mark Hopkins Hotel on Nob Hill, where Ross is spotted in the lobby near the start of the film; a fancy house at 2700 Vallejo Street in the Pacific Heights district, which stood in for the home of scheming district attorney Walter Chalmers (Robert Vaughn); the Kennedy Hotel off the Embarcadero near the end of Howard Street, standing in the shadow of the Oakland Bay Bridge and serving as the Daniels Hotel, the second-class dive where Ross is stashed and eventually shot; an apartment at 1153–1157 Taylor Street, near the corner of Clay Street, which was Bullitt's home; San Francisco General Hospital on Potrero Avenue, where the wounded Ross was tended to and where Bullitt chased away the assassin intending to finish to job he had started at the Daniels; Grace Cathedral on Taylor Street, where Chalmers served a writ to Captain Bennett (Simon Oakland) as he was on his way to mass with his family; and

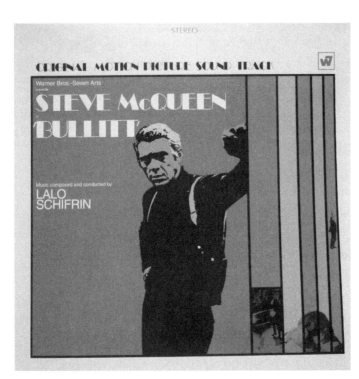

The Warner Bros.–Seven Arts soundtrack album for *Bullitt* added some groovy colors to the movie's famous image of Steve McQueen at his coolest.

Enrico's, a restaurant at Broadway and Kearney Street where Bullitt stops to pick up some information from his informant, Eddy (Justin Tarr). Outside the city proper, *Bullitt* was filmed at the Thunderbird Hotel (later changed to the Clarion) in Millbrae, where the body of the ill-fated Ann Renick is located by the police; and the San Francisco International Airport, which included a chase on the runway and a bloody finale inside one of the terminal buildings.

Running on foot through the seemingly deserted lower bowels of a hospital and dodging planes on a runaway made for some tense action moments, but McQueen had a grander idea for that car chase. It would be set smack in the middle of the picture and take place partially on the streets of San Francisco. (Yates would claim that it was D'Antoni who really pushed for the chase.) McQueen didn't want rear projection used, nor speeded-up camerawork that allowed the vehicles to look as if they were zipping along at a faster pace. As he envisioned it, this would be the most realistic chase yet put on film, and so one of the chief stunt coordinators in the business, Carey Loftin, would help stage it. The chosen vehicles were a 1968 Mustang GT for McQueen's character and a 1968 Dodge Charger for his pursuing (and then fleeing) enemy, the hired killers who had tried to knock off Ross. After much convincing, careful planning, and assurance of complete safety, Yates and his team received full cooperation from the city council, though they were restricted to certain streets and were required to complete the sequence on the roads outside the city limits. McQueen, who was an auto fancier, wanted very badly to do most, if not all, of his own driving, but after proving himself inadequate in pulling off certain moves, he reluctantly handed the bulk of the racing over to a professional, Bud Elkins, with additional work done by Loftin himself. Bill Hickman drove the Dodge; it and the Mustang were followed by a third car in which Pat Houstis drove cinematographer William Fraker. A pair of cameras were also strapped inside the two onscreen cars, an arrangement that made for the most breathtaking moments—the audience felt the drop and thump of the tires as the automobile swooped down the San Francisco hills. Key moments in the scene were shot at Army Street (the U-turn where the chase began), Taylor Street, Filbert Street, and Chestnut Avenue before the film moved on to Marina Boulevard,

Mansell Street, and Guadalupe Canyon Highway. This scene, which took two weeks to shoot, would be a major reason the picture ran $500,000 over budget, but turned out to be worth every penny.

If indeed it was the chase that got more and more people to see the picture, so be it. *Bullitt* went from strong performer to flat out blockbuster, taking in more than $35 million at U.S. box offices. That made it far and away McQueen's highest-grossing picture to date, with only *My Fair Lady* (1964) topping it among Warners' moneymakers of the decade. The movie became one of the most talked-about releases of its time, the image of speeding cars instantly bringing it to mind for an entire generation. McQueen had reached an undreamed-of level of popularity, and Yates had successfully launched his American career.

STAR!

Academy Award Nominee: Supporting Actor (Daniel Massey); Art Direction–Set Decoration; Cinematography; Sound; Song ("Star!"); Score of a Musical Picture—Original or Adaptation; Costume Design

Opening date: October 22, 1968.

Twentieth Century-Fox.

Director: Robert Wise. Producer: Saul Chaplin. Screenplay: William Fairchild. Photography: Ernest Laszlo. Production Designer: Boris Leven. Set Decorations: Walter M. Scott, Howard Bristol. Costumes: Donald Brooks. Music Supervisor and Conductor: Lennie Hayton. Songs: "Star!," by Sammy Cahn and James Van Heusen; "Down at the Old Bull and Bush," by Harry Von Tilzer, Andrew B. Sterling, Russell Hunting, P. Krone; "Piccadilly," by Walter Williams and Paul Morande (music) and Bruce Seiver (lyrics); "Oh, It's a Lovely War!," by Maurice Scott (music) and J. P. Long (lyrics); "In My Garden of Joy," by Saul Chaplin; "Forbidden Fruit," by Noël Coward; "'N' Everything," by Buddy De Sylva, Gus Kahn, and Al Jolson; "Burlington Bertie from Bow," by William Hargreaves; "Parisian Pierrot," by Noël Coward; "Limehouse Blues," by Philip Braham (music) and Douglas Furber (lyrics); "Someone to Watch Over Me," by George Gershwin (music) and Ira Gershwin (lyrics); "Dear Little Boy (Dear Little Girl)," by George Gershwin (music) and Ira Gershwin (lyrics); "After the Ball," by Charles K. Harris; "Someday I'll Find You," by Noël Coward; "The Physician," by Cole Porter; "Do, Do, Do," by George Gershwin (music) and Ira Gershwin (lyrics); "Has Anybody Seen Our Ship?," by Noël Coward; "My Ship," by Kurt Weill (music) and Ira Gershwin (lyrics); "The Saga of Jenny," by Kurt Weill (music) and Ira Gershwin (lyrics). Dances and Musical Numbers Staged by Michael Kidd. Editor: William Reynolds. Deluxe Color. Todd-AO. 175 minutes (including overture and entr'acte).

CAST: Julie Andrews (Gertrude Lawrence), Richard Crenna (Richard Aldrich), Michael Craig (Sir Anthony "Tony" Spencer), Daniel Massey (Noël Coward), Robert Reed (Charles Fraser), Bruce Forsyth (Arthur Lawrence), Beryl Reid (Rose), John Collin (Jack Roper), Alan Oppenheimer (Andre Charlot), Richard Karlan (David Holtzman), Lynley Laurence (Billie Carleton), Garrett Lewis (Jack Buchanan), Elizabeth St. Clair (Jeannie Banks), Jenny Agutter (Pamela Roper), Anthony Eisley (Ben Mitchell), Jock Livingston (Alexander Woollcott), J. Pat O'Malley (Dan), Harvey Jason (Bert), Damian London (Jerry Paul), Richard Angarola (Cesare), Matilda Calnan (Dorothy), Lester Matthews (Lord Chamberlain), Bernard Fox (Assistant to Lord Chamberlain), Murray Matheson (Bankruptcy Judge).

PLOT: Gertrude Lawrence relates the story of how she rose from entertaining in the music halls to become one of the great musical and dramatic actresses of both the London and New York theater.

Gertrude Lawrence (1898–1952) had been one of the few stars to achieve an equal degree of success on both the West End and the Broadway stage. As was so often the case with some of the immortal entertainers of the live theater, she did not fare so well in motion pictures. None of the handful she made suggested that audiences were in the presence of a peerless talent. Hollywood never had any hesitation about putting together lavish biopic musicals of both performers and composers from the theater whose familiarity to the average moviegoer might be peripheral or minor, mainly because the résumés of these people often provided an excuse to delve into a catalog of wonderful show tunes. When Saul Chaplin and Robert Wise struck on the idea of a Lawrence biopic, it was not so much because of a need to bring the lady back into the spotlight as it was a chance to give the woman they had adored working with on *The Sound of Music* (Twentieth Century-Fox, 1965), Julie Andrews, a great showcase in which to sing up a storm, act both sophisticated and bawdy, handle some tear-jerking melodramatics that were the staples of the genre, and prove her prowess in comedy. Andrews had another contractual commitment to Fox, after all; but she had enjoyed Wise and Chaplin's company as much as they had hers and was very excited by the challenge. According to her large fan base, however, Lawrence possessed a magic singularly her own that bore little resemblance to Andrews's very special talents. Andrews was also a far better vocalist and more physically attractive. Not unlike so many biopics before or after, it was almost a given that this was not going to be an example of astonishing mimicry or impersonation, but of one great musical star giving her "suggestion" of another. Because *The Sound of Music* was Fox's most treasured release, bringing in astronomical figures that became the stuff of legend, the studio had no qualms about Wise and Andrews doing pretty much whatever they pleased, budget be damned. Called simply (yet excitingly) *Star!*, the film became one of the company's most lavish, no-expense-spared items of the decade. Andrews would receive $625,500 for her participation.

> "If the lady's brilliantly witty, if she makes the dialogue flash. If the lady's way with a ditty, makes the ditty seem like a smash. If her songs add up to a fancy repertoire, the chances are the lady's a star."
> —Gertrude Lawrence

There was no doubt that *Star!* was going to present Andrews front and center as pretty much the whole show, to a degree that the five romantic interests worked into the story weren't written with all that much depth, nor were they cast with the most colorful of actors. These were Richard Crenna, the best known of the bunch, as Lawrence's second husband, Richard Aldrich; Indian-born Michael Craig, who had already stood in a bigger star's shadow when he played Nick Arnstein opposite Barbra Streisand in the London production of *Funny Girl*, as Sir Tony Spencer; Robert Reed, known at the time for the series *The Defenders*, as an actor named Charles Fraser; Anthony Eisley, late of television's *Hawaiian Eye* detective series, as banker Ben Mitchell; and John Collin, whose previous work was known only, if at all, in his native England, as Gertie's first husband, Jack Roper. For legal reasons, only Aldrich's real name was used. Jack Roper was in fact Frank Gordon-Howley, to whom Lawrence was married from 1924 to 1927; Ben Mitchell's counterpart was Wall Street's Bert Taylor; Sir Tony Spencer was based on Captain Philip Astley, who would later marry actress Madeleine Carroll; and the only Broadway actor registered as Charles Fraser had appeared on the Great White Way more than twenty years before the events depicted here. Compensating for this soft lineup was Daniel Massey, the son of actor Raymond Massey, who over the years had been making a name for himself in theater and television; he had already scored in a pair of musicals, *Living for Pleasure* in London and *She Loves Me* in New York. Cast as Noël Coward (who was, in fact, Massey's godfather), he brilliantly captured the self-satisfaction, martini-dry delivery, and effete brio of this very individual personality, making it quite clear that despite his preference for men, Coward was the true love of Lawrence's life and thus the predominant male figure in the picture.

With some 3,200 costumes (with no fewer than 125 different outfits for Andrews alone) by Donald Brooks; seven soundstages worth of set designs by Boris Leven (with whom Wise had worked on both

Sound of Music and *West Side Story*); choreography by one of Broadway and Hollywood's legends in the field, Michael Kidd; and scoring by Lennie Hayton, one of the pivotal figures of MGM's golden era of the musical genre, *Star!* was given a budget between $12 million and $14 million. And it ended up looking and sounding like it was worth every cent. Principal photography began on April 12, 1967, at the Twentieth Century-Fox Studios, several numbers being among the first shot. Between May 15 and June 5, the company went east for location shooting in New York. Scenes were shot at four theaters, the Music Box (for *Susan and God*), the Cort (for *Lady in the Dark*), the Belasco (*Andre Charlot's Revue of 1924*), and the Lyceum (for *Oh, Kay!*). All of them looked authentic for the period, but none was accurate in putting the right play to the right locale. *Susan* had been done at the Plymouth, *Lady* had premiered at the Alvin, *Charlot* had been seen at the Times Square, and *Oh, Kay!* had debuted at the Imperial. Additional scenes

There was no doubt who the selling point of *Star!* was—Julie Andrews dominated the cover of Twentieth Century-Fox Records' handsomely packaged soundtrack.

were filmed at Cartier's, Central Park, Washington Square Park, and the Algonquin Hotel (playing itself). A house on Oyster Bay Road in Mill Neck, Long Island, stood in for Lawrence's English country home; Tibbets Brook Park in Yonkers became the site of the midnight swimming-and-boating party supposedly taking place in Maidenhead; and St. Thomas Church on Fifty-third Street passed itself off as the outside of a London courtroom.

After shooting at the Cape Playhouse in Dennis, Massachusetts, and at the Villa La Serena at Cap Ferrat in the south of France, Wise and his crew journeyed to London for scenes that either did not involve Andrews (who returned to Hollywood for rehearsals, avoiding her native country for tax purposes) or could be shot with a stand-in. The June 24–July 8 London locations included Isleworth Studios (where the "Down at the Old Bull & Bush" throwaway and the interior of the Italia Conti School were done), Marble Hill Park (filling in for Hyde Park Corner), Clayborn Mews (the outside of Gertie's house), Theatre

Ratford (the Swansea Music Hall), Regents Park (for Sir Anthony and Gertie's row in the lake), Marylebone Station (where young Gertie and Noël were seen embarking on their tour), Westminster School (for the exterior of the Lord Chancellor's office), and Leslie Street, as the neighborhood where Gertrude was born. Back in Hollywood, the remaining dramatic scenes were shot between July 4 and October 4. The rest of the shoot entailed the more elaborate songs, including the sensational "The Saga of Jennie" (shot over a two-week period), "Parisian Pierrot," "The Physician" (from the London production of Cole Porter's *Nymph Errant*), and "Limehouse Blues." The last brought the shoot to a close on December 14.

Fox beat the drum loudly for *Star!*, letting audiences know way in advance that they were going to have an opportunity to enjoy another great big package of songs from the *Sound of Music* team, although the two pictures couldn't have been further apart in tone or design. As if audiences already suspected as much, advance sales on the road-show attraction were not even close to what the studio had hoped, given how much cash it had spent on the project. The film became the latest high-priced musical to get razzed by the majority of critics, but Fox hoped *Star!* would overcome this harsh and frankly unwarranted negativity, just as *Sound of Music* had. Unfortunately, audiences weren't sure if they wanted to spend three hours in the company of a more stylish and savvy Andrews than they'd grown to love, so they didn't give the picture the support it needed. Very soon after its premiere studio executives began to wonder if they might solve their problems by presenting a slightly shorter version of the picture. With Wise's reluctant blessing, they removed twenty minutes from the 175-minute film, which mean that pieces of "Forbidden Fruit," "Limehouse Blues," "Burlington Bertie," and "Parisian Pierrot" were now excised, while "Someday I'll Find You" (though not the rest of the *Private Lives* re-creation) and "My Ship" were cut from the movie altogether. Needless to say, this only made those who had enjoyed the movie angry, and word began to spread that *Star!* was not worth bothering with.

It seemed positively criminal that all the negative press should affect Andrews's efforts, because she had worked harder on this movie than any other before or since, and her achievements were often glowing. She took charge of the picture from the start, managed to keep the bitchier aspects of Lawrence from turning unpleasant, and was at her peak as a singer. Simple ballads like "My Ship" and "Someone to Watch over Me" presented these great songs at their best; she and Massey were delightful performing "Has Anybody Seen Our Ship?," suggesting the pleasure with which Coward and Lawrence might have played off one another; while "Burlington Bertie" became one of Andrews's crowning moments on film. "Limehouse Blues" was staged with all the aplomb of MGM in its heyday, and "The Saga of Jennie" was, quite simply, one of the most exciting realizations of an already great song to be reimagined for a motion picture.

After its general release engagements did nothing to perk up business, a drastic step was taken that would further hurt the picture's already tarnished reputation. It was decided to pull *Star!* from distribution and hack away at the already mutilated prints until the running time was brought down to 120 minutes. An infuriated Robert Wise would have nothing to do with this desecration, asking that the credit "A Robert Wise film" be removed from the print ads as well as the film itself. As if to emphasize their increasing desperation, the movie was given an inane new title, *Those Were the Happy Times*, with an icky new ad campaign that hoped to draw comparisons with *The Sound of Music* but looked more like one of those MGM kiddie matinee posters that were prevalent at the time. Released in this butchered format a year after its once-glittering premiere, the film flopped yet again. Fox finally admitted defeat, but Wise and Andrews would be vindicated in the future. Following a showing in London in 1981 of the complete version, word began to spread that the "bomb" wasn't a bomb at all in terms of quality. The movie was far from perfect as a drama, but Andrews and the musical program were as good as they came. Additional revival theater showings turned opinion around on the picture, and it became clear that *Star!* was just another victim of the changing scene at a time when critics, eager to appear hip, needed to trash pictures that were proudly old-fashioned in tone and content. Put back together to stay once and for all on subsequent theater screenings, the laserdisc transfer, and the DVD release, there was no longer any doubt that *Star!* was something that anyone with a true appreciation of the range of Julie Andrews should cherish.

THE LION IN WINTER (United Kingdom)

Academy Award Winner: Best Actress (Katharine Hepburn); Best Screenplay—Based on Material from Another Medium; Best Original Score—For a Motion Picture (Not a Musical)

Academy Award Nominee: Picture; Actor (Peter O'Toole); Director; Costume Design

Opening date: October 30, 1968 (London: December 29, 1968).

AVCO Embassy. A Joseph E. Levine Presentation of a Martin Poll Production.

Director: Anthony Harvey. Producer: Martin Poll. Executive Producer: Joseph E. Levine. Screenplay: James Goldman, based on his 1966 play. Photography: Douglas Slocombe. Art Director: Peter Murton. Art Director (French Sequences): Gilbert Margerie. Set Decorator: Peter James. Costumes: Margaret Furse. Music: John Barry. Editor: John Bloom. Eastmancolor. Panavision. 135 minutes (including overture, entr'acte, and exit music).

CAST: Peter O'Toole (King Henry II), Katharine Hepburn (Queen Eleanor of Aquitaine), Jane Merrow (Princess Alais), John Castle (Prince Geoffrey), Timothy Dalton (King Philip of France), Anthony Hopkins (Prince Richard), Nigel Stock (Capt. William Marshall), Nigel Terry (Prince John), Kenneth Ives (Eleanor's Guard), O. Z. Whitehead (Bishop of Durham).

PLOT: King Henry II summons his family for a Christmas court at Chinon Castle, where he and his estranged wife, Eleanor of Aquitaine, quarrel over which of their sons is the most worthy successor to the throne of England.

Peter O'Toole had the distinction of giving two of the decade's greatest performances, playing the very same character in a pair of movies that had no relation to one another. In 1964 O'Toole had scorched the screen with his volatile, impassioned turn as King Henry II in *Becket* (Paramount), in which he verbally sparred with a mild-mannered Richard Burton for the monarchy's control of the English church. He earned his second Oscar nomination for his bravura work and solidified his position as one of the most magnetic actors to grace the screen in years. Four years down the line the opportunity to reprise Henry arose when producer Martin Poll proposed O'Toole join him in a property to which Poll had purchased the rights, *The Lion in Winter*. James Goldman's play, in which the author had imagined a Christmastime battle for power between Henry II and his imprisoned wife, Eleanor of Aquitaine, had opened at New York's Ambassador Theatre on March 3, 1966, with Robert Preston and Rosemary Harris in the leads. Despite earning a Tony Award for Harris, the play didn't find much favor with reviewers

> "The only thing you want to see is father's vitals on a bed of lettuce. You don't care who wins as long as Henry loses. You'd do anything. You are Medea to the teeth, but this is one son you won't use for vengeance on your husband."
> —Richard

or the general public; Goldman's crackling script did not even rate a Tony nomination that year, and the production closed after ninety-two performances. O'Toole's decision to film it would help raise its stature, and Goldman was forever grateful.

O'Toole—who was, after all, ascending to the throne for a second time—took a very hands-on approach to the whole project when it came to who was going to be sharing the opening credits with him. For the part of Eleanor, his wish list was topped by nothing less than the best, Katharine Hepburn, who was, in fact, one year shy of the exact age the queen would have been (sixty-one) at the time the action took place. Hepburn had not worked since the death of her beloved companion Spencer Tracy in June 1967, but she knew that roles this meaty for women her age did not come along every day in motion pictures and was happy to do it. O'Toole was keen on having Anthony Harvey direct the film, on the basis of the accomplished job he had done on the offbeat independent drama *Dutchman* (Continental, 1967), which ran all of fifty-five minutes and was set entirely on a New York subway car.

Insomuch as the script did not veer too far from a theater piece, Harvey gathered his cast to rehearse on the stage of the Haymarket in London's West End over a two-week period. Actual shooting commenced on November 27, 1967, at Ardmore Studios in Kilbride, Ireland, where most of the castle rooms were constructed. Art director Peter Murton made the bold move of keeping the interiors plain and devoid of the usual tapestries and glossy movie-studio sheen found in most period films. The Ardmore version of Charnin Castle actually seemed like it was constructed centuries ago, and the dank winter chill nearly leapt off the screen. For exteriors, filmed after studio shooting had finished, such ancient French structures as the Château de Tarascon, the Abbey de Montmajour, and the walled city at Carcassonne provided backdrops. Eleanor's grand arrival on the riverbank near Chinon was shot on the Rhône River aboard a specially built barge that had to be transported from Southampton to France.

While *Lion* was being filmed, AVCO Embassy was experiencing undreamed-of profits from its 1967 Christmas release *The Graduate*, which meant that it had firmly established itself as one of the new independent companies to be reckoned with. With a property as saleable and prestigious as *The Lion in Winter* on its hands, the studio decided the film would get the full

The story of a family at odds found two great actors very much in sync, as is evident in this ad for the British release of *The Lion in Winter*, which captures stars Peter O'Toole and Katharine Hepburn in a particularly dramatic moment.

reserved-seat engagement treatment, which meant adding an overture and entr'acte music, though the film's 135-minute running time was shorter than that of most motion pictures deemed worthy of this highfalutin form of exhibition. What *Lion* wound up having in its favor, unlike so many prehyped road-show extravaganzas, was mostly rave reviews. All the camera angles in the world could not disguise the fact that this was a filmed staged play that just happened to have sturdier sets, but the words and the performances were what counted, and there was much excitement listening to the actors tossing off dialogue that sounded both intelligent and surprisingly contemporary. Goldman wasn't looking to educate or suffocate with fanciful speeches, but to present a domestic drama to which anyone from a squabbling household could relate. This gave *The Lion in Winter* an extra edge of audience appeal; parents and children argued, emotionally decimated one another, made peace, lost control, regained it, and let slip their feelings of admiration, love, or indifference, just as real people did. Full of quotable lines both bitchy and clever, it hardly mattered that the construction from scene to scene seemed more than a bit disjointed, as issues were raised and unresolved throughout and emotions and motivations seemed to shift from moment to moment. In the end the very subject on which the royals came together to settle, the succession, was left hanging. It was a testament to the film's overall impact that few seemed to complain or care.

Portrait of a bickering family: (*background*) Timothy Dalton, Peter O'Toole, Anthony Hopkins, Katharine Hepburn, and John Castle; (*foreground*) Nigel Terry and Jane Merrow, in *The Lion in Winter*.

As for history, Eleanor got her way: Richard became King Richard I, having succeeded his father to the throne upon Henry's death in 1189, only six years after the events portrayed in the film. Henry, however, would find his wishes fulfilled as well: John wound up taking over the monarchy from his older brother when Richard passed away in 1199. Perhaps the homosexual inclinations hinted at in *Lion* were based in fact, for Richard never had any offspring, nor was middle brother Geoffrey, who died in 1196, around to succeed him. The youngest brother, John, became one of England's least popular rulers, and his reign ended with his death in 1216. Eleanor had passed away in 1204. Because infighting among royalty has never ceased to fascinate, it became quite the norm for theater companies to include Goldman's play among its repertoire, something the author would never hesitate to fully credit to the critical acclaim and strong box-office attendance for the movie.

FACES

Academy Award Nominee: Supporting Actor (Seymour Cassel); Supporting Actress (Lynn Carlin); Story and Screenplay—Written Directly for the Screen

Opening date: November 24, 1968.

Continental. A Walter Reade Organization Presentation.

Director-Screenplay: John Cassavetes. Producer: Maurice McEndree. Photography: Al Ruban. Art Director: Phedon Papamichael. Music Direction: Jack Ackerman. Editors: Maurice McEndree, Al Ruban. Black and white. 130 minutes.

CAST: John Marley (Richard Forst), Gena Rowlands (Jeannie Rapp), Lynn Carlin (Maria Forst), Seymour Cassel (Chet), Fred Draper (Freddie), Val Avery (Jim McCarthy), Dorothy Gulliver (Florence), Joanne Moore Jordan (Louise Draper), Darlene Conley (Billy Mae), Gene Darfler (Joe Jackson), Elizabeth Deering (Stella), George Dunn (Comedian).

PLOT: Feeling that their staid marriage has come to an end, Richard Forst walks out on his wife, Maria, believing he is now in love with Jeannie, a woman he has just met, while Maria allows herself to be picked up by Chet, a flirtatious stranger she meets at a nightclub.

Like so many actors before and since, what John Cassavetes *really* wanted to do was direct, and so he did, coming up with a crude, improvisational effort called *Shadows* (Lion International, 1960). Nonetheless, it impressed many in the industry for its attempt to get as far away as possible from the staged, scripted feel of a traditional Hollywood movie. As his reward, Cassavetes was allowed to direct two studio features, *Too Late Blues* (Paramount, 1961) and *A Child Is Waiting* (United Artists, 1963), but he was unhappy with the meddling of outside forces and lack of freedom allotted him on these pictures. He wanted nothing more than to return to the free-form guerilla filmmaking he'd experienced his first time behind the camera. Along with his *Shadows* editor-producer, Maurice McEndree, Cassavetes began formulating an idea for a domestic drama that he would bankroll himself, shooting it on his own time with actors who were willing to work simply for the love of it, including his wife, Gena Rowlands. Armed with a very loose script, Cassavetes managed to coax several friends, family members, and acquaintances to participate in the project, explaining to them that this would have to be done out of dedication, with potential financial rewards somewhere down the end of the line.

> "Nobody has the time to be vulnerable to each other."
> —Chet

With borrowed equipment, including two loaned, 16mm Éclair cameras, Cassavetes and his crew started shooting their black-and-white picture (alternately referred to as *The Marriage* and *Inside-Out* during production, until the director settled on *Faces*) in January 1965. The Cassavetes home stood in for John Marley's house and Gena Rowlands's mother's residence was used for her daughter's character's apartment, while such Los Angeles locales as the Whisky a Go Go and Losers, a club on La Cienega Boulevard, allowed the filmmaker to shoot there. Because Cassavetes was not able to film on a steady, uninterrupted schedule (most of the movie was shot at night, since many of the participants had day jobs) and because he encouraged so much improvisation, with scenes being done over and over again, the filming continued off and on until July of that year. (There would be some additional reshoots in 1967.)

By the time Cassavetes finished shooting, more than 115 hours of footage had been printed. Editing took place at his house, in a converted carport, over the next three years. At one point, in a moment of temporary madness, Cassavetes considered putting out an eight-hour cut of the movie, so satisfied was he with what he was seeing. Instead, the version he finally showed to his cast and crew in early 1968 clocked in at three hours and forty minutes. Wisely, he kept clipping away at the length, whittling it down to 114 minutes by June of that year, only to restore 16 minutes, bringing his final print to 130 minutes—the first of too many examples of a Cassavetes movie that went on far too long for its own good. The 16mm negative was reprinted as a 35mm film, and early showings of the movie garnered favorable word of mouth. Cassavetes tried to get it submitted as an entry at the Venice Film Festival, only to find that he did not make the deadline. The judges, however, changed their minds, simply on the basis of the picture's merits, and allowed *Faces* to compete. It earned a Best Foreign Film award as well as an acting mention for John Marley, and its inclusion in the New York Film Festival that year was crucial in bringing it the sort of critical praise that helped a small movie get noticed. *Faces* was not, however, the sort of raw experiment that any of the studios would touch. Instead, the independent Walter Reade Organization picked it up for distribution, paying $250,000 for the rights to release it in America under the Continental banner.

Faces seemed like such a nose-thumbing in the face of conventional and safe Hollywood filmmaking that it generated excitement among a certain faction of moviegoers who were looking for something fresh, original, and difficult. This was just about the closest thing to home-movie making, blown up for the big screen, with an occasionally inaudible soundtrack (despite postproduction attempts to

The *Faces* on hand in this ad for John Cassavetes' raw drama are Seymour Cassel (pictured twice), Lynn Carlin, and Mrs. Cassavetes, Gena Rowlands.

fix the mistakes), overexposed film, and a jittery camera that seemed to cross the boundaries of decorum, exposing the characters' deepest emotional and physical imperfections with merciless close-ups. To some this was the ultimate breakthrough in recording human behavior in all its painful grasping for contact and understanding. Nothing seemed mapped out or planned, and the dialogue erupted from the principals' mouths as if it really were being made up on the spot. Cassavetes was championed for putting an end to cinematic artifice and gloss, and his very personal style of directing turned him into a cultural hero of independent movie making. This was not, however, in any way akin to widespread admiration. Although *Faces* became one of the great successes of the art-house circuit, it was all too loose and maddening to appeal to the general public. For every serious cinema fanatic who praised the picture as groundbreaking, there were those who decried its formless lack of discipline, repetitious improvisational riffs, extended running time, and overall self-indulgence.

With *Faces* on his résumé, Cassavetes once again found Hollywood beckoning. His next two features, *Husbands* (1970) and *Minnie and Moskowitz* (1971), were made on his terms for Columbia and Universal, respectively. Although moviegoers displayed some degree of interest in these two oddities, it became all too apparent that this sort of edgy, improvisational material was never going to go down well with a mass audience, and neither studio saw much point in continuing a relationship with the director. Not surprisingly, therefore, Cassavetes took his desire for independence one step further, forming his own company and naming it Faces. It distributed his next three movies, *A Woman Under the Influence* (1974), for which he would receive his sole Oscar nomination for directing; *The Killing of a Chinese Bookie* (1976); and *Opening Night* (1978). By this point the camps were sharply divided between those who hailed John Cassavetes as one of the greatest of all visionary artists and those who gave his uncompromising style a wide berth.

THE FIXER

Academy Award Nominee: Actor (Alan Bates)

Opening date: December 8, 1968.

MGM. An Edward Lewis Production.

Director: John Frankenheimer. Producer: Edward Lewis. Screenplay: Dalton Trumbo. Based on the 1966 novel by Bernard Malamud. Photography: Marcel Grignon. Art Director: Béla Zeichan. Costumes: Dorothy Jeakins. Music: Maurice Jarre. Solo Violin: Zina Schiff. Editor: Henry Berman. Metrocolor. 132 minutes. Rated M.

CAST: Alan Bates (Yakov Bok), Dirk Bogarde (Bibikov, Investigating Magistrate), Georgia Brown (Marfa Golov), Hugh Griffith (Nikolai Lebedev), Elizabeth Hartman (Zinaida Nikolaevna), Ian Holm (Prosecuting Attorney Grubeshov), David Opatoshu (Latke), David Warner (Count Odoevsky), Carol White (Raisl), George Murcell (Deputy Warden), Murray Melvin (Priest), Peter Jeffrey (Berezhinsky), Michael Goodliffe (Ostrovsky), Thomas Heathcote (Proshko), Mike Pratt (Father Anastasy), Stanley Meadows (Gronfein), Francis De Wolff (Warden), David Lodge (Zhitnyak), William Hutt (Tzar Nicholas II), Alfie Bass (Potseikin), Danny Green (Prisoner Who Beats Up Yakov).

PLOT: Yakov Bok, an impoverished Jewish fixer living in Czarist Russia, is unjustly arrested for the brutal murder of a young boy and tossed into solitary confinement by the anti-Semitic authorities, who order him tortured and humiliated in an effort to make him confess to the crime.

Full of good things and good intentions, *The Fixer* wasn't able to bring its better elements together into an entirely satisfying whole. Like so many movies, it had the unenviable task of living up to an acclaimed novel read and praised by many, one that had in fact earned a Pulitzer for author Bernard Malamud. Malamud's account of the anti-Semitic hell endured by an innocent Jewish handyman in early twentieth-century Russia was so relentless in its depiction of the physical and psychological punishment inflicted upon its hapless hero that it was often difficult to read, the sort of effective writing that instills a seething anger in the reader toward every injustice, large or small, ever inflicted upon a human being. Malamud did not have to make up this kind of tale; he based his book on an actual incident

> "Do you think I'm such an idiot as to believe all these stories about the Jews? Of course not. There's no Jewish problem in Russia; nor anywhere else for that matter. There's only the problem of human nature."
> —Count Odoevsky

that had taken place in 1911 Kiev when an ex-soldier and father of five, Mendel Beiliss, was imprisoned under the false charge of having murdered a thirteen-year-old boy as part of a "Jewish ritual." Beiliss was finally acquitted, but the heinous motivations behind these trumped-up charges exposed Russia's disgraceful treatment of its Jewish population.

This is **"The Fixer"**... who didn't know he had courage... until courage was all he had left.

Based on the Pulitzer Prize–winning novel by Bernard Malamud.

Metro·Goldwyn·Mayer presents
the John Frankenheimer·Edward Lewis Production of

the fixer
starring Alan Bates
Dirk Bogarde, Hugh Griffith, Elizabeth Hartman,
Ian Holm, David Warner, Carol White
Screenplay by Dalton Trumbo, Based on the novel by Bernard Malamud,
Produced by Edward Lewis, Directed by John Frankenheimer

Alan Bates was very much the focus of attention in this ad for *The Fixer*, although he ended up looking a great deal shabbier in the film itself than either image of him shown here.

Producer Edward Lewis and director John Frankenheimer saw that, grim as it was, *The Fixer* had the makings of a powerful movie, and they purchased the rights to the book in October 1966. Because the team was toiling away at the time on MGM's big Christmas attraction for that year, *Grand Prix*, they turned to that studio for financing, getting a $3 million commitment. Frankenheimer announced to the press that he would be shooting the film on location in the Soviet Union and that his chosen scriptwriter, Dalton Trumbo, would deviate very little from Malamud's text, simply because they didn't think the material needed much alteration. However, whereas the book had begun with the announcement of the boy's murder, then flashbacked to the events leading up to it, the movie would tell the tale chronologically. Although Frankenheimer had intended to include as much of Malamud as possible, a good deal of the footage he filmed ended up on the cutting-room floor. The finished movie did not contain the reading of Nikolai's deposition condemning Yakov's actions, making the character appear somewhat more benign than Malamud had intended; nor did it include the arrival of a letter from the slain boy's mother insisting Yakov confess to the murder so people would stop suspecting her of any involvement, a most effective incident that had spoke volumes about the woman's guilt. Missing, too, was the character of Yakov's simple but good-hearted father-in-law (played by Jack Gilford in the deleted scenes) and the emphasis on the political upheaval about to take place in Russia as the story ends.

Frankenheimer ended up shooting the movie not in the Soviet Union, but in Hungary, making this the very first American picture to be filmed there in its entirety. He used the Mafilm Studios and a twenty-square-block area of Budapest that for the sake of tourism had been kept looking pretty much as it had prior to World War I. The old Buda Prison was used for Alan Bates's incarceration. *The*

Fixer began principal photography on October 9, 1967, and continued for another four months. It was an uncomfortable shoot that found Frankenheimer and Trumbo at odds over their interpretation of the piece; furthermore, the director considered actor Dirk Bogarde a most disagreeable presence on the set, despite his fine work. The overseas filming had managed to keep the budget down, and the movie certainly looked like an impressive prestige item, which encouraged MGM to hold it for a select booking in December 1968. Although Frankenheimer's first screening of the picture (after having hacked away at its considerable length) had been greeted rapturously, the paid critics were far less supportive than anticipated. Metro now had a very bleak movie on its hands without the benefit of across-the-board raves to help it along. Bates ended up as one of the five finalists for the Best Actor Oscar (curiously, the only time he would ever receive such recognition), but *The Fixer* was looked upon by most as having fallen short of its source material. Frankenheimer conceded defeat on this project, chalking it up as one of his failures.

OLIVER! (United Kingdom)

Academy Award Winner: Best Picture; Best Director; Best Art Direction-Set Decoration; Best Sound; Best Score of a Musical Picture—Original or Adaptation; Special Award: Choreography

Academy Award Nominee: Actor (Ron Moody); Supporting Actor (Jack Wild); Screenplay—Based on Material from Another Medium; Cinematography; Film Editing; Costume Design

Top 10 Box Office Film

Opening date: December 11, 1968 (London: September 26, 1968).

Columbia. A Romulus Production. Produced by Arrangement and in Association with Donald Albery.

Director: Carol Reed. Producer: John Woolf. Screenplay: Vernon Harris. Based on the 1962 musical with book, music, and lyrics by Lionel Bart, from the 1838 novel *Oliver Twist*, by Charles Dickens. Songs by Lionel Bart: "Food, Glorious Food," "Oliver!," "Boy for Sale," "Where Is Love?," "Consider Yourself," "Pick a Pocket or Two," "It's a Fine Life," "I'd Do Anything," "Be Back Soon," "Who Will Buy?," "As Long as He Needs Me," "Reviewing the Situation," "Oom-Pah-Pah." Music Supervisor, Arranger, Conductor, Orchestrator, and Choral Arranger: John Green. Photography: Oswald Morris. Production Designer: John Box. Art Director: Terence Marsh. Set Dressers: Vernon Dixon, Ken Muggleston. Costumes: Phyllis Dalton. Choreographer and Musical Sequences Staged by Onna White. Editor: Ralph Kemplen. Technicolor. Panavision. 153 minutes (including overture, entr'acte, and exit music). Rated G.

CAST: Ron Moody (Fagin), Shani Wallis (Nancy), Oliver Reed (Bill Sikes), Harry Secombe (Mr. Bumble), Mark Lester (Oliver Twist), Jack Wild (the Artful Dodger), Hugh Griffith (Magistrate), Joseph O'Conor (Mr. Brownlow), Hylda Baker (Mrs. Sowerberry), Leonard Rossiter (Mr. Sowerberry), Sheila White (Bet), Peggy Mount (Widow Corney), Megs Jenkins (Mrs. Bedwin), James Hayter (Jessop), Kenneth Cranham (Noah Claypole), Wensley Pithey (Dr. Grimwig), Robert Bartlett, Jeff Chandler, Chris Duff, Nigel Grice, Ronnie Johnson, Nigel Kingsley, Robert Langley, Peter Lock, Clive Moss, Ian Ramsey, Billy Smith, Kim Smith, Freddie Stead, Raymond Ward, John Watters (Fagin's Boys).

PLOT: Orphaned Oliver Twist flees to London, where he is taken under the wing of Fagin and his gang of young pickpockets.

Although the British had always taken great pride in their contribution to world theater, there was one area in which they had to concede defeat when it came to competing with the Americans, and that was in creating successful, traditional book musicals. It was up to Lionel Bart to put an end to that with his third West End effort, adapting Charles Dickens's classic novel *Oliver Twist* into the singing-and-dancing format. (Dickens's book, like many of his most famous novels, had first been published serially, in *Bentley's Miscellany*, between February 1837 and April 1839. It was then published in three volumes in 1838, before the last installment in the series appeared.) Officially crediting Dickens as its source, Bart in fact owed a great deal of the structure of his adaptation to the much-admired 1948 film version of *Oliver Twist* directed by David Lean. Bart made sure he toned down some of the grimmer aspects of the original story, like Oliver being shot while forced to participate in a bungled break-in and Fagin's execution for his crimes, though the brutal killing of Nancy was deemed too essential to the story line to tamper with. Bart, like Lean, kept only Mr. Brownlow as the one link to Oliver's past, leaving out the novel's characters of Mrs. Maylie and Rose (who turned out to be the sister of Oliver's late mother). The character of Monks, Oliver's half brother, who enlists Fagin and Bill Sikes to eliminate the boy so that he may be the sole heir to the lad's inheritance, was also removed from the musical version, while Oliver's young nemesis during his stay with the Sowerberrys, Noah Claypole, no longer returned to the tale as a member of Fagin's gang, as he had in the Dickens book.

Opening on June 30, 1960, at London's New Theatre (which would later change its name to the Albery), *Oliver!* starred Ron Moody as Fagin, Georgia Brown as Nancy, Keith Hamshere as Oliver, Martin Horsey as the Artful Dodger, and Danny Sewell as Bill Sikes. Under the direction of Peter Coe, with an innovative rotating set by Sean Kenney, the show became the smash hit of the season, and Bart was hailed for his rousing and melodic songs. Seeing no imminent closing date, producer David Merrick purchased the rights to bring the show to America, starting it off in Los Angeles in the summer of 1962. After stopovers in San Francisco, Toronto, and Detroit, *Oliver!* opened at New York's Imperial Theatre on January 6, 1963, and ran for 774 performances, finally closing on November 14, 1964. Brown and Sewell repeated their West End roles, as did Hope Jackman (as Mr. Corney)

> "In this life, one thing counts, in the bank large amounts. I'm afraid these don't grow on trees; you've got to pick a pocket or two."
> —Fagin

and Barry Humphries (as Mr. Sowerberry). Bruce Protchnick, who had been one of the cast replacements in London, was the Broadway Oliver, while the new Fagin, Clive Revill, was among the show's Tony nominees. Bart, Kenney, and conductor Donald Pippin all took home awards. After a nine-month tour, the show returned east to play at the Martin Beck Theatre for another 64 performances in 1965. Meanwhile, the London production kept on breaking records. It finally closed in September 1966 after a six-year run of 2,618 performances, making it the longest-running British musical up to that time. Less than a year later the show was back in the West End at the Piccadilly Theatre, with Humphries now promoted to the role of Fagin and future pop star Phil Collins as the Artful Dodger.

Knowing he had a desirable property on his hands, Bart held out for the most lucrative movie offer, turning down esteemed British director Carol Reed, among others. The Mirisch Corporation tried to put in its bid in 1963, hoping to cast Georgia Brown opposite Peter O'Toole as Fagin, but that intriguing prospect fell through. The following year Brookield Productions, the company Peter Sellers and John Bryan had just created, announced that it had secured the rights in order to provide Sellers with another vehicle to display his chameleonlike versatility. Although Bart was in favor of this transaction, the show's original producer, Donald Albery, insisted that he was in a position to override the Brookfield deal if a better offer came along, which he got from Romulus Films. Sellers was out, and the Woolf Brothers, John and James, won the coveted deal. Romulus's most notable recent credit had been the Leslie Caron drama *The L-Shaped Room*, and the same distributor responsible for that 1963 release, Columbia, struck a deal to distribute *Oliver!* as well. Despite the announcement that *Alfie* director Lewis Gilbert would get the job of helming and adapting the piece, the final choice was none other than Carol Reed, who was overjoyed to find the property he had once failed to grab hold of end up in his hands after all.

Initially it looked as if Peter Sellers was also going to get a reprieve when the Columbia brass suggested Romulus still use him for Fagin. Reed, however, was adamantly against this casting, favoring the originator of the part, Ron Moody. *Oliver!* wound up bucking the typical practice of filling the original stage roles with star names and was cast with virtually no consideration whatsoever for marquee value. Moody, who had displayed his comic finesse in such movies as the Miss Marple mystery *Murder Most Foul* (MGM, 1964) and the satire *The Mouse on the Moon* (United Artists, 1963; he played the part created by Sellers in *The Mouse That Roared*, Columbia, 1959), was far from well-known in the United States. This was also true of Shani Wallis, a cabaret singer and West End musical star, who nabbed the role of Nancy. Although the casting reeked of nepotism, Reed's real-life nephew, Oliver Reed, was suggested for the part of brutish Bill Sikes not by the filmmaker, but by producer John Woolf. He was so

Jack Wild (*bottom right*) and the rest of Fagin's boys attempt to distract their mentor (as played by Ron Moody) as he demonstrates the joys of pickpocketing in *Oliver!*

right for the character, however, that all question of favoritism vanished. Carol Reed chose snub-nosed fourteen-year old Jack Wild, who had appeared as one of Fagin's nameless boys during the original West End run, for the charismatic Artful Dodger, and went with angelically blond Mark Lester (who turned nine during the shoot) for the title role. Lester had played one of Dirk Bogarde's brood in the disturbing *Our Mother's House* (MGM, 1967) and had the perfect sympathetic countenance, even if he was incapable of carrying a tune. Although it was kept a secret for years, Lester's breathy, rather strained vocals were provided by a female ghost singer, twenty-year-old Kathe Green, the daughter of the film's musical director, John Green.

Screenwriter Vernon Harris was asked to make some alterations in bringing the work to the screen. The principal changes involved the elimination of songs performed by some of the supporting characters: "I Shall Scream," a comic duet for Mr. Bumble and Widow Corney presented prior to the former's singing of "Boy for Sale"; and "It's Your Funeral," a solo for the undertaker, Mr. Sowerberry, which had not even been included on the Broadway cast recording. Two of Nancy's numbers, "It's a Fine Life" and "Oom-Pah-Pah," were given more comfortable positions in the story line. The former was moved from Fagin's lair (where it had come too close to Nancy's singing of "I'd Do Anything") and became a rousing entertainment for the patrons at the Three Cripples tavern. The latter now provided tension as a diversion staged by Nancy in an effort to get Oliver away from Sikes. Perhaps the most important and beneficial revision was to bring Sikes into the story earlier and to cut his song, "My Name," inasmuch as the scowling manner in which Reed played him hardly made Sikes the sort of fellow who'd be found chirping a tune. The decision to eliminate his music made him that much more threatening and unpleasant.

Given a no-expense-spared budget of $10 million, *Oliver!* took over the Shepperton Studios, where no fewer than six soundstages were filled with John Box's smashing sets. In the meantime, re-creations of the London slums and a lovely crescent in Bloomsbury rose on the studio's back lot. The film started shooting on June 23, 1967, after eight months of preparation and rehearsals, and it continued to dominate the facility for the next seven months. Looking at the finished print, Columbia couldn't have been happier. Every casting choice, every revision from the play, and every set design, dance step, and line of dialogue had been carefully and tastefully chosen, and now the film worked even better than the stage original had. The studio decided to delay the movie's U.S. opening so that it could be their big Christmas 1968 release. Pretty soon after the six-month postproduction period, *Oliver!* was booked to open in London on September 26, 1968, where it was instantly hailed as every bit as exciting as its stage predecessor. English audiences began queuing up in record numbers, and the movie was a sold-out sensation by the time it began its reserved-seat American engagement. (In New York it opened the brand new twin cinema the Loews State, in Times Square.) Unlike most of the expensive musicals that were showing up in cinemas during the late '60s, the critics of the day actually loved *Oliver!*, praising Reed's exuberant yet loving direction, which never let the spectacle outshine the heart of the story. The film managed to maintain the grittiness of the novel without ever turning off those in search of a rollicking good time. The deaths of Sikes and Nancy were nightmarish and yet never detracted from the musical-comedy feel of the picture, and any worries over an anti-Semitic interpretation of Fagin were quelled by Moody's tremendously enjoyable performance.

Each and every one of the cast principals was championed as a bright "new" screen talent, and Moody and Wild ended up in the running for Oscars. *Oliver!* entered the Academy race with eleven nominations, including that for best picture, which meant it was competing with yet another lavish musical hit from Columbia, *Funny Girl*. Despite indications that *The Lion in Winter* (AVCO Embassy), had the inside track, it was *Oliver!* that ended up with the Best Picture award—a signal of sorts that Hollywood wasn't ready quite yet to make a complete and total leap into the more free-spirited, adult-themed cinema being heralded in movies like *Alfie* or *The Graduate* (AVCO Embassy, 1967). Coming less than two months after the creation of the MPAA rating system, *Oliver!* became the first, and, to date, the only G-rated movie to win the top Oscar honor. Select cynics from future generations would try to argue against a movie culture that allowed such an old-fashioned a picture to trump the bleak *Rachel, Rachel* (Warner Bros.), as well as the groundbreaking and cryptic *2001: A Space Odyssey* (MGM), which did not even rate a spot among the five finalists. But there was no denying that *Oliver!* was nothing less than superb in what it set out to be. Its already plentiful U.S. box office soared after its Academy triumph, and it became one of the year's Top 10 hits. Back in London, the picture ran for more than a year at its premiere venue. Carol Reed, Bart, and company had created what would be commonly recognized as the greatest and most enduring of the small number of British motion-picture musicals.

ISADORA (United Kingdom–United States–France)

Academy Award Nominee: Actress (Vanessa Redgrave)

Opening date: December 18, 1968 (London: March 5, 1969; New York: April 27, 1969, as *The Loves of Isadora*).

Universal. A Robert and Raymond Hakim Production.

Director: Karel Reisz. Producers: Robert Hakim, Raymond Hakim. Screenplay: Melvyn Bragg, Clive Exton. Additional Dialogue: Margaret Drabble. Adapted for the screen by Melvyn Bragg. Based on the books *My Life* (1927), by Isadora Duncan, and *Isadora Duncan: An Intimate Portrait* (1928), by Sewell Stokes. Photography: Larry Pizer. Production Designer: Jocelyn Herbert. Set Dressers: Bryan Graves, Harry Cordwell. Wardrobe: Ruth Myers, John Briggs, Jackie Breed. Music: Maurice Jarre. Music for Dance Sequences and Period Dance Music, Classical and Dance Music Arranger and Conductor: Anthony Bowles. Songs: "Bye Bye Blackbird," by Ray Henderson and Mort D. Dixon; "I Wonder Where My Baby Is Tonight," by Gus Kahn and Walter Donaldson. Choreographer: Litz Pisk. Editor: Tom Priestley. Eastmancolor. 157 minutes (including overture, entr'acte, and exit music; later cut to 138 and then to 131 minutes). Rated M.

CAST: Vanessa Redgrave (Isadora Duncan), James Fox (Gordon Craig), Jason Robards (Paris Singer), Ivan Tchenko (Sergei Essenin), John Fraser (Roger Thornton), Bessie Love (Mrs. Duncan), Cynthia Harris (Mary Desti), Libby Glenn (Elizabeth Duncan), Tony Vogel (Raymond Duncan), Wallas Eaton (Archer), John Quentin (Pim), Nicholas Pennell (Martin Bedford), Ronnie Gilbert (Miss Chase), Christian Duvaleix (Armand, Pianist), Vladimir Leskovar ("Bugatti").

PLOT: Fiercely individualistic Isadora Duncan becomes one of the great influential and controversial figures in the arts, with her free-form manner of expressionistic dance, as she leads a frantic life filled with shattered love affairs and tragedy.

Universal's risky biopic *Isadora* was intended both to celebrate and to explain the curious and tragic life of Isadora Duncan, who revolutionized dancing while championing individuality in the face of a frequently puzzled and outraged society. There had been talk (but nothing more than that) over the years of Duncan's being the subject of a movie bio, with names as varied as Greta Garbo and Shirley MacLaine tossed about as the star. It was highly unlikely that had such a movie gotten made in earlier years, it would have been a faithful dramatization of the dancer's life. That life was so steeped in unhappiness and ended so horribly that it would have been difficult to cobble a conventional, uplifting studio bio movie from the facts. Not only did Duncan suffer the unbearable loss of both her small children in a freak auto accident, but she had borne them out of wedlock while living with two different men. She was an outspoken advocate for free love and women's rights; dressed freakishly to simulate flowing classical Greek garb; had a volatile, out-of-control marriage to a boorishly rude, self-indulgent Russian poet; and caused a stir when she exposed her breasts to a stupefied Boston audience in the middle of one of her expressive dance pieces. Her death was so unpleasant that nobody would ever dare to stage it authentically: Isadora's long, flowing scarf had accidentally become tangled in the wheel spokes of a moving sports car; the force broke her neck and yanked her from the vehicle, hurling her body violently to the pavement, and the corpse was dragged several yards before the driver was aware of what had happened. Now that it was the late '60s, things were freer, rebels were in fashion, and independent women were an important part of the sexual revolution. Isadora Duncan could be looked upon as a pioneering hippie of sorts, and suddenly her story seemed very feasible, very relevant.

The brothers Robert and Raymond Hakim, who owned the rights to both Duncan's own posthumously published autobiography and a biography written shortly afterward by Sewell Stokes, decided that they had not only the right actress but also the right director in mind for their long-overdue project after seeing the whimsical British black comedy *Morgan!* (Cinema V, 1966). They had been enchanted by the effervescent charms of Vanessa Redgrave and were highly impressed by the snappy, offbeat directorial touches of Yugoslavian-born Karel Reisz. The wait had been well worth it, for in Redgrave they found an individualistic, fearless, graceful, and magnetic actress who seemed very much in tune with everything Duncan represented or hoped to achieve in her passion, her art, and her life.

Unfortunately, no clear full-length footage of Isadora in performance was available, nor had she bothered to give a detailed description of her dancing style in her book. To prepare for her role, Redgrave tracked down a grainy, badly faded amateur movie, approximately fifteen minutes long, that had been shot by a Russian cameraman. With these brief flashes for references and calling on some ballet training she had had during her youth, Redgrave ventured with total commitment into the part, rehearsing the movements with Litz Pisk over a six-month period prior to shooting; her training continued throughout the production.

> "Art and love destroy each other. . . . Oh, I suppose it might be possible, for a short time, with some people . . . but you have to have a real run of luck."
> —Isadora Duncan

Financing for the $4 million film came from the Egyptian Hakim Brothers, Universal, and French-based Paris Film. Although Duncan was American born, spent a pivotal part of her life in Russia, and died in Nice, none of the movie was shot in any of those places. Instead, the picture divided most of its time between England and Yugoslavia. In the United Kingdom, Reisz used the famous Wilton Music Hall at 1 Grace's Alley, Wellclose Square, London, to substitute for an American vaudeville stage in which Duncan made an appearance under the unlikely name "Peppy Dora"; the Victorian Waddesdon Manor, outside of Aylesbury, Buckinghamshire, to stand in for Bellevue, the French school millionaire Paris Singer purchased for Duncan so that she could teach dance to young girls; the Royal Albert Docks for the sequence in which Duncan and her husband Essenin are protested upon their return to America; the British Museum, where Duncan finds herself inspired by the Elgin Marbles, originally part of the Parthenon; Metron Park, Surrey, where the fight scene between Duncan and Essenin was so realistically staged that Redgrave wound up breaking a toe; the Theatre Royal, Drury Lane; the Wimbledon Theatre, for the notorious "topless" scene (the extras supposedly were not informed of what they were about to witness so that the film could capture the true shock from their faces); and the actual Singer estate of Oldway Mansion in Paignton, Devon, which later became the Paignton Civic Center. Figuring that Nice no longer looked as it had in the late 1920s, Reisz went scouting throughout Europe and decided that the Opatija, along the Croatian coast on the Adriatic Sea, was the perfect substitute. This find prompted him to choose other locations there as well, including Ptuj, where a sixteenth-century castle high above the town became Isadora's Russian dancing school; and Rijeka, whose National Theatre became the scene of

Duncan's 1910 triumph at the Berlin Theater. Principal photography began in England on September 1, 1967. The company then traveled to Yugoslavia and then back to England before wrapping the eighteen-week shoot.

If *Isadora* was a bit too artsy for mainstream acceptance, it did have controversy working in its favor. Universal decided that there was artistic justification for a discreet moonlit nude scene of Redgrave after a bit of lovemaking with James Fox and, most important, for that breast-bearing display, which was, after all, one of the key moments of infamy for the dancer. The studio was so sure it had a great work on its hands that it encouraged Reisz to stretch it out to three hours so it could be given the full road-show treatment. Reisz reluctantly complied, handing the studio a 177-minute print that was previewed to mixed reactions. Twenty minutes were sliced from that version for the scheduled opening in Los Angeles in December 1968, which would include an overture and intermission. Banking on critical raves to ensure for itself Oscar nominations and prestige galore, Universal was horrified when the *Los Angeles Times* panned the picture, making it look very unimportant indeed during the all-important year-end awards season. As other reviews began to trickle in, it was clear that this picture was prompting a sharply divided reaction. Reisz's decision to jump frequently between the older Isadora, on the last day of her life, to the past was championed by many as keeping the picture alive and contemporary, with flashy edits, but for also becoming a meditation of sorts, coming directly from the subject's mind. Others found this more than a bit confusing and were put off by the film's extended length. Nobody had any complaints about Redgrave, however, who was breathtakingly good. She played Duncan as borderline possessed in both a good and a bad sense, a singularly individual talent of such striking influence and originality that her gifts appeared unearthly, and yet a creature so dangerously at odds with an oppressive, rational society that she seemed

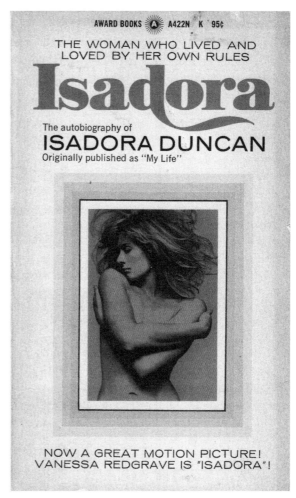

Isadora Duncan's none-too-dependable autobiography *My Life* was reissued by Award Books in conjunction with the release of *Isadora*. It placed the film's provocative image of Vanessa Redgrave on its cover for maximum sales appeal.

forever on the brink of collapsing into mental despair. In a very short time Redgrave had proven that she was a great actress, if not one of the greatest to illuminate movie screens of the late '60s, and *Isadora* remained, in many ways, her greatest motion-picture triumph.

Paying customers, however, were sending the message that, great performance or not, they were simply not interested. The Los Angeles engagement was proving to be such a failure that Universal, who earlier that year had insisted on bigger and longer, now demanded that Reisz do a bit more surgery on the picture in hopes that shortening *Isadora* would make it more attractive. Reluctantly, he cut another 19 minutes, most of it consisting of the older Isadora, which meant fewer flash-forwards, and, hopefully more clarity to the easily confused. While the 138-minute version (which still included an overture and entr'acte) of *Isadora* continued to play in Los Angeles, the Hollywood Foreign Press weighed in first, bestowing a Golden Globe nomination upon Redgrave. When the Oscar nominations were announced that year, Vanessa Redgrave was, indeed, among the five finalists, which normally would have ensured an opening in the rest of the major U.S. markets by that point. Instead, the film next appeared in its shortened form in London, where it opened on March 4, 1969. This was unprecedented: *Isadora* would spend the entire Oscar campaigning season playing only in the Los Angeles area, with interested reviewers and filmgoers in the rest of America denied seeing one of the year's nominated (not to mention best) performances right up to the night when the winner*s* were announced.

When at last the picture received its New York premiere, thirteen days after the Oscar ceremony, those anticipating its arrival were horrified to learn that not only were they getting the aborted cut, but it now had a very desperate title change—*The Loves of Isadora*—as if to ensure the more simpleminded viewers that they were getting pretty much what they had come to expect from a standard biopic. *Isadora* stubbornly was *not* a standard biopic; but despite its virtues, and although it was the best work of Reisz's erratic career, it was chalked up as a resounding failure in its day. Redgrave constantly rose above these condemnations, however: she won a Best Actress Award at the 1969 Cannes Film Festival and received the National Society of Film Critics Award later in the year. *Isadora* became one of those movies that the appreciative sought out and championed. After many years it was finally restored to its correct 157-minute length, which proved that all those edits had done nothing but damage its complex structure.

1969

THE PRIME OF MISS JEAN BRODIE (United Kingdom)

Academy Award Winner: Best Actress (Maggie Smith)

Academy Award Nominee: Song ("Jean")

Opening date: March 2, 1969 (London: February 25, 1969).

Twentieth Century-Fox.

Director: Ronald Neame. Producer: Robert Fryer. Screenplay: Jay Presson Allen. Based on her 1966 play from the 1961 novel by Muriel Spark. Photography: Ted Moore. Production Designer: John Howell. Art Director: Brian Herbert. Set Dresser: Pamela Cornell. Costumes: Elizabeth Haffenden, Joan Bridge. Music: Rod McKuen. Editor: Norman Savage. Deluxe color. 116 minutes. Rated M.

CAST: Maggie Smith (Jean Brodie), Robert Stephens (Teddy Lloyd), Pamela Franklin (Sandy), Gordon Jackson (Gordon Lowther), Celia Johnson (Miss Mackay), Diane Grayson (Jenny), Jane Carr (Mary McGregor), Shirley Steedman (Monica), Lavinia Lang (Emily Carstairs), Antoinette Biggerstaff (Helen McPhee), Margo Cunningham (Miss Campbell), Isla Cameron (Miss McKenzie), Rona Anderson (Miss Lockhart), Ann Way (Miss Gaunt), Molly Weir (Miss Allison Kerr), Helena Gloag (Miss Kerr), John Dunbar (Mr. Burrage), Heather Seymour (Clara), Leslie Patterson (Prefect).

PLOT: At Edinburgh's Marcia Blaine School for Girls, independent instructor Jean Brodie voices her own controversial opinions on fascism and politics in an effort to leave her imprint on her impressionable charges.

Decidedly *not* in the tradition of inspirational stories about individualistic teachers who guide their students toward better lives, *The Prime of Miss Jean Brodie* featured a protagonist who certainly was unlike any other instructor previously seen onscreen. Jean Brodie was fiercely original in her approach to education, defiantly unconcerned with image, and dangerously misguided in the spell she could weave over her malleable charges. Brodie was, politically speaking, a fascist. This charismatic, unforgettable, and decidedly infuriating character had come from the pen of Muriel Spark, whose background included having attended a girls' school (James Gillespie's), not unlike the fictitious Marcia Blaine institution of her book, and doing some teaching along the way. *The Prime of Miss Jean Brodie*, her sixth published work, arrived in 1961 and was short enough to be run in its entirety in the *New Yorker* magazine that year. Writer Jay Presson Allen was fascinated by the story and believed it could be restructured as a dramatic piece for the stage, spending close to four years on the adaptation. Spark's version had been very much an examination of the characters of Brodie and six of her "set," formidable schoolgirls who grew from the ages of ten or eleven to the age of eighteen during the course of the book. Spark would jump randomly ahead in the narrative, revealing the fates of her principals, so

> "You're not in your prime, Jean. You're a frustrated spinster taking it out in idiot causes and dangerous ideas; a school marm."
> —Teddy Lloyd

as to shortchange the dramatic suspense of the narrative, something that would not have worked in the theater. Allen pared down the number of schoolgirls to four, spreading the characteristics of the original six among them and shifting names, all the while keeping the key character of Sandy pretty faithful to the way Spark had conceived her. Allen carried over the idea of Sandy later becoming a nun, structuring the play so that it was a flashback, with Sister Helena (Sandy) telling the story from her cell at the convent to an inquisitive reporter. Such Spark characters as the grim teacher, Miss Gaunt, and Teddy Lloyd's wife, Dierdre, were no longer part of the narrative. And it seemed far too problematic to have an actor portray Teddy as a one-armed veteran of World War I, as Spark had depicted him, so the character was given a full set of appendages for the stage.

The Twentieth Century-Fox Records soundtrack for *The Prime of Miss Brodie* gave special emphasis to trendy poet Rod McKuen's contribution to the film, though what really grabbed one's attention was an illustration of the cast principals by the great Al Hirschfeld.

The West End production debuted on May 5, 1966, at the Wyndham Theatre under the direction of Peter Wood and featured one of the most talked-about new talents as the lead, Vanessa Redgrave. Robert Fryer, who had just produced *The Boston Strangler* for Twentieth Century-Fox, persuaded studio chief Darryl F. Zanuck to purchase *Brodie* prior to its Broadway transfer. The American version arrived at the Helen Hayes Theatre on January 16, 1968, starring Zoe Caldwell. The play ran for 367 performances, closing in December of that year, by which time the movie of *Jean Brodie* was already in the can. Because the material was neither a conventional love story nor particularly uplifting, Zanuck had wanted some sort of box-office insurance, so he offered the lead to Julie Andrews. But Andrews, who didn't feel she could pull off the Scottish accent required, turned it down. Instead, the name of Maggie Smith came up. The brilliant actress had actually been the first choice for the West End *Jean Brodie* but had had to pass because of scheduling conflicts.

Jay Presson Allen was enlisted to adapt Sparks's work, which meant that pretty much all the dialogue that had sparkled and provoked onstage would be up there on the screen. Wisely, the distracting present-day sequences with the humorless Sister Helena were deemed unnecessary, and the movie was told in a straightforward chronological fashion beginning in 1932—one year after the play was set and two years after the book. The few changes included cutting a scene in which Miss Mackay combs the dictionary to find out that Brodie's self-righteous translation of the word "education" is, in fact, inaccurate; and one in which Sandy visits the headmistress to suggest trapping the irresponsible Brodie by taking her political leanings into consideration. It was decided that the surprise of Brodie's betrayer be held until the confrontation between Jean and Sandy in the classroom (moved from Sandy's home, where it took place in the play). Although the film had no qualms about bringing up all manner of adult themes, a discussion about birth control between Jean and Lowther was omitted, as was Brodie's favorable endorsement of Adolf Hitler; her rapturous praise of Benito Mussolini was considered quite controversial enough.

Shooting began on April 29, 1968, at Shepperton Studios, where all the school interiors were done over a ten-week period prior to moving the production to Edinburgh in the middle of July. There, an Early Tudor house on Candlemaker Row became Teddy's art studio, and a small late Victorian home in Admiral's Row stood in for Jean's house, from which she embarked on her bicycle at the start of the picture. The thirteenth-century Barnbougle Castle, located in Cramond on the shores of the Firth of Forth, became Gordon Lowther's inherited estate, to which Brodie escapes for her carnal pleasures with the mild-mannered music teacher. To stand in for the façade of the Marcia Blaine School for Girls, the Donaldson School for the Deaf was chosen.

The Prime of Miss Jean Brodie was not to be everyone's cup of tea, for indeed an inherent sadness seemed to overwhelm the characters throughout, and the conclusion provided little sense of triumph or happiness for any of the principals. Audiences were confronted with a complex and unrelentingly exasperating central figure whose very flamboyant individualism drew the unsuspecting into her web, from which only those wise enough to realize the danger were able to escape in time. It made for an unsettling experience for many, a darkly fascinating one for others. There was no doubt, however, that this was Maggie Smith's finest hour onscreen to date. Alternately maddening in her stubborn resolve to march to her own tune, and yet admirable in her independent streak of self-preservation, Smith revealed a foolish and frightened woman under the bravado, but not before she dared to inch close to self-parody, with Brodie's whimsically overboard flights of self-involved romanticism and fancy. In its own way it was one of the most daringly executed performances of the decade, one that could have easily been smashed to pieces in the hands of a less adept actress.

THE LOVE BUG

Top 10 Box Office Film

Opening date: March 13, 1969.

Buena Vista. A Walt Disney Productions Presentation.

Director: Robert Stevenson. Producer: Bill Walsh. Screenplay: Bill Walsh, Don DaGradi. Based on a story by Gordon Buford. Photography: Edward Colman. Art Directors: Carroll Clark, John B. Mansbridge. Set Decorators: Emile Kuri, Hal Gausman. Costumes: Bill Thomas. Music: George Bruns. Editor: Cotton Warburton. Special Photographic Effects: Eustace Lycett, Alan Maley, Peter Ellenshaw. Special Effects: Robert A. Mattey, Howard Jensen, Dan Lee. Driving Sequences Supervisor: Carey Loftin. Technicolor. 108 minutes. Rated G.

CAST: Dean Jones (Jim Douglas/Hippie in Van), Michele Lee (Carole Bennett), Buddy Hackett (Tennessee Steinmetz), David Tomlinson (Peter Thorndyke), Joe Flynn (Havershaw), Benson Fong (Mr. Wu), Joe E. Ross (Detective), Barry Kelley (Police Sergeant), Iris Adrian (Carhop), Andy Granatelli (Association President), Ned Glass (Toll Booth Attendant), Robert Foulk (Bice), Gil Lamb (Policeman in Park), Nicole Jaffe (Girl in Hot Rod), Russ Caldwell (Boy in Hot Rod), P. L. Renoudet, Herb Vigran (Policemen on Bridge).

PLOT: Realizing that the Volkswagen he's purchased has a mind of its own, Jim Douglas turns the anxious little Beetle into a champion competitive race car.

Despite the fact that its origins were rooted in the early years of Nazi Germany, nobody held this against the Volkswagen, which was, by general consensus, the cutest of all automobiles and certainly one of the most popular. Originally conceived as an affordable means of transportation for the general public, the Beetle prototype was first introduced in Germany during the 1930s, but the car had to wait until the end of World War II and the demise of National Socialism to reach the international market. It took another two decades and the imagination of the Walt Disney Company to make a film that took full advantage of audiences' affection for this compact and inadvertently funny-looking vehicle.

> "Most guys spend more love and time and money on a car in a week than they do on their wife and kids in a year. Pretty soon, you know what?—the machine starts to think it is somebody."
> —Tennessee

Shortly after joining the studio as one of its roster of stock players, Dean Jones approached Walt Disney with the idea of doing a film about the first sports car brought to America. Disney, whose commercial sense had made him the entertainment giant he was, had a different property in mind: a story by Gordon Buford entitled *Car Boy Girl*, which involved an automobile with a mind and heart of its own.

Disney regular Robert Stevenson was assigned to direct but left all of the second unit material to be done by others more experienced in the field of automobile stunt work. Carey Loftin, who had done some impressive rubber burning in such movies as *It's a Mad Mad Mad Mad World* (United Artists, 1963) and *Grand Prix* (MGM, 1966), was given the job of coordinating the driving sequences and handled Herbie the Volkswagen's principal stunts, perhaps the most eye-popping of which involved the bug's driving around a hairpin curve on just three wheels, an image that was used in a great deal of the advertising. Arthur J. Vitarelli was placed in charge of the second unit footage, which was shot first. Filming began on April 1, 1968, at such California locations as the Riverside Raceway in Riverside, where Herbie

was allowed to be photographed participating in an actual race; Willow Springs Raceway in Rosamund; Big Bear, which required Herbie to come zooming down the side of a mountain; the Golden Oak Ranch, where Herbie's memorable bounce over the lake was created; and some select areas of San Francisco, including Union Square (the final shot in the film) and, of course, the zigzagging Lombard Street. Studio work on the Disney soundstages in Burbank was completed in mid-July 1968. Eight different Herbie models were used, including a hydraulic Herbie and a shaking Herbie; while the racing Herbies utilized a Porsche engine, brakes, and tires.

Being made at the height of the "hippie era" of the late '60s, the film made sure that it featured such characters among its cast, which, of course, kept it very much a product of its time, as did such expressions as "groovy," "out of sight," and "fuzz." The Disney folks wanted to emphasize this inclu-

Buddy Hackett practices his Chinese alphabet for Benson Fong in *The Love Bug*.

sion of the flower-power generation, a choice that turned out to be instrumental in the title finally chosen for the picture, *The Love Bug* (it was certainly preferable to such other choices as *The Magic Volksey* and *Beetlebomb*). With an ad campaign that included Buddy Hackett with a medallion around his neck and a scattering of bright flowers, *The Love Bug* seemed like the hippest thing the Disney folks could have come up with at the time, at least as far as family audiences were concerned. If there was one Walt Disney gimmick comedy that hit the public nerve with a resounding bang, it was this film, and the public started flocking to Herbie as soon as the film opened in mid-March 1969. Although Disney could depend upon a certain loyal family audience to come to most of their offerings, *The Love Bug* became that rare feature from the studio that crossed over into something bigger, attracting an eclectic group of moviegoers who were hoping for a lighthearted time at the movies. Nobody was fooled into believing that this was all that much different from most of the slapstick-ridden comedies that had become a staple of the company during the decade, but it kept enough indiscriminate viewers smiling to become a box-office sensation of unexpected proportions. By the end of 1969 it had outgrossed all the other moneymakers of that year. It was not surpassed until sometime early in 1970, when *Butch Cassidy and the Sundance Kid* (Twentieth Century-Fox), overtook *Bug* as the top-grossing 1969 release. *The Love Bug* wound up ranking second on Disney's list of all-time box-office champions, bested only by *Mary Poppins*.

GOODBYE, COLUMBUS

Academy Award Nominee: Screenplay—Based on Material from Another Medium

Top 10 Box Office Film

Opening date: April 3, 1969.

Paramount. A Stanley R. Jaffe Production.

Director: Larry Peerce. Producer: Stanley R. Jaffe. Screenplay: Arnold Schulman. Based on the 1959 novella by Philip Roth. Photography: Gerald Hirschfeld. Art Director: Manny Gerard. Costumes: Gene Coffin. Miss MacGraw's Wardrobe: The Villager. Music: Charles Fox. Songs written and performed by the Association: "Goodbye, Columbus," "It's Gotta Be Real," "So Kind to Me." Editor: Ralph Rosenblum. Technicolor. 102 minutes. Rated R (later changed to PG).

CAST: Richard Benjamin (Neil Klugman), Ali MacGraw (Brenda Patimkin), Jack Klugman (Ben Patimkin), Nan Martin (Mrs. Patimkin), Michael Meyers (Ron Patimkin), Lori Shelle (Julie Patimkin), Monroe Arnold (Uncle Leo), Kay Cummings (Doris Klugman), Sylvie Straus (Aunt Gladys), Royce Wallace (Carlotta), Anthony McGowan (Boy in Library), Mari Gorman ("Simp," Laura Simpson Sockaloe), Jan Peerce (Uncle Manny), Max Peerce (Uncle Max), Ray Baumel (Uncle Harry), Delos Smith (Mr. Scapello), Gail Ommerle (Harriette), David Benedict (Rabbi), Michael Nouri (Don Farber), Betty Greyson (Aunt Molly).

PLOT: Neil Klugman falls in love with the beautiful Brenda Patimkin, fully aware that her well-to-do parents don't approve of their pampered daughter carrying on with someone they believe is beneath them.

In 1959 readers were introduced to the work of Philip Roth, a former teacher and part-time film reviewer who published his first novella, *Goodbye, Columbus*, along with five other stories, all of them poking fun at the manners and mores of postwar middle-class American Jews. For everyone who recognized the honesty with which Roth looked askance at this world of class warfare and false values, there were those who felt his portrayal of suburban Jewish life was perhaps a bit harsh in the way it exposed the tackier side of the nouveau riche and their inability to let go of the more gauche habits of the upbringing they had supposedly left behind. In truth, Roth's ability to shed light so astutely upon parental dominance, spoiled children, and the corrupting nature of money was and remains potent and relevant, even putting aside the Jewish heritage of his characters. Although the novella had been much read and much admired within the movie industry, there was that whole touchy "Jewish" thing that had kept anyone from transferring it to the big screen for ten years. There had been enough slander and negativity tossed at the Jewish community by the rest of the world, so why would Hollywood, which was run predominantly by Jews, want to rock the boat any harder by taking a backhand to their own kind? In addition, the book was certainly very adult, insomuch as the final plot point hinged on the heroine's having her diaphragm discovered by her meddling parents. Among those who championed a film adaptation was Stanley R. Jaffe, the son of Columbia Pictures president Leo Jaffe, who, having purchased the rights in March 1967 under his company's Willow Tree banner, wanted to use Roth's work for his first project as a producer. Knowing full well that Jews were a loyal audience where movies were concerned and that the fall of the Production Code meant that this picture could be very saleable as something sexy and appealing to the young, Jaffe was able to make a deal not with his father's studio, but with Paramount.

It was decided from the outset that there was no conceivable reason to keep *Goodbye, Columbus* set in the past. The attitudes and behavior depicted were not at all dated relative to the late '60s. However, the producers chose not to keep Roth's New Jersey setting, moving the action out of Newark and Short Hills to New York state. That the book he had to work with was relatively brief in the first place meant that screenwriter Arnold Schulman was able to keep much of the story line intact for the film, removing a sequence in which Mrs. Patimkin expresses her disappointment in Neil for not taking more interest in his synagogue and for not knowing whether his mother belongs to the Jewish women's group Hadassah, and getting rid of scenes in which Brenda insists on going running with Neil in the mornings in order to time him to see how good he is in competition. There was also a delay in *when* Brenda and Neil would finally have sex with one another. In the book it happened when the two had stayed home to babysit Brenda's sister, but in the film it occurs later, in a scene in her family attic. Because Schulman chose not to have Neil narrate the story, as he had done in Roth's version, the writer was able to add two crucial moments that enhanced the work: having Brenda's father remark with assurance after his initial introduction to Neil that Brenda would "grow tired" of him (this summed up Mr. Patimkin's measured disdain brilliantly) and giving Mr. Patimkin a brief moment at his son's wedding in which he tells Brenda how proud he is of her, thereby providing her with even greater motivation to feel ashamed when her sexual activities become known to her parents.

> "How can a sensible, middle-class Jewish girl go to bed night after night with somebody and not use any kind of precaution whatsoever? Don't you know they make babies that way?"
> —Neil Klugman

Just as Jaffe had gone for a Jewish writer, he also decided to offer the job of directing the picture to someone who not only had a Jewish background, but who had also grown up in the New York Metropolitan area, Larry Peerce. Handed a literate script, Peerce did work of the highest caliber, never hammering laughs but instead letting them come through subtle observation. He was also helped by some splendid casting, chiefly that of his leading man, Richard Benjamin, who was nice-looking without being overwhelmingly handsome, had the requisite Jewish heritage, was extremely affable, and could produce big laughs with some very sharp, deadpan line readings. It was, by and large, one of the most brilliant motion-picture debuts of the decade. Curiously, though, it was not heralded as such. Instead, an "introducing" credit line was given to Benjamin's costar, Ali MacGraw, despite the fact that this was *not* her debut. MacGraw, who had at first been rejected as "not Jewish" enough, had started out as a hotel waitress in Atlantic City back in the 1950s before she took up fashion design. Soon her looks earned her a place in front of the cameras as she began modeling for magazine ads and television commercials. This had led to a brief role in a Kirk Douglas thriller, *A Lovely Way to Die* (Universal, 1968), a credit that was so obscure Jaffe felt justified in presenting her as someone audiences hadn't seen before.

Because of the lack of name stars, Paramount wasn't obliged to spend much more on *Columbus* than absolutely necessary, allotting a pretty meager $1.5 million budget. Peerce began filming on July 8, 1968, utilizing the Biograph Studio in the Bronx for interiors. He also used some exteriors in that borough as well to serve as Neil's neighbor-hood. A private home in Purchase, New York, in Westchester County, became the Patimkin house, and the Old Oaks Country Club supplied the pool where Neil and Brenda first meet. Neil was seen toiling at the Carnegie Public Library in Yonkers, where some of the nicest scenes in the picture took place, involving his friendship with an eager-to-learn little boy. New York City locations included the Grand Ballroom at Del-monico's Hotel on Park Avenue for the big wed-ding reception scene, which provided the movie with some of its most astute observations about the often strident and grotesque nature of this ritual. Principal photography concluded in Sep-tember after a tight sixty-three-day schedule.

Goodbye, Columbus captured everything Roth had set out to accomplish in his book, a magnifi-cent and wise adaptation of a terrific novel that was, quite simply, one of the most satisfying of the new, bolder forms of social comedy to come out of Hollywood and as good in its own way as *The Graduate* in thumbing its nose at the pre-

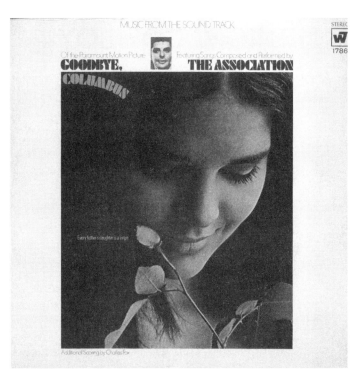

Giving the Association prominent billing on the soundtrack for *Goodbye, Columbus* made sense, since the LP was on the group's Warner Bros.–Seven Arts label. The album did not, however, produce any hit singles for the group, whose time on the top of the pop charts had already passed.

tensions of the lowbrow upper class. Few movies have so brilliantly captured how easily love is sacrificed to position and status, as MacGraw (in what would turn out to be her most accomplished movie per-formance) embodied everyone's worst nightmare of the too-good-to-be-true golden girl who opens her arms and legs for carnal pleasures, never once believing that she will also open her heart to someone so clearly "beneath" her station in life. Because of the very casual manner in which this emotional tragedy was played out, *Columbus* was not only savagely funny but equally disturbing in its depiction of ideals abandoned in favor of empty materialism. Brenda's attraction to Neil is nothing more than a minor form of rebellion toward her parents before her inevitable resignation to becoming just like them, shallow and narrow-minded, as she assumes her position in society of "respectability." Whether it was the enticing come-on line used extensively in the ad campaign ("Every father's daughter is a virgin") or the fact that this was one of the smartest pictures to capture the inherent pain of a shattered first romance, *Goodbye, Columbus* performed even beyond expectations to become one of the top moneymakers of the year.

MIDNIGHT COWBOY

Academy Award Winner: Best Picture; Best Director; Best Screenplay—Based on Material from Another Medium

Academy Award Nominee: Actor (Dustin Hoffman); Actor (Jon Voight); Supporting Actress (Sylvia Miles); Film Editing

Top 10 Box Office Film

Opening date: May 25, 1969.

United Artists. A Jerome Hellman–John Schlesinger Production.

Director: John Schlesinger. Producer: Jerome Hellman. Screenplay: Waldo Salt, based on the 1965 novel by James Leo Herlihy. Photography: Adam Holender. Production Designer: John Robert Lloyd. Set Decorator: Phil Smith. Costumes: Ann Roth. Editor: Hugh A. Robertson. Music: John Barry. Song: "Everybody's Talkin'," by Fred Neil, performed by (Harry) Nilsson. Additional Songs: "A Famous Myth," by Jeffrey Comanor, performed by the Groop; "Tears and Joys," by Jeffrey Comanor, performed by the Groop; "He Quit Me," by Warren Zevon, performed by Lesley Miller; "Jungle Jim at the Zoo," by Richard Sussman, Richard Frank, and Stan Bronstein, performed by Elephant's Memory; "Old Man Willow," by Richard Sussman, Michal Shapiro, Myron Yules, and Stan Bronstein, performed by Elephant's Memory. Deluxe color. 113 minutes. Rated X (later changed to R).

CAST: Dustin Hoffman (Enrico "Ratso" Rizzo), Jon Voight (Joe Buck), Sylvia Miles (Cass), John McGiver (Mr. O'Daniel), Brenda Vaccaro (Shirley), Barnard Hughes (Towny); *Texas*: Ruth White (Sally Buck), Jennifer Salt (Annie), Gil Rankin (Woodsy Niles), Gary Owens, T. Tom Marlow (Little Joe), George Eppersen (Ralph), Al Scott (Cafeteria Manager), Linda Davis (Mother on the Bus), J. T. Masters (Old Cow-hand), Arlene Reeder (Old Lady); *New York*: Georgann Johnson (Rich Lady), Jonathan Kramer (Jackie), Anthony Holland (TV Bishop), Bob Balaban (Young Student), Jan Tice (Freaked-Out Lady), Paul Benjamin (Bartender), Peter Scalia, Vito Siracusa (Vegetable Grocers), Peter Zamagias (Hat Shop Owner), Arthur Anderson (Hotel Clerk), Tina Scala, Alma Felix (Laundromat Ladies), Richard Clarke (Escort Service Man), Ann Thomas (Frantic Lady), Waldo Salt (Voice of Maury); *The Party*: Viva (Greta McAlbertson), Gastone Rossilli (Hansel McAlbertson), Ultra Violet, Paul Jabara, International Velvet, William Dorr, Cecelia Lipson, Taylor Mead, Paul Morrissey (Party Guests); *Florida*: Joan Murphy (Waitress), Al Stetson (Bus Driver).

PLOT: Believing he can make a fortune bedding rich ladies for money, naive Joe Buck leaves behind his simple Texas life and heads for Manhattan, where he is quickly undone by the unforgiving nature of urban life, instead finding an unexpected soul mate in crippled, two-bit con man Ratso Rizzo.

Following the establishment of the Motion Picture Association of America ratings system in late 1968, the field was wide open for Hollywood to show just how daring it was going to be when tackling formerly taboo subjects. Perhaps no movie during this period better demonstrated the gigantic leap forward than *Midnight Cowboy*. The rights to James Leo Herlihy's unflinching novel, in which a would-be male hustler was the central character, had been purchased by producer Jerome Hellman in 1966, though at the time the author himself was shocked to think that it might be adapted faithfully into a motion picture. Having been impressed by John Schlesinger's dazzlingly modern directorial touches on *Darling* (Embassy, 1965), Hellman's idea was to entice him to make the leap from the British New Wave to American filmmaking, hoping that he'd be able to bring the same degree of emotional depth, fluid visual sense, and caustic adult wit to the piece. Schlesinger had greatly admired Herlihy's novel and loved the idea of tackling something so dangerous, knowing it would be a challenge to bring the right level of grit and frankness to the drama without lapsing into exploitation or turning it into some sort of freak show. It would therefore be essential to emphasize the humanity that would keep audiences engaged. If, however, Hellman wanted him, he would have to wait; Schlesinger had already decided to take advantage of his newly exalted position in the industry by convincing MGM to let him film *Far from the Madding Crowd*. Putting *Cowboy* on hold while he went off to do his costly period picture proved beneficial, since the two-year delay between the purchase of the property and the actual start of filming saw the fall of the Production Code and Hollywood's long-overdue leap into maturity.

> "You were gonna ask me for money? Who the hell do you think you're dealing with—some old slut on Forty-second Street? In case you didn't happen to notice it—ya big Texas longhorn bull—I'm one helluva gorgeous chick!"
> —Cass

Hellman got hold of a screenplay about a draft dodger by writer Waldo Salt and found himself caught off guard by how fresh and contemporary it sounded, coming from someone whose career dated back to MGM in its late 1930s heyday. Hired to do the *Cowboy* script, the veteran writer did a surprisingly faithful job of bringing the situations and characters to life. He compressed much of the background of the main protagonist, Joe Buck, into a series of flashbacks that were, as filmed by Schlesinger, sometimes a bit confusing to those not familiar with the source material. Omitted was a mysterious hustler named Perry, who introduces Joe to marijuana and takes him to a Houston whorehouse presided over by overbearing madam Juanita and her grotesque offspring, who ends up forcing himself on Joe. Instead, Joe's assault was dramatized in the screenplay as having occurred when a gang of youths attacked him and his girlfriend, Annie. In the novel she was portrayed as an unapologetic slut, while her few brief scenes onscreen made her seem more like a hapless victim. Also added for the movie was a sequence in which Ratso comes up with the idea of passing Joe off as an escort for an occupant of the Berkeley Hotel for Women, a miscalculation that ends in humiliation. United Artists was excited enough with what they read to agree to back the film, though they hardly envisioned blockbuster business and offered no more than $1 million to get it made. Hellman's request that they more than double that amount was agreed upon as long as he, Schlesinger, and Salt were willing to take salary cuts up front and accept a percentage of the profits instead. Their decision to do so not only showed their faith in the property, but would bring them each a nice fat reward down the line, greater than any of them had anticipated.

As far as Hellman was concerned, he had only one actor in mind to embody *Cowboy*'s grotesque, two-bit hustler Ratso Rizzo: an unknown he'd seen perform in the quirky off-Broadway comedy *Eh?* Dustin Hoffman was so excited about the role that he was willing to cancel any other potential project or offer. Once again the delay ended up benefiting the picture, for in the meantime Hoffman, having landed the leading role in the most popular and influential film comedy of its day, *The Graduate* (AVCO Embassy, 1967), went from being just another of the New York theater's talented but struggling thespians to nothing less than a show-business superstar. United Artists was only too happy to have the most in-demand performer of the moment taking one of the leading roles in their iffy project. Schlesinger was resistant to this casting idea, having no other image of Hoffman outside of the shy, affable, clean-cut southern California rich boy he'd seen him play onscreen in Mike Nichols's smash hit, which couldn't have been further from the character of the slimy, scheming Ratso. So eager was Hoffman to prove him wrong that he met the director in full character, unshaven and filthy, winning him over with his versatility and thorough analysis of every facet of Ratso as he intended to play him. That his status had changed in two years was clearly reflected in his paycheck: Hoffman received $250,000 for *Midnight Cowboy*, far more than the $75,000 he'd gotten for *The Graduate*.

Hoffman was so dedicated to the project that he was perfectly willing to rehearse and do screen tests with all final candidates for the role of naive Texas greenhorn Joe Buck. After dismissing such stars as Warren Beatty and Robert Redford as unsuitable, Schlesinger narrowed it down to a little-known television player, Kiel Martin; one of the busiest young talents on the scene, Keir Dullea, who had caused a stir playing the disturbed young man in *David and Lisa* (Continental, 1963); Canadian Michael Sarrazin, who had recently signed a contract with Universal Studios; and theater actor Jon Voight. In the end it was decided that Sarrazin came off best of the bunch, but Universal chose to be difficult about releasing him, asking for more money than originally agreed upon. The move wound up costing him the part. Hellman and Hoffman were meanwhile campaigning for Voight and convinced Schlesinger to audition him once again. The second audition led the director to do a complete about-face over his initial objections, and he realized that Voight was the ideal choice after all. It is no slight to Sarrazin's talents to say that Schlesinger, Hellman, and all involved in *Midnight Cowboy* were very soon convinced that Universal had done them a big favor. Hoffman and Voight made for a remarkable duo onscreen, and the director encouraged them to improvise many of their scenes together during rehearsals. These were in turn tape recorded by Waldo Salt, who fashioned these acting exercises into playable dialogue.

Shooting on location was essential for the feel of the film, and the Times Square and Forty-second Street captured by Adam Holender's camera was filled with rotting movie palaces, grubby eateries, harsh neon signs, and desperate souls in search of sex, drugs, and quick cash during a time of decay that would stretch well into the following decade. Sets were created at the Filmways Studio in East Harlem, a busy facility that would shut its doors in the 1980s owing to the deterioration of the surrounding neighborhood. There the interior of an abandoned building from Manhattan's Lower East Side was gutted and rebuilt by art director John Robert Lloyd within the soundstages, giving the squatter's apartment shared by Joe and Ratso an authenticity that might not have been possible had it been constructed from scratch. The Claridge Hotel on Broadway between Forty-third and Forty-fourth Streets was used for Joe's first New York residence, shortly before it gave way to the wrecking ball; 114 East Seventy-second Street was Cass's swank apartment building; the Berkeley Hotel for Women on Fifty-fifth Street and Fifth Avenue (since converted into the Peninsula) saw Joe tossed from the premises; and the crosswalk at Fifty-eighth Street and Sixth Avenue was the setting for the film's most parodied moment, as Ratso barks "I'm walkin' here!" at an inconsiderate cab driver who nearly runs him down. Additional shooting took place at a cemetery on Long Island; in Texas, in Big Spring (where Joe leaves his dishwashing job at Miller's Restaurant) and Stanton (where many of the flashback sequences were shot); and Florida's Coral Gables, Hollywood, and Miami. Principal photography began on May 6, 1968, and continued throughout the summer months. By the time it wrapped in September, *Midnight Cowboy*'s cost had climbed to $3.6 million.

Schlesinger, searching for contemporary music to underscore the picture, rejected Harry Nilsson's "I Guess the Lord Must Be in New York City" but asked if he might instead use another tune Nilsson had sung but not written. Fred Neil had composed "Everybody's Talkin'" for his self-titled 1966 album, and Nilsson had covered the tune for his second LP, *Aerial Ballet*, in 1968. This mournful ballad so beautifully captured the sense of illusory freedom that drove Joe Buck that it was hard to believe it was not written with *Midnight Cowboy* in mind. While the picture tossed in snatches of songs by the Elephant's Memory and Warren Zevon, among others, it was the Neil-Nilsson cut that made all the difference. It came to be inextricably associated with the movie, reaching the number 6 position on the *Billboard* charts in September 1969 and earning Nilsson a Grammy Award for Best Male Pop Vocal Performance.

With glimpses of nudity, an uncompromising depiction of the urban underbelly of society, and an unexpected oral sex sequence, Schlesinger and company were boldly venturing into hitherto unexplored territory, which they actually hoped would bring them an X rating. The MPAA board initially granted the picture an R, but Schlesinger wanted the finished film to be something that only adults were permitted to see. Eventually he got his X, making *Midnight Cowboy* the first major studio production to receive this rating. The rating had not yet acquired the undesirable, pornographic connotation it would get in only a few short years, and it made 1969 audiences more than eager to see what they couldn't see elsewhere. Schlesinger and company made a movie that not only asked Americans to empathize with a pair of misbegotten misfits fighting against an uncaring society, but to be thoroughly engrossed in a story that dealt principally with the issue of loneliness, never a hot box-office topic. Throughout the film

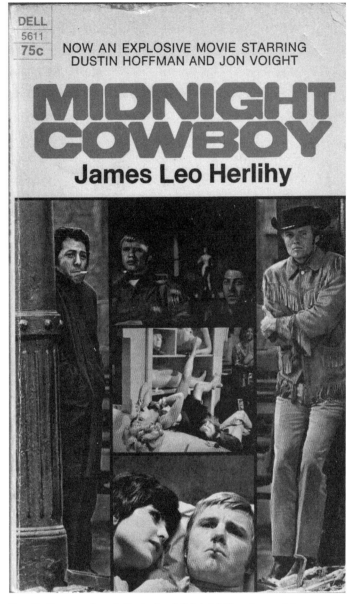

The Dell paperback tie-in for *Midnight Cowboy* of James Leo Herlihy's very adult novel.

Joe faced a world of savvy operators, quicker and faster to act than the dim-witted cowboy and far more self-absorbed. It made for one of the most honest, compelling dramas of the decade, and those who appreciated that the graphic manner in which it was depicted was necessary, not exploitative, realized that there was no turning back. Motion pictures were growing up, capturing real life and genuine human behavior without the inhibitions or rules of decorum that had been imposed upon them for years. *Midnight Cowboy* paved the way for a less restrictive approach, even to films with tamer subjects.

The real sign of the total acceptance of the picture and its themes within the industry was the seven Oscar nominations it received, including that for Best Picture. While its fellow nominees represented both traditional Hollywood (Universal's *Anne of the Thousand Days* and Fox's *Hello, Dolly!*), and the cinema vérité of foreign cinema (Cinema V's *Z*), its chief competitor was considered Fox's *Butch Cassidy and the Sundance Kid*, which had brought the western into modern times with a lighthearted brio that turned it into nothing less than a box-office sensation. In the end it was *Midnight Cowboy* that triumphed, making it the first (and only) X-rated motion picture to receive the coveted top honor from the Academy. As such, it was looked on as an important breakthrough by mavericks within the industry who were hoping to bury forever what they perceived as safer and more generic mainstream studio fare.

Two years after its success *Midnight Cowboy*, without having so much as a single frame removed from it, was granted an R rating. Hollywood no longer responded so hysterically to anything that challenged the norm. In time, most of what had been perceived as shocking in the work grew less so as movies delved into a variety of subject matters with far less taste and subtlety, while its strengths as a probing character study remained solid.

LAST SUMMER

Academy Award Nominee: Supporting Actress (Catherine Burns)

Opening date: June 10, 1969.

Allied Artists. An Emanuel L. Wolf Presentation of an Alfred Crown–Sidney Beckerman Production.

Director: Frank Perry. Producers: Alfred W. Crown, Sidney Beckerman. Screenplay: Eleanor Perry. Based on the 1968 novel by Evan Hunter. Photography: Gerald Hirschfeld. Art Director: Peter Dohanos. Costumes: Theoni V. Aldredge. Music: John Simon. Songs by John Simon: "Temptation, Lust and Laziness" (performed by Aunt Mary's Transcendental Slip & Lurch Band), "Drivin' Daisy" (Cyrus Faryar), "Cordelia" (Buddy Bruno), "Sonuvagun" (Buddy Bruno), "Hal, the Handyman" (John Simon), "Lay Your Love on Me" (Ray Draper), "Magnetic Mama" (the Electric Meatball), "Safari Mary" (Henry Diltz). Editor: Sidney Katz. Eastmancolor. 97 minutes. Rated X (later edited to an R).

CAST: Barbara Hershey (Sandy), Richard Thomas (Peter), Bruce Davison (Dan), Catherine Burns (Rhoda), Ernesto Gonzalez (Anibal Gomez), Peter Turgeon (Mr. Caudell), Lou Gary, Andrew Krance, Wayne Mayer (Town Hoods), Lydia Wilen (Waitress).

PLOT: While spending summer vacation with their families, Dan and Peter encounter the free-spirited Sandy, who delights in dictating the rules in their relationship, making it her pet project to help an injured seagull and bring the socially inept Rhoda out of her shell.

In a decade filled with teenage romps set at the beach, Hollywood never really approached this genre with much in the way of serious intent, frivolity being the order of the day when it came to putting youth on the shore. Writer Evan Hunter had something altogether different in mind when he wrote *Last Summer*. The man who had given '50s audiences a scare with *Blackboard Jungle*, his comment on the shocking levels of violence among urban school teenagers, now took a look at four seemingly normal teens spending a lazy summer at a fictionalized island community called Greensward where their efforts to amuse themselves lead to cruelty and the dangerous unleashing of the underlying sexual tension festering within all people of that age. A pair of novice would-be producers, Alfred Crown and Sidney Beckerman, purchased the rights to the book prior to its publication for $150,000, hoping to make it their first effort in what they envisioned as a lucrative career making movies. The unpleasant nature of the subject matter was a bit of a hard sell, so Crown and Beckerman were grateful to finally get a firm commitment from the independent Allied Artists. To transfer the difficult work to the screen, the producers made the brilliant choice of hiring the husband-and-wife filmmaking team of Frank and Eleanor Perry, who were given a fairly skimpy $1 million budget and minimal shooting time.

Figuring he was under no obligation to use name actors for his four principals, and realizing that he wasn't in any position to pay someone who wanted a substantial salary, Perry was free to cast according to talent. The results of his auditions brought him Bruce Davison, who had just appeared as part of the Lincoln Center Repertory Company in a production of *Tiger at the Gates*; Catherine Burns, who had played one of Zoe Caldwell's impressionable students in the Broadway version of *The Prime of Miss Jean Brodie*; Richard Thomas, who had been acting onstage and television since he was a child and had credits as diverse as the children's series *1,2,3 Go* (NBC, 1961–62) and two separate productions of *Richard III* to his name; and Barbara Hershey, who had starred on an unsuccessful television series, *The Monroes* (ABC, 1966–67). Burns, at twenty-three, was the oldest, followed by Davison (twenty-two), Hershey (twenty), and Thomas (seventeen). It was their picture to carry, the few other roles being subordinate to theirs.

> "She acts awfully sexy, the way she's always taking off her top."
> —Dan
>
> "I don't think she does it to be sexy. I think she does it to be chummy, ya know? Sort of a friendly gesture."
> —Peter

Hunter's structuring of the story and his dialogue were good enough to keep intact for much of Eleanor Perry's script, but some changes were required. The age of the principals on the page was approximately sixteen, whereas the movie kept this information pretty vague, so there would be no questioning of whether these older performers were really passing for younger. The book had been narrated by Peter, who had an unfortunate habit of using highly homophobic slang, as insensitive, randy teens were apt to do. Although the movie was told pretty much from his point of view, his voice-over observations were deemed unnecessary. Dropped from the screenplay were a trip by the three friends to a deserted island where they took the time to go snorkeling; a plump lady named Violet who has the hots for David (his name became Dan for the film); a party sequence in which Rhoda makes a spectacle of herself by getting up in front of the crowd to sing; a bizarre dream sequence following the humiliation of Anibal, in which Peter imagines none other than Alfred Hitchcock (!) warning him not to go into a mysterious room; and a very telling scene in which Rhoda explains her own dream, in which she debates whether to join a party she doesn't want to be a part of and yet cannot help but desire. Sandy's story of being hit on by an older man now involved a town alderman instead of her mother's boyfriend, which certainly had made for a more unnerving atmosphere in her household; it was wisely decided not to have Peter and David/Dan also smash the poor seagull with a rock after finding it bludgeoned by Sandy, since the whole situation was upsetting enough without turning audience sympathy away from the boys as well; rather than have Peter and Rhoda be startled by the sight of two men kissing, the scene was given over to Dan and Sandy, the latter once again showing her unexpected fascination with the forbidden by insisting on watching; and a believable bit of late-'60s mind alteration was inserted into the story by having Peter, Dan, and Sandy smoke pot prior to Rhoda's big speech about her mother's drowning.

The Perrys were in need of a beach, and to minimize the amount of interference between the filmmakers and the public, it was decided to let the cameras roll as soon as the summer season had come to a close on Fire Island. Shooting began there on September 9, 1968, and continued for nine weeks, mostly in the communities of Seaview and Ocean Beach. Although most of the movie took place out of doors, Perry was insistent on shooting inside actual homes when the script required an interior. In all, only three days were done in a closed set, using the Focus Studios in Manhattan. For the brief trip to the mainland in which the young principals enact their cruel date with Anibal and face a group of persistent thugs, Bayshore, Long Island, was chosen.

Last Summer was a devastatingly adult film, but Perry wasn't expecting the MPAA to slap an X on it. The harrowing rape scene that climaxed the movie was simply too graphic and featured too much flesh, as far as the ratings board was con- cerned. At first Allied Artists accept- ed the rating; after all, it hadn't hurt *Midnight Cowboy* (United Artists), which had gone into release a month before *Last Summer*'s opening in June 1969. Helped by strong reviews, the picture began a respectable run in se- lect theaters, but Perry finally decided he would willingly make a few trims to ensure that it could play to a wider audience. A little more than a month after its premiere, the film was rerated R, and it was that version that became the final one for all future versions, including home video.

Barbara Hershey gives her new friends, Richard Thomas and Bruce Davison, equal attention in *Last Summer*.

The cuts hardly lessened the im- pact of the picture, which was just about the most honest and unsettling take on the inherent bad lurking under adolescent repression that had ever been presented onscreen. Perry had gotten ace performances across the board from his principals, who enacted the characters' hedonistic and often thoughtless behavior with an edge of cruelty that was all too easy to relate to for anybody who remembered the darker aspects of their teenage years. Given its uncompromising nature, *Last Summer* never broke out beyond modest success at the box office and, unfairly, dropped off the radar with the passing decades, while less accomplished movies from the same period continued to be well known. Spare in its look, rich in characterization, utterly convincing in its portrayal of the unpre- dictability of human nature, *Last Summer* was not just one of the cinema's best dramatizations of teenage behavior and Frank and Eleanor Perry's crowning achievement, but, beyond a doubt, one of the finest movies of the 1960s.

TRUE GRIT

Academy Award Winner: Best Actor (John Wayne)

Academy Award Nominee: Song ("True Grit")

Top 10 Box Office Film

Opening date: June 11, 1969 (New York: July 3, 1969).

Paramount. A Hal Wallis Production.

Director: Henry Hathaway. Producer: Hal B. Wallis. Screenplay: Marguerite Roberts. Based on the 1968 novel by Charles Portis. Photography: Lucien Ballard. Production Designer: Walter Tyler. Set Decorators: Ray Moyer, John Burton. Costumes: Dorothy Jeakins. Music: Elmer Bernstein. Title song by Elmer Bernstein (music) and Don Black (lyrics), performed by Glen Campbell. Editor: Warren Low. Technicolor. 128 minutes. Rated G.

CAST: John Wayne (Marshal Reuben J. "Rooster" Cogburn), Glen Campbell ("La Boeuf"), Kim Darby (Mattie Ross), Jeremy Slate (Emmett Quincy), Robert Duvall (Lucky Ned Pepper), Dennis Hopper ("Moon"), Alfred Ryder (Goudy, Defense Attorney), Strother Martin (Col. G. Stonehill), Jeff Corey (Tom Chaney), Ron Soble (Capt. Boots Finch), John Fiedler (Lawyer J. Noble Daggett), James Westerfield (Judge Parker), John Doucette (Sheriff), Donald Woods (Barlow), Edith Atwater (Mrs. Floyd), Carlos Rivas (Dirty Bob), Isabel Boniface (Mrs. Bagby), H. W. Gim (Chen Lee), John Pickard (Frank Ross), Elizabeth Harrower (Mrs. Ross), Ken Renard (Yarnell Poindexter), Jay Ripley (Harold Parmalee), Kenneth Becker (Farrell Parmalee), Stuart Randall (McAlester).

PLOT: Determined to see the man who murdered her father brought to justice, Mattie Ross hires ornery, one-eyed Marshal Rooster Cogburn to get the job done, insisting on joining him on his manhunt, against the lawman's better judgment.

If there was one star who could be called the dominating force of '60s American cinema it was John Wayne, who was still a towering and popular presence on the scene forty years after he first arrived in Hollywood. It was only fitting that he should cap the decade with the sort of showcase that celebrated and summed up all facets of his appeal, *True Grit*. A part that seemed written with no one else in mind, one-eyed Deputy Marshal Reuben J. "Rooster" Cogburn came from the pen of Arkansas-born reporter-turned-novelist Charles Portis. *True Grit* caught the attention of several Hollywood studios while it was still in galleys, but not all of them were willing to cough up Portis's hefty $300,000 asking price. One who didn't seem to mind the expense was independent producer Hal Wallis, who scored the rights. Wayne's own production company, Batjac, had actually been willing to go higher, if necessary, but was too late with its bid. Wayne needn't have worried; Wallis had him and only him in mind to play Rooster, so Wayne not only got the coveted role, but did so without having to pay an up-front price. Rooster was the showy part, but Mattie Ross, the fourteen-year-old narrator of the tale and present in every scene, was the real centerpiece of the story. Wallis was not aiming to cast an actress of that actual age, planning instead to find someone who could pass for a young lady of indeterminate teen years.

Wallis managed to catch young Kim Darby in one of the many television appearances she had been making at the time and decided that he had found a far better Mattie Ross than Paramount's original choice of Mia Farrow could ever have been. Darby had, in fact, just played young women out west in episodes of both *Gunsmoke* and *Bonanza*. The former pitted her against actor James Stacy, who had since become her husband. This recent union almost kept Darby from accepting the *True Grit* role, since she had settled into married life and thought she might want to take time off from acting. Wallis therefore found himself going out of his way to accommodate the demands of an actress who was basically an unknown, with only a handful of motion pictures (notably Universal's 1965 drama *Bus Riley's Back in Town*) to her credit.

Insomuch as the story was told from the point of view of a female, a woman writer was hired, Marguerite Roberts, who had been blacklisted during the '50s. Still, that apparently did not put her on the bad side of Wayne, who had been a vocal anticommunist and a supporter of McCarthyism. Roberts knew that Portis had written a very cinematic tale and did very little in the way of changing what had worked so wonderfully on the written page. Mattie's first meeting with Rooster now came during his arrival at the jail while he is unloading a wagon of prisoners, whereas in Portis's book she did not see him before she dropped by the courtroom. Wisely, any derogatory remarks about minorities were dropped, so Ned Pepper's fellow outlaw was now referred to simply as "The Original Mexican" rather than "The Greaser," as Portis had named him. And a scene in which Capt. Finch rides out to inform Rooster that the man he testified against has escaped from jail was eliminated simply because there had been no payoff to this pronouncement. The most drastic changes all came at the end. In the novel Rooster had taken the snakebitten Mattie all the way back to Fort Smith (in the movie the McAlester outpost seemed a more plausible destination for the film) in one swift ride; La Boeuf had actually survived the conk on his skull (another instance in which a motion picture opted for a character's dying over the happier results of the book, though Hollywood was always accused of quite the opposite); Mattie's injury had necessitated having her arm amputated, a fate deemed far too gruesome for the heroine of a movie; and Rooster was eventually stripped of his marshal's badge. The finale that Portis had created took place twenty-five years after the adventure: Rooster dies just days before Mattie's long-overdue visit, the ex-lawman having been reduced to performing in Wild West Shows with Cole Younger and Frank James. Mattie, who never married, had Rooster's body brought back to her farm and buried in the family plot. This was much too glum for a movie ending, so Roberts came up with the very touching farewell between Rooster and Mattie at the Ross family's gravesite, punctuated by Wayne's wonderful exit line and grand gesture of jumping his horse over a fence.

The majority of *True Grit* was filmed in southwestern Colorado, taking in such locations as Montrose; the Adams Ranch in the San Juan Mountains; Ridgway, where the town scenes set in Fort Smith were

> "I mean to kill you in one minute, Ned. Or see you hanged in Fort Smith at Judge Parker's convenience. Which'll it be?"
> —Rooster Cogburn
>
> "I call that bold talk for a one-eyed fat man."
> —Ned Pepper

shot; the Ouray County Courthouse, in Ouray; and Owl Creek Pass, east of Ridgway, which included the meadow in which perhaps the movie's most famous sequence was filmed: Rooster's gun battle with Ned and his thugs, the old lawman chomping the horse's reins between his teeth as he opened fire on his enemies. Shooting took place between September 5 and December 1968, and the exciting footage being seen in the dailies compensated for the fact that Wayne was none too fond of his twenty-one-year-old leading lady, who was behaving more like a temperamental established star than a motion-picture novice.

Paramount managed to get *Grit* booked as one of the summer attractions at the then-coveted Radio City Music Hall, the first John Wayne movie to do so since MGM's *The Wings of Eagles* twelve years earlier. In May of 1969 the MPAA gave the picture an M rating, which was acceptable for a movie playing at the family-oriented theater (the Hall had already shown a few M features in the first several months of the newly established rating system). There was still an adult stigma about such a rating, however, and Paramount, hoping to sell the picture as a "family" attraction, appealed to the association and managed to get a G, which meant that audiences of all ages could hear Glen Campbell say "bastard"; see Dennis Hopper have his fingers chopped off with a hunting knife, and witness to Wayne's famous "Fill your hand, you son of a bitch" remark to Robert Duvall. Clearly the ratings system was having trouble establishing its boundaries, something they never have seemed to be able to straighten out.

The Capitol Records soundtrack for *True Grit* included two versions of Glenn Campbell's recording of the title tune, but despite his popularity at the time and the fact that the song earned an Oscar nomination, it only reached number 35 on the *Billboard* charts.

Obviously, Wayne was one old-time star audiences took great delight in seeing mouth off in such a manner, for *True Grit* did tremendous business, even beyond what was expected for a John Wayne western. Helped by an unexpected display of critical support, with reviewers championing the picture as some sort of career testimonial to one of the most enduring of all actors, *True Grit* found itself attracting even those who had made it a policy to skip most of Wayne's vehicles in recent years. Wayne, who had always been a better actor than most critics gave him credit for, had opened up even further than before, showing levels of subtle emotion and good-natured self-effacement in the part, allowing himself to look like hell and be judged as such. Even on the heels of his controversial and much-hated conservative stance on the Vietnam War, *The Green Berets* (Warner Bros., 1968), the motion-picture industry found itself very much in love with Wayne again, and the campaign was on to crown his lifetime of achievements with an Oscar. With all this Duke adoration and praise, poor Kim Darby almost got lost in the shuffle, though the bulk of the picture really did belong to her and her performance was everything the part called for and more. Her plucky Mattie Ross was a marvelously original creation, a well-mannered lady who was also more than part tomboy, her outspoken criticism of her uncouth and self-righteous male cohorts a marvelous display of free-thinking spirit.

With the general feeling that 1969 was the year in which the "new" and "younger" Hollywood of such pictures as *Midnight Cowboy* (United Artists) and *Easy Rider* (Columbia) was wiping away the more old-fashioned approach to cinema, it appeared that *True Grit* stood to get overlooked come awards time. Although it had proven to be one of the most appealing examples of solid, uncluttered storytelling to come along in years, the accolades sent in its direction prior to the Oscar ceremonies were few, with Wayne copping a Golden Globe for Best Actor, Campbell receiving a Promising Newcomer trophy from the same organization, and Roberts earning a mention from the Writers Guild. But it was the Academy Award that mattered to Wayne, and his victory that year (beating *Midnight Cowboy* stars Dustin Hoffman and Jon Voight, as well as Welshman Richard Burton and Irishman Peter O'Toole) was indeed the icing on the cake.

THE WILD BUNCH

Academy Award Nominee: Story and Screenplay—Not Based on Material Previously Published or Produced; Original Score

Top 25 Box Office Film

Opening date: June 18, 1969 (New York: June 25, 1969).

Warner Bros.–Seven Arts. A Phil Feldman Production.

Director: Sam Peckinpah. Producer: Phil Feldman. Screenplay: Walon Green, Sam Peckinpah. Story: Walon Green, Roy N. Sickner. Photography: Lucien Ballard. Art Director: Edward Carrere. Wardrobe: Gordon Dawson. Music: Jerry Fielding. Editor: Louis Lombardo. Technicolor. Panavision. 145 minutes (later cut to 134 minutes) Rated R.

CAST: William Holden (Pike Bishop), Ernest Borgnine (Dutch Engstrom), Robert Ryan (Deke Thornton), Edmond O'Brien (Freddie Sykes), Warren Oates (Lyle Gorch), Jaime Sanchez (Angel), Ben Johnson (Tector Gorch), Emilio Fernandez (Gen. Mapache), Strother Martin (Coffer), L. Q. Jones (T. C.), Albert Dekker (Pat Harrigan), Bo Hopkins (Crazy Lee), Dub Taylor (Wainscoat), Paul Harper (Ross), Jorge Russek (Zamorra), Alfonso Arau (Lt. Herrera), Chano Urueta (Don Jose), Sonia Amelio (Teresa), Aurora Clavel (Aurora), Elsa Cardenas (Elsa), Bill Hart (Jess), Rayford Barnes (Buck), Steve Ferry (Sgt. McHale), Enrique Lucero (Ignacio), Elizabeth Dupeyron (Rocio).

PLOT: Realizing their outlaw days are coming to an end and needing to pull off one last job in order to retire, Pike Bishop and his gang agree to rob an arms shipment for corrupt *federale* officer Mapache.

Director Sam Peckinpah's combustible film *The Wild Bunch* definitely separated the men from the boys. The movie seemed to declare, in most unsubtle terms, that all westerns up to that point, even the toughest and meanest of them, had been quaint tea parties in comparison. If *Bonnie and Clyde* had raised the bar on depicting cinematic violence with its shocking finale, which found its eponymous outlaws brought down in a hail of graphic gunfire, Peckinpah's film went it one better by having his protagonists shoot back in response, loudly, fiercely, and most explosively.

It should have been no surprise to expect something so revved up and controversial from a filmmaker who had never made himself a welcome participant in the Hollywood mainstream. A confrontational hellraiser, Peckinpah fought to do things his way, which constantly put him at odds with studio bosses, financiers, and actors, from the time he directed his first feature, *The Deadly Companions* (Pathé-American) in 1961.

The story outline for what would become *The Wild Bunch* (an uncredited reference to the name of Butch Cassidy's outlaw gang) came from a Hollywood stuntman, Roy N. Sickner, whose ideas were expanded upon by documentary filmmaker Walon Green. Green wrote a screenplay that ended up with Peckinpah, who was very excited by the idea of a group of aging gunmen facing their final showdown (having already visited such territory in his elegiac *Ride the High Country* [MGM, 1962]) and began to sketch out his own additions and ideas, rewriting Green's script with assistance from Jim Silke. Warner

Bros.–Seven Arts saw the picture as a saleable action piece as long as Peckinpah (who would be paid $75,000 for his work on the script, $100,000 for directing) could get some star names attached to it. William Holden (who received $250,000) turned out to be an acceptable substitute for Peckinpah's original choice, Lee Marvin, who was unavailable. Holden had thirty years of stardom behind him, even though his recent box-office track record had been soft at best. He was backed up by Ernest Borgnine (earning $120,000), who had a high recognition factor, though he had never been a draw per se, and there was guaranteed journeymen work to be gotten from the likes of the customarily excellent Robert Ryan, Edmond O'Brien (who had acted for Peckinpah on an episode of *Zane Grey Theater*), and two underrated character actors with whom Peckinpah had worked with previously in *Major Dundee* (Columbia, 1965), Ben Johnson and Warren Oates, here cast as brothers. Warners was willing to put up $3.5 million to make the movie, which was admirable insomuch as the majority of the leads were past fifty and there was no genuine romantic interest, the closest thing to a leading lady being a Spanish-speaking actress who was required to be promptly shot down by her spurned lover.

Shooting began on March 25, 1968, at Parras, Mexico, which became the town where the opening robbery-gone-wrong would turn into a bloody free-for-all. Landscapes like the Duranzo Arroyo in Torreón and El Romeral provided the Panavision backdrops for some of the action, while El Rincón del Montero was used for Angel's poverty-stricken village. The river crossing and bridge explosion took place on the Río Nazas, and the deftly executed railroad robbery was staged at La Goma, near Torreón. The setting for the stunning finale that few were prepared for, set at Aqua Verde, was shot at the Hacienda Cienega del Carmen. Far away from the watchful eye of Warners, Peckinpah ran his set as he pleased, encouraging improvisation, making sure his cast

> "We gotta start thinkin' beyond our guns. Those days are closin' fast."
> —Pike Bishop

and crew partied as heartily as they did in the picture, and in his famously antagonistic manner demanding nothing less than the best from each of his actors, earning respect from some and clashing with others, such as Robert Ryan, who ended up giving the most dignified performance in the picture, but at a very high price.

Figuring the very same studio for which he was working had OK'd the extreme violence of *Bonnie and Clyde*, Peckinpah had no intention of reining in the blood in his film. Determined to give moviegoers an experience they could not walk away from easily, he had his special effects crew rig up more squibs than had ever been used before, asking them to mix in slices of raw steak to ensure that when the blood spurted from the wounded actor it would look as if actual tissue were being torn from the body. This fearless effect was so horrifying, so unexpected, that it changed the course of motion-picture violence forever. Warners got panicky when *Bunch* did not meet its scheduled May 10 finish date, but Peckinpah was certain he was creating something far too special to worry about meeting deadlines or budget cutoffs. Impressed by what he was doing, the studio had no choice but to keep shelling out the cash, allowing the cost to escalate to $6 million. The production finally wrapped on June 27, 1968.

Unrealistically, Peckinpah was envisioning his picture as something grand and important enough to rate possible special treatment, with a reserved-seat opening and an intermission. For the next several months he chopped the first cut down from five hours in length to three hours and forty-five minutes and then to three. This was not what Warners had in mind, however, and he was obliged to bring it down closer to two and a half hours. The studio wasn't quite sure what it was about to bestow upon the general public, because just as many people seemed to tremble with excitement over what they saw as were sickened by it all. When Warners began previewing the picture, they found that the movie polarized the critics to such extremes that a battle began to see who could condemn or champion it with more passion. This sort of controversy appeared to be just the ticket Warners needed to make a profit on something so risky.

For its premiere engagements in the United Kingdom, *The Wild Bunch* was given the royal treatment: reserved seats and road-show prices were offered for intrigued patrons who might have heard of its controversial reception back in the United States.

The Wild Bunch raised the issue of just how far a filmmaker should or would go in depicting bloodshed onscreen, with supporters finding something almost cathartic and poetic about the spurts of plasma, the bodies wrenching in slow motion, and the rapid cutting that made certain ungainly images seem almost sublime. There was no getting around the fact that this was one mean movie. That was evident from the opening scene, which included gleeful children torturing a scorpion, innocent people being slaughtered and callously left to die or have their corpses ransacked, and some very unsentimental reactions to fallen comrades by pretty much everyone participating in the

mayhem onscreen. Within the first fifteen minutes most people were either revolted by the whole thing with no intention to forgive, no matter what might happen throughout the remainder of the picture, while others were so hopped up by this virtuoso piece of filmmaking that they couldn't wait to see what else was in store. Surprisingly, for an opening that seemed to suggest nonstop action, there was lots of introspective brooding for a good deal of the story, and it became clear that there would be as much melancholy as there was blood and guts. In the middle of the picture came a smashingly executed train robbery, which proved just how expertly Peckinpah could stage a scene that didn't necessarily depend on an abundance of flesh wounds. Everything paled, however, next to the shoot-out that capped the film, a five-minute explosion of gore staged with such cinematic finesse and disregard for weak stomachs that it very quickly took its place among the most legendary scenes in the history of movies. *The Wild Bunch* was closing the chapter on the old west, and judging from the unpleasantness of it all, this didn't seem like such a bad thing. With lawmen and soldiers behaving as badly as the outlaws, the cowboys of a thousand myths never seemed so malignant or devoid of heroism.

Still worried that they were releasing a movie that ran much too long (as indeed it did), Warners managed to talk Peckinpah into removing some footage. After two weeks in exclusive release, four sequences were excised: the flashback to how Ryan's character was captured as Holden got away; another flashback indicating how Holden got his gimpy leg; a scene in which O'Brien revealed that Bo Hopkins's character was his grandson; and a three-and-a-half-minute scene with Mapache under attack by Pancho Villa's forces. It was not until after Peckinpah's death that *The Wild Bunch* finally had its missing pieces restored, by which time the picture was part of western-movie folklore, hailed as a bona fide classic. Because time hasn't diminished the repulsive impact of so much of its cruelty, it is safe to say that the film still divides viewers sharply from the moment that hapless scorpion first appears onscreen.

EASY RIDER

Academy Award Nominee: Supporting Actor (Jack Nicholson); Story and Screenplay—Not Based on Material Previously Published or Produced

Top 10 Box Office Film

Opening date: July 14, 1969.

Columbia. A Pando Company in association with Raybert Productions Presentation.

Director: Dennis Hopper. Producer: Peter Fonda. Screenplay: Peter Fonda, Dennis Hopper, Terry Southern. Photography: Laszlo Kovacs. Art Director: Jerry Kay. Editor: Donn Cambern. Songs: "The Pusher," by Hoyt Axton, performed by Steppenwolf; "Born to Be Wild," by Mars Bonfire, performed by Steppenwolf; "Wasn't Born to Follow," by Gerry Goffin and Carole King, performed by the Byrds; "The Weight," by Jaime Robbie Robertson, performed by the Band; "If You Want to Be a Bird," by Antonia Duren, performed by the Holy Modal Rounders; "Don't Bogart Me," by Elliott Ingber and Larry Wagner, performed by Fraternity of Man; "If Six Was Nine," written by Jimi Hendrix, performed by the Jimi Hendrix Experience; "Let's Turkey Trot," by Gerry Goffin and Jack Keller, performed by Little Eva; "Kyrie Eleison," by David Axelrod, performed by the Electric Prunes; "Flash, Bam, Pow," by Mike Bloomfield, performed by the Electric Flag; "I'm Alright Ma (I'm Only Bleeding)," by Bob Dylan, performed by Roger McGuinn; "Ballad of Easy Rider," written and performed by Roger McGuinn. Executive Producer: Bert Schneider. Technicolor. 94 minutes. Rated R.

CAST: Peter Fonda (Wyatt), Dennis Hopper (Billy), Antonio Mendoza (Jesus), Phil Spector (the Connection), Mac Mashourian (Bodyguard), Warren Finnerty (Rancher), Tita Colorado (Rancher's Wife), Luke Askew (Stranger on Highway); *The Commune*: Luana Anders (Lisa), Sabrina Scharf (Sarah), Sandy Wyeth (Joanne), Robert Walker (Jack); *Jail*: Jack Nicholson (George Hanson), George Fowler Jr. (Guard), Keith Green (Sheriff); *Cafe*: Hayward Robillard (Cat Man), Arnold Hess Jr. (Deputy), Buddy Causey Jr., Duffy Lafont, Blase M. Dawson, Paul Guedry Jr. (Customers); *House of Blue Lights*: Toni Basil (Mary), Karen Black (Karen), Lea Marmer (Madame), Cathé Cozzi (Dancing Girl); *Pickup Truck*: David C. Billodeau (Driver), Johnny David (Roy).

PLOT: After selling their stash of cocaine, Billy and Wyatt head out on their motorcycles for Mardi Gras, encountering much hostility along the way from those who scoff at their long hair and free-spirited lifestyle.

Peter Fonda had earned his niche in the movie industry by the late '60s, having starred in several pictures since his 1963 debut in the Universal fluff *Tammy and the Doctor*. His films included one unexpected box-office hit, *The Wild Angels* (American International Pictures, 1966), a motorcycle pic for the drive-in trade that made some $10 million on a minuscule investment. Fonda was not, however, happy with his lot in life, dwelling on the opposite end of the spectrum from the glamorous movie-star world his father, Henry Fonda, had been a part of since the 1930s. Young Fonda was instead very much a part of Hollywood's counterculture drug scene, bad-mouthing the studio system and deriding most American mainstream product as out of touch and old-fashioned. There were others of his age group who shared his cynical view, notably Dennis Hopper, who had been acting in films since appearing in *the* big teen angst picture of its era, *Rebel without a Cause* (Warner Bros., 1955). Since that time Hopper had built up a reputation as a volatile and often difficult presence on film sets, and his disenchantment with the state of motion pictures was even more pronounced than Fonda's. The two actors first worked together on one of Roger Corman's low-budget attempts to tap into the drug scene, *The Trip* (American International Pictures, 1967), which boasted a script by B-movie actor Jack Nicholson. During the shoot, while Corman was preoccupied with other duties, he sent Fonda and Hopper off to shoot footage for the film's LSD sequence, giving them their first movie-making experience together.

Fonda soon afterward came up with a story line for a biker picture that he hoped would be something more than those Corman and his ilk were churning out. He envisioned a modern-day western of sorts, with himself and Hopper as the heroes, although these heroes would start their trek across the American landscape after scoring a major cocaine transaction. They would experience the hostility most of America felt toward those daring enough to drop out and do their own thing, allowing Fonda to make his statement against "square" society. He would serve as producer, and Hopper would fulfill his long-cherished dream of directing. Hopper was thrilled by the prospect, though he was well aware that the two novice moviemakers would have to bring in a professional writer to help shape their joint vision into something filmable. Fonda's choice was Terry Southern, one of the iconic figures of the counterculture movement. Southern had penned the satirical novels *Candy* (with Mason Hoffberg) and *Blue Movie* and collaborated with Stanley Kubrick on one of the hippest screenplays of the era, *Dr. Strangelove* (Columbia, 1964).

Fonda and Hopper conceptualized their own characters. Hopper also came up with the idea of the lawyer who joins the two bikers on their trek, and Southern developed the

> "It's real hard to be free when you are bought and sold in the market place. 'Course don't ever tell anybody that they're not free, 'cause then they're gonna get real busy killin' and maimin' to prove to you that they are."
> —George Hanson

whole thing into a working screenplay. The script was certainly loose, with a very off-the-cuff feel to much of the dialogue. It would hardly be considered the sort of stellar writing that could stand on its own without the visualization Hopper brought to it. Starting with a twelve-page treatment, Hopper and Fonda shopped the project around Hollywood, without much luck. They had wanted to avoid falling back on Corman and American International Pictures, considering the director narrow of vision and out of sync with what they had in mind. Jack Nicholson, who had just written the screenplay for the Monkees' movie, *Head* (Columbia, 1968), suggested Hopper and Fonda approach the company behind the Monkees' television series, Raybert, about getting their financing. Bert Schneider and Bob Rafelson, the two men in charge of this organization, saw *Easy Rider* as just the sort of youth-orientated commentary they wanted to make and agreed to put up the $370,000 needed. Because of their established relationship with Columbia Pictures, they approached the studio about distributing the film. Columbia viewed the project as a relatively low risk, given that Fonda's then-bankable name would be attached to a genre he'd already proven himself in, and gave the OK.

The first step was to get footage of the actual Mardi Gras festivities, so Hopper and his guerilla crew flew to New Orleans during the last week of February 1968 for the needed shots. He and Fonda quarreled from the beginning. Hopper seemed to have very little idea of what he was doing, being heavily into booze, acid, and pot at this stage in his life, often directing while in an altered state and pretty much filming on the fly. After he returned to Raybert with his crude-looking Mardi Gras footage, Schneider and his cohorts had reason to panic. They were hoping for something audacious and original, but they weren't expecting it to look this amateurish. What exactly Hopper was aiming for wasn't quite clear, but after a break the of-

Despite reports of dissension, director Dennis Hopper and producer Peter Fonda show an easy rapport on the set of *Easy Rider*.

ficial filming began in March, with the journey from California to Louisiana being shot pretty much in sequence. By this point Rip Torn, the actor originally chosen to play alcoholic lawyer George Hanson, had had a falling out with Hopper (Hopper had wanted him to defer his salary to keep the budget down) and walked off the picture. When the suggestion arose of having Jack Nicholson serve as an on-location liaison between Raybert and Hopper, someone had the brilliant idea of Nicholson's taking over the role of Hanson as well. Fonda liked the casting, but Hopper didn't think he was right for the part. Fonda, as official producer, overruled his director, and the deci-

sion to put Nicholson into the movie turned out to be the smartest thing the filmmakers did.

Hopper continued his loose directorial approach over the seven weeks it took to shoot the movie, only now he was working with a larger behind-the-scenes crew. The picture progressed from the Los Angeles Airport, where the opening drug deal (with legendary record producer Phil Spector in a cameo as the buyer) was filmed; on to the ghost town of Ballarat, California, near Death Valley, where Fonda made his freedom gesture of tossing away his watch; and then across the California-Arizona state line at Needles. The Pine Breeze Inn in Bellemont, Arizona, near the fabled Route 66, was the location for the sequence in which a conservative older man refuses to rent rooms to the two bikers. Backdrops of historic Monument Valley made Fonda's "western" comparison a reality, this area having been the setting for so many of John Ford's best-known features, including *Fort Apache* (RKO, 1948), which had featured Peter's father. In Taos, New Mexico, a growing artists' community (which contained the gravesite of D. H. Lawrence), Hopper shot the opening junkyard scene and the interiors of the jail in which Billy and Wyatt meet Hanson. The exterior of the jail was found in nearby Las Vegas, New Mexico, whose main street was used for the scene in which the bikers crash a parade, the defiant act that puts them behind bars. The tense scene in which the trio of motorcyclists meets with hostility at a roadside café from a bunch of rednecks, played by actual locals, was shot in the small town of Morganza, Louisiana. Outside of that same town was staged the devastating finale on State Highway 1, by the banks of the Mississippi River.

It is safe to say that when *Easy Rider* was finally screened for the Columbia brass, there were just as many who were puzzled by the movie as there were those who were excited by its raw, often defiantly crude structure and its urgent cry against conformity and violence. Within the industry word began to spread that Hopper had thumbed his nose at the studio system and come up with something well worth the struggle. Columbia scheduled the movie for a mid-July opening (with one of the great ad lines of the decade: "A man went looking for America and couldn't find it anywhere") and were thrilled to see that for every critic who considered it choppy, pretentious, vague, and amateurish, there were those who took the whole thing very seriously, treating it as some sort of important comment on the sorry state of the country and a groundbreaking breath of fresh air in its sometimes chaotic, often poetic rendering of a doomed journey into the ugly underbelly of the land of the free. More importantly, just as everyone behind the project hoped, they had tapped into a vital nerve of the American youth, who began flocking to the picture. As far as they were concerned *Easy Rider* had gotten it right, speaking honestly about the unrest between the generations and the alienation kids were facing from an oppressive, narrow-minded society as they sought answers and individual freedoms in their own country. Hollywood was thrown for a loop by the staggering box-office success of the picture. Millions flowed back into Raybert's (since renamed BBS), Fonda's, Hopper's, and Columbia Pictures' bank accounts. Suddenly it was time to re-evaluate just what paying customers wanted to see, how they wanted it presented, and how important the cultural and sociological interests of America's youth were to themes in upcoming motion pictures.

Because *Easy Rider* had rapidly grown from a mere hit film into a cultural landmark, Hopper was hailed as some sort of counterculture hero and icon of the period. Exactly how talented he was as a film-maker was open for debate, insomuch as his lack of focus in piecing the film together often caused it to teeter on the brink of disaster. *Easy Rider* frequently played at a lazily underwhelming tempo during its early scenes, with some terrific music, stunning vistas, and an occasional passing statement capturing one's attention. Fonda's stonily unflappable reserve was greeted by many fans as the epitome of cool, when in fact it was the very worst example of this limited actor's inability to express himself or suggest much nuance or complexity. Hopper was certainly the more engaging of the two protagonists, although his chattering and incessant use of the word "man" made him more amusing than three-dimensional, not unlike an eccentric sidekick from an old western serial.

What brought the movie to a higher level was the arrival of Jack Nicholson's weary dropout of a lawyer. Suddenly there was somebody of value onscreen whom people could really latch on to and care about. Unlike Fonda and Hopper's characters, he was not aimless, angry, or monosyllabically deadened in his form of expression. Nicholson's Hanson was as disillusioned as the other two main characters, but he seemed the sort of person who was more inclined to do something about the disorder rather than merely sitting around smoking dope. His senseless murder made audiences sit up in their seats, and suddenly there was a greater understanding of the dangerous polarization going on in the country between the freethinkers and those stubbornly rooted in fear, hostility, and backward ideals. As if this sequence wasn't enough to send audiences home in deep thought, the unexpected violence that brought down the two leads in the finale was another punch to the gut. Because of it, no matter what the feeling about the often ragged series of events that proceeded, *Easy Rider* did indeed earn its stripes as an important motion picture.

ALICE'S RESTAURANT

Academy Award Nominee: Director

Opening date: August 20, 1969 (New York: August 24, 1969).

United Artists. A Florin Production.

Director: Arthur Penn. Producers: Hillard Elkins, Joe Manduke. Screenplay: Venable Herndon, Arthur Penn. Based on the 1966 song "The Alice's Restaurant Massacree," by Arlo Guthrie. Photography: Michael Nebbia. Production Designer: Warren Clymer. Set Decorator: John Mortensen. Costumes: Anna Hill Johnstone. Music: Arlo Guthrie. Songs: "One Lung Rag," written and performed by Arlo Guthrie; "Pastures of Plenty," by Woody Guthrie, performed by Pete Seeger; "Car Song," by Woody Guthrie, performed by Pete Seeger; "You're a Fink," by Arlo Guthrie and Garry Sherman, performed by Arlo Guthrie; "Songs to Aging Children," by Joni Mitchell, performed by Trigger Outlaw; "Amazing Grace," adapted by Arlo Guthrie and Garry Sherman. Musical Supervision and Additional Music Composer and Arranger: Garry Sherman. Editor: Dede Allen. Deluxe color. 111 minutes. Rated R.

CAST: Arlo Guthrie (Arlo Guthrie), Pat Quinn (Alice Brock), James Broderick (Ray Brock), Michael McClanathan (Shelly), Geoff Outlaw (Roger Crowther), Tina Chen (Mari-chan), Kathleen Dabney (Karin), William Obanhein (Officer Obie), Seth Allen (Evangelist), Monroe Arnold (Bluegrass), Joseph Boley (Woody Guthrie), Vinnette Carroll (Lady Clerk), Sylvia Davis (Marjorie Guthrie), Simm Landres (Private Jacob), Eulalie Noble (Ruth), Louis Beachner (Dean), MacIntyre Dixon, Rev. Dr. Pierce Middleton (Deconsecration Ministers), Donald Marye (Funeral Director), Shelley Plimpton (Reenie), M. Emmet Walsh (Group W Sergeant), Judge James Hannon, Pete Seeger, Lee Hays (Themselves), Graham Jarvis (Mr. Binkley, Music Teacher), Frank Simpson (Sergeant), Alice Brock (Suzy).

PLOT: Musician Arlo Guthrie leaves college and heads for Massachusetts, where his friends Ray and Alice Brock have purchased a deconsecrated church that they plan to turn into a communal living space.

Having placed most of Hollywood at his feet after the tremendous commercial response, not to mention cultural impact, of *Bonnie and Clyde* (Warner Bros., 1967), director Arthur Penn was in the enviable position of pretty much picking whatever he pleased as his follow-up project. As if to throw everyone a curve ball, he decided that his next picture would be based on a song, of all things. The tune in question, officially titled "The Alice's Restaurant Massacree," was not your average ballad, but something best described as a talking blues record. Eighteen minutes and twenty seconds in length, it recounted the true story of the arrest of musician Arlo Guthrie and his buddy

> "I mean I'm sittin' here on the Group W bench, 'cause you want to know if I'm moral enough to join the Army, burn women, kids, houses and villages, after bein' a litter bug."
> —Arlo

Richard Robbins for dumping the remains of a Thanksgiving dinner down the side of a hill on the outskirts of the town of Great Barrington, Massachusetts, on November 28, 1965. Because the local authorities made a big deal about this incident, and because it led directly to Guthrie's disqualification from the draft, with the army declaring that someone who littered was unfit to kill Vietnamese, Guthrie took great satirical delight in writing it all down and setting it to music. The song appeared on Guthrie's 1967 debut album, *Alice's Restaurant*, and brought him a following among young Americans who related to the irony of the situation. Because the extensive length of the piece made it difficult to play on the radio airwaves, the "Massacree" became not a chart hit, but more of a cult favorite. Penn's proposal to dramatize it on film helped it and its author to become that much better-known.

Penn's plan for transferring the novelty song from disc to screen was to go right to the source, getting feedback and ideas from Guthrie and other parties involved in the affair, including the titular character, Alice Brock, and her husband, Ray, both of whom had turned the deconsecrated Trinity Church on Van Deusenville Road in Great Barrington into a commune of sorts where the Thanksgiving dinner in question had taken place. For the first (and only) time in his career, Penn actually worked on the screenplay of one of his pictures, writing the first treatment before getting playwright Venable Herndon involved, on the basis of a 1966 off-Broadway piece he had written called *Until the Monkey Comes.* . . . There was no doubt in Penn's mind that Guthrie should portray himself; Arlo possessed an affable personality that Penn rightly theorized would make for a very engaging figure onscreen. He was no actor, to be sure, and never presented himself as such, so he simply mellowed his way through the role, which made no unreasonable demands on his limited thespian talents.

Taking authenticity one step further, Penn planned to use as many of the actual locations from the real incident as possible. Starting on October 1, 1968, he and his company spent five weeks shooting in and around Stockbridge, Pittsfield, and Great Barrington, using the hundred-year-old once-Episcopalian Trinity Church, a motorcycle track, the Prospect Hill town dump, and the police station exterior. The scene between Arlo and the

Doubleday published the screenplay for *Alice's Restaurant,* which marked the only time either playwright Venable Herndon or director Arthur Penn received a screenwriting credit.

college dean was shot at the Jesuit Administration's office at Cranwell College. Because the actual Alice's Restaurant (the official name of which had been the Back Room, located behind a grocery store at 40 Main Street in Stockbridge) had already closed down by the time the film was made and would have proven too small for extensive shooting anyway, the interior was recreated on a specially built soundstage converted from an enormous former printing plant in Stockbridge. Other sets built there by production designer Warren Clymer included the inside of the police station, a radio station sound booth, a Greenwich Village hippie nightclub, and the New York draft board induction center. One week was spent filming in New York, including the city sanitation sheds and the outside of the draft board on Whitehall Street.

Although United Artists sold the film as something quirky that young audiences would want to see, it didn't take much to realize that *Alice's Restaurant* was not the celebration of youthful freedom versus authority that some had anticipated, but rather a melancholy meditation on shattered idealism and the promise of a perfect, communal society gone awry. Penn's direction was low-key and deliberate in unfolding a story that seemed at first to be a series of disjointed moments in the life of restless societal dropout Guthrie. This easygoing way of life soon segued into a hopeful gathering of other misfits, outsiders, and free spirits who had come together to form a nonjudgmental coexistence wherein folks could do as they pleased. *Alice's Restaurant* was probably the closest a picture from that era came to capturing the sincere outreach for harmony that came to symbolize the better efforts of America to fulfill some greater purpose, while also catching its unfocused, dangerously unpredictable rhythms. Audiences felt very comfortable with this sometimes lazy, not always compelling, but undeniably evocative movie, and it became a prize moneymaker at the time. It did not, however, continue to endure as a time capsule of 1969 as solidly as did the even less polished *Easy Rider* (Columbia). It seemed to speak more powerfully to those who actually lived through the decade than to those later generations looking back upon it. Nevertheless, Arthur Penn had set out to speak about the times and had accomplished just that, bringing a good deal more respect to the issues on hand than a less revered director might have done with a similar film.

BUTCH CASSIDY AND THE SUNDANCE KID

Academy Award Winner: Best Story and Screenplay—Not Based on Material Previously Published or Produced; Best Song ("Raindrops Keep Fallin' on My Head"); Best Cinematography; Best Original Score

Academy Award Nominee: Picture; Director; Sound

Top 10 Box Office Film

Opening date: September 23, 1969 (New York: September 24, 1969).

Twentieth Century-Fox. A Newman-Foreman presentation of a George Roy Hill-Paul Monash Production.

Director: George Roy Hill. Producer: John Foreman. Screenplay: William Goldman. Executive Producer: Paul Monash. Photography: Conrad Hall. Art Directors: Jack Martin Smith, Philip Jefferies. Set Decorators: Walter M. Scott, Chester L. Bayhi. Costumes: Edith Head. Music: Burt Bacharach. Song by Burt Bacharach (music) and Hal David (lyrics): "Raindrops Keep Fallin' on My Head," performed by B. J. Thomas. Editors: John C. Howard, Richard C. Meyer. Deluxe color. Panavision. 111 minutes. Rated M.

CAST: Paul Newman (Butch Cassidy), Robert Redford (the Sundance Kid), Katharine Ross (Etta Place), Strother Martin (Percy Garris), Henry Jones (Bike Salesman), Jeff Corey (Sheriff Ray Bledsoe), George Furth (Woodcock), Cloris Leachman (Agnes), Ted Cassidy (Harvey Logan), Kenneth Mars (Marshal), Donnelly Rhodes (Macon), Jody Gilbert (Large Woman Passenger), Timothy Scott (News Carver), Don Keefer (Fireman), Charles Dierkop (Flat Nose Curry), Francisco Cordova (Bank Manager), Nelson Olmstead (Photographer), Paul Bryar, Sam Elliott (Card Players), Charles Akins (Bank Teller), Eric Sinclair (Tiffany's Salesman), Percy Helton (Sweet Face), José Chávez (Bolivian Police Commander).

PLOT: Following a botched train robbery, outlaws Butch Cassidy and the Sundance Kid find themselves pursued by a relentless posse, leading them to wonder whether it might be time to give up their criminal ways.

Outlaws Butch Cassidy and the Sundance Kid owe the world's enduring image of them almost entirely to how Paul Newman, Robert Redford, William Goldman, and George Roy Hill chose to present them in their none-too-serious, mostly fabricated take on their exploits, entitled, quite directly, *Butch Cassidy and the Sundance Kid*. To those who had attended B-westerns throughout the '50s, these real-life badmen were hardly unfamiliar characters, having popped up together in many a low-budget oater. All of these stories took liberties with the actual tale, which had so many missing pieces and contradictions that writers couldn't help but feel obliged to make up what they could. Cassidy was born Robert Leroy Parker in Beaver, Utah, in 1866, while Sundance, christened Harry Longabaugh (the first "a" in his last name was dropped in the Goldman script, for reasons unknown) arrived the following year, though his place of birth seems uncertain, some sources citing Plainfield, New Jersey, and others insisting on Mont Clare, Pennsylvania. After leading separate lives of crime punctuated by periods of incarceration, the two men joined forces in the late 1890s, with Butch taking charge of an outlaw gang he called "The Wild Bunch." Their hideaway was at the Hole-in-the-Wall ranch in central Wyoming. There *was* a train robbery of the Overland Flyer, as recreated (twice) in Goldman's script (under the name Union Pacific Flyer), and the two outlaws, along with Sundance's lady love, Etta Place, did indeed hightail it to South America in 1903. Five years later Butch and Sundance were ambushed while in San Vicente, Bolivia, but whether or not the two men died on November 4, 1908, was something that historians would debate for years to come. Some contend that they were gunned down by the local authorities, while others are certain both men took their lives to avoid capture. Decades later Butch's sister, Lulu Parker Betenson, swore that her brother returned to the United States and lived in anonymity, going in for prospecting, among other jobs, until his death in Spokane, Washington, in 1937. There is also a strong possibility that Sundance too found his way back to America, dying in Casper, Wyoming in 1957. What exactly happened to Etta Place following the fateful standoff in 1908 is even less clear, all records of her existence having produced no certain answers.

> "I never met a soul more affable than you, Butch, or faster than the Kid. But you're still nothin' but two-bit outlaws on the dodge. It's over, don't you get that? Your times is over and you're gonna die bloody. And all you can do is choose where."
> —Sheriff Bledsoe

William Goldman took a few elements of fact, deliberate fiction, speculation, and legend and stirred them all up into a screenplay that made the two criminals into good-natured fellas who took great delight in thwarting authority but really had little intention of harming anybody. Goldman completed his script during a stint as an instructor at Princeton and began shopping it around in Hollywood with the idea of having Paul Newman's name attached to it, since he had just done a commendable job of writing one of the star's recent hits, *Harper* (Warner Bros., 1966). Newman was very pleased with what he read and was told that it was being proposed as a possible teaming between himself and Steve McQueen. McQueen, however, wasn't too sure that he wanted to share equal screen time with an actor of even greater stature than himself and passed on it. George Roy Hill, who was engaged to direct, wanted Robert Redford to do it, but Twentieth Century-Fox was not convinced that he was a big enough name, despite his having just played the lead in Paramount's top-grossing film of 1967, *Barefoot in the Park*. Once Hill managed to convince Newman and Goldman that Redford would be ideal, this creative force became too strong and insistent for Fox to battle, and the studio gave in.

With Newman the bigger star, one thing was certain: the original title of Goldman's script, *The Sundance Kid and Butch Cassidy*, would have to be changed, and so the two names were simply swapped around, which had an easier sound to it anyway. Principal photography began on September 16, 1968, with the staging of the Flyer train robbery aboard a real operating narrow-gauge rail line between Durango and Silverton, Colorado. The company stayed in the area to shoot the beginning of the famous cliff dive, done by Newman and Redford at the Animas River near Durango, with the two actors landing on a platform a few feet below them. The remainder of the scene, with two stunt men plummeting off the rocks and landing in the river, was finished at the Fox Ranch in Malibu. Most of the rest of the American sequences were shot in the southwestern corner of Utah against the backdrops of Zion National Park, St. George (where much of the chase between the posse and the outlaws was filmed), and the small town of Grafton, where an abandoned Mormon community outside of Rockville filled in for the schoolhouse and farm of Etta Place. It was here that one of *Butch Cassidy*'s most joyful and defining moments, the bicycling montage with Etta and Butch, was shot.

The company then traveled to Hollywood, where the western street outside of Fanny Porter's whorehouse was constructed on the Fox back lot, while a western town over at Warners was rented for the opening sequence, in which Butch cases the bank. While at Fox, Hill had hoped to utilize the enormous turn-of-the-century New York set that had been built for the studio's lavish musical *Hello, Dolly!*, for the scene in which Etta and the two men visit Manhattan en route to South America. Zanuck quickly nixed this idea because it meant that this impressive achievement would first be seen in *Butch Cassidy* rather than in the movie for which it was constructed, since *Dolly* was not scheduled to open until Christmas of 1969, three months after *Sundance*. To compensate, Hill came up with the idea of showing the trip through a montage of old photographs into which the actors' images were cleverly inserted. The final location stop was Taxco, a town southwest of Mexico City, which passed for Bolivia, and where the magnificently staged gunfight between the two outlaws and their South American nemeses took place. *Butch Cassidy* finished shooting on January 8, 1969.

Bantam Books published William Goldman's original screenplay for *Butch Cassidy and the Sundance Kid*, making prominent mention of the author's Academy Award as well as his 1964 novel *Boys and Girls Together*.

Having started out with a script that needed next to no alterations, and having gotten exactly the stars he believed all along would bring immeasurable sympathy and smarts to the project, Hill was never more confident that he had produced a solid hit. Therefore, he and Goldman were more than a bit taken aback by some of the middling and even near damning reviews that began showing up once the picture started screening in the fall of 1969. This was, however, one case in which whatever negative press the movie received was quickly forgotten, as word of mouth turned *Butch Cassidy* into one of the more solid box-office performers of the autumn season.

The enthusiasm, however, did not end there. This was not just a film that people recommended to their friends, but something than engendered an enormous amount of goodwill. Many of the critics may have missed the boat, but general audiences could tell that this was a picture so well crafted that it managed to mix humor, adventure, and tragedy without missing a beat. Not unlike *Bonnie and Clyde* (Warner Bros., 1967), this was a film that appeared to make light of, indeed celebrate, the initial crime-spree exploits of its protagonists, only to slowly turn 180 degrees until it was evident that no good was going to come from the outlaw life. Audiences found themselves laughing at both the misfortune of the gang's "victims," but also at the frequently clumsy efforts of Butch and Sundance to pass themselves off as the desperadoes they weren't really at heart. Moviegoers began talking excitedly about such set pieces as the cliff jump, the notorious kick in the groin, the overdynamited train robbery, and the dazzling, doomed shoot-out that concluded with an unforgettable, and somehow poignant, freeze-frame. Hill and his leads graciously credited Goldman for having done all the hard work, but it was evident that the pairing of Newman and Redford went several steps beyond chemistry to become one of the great male-male teamings in cinema history. Because they seemed so effortlessly in step with one another, with not even the vaguest suggestion of a homosexual relationship—a point that helped to put more nervous moviegoers at ease—the actors made the bonding between these two men, racing against time to beat the fast-changing world, the important factor in what made the whole thing click.

Yet another masterstroke on Hill's part had been one that might have backfired and wrecked the entire movie: the decision to hire Burt Bacharach to do the score. Bacharach had made his name with a very contemporary, brassy sound, but Hill felt that the already hip feel of the movie would be emphasized all to the better with music that placed it firmly in the decade in which it was released. Bacharach's bouncy themes added tremendously to the tongue-in-cheek tone of much of the picture and his addition of a song, written with his longtime collaborator, lyricist Hal David, turned the already charming bicycle scene into something magical. On first hearing, "Raindrops Keep Fallin' on My Head" didn't seem to have a whole lot to do with Butch, Sundance or the Old West, but there was a lazy, sunny feeling to it so perfectly in tune with the late '60s that upon a single listening it caught you and held you.

Butch Cassidy and the Sundance Kid became not only the highest-grossing movie released in 1969, but also landed among the top five box-office moneymakers for the entire decade. The film not only helped create an entire genre of jokey westerns, but turned Robert Redford from a good-looking lead actor into one of the true superstars of the following decade. He and Newman, who had bonded as well offscreen as they did on, let it be known that they were very interested in going another round if the screenplay was right. Four years later they found the right property in a lighthearted confidence caper penned by David S. Ward, *The Sting* (Universal). Under Hill's direction once again, that movie, though not as polished as the first film, hit just the right notes for the same audiences and became an even bigger moneymaker than *Butch Cassidy*, taking home seven Academy Awards, including those for Best Picture and Best Director.

BOB & CAROL & TED & ALICE

Academy Award Nominee: Supporting Actor (Elliott Gould); Supporting Actress (Dyan Cannon); Story and Screenplay—Not Based on Material Previously Published or Produced; Cinematography

Top 10 Box Office Film

Opening date: October 8, 1969.

Columbia. A Frankovich Production.

Director: Paul Mazursky. Producer: Larry Tucker. Screenplay: Paul Mazursky, Larry Tucker. Executive Producer: M. J. Frankovich. Photography: Charles F. Lang. Art Director: Pato Guzman. Set Decorator: Frank Tuttle. Costumes: Moss Mabry. Music: Quincy Jones. Songs: "Hallelujah Chorus," by George Frederic Handel, performed by chorus; "What the World Needs Now Is Love," by Burt Bacharach (music) and Hal David (lyrics), performed by Jackie DeShannon. Editor: Stuart Pappé. Eastmancolor. 106 minutes. Rated R.

CAST: Natalie Wood (Carol Sanders), Robert Culp (Bob Sanders), Elliott Gould (Ted Henderson), Dyan Cannon (Alice Henderson), Horst Ebersberg (Horst), Lee Bergere (Emilio), Donald F. Muhich (Alice's Psychiatrist), Noble Lee Holderread Jr. (Sean Sanders), K. T. Stevens (Phyllis), Celeste Yarnall (Susan), Lynn Borden (Cutter), Linda Burton (Stewardess), John Brent (Dave), Garry Goodrow (Bert), Carol O'Leary (Sue), Constance Egan (Norma); and *Institute Group*: Gregg Mullavey (Leader), Diane Berghoff (Myrna), Andre Philippe (Oscar), John Halloran (Conrad), Susan Merin (Toby), Jeffrey Walker (Roger), Vicki Thal (Jane), Joyce Easton (Wendy), Howard Dayton (Howard), Alida Ihle (Alida), Paul Mazursky (Screaming Man).

PLOT: Having gotten in touch with their true feelings after attending a twenty-four-hour session with an encounter group, Bob and Carol Sanders hope to share their newfound inner peace and freer lifestyle with their more uptight friends Ted and Alice.

One of the trendy topics talked about with a suggestive leer during the late '60s was "wife swapping." The rules weren't exactly the same ones that applied to the swapping of baseball cards; it meant that couples, freed by the "sexual revolution," were turning to good friends and wondering if a onetime change of partners might be an enlightening and stimulating experience. Journalists wrote articles about it, comedians told jokes about it, and everyone wondered if anybody they knew would really do something so outrageous. Paul Mazursky and Larry Tucker decided to write a screenplay about it and came up with the first, foremost, and final word on the subject, *Bob & Carol & Ted & Alice*, one of the best comedies of its era, one that didn't depend on punch lines for cheap laughs, but let the humor develop by simply confronting the issue without fear. The collaborators circulated a five-page treatment that involved two couples exploring the possibilities of sexual freedom, leading up to their jumping into bed together. Although Hollywood was looking for risqué adult fare at the time, this seemed to cross the boundaries of good taste for most people, and it was not until producer Mike Frankovich got hold of it that he agreed to put it on his slate of upcoming films.

Mazursky had used his own experiences as the launching point for the story. The opening sequence was based on a trip he took with his wife to Esalen, an institute established in 1962 along the coastline of Big Sur, California, that encouraged self-exploration, sensory awareness, and meditation, among other things. He and Tucker then improvised the rest of the script, which took on the challenging subject of extramarital sex and presented it not as the unforgivable act it had always been perceived as throughout the history of entertainment, but as nothing more than another step in personal growth, a natural human inclination. Each scene consisted of long and probing discussions about why we stray, just how morally repugnant the act is to some and not to others, and the possibilities of an open relationship that understands the difference between physical release and love. Mazursky and Tucker's writing was so smart that it did not openly mock the touchy-feely tactics of the encounter group, but allowed audiences to decide for themselves just how silly or how enriching these techniques seemed, depending on your stance on the subject. There was much mileage to be gotten out of the very liberated belief that sexual fulfillment need not stop at marriage, and the film pushed enough hot buttons to keep audiences laughing, shifting in their seats with discomfort, aroused with a certain degree of titillation, and pondering the whole thing afterward (as the film's ad line suggested, "Consider the possibilities"). Frankovich was astute enough to know that he could have an explosive hit on his hands and gave Mazursky the green light not only to proceed but to make his directorial debut as well.

> "I wanna share something beautiful with you: Bob had an affair when he was in San Francisco. It . . . it wasn't an affair, it was . . . it was just sex. But he told me about it. And I just . . . I had to share it with you, because it's so beautiful."
> —Carol

Bob & Carol began filming on October 7, 1968, with all interiors (including the restaurant, the Sanders residence, Ted and Alice's bedroom, and the hotel room where the film's most notorious image, of the four principals sitting up in bed together, took place) shot on the Columbia Studios lot. Because Esalen would not allow Mazursky to film on the premises, an isolated hilltop site was chosen some sixty miles north of Hollywood in the San Gabriel Mountains at Angela's Crest, which included some provocative nudity glimpsed during the opening credits. An El Taco restaurant in Hollywood included a vocal cameo by Howard Koch Jr.; a residence in Pasadena provided the pool and front exterior of Bob and Carol's house; the actual editing rooms at Columbia were glimpsed for a scene of

What LP offered the "Hallelujah Chorus" from Handel's *Messiah* alongside Burt Bacharach? The Bell Records soundtrack for *Bob & Carol & Ted & Alice,* with its groovy-colored logo capturing the spirit of the late '60s and the film's endorsement of free love.

Bob flirting with a fellow employee; and the slot room, lobby, and parking lot of the Riviera Hotel in Las Vegas were used for the finale. Shooting wrapped on December 16 of that year.

Mazursky's film was done with wit, taste, and style, but Columbia figured it was best to sell it as provocative and "dirty" because that was the kind of advance press that got the public to buy tickets. Once word got out that it involved wife swapping, *Bob & Carol & Ted & Alice* was a title simply too irresistible for the press to avoid and, due to the picture's box-office success and the media's constant mention of the name for titillation and cheap humor, it came to symbolize something far more salacious than anything that appeared onscreen. The movie gave audiences plenty to think about, but also granted the more old-fashioned viewers the consolation of a happy, morally sound ending that assured them that even the sexual revolution had its limits when it came to breaking boundaries.

PAINT YOUR WAGON

Academy Award Nominee: Score of a Musical Picture—Original or Adaptation

Top 10 Box Office Film

Opening date: October 15, 1969.

Paramount. An Alan Jay Lerner Production.

Director: Joshua Logan. Producer-Screenplay-Lyrics: Alan Jay Lerner. Adaptation: Paddy Chayefsky. Music: Frederick Loewe. Music for Additional Songs: André Previn. Based on the 1951 musical by Alan Jay Lerner and Frederick Loewe, presented on the stage by Cheryl Crawford. Photography: William A. Fraker. Production Designer-Costumes: John Truscott. Art Director: Carl Braunger. Set Decorator: James I. Berkey. Choral Music Conductor: Roger Wagner. Orchestral Music Scored and Conducted by Nelson Riddle. Choral Arrangements and Music Assistant to the Producer: Joseph J. Lilley. Songs by Lerner and Loewe: "I'm On My Way," "I Still See Elisa," "Hand Me Down That Can o' Beans," "They Call the Wind Maria," "Whoop-Ti-Ay! (Shivaree)," "I Talk to the Trees," "There's a Coach Comin' In," "Wand'rin' Star." Songs by Lerner and Previn: "The First Thing You Know," "A Million Miles Away behind the Door," "The Gospel of No Name City," "Best Things," "Gold Fever." Choreographer: Jack Baker. Editor: Robert C. Jones. Technicolor. Panavision. 166 minutes (including intermission and exit music; later cut to 137 minutes). Rated M.

CAST: Lee Marvin (Ben Rumson), Clint Eastwood ("Pardner"—Sylvester Newel), Jean Seberg (Elizabeth Woodling Rumson), Harve Presnell ("Rotten Luck Willie"), Ray Walston ("Mad Jack" Duncan), Tom Ligon (Horton Fenty), Alan Dexter (Parson), William O'Connell (Horace Tabor), Ben Baker (Haywood Holbrook), Alan Baxter (Mr. Fenty), Paula Trueman (Mrs. Fenty), Robert Easton (Ezra Atwell), Geoffrey Norman (Foster), H. B. Haggerty (Steve Bull), Terry Jenkins (Joe Mooney), Karl Bruck (Schermerhorn), John Mitchum (Jacob Woodling), Sue Casey (Sarah Woodling), The Nitty Gritty Dirt Band (Band).

PLOT: After striking gold, Ben Rumson and Pardner settle in the makeshift mining town of No Name City, where they set up a rather unorthodox household, allowing them to "share" Elizabeth, a Mormon woman Ben has purchased as his bride.

Thanks to the tremendous financial and critical success of *My Fair Lady* (Warner Bros., 1964), the songwriting team of Alan Jay Lerner and Frederick Loewe was a hot property. Only problem was, it was a hot property that was a thing of the past, the two men having parted ways after the Broadway presentation of *Camelot* in 1960; Loewe retired from the field altogether. While making the 1967 Warner Bros. film adaptation of *Camelot*, Lerner hoped to get the studios interested in one of the team's stage works that had slipped through Hollywood's hands, *Paint Your Wagon*. The original Broadway version had opened on November 12, 1951, at the Shubert Theatre and ran a respectable 289 performances. Several film companies had considered buying the property at the time (including Paramount, which envisioned it as a vehicle for Bing Crosby), and it had made it so far as to end up with former MGM chief Louis B. Mayer, who planned to make it his first independent production, though that dream never materialized. Set during the California Gold Rush of 1853, the musical revolved around miner Ben Rumson (James Barton) and his sixteen-year-old daughter, Jennifer (Olga San Juan). Rumson finds gold, names a town after himself, and ends up purchasing a Mormon bride (Marijane Maricle) eager to part from her husband, who has a second wife of his own. Jennifer winds up falling in love with the mining town's outcast, a Mexican named Julio (Tom Bavaar).

Nobody was ever terrifically pleased with the show's book, including Lerner himself, who tinkered with it so much during out-of-town tryouts that the liner notes on the original cast album gave an inaccurate plot description of what New York audiences actually saw. The score, however, was the thing, and it brought forth its share of pleasures. When it came time to sell the idea of a movie adaptation, Lerner hoped to get his *Camelot* director, Joshua Logan, on board by assuring him that the original book would be almost entirely reconceived and that the job of adapting the troubled script would be handed over to the esteemed Paddy Chayefsky. In addition to some dance instrumentals, nine tunes from the original score were discarded: "Rumson," "What's Goin' On Here?,"

> "Sodom was vice and vice-a-versa, you wanna see where the vice is worser? Here it is! I mean here it is!"
> —Parson

"Strike," "How Can I Wait?," "In Between," "Movin'," "Carino Mio," "Another Autumn," and "All for Him." With all of these songs gone, Lerner needed to come up with some brand new ones. Since Loewe was out of commission, he opted for André Previn as his collaborator, and together they penned five numbers. The names Ben Rumson and Elizabeth Woodling were retained from the original script for two of the principal characters, and the plot point about Elizabeth's being one of two wives happily purchased from a Mormon was kept intact. Beyond that, the finished screenplay bore next to no resemblance to what audiences had seen onstage back in the early '50s. Between Lerner and Chayefsky, the two writers came up with an apocalyptic finale in which the mining town literally collapses from greed and, more significantly, added a very late '60s touch by having the three principals set up a ménage à trois of sorts, sharing house and bed and extolling an advanced form of free love.

Lerner's decision to allow Joshua Logan to direct *Paint Your Wagon* was a fatal one that damaged whatever potential the property had in the first place. Apparently having no objections to Logan's inadequate handling of not only *Camelot* but of Rodgers and Hammerstein's *South Pacific*, Lerner begged the director to come aboard, even though Logan was none too enchanted with the material. Whereas Lerner had been an off-set collaborator on *Camelot*, this time, as credited producer, he insisted on having his say on virtually every aspect of the production, a move that led to his instantly locking horns with Logan. Wanting the movie to have an authentic, outdoor feel, Lerner insisted nearly all of it be shot on location. The site selected was the beautiful Eagle Creek section of Wallowa National Forest, forty-seven miles northeast of Baker, Oregon. Because of the isolation of the area, cast and crew had to either trek over miles of dirt roads or be flown there by helicopter. Logan wanted the built-up version of No Name City to be constructed at Paramount in order to save money, but Lerner and production designer John Truscott had more elaborate ideas for the set, rightfully figuring that a complex system would have to be built for the finale in order to collapse the structures into the ground on cue, something that would have been difficult to pull off in the confines of a back lot. Shooting began on June 28, 1968, at the Oregon location and was supposed to be finished after three months. Multiple problems interfered with their plans, and by October the crew was still stranded up in the woods. With cold weather setting in, the

The packaging for Paramount Records' *Paint Your Wagon* soundtrack customarily allowed the logo with its images of the movie's three stars to slip off once the plastic was removed, leaving buyers with a title-free painting of the old west.

company finally hightailed it back to the Paramount soundstages, where such interior sets as the Grizzly Bear Saloon were built.

The allotted budget of $9 million quickly ballooned out of control, and the final cost on the picture was a staggering $19 million, $5 million short of the small fortune spent around the same time on *Hello, Dolly!* (Twentieth Century-Fox, 1969). Logan blamed Lerner's meddling and Truscott's perfectionism for much of the cost overruns, and he had few regrets about handing the footage over to Lerner for final edit. Perhaps it was Lerner who managed to salvage some of the film, hoping to bring attention to the one aspect that deserved praise, the melodic score he, Loewe, and Previn had come up with. Despite Logan's sometimes inept staging, the orchestrations by Nelson Riddle did full service to such splendid tunes as "I'm On My Way," "There's a Coach Comin' In," and "Gold Fever." Eastwood's soft, introspective interpretation of "I Talk to the Trees" turned out sounding quite pleasant, while Marvin's husky croaking on the most beautiful composition, "Wand'rin' Star," added a certain haunting quality to it. (In England a single of this rendition actually managed to land on the charts!)

Despite the fact that most critics proclaimed *Paint Your Wagon* a disaster, it garnered its share of ticket buyers, though not enough to cover its whopping cost. Hoping to get more customers in the seats, Paramount twice tried to appeal the M (mature) rating slapped upon the picture and have it designated a G, but the ratings board stood its ground, citing the use of such words as "bastards" and "Goddamn," not to mention the depiction of prostitution and polygamy. Although the free-spirited live-in arrangement of the three principals gave the movie a provocative modern slant the original play script did not have, the authors hadn't the guts to let it play out with any daring. Elizabeth was ultimately influenced by the narrow-minded thinking of the pious Fenty family, throwing both her men out and ultimately deciding that a monogamous relationship is the only viable one (even though, until outside forces expressed their disapproval, this arrangement had in fact seemed to be working out very nicely). Similarly, despite its portrayal of No Name City as something akin to a hippie commune for hedonists in search of pleasures, no questions asked, the final act inflicted a punishment upon them worthy of Cecil B. DeMille, the earth literally swallowing up the degradation.

THE STERILE CUCKOO

Academy Award Nominee: Actress (Liza Minnelli); Song ("Come Saturday Morning")

Opening date: October 22, 1969.

Paramount. An Alan J. Pakula Production.

Director-Producer: Alan J. Pakula. Screenplay: Alvin Sargent. Based on the 1965 novel by John Nichols. Photography: Milton R. Krasner. Art Director: Roland Anderson. Set Decorator: Charles Pierce. Ladies' Wardrobe: Jennifer Parsons. Men's Wardrobe: John Anderson. Executive Producer: David Lange. Music: Fred Karlin. Song: "Come Saturday Morning," by Fred Karlin (music) and Dory Previn (lyrics), performed by the Sandpipers. Additional Songs: "Greensleeves" (traditional), "House of the Rising Sun" (unknown), and "Hey Liley Liley Lo," by Elizabeth Austin and Alan Lomax. Editors: Sam O'Steen, John W. Wheeler. Technicolor. 107 minutes. Rated R.

CAST: Liza Minnelli (Marianne "Pookie" Adams), Wendell Burton (Jerry Payne), Tim McIntire (Charlie Schumacher), Elizabeth Harrower (Landlady), Austin Green (Pookie's Father), Sandy Faison (Nancy Putnam), Chris Bugbee (Roe), Jawn McKinley (Helen Upshaw).

PLOT: During his freshman year at college, shy Jerry Payne finds himself falling in love with needy, extroverted Pookie Adams, who tries to coax him out of his shell and leave conformity behind.

By the late 1960s most people following the entertainment scene knew who Liza Minnelli was. Aside from being the offspring of two of the most admired names in show business, singer-actress Judy Garland and director Vincente Minnelli, she was very much an A-list professional in her own right, prominent throughout the '60s on television, stages, and recordings. Having pulled off a supporting role in Albert Finney's offbeat directorial bow, *Charlie Bubbles* (Universal, 1968), Minnelli felt it was time to see if she could make as big an impact in motion pictures as her parents had. Her chance came when producer Alan J. Pakula bought the rights to John Nichols's first novel, *The Sterile Cuckoo*, in 1965. Minnelli read the book and was so sure that she could pull off playing its quirky, loquacious, fragile heroine, Pookie Adams, that she contacted Pakula directly to offer her services. Once Pakula finally decided to go ahead with *Cuckoo* in 1968, he not only handed Minnelli her dream part but had grown so fond of the property that he decided that he himself would be directing the picture, his first effort behind the cameras in this capacity.

It was just as important to find the right actor to portray the other key role—that of shy, guileless Jerry Payne, the narrator of Nichols's book. Since Liza's extensive media exposure made her the "name"

> "Somehow or other, when everything's a little bit perfect, I just get nervous. I mean, it can't last."
> —Pookie Adams

attached to the picture, Pakula was free to go with whomever he wanted for his leading man. He chose a total newcomer, Wendell Burton, after seeing him play the most guileless character of them all, Charlie Brown, in a San Francisco production of the musical *You're a Good Man, Charlie Brown*. Minnelli and Burton would carry the bulk of the picture, which was shaped into a mostly two-character love story, the only other actor to get billing at both the front and the end of the movie being Tim McIntire as Burton's blustering college roommate.

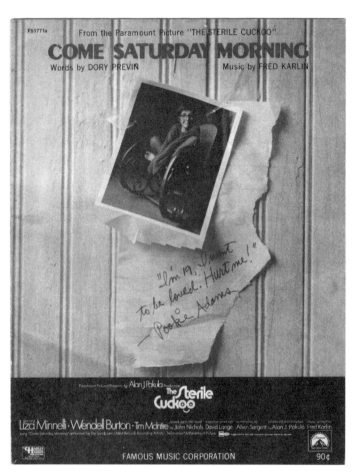

The sheet music for one of the many attractions of *The Sterile Cuckoo,* Dory Previn and Fred Karlin's beautiful "Come Saturday Morning," which became a hit for the Sandpipers.

To adapt the book, Pakula called on Alvin Sargent, who had just done a less-than-stellar job on the last picture Pakula had produced, the Gregory Peck western *The Stalking Moon* (National General, 1969). Sargent chose to carry very little over from page to screen outside of the general premise: overly needy Pookie becomes romantically involved with timid college boy Jerry. Among the few moments to make the transition were a humorous scene in which the two virginal teens hesitantly disrobe for one another in a freezing cold motel cabin; Pookie's insistence on spending spring break with Jerry, while he hopes to study and improve his dropping grades; and Pookie's speech about how only a minute of our lives is spent being truly happy. Nichols's book had the pair meeting as Jerry is beginning college and Pookie is finishing off her stint in high school. Sargent changed this so that they were attending college at the same time, at presumably nearby schools. The story now took place during the course of one school year, not several. In the film it was up to Pookie to (more characteristically) track Jerry down after their initial meeting and correspondence, whereas Nichols had Jerry pursue Pookie to her school after seeing her picture in a campus publication; Jerry would not be distracted from his relationship by pledging a fraternity, the character being far more socially inhibited onscreen than he was in print; Pookie would not be involved in a horrid car accident of which she is the only survivor, but would instead be wracked with guilt because her mother had died giving birth to her; and there was no trip to New York City, which had provided the climax of the book and the incident that brought the couple to the realization that their happiness with one another had vanished. While Sargent kept the sad theme of the gradual decline of a love affair in which two people simply cannot remain simpatico with each other because they have changed, he did not wish to journey too deeply into potentially depressing areas. In the book, Pookie very nearly talked Jerry into a suicide pact (with an overdose of aspirin!) and might even have gone through with her end of the bargain, since the final chapter consisted of Jerry reading a note from her in which she proposes offing herself.

Although the whereabouts of the college in the book had been deliberately kept vague, Pakula liked the idea of setting his film at the very school from which Nichols himself had graduated, Hamilton (as in Alexander) College, in Clinton, New York, outside of Utica. *The Sterile Cuckoo* might not be a faithful rendering of Nichols's book, but at least it would have the right setting. Additional filming took place in that same area at nearby Vernon Center, which included the bus stop where Pookie and Jerry part for their respective schools near the start of the film; and at Sylvan Beach on Lake Oneida, which provided the tourist cabins for Jerry and Pookie's first sexual encounter and the subsequent beach scenes. After a six-week shooting period that began in this area on September 11, 1968, the company went west to shoot interiors at the Paramount studio lot. While on the West Coast, the brief glimpse of Jerry and his roommate, Charlie, sledding on their winter break was shot at Big Bear Lake in the San Bernardino Mountains. In the nearby town of Ontario, California, was filmed the opening sequence, in which Pookie and her father wait silently at a bus stop in front of a dilapidated building.

Pakula's decision to go with the persistent Minnelli turned out to be a smart move. She was absolutely perfect in the part, preventing this potentially overbearing character from slipping into obnoxiousness, always suggesting hints of desperation or loneliness just beneath the surface. It was a tough task to find the right balance in making Pookie's independence alternately enviable and pitiable, suggesting that this was not so much a life chosen as one she had become resigned to because of her inability to fit in, but Minnelli managed to pull it off. She was so good and such a focus of the reviews that Wendell Burton was unfortunately neglected or underrated for his superb performance as a well-meaning, awkward young man who is equally confused and defeated by his first love affair. The audience response was enthusiastic; here was an unpretentious little movie that was just as honest in depicting the first stages of romance as it was in painfully spelling out the clash of complex personalities that can destroy what once seemed to be a perfect thing.

GOODBYE, MR. CHIPS

Academy Award Nominee: Actor (Peter O'Toole); Score of a Musical Picture—Original or Adaptation

Opening date: November 5, 1969.

MGM. An Arthur P. Jacobs Production.

Director: Herbert Ross. Producer: Arthur P. Jacobs. Screenplay: Terence Rattigan. Based on *Goodbye, Mr. Chips* by James Hilton, originally published in *British Weekly* in 1933 and then as a novella in 1934. Photography: Oswald Morris. Art Director: Maurice Fowler. Production Designer: Ken Adam. Costumes: Julie Harris. Editor: Ralph Kemplen. Songs by Leslie Bricusse: "Fill the World with Love," "Where Did My Childhood Go?," "London Is London" "And the Sky Smiled," "Apollo," "When I Am Older," "Walk Through the World," "What Shall I Do with Today?," "What a Lot of Flowers," "Schooldays," "You and I." Music Scoring: John Williams. Associate Musical Director: Ian Fraser. Associate Choreographer and Special Assistant to Mr. Ross: Nora Kaye. Metrocolor. Panavision. 151 minutes (including overture, entr'acte, and exit music; later cut to 133 minutes). Rated G.

CAST: Peter O'Toole (Arthur Chipping, "Chips"), Petula Clark (Katherine Bridges Chipping), Michael Redgrave (Headmaster), Siân Phillips (Ursula Mossbank), Alison Leggatt (Headmaster's Wife), Michael Bryant (Max Staefel), George Baker (Lord Sutterwick), Jack Hedley (William Baxter), Clinton Greyn (Bill Calbury), Barbara Couper (Mrs. Paunceforth), Michael Culver (Johnny Longbridge), Elspeth March (Mrs. Summersthwaite), Clive Morton (General Paunceforth), Ronnie Stevens (Algy), Mario Maranzana (Pompeii Guide), John Gugolka (Sutterwick Jr.), Michael Ridgeway (David), Tom Owen (Farley), Craig Marriott (New Boy), Elspet Gray (Lady Sutterwick), Jeremy Lloyd (Johnson), and the Boys of Sherborne School.

PLOT: Arthur Chipping, a timid, socially awkward classics teacher at Brookfield School, blossoms when he falls in love with Katherine Bridges, an exuberant music-hall entertainer who takes a fancy to his gentility and lack of pretense.

Agent-turned-producer Arthur P. Jacobs decided he wanted to remake MGM's classic 1939 tearjerker *Goodbye, Mr. Chips* as a musical, but not in the traditional sense. Rather than present large-scale numbers or love duets for this revision of James Hilton's novella, he envisioned something more appropriately intimate. A score by André and Dory Previn was commissioned, and both Vincente Minnelli and Gower Champion joined up and dropped out along the way as potential directors. While all of this planning and negotiating was adding up to naught, Jacobs produced the much-hyped children's musical, *Doctor Dolittle* (Twentieth Century-Fox, 1967), which boasted Herbert Ross as its choreographer and Leslie Bricusse as songwriter. Since Ross was the only one

> **"Fourteen weeks of school cap tipping, filthy food, and Mr. Chipping."**
> **—Brookfield student**

who seemed to understand what Jacobs had in mind for *Chips*, he was given the assignment of directing the property, his debut behind the cameras in this capacity. Bricusse was hired in early 1968 to write the score, by which time both Peter O'Toole and former child actress–turned–pop singer Petula Clark had both agreed to star. O'Toole had initially balked at the idea of a musical *Chips* until he was told that distinguished playwright and screenwriter Terence Rattigan would be responsible for the script. O'Toole needn't have worried that he'd be risking failure or folly by singing and dancing, because there was precious little of the former and none of the latter for his character. Ross and Rattigan had conceived of most of the tunes as interior monologues, sung in voice-overs that occasionally segued into the character's actually singing onscreen. O'Toole's croaky chirping seemed fitting for the timid schoolteacher he was portraying. Clark, being the true vocalist on hand, was given the bulk of the songs.

Hilton's book had been written in a mere four days in November 1933, in order to be included in time for the *British Weekly*'s Christmas issue. The following year, the story showed up in *Atlantic Monthly* and, finally, in book form. It met with a mild response in England initially, finding greater success in America. Ultimately, the British embraced this very simple but touching story of a shy schoolmaster who looks back on his life as an instructor at Brookfield School, starting from his arrival in 1848, through his two terms as acting headmaster, his retirement following World War I, and his final years spent as a beloved figure living adjacent to the school grounds. The important catalyst in his growth from stodgy, disliked instructor to a man admired and loved by his pupils was his free-thinking and kindly wife, Katherine, whom he meets on a holiday in the Lake District and promptly marries, only to lose her in childbirth

Peter O'Toole protects himself from the English weather while novice director Herbert Ross endures the elements on the set of *Goodbye, Mr. Chips*.

two years later. The first dramatization of Hilton's story was, in fact, British, a 1937 West End production with Leslie Banks as the schoolmaster. The 1939 MGM film was shot in England and starred Robert Donat in his Academy Award–winning performance and Greer Garson in her motion-picture debut.

Filming on the new *Chips* began on July 16, 1968, at the Sherborne School in Dorset, with 250 of the students staying on during the summer break to play the Brookfield boys. The filmmakers utilized not only the school grounds, but also its classrooms and dormitories, the adjoining village, and the railroad station, as well as the vicarage, which served as the Chipping home. Additional filming went on at the Great Theatre in Pompeii (it was the first motion picture given permission to film there); the Greek temples at Paestum, at which Katherine sings "And the Sky Smiled"; and the fishing village of Positano, for the song "Apollo." The unit then moved on to London to film at Syon Park, the Salisbury Pub, and the Thames walking path east of Kew Bridge. Three major sets were built at MGM Studios in Borehamwood: the ballroom of the Savoy Hotel, where Chips first meets Katherine; the Assembly Hall of Brookfield, where Katherine joins the boys for a reprise of "Fill the World with Love" and, later, for the rollicking "Schooldays" presentation at Founder's Night; and the London Music Hall, at which Katherine is seen performing "London Is London." The updating for the new film meant that the story line would begin in 1924, then be brought up to World War II and its aftermath, with a coda set in the present.

Readers of Hilton's minuscule novel were no doubt taken aback by the 151 minutes Ross and company took to tell this small tale. Despite Rattigan's intelligent and loving script, the movie often gave the feeling of something dragged out way beyond the breaking point. The road-show musical was very much the norm at the time, and MGM theorized that if *Chips* was to be treated as an important attraction it had to include an intermission, meaning it needed to run long enough to warrant one. Even more harmful, Jacobs and Ross's muted approach to the songs pretty much backfired. Many of the tunes seemed underwhelming and too casually tossed off, robbing the film of the feel of a musical; it played more like a drama that happened to have some songs thrown in as an afterthought.

As far as the acting went, O'Toole and Clark did themselves no shame. O'Toole, going up against Donat's much-loved performance from the original film, managed to portray an emotionally reserved, dull man in a sympathetic and understandable manner, no easy feat. Clark ended up with the best role of her all-too-short film career as an adult, the part having been expanded for her benefit from the relatively brief time Greer Garson had been given in the earlier film and from Katherine's equally limited appearance in the book. O'Toole received his fourth Oscar nomination and wound up being the one aspect of the film that, in the year of its release, kept it from being written off as a misfire altogether by the many critics and audiences who denounced it as out-of-date. The poor turnout for *Goodbye, Mr. Chips* was a devastating blow to MGM, which decided to trim eighteen minutes from it when the movie went into general release in April 1970. Since select songs were among the cuts, it was clear that the original concept had not worked and was certainly not the main reason anyone wanted to see the film.

Z (France–Algeria)

Academy Award Winner: Best Foreign Language Film; Best Film Editing

Academy Award Nominee: Picture; Director; Screenplay—Based on Material from Another Medium

Opening date: December 8, 1969 (Paris: February 26, 1969).

Cinema V. A Valoria Films Presentation of a Coproduction of Reggane Films (Paris) and Office National pour le Commerce et l'Industrie Cinématographie (Algeria).

Director: Costa-Gavras. Producers: Jacques Perrin, Hamed Rachedi. Screenplay: Jorge Semprún, [Costa-Gavras]. Dialogue: Jorge Semprún. Based on the 1966 novel by Vassili Vassilikos. Photography: Raoul Coutard. Production Designer: Jacques D'Ovidio. Costumes: Piet Bolsher. Music: Mikis Theodorakis. Editor: Françoise Bonnot. Eastmancolor. 127 minutes. Rated M.

CAST: Yves Montand (the Deputy), Irene Papas (Helene, the Deputy's Wife), Jean-Louis Trintignant (the Examining Magistrate), Charles Denner (Manuel), Georges Geret (Nick, the Witness), Jacques Perrin (the Journalist), François Périer (the Public Prosecutor), Bernard Fresson (Matt), Pierre Dux (the General), Julien Guiomar (the Colonel), Marcel Bozzufi (Vago), Magali Noël (Nick's Sister), Renato Salvatori (Yago), Jean Bouise (Georges Pirou), Clotilde Joanno (Shoula), Maurice Baquet (the Bald Man), Hassan Hassani (the General's Chauffeur), Gérard Darrieu (the Baron), Jean-Pierre Miquel (Pierre), Van Doude (the Hospital Director), Jean Daste (Illya Coste), Gabriel Jabbour (Bozzini), Jean-François Gobbi (Jimmy the Boxer), Guy Mairesse (Dumas), Andrée Tainsy (Nick's Mother), Eva Simonet (Niki).

PLOT: The examining magistrate demands a full-scale investigation to find out how the president of a pacifist organization ended up being assaulted after a political rally and just which parties are responsible for the suspicious attack.

The final word (or, in this case, the final letter) on political conspiracy thrillers, Z was just about the summit in terms of what most critics were looking for in late '60s cinema. Shot with a raw, documentary-like feel, bristling with open anger at the current political situation not only in Greece but in regard to those willing to support that country's military dictatorship, this was not just a movie but a statement against oppression, injustice, and governmental fraud; and as far as its maker, Costa-Gavras, was concerned, it affected every single one of us. It was while visiting Athens in the early spring of 1967 that Gavras got hold of Vassili Vassilikos's novel Z (the title, which stood for the Greek word zei, means "he lives"), a thinly disguised exposé of the corrupt investigation into the death of Gregorios Lambrakis, a left-wing member of the Greek parliament who had been run over by a pickup truck in Salonika on May 22, 1963. In time, it came to light that this was no accident, but a political assassination orchestrated by the country's right-wing forces. Upon returning to his adopted country of France, Gavras was dismayed to learn that a military junta had overthrown the civilian government in Greece and taken power on April 21, 1967. He was now more determined than ever to turn Z into a motion picture and bought the rights to the book prior to its publication in France.

To help him write the screenplay, Gavras enlisted another man who had left his native land for France, Jorge Semprún, a Spanish political activist and writer who had just earned an Oscar nomination for writing Alain Resnais's dense *La guerre est finie* (United Artists, 1967). Believing they could implicate Greece without actually making it clear just where their movie was being set, they chose to remove any of the book's direct references to the precise location of the events. Vassilikos's novel had referred to the slain parliament member as "Z" (called "the Deputy" onscreen) and had most specifically mentioned the real date of the assassination as well, whereas the film kept this vague. Perhaps feeling that they had enough villainy going for them, the filmmakers made the death squad hired to do the murder no longer pro-Hitler and flat-out anti-Semitic, as Vassilikos had depicted them, nor was their chief assassin, Vago, keen on seducing little boys, but a homosexual interested in men closer to his own age. The screenplay added a tense scene in which Vago tries to bump off a key witness with his cane, while the book had left him laid up in bed. The film eliminated the sidebar stories of some of the participants in the events, including a student who ends up having his hair clipped by the police while trying to put flowers on Z's grave—an unfortunate omission in terms of sociological topicality, insomuch as the world's youths were finding a surprising degree of opposition because of their decision to let their hair grow. Gavras and Semprún also chose to minimize the role of the Deputy's wife; she had been featured in several lengthy passages in the book in which she reflected upon how much she missed her husband.

> "Around the world too many soldiers are ready to fire on anything moving toward progress."
> —The Deputy

Nobody was fooled into thinking that *Z* was anything less than an incendiary condemnation of Greek politics, a fact that scared off several potential backers Gavras had been counting on. Once Gavras realized he couldn't depend on funding from European or American distributors, one of his cast members, Jacques Perrin, took on the job of finding it. The French government agreed to put up $80,000, while Perrin managed to entice Algeria to not only provide them with their outdoor locations but to join in as coproducers, making this the very first cinematic collaboration between France and its former colony. Independent producer Hercules Mucelli put up another $200,000. To help keep the cost down, many of the cast principals agreed to work on spec. In the summer of 1968 Gavras began shooting throughout Algiers, including some interiors, with the rest of the indoor filming to be done in Paris. A total of $750,000 was spent over the ten-week period of principal photography.

When it premiered in France in February 1969, *Z* was championed as an explosive statement against dictatorial government practices and a criticism of the shameful complicity of all world leaders who put power before humanity. Gavras had not sacrificed the thriller aspect of his picture, though he certainly allowed for a great deal of talk to dominate the proceedings. It was talk worth listening to, however—worth arguing about and contemplating. The time was just right to tell people that they could no longer depend on heroes to save them, that injustice was waiting to sneak up and seize control at every possible chance. The film quickly began building an audience, and public support increased once word spread that Greece absolutely refused to allow *Z* to be shown there. Despite the fact that the movie had engendered so much discussion, the big companies were still terrified of it, so it was up to

Don Rugoff's tiny independent, Cinema V, to finally bid for U.S. distribution rights.

Rugoff mounted an $80,000 ad campaign, unprecedented for the American release of a movie in another language. The poster image of the tattered letter "Z" hovering over a dead body was nothing if not intriguing, and the distributor could not have hoped for more critical support than he ended up receiving from American reviewers, who fell all over themselves trying to come up with superlatives to describe Gavras's assured mix of intellectual intrigue and anger. The picture was booked to open during the Christmas season to ensure that the favorable press would also lead to awards. That tactic worked, and Z became the very first foreign-language picture to grab the Best Film prize from the New York Film Critics. If the Oscars were looking for an "important" movie to honor, they couldn't have earned more respect from the critical factions when they not only selected Z to be among the Foreign Film nominees, but also chose it as one of the five finalists for the coveted Best Picture award. This marked the first time a movie had been given nominations in both these categories and made Z the very first foreign film since *Grand Illusion*, thirty-one years earlier, to be in the running for the Best Picture Oscar. Z kept doing excellent business as it expanded the number of its bookings. Figuring they might be able to entice a wider demographic, Rugoff received permission from Gavras to show the movie in a dubbed print as well. Many of the cast principals agreed to do the job, knowing that the picture could withstand this unholy practice if it meant getting a few more skeptics to hear its message.

The Ballantine Books paperback tie-in of Vassilis Vassilikos's explosive novel *Z* contained the simple but potent tattered logo of the title that was used in all of the film's advertising.

THEY SHOOT HORSES, DON'T THEY?

Academy Award Winner: Best Supporting Actor (Gig Young)

Academy Award Nominee: Actress (Jane Fonda); Supporting Actress (Susannah York); Director; Screenplay—Based on Material from Another Medium; Art Direction–Set Decoration; Score of a Musical Picture—Original or Adaptation; Film Editing; Costume Design

Opening date: December 10, 1969.

Cinerama. An ABC Pictures Presentation of a Palomar Picture. A Chartoff–Winkler/Pollack Production.

Director: Sydney Pollack. Producers: Irwin Winkler, Robert Chartoff. Screenplay: James Poe, Robert E. Thompson. Based on the 1935 novel by Horace McCoy. Photography: Philip H. Lathrop. Production Designer: Harry Horner. Set Decorator: Frank McKelvy. Costumes: Donfeld. Executive Producer: Theodore B. Sills. Associate Producer–Music: Johnny Green. Songs: "Easy Come, Easy Go," by John Green (music) and Edward Heyman (lyrics), performed by Lynn Willis; "The Best Things in Life Are Free," by Buddy G. DeSylva, Lew Brown, and Ray Henderson, performed by Bonnie Bedelia. Orchestral Arrangements: John Green, Albert Woodbury. Marathon Dancers Supervisor: Tom Panko. Editor: Fredric Steinkamp. Deluxe color. Panavision. 120 minutes. Rated M.

CAST: Jane Fonda (Gloria Beatty), Michael Sarrazin (Robert Syverton), Susannah York (Alice LeBlanc), Gig Young (Rocky Gravo), Red Buttons ("Sailor," Harry Klein), Bonnie Bedelia (Ruby Bates), Bruce Dern (James Bates), Michael Conrad (Rollo Peters, Floor Judge), Al Lewis (Turkey), Robert Fields (Joel Girard), Severn Darden (Cecil), Allyn Ann McLerie (Shirl Clayton), Madge Kennedy (Mrs. Laydon), Jacquelyn Hyde (Jackie Miller), Felice Orlandi (Mario Petrone), Arthur Metrano (Max), Gail Billings (Lillian), Lynn Willis (Coley James), Maxine Greene (Agnes), Mary Gregory (Nurse), Robert Dunlap (College Boy), Paul Mantee (Jiggs, Floor Judge), Tim Herbert (Doctor), Tom McFadden, Noble "Kid" Chissell (Trainers).

PLOT: Badly in need of money during the Depression, Robert Syverton enters a dance marathon where he is partnered with the embittered Gloria Beatty, who has nothing but contempt for the public spectacle in which they are forced to participate.

If every unique subject deserves its definitive film dramatization, then the dance marathon craze of the 1930s got just that with *They Shoot Horses, Don't They?* Something of a sadomasochistic fad, in which couples were expected to dance in competition for cash prizes for hours, days, and even weeks on end, with minimal breaks allowed simply to ensure that they would not drop dead, marathons were eventually phased out by concerned citizens' groups, who saw them as exploitative and degrading displays. Despite (or more likely because of) the humiliation involved, spectators showed up to watch these determined souls sway and shuffle around the dance floor, most of the participants badly in need of money in the Depression years. Horace McCoy had experienced the grit and anxiety of these public events firsthand, having served as a bouncer at the Aragon Ballroom at Ocean Park in Santa Monica in the early 1930s. He wrote his short, very bleak, and hauntingly titled novel about the subject, *They Shoot Horses, Don't They?*, in 1931, but had to wait five years before it finally received a limited publication. Supposedly Charlie Chaplin expressed interest in buying the rights to the book; other stories claim that

McCoy sold away those rights for a mere $200 and a drink. Whatever the truth, no film version would be developed in McCoy's lifetime: the author died in Hollywood, in dire financial straits, of a heart attack on December 15, 1955, at the age of fifty-eight.

It was screenwriter James Poe who finally got the property out of the dormant stage and closer to becoming an actual film. It remained, however, a hard sell to the studios, who were put off by its relentlessly downbeat nature, so Poe took his adaptation to the newly formed independent producing team of Irwin Winkler and Robert Chartoff. The two managed to get backing for *They Shoot Horses* from the American Broadcasting Company, which had just recently started a motion-picture unit, ABC Pictures, and had scored a pair of hits in 1968 with *Charly* and *Candy*. Additional support came from Palomar Pictures International. Budgeted at $4 million, the picture was supposed to mark Poe's directorial debut, but three weeks into the December 1968 start date he was fired from the project.

His replacement was Sydney Pollack, who immediately sought another writer to do a pretty thorough overhaul of the script. He settled on Robert E. Thompson, whose prior assignments had been exclusively on television. Poe would retain his onscreen credit, however, though Pollack, who had worked on the screenplay as well, received no up-front

> **"Yowza! . . . Almost fifteen hundred hours of continuous dancing—and yet they're still out there, each one of them fighting, struggling to stay in the race."**
> **—Rocky**

mention. The adaptation of the novel dumped the flashback idea. The book told readers right from the start that Robert had shot Gloria and was standing trial, and each chapter was separated by a page of courtroom phraseology building up to Robert's sentencing. For the film, Pollack inserted cryptic flash-forwards of Robert facing trial to indicate that something ominous was going to happen. The movie decided against placing much or any emphasis on several peripheral contestants from the novel, including Mario, who was forced to flee the marathon because he was wanted by the police; Freddy, who also made tracks from the competition once it was discovered that his girlfriend was underage; and Pedro, who tried to shoot Rocky because he believed the emcee had seduced his partner. Gone too were the self-righteous women's group that successfully campaigned to get the marathon closed down and the marathon's manager, Socks Diamond. Added were an old sailor whose determination leads to his collapse during a derby run and Alice, a deluded starlet who begins to crack up under the strain of it all. The characters of James and his pregnant wife, Ruby, were allowed to stay on to the end of the film, though in the book the couple had been dismissed because of her physical condition. The gruesome accidental shooting of the kindly marathon groupie Mrs. Laydon was written out of the script, the writers perhaps correctly figuring that one gunshot in the head was enough for any film. A decided improvement from page to screen was having Gloria and Robert thrown together at the marathon out of convenience because her sickly partner has been disqualified; in McCoy's book they had met in Hollywood and agreed to participate in the contest. Giving them no prior history together made their partnering on the dance floor a better example of the randomness of the ritual.

Most of the action was confined to the interior of the ballroom. Harry Horner's impressive and detailed set design, which was patterned after the original Aragon Ballroom, was built on Stage 4 of the

Warner Bros.–Seven Arts Studio, where filming began on February 17, 1969. In order to keep his lens close to the action, Pollack often placed himself right on the dance floor, following the actors with a camera strapped to a helmet while wearing roller skates. During the shoot, Jane Fonda and Red Buttons threw themselves into the project by hitting the floor for an eighteen-hour stretch in order to experience the feeling of exhaustion they were supposed to be conveying onscreen. Both actors gave among their finest performances, as was the case with pretty much everyone involved. Fonda, who had been both a delightful comedic actress and a commendably serious one who hadn't had much luck in participating in any worthwhile dramas, surpassed anything else she had done up to this point. With her edgy and strongly committed work, she managed to make the relentlessly pessimistic character far more understandable and pitiable than she had been in McCoy's book. Perhaps the strongest individual moment in her performance could be found in a scene without a single word, when Gloria is seen dancing alone, hugging herself protectively and with fierce need, suggesting resilience in the face of inevitable defeat.

The ABC Records soundtrack for *They Shoot Horses, Don't They?* featured versions of many period tunes, but it belonged first and foremost to Johnny Green, who not only did the arrangements and tinkled the piano keys, but slipped in his own song, "Easy Come, Easy Go," written *after* the events in the story took place.

They Shoot Horses, Don't They? was hailed for its refreshingly unsentimental look at the past, wiping away all earlier, nostalgic re-creations of the era with its unsparing dissection of an exploitative and brutal event, of beaten souls losing what remaining dignity they possessed while clinging to a hopeless goal. The metaphor of the dance as life itself was plainly there for all to see, yet the film didn't lapse into heavy-handed allegory, thanks to Pollack's incisive touch. Pollack and his team had also accomplished the task of staying true to the spirit of McCoy's much-admired work while making compelling cinema within a potentially limited framework. As a much-lauded year-end release, the movie seemed like a sure lock for one of the Academy's Best Picture slots. Yet although *Horses* had taken the National Board of Review award in this category, the nine Oscar nominations the movie received did not include the top spot, which meant it entered the record books as the film to receive the most Academy Award nominations ever without securing a Best Picture mention.

MAROONED

Academy Award Winner: Best Special Visual Effects

Academy Award Nominee: Cinematography; Sound

Opening date: December 11, 1969 (New York: December 18, 1969).

Columbia. A Frankovich-Sturges Production.

Director: John Sturges. Producer: M. J. Frankovich. Screenplay: Mayo Simon. Based on the 1964 novel by Martin Caidin. Photography: Daniel Fapp. Production Designer: Lyle R. Wheeler. Set Decorator: Frank Tuttle. Costumer: Seth Banks. Editor: Walter Thompson. Special Visual Effects: Robie Robinson, Lawrence W. Butler, Donald C. Glouner. Eastmancolor. Panavision. 133 minutes. Rated G.

CAST: Gregory Peck (Charles Keith), Richard Crenna (Jim Pruett), David Janssen (Ted Dougherty), James Franciscus (Clayton Stone), Gene Hackman (Buzz Lloyd), Lee Grant (Celia Pruett), Nancy Kovack (Teresa Stone), Mariette Hartley (Betty Lloyd), Scott Brady (Public Affairs Officer), Craig Huebing (Flight Director), John Carter (Flight Surgeon), George Gaynes (Mission Director), Tom Stewart (Houston Cap-Com), Frank Marth (Systems Director), Duke Hobbie (Titan Systems Specialist), Dennis Robertson (Launch Director), Vincent Van Lynn (Aerospace Journalist).

PLOT: When the *Ironman-1* finds itself stranded during its attempted return to earth, NASA officials must act quickly to rescue the three astronauts on board before their oxygen runs out.

Perhaps it was the excitement over the space program that enveloped much of America during the 1960s, that made anybody believe a movie could be made from one of the first novels to examine the field, Martin Caidin's *Marooned*. This astonishingly boring book seemed more like a technical manual than a work of fiction, with endless minutiae about how everything in a space capsule worked, what it took to make a rocket launch, and far too much information about each step taken to test a man before he could be sent into space. Surprisingly, it was Frank Capra who was first drawn to the property while researching space details for a short movie, *Reaching for the Stars*, to be shown as the opening exhibit at the New York World's Fair's Hall of Science. Capra obtained an option on the book and brought it to the attention of Columbia head Mike (M. J.) Frankovich, who made sure his studio purchased the rights and targeted a May 1965 start date. Frankovich hired Walter

> "The hell with waitin' for a bunch of slide rule jockeys. We used to fix the airplanes we flew with paper clips. Let's get into our hard suits and fix this bird."
> —Jim Pruett

Newman to write a screenplay, but Capra postponed the initial launch until January 1966, by which time he and Frankovich were at odds over the budget. Eventually, after nearly three years' involvement with the property, Capra backed out, believing that the movie could not be made, or at least not as he envisioned it. Columbia had already spent money filming all of the rocket launches from Cape Kennedy over the past three years, knowing there would be nothing comparable to the real thing when it came to showing these sequences on the big screen.

No doubt spurred on by the gigantic success of MGM's eye-popping *2001: A Space Odyssey* (1968), Frankovich was more determined than ever to get in on the space craze, and *Marooned* now became a personal production of his independent company, which released through Columbia. With Capra not only off the project but now retired, Frankovich offered the job of director to John Sturges, while Mayo Simon was given the difficult task of turning the action-free book into something that would move onscreen. Caidin's original novel had begun with a solo astronaut, Richard Pruett, coming to the realization that the retro rockets on his orbiting capsule have failed to ignite, leaving him to float in space until his oxygen gives out. He then flashed back to his training in the air force and his gradual induction into the space program, which was basically an excuse for the author to give a brief history of how the actual *Mercury* astronauts came to be. Simon's script had Pruett (whose name was changed from Richard to Jim) joined in his once lonely trek by two other astronauts, and it no longer made their rescuer, Ted Dougherty (Jim in the book), Pruett's dearest friend from his flight-school days. The film retained the idea of the Russian cosmonaut's lending a hand, gave all the stranded fliers distraught wives, and kept

David Janssen (*center*) and director John Sturges (*right*) on the set of *Marooned* with the behind-the-scenes helicopter crew.

the character of NASA director Charles Keith; but it was no more successful in fleshing out these people, not to mention members of the ground-control rescuers, than Caidin had been.

Ironically, since Capra had dropped out owing to escalating expenses, Frankovich now wanted to spend a great deal of money on the picture, giving Sturges an $8 million budget with which to work. Close to $3 million was spent on constructing the sets, which included an exact replica of Houston's Missile Space Control Center, built on the Columbia lot. *Marooned* was so big in concept, however, that the film's main set would not even fit on the studio's soundstages. Therefore, MGM's largest facility, Stage 27, was rented. It was here that principal photography began on November 18, 1968, with space scenes utilizing a blue-backing matte process shot against a huge eighty-by-forty-foot blue screen using a full-scale space craft. The scenes of *Ironman-1* (a new name for *Mercury Seven*, as it was called by Caidin) floating in the silence of dark space that were staged on this set were done with total conviction by Robie Robinson, Donald C. Glouner, and their special-effects team. This turned out to be the most satisfying aspect of the picture. Outside of the studio locales, an additional three weeks were spent at Cape Kennedy for maximum authenticity with the production wrapping in mid-April 1969.

Unfortunately, authenticity seemed to take priority over entertainment. *Marooned* strove so hard to seem like the sort of science fiction that could actually happen that it had a dead serious, lumbering feeling, with facts and figures trumping characterization and emotional involvement. Sturges and Simon had failed thoroughly to turn Caidin's book into cinema, and word very quickly got around that Columbia had spent too much money on a better-looking version of what audiences saw on television during the actual space flights—which at least had breaks for commercials, giving viewers the ability to tune out when things got too dull. By the time *Marooned* premiered as a big 1969 Christmas attraction, NASA had already put a man on the moon, which seemed to bode well for audience interest. Selected as the movie to open New York's prestigious new Ziegfeld Theatre on Fifty-fourth Street, *Marooned* could not battle the scathing reviews heaped upon it, and it struggled at the box office. The film ended up (justifiably) getting noticed for its special effects at the Oscar ceremony and only rated mention later on, after its theatrical run, as being somewhat prescient when the actual *Apollo 13* crew faced a similar situation with its three-man crew. That story, however, was told with far more finesse and interest by director Ron Howard with the 1995 Universal release *Apollo 13*, which turned out to be, critically and financially, everything that *Marooned* had hoped to be and wasn't.

CACTUS FLOWER

Academy Award Winner: Best Supporting Actress (Goldie Hawn)

Top 10 Box Office Film

Opening date: December 16, 1969.

Columbia. A Frankovich Production.

Director: Gene Saks. Producer: M. J. Frankovich. Screenplay: I. A. L. Diamond. Based on the 1965 play by Abe Burrows, from the 1963 French play *Fleur de cactus* by Pierre Barillet and Jean-Pierre Grédy. Photography: Charles E. Lang. Production Designer: Robert Clatworthy. Set Decorator: Ed Boyle. Costumes: Moss Mabry. Men's Wardrobe: Guy Verhille. Music: Quincy Jones. Songs: "A Time for Love Is Anytime," by Quincy Jones (music) and Cynthia Weil (lyrics), performed by Sarah Vaughan; "I Needs to Be Bee'd With," by Quincy Jones and Ernie Shelby, performed by Johnny Wesley. Editor: Maury Winetrobe. Eastmancolor. 104 minutes. Rated M.

CAST: Walter Matthau (Dr. Julian Winston), Ingrid Bergman (Stephanie Dickinson), Goldie Hawn (Toni Simmons), Jack Weston (Harvey Greenfield), Rick Lenz (Igor Sullivan), Vito Scotti (Señor Sánchez), Irene Hervey (Mrs. Durant), Eve Bruce (Georgia), Irwin Charone (Mr. Shirley, Record Store Manager), Matthew Saks (Stephanie's Nephew), Sandy Balson (Marsha).

PLOT: Anxious to dump his younger girlfriend, dentist Julian Winston causes all sorts of complications and misunderstandings when he tries to pass off his nurse, Stephanie Dickinson, as his wife.

Somebody at Columbia Pictures seemed to smell a hit, because Abe Burrows's American adaptation of the French comedy *Fleur de cactus* was purchased by the studio in November 1965, a month before it had its official Broadway opening. The playwright received an impressive $250,000 upfront, with an escalator payment not to exceed $750,000. As fate would have it, *Cactus Flower* had something very appetizing in its favor: the addition of Lauren Bacall to the cast. For it was her presence that no doubt caused New York audiences to start lining up in big numbers at the box office for this sweet, unremarkable bit of romantic fluff. Bacall was joined in the original cast by Barry Nelson as the object of her affections; newcomer Brenda Vaccaro as Nelson's younger lover; Burt Brinckerhoff as inquisitive neighbor Igor; future director Robert Moore as obnoxious, unemployed actor Harvey Greenfield; and Arny Freeman as the salacious Señor Sanchez. Premiering December 8, 1965, at the Royale Theatre, the comedy ran for an unexpected three years, finally closing on November 23, 1968, with a total of 1,234 performances. The property ended up in the lap of former Columbia executive Mike Frankovich, who had actually seen the play in its French incarnation and had recently moved over to independent production, making *Cactus Flower* one of the first of his properties. His request that Billy Wilder's writing partner, I. A. L. Diamond, adapt the play was met with much favor, as was hiring Gene Saks to serve as director, the onetime actor having just knocked off two hits in a row for Paramount with the stage-to-screen transfers of *Barefoot in the Park* (1967) and *The Odd Couple* (1968). What is more, Saks would be reunited with one of the stars of the latter, Walter Matthau, an ideal choice for the libidinous dentist who isn't the catch he thinks he is.

It seemed like pretty much of a sure thing that Bacall would be asked to repeat her stage triumph, since she had become something a Hollywood legend by that stage of her career. She and half the theater community were therefore nothing short of flabbergasted when Frankovich decided he did *not* want her. Having given her the thumbs down, Frankovich was pressed to come up with somebody pretty damn special as a replacement. This he did, inviting Ingrid Bergman to make her first Hollywood movie since the Alfred Hitchcock misfire *Under Capricorn* (RKO) twenty years prior. Bergman had initially balked at the offer, wondering if she might come off as too old in the part and asking for a screen test. Columbia complied, everyone was happy with the results, and Bergman wound up being paid a very handsome $800,000 for her services.

> "Right now she's surrounded by her husband, her ex-boyfriend, her current boyfriend and maybe her future boyfriend."
> —Toni Simmons

To play Matthau's needy girlfriend, Frankovich had the brilliant idea of hiring one of the brightest names on the television screen, the delectable Goldie Hawn, whose giggling, infectiously goofy charms had made her one of the standout new stars of the smash hit variety show *Rowan & Martin's Laugh-In*. This masterstroke of casting brought even greater attention to the film. Columbia set out to hype Hawn as the next big addition to screen comedy, slapping an "introducing" credit before her name in the opening titles despite the fact that she had already shown up, as "Goldie Jeanne Hawn," in the Disney musical *The One and Only, Genuine, Original Family Band*, released shortly after *Laugh-In* hit the airwaves in early 1968.

Though fans of the play might have missed Bacall, they had little to complain about when it came to fidelity to Burrows's screenplay. Diamond didn't do much more than drop a line here and there, open certain scenes up for the outdoors, and change some minor details. And to let people know that this property was no longer a part of 1965 but very 1969, a hippie was seen placing flowers on people's windshields in the opening scene. Interestingly, some lines that compared Stephanie to playing "Joan of Arc" were deleted, which meant that the film missed a chance for an amusing inside joke: Bergman had played the famous martyr in the RKO film *Joan of Arc* two decades earlier.

After three weeks of rehearsal, *Cactus Flower* began shooting at the Columbia Pictures studio on February 10, 1969. Cast and crew spent most of their time there before traveling to New York in April for six days of exteriors. These locations included the Genesco (later Crown) Building at Fifth Avenue and Fifty-seventh Street, where Matthau and Bergman were required to enter the lobby from opposite sides; the recently opened General Motors Building on Fifth Avenue, where Matthau and Hawn had a discussion in its automobile showroom; the Plaza Theatre on Fifty-eighth Street, where Hawn and Matthau were seen attending a showing of Paramount's hit *Romeo and Juliet*; the entrance to Trude Heller's, a trendy disco at Sixth Avenue and Ninth Street, renamed "The Slipped Disc" for the picture; lower Eighth Avenue across from Stereo Heaven, used for Hawn's place of employment; the Guggenheim Museum, where Hawn and Matthau argued while assessing some sculptures by David Smith; and an apartment on West Eleventh Street in the Village, where Hawn was first seen mailing a suicide letter in front of the building. The production wrapped in early May.

Cactus Flower had never been a particular critics' favorite, so it didn't come as much of a surprise when the reviews ranged from lukewarm to hostile. This was the sort of gentle, mildly funny adaptation of a bright and far from ground-breaking stage comedy of the sort that wasn't asking to win awards, only to send its audiences home with smiles on their faces, even if they forgot pretty much everything about the plot by the time the next day dawned. The film captured everything that had made the show work onstage and had the advantage of three marvelous performances, with Matthau once again proving himself a master of this sort of artificial yet amusing style of farce. Bergman was an absolute delight and seemed to be having the time of her life, tossing off one-liners with her own brand of wit, making even the ones that read like duds on the written page sparkle from her lips. The critics were very kind to these two

Goldie Hawn made a successful leap from small screen to big with *Cactus Flower* and ended up with an Academy Award.

performers but were positively rapturous in their praise of Hawn. With this role she had taken her pin-headed, pixyish caricature from television and adapted it carefully to a more fully dimensional comic character, keeping Toni from appearing downright insufferable in her cluelessness and finding only her guileless charm. All three of these actors had their legions of supporters, and the combination proved irresistible: audiences showed up in huge numbers, turning this very likable and undemanding picture into one of Columbia's highest-grossing movies of the decade. And just to prove that Frankovich and Saks had made the right choice in plucking Hawn off the small screen, she ended up winning the Academy Award for Best Supporting Actress of 1969, launching her as one of the brightest additions to the motion-picture scene for the next three decades.

HELLO, DOLLY!

Academy Award Winner: Best Art Direction-Set Decoration; Best Sound; Best Score of a Musical Picture—Original or Adaptation

Academy Award Nominee: Picture; Cinematography; Film Editing; Costume Design

Top 10 Box Office Film

Opening date: December 17, 1969.

Twentieth Century-Fox. An Ernest Lehman Production.

Director: Gene Kelly. Producer–Screenplay: Ernest Lehman. Based on the 1964 musical stage play produced on the New York Stage by David Merrick, with book by Michael Stewart, music and lyrics by Jerry Herman. Based on the 1938 play *The Matchmaker*, by Thornton Wilder. Photography: Harry Stradling. Production Designer: John DeCuir. Art Directors: Jack Martin Smith, Herman Blumenthal. Set Decorators: Walter M. Scott, George Hopkins, Raphael Bretton. Costumes: Irene Sharaff. Songs by Jerry Herman: "Just Leave Everything to Me," "It Takes a Woman," "Put On Your Sunday Clothes," "Ribbons Down My Back," "Dancing," "Before the Parade Passes By," "Elegance," "Love Is Only Love," "Hello, Dolly!," "It Only Takes a Moment," "So Long, Dearie." Music Scored and Conducted by: Lennie Hayton, Lionel Newman. Orchestrations: Philip J. Lang, Lennie Hayton, Herbert Spencer, Alexander Courage, Don Costa, Warren Barker, Frank Comstock, Joseph Lipman. Choreographer: Michael Kidd. Associate Producer: Roger Edens. Editor: William Reynolds. Deluxe color. Todd-AO. 149 minutes (including overture, entr'acte, and exit music). Rated G.

CAST: Barbra Streisand (Dolly Levi), Walter Matthau (Horace Vandergelder), Michael Crawford (Cornelius Hackl), Louis Armstrong (Orchestra Leader), Marianne McAndrew (Irene Molloy), E. J. Peaker (Minnie Fay), Danny Lockin (Barnaby Tucker), Joyce Ames (Ermengarde), Tommy Tune (Ambrose Kemper), Judy Knaiz (Gussie Granger, "Ernestina Simple"), David Hurst (Rudolph Reisenweber), Fritz Feld (Fritz, German Waiter), Richard Collier (Joe, Vandergelder's Barber), J. Pat O'Malley (Policeman in Park), James Chandler (Sullivan, Ticket Clerk), Scatman Crothers (Mr. Jones, Porter).

PLOT: In turn-of-the-century New York, matchmaker Dolly Levi helps clerks Cornelius Hackl and Barnaby Tucker find romance, all the while hoping to land their wealthy boss, Horace Vandergelder, for herself.

The origins of one of the best-loved musicals of the twentieth century could be traced to a long-forgotten British farce, *A Day Well Spent*, written by John Oxenford and produced on the London stage in 1834. Oxenford's play, about the enjoyment experienced on a simple trip away from the grind of daily work, inspired an Austrian adaptation by Johann Nestroy, *Einen jux will er sich machen* (*He Wants to Make a Joke*), which premiered in Vienna eight years later. Following the acclaim he received for *Our Town*, Thornton Wilder (1897–1975) penned his first adaptation of Oxenford's piece and entitled it *The Merchant of Yonkers*. Starring Jane Cowl as the meddling, life-affirming Mrs. Levi, the play premiered on December 28, 1938, and was quickly deemed a flop. Undeterred, Wilder was sure there was something worthwhile to be culled from his story line and tinkered with it over the years until he finally got it right. His newly retitled adaptation, *The Matchmaker*, debuted at the Royale Theatre on December 5, 1955, with Ruth Gordon as Mrs. Levi. It was an instant hit and ran 486 performances.

Theatrical impresario David Merrick thought that Wilder's property would lend itself very nicely to being adapted into a stage musical and hired an enthusiastic Jerry Herman to write the score. Starring Carol Channing as Dolly, with David Burns as her cranky marital goal, Horace Vandergelder; Charles Nelson Reilly as the oppressed store clerk Cornelius Hackl; and Eileen Brennan as the widowed Irene Molloy; with direction by Gower Champion and book by Michael Stewart, *Hello, Dolly!* opened at the St. James Theatre on January 16, 1964, and became the surprise Broadway sensation of the decade. It made Channing a household name, earned a (then) record ten Tony Awards, and, with its rousing title song, introduced one of the great chart-topping numbers to come from the New York stage. It gave the irrepressible Louis Armstrong a hit single, with Grammy Awards going to both Satchmo and to Jerry Herman for Record of the Year. The show ran an astounding 2,844 performances, and Dolly became one of the most coveted roles for middle-aged actresses, allowing an impressive line-up of *grande dames* to follow Channing in the part: Ginger Rogers, Martha Raye, Pearl Bailey (heading a much-publicized all-black cast), Phyllis Diller, and Ethel Merman, who, ironically, had turned down the role in the first place.

> "I have always been a woman who arranges things, for the pleasure and the profit it derives. I have always been a woman who arranges things, like furniture, and daffodils . . . and lives."
> —Dolly Levi

In 1965 Twentieth Century-Fox became the lucky studio to purchase the rights to what seemed like a sure thing for adaptation to movie screens. That same year they had brought forth *the* gargantuan musical hit of the decade, *The Sound of Music*, and were anxious to spin some more gold from Broadway melodies. There was, however, a clause in the contract they had signed with producer David Merrick specifying that a film version of *Hello, Dolly!* could not open until *after* the show had ended its Broadway run; and in 1965 there was no end in sight for the smash hit. So plans for a *Dolly* film were put on the back burner for a while. When, in 1967, the film's producer and screenwriter, Ernest Lehman, finally got the property up and running again, he was faced with finding a middle-aged actress who was considered enough of a hot box-office attraction to carry what Fox planned as a very expensive motion picture. Needless to say, Channing was rejected outright; she had little film experience (despite her 1967 Oscar-nominated triumph in Universal's *Thoroughly Modern Millie*), and her persona was considered too large or perhaps too bizarre for her to be given a leading role on the big screen. Nor were any of her stage successors given much serious consideration, most of them being thought of as names from the past or too "inexperienced" on the big screen. Certainly the most suitable middle-aged musical performer to retain her standing as one of Hollywood's great stars, and one who would have made for a sublime Dolly, was Judy Garland, but her much-publicized expulsion from Fox's *Valley of the Dolls* pretty much quashed that possibility. But there was one singer who, by the time the film was ready to roll, had become just about the most famous female name in the industry, so Fox decided that Barbra Streisand (for a $750,000 salary) would be the cinematic Dolly Levi, even though she was only twenty-six years old when the movie went into production. This inappropriate bit of casting caused a great deal of backlash against the picture even before a single frame was shot, especially by members of the Broadway community, who looked upon it as yet another example of Hollywood tampering with a stage property in order to ensure financial success. Streisand herself began to regret her decision to accept the part, and her insecurity caused its share of tension during the long shoot.

Far more ideal was the casting of Walter Matthau, a letter-perfect choice to play the cantankerous Vandergelder and an increasingly bankable attraction following his Oscar-winning triumph in *The Fortune Cookie* (United Artists, 1966) and his successful transition to leading man with Fox's sly comedy *A Guide for the Married Man* (1967). An equally brilliant idea was to hire the director of the latter film, Gene Kelly, to helm the gargantuan production, since Kelly was responsible (along with Stanley Donen) for the most cherished film musical of them all, *Singin' in the Rain* (MGM, 1952). *Dolly* turned out to be a wonderful opportunity, bringing out the very best in his talents behind the camera. It was hands down Kelly's most impressive noncollaborative achievement in this field.

Lehman's adaptation of the Michael Stewart book stayed pretty close to the structure of the play, the most notable elimination being the trial that had followed the pandemonium at the Harmonia Gardens restaurant, so that the two numbers from this scene, "It Only Takes a Moment"

Barbra Streisand takes it easy on the set while filming the massive parade sequence from *Hello, Dolly!*

and "So Long, Dearie," were performed instead in a park and in front of the dining establishment, respectively. One song was dropped altogether, "Motherhood," which Dolly had sung in Mrs. Molloy's hat shop in order to distract Horace from finding his employees on the premises; and Dolly's opening number, "I Put My Hand in Here," kept its lead-in ("call on Dolly"), but the remainder of the song was discarded in favor of a more driving number, "Just Leave Everything to Me," which Herman had written especially for Streisand's dynamic personality. Also, in order to give the star some pensive ballads to sing, he dug up a trunk song cut from *Mame*, "Love Is Only Love," and gave Barbra her own, more reflective version of "It Takes a Woman" to follow Matthau's comical one.

Even with $20 million allotted for the budget, Fox needed to cut corners wherever it could and decided that John DeCuir and his team of designers should build their lavish re-creation of 1890s New York City not at the company's Malibu Ranch, as originally planned, but right there on the studio back lot, or rather the front lot. Ingeniously, DeCuir came up with the idea of utilizing the Fox offices at the entrance to the studio and adorning them with false fronts to resemble old Manhattan. Therefore, Fourteenth Street, with its Harmonia Gardens, as well as Mrs. Molloy's hat shop, and various backgrounds used for the "Elegance" number, were constructed at a cost of nearly $2 million. Filming began on the Fox soundstages on April 15, 1968, before the company moved east in early June to the tiny, picture postcard town of Garrison's Landing, New York (located directly across the Hudson River from West Point), which stood in for nineteenth-century Yonkers.

Returning to Hollywood in July, the production finally wrapped in early September, having endured its share of bumps along the way. Most notable of these was the animosity that developed between its two stars, who simply could not stand one another. Their frequent sniping on the set became the stuff of headlines, and Kelly did everything in his power to establish peace between the two outspoken performers. Streisand, ever the hands-on perfectionist, made herself unpopular by making suggestions to Kelly about how the picture should be made. Although some of her ideas may have been valid ones (it was her suggestion that Kelly pull back the camera as she held the dazzling final note on "Before the Parade Passes By"), she was dead wrong when she balked at the idea of having Louis Armstrong added to the cast to chime in on the title number, Streisand thinking it was a cheap gimmick to cash in on Satchmo's hit recording. As it turned out, Armstrong's brief appearance was one of the undisputed highlights, even for those critics who derided the movie otherwise. Kelly and his team exploited the opportunity in the best possible sense, bringing together two unique and gifted performers with sensational results. It would turn out to be the final onscreen appearance of the great trumpeter and singer, who died on July 6, 1971.

With a final price tag of $24 million, Twentieth Century-Fox had the dubious distinction of having produced the most expensive musical in the history of the genre, only to realize that they still could not release it. With the stage version still packing in the crowds, the studio was obliged to honor David Merrick's wishes that the picture be held from distribution, and they did so until they started to fear that further delays might leave them with spoiled goods on their hands. Insistent that the movie open by Christmas of 1969, Fox paid an additional amount to Merrick to compensate for any lost revenue. (The stage *Dolly* finally closed on December 27, 1970, making it, at the time, the longest-running Broadway musical ever and the third-longest-running show in Broadway history.) More than five years had passed since *Hello, Dolly!*'s New York opening and the film's road-show premiere, and the country had changed at a head-spinning pace during that time, musically, cinematically, and sociologically. It no longer seemed possible that Herman's title track could snatch a Grammy Award away from a rock record, as it had in 1964, and the blatantly old-fashioned tone of the piece was viewed by many as woefully out of date and irrelevant when blown up on the big screen. Kelly and company had proudly crafted a family-oriented musical in the style of their best work from MGM's heyday in the genre, but several critics decided to hold up *Hello, Dolly!* as an example of Hollywood's failure to move with the times. In light of the success of such antiestablishment pictures as *Midnight Cowboy* (United Artists) and *Easy Rider* (Columbia), many felt obliged to criticize the film not for what it was, but for what it never set out to be.

Boasting one of the most familiar titles of the decade and coming in the wake of Streisand's Academy Award–winning triumph in *Funny Girl*, the film couldn't help but attract a healthy number of customers. But it was not enough to allow Fox to rest easy where their costly investment was concerned. Despite ending up as one of the highest-attended of all 1969 releases and earning an Oscar nomination for Best Picture, *Hello, Dolly!* was quickly and unjustly branded a flop by the naysayers, eager to see the end of similarly costly, traditional extravaganzas. It was only in retrospect that more people began to look back on the film without all the baggage surrounding its initial release and realize that Kelly had done an exemplary job in transferring the piece to the big screen, giving it all the energy and professionalism it deserved and making it one of the most satisfying and tuneful of all the lavish screen musicals of the era.

ANNE OF THE THOUSAND DAYS

Academy Award Winner: Best Costume Design

Academy Award Nominee: Picture; Actor (Richard Burton); Actress (Geneviève Bujold); Supporting Actor (Anthony Quayle); Screenplay—Based on Material from Another Medium; Cinematography; Art Direction–Set Decoration; Sound; Original Score

Opening date: December 18, 1969 (New York: January 20, 1970).

Universal. A Hal Wallis Production.

Director: Charles Jarrott. Producer: Hal B. Wallis. Screenplay: Bridget Boland, John Hale. Adaptation: Richard Sokolove. Based on the 1948 play by Maxwell Anderson. Photography: Arthur Ibbetson. Production Designer: Maurice Carter. Art Director: Lionel Couch. Set Decorators: Peter Howitt, Patrick McLoughlin. Costumes: Margaret Furse. Music: Georges Delerue. Song: "Farewell, Farewell," by Georges Delerue and John Hale. Editor: Richard Marden. Makeup: Tom Smith. Technicolor. Panavision. 145 minutes. Rated M.

CAST: Richard Burton (King Henry VIII), Geneviève Bujold (Anne Boleyn), Irene Papas (Queen Catherine), Anthony Quayle (Cardinal Wolsey), John Colicos (Thomas Cromwell), Michael Hordern (Thomas Boleyn), Katharine Blake (Elizabeth Boleyn), Peter Jeffrey (Norfolk), Joseph O'Conor (Bishop Fisher), William Squire (Thomas More), Valerie Gearon (Mary Boleyn), Vernon Dobtcheff (Mendoza), Gary Bond (Smeaton), Terence Wilton (Lord Percy), Denis Quilley (Weston), Kate Burton (Serving Maid), Liza Todd Burton (Beggar Maid), Michael Johnson (George Boleyn), Esmond Knight (Kingston), Nora Swinburne (Lady Kingston), T. P. McKenna (Norris).

PLOT: King Henry VIII makes the controversial decision to declare himself head of the Church of England so that he can divorce Catherine of Aragon and wed Anne Boleyn.

Of all the wives King Henry VIII racked up during his thirty-eight-year (1509–47) reign over England, spouse number 2, Anne Boleyn, always held the most fascination for the public. She had been, after all, wooed and wed, only to be sent unjustly to the chopping block, but not until she had given birth to the girl who would become the country's most powerful, influential, and famous monarch of them all, Elizabeth I. Perhaps because of the story's inevitable unhappy ending, Hollywood had steered away from giving the hapless queen her own showcase. But by 1969 it was time to put Anne front and center in her own lavish costume drama, and she received her due, by way of independent producer Hal B. Wallis, with *Anne of the Thousand Days*. Wallis had been in possession of this property for quite some time, the original Maxwell Anderson play having debuted on Broadway twenty-one years before the film version made it to the screen. Under the direction of H. C. Potter it had opened on December 8, 1948, at the Shubert Theatre with Rex Harrison as Henry, Joyce Redman as Anne, and John Williams as the Duke of Norfolk. By the time it closed on

> "Divorce is like killing; after the first time it doesn't seem so difficult."
> —King Henry VIII

October 4, 1949, after 288 performances, it had earned Tony Awards for Harrison and for scenic designer Jo Mietziner.

Shortly after Wallis's acclaimed film *Becket* (Paramount, 1964) proved that the general public was very interested in well-scripted tales of bickering rulers and scheming court flunkies, he proposed a

The sheet music for "Farewell, Farewell," a tune that made little impression amid the historical treachery in *Anne of the Thousand Days*.

screen adaptation of *Anne*. His initial idea was to get Peter O'Toole, who had scorched the screen in *Becket* as Henry II, to return to the Throne Room and portray the charismatic, egomaniacal Henry VIII. When O'Toole proved unavailable, Wallis decided to offer the starring role to *Becket*'s other male lead, Richard Burton, who frankly wasn't all that excited about the project. He did, however, love the idea of being paid $1 million up front plus 10 percent of the gross, and so he agreed to come aboard. Several young British actresses were initially tested for the role of Anne, but twenty-six-year-old French Canadian actress Geneviève Bujold got the part. After all, the real Anne had spent many of her formative years in France and spoke the language fluently, which could plausibly account for the actress's accent. By the time the project finally moved from the planning stages to reality, Wallis's twenty-four-year distribution deal with Paramount Pictures was coming to a close. *Anne of the Thousand Days* would be his first production as part of his new pact with Universal Pictures, the studio at which he would bring his long and prestigious career to an end.

Placed in charge of the picture was Charles Jarrott, whose participation was perhaps its weakest aspect, since there was very little style or originality in his direction. He bestowed upon the movie a professionalism that fell short of inspiration. The film script got rid of Anne and the king's stagy solo monologues; a scene bringing Anne and her successor, Jane Seymour, together for the first time was discarded, the latter being brought into the drama at a later date; and mention of the death of Anne's original betrothed, Northumberland, was no longer included in the dialogue. Wisely, a good deal of Anderson's lines were retained, his script having been both clever and informative without sacrificing the stuff of good, incisive drama. The most important addition to the screenplay was the actual inclusion of the first of Henry's long line of wronged wives, Catherine of Aragon, who had been frequently mentioned but never seen onstage. Figuring any foreign accent could pass for Spanish, Greece's chief tragedienne, Irene Papas, got the part; Jarrot knew well that few could carry the burden of neglect as dramatically as she could.

Given a $3.5 million budget, *Anne* began shooting in England in late May 1969, wrapping at the end of August. Soundstages at Shepperton housed the interior sets, while re-creations of the streets of sixteenth-century London were constructed on the back lot of Pinewood. The real Hever Castle, the Boleyn home located near Sevenoaks in Kent, made itself available for filming, while Penhurst Place, also in Kent, stood in for Henry's Greenwich palace. Hunting scenes were shot at Richmond Park in London.

Most bookings for the two-and-a-half-hour picture were scheduled for early 1970, but Wallis and Universal decided their movie was the sort that might appeal to Academy voters if it made it under the wire with a December run in Los Angeles. The move proved most beneficial. Opening on a reserved-seat basis, *Anne* scored ten Oscar nominations. This sort of attention worked magic at the box office, and the film played off these honors to become one of the top moneymakers of the year.

Although there were plenty of complaints about overly familiar material and old-fashioned film-making that was out of sync with some of the grittier fare being attempted, *Anne of the Thousand Days* was solid storytelling, and a good story at that. Dialogue crackled between the two principals, the court intrigue was appropriately juicy, and the movie always entertained. Burton, for all his initial disinterest, was on the mark in capturing the King's self-righteousness, charisma, and borderline-psychopathic be-havior. Bujold matched him step for step, if not indeed surpassing him, playing a strong-willed woman who was just the sort of lady a less pigheaded and chauvinistic monarch might have realized was the ideal companion, both romantically and for her leadership skills. This was the tragedy of a woman who had the capacity for doing great things, only to be destroyed by a tyrant who was unable to treat a female as his equal. Wallis, very pleased with the reception for the film, set out to produce yet another tale of British royals, hiring Jarrott to direct *Mary, Queen of Scots* (Universal), two years later. While a good film in its own right, there was less and less interest for this sort of product as the '70s progressed, and the box office for *Mary* was middling at best.

THE HAPPY ENDING

Academy Award Nominee: Actress (Jean Simmons); Song ("What Are You Doing the Rest of Your Life?")

Opening date: December 21, 1969.

United Artists. A Pax Enterprises Production.

Director-[Producer]-Screenplay: Richard Brooks. Photography: Conrad L. Hall. Costumes: Rita Riggs. Music: Michel Legrand. Songs by Michel Legrand (music) and Alan and Marilyn Bergman (lyrics): "What Are You Doing the Rest of Your Life?," performed by Michael Dees; "Hurry Up and Hurry Down," performed by Bill Eaton; "Something for Everybody," performed by Bill Eaton. Editor: George Grenville. Technicolor. Panavision. 112 minutes. Rated M.

CAST: Jean Simmons (Mary Wilson), John Forsythe (Fred Wilson), Lloyd Bridges (Sam), Shirley Jones (Flo), Teresa Wright (Mrs. Spencer), Dick Shawn (Harry Bricker), Nanette Fabray (Agnes), Robert Darin/Bobby Darin (Franco), Tina Louise (Helen Bricker), Kathy Fields (Marge Wilson), Karen Steele (Divorcee), Gail Hensley (Betty), Eve Brent (Ethel), William O'Connell (Minister), Barry Cahill (Handsome Man), Miriam Blake (Cindy).

PLOT: Desperately unhappy with her life, Mary Wilson walks out on her sixteenth wedding anniversary celebration, impulsively flying off to the Bahamas as she looks back on what went wrong in her marriage.

The very ironically titled *The Happy Ending* looked at marriage in the '60s and came to the conclusion that pretty much everybody was miserable, having dreamed early on of eternal fulfillment and instead having accepted, somewhere along the way, a life of compromise, surrender, and numbing routine. Director-writer Richard Brooks had conceived the film as a showcase for his wife of nine years, Jean Simmons, believing that she was long overdue to actually carry a feature film, something she had seldom done throughout her career, usually being the leading lady to a more bankable male star. The role of Mary Wilson allowed her to plunge into moments of self-reflection, depths of despair, and situations of supreme discomfort as she let herself unravel through an alcoholic haze of depression and self-pity over her empty life.

Brooks got his cast to work for a fraction of their salaries, and they trusted him enough to consent to doing their roles without seeing a finished screenplay. Instead, he handed them only two pages of dialogue each day, keeping the outcome of their characters a secret, since he himself hadn't come up with any final conclusions, tinkering with the writing all during the shoot. Going for a location that had not been overused in movies, Brooks chose Denver, Colorado, as his chief setting. Shooting

> "American husbands are so blind. Always they wish to remember the way love was. But . . . nothing is the way it was . . . not even then. Remembering is the end of love. Love is always now."
> —Franco

began there on January 15, 1969, before cast and crew moved west to Los Angeles, where a rented Beverly Hills home was used for the interiors of the Wilson house, and then on to Paradise Island in the Bahamas, where Simmons's character traveled in hopes of sorting things out. The Miami airport was used for all airline scenes. Working hastily, Brooks managed to reduce the original budget from $2 million to $1.7 million, bringing the picture in a miraculous 28 days under its designated 102.

The Happy Ending certainly did let Simmons have an acting feast and featured plenty of scathing and profound observations on the seemingly hopeless nature of supposed marital bliss. Unfortunately, there was also something relentlessly downbeat in all this self-examination; there was no sense of accomplishment or progression in Mary Wilson's story, only a feeling of unsatisfying defeat. The picture opened to mostly negative reviews that declared it often hollow and ultimately tiresome, and the box office suffered accordingly. As for Richard Brooks, he turned out to have been surprisingly close to the mark

The United Artists soundtrack for *The Happy Ending* contained the movie's grim logo of an anniversary cake tossed in the trash, but it also included a lovely ballad by Michel Legrand and Alan and Marilyn Bergman, the enduring "What Are You Doing the Rest of Your Life?"

when he chose to examine a marriage that started falling apart after sixteen years. In 1977 he and Simmons went their separate ways; they had been wed for seventeen years.

THE REIVERS

Academy Award Nominee: Supporting Actor (Rupert Crosse); Original Score

Opening date: December 25, 1969.

National General Pictures. A Cinema Center Films Presentation of an Irving Ravetch–Arthur Kramer Production in Association with Solar Productions.

Director: Mark Rydell. Producer: Irving Ravetch. Screenplay: Irving Ravetch, Harriet Frank Jr. Based on the 1962 novel by William Faulkner. Executive Producer: Robert E. Relyea. Photography: Richard Moore. Production Designers: Charles Bailey, Joel Schiller. Set Decorator: Phil Abramson. Costumes: Theadora Van Runkle. Music: John Williams. Editor: Thomas Stanford. Winton Flyer by Von Dutch. Technicolor. Panavision. 108 minutes. Rated M.

CAST: Steve McQueen (Boon Hogganbeck), Sharon Farrell (Corrie), Will Geer (Boss McCaslin), Michael Constantine (Mr. Binford), Rupert Crosse (Ned McCaslin), Mitch Vogel (Lucius McCaslin), Lonny Chapman (Maury McCaslin), Juano Hernandez (Uncle Possum), Clifton James (Sheriff Butch Lovemaiden), Ruth White (Miss Reba), Dub Taylor (Dr. Peabody), Allyn Ann McLerie (Alison McCaslin), Diane Shalet (Hannah), Diane Ladd (Phoebe), Ellen Geer (Sally), Pat Randall (May Ellen), Charles Tyner (Edmonds), Vinnette Carroll (Aunt Callie), Gloria Calomee (Minnie), Sara Taft (Sarah), Lindy Davis (Otis), Raymond Guth (Uncle Ike), Shug Fisher (Cousin Zack), Logan Ramsey (Walter Clapp), Burgess Meredith (Narrator).

PLOT: Left to care for Boss McCaslin's new Wynton Flyer, handymen Boon Hogganbeck and Ned McCaslin sweep the boss's impressionable grandson Lucius off to St. Louis in hopes of showing the boy the good life.

By the late '60s Steve McQueen was sitting on top of the world as one of the hottest and highest paid names in the motion-picture industry, pretty much able to make whatever picture he pleased. He had risen to these heights by cultivating the image of an introspective loner, a man of infinite cool, but he was itching to find out if his fans would accept him at something a bit less predictable, something highly uncharacteristic of him, and decided he would like to play the impulsive, extroverted, low-brow farm hand Boon Hogganbeck in an adaptation of William Faulkner's *The Reivers*. This came as a surprise, not only because Hogganbeck did not in any way match the physical description of McQueen (someone like George Kennedy more readily came to mind when reading the book), but because he was not the main figure of attention, being very much a supporting role, something more suited to a character player than a star. It was just this sort of challenge, plus the fact that his last attempt at broad comedy, *Soldier in the Rain* (Allied Artists, 1963), had ended up such a failure, that made McQueen that much more determined to do it, so *The Reivers* was lined up as the first project between his own production company, Solar Pictures, and the newly formed Cinema Center Films, an offshoot of CBS Television.

> "If ya ever wanna reach your manhood, sometimes you gotta say 'goodbye' to the things you know and 'hello' to the things you don't."
> —Boon Hogganbeck

Faulkner's book had been the last of his works to be published in his lifetime, debuting in June 1962, only a month before the author's death. Originally given the cumbersome title of *The Horse Stealers: A Reminiscence*, Faulkner then changed it to *The Reavers*, from the word *reave*, which meant "to rob or plunder." This didn't satisfy him either, so he decided to go with the Scottish spelling of the word, hence the seemingly incorrect ("i" after "e," going against the standard rules of spelling taught to all schoolchildren) *The Reivers*. Despite the fact that his dense, overly wordy, and often turgid style of writing did not make his books easy to transfer to film, multiple attempts had been made, but the results had been varied—*The Story of Temple Drake* (Paramount, 1933) and *The Sound and the Fury* (Twentieth Century-Fox, 1959) had little to do with the author's original intentions. One of the more accessible and financially successful adaptations had been Fox's 1958 rendition of *The Hamlet*, re-titled *The Long Hot Summer*, and therefore the very same people, Irving Ravetch and Harriet Frank Jr., were engaged to turn *The Reivers* into a commercial motion picture.

The first line of duty in the adaptation was to make sure that Boon was front and center through as much of the story as possible, though he had dropped out of sight multiple times in Faulkner's original. Several minor characters, including other employees of the McCaslin farm and Lucius's three younger brothers, were considered superfluous and dropped, as were the McCaslin family's trip to a funeral in Bay St. Louis; a stay at Ballenbaugh's, a ferry stop that catered to criminals on the run; an entire sequence in which hooker Corrie gets one of her johns, Sam, a flagman for the train line, to smuggle a racehorse into a baggage car; and a plotline in which a prostitute named Minnie has her gold tooth stolen while sleeping. In order to build things up more suspensefully to one big race, the two competitions were no longer split up by the arrest scene, which was moved earlier. Whereas in the book Lucius had lost the race, simply because he wasn't fast enough, this did not seemed dramatic enough for a commercial film that was looking for audiences to get deeply involved in the event, so it was decided to have a rival jockey cheat, prompting an outcry from the spectators. Wisely, the writers also felt it necessary to bring the character of Ned into the more progressive light of the late '60s, making him more cunning rather than the simpleminded, stereotypical, backward, and fairly obnoxious black man he had been in the book. Faulkner's southern upbringing meant that he was always forthright about depicting the racial unrest

Steve McQueen approves of his messy state while filming the mud scene from *The Reivers*.

among his characters, but it wouldn't fly to allow this sort of demeaning attitude to remain in 1969 without pointed commentary. Therefore the villains were clearly delineated as racist and any insults made by Boon toward Ned in no way reflected a genuine disdain, but a barely concealed mutual affection. As much as it was plausible to do so, Ned was now seen as something of an equal to Boon and Lucius.

As had been the case with most of his movies, McQueen proved to be very demanding on the set, making sure that everybody knew exactly who the muscle was on the project. He was so unhappy with the dailies that he tried his best to have director Mark Rydell fired, but the executives at Cinema Center overrode the star's request and Rydell stayed on, doing a professional job yet one that was hardly ever inspired, which was often the case with this director. The film rolled on September 30, 1968, with the bulk of principal photography taking place in tiny Carrollton, Mississippi (population 500). The town's appropriately quaint, early twentieth-century feel meant there was almost no need to build period sets from scratch. The horse-race sequences were shot at the Disney Ranch in California, with interiors done at the CBS Studio Center. The Yellow Winton Flyer was built specially for the movie by famed customized car designer Von Dutch (real name: Kenny Howard) so that it could be driven with modern efficiency.

Although McQueen got top billing and Rupert Crosse got the best reviews, it was twelve-year-old Mitch Vogel who really carried the picture on his shoulders. His very engaging work, which included some terrific acting opportunities along the way, most notably in his final tearful confession to his grandfather, is what really pulled *The Reivers* above the ordinary. It was a testament to how good he was in the part that when he broke his leg during filming, there was no consideration whatsoever of replacing him.

Held for the prestigious Christmas Day spot at the close of the decade, *The Reivers*, despite the inclusion of hookers and some rough talk, was blatantly old-fashioned. But that didn't seem to bother certain critics, who gladly recommended the picture as good natured, lightweight fun. The movie was sold strictly on McQueen's image, with a great big close-up of the star nibbling on some wheat, looking very cheeky and sporting longer hair than was his custom—after all, it *was* the late '60s. Happily for McQueen and his company, *The Reivers*, on which $5 million had been spent ($700,000 going to McQueen), was a box-office success, taking in $17 million in American theaters, though it held little appeal in other countries. McQueen had definitely done his share of shameless overemoting in the part, but hardly to the detriment of a picture that didn't leave much of a lasting impression, being best described as pleasant, no more, no less. Even if the movie came through financially, it wasn't enough for the customarily prickly and hard-to-please star, who felt that he had mucked things up yet again. For his next picture, *Le Mans* (National General, 1971), he figured he'd play it safe, doing what he felt more comfortable with: racing cars. Cinema Center Films would stick around for only another four years, *The Reivers* proving to be the most popular release on their small slate of films.

bibliography

Adamson, Joy. *Born Free: A Lioness of Two Worlds*. New York: Bantam, 1967.

Agel, Jerome, ed. *The Making of Kubrick's 2001*. New York: Signet, 1970.

Albee, Edward. *Who's Afraid of Virginia Woolf?* New York: Pocket Books, 1966.

Allen, Jay Presson. *The Prime of Miss Jean Brodie*. New York: Samuel French, Inc., 1969.

Anderson, Maxwell. *Anne of the Thousand Days*. New York: Dramatists Play Service, 1976.

Ball, John. *In the Heat of the Night*. New York: Bantam, 1967.

Barnes, Alan, and Marcus Hearn. *Kiss Kiss Bang! Bang!: The Unofficial James Bond Companion*. London: BT Batsford, 2000.

Barrett, James Lee, Peter Udell, and Philip Rose. *Shenandoah*. New York: Samuel French, Inc., 1975.

Beardsley, Helen. *Who Gets the Drumstick?* New York: Bantam, 1968.

Benchley, Nathaniel. *The Off-Islanders*. New York: Popular Library, 1961.

Benedictus, David. *You're a Big Boy Now*. New York: Bantam, 1967.

Bergman, Ronald. *The United Artists Story*. New York: Crown, 1986.

Bolt, Robert. *A Man for All Seasons*. New York: Scholastic Book Services, 1967.

Boulle, Pierre. *Planet of the Apes*. New York: Signet, 1968.

Bragg, Melvyn. *Richard Burton: A Life*. New York: Warner Books, 1988.

Braithwaite, E. R. *To Sir, with Love*. New York: Pyramid, 1967.

Burrows, Abe. *Cactus Flower*. New York: Samuel French, Inc. 1966.

Caidin, Martin. *Marooned*. New York: Bantam, 1965.

Chanslor, Roy. *The Ballad of Cat Ballou*. New York: Signet, 1965.

Dickens, Charles. *Oliver Twist*. New York: Lancer Books, 1968.

Duncan, Isadora. *Isadora: The Autobiography of Isadora Duncan*. Originally published as *My Life*. New York: Award Books, 1968.

Eames, John Douglas. *The MGM Story*. New York: Crown, 1979.

———. *The Paramount Story*. New York: Crown, 1985.

Ely, David. *Seconds*. New York: Signet, 1966.

Faulkner, William. *The Reivers*. New York: Signet, 1969.

Finstad, Suzanne. *Natasha: The Biography of Natalie Wood*. New York: Three Rivers Press, 2001.

———. *Warren Beatty: A Private Man*. New York: Harmony Books, 2005.

Fishgall, Gary. *Against Type: The Biography of Burt Lancaster*. New York: Holiday House, 1995.

Fleming, Ian. *Thunderball*. New York: Signet, 1963.

———. *You Only Live Twice*. New York: Signet, 1965.

Fonda, Peter, Dennis Hopper, and Terry Southern. *Easy Rider*. New York: Signet, 1969.

Forster, Margaret. *Georgy Girl*. New York: Berkley Medallion, 1966.

Foster, Allan. *The Movie Traveler: A Film Fan's Guide to the UK and Ireland*. Edinburgh: Polygon, 2000.

Fowles, John. *The Collector*. New York: Dell, 1968.

Fry, Christopher. *The Bible*. New York: Pocket Books, 1966.

Gardner, Herb. *A Thousand Clowns*. New York: Samuel French, Inc., 1965.

Garrett, George P., ed., et al. *Film Scripts Four:* Darling, A Hard Day's Night, The Best Man. New York: Irvington Publishers, Inc. 1989.

Gilroy, Frank D. *The Subject Was Roses*. New York: Dell, 1968.

Godfrey, Lionel. *Paul Newman: Superstar*. New York: St. Martin's Press, 1978.

Goldman, James. *The Lion in Winter*. New York: Dell, 1968.

Goldman, William. *Butch Cassidy and the Sundance Kid*. New York: Bantam, 1969.

Gordon, Mildred, and Gordon Gordon. *That Darn Cat*. Originally published as *Undercover Cat*. New York: Bantam, 1965.

Goudsouzian, Aram. *Sidney Poitier: Man, Actor, Icon*. North Carolina: University of North Carolina Press, 2004.

Grosman, Ladislav. *The Shop on Main Street*. Garden City, NY: Doubleday & Company, Inc., 1970.

Harburg, E. Y., and Fred Saidy. *Finian's Rainbow*. New York: Berkeley, 1968.

Harvey, Stephen. *Directed by Vincente Minnelli*. New York: Harper & Row, 1989.

Herlihy, James Leo. *Midnight Cowboy*. New York: Dell, 1969.

Herndon, Venable, and Arthur Penn. *Alice's Restaurant*. Garden City, NY: Doubleday & Company, Inc., 1970.

Hirsch, Julia Antopol. The Sound of Music: *The Making of America's Favorite Movie*. Chicago: Contemporary Books, 1993.

Hirschhorn, Clive. *The Columbia Story*. New York: Crown, 1989.

———. *The Hollywood Musical*. New York: Crown, 1983.

———. *The Universal Story*. New York: Crown, 1983.

———. *The Warner Bros. Story*. New York: Crown, 1979.

Hofstede, David. *Audrey Hepburn: A Bio-Bibliography*. Westport, CT: Greenwood Press, 1994.

Hunter, Evan. *Last Summer*. New York: Signet, 1969.

Jewison, Norman. *This Terrible Business Has Been Good to Me*. New York: Thomas Dunne Books, 2005.

Kata, Elizabeth. *A Patch of Blue*. Originally published as *Be Ready with Bells and Drums*. New York: Popular Library, 1965.

Keyes, Daniel. *Flowers for Algernon*. New York: Bantam, 1970.

Kipling, Rudyard. *The Jungle Books*. New York: Signet Classics, 1961.

Laurence, Margaret. *Rachel, Rachel.* Originally published as *A Jest of God.* New York: Popular Library, 1968.

Le Carré, John. *The Spy Who Came In from the Cold.* New York: Dell, 1965.

Lelouch, Claude. *A Man and a Woman.* London: Lorimer Publishing, 1971.

Levin, Ira. *Rosemary's Baby.* New York: Dell, 1967.

Lindsay, Howard, and Russel Crouse. *The Sound of Music.* New York: Bantam, 1967.

Malamud, Bernard. *The Fixer.* New York: Dell, 1967.

Maltin, Leonard. *Leonard Maltin's Movie & Video Guide,* 2008 edition. New York: Signet, 2007.

McCarty, John. *The Complete Films of John Huston.* Secaucus, NJ: Citadel Press, 1987.

McCoy, Horace. *They Shoot Horses, Don't They?* New York: Avon, 1970.

McCullers, Carson. *The Heart Is a Lonely Hunter.* New York: Bantam, 1970.

McKenna, Richard. *The Sand Pebbles.* New York: Fawcett Crest, 1968.

Menzel, Jiří, and Bohumil Hrabal. *Closely Watched Trains.* New York: Simon & Schuster, 1971.

Michael, Paul. *The Great American Movie Book.* Englewood Cliffs, NJ: Prentice-Hall, Inc., 1980.

Michener, James A. *Hawaii.* New York: Bantam, 1961.

Moore, Robin. *The Green Berets.* New York: Avon, 1966.

Nathanson, E. M. *The Dirty Dozen.* New York: Dell, 1966.

Naughton, Bill. *Alfie.* London: Samuel French, 1963.

Nichols, John. *The Sterile Cuckoo.* New York: Avon, 1970.

Nicolson, Robert. *The Whisperers.* New York: Alfred A. Knopf, 1961.

O'Brien, Daniel. *The Frank Sinatra Film Guide.* London: BT Batsford, 1998.

O'Rourke, Frank. *The Professionals.* Originally published as *A Mule for the Marquesa.* New York: Avon, 1966.

Pasternak, Boris. *Doctor Zhivago.* New York: Signet, 1965.

Perry, Danny. *Cult Movies: The Classics, the Sleepers, the Weird, and the Wonderful.* New York: Dell, 1981.

———. *Cult Movies 2: Fifty More of the Classics, the Sleepers, the Weird, and the Wonderful.* New York: Dell, 1983.

———. *Cult Movies 3: Fifty More of the Classics, the Sleepers, the Weird, and the Wonderful.* New York: Dell, 1988.

Pike, Robert L. *Bullitt.* Originally published as *Mute Witness.* New York: Avon, 1968.

Porter, Katherine Anne. *Ship of Fools.* New York: Signet, 1963.

Portis, Charles. *True Grit.* New York: Signet, 1969.

Raphael, Frederic. *Two for the Road: A Screenplay.* New York: Holt, Rineheart and Winston, 1967.

Reeves, Tony. *The Worldwide Guide to Movie Locations.* London: Titan, 2006.

Riese, Randall. *Her Name Is Barbra: An Intimate Portrait of the Real Barbra Streisand.* New York: Birch Lane Press, 1993.

Roberts, Randy, and James S. Olson. *John Wayne: American.* New York: Free Press, 1995.

Roth, Philip. *Goodbye, Columbus.* New York: Bantam, 1969.

Sackett, Susan. *Hollywood Sings!: An Inside Look at Sixty Years of Academy Award–Nominated Songs.* New York: Billboard Books, 1995.

Shakespeare, William. *Othello*. New York: Signet Classics, 1963.

———. *Romeo and Juliet*. New York: Scholastic Book Services, 1969.

Shipman, David. *The Great Movie Stars: The International Years*. New York: St. Martin's Press Inc., 1972.

———. *The Great Movie Stars 1: The Golden Years*. Boston: Little, Brown and Company, 1989.

———. *The Great Movie Stars 2: The International Years*. Boston: Little, Brown and Company, 1989.

Simon, Neil. *The Comedy of Neil Simon*. New York: Random House, 1971.

———. *The Odd Couple*. New York: Scholastic Book Services, 1968.

Solinas, Franco. *Gillo Pontecorvo's* The Battle of Algiers*: The Complete Scenario*. New York: Charles Scribner's Sons, 1973.

Spark, Muriel. *The Prime of Miss Jean Brodie*. New York: Laurel, 1971.

St. Charnez, Casey. *The Complete Films of Steve McQueen*. Secaucus, NJ: Citadel, 1992.

Stewart, Michael, and Jerry Herman. *Hello, Dolly!* New York: Signet, 1964.

Susann, Jacqueline. *Valley of the Dolls*. New York: Bantam, 1971.

Trevor, Elleston. *The Flight of the Phoenix*. London: Pan Books, Ltd., 1964.

Walker, Alexander. *Fatal Charm: The Life of Rex Harrison*. New York: St. Martin's Press, 1992.

Wallant, Edward Lewis. *The Pawnbroker*. New York: Macfadden-Bartell, 1964.

Webb, Charles. *The Graduate*. New York: Signet, 1967.

Westheimer, David. *Von Ryan's Express*. New York: Signet, 1965.

Wilder, Billy, and I. A. L. Diamond. The Apartment *and* The Fortune Cookie: *Two Screenplays by Billy Wilder and I. A. L. Diamond*. New York: Praeger, 1971.

Wiley, Mason, and Damien Bona. *Inside Oscar: The Unofficial History of the Academy Awards*. Tenth Anniversary Edition. New York: Ballantine Books, 1996.

Willis, John. *Screen World*. Vols. 16–20 (1965–69). New York: Crown, 1966–70.